Talleyrand-Périgord

PAIRS DE FRANCE · PRINCES DE CHALAIS ·
DUCS DE PÉRIGORD · DUCS DE TALLEYRAND ·
DUCS DE MONTMORENCY ·
PRINCES DE BÉNÉVENT · DUCS DE DINO ·
PRINCES DE SAGAN ·
GRANDS D'ESPAGNE DE IÈRE CLASSE ·
MARQUIS D'EXCIDEUIL ·
COMTES DE GRIGNOLS, DE MONTIGNAC, ETC.

COAT OF ARMS: *Red shield, three armed gold lions,*
passant and crowned in azure

MOTTO: *Réqué Diou*

Jean Baptiste Colbert
1619–1683

Duc de Mortemart + DAUGHTER

Marie Françoise
de Rochechouart–Mortemart
+ Duc de Chalais

André + Marie de Courbon
NOBILITY CONFIRMED IN 1688 BY 1475 PROOF.

Daniel ══════ MARRIES (2) *Marie–Elisabeth Chamillart*
MARQUIS DE TALLEYRAND-PÉRIGORD.

Charles–Daniel
1734–1788
COMTE DE PÉRIGORD.
MARRIES VICTOIRE-ELÉONORE
DE DAMAS D'ANTIGNY.

Gabriel–Marie
1726–1795

Louis–Marie
BARON DE PÉRIGORD.

Alexandre–Angélique
ARCHBISHOP OF RHEIMS;
CARDINAL-ARCHBISHOP OF PARIS
(1821).

Charles Maurice
de Talleyrand–Périgord
1754–1838
MARRIES CATHERINE-NOËL WORLÉE,
MME GRAND.

Archambaud
1762–1838
DUC DE TALLEYRAND 1817.
MARRIES MADELEINE DE SÉNOZAN.

Boson

Louis
D. IN BERLIN 1808.

Edmond
DUC DE DINO, DUC DE TALLEYRAND.
MARRIES DOROTHÉE DE COURLANDE.

Mélanie
MARRIES JUST DE NOAILLES,
PRINCE DE POIX.

Napoléon–Louis
DUC DE VALENÇAY.

Alexandre–Edmond
DUC DE DINO.

Pauline
MARRIES HENRI DE CASTELLANE.

Talleyrand

Talleyrand

THE ART OF SURVIVAL

Jean Orieux

TRANSLATED FROM THE FRENCH
BY PATRICIA WOLF

Alfred A. Knopf New York
1974

THIS IS A BORZOI BOOK
PUBLISHED BY ALFRED A. KNOPF, INC.

Library of Congress Cataloging in Publication Data:

Orieux, Jean, date.   Talleyrand; the art of survival.

Bibliography: p.   1.   Talleyrand-Périgord, Charles
Maurice de, prince de Bénévent, 1754–1838.
DC255.T307513 1974   944.04′092′4 [B]   73–8989
ISBN 0–394–47299–3

Manufactured in the United States of America
First American Edition

*To Mesdames M. Chibois and J. Pefferkorn
and to "our little universe"*

Contents

Preface

Few personalities have aroused greater hatred and greater admiration than Talleyrand. The impassioned curiosity kindled by this passionless man cannot be extinguished, for he resolved to be enigmatic and he succeeded.

The problem was to uncover the man behind the masks, a bewildering enterprise. I relied on all those who knew him, who heard him speak, who had painted him or sounded him out. There were innumerable witnesses; I had to round them up. The historian Marc Ferro gave me access to the best sources. The search for my hero was particularly perplexing at the time he linked his fate to that of Napoleon Bonaparte. Relations between those two personalities take on an entirely different aspect if history, rather than the everlasting "Napoleonic legend," is consulted. When, Marc Ferro, will a team of young historians give us the real record of the Consulate and the Empire? A study such as *L'Opposition à Napoléon* by Louis de Villefosse and Jeanine Bouissounouse casts new—and welcome—light on the Napoleonic adventure. Thanks to them, Talleyrand's role appears less mysterious and less blamable. Emile Dard's *Napoléon et Talleyrand* was of equal help to me. Michel Poniatowski's *Talleyrand aux Etats-Unis* is full of revelations concerning Talleyrand's financial activities, his courage, and his scrupulousness. *Talleyrand's Last Duchess: The Duchess of Dino,* by Françoise de Bernardy, is an intimate glimpse of Talleyrand's last twenty years. In *The Reconstruction of Europe: Talleyrand and the Congress of Vienna 1814–1815,* the historian Guglielmo Ferrero pays tribute to Talleyrand's European outlook, as Duff Cooper also has done. The *Correspondence* edited by G. Pallain dealing with the Congress of Vienna and Talleyrand's diplomatic missions to London is a valuable source, as are the *Lettres de Talleyrand* edited by Pierre Bertrand. I found myself constantly consulting Bernardine Melchior-Bonnet's *Dictionnaire de la Révolution et de l'Empire.*

Finally, we have the *Memoirs,* far less mendacious than claimed, in which Talleyrand, with cloak drawn close, picks his way gingerly among events he "neglects" to observe. A sudden burst of sincerity escapes him: seize it before it vanishes! In the long run, this practice of "forgetting" is more illuminating and less dishonest than weak excuses.

After spending three years investigating my hero and his times, I turned to Lacour-Gayet's *Talleyrand* (Payot, 1928), a veritable monument of research and historical discovery. The richness, precision, and integrity of such a work compels admiration. It confirmed much of the material I had compiled from other sources. Wherever possible throughout my book, I have acknowledged it as an indispensable guide. Of course, Lacour-Gayet's *Talleyrand* appeared fifty years ago and presents a portrait which subsequent studies have interpreted in various ways, including Dr. René Laforgue's *Talleyrand, l'homme de la France,* the psychoanalysis of a nation, and Michel Missoffe's *Le Coeur secret de Talleyrand.*

The true face of Talleyrand began to emerge in my conversations with Madame de Montgomery-Bethouart, who has my gratitude and admiration. In the trying moments Talleyrand made me endure, I was cheered by the good taste, the wit, and occasionally the patience of my friends Mesdames Chibois and Pefferkorn. I am glad they allowed me to dedicate this book to them.

The main problem was to establish my hero's features: they could not have been more immobile or elusive. He is so multifaceted, so iridescent, that during the four years of our co-existence I seemed to rediscover him every day and was sorely tempted to redefine him on each page. It would have been a great mistake. Rather than being defined, Talleyrand is meant to be accompanied. The journey through eighty-four tumultuous years is fascinating, from the seminary to the boudoir, from the altar to the gambling table, from Versailles to the shabbiest nests of intrigue. Wherever you find him, he is like silk, shimmering; the luster is evanescent, the fabric remains. Talleyrand's shimmer is at times pure scandal, at times mere escapade; it may alarm us, but the play of light is always fascinating.

No particular historian or biographer has induced this perturbing face to declare itself more openly. Rather, we must thank the contentious, anarchistic climate of our times, with its power to tear off masks. Talleyrand, who saw no danger in his "liaisons dangereuses," felt alienated by the bourgeois society of Joseph Prud'homme. His utter boredom is manifest in certain biographies published during that dreary period; by the same token, he eluded those authors, retaining his sphinxlike mask. We look at things differently now, and see the bishop, the Assembly deputy, the dissident minister as more at home in our present-day climate of dissent than among the bourgeois coattails of 1838.

The time was ripe to sit down and have a chat with Monsieur de Talleyrand. Because I refrained from preaching to him, perhaps he has shown his true face.

An African proverb says: "You are the child of your times more than the child of your father." Talleyrand is the child of several eras and several societies. Once one has pierced the mask of his impassivity, his face, for all its gentle humanity, hints at shadowy clefts untouched by the radiant light of Louis XV's century. Talleyrand is at once the contemporary of Voltaire, Mirabeau, Napoleon, Lamartine, and Balzac. He speaks Voltaire's language, operates with Mirabeau's venality, and winds up hobbling into the *"Ténébreuses Affaires"* of Balzac's *Comédie humaine*.

Though committed to the present, he is always immutable. In every historic upheaval, he was the vital vehicle of the grandeur, vices, elegance, and charm of former times. Faithful to the wig and to the social strictures of the Enlightenment, he was unfaithful to whatever seemed ephemeral in the society born of the Revolution: the politicians, their makeshift governments, their rhetoric and solemn promises. For him, the one thing transcending individuals, even Napoleon, was civilization—Voltaire's civilization, based on freedom, the arts of peace, trade, and prosperity. He regarded France as the incarnation of this civilization and therefore more sublime than her governments, rulers, or acrobats. He treated them all accordingly, without apology. Sarcasm, not his vices, made enemies for him. People objected to his behavior—his limp as well as his conduct. Both are plainly sinuous; like the universe itself, our hero's life is a series of curves. An infallible instinct had cautioned him that meandering was the smoothest, surest path to success. Through anxious, violent years we follow his leisurely, perfumed wake, which hugs the peaks of European society. Buzzing wasps surround him, and we hear: "Betrayal! Betrayal!" Whom has he "betrayed"? For what purpose? In politics, innovation is always betrayal. I have used the word in quotation marks as I feel it belongs to the pamphleteer's arsenal rather than the psychologist's vocabulary. Needless to say, I have not masked his failings, especially the ones he dodged so nimbly. I have caught him red-handed in the shadiest operations, in company with prominent figures of his day—including some distinguished moralizers. Bourrienne writes: "History will speak as well of M. de Talleyrand as his contemporaries have spoken ill." In fact, for a century people have been content to repeat things that envy prompted his most illustrious contemporaries to say. Bourgeois politicians have made a practice of vilifying one of the greatest servants of France and Europe. Flaubert scorns this stupidity on the French public's part in his *Dictionnaire des idées reçues* (*Dictionary of Prevailing Notions*): "Prince de Talleyrand: run him down." Homais, Badinguet, Joseph Prud'homme, and all their bourgeois counterparts obeyed like robots. I have preferred to listen to Talleyrand. Day after day I have watched him live. Few persons are more seductive than this great, benevolent aristocrat of profound and secret sensibilities. When discussing his own ideas, he was too wonderfully intelligent to bore anyone and left that to less gifted souls; savoir-faire was his private reserve. From his own century he derived the taste for gracious living and surrounded himself with all the comforts of it. He was supremely generous to his family, his servants, his diplomatic staff, his retainers at Valençay and in Benevento, and his lifelong friends. At close range Talleyrand turns out to be of "doubtful immorality."

Will "rehabilitation" be the next word? It would not offend me, though my aim was neither to rehabilitate nor to condemn him, but simply to let him live for a spell. If I succeeded, he needs no more judges; alive, he will rehabilitate or condemn himself. In any event, neither death nor neglect can erase the features of a man sprung from the roots of history. He belongs to a timeless breed whose wisdom, coated with vice, old as the world, will live on as long as there *is* a world.

Part One
1754–1796

Golden Lions Crowned Azure on a Blood-Soaked Field

Some lives are shaped in childhood, others in the course of time; still others must reach the threshold of advanced age before their purpose is ˉclear. But not the life of Charles Maurice de Talleyrand-Périgord, born on February 2, 1754, whose family bore an illustrious name and had held a pre-eminent rank in society since the ninth century. At birth, his life pattern was set: opulence and renown, coupled with spiritual privation. He limped from the start, yet he was destined to go far.

For Charles Maurice, everything began at the beginning. No victim of some absurdly romantic twist of fate, he had instead an inner drive that he tried to master through reason and through the self-image he firmly maintained, though his detractors call him a chameleon.

He was born a Talleyrand-Périgord—the vital secret of his career, which must not be underestimated simply because only once during his long life did he allude to his noble blood. "Never to be discussed but remembered always" was the key to his attitude. We cannot possibly understand the man if we disregard his ancestry and the immense pride he took in it. He hid his feelings about such matters—and others—making his conduct at times seem enigmatic; yet certain aspects of it become clear once we see what the Périgord family was like and what Charles Maurice knew about his forebears. Talleyrand belonged to the most ancient and irreproachable French nobility. The direct descent of the Talleyrands from the sovereign counts of Périgord had been confirmed by royal patents in 1475, and again in 1613, when the castellanies of Grignols and Excideuil became respectively a county and a marquisate; it was reconfirmed in 1688 and once more in the eighteenth century. Wilgrin, first count of Périgord and Angoulême, received his title from a relative, Charles the Bald. Wilgrin died in 886. His family thus was

3

related to the Carolingian dynasty. The lineage was transmitted through the eldest male heirs down to the year 1440.

The history of the counts of Périgord is terrifying. In the six hundred years between the ninth century and the fifteenth, the chronicle of their county is an endless record of pillage, murder, rape, torture, and kidnapping. Hélie I had the bishop of Limoges's eyes gouged out. The vicomte de Limoges managed to capture Hélie and would have repaid him in kind had the count not escaped after seducing the jailer's daughter. So the vicomte gouged out the eyes of one of Hélie's cousins, who was on hand.

In 990, in Tours, Adalbert, comte de Périgord, defied his suzerain Hugh Capet, comte de Paris—also king of France, a title acquired all too recently, no doubt, to please the irascible lord of Périgord—whose insolence had elicited Hugh Capet's reminder: "Who made thee count?" Adalbert flung back his historic retort: "Who made thee king?" Hugh Capet was reluctant to tangle with so powerful a rival. Our Talleyrand knew that; Capet's descendants also knew it.

The Périgords' insubordination, rapacity, and pride were a plague upon their vassals. They plundered their own capital. Périgueux included two communities: the town and the château. Peasants and artisans cowered behind the town walls in fear of their lives, seeking refuge from their lord, whose normal duty was to protect them.

The period of the Hundred Years' War was sheer disaster. The counts of Périgord—and they were not unique—deserted the French camp for the English, or, more precisely, the Capetians for the Plantagenets. As a result, towns and countryside were devastated time and again by the warring factions.

Hélie V of Périgord joined forces with Bertrand de Born, a troubadour whose lyric moods were wholly unreliable, and with the seigneur de Hautefort against Richard the Lion-Hearted, governor of Aquitaine. Hélie's allies deserted him because he was "flac et vil"—cowardly and vacillating. Later, the three became reconciled for the sole purpose of pressing Richard to revolt against his father Henry II Plantagenet, and were aided by the beautiful and formidable Eleanor of Aquitaine, Henry's estranged wife. Blood never stopped flowing in that unhappy region.

The Périgords rallied to the English crown. Archambaud V pledged support to his friend the Black Prince, governor of Guyenne, and sent his brother Talleyrand to Paris to bargain for an agreement with Charles V (the Wise)—at a price. Preferring negotiation to bloodshed, Charles paid 40,000 livres, an astounding sum. Even then the Talleyrand name fetched a high price, a family tradition thereafter. The Talleyrand of that day received a commission of 10,000 livres. As far back as the fourteenth century, then, the family managed to make quite a handsome living by wagering on heraldic leopards or lilies, as the occasion demanded.

The Talleyrand of those times also made war now and then. He joined forces with Duguesclin to recover the rich and powerful abbey of Chancelade, near Périgueux, from the English. The valiant Breton and the crafty Périgord made a success of the venture; but while Duguesclin was splitting English skulls, his ally stripped the abbey bare, leaving the walls intact only because he could not take them with him. By the fifteenth century, the wretched county was reduced to bloody ruins and ravaged fields; the violence and predation of the last two counts, Archambaud V and VI, set a new family record.

They organized and led robber bands that preyed on their own domain. The peasants pleaded for the king's aid, but Paris was far away. The French kings did intercede a number of times, but never strenuously enough. Charles VI finally put an end to the grim saga of the elder branch. Archambaud VI, defeated and deserted by all his cohorts, died in Bordeaux in 1440, banished and dispossessed of his titles and estates.

The county was awarded to Louis d'Orléans, the king's brother, whose fortune it did not enhance, for he was assassinated in the rue Barbette in Paris by the duc de Bourgogne. The county then passed to his personable son, taken prisoner at Agincourt, the delightful poet Louis d'Orléans, who in his dismal dungeon, far less concerned for Périgord than for the miserable weather outside, wrote: "Le temps a laissé son manteau de vent de froidure et de pluie."

The county was sold to Jean de Blois, comte de Penthièvre, of the House of Brittany—royal blood. Through marriage, it passed to the d'Albret family and to Antoine de Bourbon—royal blood again—and finally was transferred, with the visconty of Limoges, to Henry IV, who possessed both for the French crown. Our Talleyrand knew that the destiny of Périgord and its counts, descendants of Carolingian stock, the very essence of France, had paralleled—with no less eminence—the fortunes of the counts of Paris and their lineage. Talleyrand always believed it was his birthright to have a voice in the vital affairs of France, which were, after all, merely an extension of his family affairs.

Charles Maurice was not a descendant of the aforesaid counts.[1] His link with the main branch of the family goes back to 1166, to comte Hélie V de Périgord, known as Talleyrand. Hélie's eldest son, Archambaud, inherited the county and perpetuated his appalling line until 1440.

5

His second son, Hélie, seigneur of Grignols, initiated the younger branch from which our Talleyrand descends. Hélie de Grignols died in 1205 in the Holy Land; his grandson's marriage to Agnès de Chalais brought that branch into hereditary possession of the seignory of Chalais and, in the fifteenth century, the title prince of Chalais.

Among those bestial seigneurs, real lions armed and crowned—like the rampant charges on the family coat of arms, claws bared, on a crimson field—were two Talleyrands of opposite, but not conflicting, temperaments. Their pride and ambition made them true Talleyrands, but their dominating and acquisitive impulses changed, or rather, took on a pattern. They were "lions crowned azure," foreshadowing in a striking way their grand-nephew.

The first was Hélie de Talleyrand, son of comte Hélie VII and Brunissende de Foix. He was born in Périgueux in 1301 and died in Avignon in 1364. A churchman, he became archdeacon of Périgueux, dean of Richmond, the county of York's diocese, abbot of Chancelade, bishop of Limoges, and ultimately was raised to the cardinalate in 1331 by a kinsman, Pope John XXII. His personality is more interesting than his titles. He played an important role in the church, and could have been Pope, had he not refused the office. Petrarch said of him: "He found it more satisfying to be a Pope-maker than a Pope." For him, the business and intrigue of courts, ecclesiastic councils, and armies had greater appeal. He performed heroic services, forestalling war and violence at the risk of his life. One of the most remarkable transactions he conducted, and which would have spared France a disaster had King John the Good heeded him, took place before the Battle of Poitiers. Hélie sided with the French, but remained dean of Richmond and a friend of the prince of Wales, commander of the English army. Back and forth he shuttled between the two camps, trying to avert bloodshed. He knew the French were unprepared for battle, and that their disarray and blustering would only bring them to ruin. At last he persuaded the prince of Wales to refuse combat and withdraw, provided the French king would do likewise and agree to discuss peace.

John the Good and a party of harebrained knights jeered at cardinal de Talleyrand and flung themselves at the foe. The rest is history. Despite the rebuff, the cardinal ordered his men to stand by King John. The English disregarded his role in the affair and bore him no grudge. He parleyed once more in an effort to mitigate the disastrous defeat. A remarkably cultured man, he had a keen, discriminating, and searching mind. Petrarch admired him. His broadmindedness was legendary. In Toulouse he founded a school which reserved half its enrollment for children from Périgord. New applicants customarily were proposed by the count, but were admitted only if the student body found them acceptable. What is more, the administrative chaplains were elected by a two-thirds vote of the students—like popes in the electoral conclave. Monseigneur de Talleyrand was, in the fourteenth century, incredibly avant-gardist.

His critics censure him, however, on several accounts: he was fond of luxury and fond of money; and with all his generosity and lavish spending, he still managed to shower a colossal fortune upon his nephews. Since such a fortune was not amassed from the miserable dues of his miserable vassals, it was rumored that he had a hand in commercial ventures not strictly in keeping with the dignity of his office, and that his prodigious diplomatic transactions hinted strongly at lucrative financial operations. He was also said to have been involved in the kidnapping of Marie d'Anjou, the queen of Naples's sister, perpetrated by his own nephew the comte de Duras, whom the cardinal afterwards dragged out of prison and tortured. But is there anything one cannot say about a Talleyrand at once cardinal, diplomat, educator, and financier, even though he performs all those functions admirably? In religious fervor alone was he markedly deficient.

Whom did he resemble? Surely not his father; perhaps a grand-nephew named Charles Maurice.

At the end of the fifteenth century and the beginning of the sixteenth, another Talleyrand, a direct ancestor of our hero, deserves an accolade. Jean de Talleyrand, seigneur of Grignols and of Chalais, vicomte de Fronsac, was known as Monsieur de Grignaux (for Grignols) at Charles VIII's court, where he was chamberlain (his descendant our Charles Maurice was chamberlain, too, under Napoleon, Louis XVIII, and Charles X). Brantôme knew him and also referred to him by that name.*

In addition to being high steward of the royal household and knight of honor to Queen Anne, Jean de Talleyrand was delegated by the nobles of Périgord to represent them in the Estates-General of 1484. After the death of Charles VIII, he pursued his duties (and his fortune) under Louis XII. Brantôme praised him and the friendship he shared with the king warmly, saying that Jean was a born host, a delightful conversationalist in French and in other languages, and a great success in the diplomatic missions he undertook. Behind the scenes, he would

---

* In 1834, an enemy of Talleyrand's seized upon the name to declare that he was not of the nobility, and that his ancestry could be traced to someone named Grignaux.

manage to play rather harmless pranks with not the slightest reverence for royalty. Queen Anne asked him to teach her a few words in Spanish to greet the Spanish ambassador. Brantôme writes: "M. de Grignaux produced a smutty little phrase that she promptly memorized . . . M. de Grignaux told this to the king, who approved, knowing his [chamberlain's] lively and jesting wit." But when the queen found out the meaning of what she was going to say to the ambassador, she became so angry that "she threatened to cashier M. de Grignaux."

Jean de Talleyrand performed a special service in Louis XII's household. When no male heir came of his union with Anne of Brittany, the king married the sixteen-year-old sister of Henry VIII. That was no solution, however, for Louis had aged prematurely. Furthermore, the idle young queen was a threat, and no one realized it sooner than Louise of Savoy, whose son François d'Angoulême was presumptive heir to the throne. If the king was impotent, might they not induce some willing gentleman to stand in for him? Because Louise wanted her son to be king, she charged Talleyrand de Grignaux to spy on the young queen and to keep anything in breeches out of her path.

A herculean task, for Henry VIII's sister was, as he put it, with greater accuracy than respect, "more a madwoman than a queen." She loved the duke of Suffolk and had him made ambassador to Paris. Talleyrand needed all his wits to thwart the lovers' schemes. On many a sleepless night he roamed the palace corridors; his vigilance was repaid, for at Louis XII's death, Louise of Savoy's cherished son took the throne as Francis I. From the start, Monsieur de Talleyrand de Grignaux was therefore on excellent terms with the new monarch, as he had been with the two previous ones. Needless to say, finding favor with three sovereigns was not the customary fortune of most courtiers.

Resourcefulness was plainly a family characteristic. Nevertheless, when the elder branch was dispossessed, the younger one, lords of Grignols, Chalais, and Excideuil, was unable to reclaim the county. They retained their titles and first names—Hélie, Archambaud, Adalbert—which recur over and over in succeeding generations from the ninth century to the twentieth. As late as the nineteenth century, there were a number of Hélies in Périgord. The name "de Talleyrand" came to be the established patronymic. The first two counts had been given the surname "de Taillefer"; "Taille rang," or "Talleran," appeared in the tenth century before changing to "Talleyrand," and was pronounced Tay-rawn or Tal-rawn. In present-day Périgord it is still pronounced Tay-rawn; and in Rheims, people speak of Monseigneur de Tay-rawn. A police report dated 1792 records the name "Tailleran," indicating the way it was pronounced in Paris.

The titles and first names are only part of the legacy. Certain predilections also were passed down: fearless audacity, combined with a flair for negotiation and acting as go-between; also, an overwhelming urge for luxury, financed by astute dealings—in short, the velvet paw, razor-clawed, of the king of beasts. These ingredients, in whatever proportions heredity chanced to dispense them, produced a variety of personalities, all marked however by at least one dominant feature: arrogance. "Rien que Dieu" was their motto; its meaning, given the humor of those "lions armed and crowned," is scarcely open to doubt: God in Heaven is not likely to be a nuisance, and the king in Paris is nearly as far away. Leaving only Périgord—where no one else counts. "Rien que Talleyrand" is their true motto, far more honest than the other.

In 1613, the head of the clan was Daniel de Talleyrand, prince de Chalais, comte de Grignols, marquis d'Excideuil, baron de Beauville and Mareuil, all those estates in Périgord. He had married Jeanne de Montluc, daughter of the illustrious marshal. The comte de Chalais, one of their sons, who was a friend of Louis XIII and of Gaston d'Orléans, tried twice to murder Richelieu. His first attempt was pardoned; the second cost him his head. Royal intervention spared him from torture, but the novice headsman who decapitated him at Nantes in 1626 swung his ax over thirty times. There were always decided drawbacks to being a Talleyrand. Gabriel, their great-grandson, was killed at the siege of Barcelona; their grandson, the marquis de Talleyrand-Périgord, fell at the siege of Tournai in 1745. The marquis had married Marie-Elisabeth Chamillart, whose grandfather had been Louis XIV's minister of finance, and whose mother, Marie-Françoise de Rochechouart-Mortemart, was the daughter of the duc de Mortemart, who had wed Colbert's daughter. Talleyrand's ancestors thus were Colbert and Chamillart, and his extraordinary business acumen cannot have suffered from their legacy. The Mortemart-Rochechouart vein of the family conferred noble blood as prestigious as his own, as well as a singularly brilliant and caustic wit—known as "the Mortemart wit"—which our hero's great-great-aunt, the marquise de Montespan, applied so effectively to her dealings with the Sun King. Two of his ancestors died in battle, thus proving that the Talleyrand-Périgords paid with their lives. Their fortune, however, matched neither their valor nor their pedigree. It seems that in the antechambers of Versailles, their ministerial enterprise brought far shabbier rewards than did their wartime exploits. Though it dimmed their glory not one bit, it probably inspired their grandson Charles Maurice, whose story we are approaching, to meditate on the glaring discrepancy between the splendid service of his ancestors and their paltry returns therefrom. He would succeed in overcoming the shameful neglect which governments dispense to those who serve them too well—by getting paid in advance.

The eldest child of the marquis de Talleyrand and Marie Chamillart was Charles-Daniel, comte de Talleyrand-Périgord, born in 1734 and the father of our hero. Their third son was Alexandre-Angélique, of whom we shall hear as coadjutor of the ducal archbishop of Rheims, then as archbishop of Rheims, and finally as cardinal and archbishop of Paris at his death in 1821. He was Charles Maurice's uncle. In 1751, at the age of sixteen, Charles-Daniel married Alexandrine Marie-Victoire de Damas d'Antigny. Her noble Burgundian pedigree was impeccable, but her dowry, alas, was a mere 15,000 livres, no more than her husband possessed, though the eldest son of such a large family. For persons of their rank, the sum was trifling. She was six years older than he. They fell in love, and stayed in love. Their marriage, in that licentious era, was nothing short of miraculous, for they were faithful to the end. The comte de Périgord commanded a regiment; the countess had a place at court. They were wed in Paris in the new and gleaming white Church of Saint-Sulpice, near which they were to live with their mother, the marquise de Talleyrand, at 4, rue Garancière. In that house, now altered but still standing, their four children were born. The first boy died in infancy; the second, Charles Maurice, born on February 2, 1754, became the eldest son; then came Archambaud, in 1762; and Boson, in 1764.

The Lioncel Is Treated Like an Alley Cat

Charles Maurice was baptized on the day he was born; his godfather was his uncle, the future archbishop. From the baptistry of Saint-Sulpice the infant went directly into the care of a wet-nurse, who took him home with her to the faubourg Saint-Jacques. That was all he saw of his parents' roof. Four years later, they still had not inquired of him. Nobody learned of the accident that lamed him. When he was only a few months old, his nurse had put him on top of a chest of drawers; he fell, breaking his foot. The poor woman did nothing about the injury, and when the damaged bones eventually knit, he was clubfooted for life. His affliction is known as "accidental varus." This appalling accident, which one might expect to have evoked pity, has given rise instead to the most malevolent insinuations. Certain biographers suggest that his deformed foot was hereditary—not an infirmity, but a taint. How convenient! Dr. Cabanis asserts that a hereditary clubfoot is associated with certain mental and moral anomalies, a theory which enabled apologists of the Restoration to attribute the ex-bishop of Autun's apostasy to mental instability. That diagnosis won faint support, however, for among the many vices one might ascribe to Talleyrand, feeblemindedness—even periodic—would be hard to prove. So much for the learned opinion of Dr. Cabanès, who appears to refute Talleyrand's dictum: "Fools are not rare, only quacks."

The clubfoot was not congenital. In a letter to her mother in 1755, while her first-born was still alive and the year-old Charles Maurice in the care of a wet-nurse, Madame de Talleyrand said: "I hope you will enjoy seeing your grandchildren. My brother's children are perhaps prettier, but mine are lively and good-natured. . . . " She did not know, obviously, that her second son was lame.

From infancy, he was unable to walk without the aid of a makeshift crutch. Talleyrand's shoes may be seen in Valençay and in the Carnavalet Museum in Paris. His right foot was deformed; the shoe, shaped like an elephant's foot, had a metal brace supporting an iron rod which passed up the inside of his leg and attached to a leather band fastening just below the knee. An exquisite device for torture.

The accident brought tragedy to Talleyrand's life, abruptly twisting the child's whole future.

Like all autobiographers, Talleyrand defended himself in his *Memoirs*. This we acknowledge, and also the fact that most of what he says is credible; on the other hand, what he leaves unsaid is highly disturbing. Except on rare occasions—to be noted as they occur—he lied only by omission. His statements are true because a flawless lie has yet to be invented and because elaborating a lie is stupid, vulgar, and utterly useless—the antithesis of Talleyrand. He believed in the virtue of dissimulation, and told the truth to conceal important and dangerous information that still remains secret. His sincerity fooled the public, just as he intended.

The account of his childhood in the *Memoirs* is accurate. He was put out to nurse for four years with a poor woman who struggled to live. Talleyrand never uttered a reproach against her. But on several occasions he dared to suggest that no one gave him enough love, a confession for which he has been criticized. Yet how timid were those regrets—blaming no one—that he was not looked after properly and assured a happy childhood. He had the temerity to yearn for his mother's love. Nothing suggests that Talleyrand was wrong. His parents were so attached to each other that the children scarcely counted. Their neglect is also partly explained by the current child-rearing practices of their peers. Charles Maurice's parents were among the select group of courtiers attending the dauphin and the daughters of Louis XV, a notoriously rigid circle, bound by ceremony and convention and utterly opposed to change. To blame them without weighing the circumstances would be unfair; nor should their "severity" be taken to task, for it was the general rule. "Sensibility" had not yet wrought its havoc on human hearts. A son of the maréchal de Noailles relates that when visiting his father's apartment at Versailles, he got up at five in the morning, gulped down some soup, did lessons with his tutor, rode horseback, had a second plate of cabbage or turnip soup with some boiled beef or pork, resumed his studies, and was so hungry at times that he would try to snatch a scrap of meat off the gold platters returning from his father's table—a theft which, had the servants reported it, would have cost him a whipping. But that boy at least lived with his parents, saw them, spoke to them, and was whipped by them: he knew they cared for him. Twenty years later, Rousseau was the rage, and ladies who had never rocked a baby's cradle could be seen nursing their infants in opera boxes: that was the fashion. It did not make them any better mothers.

Charles Maurice's parents had time-consuming duties at court; the count attended the dauphin, the countess was lady of honor. Their circuit between Paris and Versailles may not have left them much time to think about their own children. In any event, the comte and comtesse de Périgord were singular in one respect: they treated their lame son differently from their other children. Severity can be explained, but not injustice, and if any scandal existed, it involved the double standard, not the harsh discipline. The scandal is nothing new and was brought to light by the count's own brother, the bailli de Périgord. Something shocking must have affected his nephew if Charles Maurice's uncle went to such lengths to teach his sister-in-law a drastic lesson.

The incident took place while the boy was living with his nurse in the faubourg Saint-Jacques. His elder brother had just died and Archambaud was not yet born, making Charles Maurice the sole family heir.[1] His uncle, the bailli de Périgord, a naval officer, returned from a long voyage and wanted to meet his nephew. He was directed to the village where the child had remained virtually forsaken.

He found him in a snowbound field chasing larks with his foster brother, a pair of little ragamuffins. The indignant naval officer caught the boy

Maurice and took him, rags and all, straight into his mother's drawing room where she was receiving formal calls. "Sister," he said, "here is the direct descendant of the princes of Chalais, whose coat of arms bears gules, three lions rampant or langued, armed, surmounted by a prince's coronet on the shield, a ducal coronet on the mantle, with the motto *Réqué Diou.*

"So now, your highness," he said to the boy, "kiss this lady who is your mother."

A rather appalling scene, certain details of which are fabricated, of course: the lark-chasing by a four-year-old crippled boy and the little prince in tatters entering his mother's visitor-filled salon are probably the narrator's own whimsy; the final kiss is appended to embarrass the mother, but in reality it was never given. The truth is more dreadful: Talleyrand was never embraced by either his mother or father. Apart from that, the anecdote is basically accurate.

Talleyrand himself, exiled to London in 1792, a ruined outcast, was the one who, in a rare mood of depression, made that disclosure to an all too sympathetic ear. Why, when he detested private confessions and barred them from his *Memoirs*? Because, in a trying moment of his life, he returned to the central source of his grief: parental neglect and the crippling injury resulting from it. If they had provided medical care soon enough, could he not have been cured?

How can we believe that his parents were fond of him when they turned over the lame child to his great-grandmother shortly after his elder brother's death? He was taken out of the desolate Paris suburbs and placed in the care of a governess—conscientious, to be sure, and whom he loved and respected just as he had loved his foster mother. Talleyrand never reproached those who served him; he was, in contrast, kind, grateful, and even affectionate.

At the age of four, the boy was packed off with his governess in the Paris-Bordeaux coach, actually a public rattletrap invariably crammed with the most ordinary travelers. It was the cheapest means of transport. The coach was to let them off at the château de Chalais, his great-grandmother's home. They were carted along for seventeen days in making the 260-mile trip. Mademoiselle Charlemagne was his governess's name —perhaps destiny's touch of flourish to that sordid journey which, for the young seigneur, was merely exile.

His parents had already made their decision: the lame boy, though now the eldest, was not to be their heir. The Chalais journey was symbolic. This child, who never laughed, never played, never was hugged, and never lived with his parents, this pathetic child had sensed that he was "different." Maurice by now was grievously wounded. He had been effaced from the family circle; no one had spelled it out, of course, but a gnawing despair warned him of his fate. A terrible sense of frustration and injustice compounded the curse of being crippled—and painfully crippled. We cannot forget that, until his dying day, Talleyrand's every step recalled the pain not only of his infirmity but also of the forfeit imposed on him in infancy. The tragedy of this keenly intelligent, sensitive, and perceptive boy was to have had the indelible disgrace inflicted on him by his own parents. They were the first to make him feel he was not like other children, not really their son, or the brother of their other sons. All the rest follows. The affronts, the perils, the insults lying ahead of him were blunted by his incurable despair. He never recovered from the denial of love and justice. Most of his contemporaries, his antagonists, and his biographers have ignored, or tried to ignore, the private grief of his deplorable childhood. Talleyrand was molded into an unnatural son. His sole offense was having parents who treated him like an intruder. Their reasons, however one chooses to judge them, reduce to a single principle: no son of theirs was entitled to both a clubfoot and the Talleyrand name. They would not let him forget it.

Fundamentals of the Enjoyment of Living

He had experienced the most abject childhood until his departure for Chalais; adolescence would deepen the wound. But in the interval, he came to know the springtime of Chalais. His great-grandmother Marie-Françoise de Rochechouart-Mortemart, daughter of the duc de Mortemart, and granddaughter of Colbert, was seventy-two in 1758 when four-year-old Maurice came to live with her. The boy entered an enchanted world, spending nearly two years with that great lady who had known the splendor of Louis XIV's court. For still another reason he found her incomparably glamorous and charming: she loved him. For the first time, someone not a nurse, or governess, or servant loved him. He bloomed. A great-grandmother's smile and kiss, his first tokens of love, were a soothing balm on the incurable wound deep within him. "My stay at Chalais made a profound impression on me," he said in his *Memoirs*. That tender, undemonstrative affection had the face, voice, and elegant bearing that stirred the young lord's deepest yearnings and inclinations. Unconsciously, he found his own identity. By observing and listening to his great-grandmother and her little court, he slipped into the way of life to which he was born and which he could see at last with his own eyes. There at Chalais, between the ages of four and six, he formed a certain image of society and of himself based on an instinctive and solid conviction that he was meant to enjoy the same enduring splendor as the venerable princess, and to become a great nobleman. Whether he were prince of Chalais or elsewhere—or nowhere—did not matter; he resolved to be and to appear a prince of decorum at all times and in all situations, regardless of fashion, public opinion, criticism or flattery, of revolutions, and even of success. To be a Talleyrand-Périgord was the rarest birthright. His idea of nobility was not to parade his pedigree, but to impose his superiority and to educate others by his presence alone.

It was she who initiated him into that private cult of aristocracy. "Madame de Chalais was a person of great distinction; her mind, her speech, her bearing, and the timbre of her voice were most enchanting. She had the celebrated wit of the Mortemarts, her own name." The admission that followed is to the point, and startling: "She liked me." A modest commonplace at once revealing and concealing the depths of his unclaimed affection, his speechless delight, the rapture engulfing a child's heart—a highly sensitive, withdrawn, and sorrowful child. "She gave me the kind of affection I had never known. She was the first woman in my family to show me tenderness." Only by omission does Talleyrand mourn the love his mother never gave him. To have blamed or rebuked her would have won him less sympathy; although some biographers choose to call that an insult to his parents, it is more likely the voice of his intense bitterness.

Toward the end of his life, still radiant with the warmth of his single childhood love, he wrote in his *Memoirs:* "She was also the first to teach me the joy of loving—bless her for it! Yes, I loved her dearly. I treasure her memory. How often have I missed her throughout my life. How often and how bitterly have I realized the value of true affection from one's own family. . . ."

He delighted in the somewhat feudal and pleasantly urbane little court attending his great-grandmother: "A number of gentlemen of the ancient aristocracy [he does not neglect their titles] made up my grandmother's little court, where feudal servility had no place, and courteous conduct accompanied the loftiest sentiments." Those were his prime values: courteous conduct and lofty sentiments. They were the heart of social intercourse; but for them, society would be a jungle. Talleyrand was so profoundly influenced by the court at Chalais, small as it was yet highly refined in speech and decorum, that throughout his life and wherever he went, he tried to re-create that magical miniature universe. He

15

succeeded, toward the end, at Valençay, which was the last "court" France would ever have. He recorded the names of those venerable nobles—some of whose families still exist in Périgord—"whose pleasure it was to escort her to Sunday Mass in the parish church, attending her with the utmost dignity and courtesy. Next to my grandmother's prayer bench was a little chair for me." Recalling those figures out of the past, he said: "Like their ancestral châteaux, they were imposing and solid; though the light was dim, it reached in with a soft glow: with leisurely dignity, they proceeded toward a more enlightened civilization." Genuine wisdom: the unhurried evolution toward a more enlightened civilization; the voice is that of Voltaire. No earthly paradise, but rather the arduous and purposeful advance of a nation toward increasing ease and liberty, aided by an informed and sympathetic nobility. Calm, deliberate progress: at the age of five, he sensed already the tempo of his whole life.

He was both observer of and actor in the spectacle of that extremely cultivated little world which served as his introduction to court life. There he trained to become Europe's most polished grand chamberlain by watching those elderly nobles attend his great-grandmother. Could a soulless and heartless child have been so sensitive to the refinements of ceremony and courtly grace?

At the age of five, like a chief of protocol he was already noting details of the princess's attire when, on her return from Mass, she would receive the poor in the château's apothecary: "My grandmother sat in a great velvet armchair behind a large black lacquer table; her silk gown was lace-trimmed with folds of ribbons and bows along the sleeves, according to the season, and three tiers of boldly figured cuffs; a tippet, a bonnet with a butterfly bow, and a black coif tied under her chin completed her Sunday costume, more elaborate than her daily one. . . ."

Another delightful discovery he made was that the common folk of Chalais had respect and affection for him. His aristocratic pride obviously thrived on that, as well as his need for kindness and sympathy. Ordinarily so reserved, he confessed astonishment at hearing the peasants express fondness for his family, extending to him. They often spoke to him about the generosity of Chalais's lords: one peasant owed his plot of land to them; another, his house; still another, a precious object; one count built the church, another, the market place. "Good trees don't deteriorate," a peasant told him, "you too will be good." Here is the aging prince de Talleyrand's warm recollection of the people of Chalais: "If, in my life, I have maintained a certain dignity without arrogance, if I love and respect my elders, I have Chalais and my grandmother's presence to thank for revealing to me the good feelings lavished on my relatives in that region, and which delighted them. . . ."[1]

He also noted—a sign of his keen sensitivity—that his contact with those good people taught him to communicate to simple folk "feelings, not overly familiar, of affection and even tenderness." It is quite true that he avoided familiarity on his own part and discouraged others from it. Familiarity, in his eyes, was not a measure of sensitivity, but a vulgar means of flattering subordinates or an attempt to outdo one's peers or superiors. When an occasion seemed to demand flattery, imposture, and deceit, he chose other means to achieve his purpose.

At Chalais he learned to read and write and even to speak a bit of the local dialect. He could undoubtedly cite and understand the Talleyrand motto "Réque Diou." In that secure, warm little world, no one ever made him conscious of his infirmity. He limped, as in Paris, but here the suffering was confined to his foot. He basked in tenderness.

After less than two years, he was sent back to Paris. Tearfully, he said good-bye to his great-grandmother. He never saw her again, though they were always together in spirit. In his heart, the princesse de Chalais remained the radiant image of love, nobility, and kindness. Mademoiselle Charlemagne came with him again on another exhausting trip in the same old coach, which reached Paris at dawn on September 1, 1760. He was six and a half. He had been happy—his last happiness.

"Be a Good Boy" . . . *and Not Too Conspicuous*

Suddenly he was handed over to destiny. An old family servant awaited him on the rue d'Enfer when the Bordeaux coach arrived. "He took me straight to the Collège d'Harcourt. At noon I was at the refectory table." What a reception: after seventeen days spent rattling around the countryside, and two years of separation, his parents were not concerned about his health, or his lameness, or how he was getting along. They were not even curious enough to find out what their eldest son was like. They imprisoned him like a criminal.

At school, he struck up a friendship with Auguste de Choiseul-Gouffier, two years his senior, which was to be lifelong. "He shared, and still shares, all the anxieties, the pleasures, and the hopes that stirred me throughout my life." Talleyrand must have liked school because his teachers and classmates were fonder of him than was his family. It was not the same as Chalais, of course, but then he realized the uniqueness of Chalais and, without a murmur, adjusted to boarding school just as he had to the faubourg Saint-Jacques.

His philosophy instructor was a certain abbé Duval, whom he did not take too seriously. He observed ironically, without enlarging on the point: "He had issued his little tract against Newton." Voltaire would have ridiculed the pamphlet, which neither dislodged Newton's theory nor enhanced the abbé's prestige in the eyes of his alert pupil. Another instructor, abbé Hardy, gave lessons to him and his cousin De La Suze. He learned little from either the abbé or his cousin, who were nondescripts.

After the incompetent abbé Hardy, he had a tutor named Monsieur Hullot, mad as a hatter and shortly replaced by Monsieur Langlois, whose sole interest was French history and the daily calendar of court ceremonial. This amiable man filled the boy's head with a pack of nonsense, including the date of every court ball. Never critical, Talleyrand observed wryly: "If, in later life, I yielded to the attraction of taking part in great public affairs, the urge was not inspired by Monsieur Langlois." Surely not, judging from the mental equipment he furnished the boy. Langlois was forgiven nonetheless, and his name is on record as one of the prince de Talleyrand's intimate callers in the year 1828. In every drawing room along the rue Saint-Florentin, the old tutor was a familiar sight in his silk habit and glass buttons, with his buckled shoes, spindly legs encased in black stockings, the tobacco pouch the size of a sugar bowl which he waved about, and the huge checkered handkerchief into which he spouted learning as flimsy as the powder on his wig. No matter, for Talleyrand cherished friendships, even that of his inept teacher, because Langlois was a kindly soul, like the people of Chalais, and because good breeding and social poise were his supreme values. Also, Langlois's penury was sufficient cause for his former pupil to aid him. The comte and comtesse de Périgord had their son and his teacher to dinner once a week during his school years. "After the meal," Talleyrand relates, "we returned to school always with the same message in our ears: 'Be a good boy, and please Monsieur l'abbé.'" That was the viaticum. What was wrong with it? Were they not giving him good advice? Monotonous, some would say, but sound.

If further proof is needed of the child's consistent moral neglect, it is the total absence of "sayings" and "habits" which families and intimates love to relate (or invent) and which they cherish as marks of extraordinary intelligence in men of renown. For Talleyrand, the record is blank. Are we to assume that such an exceptional child passed unnoticed? Or that no one remarked his gifts? Both are probably true. He was still withdrawn, for the only people he might like to have attracted were not drawn to him. Today we know that the most paralyzing force on a young mind is an abnormal emotional environment, and that children who lack affection are often poor students. Talleyrand relates that he never received any award for scholarship. He admits that he could have done better work, which is not hard to believe. To please whom? He was no fool: "The faint praise I received in order to avoid drawing attention cast a pall on my early years."

He was said to be a depraved child, a myth that gained credit, for how could an apostate priest and bishop have been good, submissive, and chaste in his youth? He was in fact an exceedingly docile boy, somewhat withdrawn, sad, and spiritless. Not depraved, but secretive. He did not display his intelligence or his penetrating mind, memory, and observation. Others ought to have discovered those gifts—and would have, with a little love. The story that follows was published in 1834 as the "truth" about the prince de Talleyrand's childhood—raving nonsense unworthy of repetition, were it not the now accepted picture of him. It is a pure witch's tale, involving a fictitious tutor named Fouquet, no trace of whom has ever been found. This imaginary character is endowed with no less than prophetic insight, and on first meeting his pupil is supposed to have declared: "You will never amount to more than an amiable rake." A strange way to begin a semester. He is said to have launched the rumor that the fifteen-year-old Maurice de Périgord, a boarder at the Collège d'Harcourt and under his supervision (how lax will become evident) managed to have his way with three young girls. Three! And sisters, at that. No small feat for an adolescent cripple in a strict school, under the watchful eye of his tutor. The crowning touch was that the girls were the three daughters of a Swiss captain who, with his last breath, had entrusted his Helvetian virgins to the bosom of his sterling widow, which bastion of virtue the monstrous schoolboy demolished with a flick of his crutch. Or perhaps his pitchfork. Ludicrous: a boy who could do that could do anything! This story circulated in Paris during Talleyrand's own lifetime, establishing the deplorable reputation of a man "who possessed every vice" on top of all those attributed to him by the pillars of decency. We will find Talleyrand tarnishing his reputation more than once, with the help of his own unerring insolence— described as cynical, which it was; but then he made no pretense of virtue. His detractors, however, bent on building their own credit by promoting his defects, all too often stoop to calumny and sheer absurdities.

He came down with smallpox at school. Instead of being cared for at home, he was lodged with a hired nurse on the rue Saint-Jacques, the only person who looked after him during his illness. He recovered, miraculously, and his fine face was not pitted, unlike that of his friend Mirabeau. He noted sadly that "such slight interest was taken in my illness." Nothing more.

Archambaud and Boson had not been put out to nurse on the day they were born and then abandoned for four years; they lived with their parents, saw them every day, spoke to them (receiving perhaps an occasional hug), and, in short, felt themselves to be members of a family. A glaring and unpardonable injustice. In his feverish solitude, the sick boy suffered another cruel blow, realizing that he was not loved and that his brothers were. "I felt isolated, helpless, persistently rejected; I do not complain for I believe those forced withdrawals into myself hastened my intellectual growth. A painful childhood caused me to exercise my mind at an early age and to accustom myself to thinking serious thoughts, which I might not have done had I known merely trivial satisfactions. . . ."

His restraint cannot hide the depth of his grief. After such a childhood, Talleyrand's foot was not the only crippled part of him. The most revealing phrase is: "I do not complain." A sigh escapes, after which he collects himself, either through self-esteem or a sense of propriety. Suffering steeled his pride and, as he discovered, built endurance: solitude had accustomed him to reflection and to silence. Throughout his life he habitually concealed whatever hurt or disturbed him, refusing to admit failure or insult. That did not prevent him from "thinking seriously" and trying to transform some failure or insult into a new source of power and pride—or simply profit—and learning from it. For instance: Why had his parents rejected him and barred him from their house? What principles were they obeying? What code of ethics, religion, or self-interest dictated their conduct? And what human value was to be derived from a religious or ethical system sanctioning the cruel injustice to which he had succumbed?

As a result of such solitary musings fostered by the galling injury inflicted on him, a child of utterly conventional background grew into a revolutionary statesman who remained nonetheless tradition-bound. The entire drama of his life lies in that desire to reconcile the irreconcilable.

The worst was still ahead. He did not know what had been decided for him. Before relating the cruelest discovery he was to make about his own future and his parents' designs, he made excuses for them—which they dearly needed, as a matter of fact. "I now realize that once my parents decided, according to their idea of the family interest, to send me into a profession for which I was entirely unsuited, they were afraid

of losing the courage to carry out their plans if they saw me too often."
He certainly was not critical of his parents.

The "profession" he dared not even mention was the priesthood.
His benevolent father and mother were making sure they would not
waver and change heart the day they would have to condemn him to the
"career" he did not, and would never, want. A superb illustration of parental defense against the threat of loving a child. Little effort was
needed, for Maurice had been banished from their hearts long before.
In the name of "family interest" they had buried him alive. It was as
simple as that.

With veiled bitterness and irony, however discreet, he added:
"Their fear is a mark of tenderness for which I am grateful."

Where Does the Seminary Lead: Heavenward or to Fortune?

After his fifteenth birthday in 1769, his parents spent a modest sum to
send Talleyrand on a visit to his uncle, coadjutor to the ducal archbishop
of Rheims, cardinal de la Roche-Aymon. No vacation, the trip was
meant to expose him to the idea of becoming a priest. That was part of
the plan. Once again he was packed off without a word, but not in the
public coach this time—a point that did not escape him. "Since it would
not befit my family for me to arrive in the archdiocese in a common
coach, a more comfortable journey was arranged than the one to Chalais.
A post-chaise called for me at the Collège d'Harcourt and took me to
Rheims in two days."

Was it also to preserve the family reputation that, immediately
upon arrival, he was told to don the cassock? The rude shock banished
any doubt of what was in store. He may have suspected it all along, but
now the dreadful certainty loomed. There was no word of explanation;
they knew he would understand and, in the end, submit. Relentlessly,
from a shabby cottage in the faubourg Saint-Jacques they drove him
straight to the archepiscopal palace of Rheims. Step by step he was slipping down the path to his final vows and eternal bondage—for "the
family interest."

He showed no dismay or reluctance, being well practiced in disguising emotions that no one cared to learn. Considering the matter
closed, his mother wrote blithely: "My son is well adjusted to his new
profession." What profession? Buttoning a cassock over one's ordinary
dress and playing choirboy is not a profession, Madam, it is a travesty.
We should settle that here and now.

In your view, Madam, the whole thing is perfectly fitting and proper, decreed by tradition and by the church. But, as you well know, faith is its own master and will not serve family interests, even yours. You have deceived your fifteen-year-old son, deceived him and God; you, a devout woman, have committed thereby a supremely irreligious act. You have gone about it with easy conscience, so easy that you are beyond reproach, having the church, your principles, your traditions, and society itself to vindicate your rights. All matched against a fine and sensitive young boy, who obeys you into the bargain. His obedience is very plain. He did not rebel—pride prevented him. A Talleyrand-Périgord does not disobey his father. He did not rebel because that would have dishonored him and you. He yielded. You thought it natural that he should do so; it was not. You deceived him and he lied to you. Because the stuff of lies is highly perishable, you are responsible for the moral disaster that occurred. Of course, you and yours put all the fault on his shoulders. You forced him to employ dissimulation; he became master of it. You rejected your son; he rejected his mother. He never condemned you, and he never forgave you. He was the victim.

You did an astounding thing, Madam: without knowing it, you turned your rejected son into the most illustrious member of your race, and France's most illustrious statesman, who remains misunderstood and unloved by the nation he served so brilliantly. Measured against a mother's initial betrayal, all subsequent betrayals were insignificant.

Those things must be said, for they are the seeds of everything to come—up to and including Talleyrand's final hour.

The archbishop of Rheims's lavish court gave young Talleyrand a number of far different ideas from those his parents had anticipated. They had expected the sumptuous elegance, the rites and honors surrounding a great prelate to dazzle Charles Maurice and set the pattern of his own aspirations. His name and the family's influence at court, combined with the boy's intelligence and innate aristocratic bearing, were certain to produce another cardinal de Périgord—a Richelieu, a Mazarin, a Fleury. In any event, would not his uncle, the coadjutor, open the door for him? A young abbé de Périgord entering the priesthood in the auspicious circle of scarlet-robed bishops would not have to wait long to exchange his black cassock for a purple one—and then the crimson robe. It was not idle fancy but accepted procedure, the normal course of events for those times and that family.

In defiance of all social, moral, and religious strictures operative in 1764, young Talleyrand "protested." The ramparts of tradition shuddered. Bitterness born in desolate solitude and his keen intelligence made him question and condemn a society and a religion that crushed his freedom and individuality. Twenty years later, calmly and deliberately, with the control and astounding insight typifying his style of argument— as opposed to the frenzied passion of contemporary debate—he applied, with devastating logic and accuracy, the principles arrived at in his youth to the institutions that had made him suffer. He destroyed them.

Who, in the archdiocese, could have detected the menace lurking behind such a handsome young face? At sixteen he was indeed extremely good-looking. Even Chateaubriand, who detested him, wrote (perhaps not as a compliment) that the abbé de Périgord was very pretty. The slender priestling with his thick, wavy blond hair, his bright blue-gray eyes, a bit cold and scrutinizing yet serene, and his fresh and fair complexion, had an air of distinction and somewhat distant reserve. He treated the prelates, the ladies, and all members of cardinal de la Roche-Aymon's court with the utmost respect. His painful lameness often restricted his movements, making him appear withdrawn, which was all to the good in that ecclesiastical setting where modesty was wholly becoming. Who would have suspected that the coadjutor's nephew, bearing one of the most celebrated names in France, had suddenly planted himself like a bomb in the bosom of the church? Talleyrand was not aware of the fact, but he would have understood the confession of François Mauriac's *Adolescent d'autrefois*: "I know that what the dean preaches and what my mother believes has nothing to do with reality. I know they do not have the faintest notion of justice. I loathe the religion they practice." Almost two centuries earlier, young Talleyrand had voiced the same execrations: "I could not endure a life of ritual. At fifteen, when one's emotions are still genuine, it is hard to see circumspection—which is the art of revealing only one facet of one's existence, thoughts, and feelings—as the supreme virtue. I came to realize that all cardinal de la Roche-Aymon's splendor was not worth the sacrifice of sincerity demanded of me." Quite an admission. He had been taught to revere the art of dissimulation; its precepts remained with him forever, but he deplored the fact that at sixteen he had not been allowed to be honest with himself and with others. "Youth," he wrote, "is the time of life when we have the most integrity." He, however, was offered a life of luxury for the price of hypocrisy. At his age, pacts of that sort are monstrous. His parents arranged them for him.

He stayed at Rheims for a year in the false role he abhorred. Some say there must have been something wrong with him if he objected to living in the archepiscopal palace, or at the abbey of Hautvilliers, a benefice of his uncle. Housed, dined, and waited upon in regal splendor, he was in the company of eloquent prelates, polished ecclesiastics, and even his parents. Certainly his mother and father would come to visit and to check on their son's progress in his dubious profession. But one would have to be totally ignorant of what goes on in the mind of a young man—especially this one—to believe or even suggest that he enjoyed being with his parents. The shock of the priesthood had opened his eyes: seeing his mother and father only sharpened his exasperation. We can picture his inscrutable gaze, his respectful—if not aloof—composure in their presence; how painful their insidious queries must have been, their feigned and remote interest in his life. At sixteen, a conflict of this nature, even a secret one, has tragic implications: the fledgling priest was concealing everything. Madame de Genlis met the cassocked boy and wrote of him: "He had a slight limp and was pale and reticent, but his good looks and observant manner impressed me." She had read the meaning in his eyes.

Books were part of his training. Devotional literature, perhaps? Far from it, for ambition, not piety, was what they wished to inculcate in him. He read the life of Hincmar, the monk of Saint-Germain who became archbishop of Rheims and counselor and minister of Charles the Bald (a cousin of Wilgrin, first comte de Périgord); the life of Cardinal Jiménez, grand inquisitor of Castile and Ferdinand V's regent; cardinal de Richelieu's life (he, of course, was the paragon of ambition); and finally cardinal de Retz's Memoirs. Little did it matter that they provided excellent introductions to the pursuit of a political or financial career, for the real purpose was to relieve the family of his presence and to transfer his right of primogeniture to his younger brother Archambaud. Providence would take care of the rest. The boy in his integrity grappled with the dilemma: "I could not yet understand what it meant to enter one profession [the priesthood] only to carry on another [statesmanship], to adopt a perpetual attitude of abnegation only to pursue more actively an ambitious career; to attend a seminary in order to become minister of finance." The tone is straight out of Voltaire, but this was no fable.

When you are sixteen and alone, confronted by so vast a conspiracy, you lose heart. That is what happened: Talleyrand was more a reed than an oak. "After a year at Rheims, seeing that I could not escape my fate, I gave up and resigned myself to it. I let them send me to the seminary." As if to the slaughterhouse.

The Marriage of Revolution and Love
Under the Aegis of Theology

He spent five years, from 1769 to 1774, at the seminary of Saint-Sulpice. Apart from his stays at Chalais and at Rheims, his whole youth centered on that district of Paris: between the rue Garancière where he was born, the rue de la Harpe where he went to school, and the seminary occupying what is now the place Saint-Sulpice, the entrance to which was on the rue du Vieux-Colombier.

They were the saddest five years in his life. He shut himself off from the ecclesiastical world which was to be his future and for which he was entirely unsuited. He hated society for imprisoning him there. "I was considered arrogant and was frequently reproved for it . . . God knows I was neither arrogant nor scornful; simply a nice young man, bitterly unhappy and resentful." [1]

It is not hard to see that he was a "nice young man"—on his way to becoming not so nice. Had he been "sensitive," a Rousseauite, he would have moaned and wept "torrents of tears." That was not his style. Concealing grief and loathing, he assumed a haughty manner, which, regardless of what he said, was indeed scornful and was intended to wall himself off from the hated society of clerics to which he had been consigned.

"I can see myself in knee breeches and my little black cassock walking in the courtyard, reading the dates carved along its walls. . . . If anyone liked solitude and shunned companionship, surely it was I. I went through my Bonaparte stage in the seminary." Later he added: "I was the most taciturn child, but also the most eager to learn, and learning came easily to me."

He was grateful for the intellectual training provided by Saint-Sulpice. Learning was his diversion because he chose what he wished to learn and did not clutter his mind with a lot of bookish nonsense; instinct and good taste prompted him to extract the kernel and ignore the chaff. He had no use for scholarship, or for anthologists unless their texts offered valid conclusions. Sixty years after leaving Saint-Sulpice, he still felt there were "three kinds of knowledge: knowledge for its own sake, breeding, and tact—the last two usually obviating the first." The despondent seminarian turned his back on pedantry and worked out a style of his own, at once mellifluous, volatile, and mannered.

The books he chose were altogether strange for a seminarian—but then he was a strange theologist, having little acquaintance with theology. His readings suggest fascination with action, adventure, and change: he read about travel and exploration; other nations, laws, and customs interested him. He was fond of accounts of long sea voyages, storms, mutinies, collisions at sea—anything involving risk and danger. Revolutions were his favorite histories. He asked no one's leave to read what he wished, cheat the jailer if you can. "During recreation periods, I secluded myself in a library where I picked out and devoured the most revolutionary books I could find, steeping myself in history, rebellions, revolts, and uprisings all over the world."

Thus he tended the flame of his revolt and, in the process, began to shape the hazardous conviction that the society strangling him was also strangling others. History taught him that rebellion had liberated other oppressed souls. The stifling robes of the priesthood had apprenticed him to revolution. His parents' glaring dereliction had driven him to rebellion. This young nobleman, whose intelligence, ambition, pride, and capacity to attract and dominate others epitomized his aristocracy, had been turned against a society and a civilization of which he was the supreme incarnation and could have been a vigorous champion.

Reading led to participation: he held private dialogues with his secret authors. In silence and solitude, his mind was broadening. He was full of admiration, and said later in life that to begrudge this was the mark of a small mind. He never failed to acknowledge superiority—above all his own. Sensing that the world stage was his true calling, he would have liked to make others think so, but reticence and arrogance still held him back. Baron de Vitrolles misjudged the youth of sixteen, though he knew him rather well in later years, when he wrote that Talleyrand "learned at an early age to flirt with scandal and to scorn the opinion of decent people." Charles Maurice bowed to his fate precisely because he dreaded scandal and respected the opinion of the most honorable people: his parents and his uncle the archbishop. Afterwards, he sang a different tune. His experience of life, of decent people and the none-too-decent ones whom he chose occasionally to frequent, taught him to scorn utterly and silently the virtues of the former, which concealed an abyss of hypocrisy and conformity, and to disdain equally the undisguised vulgarity of the others.

Recounting those bitter memories of the seminary to his niece Madame de Dino toward the end of his life, he said: "I was indignant at society and could not understand why a childhood infirmity had robbed me of my rightful position." His rightful position was, let us not forget, that of an eldest son, in civil society, of course, not the church. Added to the misery of his confinement at Saint-Sulpice was the normal resentment of an aristocrat denied his birthright: that is, his primogeniture, his right to transfer, to protect, to enrich, and to shed renown on the name and the glory vested in him. Though deprived of his natural rights in favor of his younger brother Archambaud, Talleyrand was never jealous of him, as he proved on many occasions. This refined sensitivity was an outgrowth of the "arrogance" for which he has often been taken to task. If some of his critics cannot value this, they should at least acknowledge it.

The condemned seminarian's life was not altogether black. Later on, in 1815, he admitted privately to Alexis de Noailles that the superior general, Bourrachot, gave him good advice, and that he liked Legrand, a doctor of theology. But a man of sixty-six, thinking back on the counsel of his Sulpician masters, is likely to see them in a more favorable light than did the wretched theological student in 1770. If, while that inner rage was devouring him, someone had told him that fifty years hence he would be commending his superiors, it would have stunned him. That was his way of ingratiating himself in his *Memoirs* and is no reason to call him an imposter, as some have done.

In 1821, he spoke in praise of Monseigneur Bourlier, bishop of Evreux and a former Sulpician, an opportunistic act in all probability, for the Restoration favored those who favored the church. He also yielded to the common tendency to embellish his memories of youth, even the worst of them. Finally, he conceded his respect for clerics, a feeling that never left him. He was kind and generous to them; unfrocked or not, they clustered around him, and he aided them in dangerous times. His bitter dispute with the church as an institution did not affect his sympathies for those who served her; nor did his quarrel with the family diminish his love for his brothers and nephews. Talleyrand was a turncoat who bore no grudge against those he deserted. A rare phenomenon.

In 1771, the blond young seminarian could be seen hobbling along in his black robe on the way to prayer at Saint-Sulpice, to which normally he paid scant attention. He was then eighteen, living in the era of Voltaire and Marivaux, with a head full of exciting literature and a love for everything lovable; naturally, he was bored. He fell in love. One day at Mass he met a young girl straight out of a novel by Marivaux. Like Marianne, she was shy and elegant, with youthful innocence and a pretty face. He sat by her and for once paid close attention to his prayers. He followed her out of the chapel, but she did not seem to notice him. In the end, a sudden downpour showered its blessing on them; he offered to share his umbrella with her. She did not refuse it, or his arm as he led her down the steps, or his escort back to her apartment where no umbrella was needed. The short walk to the rue Férou had not allowed much time for talk. That first visit did not end the subject of their encounter, and it was she, he tells us, who asked him to come again. She did it, he remarks, "like a very virtuous young woman"—perhaps tired of being so. Every day for two years, he made good use of her invitation. That ray of joy brightened his leaden years at Saint-Sulpice; he was able to bear the intolerable confinement only because of Dorothée. The name Dorothée Dorinville [2] was given to her at baptism, though she was of Jewish origin. She had also been converted, against her will, to the theater and, much to her distaste, was playing minor parts at the Comédie Française under the name of Luzy. Talleyrand gently remarked that they had much in common, both having been forced into unwanted careers: he wept upon an altar at which he had no desire to pray, and she upon the boards she had no desire to tread. That gave them certain bonds—not to mention the others. Their affair was no secret either at the seminary or in the neighborhood; they were always together, the most charming couple in the parish. Talleyrand would limp back and forth from the seminary to the church, and from the church to his sanctuary on the rue Férou where he worshipped his Dorothée. By a strange coincidence, his first and tenderest love was a Dorothée and his last and most absorbing passion another Dorothée, duchess of Dino, his niece.

He made no effort to hide the affair or his dislike for the priesthood—both have been held against him. His superior ought to have expelled him, and would have done a great service thereby both to the church and Talleyrand. But he said nothing, which is not to his credit either.

Why Talleyrand was not expelled is no mystery. "Only because of overriding consideration for his birth and particularly the great esteem in which his uncle the archbishop of Rheims was held, was he not sent packing on the spot." [3]

It is said that after Talleyrand first scandalized the Sulpician community by walking in public with his mistress, a second scandal would have occurred if the son of an eminent nobleman had been roundly dismissed. And why invite trouble anyway if his masters and fellow students had observed a welcome change in the young man's unsociable behavior since his courtship of Dorothée? It was characteristic of Talleyrand's very warm and humane outlook that he could detest certain institutions, but not the men representing them, who were, in his eyes, not responsible.

In short, with or without a mistress, his parents had decreed that he should be a priest. And he became one.

On September 22, 1774, he received his theology degree from the Sorbonne after presentation of a thesis dedicated to the Virgin Mary: he could not have done less. Its subject was: *Quaenam est scientia quam custodient labea sacerdotis?* (What kind of knowledge should the lips of a priest guard?) The dissertation probably owed more to his kindly adviser, Mannay, than to Talleyrand's own efforts. He remained forever grateful to his teacher, and brought him to Valençay to live out his last years, a mark of loyalty for which no one has yet blamed him. Also thanks to Mannay, he was able to circumvent the age requirement for his degree, which he received at twenty instead of the prescribed twenty-two.

Because he speaks so little of himself in his *Memoirs,* we cannot be certain whether or not Talleyrand spent some time at the seminary of Angers, as is often suggested.[4] If he did, it must have been quite an escapade according to the accounts: he tore loose one night (a Sunday during carnival, admittedly) and then slipped a new-born infant into the superior's bed! The worthy priest's surprise cannot have been greater than ours, for the joke (if you will) is in such bad taste as to be utterly unlike the abbé de Périgord, as he was then called. In his silk robes, powdered and perfumed, he did not sit with the others in the refectory, but was served at his private table, owing to the numerous and impressive quarterings on his escutcheon. In fact, the Angers escapade, which was never mentioned by him and which survives only through hearsay, is probably a fable.

Time to Take the Plunge

For whatever reason, Talleyrand was no longer at Saint-Sulpice when he made his vows on April 1, 1775. As the archbishop's nephew, had he been allowed to live with Dorothée? Why was he not ordained with the other Sulpicians instead of separately (he was always an outsider) at Saint-Nicholas-du-Chardonnet by the bishop of Lombez, Monseigneur de Salignac de la Motte-Fénelon, Fénelon's nephew? Minor holy orders had been conferred on him the previous year, on May 28, 1774, in that same church by the bishop of Quimper. He heard the message of the sacrament: "Until this hour you are free. . . [as if he had ever been free]. Once ordained, you shall not break your vows and shall be committed forever to the service of God. . . . Think carefully while there is still time. And if you persist in your holy resolve, come forward, in the name of the Lord." Listening only to his "holy resolve," he advanced and knelt. It was over with. He had taken the plunge. His mother had won. She had not bestirred herself, nor was any family member present.

On April 12, he was appointed subdeacon of Paris with the name Carolus Mauricius de Talleyrand-Périgord. Not the least proud of it, he complained bitterly in his quiet way, behind the scenes but loud enough for all to hear: "They want to make a priest of me—well, they'll have a hard time. But I am crippled, a younger son, with no escape from my fate." [1]

No one was alarmed at that time. Later on, the Revolution offered him an escape. But there is no justification for saying that Talleyrand entered the church in order to blow it up; time and time again before taking his final vows, he made no secret of his rebellion and scorn. By parading his liaison with Dorothée in the seminary and all over Saint-Sulpice, he may well have been trying to stir up trouble for himself. Yet neither his superiors nor his parents allowed it to alter their plans; they gave him a lesson in diplomacy at his own expense.

They felt that once he had taken his final vows, he would settle down and behave himself. In the end, he behaved as he would always behave, doing and thinking what he pleased, knowing that he was expected merely to play the hypocrite and not offend decent society. He would indulge his princely and voluptuous tastes, living lavishly off his benefices and allowances. A purple robe and lace-trimmed rochets could work wonders, concealing at once his crippled foot, his rancor, and his vices. He did not embark on that course just yet: "They have forced me to be a churchman; they will regret it," he informed his superior, Monsieur Cussac, who passed the comment on.

He had been treated like a pawn, though no one realized it. The abbé de Périgord might have said the same thing about his father as the prince de Ligne, his contemporary, remarked of his: "My father did not love me, I cannot say why—perhaps because we did not know each other."

The bishop of Blois, Monseigneur de Sauzin, wrote: "I can assure you that he was in a vile temper when he was ordained subdeacon." [2] Even his teacher Langlois foresaw disaster and resisted his ordainment. But what weight had a humble man's advice, an underpaid (or even unpaid) teacher's, as opposed to the comte de Périgord's will? They did not even listen to him.

The chips were down; the fatal wheel went on turning until 1789. Church and monarchy had wagered on the black; their victim played the red—and won freedom.

How to Blot Out a Coronation, or the Art of Insolence

On June 11, 1775, the abbé de Périgord attended Louis XVI's coronation in the cathedral of Rheims. He left no record whatever of his reactions to, or impressions of, that overwhelming spectacle of ecclesiastical and royal pageantry elevating the last of the monarchs by divine right. He seems to have been wholly untouched by it. A number of reasons account for his indifference to the event. The first was his father's insistence that he attend. The Talleyrands had taken part in every coronation since the time of Hugh Capet. The comte de Périgord, the vicomte de La Roche-foucauld, the marquis de Rochechouart, and the comte de la Roche-Aymon bore the Sacred Ampulla, a signal favor doubly shared by Charles Maurice through his father and through his Rochechouart blood. He could not have cared less. His uncle was coadjutor to the archbishop of Rheims, who crowned the king. He could not have cared less. Still, he had managed to pull a few strings and have himself transferred from the Paris diocese to that of Rheims in order to enjoy the favor of France's most influential archbishop, to whom his uncle was attached. The un-earned promotion was not denied him. His parents had approved, think-ing he would be under closer supervision and would advance more rap-idly. They showed poor judgment only on the first account. Though that misunderstanding drew him somewhat closer to them, it did not spark any rush of esteem for his noble father, who was to escort the gold dais on which the Sacred Ampulla rested on its journey to the cathedral from the ancient abbey of Saint-Rémy, its repository since the coronation of Clovis, first king of the Franks. The experience of Saint-Sulpice had filled Talleyrand with disgust for any kind of religious ceremonial. Ritual appalled him, as did all the sublime and cruel traditions inex-tricably bound up with the church to which he had been sacrificed. Yet because of his innate civility, self-control, and pride, he made it a principle never to give offense or even to criticize others. With utter detachment, he simply ignored—blotted out—whatever displeased him. As an indifferent onlooker, then, he watched while the king was anointed and crowned and ascended the throne elevating him above all other men and rendering him God's instrument, sovereign lord of the land and people of France. The whole thing was as boring to Talleyrand as a clerical rendition of *Esther*. A pity, for he would have seen the king's brother, Monsieur, the comte de Provence, paunchy now, later to become the crafty, paunchier Louis XVIII; and his brother the comte d'Artois, a fine-figured fellow but inept, the shoddy future monarch Charles X whom Talleyrand accompanied to his coronation fifty years afterwards, a glorious occasion sullied by bloodshed and misery. And the duc de Chartres who, under the name Philippe Egalité, claimed the head of his cousin—this hieratic monarch on whose head they were now setting a crown weightier with tragedy than diamonds. Then there was the prince de Condé, with a three-year-old boy at his side, the duc d'Enghien, who would be shot by lantern-light in the ditches of Vincennes. Did you notice that little boy, Monsieur l'abbé, standing beneath the magnificent vaulted basilica where kings were made for thousands of years? One day you yourself will go to identify the murdered corpse. Murdered by whom, and with whose connivance? Your eyes and lips are sealed. Convenient. And sad. What strange and tragic prophecies you might have left us had you been willing to look and tell what you had seen. Your biographers depict you as untouched by the grandeur, the religious pageantry, the loftiness and even beauty of that coronation. They misjudge you. In fact, you took it all in, especially the grandeur. The pomp, the rigid and complex ritual of coronation confirmed your dedication to the difficult art of diplomacy and protocol, the acute observance of precedence—your unrivaled domain. That occasion also confirmed your proud assurance of being a superior person entitled to a hand in shaping the affairs of the nation to which you were so intimately bound.

Still, in your brief notes concerning that event, there is not a word of grandeur, monarchy, or religion. You were impressed only by the faces of three charming young ladies of the court, three graceful profiles against that whole historic fresco; amid the flood of incense, you caught only the delicate fragrance of orris and bergamot. From another pen, this might be mere frivolity; from yours, it is insolence—sheer insolence to the crown, church, and your parents. Your insolence, like your lies, operates by omission. On that day, you chose to ignore the object of your parents' devotions. You were already bound for revenge.

Your scorn and insolence are easy enough to understand, but their counterparts are also a part of your makeup. You must admit that you felt completely at ease in the coronation setting, like a grand seigneur, a court dignitary; at the same time, you were a priest bent on apostasy, a vassal seething with rebellion. You were all those things, always.

The very importance of that occasion warrants exposure of your deceit and dissimulation.

The coronation proved to be a red-letter day for the young priest. "Louis XVI's coronation marked the beginning of my relations with several women, singularly gifted in different ways, whose friendship has never ceased to enhance my life. . . ." For monsieur l'abbé, it was the opening of a *fête galante.* He wrote those lines fifty years later, when the same women were still his intimate friends. Age could not dull their tender, sparkling eyes; their graceful speech and bearing conveyed the innate elegance of the Enlightened century. Their common purpose was to share the enjoyment of living with others born to live for enjoyment— not for the Sacred Ampulla which the comte de Périgord, dour and wooden in his robes of state, guarded with drawn sword. Talleyrand names those delightful women: "I speak of the duchesse de Luynes, the duchesse de Fitz-James, and the vicomtesse de Laval."

They were to play a very intimate role in his life.

The Abbé de Périgord Begins to Step Out

Life was not altogether sad, then, for the young priest. In the closing years of Louis XV's reign, "Europe's blissful years," according to the prince de Ligne, it was indecent to be sad. With his friends Choiseul, the comte de Narbonne, and Biron, duc de Lauzun, all sons of the greatest families, all pleasure-loving, potential models for *Les Liaisons dangereuses,* he was remote from the austere world of the Périgords. He and his companions had entrée to Versailles and were Madame du Barry's intimates, attending her morning toilette and regaling her with the choicest Paris gossip from the day—and particularly the night—before. They never stopped laughing. One day after each had contributed his own scurrilous little tale, the favorite turned to a mute listener, the abbé de Périgord: "Why so silent? What's the matter, no luck with the ladies? Virtue or modesty?" Quite a compliment, considering that he had neither. What he had, however, was an unerring gift for eliciting questions, the replies to which were on the tip of his tongue—a performance he executed with supreme composure and all but a yawn, fully appreciating the humor and impact of his own nonchalance. This is the first record we have of Talleyrand's sophisticated, cavalier, and remarkably effective practice of leading a conversation to the point at which people unwittingly put themselves at his mercy—then, ever so gently, springing the trap. When Madame du Barry voiced surprise at discovering such a chaste and handsome young priest, he replied: "Ah, Madam, I am musing on a very sad thought." "What's that?" "Paris is one place where it is easier to possess a woman than an abbey."

She had a merry time with all those young rakes, in whose madness there was method, for Talleyrand soon received proof that Versailles was not like Paris and that the court could dispense abbeys: he received two sinecures. As to women, he managed well enough on his own.

The first material rewards of his obedience thus came when, on September 24, 1775, the young monarch Louis XVI gave him the abbey of Saint-Rémy in Rheims. Talleyrand thereby was assured a benefice of 18,000 livres. He has been severely criticized for this; not because he collected 18,000 livres for doing nothing, but because he was overjoyed. But having had to depend completely on his family and the seminary, why should he not rejoice in "the proud satisfaction of earning his own livelihood"? He made no secret of the fact that laying hands on his first income was "a blissful experience." The money was put to good use; he paid the balance of his tuition at the Collège d'Harcourt, which his parents had neglected to do, and also settled with his poor teacher Langlois, who had not seen a penny of his stipend in many a month. The count and countess had seen fit to spend their money elsewhere. Let the church take care of their son.

There he was, the rich beneficiary of France's most venerable abbey. Saint-Rémy had been founded by the first French king, Clovis, buried next to the saint who baptized and, one might even say, crowned him. The kings of France always held Saint-Rémy in special reverence and, on their coronation day, would descend into the subterranean passages beneath the city of Rheims to kneel at the tomb of the French monarchy's patron saint, asking his aid and protection. Joan of Arc prayed there beside her king. In that crypt resided the authority and sanctity of the monarchy.

By a curious coincidence, a Périgord helped to found the Capetian dynasty and another Périgord was the last titular of Saint-Rémy. If accounts are true, this last abbé was the one who burned down the monastery in the final days of the monarchy—like the hand of fate in a Greek tragedy.

In fact, the abbey did burn in 1774.[1] The story told in Rheims in 1844, seventy years afterwards, goes as follows. One night, two young novices decided to slip out of their room, which was locked; they left through the window and slid down the wall along a rope of sheets. Their lighted candle was forgotten, and when the wind blew open the window, the curtains caught fire. The room blazed up; soon flames were racing through the ancient building, reducing floors, rafters, and every timber to ashes. Priceless manuscripts, some dating back to Merovingian times, were housed there. Two human chains came alive, one passing buckets of water, the other rescuing books and chartularies. The fire won out, but only after many precious works were saved. The church and crypt escaped destruction. Louis XVI so prized the monastery that he had it rebuilt immediately; Talleyrand became titular of the new Saint-Rémy, which still stands today. The tale was kept to a whisper in Rheims, for one of the novices responsible for the fire was Charles Maurice de Talley-rand-Périgord, the nephew of Monseigneur de Talleyrand-Périgord, arch-bishop of Rheims. Destiny's work is awesome: a Périgord setting the cradle of the monarchy ablaze!

In the same year, 1774–5, the province of Rheims chose the abbé de Périgord as its representative to the quinquennial Assembly of the Gallican Church. The appointment may have been principally a token of esteem for the archbishop, although certain distinctive traits of his nephew cannot have gone unnoticed: his attentive manner, his rare but judicious remarks, his aristocratic bearing and good looks, as well as certain excesses that were not frowned upon. His piety was never men-tioned. He was also delegated jointly with the abbé de Vogüé, who taught him the facts of ecclesiastical finance, to defend church interests against fiscal incursions of the crown—an imbroglio involving ancient feudal investitures of the clergy which the clergy was determined to exempt from taxation, claiming that they were ecclesiastical and not feudal in origin. The distinctions were often hard to make: Talleyrand maintained that all church property should be tax-exempt. The church fathers were delighted to find the archbishop's nephew so apt at drawing fine lines. His statement defending the immunity of church property was highly praised. It won him so many admirers that the young priest—frivolous in his way—was appointed *agent général du clergé* at the age of twenty-one, the representative and permanent champion of ecclesiastical interests *vis-à-vis* the royal treasury, a clerical minister of finance, if you will. It was a great honor and a mark of confidence in a young man whose ability was plainly in the domain of finance rather than theology.

Unfortunately, he had not yet finished with theology. He was only a subdeacon; though he had taken vows, his ordainment as priest was yet to come. He could still escape. But to get the whole unpleasant busi-ness over with, he left Saint-Rémy and enrolled at the Sorbonne for his advanced degree. There he studied (if you can call it that) for two years. "During the two years I spent there, theology was the thing furthest from my mind, for pleasure is foremost in the daily life of a young bachelor." He made excuses, wholly unjustifiable, for his insouciance. Because the young bachelor was also the abbé de Saint-Rémy, in fact he was deriding his office. He had lost no time in finding a group of com-panions whose tastes blended perfectly with his own: the abbés of

Montesquiou, of Saint-Phar, of Damas, and of Coucy, all with impeccable pedigrees and deplorable morals. Woe to the priests who tried to teach him theology; their hair stood on end. One instructor, totally shocked by what he heard and saw in the midst of his disrupted lecture, cried out: "Oh, mon Dieu! What do I find in those of thy servants vowed to uphold thy laws? What do I find in those destined to wear the bishop's miter? What do I find? Men who sow the vices of our time among the clergy, among the servants of God [those satanic future bishops in fact were corrupting future parish priests by teaching them to gamble at cards right in the classroom]. Oh, mon Dieu, mon Dieu! What will become of our holy religion?" How they laughed at that poor Jeremiah bemoaning the vices of the clergy; the little band of rebels dubbed him "la grande Catau" (Queen of Strumpets). Doom was surely at hand.

To distract him from his absorbing and pious labors, Talleyrand's mother and father took him with them to the archbishop of Rheims's château in Château-Thierry. Living in the country with his parents was more than he could bear. Were they counting on that? He remained impassive, solemn, and silent; they expected nothing more.

His maternal grandmother, the marquise d'Antigny, had some Burgundy delivered to the gatekeeper at the Sorbonne, who took it to him. Old Mademoiselle Charlemagne informed the marquise of the wine's arrival: "I am afraid that if the wine is a good one, it will not stay around long," she said. "Monsieur l'abbé is extremely generous and will want to treat his friends to it," which is what happened. The abbé de Périgord loved parties, small or large, and the company of his aristocratic and licentious friends. It is worth noting that his governess knew him from childhood and credited him with being generous. He would always remain so—magnificently at times—as well as compassionate and eager to help. Those who were close to him loved him.

He received his advanced degree in theology on March 2, 1778, and promptly cut himself off from everyone at the Sorbonne. By burning the midnight oil in his own blithe fashion, he came out first among the six candidates for the degree, with the citation "nobilissimus" attached to his name. He deserved to be last on the list, but that rank was reserved for a certain abbé Borie Desrenaudes, a humble priest from Corrèze and a brilliant theologian, who ought to have been first. Abbé Desrenaudes is a name to remember, for the candidates at the top and bottom of the list became lifelong friends. Despite revolution, the commoner and the aristocrat enjoyed a warm relationship.

A casual attitude toward theology and theologians enabled Talleyrand to perfect the one ability he valued: that of grasping a problem and organizing and presenting ideas so as to persuade others, or at least intimidate them. Many dedicated students had derived from their training merely a useless and tiresome train of pedantry. In his case, however, by teaching him theology, which he promptly dismissed, the seminary and the Sorbonne turned him into a first-rate dialectician.

Ordainment in Three Stages, Two of Them Impious

The Sorbonne once had—and still has—a great genius, neglected and even derided by the mindless herd, to whose repute professors on occasion would pay timid lip service. Our abbé, being of neither camp, resolved not to leave the university before rendering proper homage to this genius. In return, he wished to extract an inspiring example which dead geniuses can always impart to anyone willing to examine the record of their achievement. The great departed's name was Richelieu. We can appreciate the extraordinary spectacle of our skirt-chasing young abbé, France's least-promising and most ambitious theologian, slipping into the chapel to greet and consult the most dynamic and stimulating of masters: the monumental cardinal in his tomb. Talleyrand related the incident in his usual offhand manner: casually resting his lame foot upon the cardinal "in his beautiful tomb," he opened an unabashed dialogue with the dead. The reply he got, far from altering his self-possession, simply convinced him that Richelieu's example "was not discouraging" for the abbé de Périgord. When the interview ended, his cassock suddenly became so weightless that it swayed with the slightest breeze, or suggestion—or hint of advancement.

Young people, if they are so inclined, plainly have much to learn from great men of the past.

That was his first benediction prior to ordainment. With spirits high, he set out to obtain the second, in the springtime of 1778, from the enthroned prophet, the pope of impiety reigning over Paris and all Europe: Voltaire. The patriarch of Ferney had just returned in triumph to the capital after three years of exile. Our young abbé sought the same blessing from him as Benjamin Franklin's grandson. Imagine the drama of our hero priest, a new degree in theology to his credit, fresh from a sublime dialogue with the ghost of Richelieu and now kneeling at the feet of *Candide*'s progenitor, feeling those bony hands upon his blond and perfumed head, hearing that sarcastic voice as the venerable sage bestowed his blessing in one trenchant phrase, its main clause resounding with the glory of mankind, its furtive subordinate hastily dispatching a cloud of incense heavenward.

When he left the hôtel de Villette, this time his cassock had dissolved completely. Only his mother, father, and uncle could prove that he still wore one. Relatives are always blind.

His visit to Voltaire was no routine call, no graceful, mannered exchange of niceties affording entertainment and conveying mutual approval between two performers, who, in this case, were peers in the art. The visit and the sacrilegious reverence expressed Talleyrand's profound esteem for Voltaire. He admired above all the tone of his speech, which, for men of his position, was far more important than the content. Talleyrand considered Voltaire's tone and style to be the earmarks of civilization, without which man could not live in dignity. But for Voltaire's world, misery, tyranny, and fanaticism would reign—in short, primitive ignorance. Not life, but slavery, ill-disguised. Whereas Voltaire's vision seemed to hold a reasonable promise of happiness based on wealth, freedom, and civilized behavior; stripped of excess, of illusion, of paradise. Talleyrand was especially fond of one of Voltaire's sayings: "Worship God, serve the king, love mankind."

In terms of ecclesiastical advancement, however, things were not going well for him. Unpleasant reports kept reaching Monseigneur de Beaumont, archbishop of Paris, on the activities and utterances of the attractive young priest. His eminent name was blacklisted. He had alarmed them enough when his teachers realized that he was beyond their control. Anger and contempt had no effect on him; it was plain that his only interest was self-promotion and the indulgence of his own whims. "You wanted me? You have me. Then keep what you took." That principle guided his behavior, which was in any case, not outlandish. His follies were always moderate and would have given him much less pleasure if his career had been jeopardized by them. The priesthood had cost him such bitterness and despair that he felt it now owed him unlimited power and fortune. This was no idle fancy, but cold calculation on the part of a born calculator.

Discredited in the Paris diocese, he asked for transfer to Rheims. His uncle had become archbishop and duke of Rheims in 1777 after Monseigneur de la Roche-Aymon's death. That simplified everything, for Talleyrand was also titular of the Chapel of the Virgin in the parish of Saint-Pierre as well as of its abbey of Saint-Rémy. The abbey was incorporated into the Rheims diocese on September 17, 1779, whereupon the bishop and comte de Beauvais, Monseigneur de La Rochefoucauld, conferred on him the deaconry, entitling him to "serve at the altar, perform baptism, and preach." As if that was what he wanted! The promotion was interesting only as a necessary step on the way to becoming a priest, and in turn a bishop.

Of course, the bishopric itself was only a beginning. The episcopal throne was not Talleyrand's ultimate goal; he saw far beyond it. When a man becomes *agent général du clergé* and is trained to handle church as well as state funds; when he has won esteem in that capacity by declaring himself on the "Inalienable Rights of the Church"—establishing that whatever contributions the church chooses to give the state are freely given, but the state cannot require them; when he has defended clerical privilege artfully and ardently against the crown, and still found time to waste preaching such nonsense as the Eucharist, Penitence, the Ideals of Lent, or even saying Mass and leading the procession of the Holy Sacrament; when a man with the name of Talleyrand has accomplished all that, he is bound to wake up one morning and find himself in possession of a red leather portfolio adorned with his blazon as minister of finance—for a start.

Why condemn him for wanting it? Was it not implied that the highest rewards awaited him if he would don his cassock meekly? His uncle the archbishop never taught him anything else. The seeds sown in fertile ground yielded an incredible harvest of ambition.

On December 18, 1779, at the age of twenty-six, he was ordained a priest. Not without drama, for at the final moment, he wavered. The proud seigneur who had wanted to become an officer and whose hopes had been crushed, rose up in rebellion for the last time. But courage failed him. He was in tears the night before his ordainment; the next morning, his friend Choiseul found him in an appalling state. Such grief, especially from someone who rarely showed emotion, was a great shock. Choiseul implored him to recant and leave the church. Talleyrand refused—for his mother's sake—not out of filial love, but so as not to disgrace her socially. "No," he told Choiseul-Gouffier. "It is too late; there is no turning back."

Afterwards, he became the priest he never wanted to be, and an aristocrat serving the Revolution—but always an aristocrat.

The bishop and comte de Noyon, Monseigneur de Grimaldi, ordained him with these words, which rang in his ears the rest of his life, even in his last agonizing hours, their impact undiminished by time, pride, or his fellow men: "With holy dread you must approach this high office, remembering that those called to it must distinguish themselves by wholly divine wisdom, unblemished morals, and the regular exercise of justice." After Mass and communion, he placed his clasped hands between those of the bishop, who asked him: "Do you promise to respect and obey your bishop?" "I promise," he murmured. Not one of his relatives was there to hear that edifying promise. (The next day, however, his parents attended his first Mass.)

He limped off at the close of the ceremony, not only dragging his painful clubfoot, but also with his hands freshly shackled. His head, to be sure, was still his own. The cassock was to be his eternal shroud.

Why, at the age of twenty-six, did he finally give in? Because he was flexible and unwilling to exert himself—two permanent features of his character. Talleyrand never faced things squarely; whether it was wisdom or a fatalistic attitude that guided him, he never confronted events, he exploited them. He never repudiated a fact or rejected a person directly. With one short burst of outrage, he could have quit the priesthood. He was incapable of it. He offered no resistance. The choice he made was distressing—but paid well.

Compensation meant a great deal to him. By tapping his own immense intellectual resources, he found out where the profit lay that could repay his loss. He knew perfectly well that a break with the church would deprive him of his social position. That, in his eyes, was worse than death, for despite his scandalous behavior, he took a very conventional view of society. What is more, he would have lost benefices totaling, in 1780, 30 million old francs. Without social position and money, life was inconceivable. As long as the monarchy warranted his titles and sinecures, and promised him even greater rewards, he would suffer. But his suffering would be compensated. If one day society could no longer guarantee the privileges owed him in return for his lost freedom, then he would review the contract between them. His commitment was temporary, as he saw it; in the eyes of the church, however, he had taken "eternal vows." The seeds of his rupture with the church lay in the pledge binding him to her.

A Stylish Abbé and His Friends in 1780

The Rheims diocese had promised advancement, but for sheer living Paris was unrivaled. There he spent the final years of the Ancien Régime. His aim was to enjoy life, which he did superbly, adding his own special flourish to the art of living.

He settled in the rue de Bellechasse amid the serenity of parks, private homes, and convent gardens. Though he described it merely as "small but comfortable," the house he took was in fact two stories, with six windows overlooking the rue Saint-Dominique and the rue de Belle-chasse just beyond the entrance to the convent of the canonesses of Saint-Sepulcre. The neighborhood was truly ideal—a fact that did not interest him in the least. Excellent taste and a fondness for elegance and luxury guided his choice of furnishings. He spent lavishly on the library; indeed, he made a lifelong habit of surrounding himself with fine and valuable books, prized both for their own sake and as investments. When times were hard, the books came to his rescue in the auction room. Classical works of literature, history, and politics lined the shelves, flanked by profane texts, erotica, and several religious treatises signed by Fénelon in superb bindings. Whether sacred or profane, each book was exquisitely papered, printed, and bound; whether read or fondled, it was part of the abbé de Périgord's library and of his design for the enjoyment of life.

The books provoked no complaint during his lifetime. Once Joseph Prud'homme took up his pen, however, the world was to learn that Talleyrand delighted in "infamous" literature. Thanks to other busy pens, we also know that he owned the remarkable *Histoire de Dom B . . . portier des Chartreux,* an illustrated and unpardonably obscene publication of 1745, which rubbed covers fittingly with the *Riches Heures de Madame la Dauphine* on our abbé's library shelf. In 1790, Gouverneur Morris, a distinguished American associated with Talleyrand, borrowed his copy of the scandalous *Histoire de Dom B . . .* Morris had the good taste to confine his remarks to his Diary: "It is more than a bit odd to receive the 'Portier des Chartreux' from a churchman." This book, widely read during the century of Enlightenment, finally was banned on four occasions in the nineteenth century by the same judges who condemned *Madame Bovary* and *Les Fleurs du mal.*

Besides books and furnishings, friends and callers filled the house. In his *Memoirs,* Talleyrand recalled late breakfast gatherings on the rue de Bellechasse. "Those were wonderful mornings that I could enjoy all over again." One can understand his yearning for a circle of intelligent, well-informed, and open-minded young friends, whose impeccable breeding ruled out any trace of familiarity or vulgarity in their conduct and discourse. They could relax and talk about anything they wished. Each contributed his own special wit, knowledge, and flair. Choiseul-Gouffier was Talleyrand's best friend: "Monsieur de Choiseul is the man I have loved most dearly." A well-advised friendship, too, for Choiseul was reliable and clever. He enjoyed a flash of celebrity following a trip to Greece in his thirtieth year, which earned him a seat in the Académie Française. Talleyrand recalled, in 1821, that Choiseul "was, in a way, both an ambassador of royalty and of the arts." To this friend, who probably saved him from suicide when he was abandoned to Saint-Sulpice, he wrote in a moment of distress: "I wish you to know from my own hand that with all my heart, and in every mood of life—happy or vexed or even miserable—I love you more than anything on earth. Good-bye; don't write more than a note, but write."

Apart from a few lines sent to General Bonaparte which will appear later on, no one ever received a declaration of that sort from Talleyrand. Such emotion is indeed surprising in so secretive a man, one who has been branded a dead soul and accused of employing cajolery in the guise of friendship.

Next to Choiseul, his closest friend was the comte de Narbonne. Brilliant, captivating, and flighty rather than an arresting personality, he collected friends and ladies' hearts. Whatever glittered or soared or glowed was drawn to him. He was a handsome aristocrat, a bastard son of Louis XV and, like his father, deserving the epithet "the beloved." Women adored him. In 1781 his mistress of record was the vicomtesse de Laval-Montmorency, who had caught Talleyrand's eye during the coronation in Rheims. Later on she shifted from Narbonne to Talleyrand and remained with him the rest of his life. Like our abbé, Narbonne fluttered effortlessly from one régime to the next, for he was indeed flighty, gliding like a butterfly on the winds of history. He changed beds as readily as he changed ministries and slept soundly under any roof, always smiling. He served in Louis XVI's government, then as ambassador under Napoleon; from courting Madame de Laval he shifted his attentions to Germaine de Staël. The whole world shifted—except for Narbonne's cheerful spirits. The nice part was that he was never truly happy unless his friends were. Narbonne was passionately devoted to his friends. Talleyrand, more guarded in forming attachments, chided him for his sudden infatuations and for rushing to the defense of others, which, in the political arena, cost him a number of stinging rebuffs. But Narbonne was incorrigible. He even won the heart of that monster Fouché, who said of him: "His conversation was so charming that I welcomed it in the midst of my tedious work." Talleyrand cautioned his charming friend against the pitfalls of impetuous friendships: "In politics, as in everything else, one must not invest one's heart, or love too passionately; it causes confusion, clouds the mind, and is not always appreciated. This excessive preoccupation with someone or something, this devotion bordering on self-sacrifice often harms the cherished object —and always the loving one—by rendering it less circumspect, less fit, and even less persuasive." [1]

Although that prudent observation concerns Narbonne, it also reveals the writer himself, and might well take its place in a collection of private reflections under the heading: "Don't mix love with business—or love with love affairs."

Narbonne never changed, Talleyrand maintained his customary reserve, and the two remained fast friends.

A third familiar face at the rue de Bellechasse belonged to Armand de Gontaud-Biron, duc de Lauzun. The Gascon blood in his veins had given him an appetite for action and adventure. He was different from the others. Seven years older than Talleyrand and a veteran of the French-American Wars, he was brilliant, romantic, utterly fearless, and something of a rebel. His country house in Montrouge was the scene of some wild nocturnal revels, attended by the imperturbable abbé de Périgord with his halting gait, his priest's collar, and his ringing repartee. For different reasons, but mainly because of the disreputable company they kept—a fierce compulsion on Biron's part, a secret but pressing imperative on Talleyrand's—they both found themselves swept far afield in the revolutionary escalade. During the Revolution itself, they were involved in an odious diplomatic venture in London. Biron returned to France and played the strutting hero, pledging his sword to the people's cause; by vaunting his republican plume in the front ranks of the Northern Army, he so antagonized party bureaucrats that they demanded his head. This he courageously delivered to Paris, where, on December 31, 1793, it was permanently removed. Talleyrand, then in London, was also summoned to deliver himself, but decided to forgo the journey— because of his crippled foot, no doubt—and thus kept his head for future use.

Another guest at the abbé's table was the celebrated abbé Delille, reputedly an inspired poet by virtue of his facility for converting Greek into vapid alexandrines, but with true mastery of style. He was polished, witty, and had a hearty appetite. He frequently dined with the queen and Madame de Polignac. His company at table was sheer pleasure; his poems are something else.

Chamfort the academician was another visitor whom Talleyrand admired greatly and whose maxims he noted: "To get on in the world, you must be willing to learn what everyone else knows." Or: "Sentiments that can be evaluated have no value." And the whole room was stunned with admiration when Chamfort declared: "Some wenches are willing to sell but unwilling to give themselves."

Now and then the guests were persons we would call "technocrats" and whom Talleyrand's circle looked upon as doctors to society—its ills they could not cure, but they performed superb autopsies. One of them was indeed a physician, the famous Barthez from Montpellier; also a certain Dupont, called De Nemours, full of ideas about money, trade, and industry, and how to combine all three so as to increase a hundred-fold the profit from each. Talleyrand listened with rapt attention, something his Sorbonne professors had never been able to evoke. At such times he must have felt a minister's portfolio under his arm.

The man Talleyrand esteemed most highly and from whom he learned the most was Panchaud, the Genevan banker who loathed another Genevan, Necker. Panchaud instilled that loathing in the abbé, and together they derided Necker's competence, his reforms, and his newly acquired fortune. When Louis XVI recalled Necker in 1788, Talleyrand declared that "the king could not have made a worse choice." Events proved that the choice was in fact most unfortunate. In contrast, England adopted Panchaud's fiscal system and flourished under it—one reason why Talleyrand admired English common sense.

The frivolity of the abbé's breakfasts was thus a matter of opinion; though the atmosphere was frothy and elegant, still it was the best political economy course to be found in Paris. Discussions on poetry, love, and gastronomy would give place to debates over the Franco-British trade agreement of 1786. Many Frenchmen condemned it; Talleyrand defended it in a memorandum submitted to his friend Mirabeau on October 12, 1786. The treaty's fundamental concept was already a cornerstone of his political philosophy: commercial treaties are indispensable to international peace—an echo of Voltairean pacifism—and peace is the prime need of civilization because it promotes economic expansion, while trade agreements unite nations under the banner of prosperity. At that time England appeared to illustrate best "those liberal ideals befitting great nations."

The American Revolution was on every tongue. Frenchmen were fascinated by that overseas experiment in independence and democracy. Talleyrand and his friend Choiseul dug into their own pockets to arm a corsair which they christened "Sainte-Cause." He never sought credit for that generous act and, at the end of his life, when someone reminded him of it, he turned away and replied: "Let's forget that; it was a youthful transgression." He may well have regarded it as such for, on the one hand, he could not condone yielding to impulse in political matters or allowing emotion to blur one's judgment and objectivity; on the other hand, arming a corsair meant contributing to an act of war, and at the age of seventy he had seen slaughter enough under the Revolution and the Empire to be convinced that war was humanity's disgrace, civilization's cancer. In his last years, any association with war was unbearable to him, so he chose to forget about the corsair.

The celebrated portraitist Madame Vigée-Lebrun received Talleyrand, and, though she did not paint him, she left this vivid verbal sketch: "He had graceful features and well-rounded cheeks; his limp made him no less elegant or attractive a man; he scarcely mentioned my pictures." [2]

Talleyrand was probably more laconic than usual because he had little feeling for that type of painting. The artist neglected to add that he had sparkling eyes, fair hair and brows, and was beardless; that he wore a high collar and held his head very erect. He was tall for the period (5 feet 8 inches is entered on his passport in 1796) and often made people feel that an intense, icy stare was descending on them from somewhere above. All the abbé de Périgord's grace and civility could not dispel one's first impression that behind the youthful charm lurked something intimidating.

That was the effect full face. In profile portraits, however, a difference can be seen: the proud aristocrat is still visible, but the blurred smile emphasizes his snub nose, which detracts somewhat from the profile by widening the distance between upper lip and nostril and giving it the alarming expression of those three heraldic gold lions, armed and crowned, the restless spirit of the counts of Périgord. What is striking about the expression is its wily intelligence, the scornful sarcasm, the bold and ready insolence, the seemingly indolent and sensuous amiability. At least that is what David's unsparing portrait sketch conveys.

As he was, women adored him. They whispered that he was depraved, and other women were eager to test the truth of it. Like Voltaire, Talleyrand preferred the company of women to that of men and not only found the female intelligence more subtle and receptive, but women in general more useful. Beyond the delights of courtship and conversation, he recognized that their incomparable devotion could advance the career of a friend or a lover.

Such activity was entirely in keeping with the times. All the fashionable women were politically minded; policy was made in the salons, not by the king or his ministers. Or perhaps we should say unmade, since everything was a target for destruction. The abbé de Périgord rightly noted: "The power of so-called society in France was unparalleled in the years preceding the Revolution. . . . Every woman had administrative matters on her mind. Between quadrilles, Madame de Staël instructed M. de Surgère in the fundamentals of Western policy, Madame de Blot voiced opinions on every officer in the French navy, and Madame de Simiane promoted the taxation of Virginia tobacco."

Our abbé would have levied a tax on anything if Madame de Simiane could have made him a minister. But she could not, so he looked elsewhere. He was a familiar visitor to Madame de Montesson's salon. She had married the duc d'Orléans secretly and lived at the Palais-Royal, receiving callers either at the door or through the window. Voltaire went there once at the age of eighty-four, but only once, for his career was already behind him. Talleyrand duly made his appearance and commented: "Her house, albeit on the very borderline of respectability, was remarkably agreeable. One of her theater boxes was always reserved for dissolute churchmen." Such divine consideration! [3]

With Madame de la Reynière, wife of the affluent farmer general, the divine touch was her table at which Talleyrand frequently dined. And he regularly attended the salon of Madame d'Héricart, "who appreciated wit, young faces, and good food."

Better still, he got to know Dampierre when visiting the duchesse de Luynes, one of the ladies whose profile had caught his fancy during the coronation and who was often seen at the comtesse de Brionne's, née Rohan, the wife of a prince of Lorraine. Talleyrand could not take his eyes off her two daughters, the princesse de Carignan and her younger sister Princess Charlotte of Lorraine. Yet her daughter-in-law the princesse de Vaudémont eclipsed every titled lady in that famous and most elegant of Paris salons. Those women idolized Talleyrand, and he thrived in the perfect setting for his self-confidence, his cleverness, and his affections. The comtesse de Brionne took it into her head to make him a cardinal, but Marie Antoinette refused, having been thwarted in some other project; the king followed suit. Talleyrand came so close to obtaining the office that the denial of it caused him some resentment. However, Charlotte of Lorraine did not refuse herself and proved a charming if ephemeral mistress; she became abbess of Remiremont and died at the age of thirty. The princesse de Vaudémont took her place, and the warm affection between them lasted the rest of their lives; it replaced the courtly love of 1787 and bound them together during the dreary years of the Restoration, when old memories, meaningful to these two alone, recalled a gracious way of life that did not survive them.

Not all the salons were outstanding. Some he attended simply to keep informed, others, to please people, which he enjoyed and made a practice of. He tried not to look bored during readings of unstageable tragedies or when music was performed to make up for the lack of amusing conversation that one could find, for instance, at Madame de Brionne's. One had to be prepared for that when visiting the Liancourt's, or the Swedish ambassador comte de Creutz's, or Madame Vigée-Lebrun's. When Madame d'Epinay's Memoirs were published in 1816, readers hoped to recapture the unique flavor of pre-revolutionary society; but Talleyrand told everyone that her world "was merely the society of financiers and philosophers. Where the company was good, she was not present." [4]

The best example of "good company" either at court, in the salons, or at home was his mother's. His description of her is not a loving son's eulogy; it is a tribute to the good taste of a woman of quality who embodied the ultimate marks of fine breeding and to a masterwork of privileged society. "I made a point of visiting my mother when she was alone in order fully to enjoy her charming company. No one could match her gift of conversation. She was totally unpretentious. Her language expressed only the finest distinctions, never witticisms, which she considered far too coarse. Wit restrains the tongue, whereas she sought to give pleasure and to liberate her ideas. A variety of simple, fresh, and always delicate expressions conveyed her thoughts." Not a realistic portrait, though it contains a good deal of truth; perhaps we should call it an interpretation.

Interpretations of the abbé, however, were not nearly so glowing. Those that reached his parents also reached the king and queen, which accounts for their somewhat jaundiced opinion of him. He was forever in Paris, never in Rheims, and in Paris he frequented the most disreputable places or else the most fashionable salons; but never a church.

In 1784 he visited the duc de Choiseul, the once-famous minister of Louis XV, at his château de Chanteloup. In every word and gesture of the old statesman Talleyrand beheld the model of his ambition; it would have gratified Choiseul—and Calonne too—to know that throughout his life Talleyrand applied creatively the precepts they taught him and which reinforced his own inclinations. The two men fascinated Talleyrand and seemed to epitomize the intellectual vigor, clarity, and agility bred by the Enlightenment, which had also left its mark on him. No tiresome moments or endless unreadable reports; only sound conclusions arrived at by exploring matters in a civilized manner: in a fireside chat, at the dinner table, between social calls, at the favorite's toilette, or in the cushioned comfort of a berlin en route between Paris and Versailles—wherever informed, discerning, and cultivated persons gathered. One learned by venturing into society, which the abbé de Périgord was doing. But what a society, and what an abbé!

At Chanteloup he met Blanc d'Hauterive, an Oratorian professor. Their first conversation stretched into a forty-year-long relationship in the ministry of foreign affairs, just as he had singled out the abbé Desrenaudes the day he received his theology degree. All three were churchmen; Choiseul assured him that the era was past when statesmen made their way up through clerical ranks. The reign of cardinals was ended; no more Richelieus, Mazarins, or Fleurys. Talleyrand was taken aback by that prophecy, for had he not entered the priesthood expressly to become a statesman? Then it was just a cheap trick! He was much more interested in a government post than in the cardinalate; what possible use was a cassock if it could warrant neither salvation nor high office?

Choiseul also told him that eminent officials ought to be worldly men and to conduct themselves and their lives accordingly. The old statesman related: "In my department I always made others work harder than I did. Don't bury yourself under piles of papers; find subordinates to sort them out. Direct your affairs with a nod or gesture. . . . I have never inflicted long reports on people but have tried to narrow the subject to what would constitute the kernel of diplomatic conversations." [5]

Talleyrand of all people could well understand such counsel and the principle of substituting conversation for files and reports. Bureaucratic details were the province of subordinates. "Make your staff work, and you will add hours to your own day," Choiseul went on. "A statesman who gets about in the world is forewarned of danger, and can sense it even in a festive setting, whereas he learns nothing walled up in his office."

The abbé was only too willing to adopt that system. He went out a great deal and so was well on the way to becoming a diplomat. Old Choiseul scrutinized the respectful young Oratorian (Hauterive) and then said to the abbé de Périgord: "I think he is one of those people who should be put to work for the improvement of business, the glory of his superiors, and even his own pocket." [6]

Hauterive's future was sealed. The abbé also looked at him carefully and did not forget him; later on he put him to work for the glory of Talleyrand and even the modest advancement of Hauterive himself.

It may seem oddly amusing to put such stress on worldliness and the art of conversation. In fact, the real importance of the frivolous—though admittedly difficult—art of conversation was knowing how to employ it and to make it serve one's interests. For someone like Choiseul, it meant beguiling, appeasing, suggesting, as well as listening and gathering information. Knowledge and experience of the world, and of the people in it, is power. Needless to say, a fool who masters the art of discourse usually remains a fool, but an abbé de Périgord becomes a Talleyrand.

Behind the Scenes of Power

One of the startling attractions at the rue de Bellechasse was Mirabeau. He had attached himself to the abbé de Périgord, yet could not claim to be as intimate as Narbonne or Choiseul, being a totally different breed. Rather to his discredit, the abbé was drawn to corrupt persons: he scorned them, amused himself at their expense, and generally relied on them to do things he would not do himself and which dishonored him all the same since his disreputable connections were public knowledge. Some of those ties involved prominent personalities such as Calonne, the king's finance minister, an amiable, shrewd, and irresponsible man with whom the abbé was on the best of terms.

In a letter to Calonne, Mirabeau included this glowing tribute to Talleyrand (more were to follow): "M. l'abbé de Périgord combines his highly developed gifts with extraordinary circumspection [always that element of reserve and secrecy]. You will find no one more reliable than he, more open to gratitude and friendship, more meticulous in his habits, or less eager to share another's credit, etc." Calonne had already formed an opinion of Talleyrand and replied to Mirabeau: "Tomorrow or the day after I will write you jointly with the amiable and excellent abbé de Périgord" (March, 1787). Apparently the abbé was penning certain letters "jointly" with the finance minister. Indeed, he had more influence on Calonne than is generally known or can be proved, owing to the fact that their collaborative enterprise was scarcely of an official nature. Talleyrand mobilized opinion behind Calonne and used Mirabeau to promote the financier's projects: "You cannot praise M. de Calonne too highly," he wrote to Mirabeau, "he deserves all our support in his efforts to bring off this important matter and every assurance that it will reflect great credit on him." The "important matter" concerned preparations for the Estates-General. The abbé was already busy in the political wings, working in his own fashion to convoke the Assembly of Notables, hoping a new society would emerge from that gathering. Unobtrusively, he was pressing Calonne's various agencies to draft tax reform proposals and other measures, such as amendment of the grain laws and settlement of the clergy's debt, which the notables would have to debate. Ambition surely spurred him, for Calonne's success would mean his own glory. He would be a statesman before they made him a bishop—bishoprics, after all, were slow to come by. But he also had the instinctive desire to improve society, and it gladdened him to be part of that effort. To his good friend Choiseul, then ambassador to Constantinople, he wrote the following, mindful of the fragility of his office yet full of hope:

> Dear friend, I send you M. de Calonne's opening address to the Assembly. It is an excellent piece of work [to which he had contributed] and covers quite adequately what knowledgeable people have been saying for several years now [around the table at the rue de Bellechasse]. There is strong opposition . . . but the king is not likely to withhold his support. In another two weeks a victory will be his. . . . Then Louis XVI will have achieved the most significant administrative reforms of any era: local government and the end of privilege. The source of all blessings.

For a Talleyrand-Périgord to write such a thing, mean it, and actively promote it was truly unconventional in the year 1787. He ended on this astonishing note: "My friend, the people will at last stand for something. . . . If the king adopts all the projected reforms, his reign indeed will have been the most brilliant and purposeful chapter in the monarchy. That is my only desire. How we miss your noble, lofty, and popular presence." [1]

The letter is extremely interesting, at once sincere and unusually warm. He hid nothing from Choiseul, "the man I have loved most dearly," and whose "noble, lofty, and popular" spirit he admired. "Popular" was a new word. They both loved the common people and wanted recognition for them. The abbé had reached the juncture of two worlds. Though severely critical of Talleyrand, Sainte-Beuve had enough sense not to condemn this letter, of which he said: "It is lively, brief, pleasant, and refreshing, revealing also the first stirrings of sincere liberalism, a concern for the people's interests which stems as much from the heart as from the mind."

But Louis XVI dashed the hopes of Talleyrand and a few other persons of rank: he dismissed Calonne and banished him to Lorraine on April 30, 1787. On July 16, the Orléanist faction demanded convocation of the Estates-General.

Calonne, the abbé, and Mirabeau undoubtedly were involved in other ventures besides the major one that failed. At a dinner party given by Calonne—during which not a word was uttered about political economy—Talleyrand arrived bearing a vial of medicine sold to him by that arch impostor Cagliostro, who touted it as the sovereign remedy for migraines. The princesse de Robecq suffered from them constantly and spent most of her waking hours prone on a divan. Talleyrand straight-way applied the miraculous substance to her forehead, rubbing so hard that he bruised the skin slightly. At the sight of this, the princess's ad-mirers became so incensed that they threatened to tear the abbé to shreds. He smiled, and when the rubbing and bruising was over the princess still had her headache. That was the lesson he wished to demonstrate to Cagliostro's disciples: the elixir was a fraud and they were all idiots.[2]

Calonne had France on the brink of bankruptcy. A born gambler, who could not resist the wildest speculation, he followed Talleyrand's recommendation and sent Mirabeau to Berlin on a diplomatic mission between 1786 and 1787. Mirabeau's reports for the whole year went directly to the abbé, who deciphered them and transmitted them to the minister—or at least transmitted what he chose to let Calonne know. Financial manipulations had always fascinated Talleyrand, and he was now coolly observing the rules of that staggering game wherein church and state funds were swallowed up, shortly to be followed by church and state proper. Mirabeau, normally bankrupt, was solvent for a change and grateful to the abbé on that score—his gratitude, in fact, was excessive and distinctly cloying. There was only one problem: Mira-beau was jealous of Talleyrand's designs on his mistress Madame de Nehra, called Yet-Lu. Mirabeau wrote to her: "He has often mentioned his passion for you, and I must admit that the deceit and treachery of it all horrifies me." Mirabeau was exaggerating as usual. Where was the treachery if the abbé made no secret of his passion? Mirabeau had only to break off relations with him. But then where would his funds come from? Besides, he kept his "horror" well hidden, and this honorable man, shocked by the taint of perfidy, wrote to the target of his horror: "My dear, ever so dear Master [servility and horror are both extravagant considering that Talleyrand was five years his junior], forgive me if my emotions run away with me, for to whom can I confide my anxiety if not to you, my friend, my consolation, my mentor and champion. You are more to me than a statesman, you for whose handshake I would renounce any throne on earth. . . ." A rhetorical soufflé to which the abbé re-sponded in kind: "Farewell, my dear count, and rest assured that my tender devotion is yours forever."

Once Calonne was gone, along with the hopes he had fostered, the abbé's influence over him ceased, and Mirabeau fell out with his "dear

Master." In a letter dated April 28, 1787, he bared his resentment to another unreliable and equally unscrupulous agent, the comte d'Antraigues:

> My position has been jeopardized by the abbé de Périgord's infamous conduct [infamous not for having stolen his lady friend Yet-Lu, but for having cut off his secret source of income] and has become intolerable. I enclose an unsealed letter for him; read it and send it to him. I repeat: send it to him [giving it all the bad publicity you like!] . . . My own misfortunes have put me into his hands [poor innocent fellow, a former prisoner in the Bastille, accursed by his father, disowned by his family, detested by his wife, and a victim of the abbé de Périgord of whom he was still terrified] . . . still I must handle this vile, greedy, base, and conniving man most carefully; money and vice are all he needs. For money he sold his honor and his friend [no notable transaction, for neither the honor nor the friendship had much initial value]. For money he would sell his soul, bartering his own dungheap for gold. Farewell, dear Count.[3]

Though pure fantasy, that explosion contained the substance and even some of the vocabulary of a tedious and unremitting litany of insults which hounded Talleyrand the rest of his life. One day soon, Napoleon, another Mediterranean spirit, would hurl the same invectives in even more devastating language.

It is interesting to contrast a contemporary opinion of Talleyrand and his friend Calonne that was far different from Mirabeau's. Its author, Lord Holland, was also a different breed of man. "Talleyrand served his political apprenticeship under M. de Calonne and acquired from that witty statesman the felicitous talent for doing business effortlessly and casually in a drawing-room corner or a window alcove. In that domain he rivaled his teacher's ability and outrivaled his intellect; yet he possessed certain qualities that Calonne never had, namely, remarkable veracity, discretion, and foresight." All one can say is that the abbé de Périgord cast a different image from every perspective.

Several months after the "dungheap" letter, Mirabeau wrote to his mistress in a wholly new vein: "Four vellum copies of my book [*The Prussian Monarchy*] have been printed for those most dear to me: you, the abbé de Périgord, the duc de Lauzun, and Panchaud." Should we listen, then, to the elegies or obloquies of such persons? Yet they cannot be ignored, for the loud and vulgar insults of a man whose fame gave him power clung to the abbé's priestly habit—permanently—though Mirabeau had forgotten them a few weeks later and probably would not have appreciated a reminder of his violent attack on "what was then dearest to him in the world." Talleyrand needs no pity and was far less upset than we by the incident. As we get to know him, we find that invariably he answered his detractors with contemptuous silence. He did so this time, and Mirabeau soon was breakfasting again at Belle-chasse. It was like inviting a thunderstorm; the whole house trembled. He gave each tear- or terror-laden performance with piercing eyes, and would say of the abbé: "He can tune himself perfectly to the pitch of others"—fairer by far than his own vulgar words.

The abbé de Périgord shared the office of *agent général du clergé* with the abbé de Boisgelin and complained that the arrangement was unfair because, as he pointed out, Boisgelin, who was madly in love with Madame de Cavanac (the former Mademoiselle de Romans and Louis XV's mistress), left him to do all the work. An ironic reproach: the abbé de Périgord, taking it upon himself to condemn a colleague's lax morals, ignores his lust but censures his laziness. To even the score, he disappeared several times to Brittany, ostensibly for study purposes, but as study was much too serious an offense in that era, the trips were charged to libertinage: he was chasing the bishop of Rheims's sister-in-law, Madame de Girac, in whose bedroom he composed the following couplet:

> What care I if her beauty be exquisite
> Having listened to reason and lost my wits.

Typically, pleasure did not prevent him from becoming informed about the political and economic situation in Brittany. Madame de Girac's petticoats were one way of acquiring the facts; there are worse ways. Such is the art of living—and learning.

In 1783 he was back in Rheims, mindful on occasion that he was indeed abbé of Saint-Rémy and titular of the Chapel of the Virgin in the Saint-Pierre parish; also that he had to pay court to his uncle the archbishop if he expected to receive a bishopric. That year he met three distinguished young Englishmen traveling for their own instruction. Their conversation and personalities attracted him; he "became attuned to them" and offered them an apartment in the château de Saint-Thierry which his uncle kept for him. They were together constantly for six weeks. One of the Englishmen was Lord Chatham's son, twenty-three, with keen political insight and a seat in Parliament; Talleyrand became interested in his ideas, especially on reform, with which he liked to compare his own. The young man was William Pitt.

Talleyrand said almost nothing of that encounter; Pitt never mentioned it. We shall see why. Pitt's visit to Rheims was not wasted—only Talleyrand's trip was, to London later on in 1792. But how well they managed to read each other's mind.

Talleyrand, typical of his times, was a Freemason: it was the thing to do, and also "philosophic." The duchesse de Chartres, the duchesse de Bourbon, and the princesse de Lamballe all belonged to Scottish lodges in France. Why should not our hero join too, as it provided excellent sources of information and broad contacts among the members of such orders? It was one of many paths to fame and fortune. He and the duc d'Orléans co-founded a lodge—Talleyrand was its chief warden—that became the famous Jacobin Club. Indeed, all his friends seemed to have the golden touch. Mirabeau returned from Germany and introduced a Bavarian rite to the "Philalethes" Lodge which his friend the abbé joined. As if that were not enough, he also belonged to the fraternal order of the "Amis Réunis" and the "Société des Trente." One could never collect too much information; it was wise to have eyes and ears in all the right places.

This limping abbé rarely stood still and was seen all over Paris, yet one house in particular seemed to claim his attention. He alone went there: it was the salon of Madame de Flahaut, his official mistress. Their serene, enduring, and quasi-conjugal relationship lasted from 1783 to 1792 when the Revolution forced them to part. She was Talleyrand's only mistress who did not remain his friend to the last—and she died only two years before him.

The high season of their love was utter perfection. And the comte de Flahaut was equally perfect. His wife, Adélaïde Filleul, was married to the offspring of a union between a wine merchant and Irène du Buisson de Longpré. In fact, it was one of those families in which nobody was the son of his father, but rather of some bird of passage. Adélaïde was the daughter of a farmer general who had become her mother's protector when that lady emerged from a visit to the Parc aux Cerfs where she had caught Louis XV's eye. She was said to have borne the king a daughter, Julie, married at the age of sixteen to Abel Poisson, whose sister had already carved her niche in history as Madame de Pompadour. Plainly, the family had impeccable credentials in the royal bedchamber. Abel Poisson became the marquis de Marigny and acquired a fortune; his wife took in the orphaned Adélaïde at the close of her convent training. She was fifteen in 1776; her sister Julie was twenty-five and mistress of the notorious cardinal de Rohan. After leaving the convent, Adélaïde was thoroughly educated in the aristocratic manner. She was gifted and turned into a very pretty and good-humored young girl, who was, at the same time, shy and inexperienced: a portrait by Greuze. Or perhaps Sainte-Beuve's description of one of her novels, *Adèle de Senange*, which brought her brief renown later on: "A pastel so pale as to be almost colorless." The critic went on to say that she was praised for "the ideals of good taste that she depicted so admirably." Good taste was as deeply ingrained in her as in her lover the abbé de Périgord; without it, could she have remained his mistress for ten years?

At the age of eighteen, for reasons that are unknown, she had been forced to marry the fifty-four-year-old comte de Flahaut. An officer of noble Beauvais blood, he was an honorable and highly respected man whose courtesy was legendary. The count's brother d'Angivilliers, superintendent of the royal buildings, presented the bride with an apartment in the Louvre where she opened her salon. Her beauty and wit, as well as the abbé de Périgord's constant attendance, made her salon's reputation. "She is more than pretty," one of her admirers wrote, "and dresses with an elegant simplicity that augments her dignity and poise. . . . There is a strange charm about her. Her face is perfectly oval; her mass of chestnut hair seems to fall in ringlets beneath the powder, framing her white skin and shining brown eyes—the most beautiful eyes in the world." The writer obviously is prejudiced yet succeeds in conveying her quiet inner warmth and radiant eyes. They are what attracted and captivated Talleyrand. Madame de Flahaut was a kind woman, without malice or ill will. True, she laughed once at a woman who began her last testament with the statement: "If I happen to die . . ." She was clever and witty yet would not turn those gifts against others. Radiantly optimistic, she was always in such cheerful spirits that Montesquiou told her: "Your good nature would be the death of more misfortunes than destiny could send your way." Indeed, the Revolution unleashed every adversity upon her, which she met with great forbearance. All except one: toward the end of the century, she had a brief fit of ill temper that Talleyrand never forgave. We will return to that later on.

For ten years they got along marvelously. Each evening the abbé (afterwards bishop) would enter the house and sit down opposite his countess for a game of whist. He was, as always, rather withdrawn and cold, yet pleasant to deal with. Never discourteous, he allowed others to act as they wished, demanding no more than they were willing to give. His poise and polish made him most attractive. He would save his salient wit for an appropriate thrust, never heavy-handed but so sure and swift that it suggested a feline spirit behind the immaculate grooming and the piercing eyes of this handsome priest. Some women found him irresistible. His relations with Adélaïde certainly involved tenderness, but not passion; he had other affairs on the side and was never faithful to one mistress at a time, nor did he require it of her. That was the fashion in 1785, and the liaison as such between Madame de Flahaut and her abbé was one of the pleasant topics of conversation in Paris. Gouverneur Morris, the American ambassador, left a voluminous correspondence on the subject. He was in love with Madame de Flahaut and courted her as relentlessly as Talleyrand, but lost heart and grew desperate periodically. The way they lived seemed simply incredible to him. One day Madame de Flahaut felt ill and asked to be put to bed. She was escorted to her bedchamber, and while a maidservant undressed her and bathed her feet, the bishop of Autun (it was 1789 and Talleyrand had just been appointed to that office) turned down sweet Adélaïde's bed, dispelling the chill with a warming pan: "I watched," wrote that respectable American, "for it was rather odd to see a churchman engaged in such a pious occupation." A Fragonard sketch from life, its principle so very simple: nothing is absurd for one who knows how to live and enjoys pleasing others.

Their semi-conjugal state was even blessed by the birth of a son. No one suggested that the child's father could be Monsieur de Flahaut, who was never around—Adélaïde went so far as to claim that her marriage had never been consummated—while everyone acknowledged the babe to be Talleyrand's, he loudest of all. Gouverneur Morris, still on the scene, noted in October, 1789: "I go to the Louvre. The bishop is with Madame de Flahaut; he has asked to dine with his son today. Truly a family dinner party. He leaves and expresses regret to Madame de Flahaut for having interrupted such a moving scene. She speaks constantly of her son and weeps. I wipe away the tears as they come."

A benevolent ambassador indeed, wiping away tears brought on by the nasty bishop, who had fathered a beautiful baby and was off God knows where with Narbonne and Lauzun instead of sitting by the hearth with his mistress and son under the tender and wistful gaze of Washington's ambassador, now recording the tableau for posterity. (A curious fact here is that Talleyrand limped and Gouverneur Morris stumped about on a wooden leg.)

Monsieur de Flahaut ignored the liaison completely; not so his brother d'Angivilliers, however, who raged against his sister-in-law, spreading word of the scandalous bastardy and "his unbounded scorn" for her and her "mitred monster." He alone seems to have been angry, for the lovers, Morris, and all Paris were blissfully content. The bishop would enter her drawing room, nodding to the company, and address the comtesse de Flahaut: "Madam, may I see my son today?" A nurse brought in the little cherub all wrapped in lace, for ideas on child rearing had progressed. Monseigneur nodded approvingly and complimented the mother, then asked to see her privately for a moment. Arm in arm, and with episcopal dignity, the couple left the room, shortly to reappear with the same stately composure. When Talleyrand's life was threatened in 1791, he left his will with Madame de Flahaut for safekeeping and made her his sole heir, acknowledging both her love and the son she bore him. One might also add her fidelity, which she maintained to the limit of her power. The credit is hers, for Talleyrand's inconstancy was no secret, nor the plain fact that she would lose him the day he tired of her. Gouverneur Morris pleaded that her lover did not deserve or even appreciate her faithfulness, and she confessed: "My heart is wedded." In 1791, Adélaïde's fidelity received its first wound: she became so jealous of Madame de Staël, whom her lover was courting ardently and openly, that her resolve gave way. Gouverneur Morris was on hand as usual to record the event, at once disappointed not to have been the favored one and delighted to find Talleyrand cuckolded. She yielded to the charms of young Lord Wycombe, the marquess of Lansdowne's son, who had been sent to lodge with her and should have considered himself the luckiest Englishman in France.

One day in 1791, referring dispassionately to the widowhood awaiting her—and slow indeed in arriving—she asked Gouverneur Morris: "Whom would you advise me to marry if I should be widowed?"

Morris's answer did not please Talleyrand at all but was perhaps simply a lure: "It is rumored that the clergy may be authorized to marry."

"Oh, I shall never marry Monsieur d'Autun: before accompanying him to the altar I would have to mention my liaison with someone else."

Talleyrand was no longer the beloved. He continued to visit her regularly, but relations between the couple were not what they had been before Germaine de Staël and Lord Wycombe entered the picture. Nevertheless, their child grew strong and handsome; he was named Charles after his natural father, and Flahaut after his legal one. We shall hear more of Charles de Flahaut.

How to Ignore One's Bishopric and Still Remain Bishop

The ecclesiastical Council of 1785 paid tribute to the abbé de Périgord's remarkable talents. His arguments supporting the inalienable rights of the church brought him acclaim and remuneration. Then and there he became the champion of tradition and privilege—a position that he reversed completely later on at the start of the Revolution. In 1785, he undertook an ambitious and important project, an inventory of the charitable and educational services performed by the church, which he, the clergy's official representative, established from a questionnaire he distributed to every French parish. The resulting survey of the church's role in France in the year 1785 indicated the number of hospitals, orphanages, and schools it maintained, and its annual operating costs, income, and capital assets. Probably the first such survey ever made, it was due to Talleyrand's own efforts and became his private possession. He did not have to be told how to exploit it, and his report on clerical matters to the Constituent Assembly caused a great stir later on. The frivolity of this priest needed watching.

The Council of 1785 listened approvingly to Talleyrand's statement, after which Monseigneur Champion de Cicé, archbishop of Bordeaux and a luminary of the Gallican church, extolled him before the assembled clerics: "This is a monument of talent and zeal assuring our everlasting gratitude to the able hands that have fashioned it." And because good feelings do not "talk" as readily as round numbers, the Council voted him a gift of 24,000 livres and two special gifts of 4,000 and 3,000 livres (a total of 30 million old francs).

That was not enough. He was thirty-one, a Périgord, and clever to boot; he should have been a bishop already. What was delaying his promotion? Priests and the king. The pillars of the church were not its worldly ecclesiastics and philosopher-prelates, and rare was the cassock cut with an eye to fashion. The great majority of churchmen stood for virtue and tradition; the turbulent minority dominated the stage, giving a false impression, for behind it rose a solid wall of resistance from the bulk of the clergy. This venerable machine, complex, ponderous, and rusty as it was, represented an indestructible force even to those who attacked it verbally. Antiquity was its shield. The ranks of tradition looked upon Talleyrand and his kind as either mad or so ambitious that pride or greed drove them to make war on the most sacred institutions. That opinion frequently reached the ears of His Most Christian Majesty —who took his title seriously; it was also shared by Talleyrand's parents and their circle at court, which, because of its rigor and piety, enjoyed special favor with the throne. The abbé de Périgord, intellectual light of the salons, was frowned upon at Versailles. Yet Monseigneur de Dillon, an influential prelate of whom the king thought well, had spoken generously of him. Moreover, church officials were so grateful to Talleyrand for defending their sinecures against the royal treasury that they were resolved to keep a financial expert in their midst. What if his piety were wanting? Truly pious souls could pray for him while he tended to the community's financial interests.

In 1785 his name was removed from the list of candidates submitted to His Majesty for nomination to vacant bishoprics. Monseigneur de Marboeuf, bishop of Autun, engineered the deed; he was fully conversant with the "art of living" practiced by Talleyrand in Paris and could not be moved.

The abbé had other endorsers: besides Madame de Brionne, her daughters and their husbands, he could count on his own family, the Rohans, and the princes of Lorraine.

In 1786, the health of Bourges's archbishop, Monseigneur Phélypeau d'Herbault, showed signs of strain—highly promising for our abbé. By spreading it about in Paris and Versailles that he was the one and obvious choice for the post, he convinced everyone that rumor and fact were identical, needing only officialdom's stamp and the royal seal. He was so sure of success that he wrote to Mirabeau, then in Berlin on a diplomatic mission: "At the moment the archbishopric of Bourges awaits me. It is a highly desirable post involving administrative functions that open doors to the Estates-General. The archbishop has had a stroke. He is not expected to live more than two or three weeks."

This archepiscopal seat was indeed an important one, with jurisdiction over a number of bishops and an income sufficient even for the needs of a Talleyrand-Périgord. Unfortunately, the archbishop of Bourges recovered his health and kept his office. One year later he suffered another stroke. This would surely finish him. Talleyrand wrote to Choiseul: "My archbishop has been gravely ill for several days. They say he is slipping away. Their best remedies have little effect on his mounting illness." Never was the death of a fellow more ardently desired, but, he added: "Time is deciding my fate. Presently I cannot imagine that the archbishopric of Bourges will not be mine. For all his malice, the bishop of Autun can scarcely prevent them from giving it to me." [1]

But the bishop of Autun's "malice" did deny Talleyrand the archepiscopal post at Bourges, perhaps because providence intended him to occupy his persecutor's seat in Autun.

He groaned aloud; it must have been a crushing blow. On October 17, 1787, he wrote to Choiseul:

So the archbishopric of Bourges has gone to the bishop of Nancy, and the bishopric of Nancy to the abbé de La Fare. Now what will happen? I do not foresee any other clerical openings for some time to come. If a vacancy occurs, will they offer me something suitable that I can accept?

All my hopes are turning out badly; this is not a happy time for me, my friend. But things will change. I shall wait, but they may decide that a man of thirty-four [a respectable age in those days], who has been active and has relied completely on his own energies [the abbé de Boisgelin was certainly no help to him] for five years, during which he has been warmly praised, deserves slightly better treatment.[2]

There was indeed something of a contradiction between the praise and emoluments heaped upon him and the obstacles thrust in the path of his career. He was infinitely superior to men like Calonne, Loménie de Brienne, or the favored abbé de La Fare. Were they trying to humiliate him? Dangerous: one did not humiliate a Talleyrand without acquiring a mortal enemy. If they had begun by integrating him in the venerable machine, he might well have reshaped it; but for nine years they kept him waiting at the gate of the episcopacy, which, of course, they had to open in the end. Did they imagine they were punishing him or teaching him a lesson? How little they understood him.

Heaven must have heard his appeal for apoplexy to strike the high clergy: on May 2, 1788, the archbishop of Lyons had a stroke. Monseigneur de Marboeuf was named to that eminent post, vacating the bishopric of Autun which then went to the abbé de Périgord. Thanks to his father: gravely ill, the count summoned his son and begged him to give up speculating, gambling, political intrigue, and companions such as Mirabeau and the duc d'Orléans. No mention of his lady friends; that sin was merely venial. Talleyrand gave his word in his own inimitable manner, with unsparing refinement and courtesy. How could he withhold it in the presence of so impeccable a gentleman as his father and at the brink of death? One good turn deserves another: his father solicited from the king the bishopric of Autun for his son. Louis XVI had great respect for the count and granted his wish. Talleyrand's mother objected. She had come to realize at last that her son was not suited for a church career. Only after he had reached the age of thirty-four, with that many mistresses behind him, having built a solid reputation for speculating and gambling, having openly consorted with persons highly objectionable to the court and clergy—only then did it dawn on her that her son might become history's supremely notorious bishop. She warned His Majesty, but he had given his pledge and, as if to disclose a saintly purpose behind it, remarked artlessly as he signed the decree naming our abbé to the bishopric of Autun: "It will reform him." That is how our priest became a bishop.

On this day, the second of the month of November, 1788, the king in residence at Versailles recognizes the honorable character and habits, the piety, scholarship, gentlemanly circumstances, and other virtuous and desirable qualities possessed by [the name attached to that list of virtues inspires either laughter or a shudder according to one's humor, but not indifference] Sieur Charles Maurice de Talleyrand-Périgord, vicar-general of Rheims; His Majesty, confident that he will devote his energy and zeal to the service of the church, has freely granted him the episcopacy of Autun, presently vacant following the resignation of its former titulary Sieur Marboeuf, with an assigned annual pension of 3,000 livres for life to Sieur Borie Desrenaudes, former vicar-general of Tulle. . . .

Thus the abbé Desrenaudes was party to the celebration, his fortune inextricably linked to the career of his patron and friend.

The new bishop had to be consecrated. Not averse to the ceremony, he agreed, at the suggestion of Saint-Sulpice's superior, to make a brief retreat at the novitiate in Issy, known as the "House of Solitude." Some say that he consented only out of politeness. Would he have done better to refuse rudely? Can anyone still think that a sudden rush of piety may have moved him? That sort of objection is hypocritical nonsense. Are his feelings not yet clear? Far from concealing them, he wore them on his sleeve. The superior, a holy man and conscientious, did his best to evoke "supernatural feelings" in the lover of Mesdames de Flahaut, de Laval, de Vaudémont . . . To attempt the impossible was his priestly duty. Humbly and sadly he confessed failure. He was right; he did what was expected of him. More unfortunate is the fact that they managed to make a bishop out of someone like Talleyrand.

The ceremony took place in the stark chapel of the novitiate and was a hastily arranged affair. Monseigneur de Noyon, who had ordained him in 1780, anointed him, assisted by the bishops of Béziers and Saint-Dié. On his knees, Talleyrand took one more vow: "I, Charles Maurice, appointed to the Church of Autun, shall be henceforth and forever loyal and obedient to Saint Peter the Apostle, to the Holy Roman Church, to our Holy Father the Pope and his legitimate heirs. It shall be my duty to preserve, defend, extend, and promote the rights, honors, privileges, and authority of the Holy Roman Church, of our Holy Father the Pope and of his successors."

Let us take a second look at that oath sworn on January 16, 1789, to preserve, defend, and extend the rights and holdings of the church; its full significance would emerge before the year was ended. In January, the time-worn, venerable, and moldering apparatus of church and monarchy was still intact. A summer storm ground it to dust on July 14. All is dust, alas, except holy vows. Talleyrand was never to forget that.

An incident occurred during the ceremony. With Talleyrand kneeling before him, the officiating prelate administered the holy unction to his head, then to the palms of his hands. The abbé Emery watched every step of the sacrament fixedly and, no doubt, with some anxiety. Just as the outstretched palms were being anointed, Emery saw the kneeling man suddenly turn ashen and slump to the floor. The solemn rite came to a halt. A few minutes later, when Talleyrand had regained consciousness, they went on with it. The episode was a cry of alarm. It seems almost incredible in the career of a man notorious for his coolness and self-control. He was afraid of no one. Why did that anointing of his hands (the motions of which were to recall, in his last hours, one final scene from his youth) so affect this man in the prime of his years as to make him flinch for the first and last time? That is the uncanny part. In the privacy of a humble chapel, Talleyrand was crushed for once in his life by a terrifying sense of sin. After all, what are a mere three minutes in a lifetime of eighty-four years? A ceremony interrupted by a falling body, a shattering crystal . . . a soul that is broken, and maybe saved . . .

None of his relatives were there. His mother made no more of an appearance than at his ordainment or when he took his vows. His father died two days after the king had signed the appointment. No uncles or brothers bestirred themselves to be at his side. The ceremony, as we know, took place in the chapel called "La Solitude". . .

In 1843, an elderly priest, a former divinity student at Issy in 1789, told the historian Renan that he had attended the bishop of Autun's consecration and had found the latter's behavior unseemly. What is that supposed to mean? How could he have behaved improperly on that occasion when no one has ever reported Talleyrand's conduct as less than decorous?

The day after the ceremony the archbishop of Paris conferred the pallium upon the new bishop, a sacred legacy of Saint Synagrius handed down to each bishop of Autun since the sixth century. Actually a white woolen band embroidered with black crosses, it was worn over the chasuble. What made it unique was the wool, from sacred sheep raised in the sacred pastures of the Convent of St. Agnes-Beyond-the-Walls in Rome. Monseigneur de Talleyrand-Périgord, bishop of Autun, shoved this signal honor into his pocket and hurried off to sup with distinguished guests at Madame de Flahaut's. Adelaide used to say good-humoredly: "Each stage of life has its own appropriate bauble." What the bishop, to whom "her heart was wedded," slipped into his pocket could not have been appropriate as he gave it no further thought.

Nor did he give much thought to his diocese except as a vehicle for making him the clergy's deputy to the Estates-General, soon to be convoked. A deputy's seat is what really interested him, and to get it he would have to win the votes of priests he had never met in a parish about which he knew nothing. Success was a gamble; it meant knowing exactly where the cards lay, discarding carefully, and collecting his gains as unobtrusively as possible. Speaking of gains, let us do some accounting. The bishopric of Autun was famed more for its historic roots and its sacred pallium than for its annual revenue of only 22,000 livres. Its holder, however, was also titulary of the abbey of Saint-Rémy and its income of 18,000 livres. For Talleyrand, that was not enough. The king awarded him the abbey of Celles, near Poitiers, another 12,000 livres. All told those benefices gave him approximately 55 million old francs yearly—barely the answer to survival! So he sought additional funds by gaming and indulging in various speculative enterprises. Sometimes he was lucky, and one can picture the cozy tableau of Dame Fortune winking at our bishop in one of the gambling houses of the Palais-Royal. But the lust for money driving him to gamble promised ruin instead of riches in the long run. It was a vicious circle of sorts: he felt compelled to "make" money, that is, cash for immediate use, which disappeared immediately. What he won at gambling went right back onto the table; the trickle of gold coins fascinated him. Indeed, money aroused this cold man. The glitter of gold stirred him bodily and mentally too, triggering feverish computations and ambitious moneymaking schemes that excited him like a drug. He loved the feeling of tense expectancy; imminent danger was thrilling because it hardened his strength of mind and mustered the self-possession that was his trademark. Gambling symbolized power, and whether he won or lost he commanded his own emotions as well as his partners', who were constantly impressed by his sphinxlike countenance. Try as they might to guess what he was thinking and how his luck was running, they were invariably wrong.

In no hurry to see his parish, he decided not to return to Autun until election time. The political activities of friends and other groups in Paris were much more absorbing. The party headed by the duc d'Orléans and known unflatteringly as the Orléanist faction had Talleyrand's support. In 1789, before the Estates-General had even convened, the main parliamentary coalitions were already planned and rehearsed. The duc d'Orléans and his following, including Talleyrand, may take credit, if credit is due, for having gerrymandered the Revolution before it happened.

To avoid trying the patience of his parishioners, the new bishop dispatched a messenger, Simon de Grandchamp, to preach and administrate in his absence. That would give them someone to look at. As he really wished to occupy their ears and tongues as well as their eyes, Talleyrand sent them a pastoral letter based on a phrase in St. Paul's Epistle to the Romans: "Desidero videre vos" (I burn with desire to see you), a paragon of pulpit rhetoric in the best taste, admirably worded, and touching on matters of current interest. One hears echoes of Fénelon. The composition and stylistic clarity are remarkable, as is the exquisite eloquence, tinged slightly with sentimentality—ever so slightly, but enough to stir hearts as if the preacher himself were inspired by divine love. "As God is my witness, I never cease to think of you," he wrote at Madame de Flahaut's rosewood writing table. "Yes, bear patiently, dear brethren, the thought that you have become our fond and unique concern." His concerns, especially the nocturnal variety, were totally different. He spent time in the commonest gambling houses or else reveling at the duc de Lauzun's country place in the outskirts of Le Maine, along with Narbonne, Mirabeau, *et al.*, and a bevy of Opera House beauties with whom they would pair up at random, then mix and match at will. It is hard to single out the most striking element of that pastoral message: our bishop's serene composure, or the persuasive vigor of his style—or perhaps the tragic fate of a society possessing every endowment except the courage to defend its own brilliance.

He also touched on serious matters that had long preoccupied him. "As we are aware of the great blessings of public education, we are no less gratified by the thought that the honorable duty of educating the youth of all social classes has been entrusted to the eminent Society of Oratorians . . ." Not empty words; he was already thinking of organized education for the common people. Then he went on to speak of his father's death, ending on the following poetic note: "When I clasped his dying hands in mine and was compelled to swallow my tears lest they fall upon him . . ." Was it true? Had he ever clasped his father's hands? Or shed a single tear since the night before his ordainment? He probably was not even at his father's bedside at the end, or at the funeral, as we have no record of it. In any event, there is little reason to think he wasted much time over such formalities, having better things to do. But his parishioners did not know that, so it could not hurt them to shed a tear or two for their bishop's grief at losing his father—a dearly loved father who was also highly esteemed by the king. How many priests voted for him because of that woeful touch? Next came a remarkable analysis of the responsibilities of a bishop to his congregation, a leader to his subordinates. He is placed over them for the purpose of binding himself to them through the sacrifice and service that authority demands of those who hold it, a reflection of his own conviction: "He courts misfortune surely who seeks high office only to satisfy the wretched claims of vanity." If Talleyrand did not seek advancement to bolster his vanity, he did it for other reasons. Vanity was not in his makeup; his noble birth was in itself far greater prestige than anyone could offer him. He went on to explain that the responsibilities of leadership are "always a dreadful bondage." He was a century ahead of his audience, insisting that a public figure is "answerable for his acts at all times, that public status requires that he surrender his privacy; that each new privilege he acquires entails a new obligation."

Autun's priesthood sensed that times were changing. Rarely had a bishop expressed such concern for his parishioners, declared himself duty-bound to them and opened his heart so eloquently.

For all its moralizing, the end of his message was no less original. He exhorted his flocks to pray for simple human virtues rather than divine insights in their bishop: "pure intentions and piety" (he was obliged to use the word at least once) and especially "the ability to judge the right time and means." In fact, those were his major assets, the marks of a statesman. Talleyrand was simply asking for more of himself. He also wanted his listeners to cultivate "gentleness that prepares the mind"; he possessed it already and used it to persuade others. Next, he recommended "force that resists obstacles," a very revealing phrase—he was speaking not of aggressive force but of "resistive force." At the height of his power, his intransigence wore out his opponents and he conquered them by attrition; his patience demoralized them. The obstacle faded away, leaving Talleyrand intact. Another quality he found desirable was "kindness," not because of its virtue but because it served individuals as well as society by staving off potential difficulties, disarming animosity, and creating friends, that is, allies. Kindness was also one of his "instruments." We must admit that there are worse. Voltaire would have appreciated his final appeal for the divine gift "of that unfailing justice which perhaps embraces everything, which is power's greatest duty and the eternal friend of human thought." His tone was solemn: justice is the first and fundamental duty of power. It is the people's prime demand upon their ruler: justice must sit at his right hand. When authority and justice are as one, peace is the reward. This pastoral letter was advance notice of the electoral candidate's political credo. In no haste to appear in Autun, he chose instead to create an image of himself with his pen. Some priests undoubtedly were nonplussed, but on one point there was no argument: everyone agreed that a superior hand had written this mandate. Whether alarmed or elated, no priest could dispute the authority of a man who expressed himself thus. Never did greater reverence attend a bishop's arrival.

Churchmen who reread the letter years later, their eyes opened by the Revolution, were either horrified or intrigued by its fresh ideas and sense of commitment. Mostly horrified, for they tended to interpret the message as a dreadful parody of ecclesiastical unction, an underhanded way of lining up the votes of a trusting priesthood. How sincere was Talleyrand? Sincerity was not one of the virtues he advocated. Ideas not yet popular in religious circles, ideas that belonged to a new generation of clergy, he coated with unction. They had made him a bishop; by God, he would behave like one!

Toward the end of his life, in a conversation with Lamartine, who was deeply hurt by certain things the prince de Talleyrand had done but who admired him all the same, the aged statesman was rebuked by the poet for approaching matters dishonestly. Not offended, Talleyrand replied: "Your honesty is not mine." To him, the important thing was not to be "honest" but to say and do what Monseigneur de Talleyrand, bishop of Autun, ought to say and do in order to win a seat in the Estates-General. He could have answered Lamartine with one of his cynical and merciless observations: Honesty is what crowns my enterprises; because of what I am, they always turn out for the good of society and progress—and, what is more, my own pocket. Such was Talleyrand's peculiar sense of honesty in the context of that peculiar pastoral letter.

He put off the trip to Autun until March 12, 1789,[3] arriving in the midst of Lent. On the fifteenth, a Sunday, he made his official appearance in the Cathedral of Saint-Lazare, at the entrance to which, according to custom, he took his oath of office. Another oath, which simply went in one ear and out the other. To "his bride the Church of Autun" he pledged to uphold her rights, liberties, statutes, and immunities. "I shall not alienate, I shall not enfeoff, I shall not barter the rights, possessions, and domains of my see . . ." With that out of the way, on to important matters.

His view was habitually long-range, and he had no desire to tour the countryside checking up on parish priests or any others. He explained the position of the abbé Desrenaudes, his vicar-general, who was not residing there but would be drawing a stipend: this deputy would be more useful in Paris since the bishop's political and financial dealings in the capital required more administration than did the simple parochial matters arising in Autun. His manner of announcing that information rather astounded the canons, but they accepted it. Next came his central topic, the preparation of *Cahiers* for the Estates-General. Autun's were among the most informative and carefully edited of any *Cahiers* submitted to the Estates-General; what they had to say was said with remarkable clarity. Talleyrand, who had never explored his diocese and had barely managed to find out the source and amount of its revenues, found his bearings in that document, which provides an excellent picture of his see. With systematic precision, chapter by chapter, it proposed eliminating various obsolete institutions and instituting corresponding reform measures. The need for reform rested on two principles. The first of these was political: representatives of the people ought always to debate public issues. That daring notion necessitated defining and establishing standards of popular representation; it would doom the monarchy forever and introduce democracy. The second principle dealt with the very foundations of society: private property and individual liberty, which had to be guaranteed absolutely, entailing a complete recasting of ideas on legality and justice. That was the revolution worked out over the breakfast table on the rue de Bellechasse.

The document also contained a chapter on finance—the ministry on which our bishop had his eye. It urged the creation of a national bank (which Napoleon later instituted, the Bank of France). It called for sharing the tax burden, a measure that might have been pure demagogy had our fiscal expert not reinforced it with a nationwide registration of property. The bishop of Autun already knew that this would expose the colossal holdings of the church alongside the paltry yield of all that stagnant capital. Such a study was bound to result in a new system of land distribution and taxation. Not a paper revolution developed by lawyers and teachers, it was to be instead a flesh-and-blood affair with private property at issue. Sainte-Beuve, no admirer of Talleyrand's, was obliged to admit: "It is apparent that the bishop of Autun was from the start one of the most cultivated and imaginative men of his era."

To summarize his style of diplomacy: he dazzled and inspired awe in his diocese. As for his style of living, it made him utterly charming and irresistible. There was open house with a groaning table at the episcopal palace. The splendid dishes, the sumptuous and abundant fare put all of Autun at his mercy. It was Lent, and he had fresh seafood brought daily from Dieppe. The dismal diocese over which Monseigneur de Marboeuf had lately presided now was a perpetual fête. Only the weather struck a cheerless note; the winter was bitter. Schools had to be shut lest masters and pupils freeze. Idle students roamed the country-side creating disturbances. Law and order began to break down. Carry-ing arms became illegal. Bandits prowled and fear took root. The *Cahiers* called for opening the doors of orphanages to care for swarms of illegitimate infants. There were tales of wolves and werewolves and bands of children wild as wolves.

Monseigneur de Talleyrand-Périgord carried on in high style, so busy that he had no time to unpack all his luggage or the gifts he had received. (In 1909, Monseigneur Villard, one of his distant successors, found a magnificent crystal service, a gift of the royal crystalworks at Creusot, in one of the unopened crates that Talleyrand had brought to Autun. This crystalware, given to the Museum of Le Creusot in the Autun region, did not survive the 1944 bombings.)

Talleyrand lost no time in getting down to business and dispatched deputies to every corner of the parish, where, like well-trained canvassers, they hustled votes for their bishop. There was no time to lose as the Estates-General was scheduled to meet on April 27.

He presided over the episcopal council on March 16. He also visited Autun's seminary, exhorting its priests and students to cultivate "mental oratory." On the Sunday of the Annunciation, March 25, as a special favor to the diocese, it was respectfully requested that he conduct High Mass. Oh, the trouble they were wishing on him; as if Monsei-gneur de Talleyrand knew anything about religious ceremonial! He could not refuse. The resulting spectacle was odd indeed, with Monsei-gneur faltering over the responses, mixing them up, and reading the office in reverse order. The canons nudged each other in disbelief, some smiling, others aghast. One thing was certain: their bishop was truly a superior man, but did not know the first thing about saying Mass.[4]

He was rewarded on April 2 with an overwhelming vote as deputy of Autun's clergy to the Estates-General. After that, the only thing on his mind was getting back to Paris. For the sake of appearance he waited a few days. On April 6 he visited the Oratorian school and had to sit through the superior's sermon on a theme probably chosen for the visi-tor's edification: "How the morality of leaders influences the minds of the people," a ticklish subject indeed. Talleyrand listened in solemn dis-traction, then congratulated the preacher for an excellent address, which had failed to interest Monsieur d'Autun in the least.

The incident illustrates a side of his nature that none of his inti-mates, and certainly none of his observers in the late nineteenth century, could understand. Talleyrand never took issue with people who disagreed with him, for several reasons. First, because any discussion amounting to an argument was not only indecorous but also useless, as neither party was ever willing to accept the other's position and both usually ended up angrier and more obstinate than before. He would not argue because it served no purpose and was vulgar. Furthermore, he did not care what others thought—except the chosen few whom he allowed to share "his world." He never wanted to be convinced by or to convince someone else. Not an ideologist, he did not believe in the absolute and enduring value of a concept or opinion. The best ideas are those that bear fruit. Why spread them about? Keep them under cover and put them to work. Events will test their worth. The ideas put forth by the Oratorian priest did not bother him in the least; they simply took up time that he would have preferred to spend elsewhere, with Madame de Flahaut, for instance. But he had no rebuke for the good priest, who was simply doing his duty and doing it well. Anyway, Monsieur de Talleyrand was deep in thought and miles away from Autun.

He left there forever on April 12, 1789—Easter Day, if you please. Lest the canons ask him to say Mass . . . He wanted no part in a ridiculous performance he had been through once already. He decamped, one might say, leaving behind half his belongings. Speed on, coachman! He spent the holy day of Easter on the road. In three weeks the Estates-General would convene. Adieu Autun. Talleyrand's active episcopacy had lasted thirty days. Still, for all its 2,000 years of history, the city has never forgotten its fugitive bishop. When a Talleyrand passes through a city, or nation, or government, he is bound to leave a mark.

Monsieur d'Autun Adopts New Ideas but Sticks to His Old Habits

Versailles, on May 4, 1789, was in a fever. A joyous fever. The Paris populace had invaded the royal town to watch the procession of deputies of the three estates as it moved from the Church of Notre-Dame to the Church of Saint-Louis. The crowds applauded endlessly, applauded everyone. They awaited a miracle: the king had convoked the nation's representatives and would soon bring paradise to earth. These deputies were eminent members of their own class. They were going to speak; they were able speakers; they would speak at great length, and every word they uttered would cure the nation's ills. Money would start pouring into strongboxes, food would be plentiful, bread free, and taxes so light that paying them would be a pleasure; in short, each speaker could promise anything and do nothing. And indeed the people received every sort of promise, from prosperity to virtue. As of the fifth of May, 1789, a day later, all up and down the social ladder people could embrace freely.

What everyone had learned from reading Rousseau and Bernardin de Saint-Pierre, what everyone was discussing, amplifying, and vulgarizing was about to come true. Talk and blind faith would make it so.

The thinking that went on under all those wigs was still a bit hazy on May 4, as we can see, but the crowds were orderly and the procession advanced with all the pomp and ceremony that the age-old traditions of the monarchy have bestowed on public events in France. It was indeed a stirring spectacle. The street throngs would point to famous dignitaries whose names they knew. Thus the bishop of Autun did not pass unnoticed. There he was in episcopal robes with his clerical bands and gold pectoral cross. You could recognize him by his limp; he used a long cane. His height was distinctive, as was his expression, at once affable and ironic. With head held high, he gazed off into space. His powdered blond hair was drawn back over his ears and the nape of the neck. No one could ignore his lordly air and the sense of superiority he radiated. Everyone knew about his "bad reputation." The idea of a skirt-chasing bishop brought smirks; but when talk shifted to his moneymaking ventures the smirks faded. People had not forgotten that Calonne's unpardonable follies had ruined the nation's credit; Talleyrand was said to be his friend and adviser, perhaps even his partner.

During the Restoration, a writer of memoirs by the name of Arnault recorded his reminiscences of 1789 and left a picture of the bishop of Autun whose life and fortunes he had followed for thirty years. The picture is hard to believe, but let us try. One fine day in 1789, Arnault was walking near the Swiss Guards' Lake at Versailles. "I had noticed a man lying under a tree, 'lentus in ombra,' who seemed lost in contemplation, preoccupied more with his own than with someone else's thoughts, although he had a book in his hands." [1] A hint of malice begins to creep into this seemingly innocent description: "His face was rather attractive. It was not so much the good features that struck me as the combination of nonchalance and spite which gave the impression of an angel's face animated by a devil's soul."

Antithesis was all the rage in 1825, and that angel-devil association grew all the more popular since it was fashionable to execrate Talleyrand. The phrase made a great hit. How discerning of this Arnault to be able to read instantly the soul of a man stretched out in the grass. He went on: "It [the face] belonged obviously to a man of fashion, a man more accustomed to employing others than to serving them." An incredibly unfair and idiotic appraisal of a man daydreaming over an open book.

Then, adding lust to corruption, the writer saw "his youth already satiated with the pleasures of the flesh." (Not satiated at all, but crying for more!) Two words manage to ring true: nonchalance and spite—although irony seems more appropriate. The rest of the portrait is too crude and pitiless. It does not compare to David's pencil sketch, which is even more merciless. But while there was genius behind the painter's hatred, here, there is only mediocrity. Still, the word "devil" got more attention than David's sketch.

Talleyrand moved from the rue de Bellechasse to the corner of the rue de l'Université and the rue de Beaune. His furnishings and friends followed. Besides Narbonne and Choiseul, new recruits appeared from the Constituent Assembly. Together they and the bishop made up the Assembly's radical wing, and from their names it is apparent that the "progressivism" of 1789 was scarcely plebeian: the duc d'Orléans, the duc de Biron, the duc de La Rochefoucauld, the duc d'Enville, the duc d'Aiguillon, the abbé Sieyès, the abbé Grégoire, the marquis de La Fayette, the marquis de Montesquiou-Fézensac, the marquis de Sillery, the marquis de Mirabeau, the vicomte de Noailles, the comte de La Marck, prince d'Arenberg, and some members of the middle class whom Mirabeau had rounded up, famous jurists, economists, and journalists such as Dumont (from Geneva), Merlin (from Douai), and Garat (from Bayonne). There was also Choderlos de Laclos, the celebrated author of *Les Liaisons dangereuses* and himself equally dangerous. They were pledged to Philippe d'Orléans, engaging in activities so anti-monarchist that a royalist pamphleteer called them "candidates for the gallows." People accused them of wanting to depose Louis XVI and the elder royal branch in order to give France a constitutional monarchy. This principle was already written into Talleyrand's *Cahiers*. Because the king and his brothers refused to rule other than by divine right, the Orléanists resolved to depose and exile him to Lorraine. Philippe would then wear the secular crown, give France a Constitution that his party was drafting, and govern alongside a parliament which he would be able to manipulate. Every move had been planned. And when it came to moves, Talleyrand knew them all. An expert at motions, debates, and public or secret ballots, he also appreciated the value of private discussions, of hints dropped in the salons or committee rooms, in alcoves or at the toilette of a fashionable lady, wherever ears were attuned to a special language, at once casual and urgent, mysterious as code to strangers, yet clear, suggestive, and inviting to the initiated.

What was Louis XVI's role in this intrigue? To be felled.

Talleyrand was unquestionably sympathetic to the Orléanists, and

71

they to him. How deep his commitment ran is not documented, for there, as in other areas, he must have acted circumspectly. But the ease and frequency of his contacts with the duc d'Orléans is evidence enough. In any event, our supercautious prelate cannot have engaged himself to the hilt even though he was among those chosen to head the projected parliamentary monarchy. Whether he was to have the ministry of finance or justice we do not know. In planning their silk-and-satin revolution, however, these bright-eyed "progressives" had completely overlooked the pikes and grapeshot of real revolution. Doomed to exile, prison, or the guillotine along with Louis XVI and the loyalists, these intellectuals were so stunned by developments that they bowed to public pressure as helplessly as Versailles to the riots which they helped to foment. They had to deal with "Jacobins," who did not gamble or wish to learn how, and who refused to be governed by any rules of the social game or the political one either. Nor was Louis XVI a gamester. He was a saintly man, another "purist" like Robespierre and Saint-Just. Two irreconcilable purities, each incompatible with the flowing humanism of "the candidates for the gallows," who advocated neither virtue nor holiness, having in mind a compromise—something not quite moral but highly practical, in the context of which vice and virtue were simply the two facets of a priceless and fragile possession: life.

Like the duc d'Orléans, Talleyrand was seen as a traitor to his class after 1789. But he was wise enough to break with the party before Philippe Egalité went to the guillotine.

July 14, 1789, came and went, then the October riots, yet Parisian social life continued as before. People still believed—though with some effort —that the "new era" would burst in on a joyous note. The civil disorders had shocked Parisians, who preferred to believe they were simply that.

Talleyrand did not believe anything. He carried on in his usual style. In the summer of 1789, Paris still had its sights, its celebrities, its circus. Besides the current attractions—La Fayette, the Bastille, and Bailly, mayor of Paris—there was one other, familiar at least to the salongoers: a writer who might have been fished out of the gutter with tongs and whom everyone was reading with rapturous disgust. Some of his books had scandalous titles such as *Le Pornographe,* or *La Paysanne pervertie,* which got off to a boring start but turned into a treasury of horrors. Another called *Lucile ou les Progrès de la vertu* reveled in primitive and unsavory acts of cruelty. This was looked upon as "nature" in the raw, layered with sentiment and appended to a core of butcher-boy's sensuality. It answered the needs of a society bored with pleasure. This

Restif de la Bretonne was hailed as a genius. Reading him was not enough; he had to be seen, heard and, on occasion, touched. That appealed to the social élite, desperate for any sort of novel diversion. One evening in November, 1789, Talleyrand was invited to dine at Senac de Meilhan's and to come in costume. Behind masks, the guests could stare at Restif de la Bretonne, who wore none. He was so ugly he did not need one. What a sight the "perverted peasant" must have been, his face exposed to all those staring eyes. Dinner was lively and stimulating. "It was an extremely witty gathering," Restif reported. Afterwards Senac de Meilhan sent him the names of his witty fellow guests: the lady who came as Madame Denis, a shopkeeper, was actually Talleyrand's mistress, the duchesse de Luynes; so was the other lady, the vicomtesse de Laval, and her son-in-law Nicodemus was Mathieu de Montmorency; the one in white was Sieyès; finally, the man with the limp and the ready sarcasm was the bishop of Autun.[2] After a day's work cooking up revolution, they managed to enjoy their evenings.

There were endless meetings. Any excuse sufficed for getting together and talking. At the Palais-Royal, or the Club des Valois—more like a salon than a radical gathering place—at the Café Foy or the Société du Palais-Royal, at the "Club de 1789" where there was talk of preserving the monarchy while destroying its power, or at the "Club des Feuillants" which opened in 1791—wherever you went you would find the bishop of Autun and his cohorts: Mirabeau, Sieyès, Biron, Chamfort, Condorcet, and Montmorin, who entered the government later, Roederer, and Dupont de Nemours. The same people in the same armchairs saying the same things about the same subjects. Their activity covered a very small area, but the fever they raised approached hothouse readings and spread throughout the entire country. When it reached the countryside in 1791, some of these keen-eared gentlemen began to hear rumblings, Talleyrand among them. Deciding that it was time to declare a halt, he put his name to a petition—somewhat belated—calling for the inviolability of Louis XVI. Royalty had been violated when Orléanists abducted the king and queen from Versailles after murdering the French guard. The whole royal family was then imprisoned in the Tuileries Palace. Two years later, these sorcerer's apprentices grew alarmed and began looking for a corner to hide under the tattered robes of royalty.

But it was too late. Still, they managed to pull a few chestnuts out of the fire. The bishop, like everyone else, but perhaps with more knowledge and better results, speculated in public funds with information he culled in the clubs. Power actually resided in the narrow oligarchy of clubs and societies; when you analyzed it, that power was verbal. Although the talk was all illusion, the government acted upon it. And right in the center of this frenzied activity and bombast was the immobile, silent, watchful presence of the bishop of Autun. He was indeed impressive. Over the winter of 1789–90, he had shed, one by one, all the insignia of his priestly calling. First the skullcap, then the clerical bands, which he replaced with a lace jabot. He continued wearing his pectoral cross, but, if necessary, could thrust it out of sight under the jabot—for decency's sake, if nothing else. Yet his friends persisted in calling him "Bishop" unceremoniously and tactlessly. Couldn't they just call him Monsieur de Talleyrand?

Saddled with a diocese he needed only for its income. Talleyrand gave it as little thought as possible. Then the cost of living rose sharply and food was short. In July he sent 600 livres to his vicars-general with instructions to distribute grain "to the neediest class" in Autun. Although it did not alleviate the hunger, it reportedly subdued some of the restlessness.

On August 8 he won the undying gratitude of his canons. To prove that he had not forgotten them in the excitement of events in Paris, he sanctioned their wearing the amice, an oblong strip of fur, usually marten or silver squirrel, suspended over the arm during Mass. They were fond of that bauble and had asked for it the very day their bishop had arrived. What a gulf separated Paris from the sacristy of Saint-Lazare Cathedral! In Autun, they took up the amice; in Paris, they took the Bastille. Also in August, Monseigneur instituted prayers throughout the diocese to calm the people. The streets of Paris were stormy, and Monsieur d'Autun announced: "Religion, dearest brethren, is the firm support of monarchies and the solid foundation of national prosperity. [And what about the Orléanist party?] Return to your homes in peace, return to your daily tasks, you have nothing to fear. Prudence and patriotic ideals will keep you safe; the invincible army of your fellow citizens surrounds you protectingly. . . ." [3] Fear and anxiety plagued the nation; instead of calm there was panic. The good shepherd of Autun preached patience in his letter of August 12, 1789. Monsieur d'Autun shortly would provide France with fresh cause for exultation and alarm, hope and terror.

Monsieur d'Autun Quietly Runs the Machinery of Revolution

Talleyrand's role in the Constituent Assembly, like his conduct in general, was indefinable but not incomprehensible. Without defining it, then, let us simply try to see how he acted, the varied tactics he employed, and what some of his secret dealings were. To the end of his life he respected the ideals of the Revolution and the Constituent Assembly's reforms, which he shaped in great part, though not in showman fashion. He made little noise, yet his impact was resounding. All his efforts were unseen. People have said that he did nothing because there was nothing for one to see. His public utterances were rare; all his talking was done offstage. He had no taste for speech-making and found it a showy, vulgar performance best left to demagogues. He would not exploit his voice with its deep, pleasant ring or soft, intimate warmth, "a velvet voice." Indeed, that voice and his flair for acting could have spellbound crowds, but he did not believe in doing things "for effect." Rhetorical acrobatics were left to his friend Mirabeau, who, as we know, performed admirably.

Once the delegates were assembled and began to compete for debating laurels, he bemoaned the Assembly's oversupply "of lawyers, the type of men whose mentality, shaped by their profession, usually renders them extremely dangerous" politically. A congress of technicians and bureaucrats would have been far better. The French parliamentary system was barely born and he already blamed its prolixity for the street violence. July 14 and the October riots made him wish the Estates-General could be dissolved and new elections called. That was beyond his power and simply indicated his mood.

In parliamentary matters he was calm and deliberate, avoiding confrontations, melting opposition. Aimée de Coigny, a friend and the inspiration for André Chénier's *La Jeune Captive,* said some years later that he "was interested solely in curbing violence, in turning each deluge into a gentle shower." Hardly a do-nothing, he pressed for reform, often the most radical sort, insisting that it be enacted legally, not decreed, and that it result from negotiations with the opposition. Such a policy was simply an extension of the basic proprieties of civilized society. It appealed to the delegates and won far more support for rational progress than was realized.

On July 14, 1789, he was appointed to the Constitutional Committee—a great honor as well as an important task. The committee was reorganized on September 15, but Monsieur d'Autun stayed on. He had a major hand in its distinguished achievements, notably the Declaration of the Rights of Man, that monument to civilized man. It was he who drafted the famous Article VI and pushed through its adoption: "Law is the expression of the general will. All citizens have the right to participate personally or through their representatives in formulating it. The law must serve everyone, those it protects as well as those it punishes. All citizens are equal in its eyes and therefore eligible for any public honor, rank, and occupation according to their abilities. . . ."

Each word was in itself a peaceful revolution; each word raised men from their knees and gave them status in a free, secure, and just society of their own choosing. "The law must serve everyone, those it protects as well as those it punishes." La Barre and Calas trembled when that visionary concept was first announced by Talleyrand and acclaimed. "All citizens are equal in its eyes and therefore eligible for any public honor . . ." True fraternity consists not in calling one's neighbor brother and weeping "torrents of sentimental tears," but in safeguarding the person and property of each individual and in guaranteeing that merit alone can win him rank and honor. This is true understanding and acknowledgment of the human condition. And because reason is supreme, each individual can expect no more than his fair share, hence the statement that citizens are entitled to recognition "according to their abilities." Yet Chateaubriand said afterwards that Talleyrand had never written anything of interest!

His rare public speeches generally dealt with financial matters as he was still representing the clergy. He kept Mirabeau busy for three days and nights drafting a report on the royal lottery. Both of them considered it immoral. Laugh if you must, but this "pillar of the gambling halls" as Talleyrand came to be known (not unjustly) had decided opinions about games of chance. If a near-unfrocked bishop lost 100,000 livres at gambling, it was only that much money lost. But if a million needy souls lost 10 livres apiece, that meant 10 million livres, one-quarter of the French economy in 1790, and pauperdom for countless families.

On August 27, 1789, he spoke in support of an 80 million livre loan. The Assembly "with all its luminaries" was quite as inept as the crown when it came to reducing the public debt. The loan went through, and that monumental deficit was the cancer that finally throttled the monarchy. The Revolution simply made things worse. Monseigneur d'Autun, however, had his own economic solutions.

It is true that on August 12, 1789, he had sent a tranquilizing message to Autun's priesthood urging patience and hope. Two months later, standing before the Assembly and in honeyed tones, he demanded that church property be confiscated. In four sentences he ruined the church totally. That was his answer to the national debt. The proposal was no improvisation; he had less faith in miracles than any churchman. But he alone knew the cash value of the church. When the hideous specter of bankruptcy, with which Mirabeau taunted France in one of his famous speeches, loomed, then Talleyrand offered his solution, the "extraordinary measures" contained in his famous motion of October 10, 1789.

We have exhausted "ordinary measures," he declared; "the people are so overtaxed that any added burden would be intolerable." Very simply he explained that because the nation had no money, money would have to come from wherever it could be found, namely, the church. Why should the people starve while one sector of society basked in luxury? What was to be done? "A single far-reaching and decisive step is, in my opinion (or else I would reject it), duly in keeping with property rights. This last resort seems to point exclusively to church holdings. . . ."

The damage was done. No decision of such revolutionary significance was ever made more cautiously. And as if the whole subject were perfectly obvious to anyone with a grain of sense, he added: "I do not believe it necessary to discuss any further the question of church property." As a matter of fact, it was still being debated in 1905 and afterwards. He then went on to defend the bill's legality: "One thing is certain: the clergy is no ordinary property owner because the properties it possesses and cannot freely dispose of were given to it not for the benefit of individuals but for the performance of services. . . ." The ex-"*agent général du clergé*" knew what he was talking about. His argument is irrefutable.

But on the lips of a Talleyrand, a bishop at that, it was treason. He was betraying his family, his king, and every religious vow he had ever taken. The good work he did later for the church and the monarchy could not mitigate his villainy. Even in the nineteenth century, people unconnected with the nobility or the clergy were still calling him Judas. Yet he had done his desperate country a great service—and perhaps the church as well. For in its poverty, the church revealed to its most devout servants "the eminent dignity of the poor." Many priests currently share the bishop of Autun's thinking.

Today we can look back on 1789 and judge the question better. In any event, the nationalization of religious holdings had to occur because it was no longer feasible for most of the arable land to remain in clerical hands. Those estates were more or less "frozen" assets of the church, poorly managed and unproductive. It is no secret that the monks, priests, and bishops of the Pompadour era bore only a faint resemblance to their counterparts in medieval times. Talleyrand had managed to sum up what had to be said: property had been vested in the clergy solely "for the performance of services." Once the state took over responsibility for economic assistance and public education, it would pay churchmen for their services—and for nothing more. Secularization of various religious functions was inevitable and already on the way. Those who advocated reforming the monarchy had it in mind. Thus Talleyrand was simply

77

carrying out the nation's will. There, as elsewhere, he did what France wished to do.

The proposal was approved by the Assembly on October 10, 1789, and Talleyrand immediately turned it over to Mirabeau. He would set the course and let others run the race. Mirabeau prepared the plan and defended it tooth and nail with every theatrical device he knew. Talleyrand simply sat back and listened. The bill was passed on November 2, 1789, dispossessing the church of vast holdings that became national property. Never did the French clergy experience so painful a Judgment Day. The speed of it all was astonishing.

So was the hatred unleashed: "Having enriched himself by foul means, he had the gall to propose stripping the clergy bare and investing himself with sanctimonious philanthropy in the eyes of the deluded masses. . . ." [1] But how did prelates at the court of Louis XV and Louis XVI use their prebends and their "charitable funds"? Talleyrand has even been accused of entering the church in order to destroy it. "Having resolved long ago to sacrifice the clergy to the nation, he felt it would be safer to betray it and became a bishop." [2] That is too much. Was he himself not betrayed by being forced to enter the church? The blow was crueler for having been dealt by a churchman of noble blood, yet one must admire Talleyrand for rising above the ideas and interests of his class in order to serve the nation and look out for its future. Not all the insults hit target; some were as ridiculous as the pun which joked that Talleyrand had three faces: lust (*luxure*), perjury (*parjure*), and usury (*usure*). Other charges were more serious: he was accused of seeking to nationalize ecclesiastical property in order to cushion the value of treasury bonds he had purchased. That is not the kind of thing he would have done. He did not endorse bills involving the nation's welfare purely to promote his own gain; of course, if a bill in the public interest also happened to serve his personal interest, that was fine. No one had to teach him how to line his pockets. Apparently he and Mirabeau (solvent again, thanks to revolution) made some money out of the affair. Talleyrand is said to have garnered some 500,000 livres from various sources. Needless to say, in the inevitable scramble for nationalized property, the peasants did not inherit the land. But that was another story—off the record, of course. Suspicion sometimes is enough to bring conviction. The amount of loot Talleyrand is supposed to have amassed—half a billion old francs—is not implausible, and is at least commensurate with his talent for confiscation and his lust for money.

A sad fact, because the sacrifice he imposed on the church and his service to his country ought to have earned him greater esteem. As it turned out, his worthiest and most meaningful achievements bore the taint of his venality.

The vengeance ascribed to him was not in Talleyrand's character. He never nursed grudges; if insulted or treated shabbily, he simply forgot about it. Brooding over such matters was in bad taste. Furthermore, the past was over and done with, and clinging to it was a failing as well as a waste of time. When the confiscation bill was adopted, it is possible that he made a barbed reference to his mother and his uncle the archbishop, but there is no proof. In any event, nothing in his speech or attitude suggests that he took villainous pleasure in knifing the church in the back.

Profit, yes; pleasure, no. His diocese reacted at once. What about the vow he had sworn on the cathedral steps? Was this the way he intended to preserve "the property of his bride the Church of Autun"?

From a certain abbé Gouttes of Autun he received a strange request: would he kindly let the church keep enough land for the priests to do some farming because, as the petitioner explained, since a priest's occupation gave him considerable leisure, "he alone had the wits to conduct agricultural experiments." Talleyrand and Mirabeau refused to endorse the union of theology and agronomy, so church lands were confiscated *in toto* through the efforts of a prelate who, four years before, had been paid by the clergy for zealously defending their interests against the crown's.

The canons took issue vigorously with their bishop. Several avenues of dissent were still open to them: "With all due respect for the dignity of his office," they wrote of Talleyrand, "and for his superb endowments, let us wage an all-out attack on his plan." Every priest in his diocese shared that view except the curé de Saint-Aubin-d'Ouroux, who raised his lone voice: "Oh, my dear Bishop, allow me to speak this once. . . . You are an inspiration to all Christians." The poor man had completely missed the point; so had the canons. Talleyrand was neither touched by the one nor angered by the others. When their protest was read before the Assembly on November 11, 1789, he replied most diplomatically: "I shall never forget the precious marks of affection you have shown me. . . . Property? Surely nothing is more sacred. But, gentlemen, none of you can ignore the fact, that we are simply administrators and, as individuals, are entitled only to that which is deemed sufficient for our subsistence. . . ."

Either they did not know or did not want to know it. Pressing their rebellion, yet failing to refute Talleyrand's argument, they attacked him waspishly. "Your tender solicitations," the canons wrote to him, "are leveled at speculators in public funds, rentiers, and capitalists; upon them you would now heap the treasured possessions of French churches and crown impious luxury with superabundance." [3]

His prestige in the Constituent Assembly grew rapidly. On February 9, 1790, his speech praising the Assembly's work was roundly applauded:

> Our task is here, Frenchmen, or rather your task, for we are simply your instruments [how cleverly he put it: the whole nation was collectively responsible for the actions of its representatives]. . . . Yet blame is upon us. Some say we have destroyed everything. Because everything needs rebuilding. . . . We have moved too hastily, while others rebuke us for having acted too slowly. . . . Our meetings are tumultuous. What does it matter if the resulting legislation is wise! Certain steps still have to be taken, and we will surely hear about them from the Revolution's critics. Guard against impulsive actions, beware of violence, for disorder can be the death of liberty.

There was logic and truth in what he said, the words reflecting his own thought processes: slow and deliberate, orderly and peaceful. Outside of that, life was adventure. . . .

Flattered by Talleyrand's praise, the Assembly elected him president on February 16. It would be interesting to have seen and compared Monseigneur d'Autun climbing the steps to the rostrum and climbing the altar steps in Autun's cathedral to celebrate Mass as best he could.

One day Mirabeau launched into a description of an ideal Assembly president. Brimming with self-importance, the people's defender swaggered about, tossing his leonine head with its bulbous nose and pockmarked flesh. The picture he presented was a highly flattering self-portrait. Monseigneur d'Autun pointed out: "Monsieur de Mirabeau's description lacks only one feature: the president of the Assembly must also be pitted." Mirabeau was not put out by such barbs or by heated arguments that left Talleyrand icily indifferent. During one of those verbal explosions he shouted at the bishop: "I'll trap you yet in a vicious circle!" "Meaning you'll embrace me?" was the unruffled rejoinder.

A fresh skirmish with Autun's priesthood occurred on April 12 when the Assembly voted to end recognition of Catholicism as the state religion. Talleyrand, pressing for total secularization, had recommended this action to the Assembly. The canons of Autun protested and begged him to add his name to the petition circulated by other deputies who had voted against the motion. Talleyrand answered them: "No, gentlemen, if I have not signed such a declaration and am absolutely opposed to ever signing it, that is because I regard it as totally impossible. . . . Yes, I believe and am convinced that their zeal has misguided them [those who signed the protest] and that yours has misled you also. It seems to me that you might have restrained your impulse; any instrument of control in religious matters is a threat to the most basic human rights. . . ." The April 29 edition of *Le Moniteur* called that rebuttal "the wisest and most honorable counsel that a citizen priest has yet addressed to his diocese."

In the eyes of his critics, his sober and determined approach to an idea now common and accepted by the church—freedom of conscience and the separation of church and state—was quite unheard of and therefore disgraceful from the pen of a bishop. An anonymous letter from Autun reopened the debate. Seething with rancor and sarcasm, it branded Talleyrand the sworn enemy of the church and of Christianity, bent on destroying religion in order to win credit in the Assembly. The writer failed to understand his own bishop and his own times. Talleyrand was neither a popular leader nor a self-enraptured politician; he was far more dangerous, and proved his effectiveness in the times ahead. We agree with Grivot's comment on the author of that distressing letter: "He ought to have held his tongue." [4]

When the Autun district denounced the letter publicly, Talleyrand showed his gratitude. Autun was tired of quartering the 175-man Brittany regiment assigned there. Talleyrand proposed to billet the troops in the episcopal palace (on the ground floor, he specified).

On January 28, 1790, he urged the Assembly to legislate the monarchy's promise of French citizenship for the Jews of Portugal and Avignon. His enemies saw their chance and devised the following flatteries: "This speculating prelate, intimately acquainted with Panchaud the Jew, after whose death he continued to protect the interests of all rich capitalists of the Jewish faith, is better qualified, in view of his sordid avarice [his irrational prodigality would have been more accurate] and his vices, to be rabbi of that sect of usurers than the Christian pontiff."

In February, 1790, confident that he would reach a compromise with the opposition, the Assembly commissioned him to compose an *Address to the French People*. In fact, they were asking him to apply on a national scale the propaganda techniques he had used so successfully in his pastoral letter of January, 1789. Frenchmen needed to grasp the significance of reforms which they did not always understand, and to learn civic responsibility as well as patience and hope. The truth was that things were going very badly and someone had to break the discouraging news to the people. Talleyrand was called on to produce a lay sermon which would be read from every pulpit at Sunday Mass. Once again the bishop of Autun honeyed a bitter pill for the nation to swallow.

In March, 1790, Talleyrand proposed a bill to establish a uniform system of weights and measures for France and England, the details of which were to be worked out jointly by the Royal Society in London and the Academy of Science in Paris. He saw in it "the basis of a political entente achieved through science." That was the first official expression of his desire for an alliance with England, a lifelong desire.

His stand on a number of financial and monetary issues was judicious enough. He despised the charlatanism then epidemic, and though he would not have refused to serve under Necker, he considered the banker a boorish and ill-bred imposter. Strongly opposed to the issuance of paper money, he said on December 4, 1789: "Paper currency drives out metal currency by replacing it, and since paper can never represent real money exactly, it ends up driving out rather than replacing metal."

He repeated that warning on September 18, 1790, in speaking against the assignats, and went so far as to urge melting down church bells to provide metal for coinage. Anything was better than paper. Again in June, 1791, he revived his war on paper money, explaining that the strength of a nation's currency depends on internal conditions: order, commercial prosperity, respect for the law and for fiscal regulations. Conditions in France were grave indeed, for the day after he made that speech, June 20, 1791, the king fled to Varennes. Both civil order and fiscal stability were dealt a heavy blow.

When it came to drafting and voting on the Civil Constitution of the Clergy, he behaved far less prudently. The law was premature, contrary to national interest, and was endorsed mainly by a noisy minority using it as a nuisance device. Though he knew that uncontrolled emotion can lead to errors of judgment, especially in the political arena, Talleyrand insisted on supporting the disastrous bill. In his *Memoirs* he noted: "I am not reluctant to admit, however much I was involved in that enterprise, that the Civil Constitution of the Clergy was perhaps the Assembly's worst political error." Only half a confession at best; the blame is chiefly his, for the Civil Constitution was his handiwork. He was entirely responsible for it. Suggesting that the Assembly was at fault, he said: ". . . it was fascinated by chimerical notions of popular equality and sovereignty." Yet it was he, fascinating in himself but never fascinated by "ideas," who created that colossal blunder. It is hard to excuse him when he knew that in top-level politics ideas do not count, only actions taken in response to circumstance. He admitted that, at the time, "so violent was the torrent of ignorance and passion that it could not be checked." The truth is that his habitual nonchalance not only kept him from lifting a finger against the torrent but allowed him to be swept on by it and even to help speed it on its way. His critics never mention that one major failing of his, far more serious than his love of gambling, women, and money: a flabby will that brought his worst instincts into play. Napoleon forgave all his faults except his alarming pliability—and he knew the man he was dealing with. The Civil Constitution was passed on August 24, 1790, and became law in November of the same year. All members of the clergy were required to swear allegiance to the Constitution. It meant breaking with Rome, civil status for churchmen, a negation of human freedom and of Talleyrand's own beliefs. And though he helped to draft the law, he would not join in the debates on it. It was too late.

Louis XVI withheld his sanction for a month, then, on December 26, yielded. What was the use, the way things were going . . . By the twenty-seventh the first group of priests were bowing to civil authority. The bishop of Autun was off somewhere, but on the twenty-eighth, without fanfare, he took the oath. One more oath, that left him neither weeping nor faint. He went through all the motions without changing his opinion of the officials in charge. It was his last public performance in a cassock, a garment already in shreds and tatters. In a letter to His Majesty which he wrote three days later, he resigned the bishopric of Autun. He did not bother to advise the Vatican. That same week the Department of the Seine had appointed him its chief adviser; the post was well paid, a distinct inducement. He gave up his episcopate then, without regret, and would have done so sooner had it not meant depriving himself of 18,000 livres. Once the Department of the Seine could assure him a comparable income, he took leave of his flock. On January 20, 1791, he informed the Autun district that because of a signal honor paid him by "my native city, where my family resides," he was resigning his see and wished to have a successor appointed, which was done on February 15, 1791.

He had already written to his canons urging them to take the oath: "You will find nothing in the oath that could alarm the most delicate conscience." Unfortunately, their consciences were more than alarmed. The vicars-general thundered their indignation. "Your apostasy comes as no shock to anyone," they wrote to their bishop, "having sunk to depths of opprobrium beyond the reach of further dishonor or degradation, you can only aspire to consummate your iniquity. . . ."

Compliments of that sort are hard to swallow even for the self-possessed. "Have you thus forgotten the solemn vow you made, the vow

to betray our holy religion, to violate the rights of the church as mercilessly as its cruelest foes, that declaration of schism, heresy, and apostasy?"

Autun's priesthood thereby invented a brutal indictment: "You are
sworn to betray." He was enshrined in treason forever, and that humiliating word followed him into the grave.

What about that enchanting Lenten season of 1789 and the charming and cajoling bishop whose sparkling wit had captivated everyone?
What of those fleeting three weeks? A visitation from the Prince of Evil!

On the other hand, Autun's aristocracy was not ready to burn its
bridges. The F.B. of Autun (Former Bishop, as he signed himself) had
not left a bad impression at all. The good citizens wrote him that they
could well appreciate his choice of Paris over Autun: "The clerical ranks
are responsible mainly for the calumnies against you. We all know that
the City of Autun escaped harm during the Revolution and managed to
retain a pale image of its former splendor only because of your kind inter-
cession, which we entreat you, sir, to continue manifesting."

The abbé Gouttes replaced the abbé de Périgord. In league with
other scoundrels like himself, the new bishop stripped the diocese bare.

The Autun district appealed once again to Talleyrand in 1800 when
Lucien Bonaparte threatened to carry off two paintings in the cathedral.
Like the abbé Gouttes and his band of thieves, the Bonapartes took
everything they could lay hands on. But Talleyrand did not intervene,
for in 1800 it was not politic to refuse Lucien Bonaparte a Van Eyck and
a Fra Bartolomeo if he fancied them. Thus ended the relations between
Autun and its former bishop.

From Oath-Taking to Bishop-Making

One must admire the ease with which our hero shed his tiresome sacer-
dotal duties and plunged into politics. This shocking act invoked thun-
derous outcries reaching all the way to Rome. But the shrieks of horror
over Talleyrand's conduct surely must have mounted to Heaven when,
on February 24, 1791, a month after his resignation, he decided to consecrate two Constitutionalist bishops whom the Catholic community had
refused to confirm. He manufactured certain dates in his *Memoirs,*
claiming to have ordained one of the prelates before resigning his own
see and hoping thus to save face by admitting only half the truth. It
really makes no difference whether he anointed only one, as he said, or
three, according to the facts (on March 24 he consecrated the bishop of

Paris as well). Once again his critics have judged him too harshly. Consecration from the hands of a former bishop, they said, was not binding. A foolish argument, for though he had renounced his episcopate, Talleyrand remained a bishop. The sacrament was permanent and indelible.

Why did he perform the ceremonies? Just to be obnoxious, as some say? No, he was caught in a vise and saw no way out. Also, he regarded the whole procedure as mere ritual and harmless, except to moribund prejudices. Furthermore, it was potentially useful to help rally a new generation of clergy and heal a divided society out of which tomorrow's social and religious structures would emerge. To repair the breach he had opened, he declared in his *Memoirs* that he had consecrated two new bishops to preserve the remnants of Catholicism in France lest it succumb to Presbyterianism. That sophistry, invented thirty years later to justify what he had done, fooled no one, even under the Restoration. Still, he never abandoned the Catholic faith and remained deeply attached to its priests and its practices, or at least his own version of them.

The consecration of the two bishops had its lighter side. To begin with, nobody was eager to claim the honor of sanctifying renegade priests who had taken the civic oath. The majority of bishops had refused it; the ones who appeared at the consecration were scarcely the flower of the priesthood. The abbé Gouttes was there. Three of the Constitution-bound bishops had to be chosen: besides Talleyrand, they were Miroudot du Bourg of Babylon and Gobel of Lyda—bishops *in partibus infidelium* —all three reputedly more fervent defenders of the Constitution than of the Christian faith.

But this new faith was a violent one. The three prelates were not invited to consecrate new bishops: they were threatened with murder if they refused. Happy visions of promotion under the new régime vanished, and they saw themselves instead as martyrs. Flirting with politics was one thing; martyrdom was something else. At first they objected, then thought it over. Talleyrand realized that by consecrating renegades they were inviting slaughter at the hands of recalcitrant priests or their supporters. The choice was Scylla or Charybdis. According to Gouverneur Morris's account, Talleyrand was so upset that he wrote out his will and had it delivered to Madame de Flahaut. The situation became intolerable when the bishops of Babylon and Lyda, cowering behind locked doors, refused to appear or to officiate. It was up to Talleyrand to convince his cringing colleagues that for the sake of the Constitution and their own skins, they had better perform the ceremony. Like a true disciple of cardinal de Retz, he mustered his savoir-faire.

First he went to the bishop of Babylon to inform him that as the bishop of Lyda was on the verge of relenting, he, Talleyrand, was not about to be mangled publicly and if Monseigneur de Babylon deserted him, he would blow out his own brains. Whereupon he drew a pistol from his pocket and, fingering it expertly, threatened to use it then and there. The effect can well be imagined. Babylon not only capitulated but agreed to perform whatever was asked provided Monsieur d'Autun would put away his weapon and persuade the assassins to do likewise. Talleyrand put up his pistol, bowed, and summoning all his dignity, limped off to play the same scene for Monseigneur de Lyda. He in turn melted at the sight of the gold- and pearl-inlaid pistol. Yet critics have dismissed the incident, saying that Talleyrand was scared to death, that he was the one to break down and yield to public pressure. That is simply not so, and the facts, if one judges them fairly, show him to have acted boldly and resourcefully.

The ceremony—if we give it its proper name—took place with an armed guard ringing the Church of the Oratory, now a Protestant house of worship on the rue Saint-Honoré. If Calvin, its founding spirit, had been there he would have likened the event to a Roman orgy. Absently mouthing the solemn service, did Talleyrand perform it properly? Did he send forth truly consecrated bishops of the Aisne and the Finistère? Talleyrand was the last person to worry about such details. As to his opinion of those controversial pontiffs whom he had just anointed duly or unduly, he thought they were rogues. From a nearby window of the Oratory, pointing out the newly made prelates as they trotted to their coaches with skirts raised high, he remarked scornfully to a friend: "Look at those rascals run!"

From Rome came lightning. A papal bull dated March 10, 1791, conveyed His Holiness's distress at the conduct of the bishop of Autun. On April 13 a second bull deprived the bishop of his authority and threatened excommunication unless he retracted his sins against the church. What was he to reply? All apostolic fulminations simply confirmed his will to sever the hated fetters of his profession.

The Pope's ultimatum was carried in *Le Moniteur* on May 13, 1791. That same day Talleyrand sent the following message to his friend Biron, duc de Lauzun, his host of so many wild nights: "You know about my excommunication. Come cheer me up and dine with me. As no one will offer me fire or water, we will have to make do tonight with cold meat and iced wine." A flippant statement if there ever was one.

On April 2, 1791, he lost his "friend" Mirabeau. Using and abusing each other, theirs was a friendship of convenience. Mirabeau was the forum, the opera, the circus; Talleyrand was Versailles, the sacristy, the boudoir. He was at the dying man's bedside and commented later: "He made a spectacle of death"—both a tribute to Mirabeau's theatrical exit challenging death, and a comment on the unseemly melodrama injected into so solemn an event. In any case, Talleyrand performed the last rites for the expiring man, and someone remarked: "Now there's the perfect confessor for that sinner."

The "confessor" was executor of Mirabeau's will and charged to deliver a final message from the departed the next day before the Assembly. Realizing at last that their champion was gone forever, the delegates were stunned. In place of a funeral oration, Talleyrand presented a decidedly perfunctory appreciation of the deceased in the Church of Saint-Eustache. Grandiloquence, after all, was not his specialty.

The crowning touch to that noble friendship was the rumor that Mirabeau died in Talleyrand's arms because the latter poisoned him. This ridiculous story is still repeated occasionally.

In his last years, Talleyrand supplied the biographical material for Colmache's *Reminiscences of Prince Talleyrand*. He recalled Mirabeau's keen mind as well as his apathy and irresoluteness, which made him a pawn in the hands of dangerous men like Pétion and Brisson, fanatical "republicans" hell-bent on a disastrous course. In 1791 Talleyrand believed that France and the monarchy were inseparable, that the country was not ripe for democracy; the French had no sense of civic duty, and abolishing the throne would not lead to parliamentary government, but instead to what he described as "a popular state under a dictator." Even in 1791 he caught wind of Robespierre and the Committee of Public Safety. Mirabeau could have fought such a dictatorship; not Talleyrand, whose eyes were open but who did not act. "From then on I saw that he was doomed, but whether foul play, as was said, or physical or nervous strain caused his death, we will never know."

Mirabeau knew that Talleyrand shared his ideas on a government for France but would not stick his neck out to promote them. Why defend princes who surrender their own interests? Yet Mirabeau entrusted him with his hopeless political testament: "I take with me the last rags of the monarchy."

Talleyrand believed him. Still, he made one last overture at court. The tribune's death left an ever-widening gulf between the throne and the radicals into which the nation was about to be violently swept. Talleyrand hoped that Louis XVI would see the danger and come to his senses. He sent the following message to the king through his district administrator Laporte: "This message comes from the bishop of Autun, who makes known his desire to serve Your Majesty. He has bid me convey that Your Majesty may test his zeal and reliability by assigning him some task either in the district or in the National Assembly. His ability to execute your wishes will prove his zeal" (April 20, 1791).

That plainly incriminating document was later discovered in the famous iron strongbox containing the king's papers which the Convention seized. There was a second note dated May 3, 1791, informing His Majesty that Talleyrand was going to address the Assembly on the use of religious buildings and would welcome the monarch's comments. No reply.

On May 7, 1791, Talleyrand gave a remarkable speech. He who had sworn to uphold the Civil Constitution now defended freedom of conscience in non-juror priests. "It is time we recognize that freedom of opinion is not a hollow phrase in the Declaration of Human Rights, that it is a genuine freedom, a real possession no less sacred or inviolate than others, and must be protected." That was his concept of liberty.

Liberty, alas, barely born, was struggling to survive. Those who had voted for the Declaration already needed reminding that freedom of speech extended to dissenters as well. We encounter this amazing stricture: "Let us hear no more of tolerance: this prevalent word is insulting and should be stricken from the vocabulary of a free and informed people." Twentieth-century talk.

Without mentioning himself, he referred to papal denunciations of oath-taking churchmen. That was his public answer to the Pope, patient but firm. Any change of attitude would have to come from Rome. "We shall await confidently either from the present disabused [to prove that he is not] pontiff or else his successors [no hurry!] the inevitable return to a cordial spirit of religion." What cheek! And doesn't it suggest that it was the Pope who had ruled out "a cordial spirit of religion"? Just as in 1802 people would get the impression that Talleyrand hatched the Concordat with Pius VI's heir.

The French nation, especially the children of the poor, owes the "former bishop of Autun" another debt of gratitude usually overlooked. Chateaubriand, who took such pains to detail his failings and vices, never mentioned it. Had Chateaubriand been less self-preoccupied and more alert to his country's needs, he probably would have read one of the most inspiring and significant statements on social justice to come out of the Revolution, the Public Education Bill. It was Talleyrand's work, something of a charter guaranteeing free schooling to all French children. No one person could have compiled such a comprehensive and fact-laden document. Talleyrand said so in his *Memoirs:* "To work out this massive project, I consulted the most distinguished specialists and scholars of our time . . . among whom were M. de Laplace, M. Monge, M. de Condorcet, M. Vicq d'Azyr, and M. de la Harpe. They all helped me. Our work gained a reputation for which each of them deserves credit."

To be associated with those famous names was certainly a great honor. His closest collaborators were the abbé Desrenaudes, as usual; Chamfort; and Guilhe, director of Bordeaux's institute for the deaf and dumb and an outstanding educator. With Desrenaudes, Talleyrand was able to sift through a mass of information and turn out a singularly solid and lucid document. But the nineteenth century managed to snuff out whatever reputation this prodigious achievement had enjoyed.

An amazing man, that bishop, seeing to it that Madame de Fla-haut's bed was warmed, doing acrobatic stunts with Lauzun, drawing aces in every gambling hall, captivating the most aristocratic and inaccessible ladies, administering extreme unction to Mirabeau as Voltaire might have done it, yet attacking with pedagogical gravity and the tender conscience of a public benefactor the problem of educating all society. He deplored "the total cultural deprivation extending to the majority of the population," and the generally poor quality of instruction due to "blind and persistent observance of long-outmoded practices." All this debris from the past convinced him of "the urgent need for a completely new system of education." Unlike demagogues who pride themselves on their record of destruction, he followed up his attack on the past with a constructive picture of what the future ought to be. Before an approving Assembly, he sketched the monumental outlines of public education, stressing that it ought to be "financed with utmost generosity because it is essential to everyone." He imagined it as a pyramid, with all French children at the base and the Institut de France at the top. "We propose the creation of a national Institute embracing the universe of the mind, the adornments of the imagination, and the full attainments of genius." When the Institut de France was founded in 1795, Talleyrand, not forgotten, was among the initial members. Is he still remembered there? He even predicted that the Declaration of the Rights of Man would become part of the elementary school curriculum, calling it "the children's new catechism." For a while it was in fact part of the standard civics course until the study of civics itself was discontinued.

Not all Talleyrand's acts were unselfish and objective by any means, but his program for public education was absolutely altruistic.

There are much faster routes to fame and fortune, as we know. The proof is that this aspect of Talleyrand's career drew praise from his contemporaries and silence afterwards. It is unquestionably his most humane and commendable achievement. One is surprised to learn that a prerevolutionary bishop of noble blood gave democratic France her strongest pillar: public education. The principle was proclaimed in 1791, but not fully implemented until 1882 under Jules Ferry, the Third Republic's statesman, who instituted Monsieur d'Autun's plan though no one mentioned its author. In 1882, a cassock, albeit frayed at the seams, was no recommendation. Here again, Talleyrand, a product of ageless nobility, was a century in advance of his times, more progressive than the nineteenth-century bourgeoisie, and committed to the future, to the nation, and to the Rights of Man.

His courage admittedly was not apt to win the acclaim of relatives and peers. To them he was a disgrace. His two uncles, the comte de Périgord and the archbishop, were appalled by his conduct. Commenting on his infamous nephew, the count said: "No matter what you thought or said about him, he would serve you if it served his interests." A harsh judgment and not inaccurate. Talleyrand never kept track of insults; his foes could scream their heads off about him and he didn't blink an eye, for one day they might be useful to him. In any event, the nephew had one advantage over the uncle, for all his honesty: the count aired his opinions publicly, whereas Talleyrand kept still, holding his tongue while all around him rose the croaking of frogs in a swamp. A rare gift, that silence.

His uncle the archbishop had emigrated. As to his mother, Talleyrand never spoke of her. Nor she of him; one wonders whether her son really existed for her. Still, in 1790 a respectable publication printed her alleged lament at having given birth to such a "monster"—a current expression of blighted hopes. In fact she had borne a very handsome, intelligent, and sociable son whose life she had ruined because he broke his foot. It was said that her shame at hearing her son disparaged by other émigrés was so unbearable that she fled to Wolfenbüttel in Germany, where she and her brother-in-law the archbishop brooded over the renegade's perversity. He, for his part, nursed no rancor; having blocked out the past and his family, he was thinking of the present and the future.

There was a lot to think about. On September 30, 1791, the Constituent Assembly disbanded, its career at an end. A curious provision made all members ineligible for re-election to the new so-called Legislative Assembly. Talleyrand was then helping administrate the Paris district, not a crucial post, but not an easy one either. Loyal to the principles he had expounded in the Assembly, yet fearful of the turn of events, he resolved to go on supporting the Revolution.

How to Organize a Festival and Learn Something from It

On June 7, 1790, the bishop of Autun proposed an idea of his to the Constituent Assembly and thus created a signal date in the history of the Revolution. Not a bloodbath for once, but a festival, the Festival of the Federation. This is what he told the Assembly, the nation, and posterity (his real talking was done afterwards in the wings, for the event was indeed pure theater): "The Committee has decided that this Fête de la Fédération, a truly national federation, should be celebrated with utmost dignity; that such a festival, by inspiring thoughts of the glorious past, by strengthening fraternal ties among citizens, and by making public the patriotism of all Frenchmen, will prove to any existing enemies of the Revolution the vanity of their attempts to destroy it."

This was simply the preface to the central theme: the festival was a propaganda device for demonstrating peacefully yet overwhelmingly the French people's unanimous endorsement of the new régime. It was meant to suggest the power behind the Revolution. A sublimely clever concept calling for a sublimely beautiful festival. Everyone who favored the Revolution or had accepted its inevitability greeted the scheme enthusiastically. The new order appealed to some who thought it really promised order—an erroneous and costly assumption. Talleyrand's gamble on their show of confidence (or at least on their hope) catapulted him overnight from local notoriety to national renown. People applauded him on the street; in the clubs, his arrival prompted a standing ovation. The drama needed a stage, a theater, and an audience. He put his theatrical and organizing talents to work.

Workmen besieged the Champs de Mars and began digging an amphitheater, its outer rim elevated, its center the base of an earthen pyramid surmounted by an altar. All Paris turned laborer; armies of shovels and wagons moved mountains of earth. In those last weeks of June, 1790, patriotism was measured by the cartload. Wheeling her own specially designed mahogany barrow, the duchesse de Luynes demurely trundled debris forming the gradins over which the multitudes would pass, singing and shouting, to pledge their faith in everlasting national unity. Our bishop, in the starring role, would officiate at the Altar of the Nation.

The holy day dawned under ugly skies. That first Fourteenth of July celebration was rain-sodden. Torrents fell upon a sea of multicolored umbrellas. Still, all was in readiness, and the vast procession set out from the Bastille at seven in the morning. Every province, city, and village was represented. The line stayed orderly as far as Cours-la-Reine, where the marchers broke ranks under the heavy downpour and, clustering under umbrellas, managed to reach the Champs de Mars across a bridge of boats strung over the Seine for the celebration. Facing the Ecole Militaire was the royal tribune hung with blue and gold velvet. Hundreds of thousands of people slowly filled the vast amphitheater. Never had such a multitude gathered on French soil, or in all Europe for that matter, and never did a crowd shiver so under the relentless rain. Enthusiasm and hope began to rise. It was a great event, an extraordinary display of confidence in an imperiled nation in the throes of radical change, which its people were determined to save. It demonstrated the love of Frenchmen for France.

The center of attention at the tip of the pyramid was the bishop of Autun, presiding at the altar in the eyes of Heaven, the king, and his country; he would celebrate the Mass of unity, fraternity, peace, and liberty. Why shouldn't the king have chosen him? He had hesitated, it is true. But Talleyrand deserved the honor; for Parisians, he symbolized the union of church, Constitution, and common people. His name was synonymous with federation: he stood for tradition invigorated with fresh ideas, he ennobled the Revolution, and he alone revolutionized the Ancien Régime. It was up to him to make a resounding success of that festival of harmony and reconciliation.

He thanked His Majesty in a letter delivered by Saint-Priest, secretary of the king's household.

The star performer had to perfect his entrance, his service, and his exit. His sacred—or sacrilegious—act would go down in history. No ordinary cripple could have seen it through. The day before, he had worked over his weakest point, the Mass, lack of attention to which had once got him into trouble in Autun, as we recall. This time a serious political drama was at stake. A rehearsal was called on the night of July 13, followed by dinner at Monsieur de Saisseval's house on the rue de Lille. The mantelpiece served as altar. The acolyte was no other than Mirabeau * who, in fact, could teach the bishop a thing or two about the Mass, which he knew backwards and forwards from all his prison years, having listened to more Masses behind bars than Talleyrand had

* Mirabeau's death, referred to in the previous chapter, took place the year after the Fête de la Fédération, that is, in April, 1791.

heard in the seminary. It was an incredible scene: Mirabeau with his pitted, leonine muzzle murmuring the responses, correcting errors, improving gestures, or snorting angrily, while the docile and unctuous bishop, heeding the cues, managed to produce just the right tone of voice, the ritual motions, the lofty and sanctimonious expression: it all came back to him easily. The dinner guests sat back and roared with glee. In his miter, his laces, and his chasuble, their friend was so convincing that even Talleyrand's faithful little dog, unable to recognize his master in episcopal trappings, began barking angrily and snapping at the hem of his robe, which sent everyone into fresh gales of laughter.

The ceremony was late in starting because of the rain. Talleyrand was at his post at the Ecole Militaire along with the clergy. The Federates had not arrived: "When will those blockheads get here?" he muttered impatiently. At last the signal came; the ecclesiastical procession approached the sacred pyramid, hundreds of priests in perfect order and the bishop of Autun with his miter and cross bringing up the rear. The clergy assembled in tiers along the sides of the pyramid; at the base stood La Fayette, grim as usual, to whom Talleyrand whispered as he passed: "For pity's sake, don't make me laugh!" The proud marquis was shocked: "A remark like that needs no comment," he wrote. It was beyond his understanding because he took for granted his own divinity, whereas Talleyrand, knowing the whole spectacle was staged, looked at it through the eyes of a Stendhal rather than a Joseph Prud'homme, his judgment unswayed by the setting, the Mass, the singing, the plumes and red banners, the transports of passion—or the dug-up terrain. It was all a show, which, if used effectively, could become the political sacrament of the new France, the seeds of the future.

Chateaubriand said that he regretted feeling feverish that day and missing the spectacle. "I shall always regret not having seen M. de Talleyrand celebrate Mass assisted by the abbé Louis, or, with his saber at his side, seen him grant an audience to the Turkish ambassador." Chateaubriand seems to have missed a number of events on which he managed to comment all the same.

The abbé Louis, soon to drop his cassock, and the abbé Desrenaudes assisted at Mass. We have already met the vicar-general of Autun who never set eyes on his vicarage. We will hear more of Louis, later unfrocked, who had no bearing on Talleyrand's career though they weathered the same storms. He was Louis XVIII's finance minister, and a good one. Of course, he was a baron at that point, not an abbé. Things do change. At the moment, however, he and Desrenaudes were busy cueing Mass for Monseigneur d'Autun, whose dramatic genius supplied the perfect climax to the service: with one gigantic, sweeping gesture embracing the king, the royal family, the army, the Federates, the provinces, and even the frontiers, which had drawn near miraculously, encircling the pyramidal altar with its tip marked by Talleyrand's miter; embracing the nation crystallized at his feet, ardent and purposeful under the centuries-old oriflamme of Saint Denis raised in the king's honor, and under the new banners of the eighty-three new départements—he, pontiff for an hour, bestowed the generous tide of his blessings, all sham, but thoroughly practical.

In his fine bass he began the *Te Deum,* which a choir of 300,000 took up, accompanied by a 1200-man orchestra. The voice of France reached the heavens that day, and every face was bathed in tears of joyful promise. Only Talleyrand was not moved, or alarmed, or excited. He was pleased with himself and with his fellow citizens. "Sing and weep for joy, today France is solidly united again, you are as one and shall remain so whatever happens—and the worst will happen. But you shall be united in the new times ahead."

In the end, Talleyrand's comic performances can entertain only himself—and in private. They are too serious to be laughed at, too pragmatic for their cynicism to offend us. What remains of all the fuss on July 14, 1790? A legend, and the memory of an awe-inspiring, peaceful spectacle, a day of hope and faith in a reconciled nation.

Having done what he set out to do and made thousands happy, he decided to devote the rest of the day to his own pleasures. His critics will not allow that: he should have meditated, flown into patriotic ecstasies, and, as they put it, communed with the Nation. It was Talleyrand's practice, however, to administer communion, not to partake of it. Removing his vestments, he headed straight for the gambling table. Did his latest success bring him good fortune? He won, and won royally, broke the bank, rose from his chair, called for his carriage and left: "My pockets bulged with gold coins, not to mention the discount notes." He exhibited the horde of gold to his stunned companions at the vicomtesse de Laval's where, giddy with the day's success, they all sat down to dinner. A splendid evening. Then, with his extraordinary gift for sensing opportunity, he decided suddenly after dinner to return to the gambling table. Luck was still with him; he broke the bank again. That kind of surprise was truly exciting. Tempting fate that way, lured by suspense and risk, stirred his blood far more than reciting Mass to an audience of 300,000. Kings and multitudes did not intimidate him, and the rank and number of his associates was immaterial; but gambling, like any flirtation with fate or death, gave him a special thrill.

After the second windfall: "I returned to Madame de Laval's and showed her the gold and the notes. I was covered with them; they were even coming out of my hat. Remember, it was July 14." [1] Yes, we already noted that. In his *Memoirs* he failed to mention it.

A Few Aspects of Monseigneur d'Autun

His reputation for gambling was beginning to work against him. The Reign of Virtue had opened with the convocation of the Estates-General; royalist pamphleteers and "patriots" gave him no peace. Camille Desmoulins's tract *Les Révolutions de France et de Brabant* contained a fierce indictment of current morality. Talleyrand was extremely sensitive to the attacks of that lay Savonarola: "How are we to curb gambling when among its pillars are three Assembly presidents: Beaumetz, Le Chapelier, and the bishop of Autun? It is true, of course, that the 500,000 francs pocketed by the latter in a session the day before yesterday did not come from some gambling den [pure coincidence!] but from Madame Montesson's house." It is perfectly possible that he gambled at Madame de Montesson's (Madame d'Orléans); he went wherever cards were dealt. Only the amount is exaggerated (it would convert to 500 million old francs), for Camille Desmoulins is like a beggar describing a rich man's fortune, stringing out the zeros in his excitement. Anyway, the bigger the sum, the bigger the scandal.

Though slander never ruffled him, Talleyrand seemed to sense the menace behind those attacks. Some critics have tried to concoct a "mystery" (one more of them) out of his utter indifference to vilification. Biographers and the French public have simply added it to his long list of discredits, thinking that anyone who swallows insults from his concierge is a monster. Thus posterity is supposed to imagine the "monster" lulling himself to sleep reading scurrilous tales of his own vice and corruption, a disgraceful, if not criminal fellow. But the Talleyrand pride was such that even as a child he learned to arm himself against scorn, envy, and even neglect. He was so insulated, so secure in his self-esteem, that the train of insults and threats following him about all his life altered his conduct and thinking no more than the trail of dust from a thoroughbred's hooves slows its race.

His adopted arrogance may make him a rarity, but not a "mystery." Let us try to understand his pride in relation to other proud men. Talleyrand certainly heard that supremely arrogant aristocrat Metternich when he remarked: "In Austria, humanity starts with the rank of baron."

Talleyrand did not reply because he had caught the unpleasant overtones of Molière's comtesse d'Escarbagnas. Had he been a haughty
man, he could have complained that the social ladder in Austria descended a bit too low, and that for him, it began with Charlemagne,
included the Capetians, and ended with Talleyrand, comte de Périgord.
So deep was the conviction that he would have found it impossible to
express; trying to do so would have shaken his rocklike faith in himself,
the strength of which relied on secrecy. The power of secrecy! Nietzsche,
another confirmed aristocrat, said: "Every superior man must wear a
mask." And who illustrates this better than Talleyrand? No, there is no
mystery. Still, he answered Camille Desmoulins's attacks—and agreed
with him! Why should he feel offended if poor Camille did not know
the correct amount of his winnings? To set him straight, he pointed out
that he had cleared only 30,000 livres (25 million old francs) and even
gave the addresses of some of his gambling haunts. But he did not pledge
never to set foot in them again. "I am correcting the facts," he was quoted
as saying in the daily *Chronique de Paris* for February 8, 1791, "without
trying to justify them." He went on to admit his frailties and asked how
anyone could be perfect. Was not the test of a man's sincerity his will-
ingness to undertake self-criticism publicly? "Therefore I reproach myself and consider it my duty to say so, for since the dawn of virtue's
reign . . . the one true way to redeem one's faults is by having the
courage to admit them."

But this is laughable: in order to erase a sin, one had only to confess
it publicly. According to Jean-Jacques's *Confessions,* he was in a state
of utter "virtue." Had he ever concealed his gambling and wenching?
No, he had aired everything; you could read it in the press. So he was
blameless and need never feel remorse.

Why all the insolent and hypocritical nonsense? He had just been
nominated for the archbishopric of Paris, a post he did not want at any
price. Bent on quitting the priesthood, he was hardly in the mood to
consider advancement in the profession he abhorred. The church was
about to capsize—as he knew better than anyone—and they were offering him the job of helmsman. Thank you very much. To discourage any
more of such good will, he confessed his sins, and in order to render
them unpardonable and himself unfit for the office proposed, he published them in the press. Seeing them in print, a royalist pamphleteer
commented: "It is common knowledge that whatever the bishop of
Autun has to say is the gospel truth." They called him a "gambler, an
oath-taker, and a thief." Thanks to enemies on the left and right, he
escaped the archbishopric.

On the other hand, he would have welcomed a government post. The nation's finances were in such sorry shape that Necker, whom the king had called in, did not know where to turn for help in managing them. To reach the father, Talleyrand besieged the daughter, Germaine de Staël. Courting her urgently and openly, his rapid progress and tangible results soon were the talk of Paris. That was the time poor Adelaide became jealous and took up with Lord Wycombe. Germaine de Staël was not a typical Talleyrand conquest. She was a big woman, built like a stevedore, her bodice powerless to subdue the mountains of flesh and muscle. Broad-shouldered, with a heavy neck and sturdy arms, her skin was swarthy, her features coarse, her eyebrows thick. Like many of her sister amazons, she had a weakness for ornate, frilly costumes and a peculiar relish for turbans, which she wound around her head haphazardly leaving clumps of shiny black locks peering out at all angles. One was forced to admit that the legendary Germaine was not a fashion plate. Still, her black eyes had depth and sparkle, her mind was brilliant, tireless, and stimulating, and she was unusually generous and sensitive. In that too capacious, too stout heart of hers dwelt a forget-me-not. She became Talleyrand's mistress and most loyal friend in the troubled times ahead. To break into the government, he was willing to put up with Germaine's somewhat bulky and bookish mentality, her bulk itself, her literary effusions and passionate enthusiasms. His strategy was plain: while Calonne held power, Necker was the worst friend a king could have. But when Necker triumphed in the twilight of the monarchy, Talleyrand thought it prudent to seek his favor and, for that purpose, to chase his daughter. Though highly recommended to Necker, Monsieur d'Autun's services were refused. Necker wrote to the king of Sweden that Talleyrand was "a brilliant and capable man, ill-served by his ambition" (and also probably by the contempt he had once displayed for Necker).

In all the confusion, Marie Antoinette, who detested Talleyrand, apparently favored his appointment and asked Vicq d'Azyr, her doctor, to see what support he could muster. When the queen's endorsement leaked out, the Assembly at once refused Talleyrand the post they had been ready to offer him as a reward for his earlier efforts in the financial domain.

An attack had worked out in his favor; a good word killed his hopes. That is life.

His own financial picture, though better than the national one, was far from sound. Talleyrand was up to his ears in debt. Still, his work in the Assembly made foreign representatives seek him out, having heard of his great discretion. From the Spanish ambassador alone he received the equivalent of 500,000 livres (not the guesswork of a pamphleteer this time) for promoting renewal of the Franco-Spanish treaty of alliance. When church property had been nationalized, he had received the same amount, making a total of a billion old francs in two years. They disappeared just as they had come. In 1791, Talleyrand borrowed Madame de Flahaut's jewels and pawned them for 92,000 livres to settle some of his debts. Where did all the money go? For lavish living, for gifts? Both. He gambled away most of it. People speak of his colossal winnings—an isolated incident compared to near-daily losses that sometimes reached the tens of millions. He pauperized himself nightly without batting an eyelash. That stolid, self-possessed indifference was part of his princely bearing and his own way of impressing people silently.

Such a life called for constant monetary refueling. During the Restoration, when he told Vitrolles: "You see, one must never be taken for a poor devil. I was always a rich one," he seemed to forget that once he was nearly destitute and contemplating suicide. With or without money, he managed to live lavishly, maintaining his usual poise and polish even when the funds ran out. Still, logic told him that the best way of upholding the Talleyrand style of life was to have lots of money even if he spent it all, for spending entered into his "art of living."

The *Galerie des Etats Généraux* contains the following portrait of Talleyrand under the suggestive name of "Amène" ("Pleasing" or "Agreeable"):

> Amène has enchanting manners that enhance virtue itself. An excellent mind is his chief asset; in judging men compassionately and events dispassionately, he possesses the moderation that distinguishes a wise man. Amène does not aspire to achieve fame overnight [a good point, for Talleyrand was never in a hurry, not even for position; his ambition operated in slow gear]. He will succeed by seizing the abundant opportunities available to one who does not force the hand of fortune.[1]

The description has many familiar features, its benevolence far more revealing than slander. But then its author Choderlos de Laclos is not inept. He ends up by telling us that a "pleasant disposition, good looks, and appealing warmth" inspired the name Amène, and that apart from his rank and education, this kind and liberal nobleman had an exceptional intellect, unique in his day except for Napoleon's. In contrast, another contemporary appraisal of Talleyrand published in 1790 under the title *Portrait d'un aristocrate* strips him of everything, including intelligence:

> Artless and dull-witted, yet highly competent
> Under Calonne at making ten for one on the Exchange
> And in his ancient harem at flouting decency
> Such was once the life of Autun's pontiff.
> . . . Coldly, callously, he rejects tradition,
> Counsels thievery, teaches perjury
> And sows discord while preaching peace.
> Over and over we hear that he can create nothing
> And is reading someone else's speeches.

[Chateaubriand was to echo the last reproach, complaining that Talleyrand could not write and was too lazy to work at it. The fact remains that he and Voltaire spoke the same language.]

> But what another man wrote he surely inspired
> Its pulse is unmistakably his.[2]

In 1834, Villemarest sought revenge for his dismissal as secretary of state by publishing his scathing *Monsieur de Talleyrand,* a treasury of slander. The author reported that, in 1790, the Tuileries (i.e., Louis XVI and Marie Antoinette) made "advances" to Talleyrand in the form, to be sure, of huge sums of money. One might expect to hear next that he leaped voraciously upon the gold, waiving all loyalties. But no, the attack was more venomous. Talleyrand is supposed to have resented the gift and spurned it with the following comment (the content, style, and tone of which deserve careful examination): "In the treasury of public opinion I shall find far greater resources than you offer me. Money obtained at court heralds disaster; and since I want more money, I shall make sure to build my fortune on firmer ground." That is a horse trader's blunt and vulgar tongue, not Talleyrand's. He would never have addressed the court or any minister on such a note. Unfortunately, however, Villemarest's slander has passed for the truth. Talleyrand's profiteering is well documented enough, as we shall see, and illustrates his greed rather than his crudity. It is not entirely false that he tried to find favor at court. One illustration of this was his meeting at Marly on the night of July 16, 1789, with the comte d'Artois. It took him fully two hours to drum into the future Charles X's head that the Bastille had fallen and royal authority in Paris was at an end. Could he not have found a more alert and responsive ear, or was there none? He picked the count because they were friends and he was a "pleasant" fellow. He could at least persuade him to tell the king how dangerous his position had become. Like the eternal dialogue of the deaf: "It is civil disorder."

"No, Sire, it is a revolution." In their second meeting, the comte d'Artois reported the results of his conversation with the king. Louis XVI would not act and would not consider spilling one drop of French blood. That was the "tyrant, the tiger thirsting for the people's blood," who was to be sacrificed on the altar of the nation. Once he realized how things stood, the comte d'Artois made his decision—not what a grandson of Henry IV and Louis XIV would have decided: "As for me," he told Talleyrand, who could not believe his ears, "my mind is made up, I shall go away tomorrow, I shall leave France." A fine example! When things went wrong, you looked elsewhere for peace and quiet. Perhaps the king's attitude had demoralized him. Like Talleyrand, he saw that the monarchy was doomed. Yet Talleyrand was the one to take a prince's stand, urging the king's brother to stay and serve as an example to others, reminding him that the sovereign would be isolated, and that he *ought* not to leave. His pleas fell on deaf ears. Talleyrand learned a lesson from the prince's conduct, a cynical one: "Then, Sire, each of us has license to consider only his own interests since the king and the princes are deserting theirs and those of the monarchy." The comte d'Artois's reply was crushing: "That is indeed my advice. Whatever happens, I shall not blame you and you may always rely on my friendship."

Talleyrand must have cast a scornful eye on the departing prince of the blood, France's future king, who, when faced with the greatest tragedy of her history, counseled desertion.

Diplomatic Feelers: England Is Harder to Conquer
than the Autun Diocese

Why did he not side with the Revolution? Though he saw its perils more clearly than anyone, still he felt that revolution was the way forward for France.

He said so—and deserves credit for it—in his *Memoirs*, written during the Restoration. Actually, in defending the position he had taken in 1791, he was attempting to prepare his readers for the spectacular reversals marking the rest of his career. That is why he endured the slander heaped on him for his notorious retractions. He said: "I thought it over carefully and came to the conclusion that I must serve France as France, whatever the situation happened to be [i.e., whatever government was in power]. One could always do some good." He came to regard government as merely a "situation," while France was a permanent fact. France must be served by serving the régime that best served her—and only as long as it was capable of serving her. In 1791, France was not in Coblenz but in Paris, and one had to serve her there no matter how much the "situation" left to be desired. Furthermore, he was alarmed by the activities in Paris of a radical faction pressing for war, not because the country was threatened from without, but because the Revolution was threatened from within. The idea of war was madness as long as there was chaos in the nation. Economic conditions were desperate, and the avalanche of reform had stirred up more confusion than enthusiasm. In practice, the new régime was proving worse than the old one.

To combat the general dissatisfaction, popular leaders found a way to rally the nation, as they had in 1789: they raised the specter of foreign invasion. If an enemy threatened her borders, France would unite behind the government. To the demagogues, war meant extraordinary powers; it was a cure-all. In a famous and rarely quoted speech, Brissot declared: "War is presently a blessing to the nation and the absence of it is the only calamity we have to fear." Such a monstrous statement seems incredible. Well, Brissot and the Girondins got their war. They paid a high price for that satisfaction, as did France.

Talleyrand summed up the decay of royal authority in his *Memoirs:* "Royalty emerging from the Constituent Assembly was merely a shadow, a fast fading shadow." He, too, had become a shadow of the old Assembly, but now that Narbonne was minister of war, a highly influential post in the new government, Talleyrand had a top source of vital information. Under pressure from the war hawks—and without relish, one may be sure—Narbonne launched a pseudo-military campaign against the elector of Trier. The operation was not referred to as "war" except for domestic consumption, and foreign governments could regard the whole performance as simply a bit of target practice.

Still, it seemed advisable to take certain precautions. Valdec de Lessart, minister of foreign affairs, chose Talleyrand for a mission to London to find out what England would do if war broke out on the Continent.

To appreciate the climate of Talleyrand's first diplomatic assignment, one must first understand the political situation in which the Assembly and its chief actors were weltering. Beginning in 1789, swarms of secret agents had converged on France from all over Europe, eager to share the spoils of the decaying monarchy.[1] We know this from the correspondence of W. A. Miles, one of Pitt's most active spies in the Paris region. Miles became friendly with an obscure journalist named Lebrun, who reappears miraculously at a later date as minister of foreign affairs. Miles was assigned to contact Mirabeau in order to scuttle the Franco-Spanish alliance. We know then that Miles and Mirabeau were on England's payroll, a fact that is also confirmed by baron de Simolin, a Russian spy from the Baltic. This plump, eagle-eyed little man was incredibly industrious. His private correspondence with Catherine the Great dispels any illusions that the French Assembly was guided by "republican virtues." Foreign powers, no longer interested in the king, instructed their agents to concentrate on manipulating members of the Committee, including eminent persons such as Talleyrand. We also learn that Talleyrand was receiving Spanish gold. By some coincidence, shortly after Simolin sent off his report that Talleyrand had hired himself out to Madrid, the same Talleyrand pressured the Assembly to vote for arming twenty-seven man-o'-wars to reinforce the Spanish fleet.

Miles went after Mirabeau, who favored the English; while Simolin worked at cross-purposes, because Russia and England were at odds over Turkey, which Pitt supported and Empress Catherine opposed. Simolin's great ambition was to win over Mirabeau, which he thought would be a heavy blow to English influence on the French "government" (if you could call it that). His dispatches told of a mysterious, fascinating person, glowingly depicted and referred to as "Mirabeau's friend." The "friend," we soon discover, was willing and eager to serve Catherine. In a report to his sovereign dated March 21, 1791, Simolin announced that he "controlled the friend" and that "the latter commanded M. de Mirabeau's thinking." It was Talleyrand. He succeeded in weaning Mirabeau from London and in getting him to support Russia against Turkey and England. On the heels of a stiff reprimand from the "friend," Mirabeau informed the Assembly that if England sent ships into the Baltic, France would retaliate. Quite an about-face. How much did it cost? There are no figures on record, but Simolin had to admit that the "friend," though estimable, was probably unreliable as long as England and Prussia could dispense princely sums to win allies in the new government. Payments were handled by Ephraim, a Jewish financier. Simolin reported that during the course of his mission in Paris, Ephraim distributed 1,002,000 livres from Monsieur de la Borde's bank, one of the leading Paris financial establishments of the time. He also commented that money would buy anything—particularly from Mirabeau. "His associate [Talleyrand] is a brilliant man and loyal to me; he would serve us exclusively if I could promise him a suitable reward, especially if the promise were fulfilled at the start."

Those dispatches cast a fearful light on the Assembly politicians. On the back of one such letter, Catherine II scribbled her reply concerning

Mirabeau, who was known to have just fallen ill: "Be generous—if he is not dead." He was. That left the "friend." Simolin gave his name: "The bishop of Autun has replaced M. de Mirabeau on the diplomatic council." It will be noticed that our hero's career has now shifted from finance to diplomacy. Still, money was always the root factor. His colleagues did not refuse their services either: all were sold or for sale, and any who were not simply had not managed to find a buyer for their mediocre wares. Talleyrand did not sell himself in the market place; he did his selling privately. With customary patience, he waited for a suitable offer to come his way. A bribe thus acquired the solemn dignity of a state affair.

In the Turkish affair, Talleyrand supported Russia because the sultan, with English and Prussian encouragement, was creating one problem after another in the eastern Mediterranean. France desired peace there; by a happy coincidence, so did Russia, and Monsieur d'Autun collected money simply for doing what he had always intended doing. If we want to view our bishop in the context of his times instead of our own, in the light of prevailing ideas rather than those of the nineteenth century or the twentieth, we ought to note what Simolin said about General Dumouriez, once a standard character in every French history textbook: "He is one of those Jacobins who, upon joining the government, has no trouble behaving like a very decent monarchist." We have to beware of casting stones at Talleyrand, or we shall end up stoning a host of others like him.

Talleyrand's collaboration with Russia ended there. Miles won the tug-of-war against Simolin because domestic conditions in France were so bad in 1792 that the French fleet could be written off as harmless and no threat to England's Eastern interests. In fact, one of the unpublicized reasons for Talleyrand's trip to London was to convince the English that France had no ambitions in the East (though she had them elsewhere) and therefore England could afford to be conciliatory and do less meddling in Turkey.

Why had he been chosen for such a strange mission? Because he was known to be an able negotiator and a long-standing advocate of an alliance with England. Had he not informed the Assembly on January 28, 1791, that it was essential "to lay the groundwork at once for eternal brotherhood between France and England"? His birth, his social poise, and his tested diplomacy all made him the perfect choice. The English could not claim that some run-of-the-mill representative had been foisted on them.

Still, the mission had no official recognition, nor was he made ambassador. He traveled as a private citizen, the idea being that as an unofficial envoy he would be received by the king and his cabinet and could discuss affairs of state. Actually, it put him in an impossible situation. In Paris it was felt that his ambiguous standing would fit him like a glove, but the glove, alas, turned out to be the wrong size.

An unpleasant surprise greeted him the moment he landed, announcing not only that he was no minister but that he was not even to be treated as a distinguished foreigner, the English having distinguished nothing beyond his deplorable reputation. Before he could contact anyone, the newspapers proclaimed that Prime Minister William Pitt had received Talleyrand and denied all his requests. The mission was a failure before it even began.

One further disgrace was the presence of Biron, who accompanied him. A fine fellow: instructed to purchase 4,000 horses for the revolutionary army—imagine the duc de Lauzun horse-trading for the Revolution!—he managed to perform the job in his own fashion. A horse dealer had him arrested for failing to pay his bill. Friends settled the debt and he was released, but the French mission was permanently tarnished. Talleyrand limped off to deliver a letter from Lessart to the latter's counterpart, Lord Grenville, at the Foreign Office and was received on January 12, 1792. The letter recommended its bearer and attempted to convince the English government that France wished "to maintain and to extend the mutual understanding between the two kingdoms."

The chief hope was that Talleyrand could bring back the assurance that England would remain neutral in the event of a conflict between France and other European countries. Public opinion in England was fiercely opposed to the Revolution, for émigrés arriving in London had painted a grim picture of the situation and had launched ugly rumors about Talleyrand and his reputation.

In a second meeting with Lord Grenville, Talleyrand did his best to persuade him that the worst was over and that France would soon reap the rewards of social progress and peace. He told him, believing it sincerely: "I have always maintained that England was our natural ally."

Highly optimistic about the mission, he needed every ounce of self-encouragement he could muster, for rebuffs were all he received. The king avoided him, and when he was announced to the queen, she ignored him. On January 20, 1792, he and William Pitt met, exchanging brief and icy civilities. Pitt made it clear that nothing could come of a mission lacking official status. His hasty reference to the time he had spent in Rheims must have caused Talleyrand to reflect on the poor memory of young English travelers who become government officials. Still, he was not hurt and could understand that temperament, which, on occasion, was something like his own. Talleyrand suspected that Pitt knew all about his secret dealings with Simolin over Turkey and his involvement with Spain that had resulted in arming a fleet against England. It is quite possible, for Pitt's agent in Paris was Miles, and Miles knew everything. That would explain Pitt's coldness.

The baffling impression he made on the English also worked against him. The sense that they were scrutinizing his every movement probably made him more standoffish than usual. Etienne Dumont, a Genevan who saw him and followed his activities in London, reported: "He remained aloof and would not expose himself. The English, generally biased against all Frenchmen, realized that he had none of his countrymen's characteristic vivacity, or familiarity, or indiscretion, or gaiety. The shell protecting his diplomatic life was his sententious tongue, his cold politeness, and his pensive manner."

Still, this diplomatic and social failure did not sour his feelings about an English alliance. Always a firm believer that time was on his side, he waited forty years, until 1833, to carry out his first assignment. His ideas and personality did not change in the interim; the English, however, came to see things differently.

He returned to Paris on May 10, 1792, to find that the Legislative Assembly had been working furiously in his absence. A whole new set of ministers was in power; Narbonne had been dismissed and Lessart arrested. Dumouriez was part of the ruling faction and had succeeded in getting Louis XVI to declare war on the king of Hungary-Bohemia. The game was taking a dangerous turn; English neutrality now being a crucial matter, it was decided that Talleyrand must return to London and obtain a formal commitment that England would not take arms.

To name him ambassador would have been so simple. But bureaucratic intrigue was far more absorbing than the threat of war, so they chose an ambassador to England who would merely act as a screen for Talleyrand's negotiations. They singled out—or rather Talleyrand did— a young man named Chauvelin, who shared his political views, did what he was told, and offered no objection to signing whatever reports were dictated to him: "He was young enough," wrote the bishop, "not to resent their coming from someone else." Reinhardt also came along as embassy secretary; we shall hear more of him later. Of course, nobody in the Foreign Office was blind to Chauvelin's purely titular function or to Talleyrand's real one. So as not to arrive empty-handed as on the previous occasion, he came armed with a letter from Louis XVI which he, Talleyrand, had dictated, a secretary had written out, and the monarch had signed. It said: "It is my impression that the last vestiges of the rivalry so detrimental to us both are gradually disappearing . . . I regard the alliance as essential to stability and domestic tranquility in our respective countries, and I would add that we, together, should be able to ensure the peace of Europe." [2]

Ill timing ruled out any chance of success for the proposed alliance. This second mission had as lame a start as the first one. Still, they had a letter from His Majesty which Chauvelin meant to use to enhance his embassy's prestige. In the diplomatic shuffle, however, the French newspapers printed the letter before Chauvelin even reached London. The English cabinet heard about the blunder, and when the French ambassador presented his letter it received as much attention as a press clipping.

Talleyrand arrived next, unhurried. Just before his departure he had received a fresh threat of excommunication from Rome. It upset him no more than the previous one. For some time now he had regarded himself as excommunicated and his own master. The official bull finally arrived, the real thing at last.

Another threat loomed, however, more dangerous than any waterlogged thunderbolt from Saint Peter's. Ribes, a deputy from the eastern Pyrenees, rose in the Assembly to denounce the duc d'Orléans and his accomplices—chief among whom was Talleyrand. As evidence, Ribes cited "the former Monsieur d'Autun's" two trips to London where he spent long hours with the duke. Ribes's speech is the first we hear of those talks. He also accused Talleyrand of using illegal favors to continue drawing an income of 72,000 livres from his bishopric. If that were true, one could well understand why he did not regret the loss of his episcopacy as he could dispense with its duties and still reap its rewards. What are we to believe? The Assembly rejected what Talleyrand contemptuously termed "indiscriminate and lunatic slander." But the Jacobins were showing their muscle, and soon even the imperturbable Talleyrand would have to heed them.

In London, he discovered almost immediately that the French mission faced formidable odds and was in slightly greater discredit than before. French troops had invaded the Low Countries, much to England's displeasure, and had been beaten, which raised English spirits and lowered French prestige. "Since this news reached here, our position has been painful," Talleyrand reported to Dumouriez. But England was so determined to have peace and Talleyrand so skillful and persevering that he succeeded in obtaining her pledge of neutrality on May 25, 1792. It was not the hoped-for alliance. But who would have signed a pact with the government then reigning in Paris? The mission was partially victorious; Dumouriez praised its chief delegate, Chauvelin, as well as his "dear associates." It was common knowledge that the "victory" was Talleyrand's. Yet all his efforts crumbled when the news of June 20, 1792, reached London. On that day the mob had invaded the Tuileries, cursing and menacing the royal family, who, unlike the palace guard, miraculously escaped being butchered. The king survived without spilling blood, but he was humiliated and reduced to utter helplessness. London's reaction to that glorious slaughter was disastrous. One incident suffices to illustrate what England's government and people thought of the French mission. Talleyrand, Dumont, and other members of the delegation were out walking one day in late June at Ranelagh. All around they could hear whispers: "Here comes the French embassy." As Dumont described the scene: "Curious and hostile stares at once fell upon our little brigade, for there were eight or ten of us, and it was soon clear that we would have plenty of walking space: at our approach they scattered left and right as if we were contaminating the very air they breathed." [3] More eloquent than any diatribe. As if nothing had occurred, Talleyrand—"le père Gambille," as Dumouriez referred to him—went on walking. But the incident made an impression on him and marked the onset of his feeling that the Revolution was bringing discredit to his country. Apt at interpreting signs, "the Man of France" as he has been called by one of the ablest French analysts and psychoanalysts,[4] read the warning: it was time to shift direction.

First Signs of a Reversal over the Matter of a Passport

On July 5, 1792, he was back in Paris. Dumouriez, of course, was no longer in power, replaced by an illustrious soul by the name of Chambonas, who suddenly asked to see Talleyrand. He was desperate. Talleyrand thus regained his seat on the Committee and, on July 6, supported the motion suspending Pétion for distinguishing himself so gloriously during the June 20 massacres, a fact which appeared to conflict with his duties as mayor of Paris. The Assembly, however, felt that Paris's mayor had every right to perpetrate butchery at the Tuileries. The Committee was headed for trouble. Talleyrand had already begun to break away from the Revolution for which he had laid the groundwork. On July 14, from the royal tribune came a gesture of encouragement directed to the Committee members and to Monsieur d'Autun in particular. That was enough to mark them for the mob's murderous vengeance. Talleyrand promptly resigned and the whole Committee after him. The buffer between the crowd and the defenseless sovereign was gone.

Talleyrand carried on his busy social life in slightly lower gear, the best salons having closed. Paris smoldered. The Brunswick Manifesto was an awful blunder that set even the moderates screaming for war. It was more provocative than Jacobin propaganda. War became a national issue: Prussia's insult had to be avenged, her challenge accepted. There was even talk of removing the king from Paris and keeping him hostage. And while a thousand orators talked their heads off to hide their own fears, Talleyrand was silent. The situation was so confused that he had no sense of direction. "I opened my mind to events, and as long as I remained a part of France anything was all right. The Revolution promised the nation a new destiny: I followed its course and ran its risks." That was only half true, for though he remained there, he had already decided to leave France. Revolutionary violence was not to his liking. But neither were sudden ruptures, so he prepared to turn about in his own quiet fashion. Foreseeing the impending social upheaval, he realized that in the aftermath someone would have to put the pieces together. He would do well to hold himself in readiness for that aftermath.

On August 8, 1792, he was acting as juror in a tribunal when someone slipped him a message from Roederer that the Tuileries was besieged and the king's safety threatened. His only reply was: "We shall see." Two days later he witnessed the tenth of August, another day of pillage and butchery. Violence, lawlessness, and mob fury triumphant— the essence of what he regarded as "inhumanity." With his rational approach to things, even to mob violence, he wrote: "The tenth of August was bound to change our thinking; maybe it saved independence and liberty in France, at least it removed and punished the traitors, yet it paralyzed us [referring to the men of 1789, formulators of the Declaration of the Rights of Man and the Public Education Bill]. Now it is no longer possible to answer for events; we must act according to a new set of rules." [1] Though he is willing to give the tenth of August credit, his last statement is still somewhat evasive. Who are the "traitors" and what "new set of rules" does he mean? It is all rather vague. However, his actions in the weeks ahead made his position clear.

First of all, he kept silent. Having seen the street mobs in action, he was not about to teach them respect for life and property. Instead of lecturing fanatics and taking useless and absurd risks, why not float with the current that was sweeping out the monarchy and civil order?

So instead of voicing his dissent, he drafted a memorandum to foreign governments advising them (in his own way) of the bloody events of August 10. The tone of it was conspicuously blunt and cold. In order to defend the insurrection, he had to attack the king, which he did with all the unction of a practiced theologian too recently excommunicated to have dropped his ecclesiastical rhetoric. "The new constitution granting the king an honorable position [had he not said that the monarch was left virtually impotent?] was quietly being undermined by him. From his coffers flowed a steady stream of corruption [and what about the $100,000 from the Spanish ambassador?] aimed at destroying or diluting the raging tide of patriotism. . . ." He went on to say that the king would brook no criticism. And this is how he depicted the mob: "The Paris populace joined with brave Federates from all over the kingdom to take arms and march to the château." There was the whole story in a nutshell, without a word of reproach against the "brave Federates." The Assembly wisely had assumed powers of which the king was unworthy and had removed him from office. Nothing illegal about that, as some European neighbors had implied; the purpose was to protect him. Then Talleyrand concluded with a laconic phrase that makes one shiver: "Today there is only one party in France."

Europe in our day knows the meaning of the single party system; in 1792, France was about to learn it. The bishop of Autun's tactful pen conveyed the message to all the courts of Europe.

How could Talleyrand, with his horror of violence and lawlessness, condone the butchery of August 10? Was he truly the "monster" that shocked every divinity student in the nineteenth century?

Actually, our bishop was on the verge of deserting the single party. His attitude toward the throne is puzzling only in terms of the unconscious sentiments we attach to things—and which Talleyrand did not, particularly in the political domain. Objectively speaking, royalty was dead and beyond resurrection. Whether one attacked or supported the king could not change the situation; what Talleyrand hoped to do was save the royal couple's life, the only thing they had left to save. For that to happen, Europe would have to recognize the régime born on August 10 and not resort to armed intervention on behalf of the fallen monarch. War would have been averted had Europe heeded Talleyrand, and the extremists would have lost their winning card.

On the other hand, what would have happened if Talleyrand had obeyed "a lofty impulse," denounced the violence and anarchy, and championed his king? The bishop of Autun's head would have graced a pikestaff beneath Madame de Flahaut's window. His own peers, safe in Coblenz, would have said laughingly that he had asked for it. History's course would not have been altered, as we say, and France would have lost a valuable head.

Pinning his hopes then on brighter days ahead, he penned that remarkably insincere yet highly practical memorandum. It dispelled the fatal suspicion gathering about his powdered aristocratic head.

His message to the English concluded on a personal note: he conveyed to the government his "sincere expression of friendship, confidence, and esteem for the first nation in Europe to win and preserve its independence." He "relies on a similar attitude on the part of the English people. . . ." Surely those feelings are earnest as well as self-serving— he made use of everything he could, including his own warm impulses. The events of August 10 made him wish to leave France as soon as possible; he decided that a third mission to London would take him a safe distance from the unruly mob whose violence he could never condone. His departure was now urgent, for too many imbeciles in Paris still insisted on calling him "Monseigneur d'Autun," or "the bishop," or even "curé." He wanted to be known simply as Monsieur de Talleyrand. Many difficult years lay ahead before the world recognized the name Talleyrand alone. In the meantime, he had to live.

And life was in London. Before considering his personal needs, he arranged for Narbonne and Beaumetz to escape over the border in his own carriage. That was no small feat, for the kindness might have cost him his head as it did Flahaut, guillotined for refusing to name the lawyer who had urged him to flee. On August 18 Talleyrand asked permission to return across the Channel and resume the negotiations he had begun. The government rejected the request, saying that his mission had been completed. He persisted and applied for a private citizen's passport indicating that the bearer was on official business, though he was really not. It was a last resort; anything was better than staying in Paris. To leave without a passport would have been the worst thing he could have done. To ask for it showed excellent foresight. He had no intention of becoming an expatriate and was simply leaving France, not deserting or emigrating. The distinction is important. He insisted on getting that passport, few of which were being issued and always with suspicious reluctance. He reminded them of his past services and patriotism, referring to himself in the third person: "To deny his request would appear to be a type of surveillance that he does not warrant." Unfortunately, the Jacobins disagreed and felt that he did warrant it. They took a jaundiced view of his conversion to the cult of virtue. But he had courted the new politicians who rose from the corpse-littered streets on August 10 to take government posts and had even found favor with, of all people,

Danton. Thus he looked to Danton for his passport and hounded him day and night. On September 1, 1792, along with Bertrand Barère, a Jacobin and loyal member of the Convention, he sat waiting in the ante-chamber of the ministry of justice hoping to catch Danton in transit. He was still there at eleven that evening. Barère described him: "In the room I met Bishop Talleyrand in boots and a pair of leather breeches, wearing a round hat and short frock coat, with his hair tied back in a knot. I had worked with him for three years in the Assembly. He was extremely cordial to me. I expressed astonishment at finding him waiting for the minister of justice at so late an hour. Because I leave for London in the morning, he told me, on instructions from the executive power; I have come for the papers that Danton will be bringing me from the executive council now in session in M. Servan's house." [2] He waited there until one-thirty in the morning without getting his passport. He would have to come back again, so great was his urge to see London. On September 7, the passport finally came through. What terrible anxiety he and others must have endured those last few days. Life and death hung in the balance; a single day's delay could have meant the end. In September, 1792, an extraordinary number of passport applicants were to sail the Channel. In less than a week it became virtually impossible to obtain one. September 2 marked the onset of the prison butcheries—gangs of criminals broke down the gates and slaughtered "suspects." What happened in Paris is beyond description.

In short, the passport signed by Danton and countersigned by five other ministers arrived none too soon. The precious document read: "Let Maurice Talleyrand pass bound for London by our order." That was how he left France in order to serve her, and her Revolution.

The journey to London was a week-long nightmare. Every road, inn, hitching post, and port was flooded with priests, women, and children all desperately fleeing the savagery.

Monsieur d'Autun had sent on his library ahead of him.

Third Trip to England: A Third Bitter Frustration

London was raising money for the émigrés and welcoming most particularly the clergy. England's concern for dissident priests finally convinced Talleyrand of her hostility to the Revolution. He ought to have been aware of it already, but was too involved in the tide of new ideas which no amount of blood and violence could dissipate. Because it existed and symbolized the France of his day—the pulse of France—

Talleyrand accepted and was willing to serve the Revolution. He wrote from London: "To a Frenchman, the idea of Prussians decreeing the law in our land is intolerable. English and French aristocrats alike are doing their utmost to undermine our unfortunate nation." Attack the Revolution and you attacked France, as he saw it. The victory of Valmy, blocking the Prussian advance on Paris, overjoyed him.

Never idle, he kept in touch with Lebrun in the foreign ministry, although he had informed Lord Grenville that his business in England was non-official. He wrote a "Memorandum on Current French Relations with the Nations of Europe," which contained some brilliant observations; rather than a doctrine (he loathed the word), one might call it a treatise of political and moral wisdom. He never altered the broad principles he sketched out in 1792. "We know now what all those ambitious notions of rank, primacy, and preponderancy reduce to. . . . At last we have learned that true primacy, the only useful and rational kind, the only kind worthy of free and enlightened men, is to govern ourselves and not entertain the absurd desire to govern others." Note the words "useful" and "rational," as well as the pragmatism of such a sensible and just policy. We can begin to understand the scorn that romantic idealists later heaped upon this man who was much too intelligent to court illusions. He also pointed out: ". . . for nations as well as individuals, wealth consists not in seizing or invading the property of others but in exploiting one's own lands."

And here is a thought for all would-be conquerors and slave masters: "We have learned that all territorial expansion, all seizures by force or by cunning . . . are merely the cruel workings of political madness and abused power, the effect of which is to increase administrative expense and confusion and to diminish the comfort and security of the governed merely to indulge the whim or vanity of their governors." Napoleon's fall is explained in that passage; indeed, the fall of every empire built on conquest.

Whether he actually believed what he wrote next is open to question. Coming as a climax to the century of Enlightenment, the Revolution had aroused passionate hopes that wisdom might one day prevail. "The reign of illusion is ended in France. Now mature, she will not permit herself to be beguiled by the political issues which corrupted and protracted her infancy so long and so deplorably. . . ." [1] This optimism seems somewhat naïve coming from a man who usually showed so little naïveté.

Unfortunately, infantile nationalism is incurable. Eight years later, mature France allowed herself to be beguiled by the greatest dream merchant in history, a certain Bonaparte, whose image Talleyrand himself set out to build. When that time comes, we will do well to recall the phrase: "The reign of illusion is ended."

Talleyrand seemed to express himself most genuinely in saying: "France therefore must confine herself to her own borders; a glorious destiny, justice, reason, and her own welfare demand it, not to mention the welfare of peoples to whom she brought freedom." An excellent plan, indeed a vision of his country's future. He foresaw that France, divided, disorganized, and seemingly incapable of mobilizing against a gathering European coalition, was less apt to become a prey than a predator converting political victory at home into a campaign of foreign aggression. That was his warning: France would jeopardize or abuse her glorious destiny, justice, reason, her own welfare and the welfare of peoples to whom she brought freedom. A wise and humane outlook, as well as a shrewd one. The reversal he had just accomplished was very skillfully camouflaged. It was hard to tell which side of the Revolution he was on.

But the Convention decided that question very quickly. Talleyrand had sent letters to Louis XVI on April 20 and May 3, 1791; when the royal strongbox was seized, a minister named Roland sorted the contents and reported them to the Assembly. In view of the two messages from Autun's former bishop, the Assembly decreed on December 5, 1792, that "charges would be brought against Talleyrand-Périgord, former bishop of Autun, and that his personal papers were to be impounded forthwith."

Things were serious. Desrenaudes, who kept a devoted eye on his affairs in Paris, plunged into the fray. He wrote a clever and courageous defense of his patron's conduct and had it printed in *Le Moniteur,* arguing that Talleyrand would have been insane to oppose the Revolution because every anti-revolutionary source had cursed him with "the kind of hatred that does him honor." And he declared boldly: "Among all the corrupt documents found in the old king's possession, I cannot find a single line or word written by him." Recalling Talleyrand's past service, "every aspect of which reflects the purest ideals of the Revolution," he ended on this hopeful note: "I am certain that the National Convention will rejoice to learn of its error and that it may always rely on a man whose loyalty it had doubted momentarily." [2]

Talleyrand also wrote to the Convention to exonerate himself and to proclaim his unswerving fidelity (a rather liberal assertion): "I have had no contact whatever either direct or indirect with the king or with M. Laporte" (only because His Majesty would not allow it). He asked them, in short, to drop the charges against him.

His letter was dignified by publication in *Le Moniteur* on December

24, 1792, but compared to the two found in the Tuileries, it is a dead letter. Only then could he really appreciate the value of the passport issued by Danton; it was fortunate that he had applied for it when he did.

The Convention listed him and seventeen members of his family, including his mother "the Talleyrand woman, widow Damas," as émigrés. They had put him in his place, among his kin.

The police were issued a warrant for his arrest with the following details:

> Taillerand [*sic*] former bishop of Autun has emigrated and is said to be on the verge of returning clandestinely to France [how little they knew him: he was bold, yes, but not stupid]. Try to get information from his relatives or from friends who may harbor him. This is a description of him from last year. Height: 5 *pieds* 3 *pouces* [he was actually taller, about 5 feet 8 inches]. Long face [not very accurate], blue eyes, average nose with a slight upward tilt. Taillerand Périgord has a limp, either in the right or left foot [at the inspector's discretion!].

How benevolent the English climate could seem to a man with a price on his head in Paris. He wrote: "I stayed in England throughout that dreadful year 1793 and part of 1794." Uneasy there, however, he felt compelled to explain his presence to Lord Grenville, saying that he was "staying on only to enjoy the peace and security afforded by a Constitution protecting freedom and property." Once again he told the prime minister that he had no political mission and was staying in London solely for the "coming sale of the rather extensive library that I shipped from Paris to London." English officials had their own ideas about this man whom Lord Grenville described as "unfathomable and dangerous"; and Grenville was the kindest critic of them all.

Talleyrand had rented a small house in Kensington Square near Hyde Park, but was rarely in it. People who limp seldom stay at home, as La Fontaine pointed out. Often he was visiting Mrs. Cosway, a painter, or Mrs. Philipps at Juniper Hall, where many French émigrés gathered. He had the fondest memories of that house, and just before leaving England, he wrote to Mrs. Philipps: "Let me express my heartfelt wishes to you, the Captain, and your children. You will find that in America you have a most willing servant. On my return to Europe I shall not fail to come to Surrey, for everything dear to my heart and soul is there." [3]

His countrymen were also there—and sorely divided. The first émigrés, royalists all, hated the "Constitutionalist" émigrés, last to arrive and looked upon as the source of all ills. No one was more heartily detested than Talleyrand. Royalists nursed their bitter remorse and, not knowing what else to do, kept hoping. They hoped for vengeance. As in Paris, they drew up lists of suspects, condemning them to every form of torture, the most civilized of which were the wheel, drawing and quartering, the stake, and the galleys. Talleyrand's name was among those doomed to be quartered according to a list in the possession of the comte d'Artois, who had once told him that he should act as he pleased; now the count singled out for quartering the man who would place him on the throne thirty years later. Whereas all this was only idle talk, in Paris the sentences were actually being carried out.

He also had his friends Narbonne, Mathieu de Montmorency, Beaumetz, Jaucourt, Lally-Tollendal, and, of course, Madame de Flahaut, living frugally and trying to make ends meet. She asked Talleyrand for help, which he could not provide, being in tight circumstances himself. That hurt her deeply. Madame de Genlis, a staunch Orléanist who lived with Mademoiselle d'Orléans—the sixteen-year-old sister of Louis-Philippe, duc de Chartres—recorded that Talleyrand offered 12,000 livres to Madame de Flahaut later on when she was in Switzerland. She refused the money. The comtesse de la Châtre was also in his circle, of whom Chancellor Pasquier said: "Her austerity was not especially impressive." Evidently, her idea of life was not to add melancholy to all the other woes she had to bear. She was Jaucourt's mistress, and delightful company. His friends of that period never forgot Talleyrand's fierce attacks on the Jacobins for having destroyed a democratic revolution, nor his caustic and entertaining wit: he would thank friends for their love feasts, "the incredible frugality of which was awesome." Though penniless, everyone managed to retain his gaiety and good humor.

One day a tempest struck them: a warm, rapturous, slightly indiscreet, slightly boisterous spirit, so keenly sensitive and intelligent that she could do no wrong—Germaine de Staël. She fell madly in love with Talleyrand and sought to snatch him forever from poor Adélaïde. Narbonne loved her also, and she him. Who knows how many others that generous heart of hers embraced. Talleyrand accepted her courtship, being too polite to appear bored, and too detached to act like a lover; he was kind and somewhat standoffish. Germaine found him unique. Indeed he was, for how many bishops would seek distraction—or maybe just peaceful silence—with a fishing rod? Our hero would spend hours on the riverbank, his motionless figure and inscrutable gaze mirrored in the calm waters. Rainy days he often spent with Madame de Flahaut, who was writing her famous novel *Adèle de Senange,* which he urged her to publish. He corrected the proofs. But sharing life with two women was not always easy. Madame de Flahaut felt that she was losing her "soulmate," while Germaine found him much too involved with her rival. Naturally, the two women were arch enemies. In her novel *Corinne,* Germaine later squared accounts by inserting a highly un-flattering portrait of Adélaïde in the person of Madame d'Arbigny, a seemingly sweet, but in reality jealous and scheming lady bent on pos-sessing a rich young Englishman who rejected her. Everyone at once could recognize Adélaïde's unhappy affair with Lord Wycombe, who was unwilling to share her with Monsieur d'Autun, whereas Germaine had no objection to dividing her favors between Narbonne and Talleyrand.

How did a man of Talleyrand's stature manage to adjust to the idle and meaningless life of an émigré, more like exile? One facet of his extraordinary personality was his plasticity, so marked that one had the impression of lack of resolve. He adapted to everything and everyone: his pliability was appalling. Without his superb intelligence to anchor him, he might well have drifted this way and that. But reason, discrimination, breeding, and a personal vision of France saved him from mediocrity. Moral invertebrate that he was, he was able still to make an enviable life for himself.

Germaine read to her friends the beginning of her philosophic-poetic-political essay *Influence des passions sur le bonheur des hommes et des nations.* Altogether different from *Adèle de Senange,* this treatise confronted the burning issues of the day. And none was of wider concern than human welfare; Robespierre, with all his unrelenting logic, was probing it in Paris. Germaine, too, wanted to share in the great achieve-ment of her era. Talleyrand marveled at her vigorous mind and brilliant prose, and she basked in his admiration, knowing his reputation as an infallible and discerning critic. For her, it meant professional acclaim coupled with a lover's caress. Her fragile happiness verged on rapture. All of them realized that events were bound to disrupt their close-knit group, ruining some of them and killing others. Germaine never forgot the warm, blissful security of those months of exile close to Narbonne and Talleyrand: "four months' escape from the shipwreck of my life." Talley-rand must have won her heart completely. Still, his mockery could hurt; he was insensitive. When he chided her, she could never deny the truth of his criticism. His own temperament kept asserting itself, and if she read aloud, he would rebuke her: "You read prose very poorly in a singsong voice that is most unpleasant. It always sounds as if you were reading verse, and the effect is not felicitous." He often said that one should not aim for effect but should read and speak in the same voice. Words should drive straight to their target, the listener, piercing his mind like shafts of light. The sound of droning dulls the mind; a flash of light rouses it.

Horrifying reports of the Terror in France angered him and aroused some strangely violent impulses: "I have a great desire to fight, I must admit," he told Germaine, "I swear that it would please me no end to give those bloody beggars a good beating." In May, 1793, Madame de Staël returned to Switzerland, heartbroken. Talleyrand had grown attached to her, intellectually more than sexually, yet he loved her as she was. Parting was painful to them both. The many letters they wrote to each other all went astray. Germaine complained bitterly. He comforted her: "Let us not reproach each other; there is no cause for it." Phrases like that overwhelmed her and unleashed a torrent of impassioned protests. In a single line he touched her heart. She was happy. Their relationship was entirely colored by politics.

Bored now with his purposeless existence, Talleyrand wrote to her on September 28, 1792: "The quiet life of an émigré can scarcely satisfy us much longer." He had the idea of using the English landing at Toulon to make that city the bridgehead for a propaganda campaign throughout Provence and establishing a constitutional monarchy there. Hopefully, Jacobin France would rally behind liberal and peace-loving forces. But where was a liberal monarch to be found? "The Bourbons are a fallen race in France. That is something to contemplate" (November 8, 1792). While Talleyrand was burying the Bourbons, they had him on their list of victims.

He would have liked to leave England for Switzerland, but the Swiss informed him that his presence was not desired. He considered going to Florence, but the grand duke asked him to refrain from jeopardizing the neutrality of that city state. He was stuck with the English.

He saw a good deal of Lord Lansdowne, whom he had met in Paris in 1783 at the signing of the Treaty of Versailles. A liberal, sympathetic to the Revolution, he had great respect for Talleyrand and won his confidence to a surprising degree. Talleyrand wrote to him on October 2, 1792, about events in Paris: ". . . those [i.e., the men of 1789] who still advocate liberty despite the mask of blood and gore that odious scoundrels have forced upon her are rare indeed." Where were those men? What had happened to them? "Repressed now for two years by terror and suspicion, the French are reduced to slaves mouthing only what is not dangerous to say. Clubs and pikes destroy human will, habituating men to dissimulation and baseness, and if this vile contagion is allowed to spread, the people will desire no more than a new tyrant. From the Jacobin leaders bowing to the headhunters right down to honest citizens, there is now an unbroken chain of foulness and deceit, the original link of which is buried somewhere in the mud." The image of dictatorship, and a terrifying commentary on France in the year 1793. That candor was proof of his high regard for Lord Lansdowne, who remained a lifelong friend.

He also met eminent men like Lord Hastings and Dr. Priestley who were extremely hospitable. Too much so for his own good. They were Pitt's chief attackers, and Talleyrand, a conspicuous émigré not above suspicion, was close enough to them to attract official comment. His abilities were well known, and Pitt feared he would pledge them to the opposition.

The other English intellectuals he frequented were all sympathetic to the Revolution: Jeremy Bentham; Canning; a son of Lord Lansdowne, Henry Petty, a cabinet member later on when Talleyrand returned to London as Louis-Philippe's ambassador; also, Sheridan, author of the famous *School for Scandal,* who, with Fox, the brilliant orator, were among Pitt's most vehement critics. One day while lunching with Fox, Talleyrand noted with some surprise the signs his host was exchanging with another young man. On learning that the latter was a deaf and mute bastard son of Fox, Talleyrand is said to have commented: "How strange to dine with Europe's most celebrated orator and find him communicating uniquely with his fingers." [4]

Not all his time was spent fishing or correcting the proofs of his mistress's novel. He also worked on a biography of the duc d'Orléans. Some say he had no gift for writing and that Beaumetz did it all. The book was never published, but the chapter on Philippe-Egalité found its way into his *Memoirs.* We also know that he sold his library. The volumes were pleasant companions; looking at them, touching and reading them provided an abstract sense of pleasure that answered his needs; their presence was comforting in his exile. But as they were also an investment, the inevitable happened: he needed money and had to auction the library. Good will occasionally pays dividends, and good books returned his original investment when he needed it most.

The sale was disastrous, however, sabotaged by London's émigré colony. None of the moneyed and cultured public attended the nine sessions from April 12 to 23, 1793. He wrote to Madame de Staël: "Today, with all my books sold, I possess outside France 750 pounds sterling to my name—how far will that take me?" He was discouraged but not defeated. As long as the money lasted, he would continue to live as he chose. But where were the benefices, the Spanish dollars, or the rubles from Simolin?

The last part of 1793 was ominous. He vegetated, or better still, hibernated, a precaution that was instinctive rather than reasoned. When the world has no place for a man of his sort, it is best not to be seen, for one man cannot stand alone against the universe. The situation would not last forever; it never does, especially an extraordinary one. The Convention and the Terror would be consumed in their own fire. Time, as always, was on his side. The main question was whether his funds would outlast Robespierre. Our hero's ambition was of a rare and dangerous kind: gentle and infinitely patient. "I agree with you completely about our present situation," he wrote. "Live quietly for several years. If a counterrevolution favors us, get involved in it [he did not suggest provoking it]. If another type, wait." Such thoughts reveal the passive side of his nature: he was shrewd enough to stay out of harm's way, but that same passivity also kept him from reaching the top. He was never the single moving force in any enterprise. Since childhood, most of his life had been spent *waiting*, as he said above. Waiting for what? For school to open, for the seminary to release him, for his cassock to fall away, for the Assembly to award him a government post, for the church to cast him out—and now for Robespierre's fall. Yet not a finger did he lift to hasten matters, telling himself always that things would change soon enough and for the best. On seeing which way the current flowed, he would plunge in and stay with it, guiding but never leading.

In London, the wait was shorter than anticipated. The £750 were dwindling rapidly, forcing him to move on. One miserable January day in 1794, Pitt sent two black-clad messengers to his house, one of whom delivered a brusque command that Talleyrand leave England within five days. In equally icy tones, he agreed to do so.

It was a harsh blow; without money, or a home, or a family to aid him, where could he go? Just forty years old now, he no longer had a career either in the church or the Assembly. At an age when success counts most, he faced utter ruin. Before obeying Pitt's order, he wanted to find out what was behind it, and whether a deal could be worked out. There was always hope if Pitt were willing to negotiate. Listening for every strand of gossip, he wrote to Madame de Staël: "The story I hear most often is that the emperor and the king of Prussia pressed for my deportation from England. Apparently the emperor and the king of Prussia are alarmed by people who fish in summer and correct proofs of novels in winter. That is what has occupied this busy mind of mine, the presence of which in Europe is so disturbing."

Treating despair with delicate irony, he neglected to mention that his chief occupation was conversation. He might write in the morning and fish all afternoon, but evenings were for talking. At Lord Lansdowne's perhaps, or in some other house where Pitt's opponents would gather. He certainly didn't talk about the weather and probably offered a suggestion or two for undermining Pitt's authority which got back to the prime minister and infuriated him. It is also possible that French exiles in London urged their émigré colleagues in Coblenz to press the courts of Vienna and Potsdam to have Talleyrand deported. If that was so, did his brothers Archambaud and Boson and his mother and uncle, all of whom were safe in Germany, come to his defense? On January 30, 1794, he wrote to Pitt for an explanation and a stay of deportation. With utmost dignity, he sought some measure of justice from a country where justice existed and pointed out the absurdity of charging him with revolutionary activities when the Convention had "decreed, accused, and outlawed me as a royalist," adding that "now I am supposed to be so vilely ungrateful as not to cherish the one charitable nation that has given me refuge." He was sincere, having loved England long before she opened her door to him. Pitt, however, convinced that what Talleyrand appreciated most about England were Pitt's enemies, ignored the letter completely—a response to which Talleyrand was no stranger. His situation was desperate.

Then this pleasure-loving, insensitive man faced misfortune squarely and was not afraid. He sent cheerful word to Madame de Staël: "At the age of thirty-nine [February 2, three days away, was his fortieth birthday] I am starting a new life; I am too fond of my friends to do otherwise." (Had he contemplated suicide?) Subtle egotist that he was, he lived for the gifted, affectionate persons who cared for him and whose lives he enhanced. "And I must also clarify what I have desired and what I have done, what I have averted and what I have regretted. I must show how I have loved liberty and love it still, and how I despise the French."

It was not a cry of disillusion. His ideal was liberty; the French rejected it and banished him, choosing instead to let a dictator flood the land with their blood. The prisons were jammed; half the population was denouncing the other half. That is what he meant in saying "I despise the French." He did not say France. Nor did he utter a word against the English for deporting him. Golden silence!

He decided to make America the land of his exile. Not the easiest choice, it meant forty days at sea and great discomfort. For an abbé accustomed to the elegance of court life, it was no small undertaking. What would he find in America? Surely not his own class of people whom he could have met in any European capital, and did in London. Yet the fierce hostility of London's émigrés sent him fleeing to "the savannas of the New World." Another reason stemmed from his profound patriotism: he did not want to be the guest of a country at war with France. America was at peace. And, in all honesty, he was also wondering what material gain that neutral and liberal country could offer him. He was poor when he left England, poorer than he had ever been, and swore that he would get rich as soon as possible. He contacted a number of London bankers before leaving; with his aptitude for politics as well as finance, the prospect of seeing a democracy in the making was interesting: "It is a country that any serious student of politics must see." He faced the adventure courageously.

Uncomplaining, this reputedly phlegmatic, deliberate man—and he was indeed that way—behaved quite differently on this occasion. Five days to prepare for such a voyage were hardly enough, however, and he asked Pitt for an extension until February 15, reserving two berths on the *William Penn*, bound for Philadelphia on that date. Beaumetz sailed with him, his cohort from the Assembly, and his valet Courtiade. He took with him a bill of exchange for $8,337.77. Madame de Flahaut served as his correspondent in London; he asked all his friends to write to him often in care of his loving Adèle—who would forward even Germaine de Staël's letters. A month's postponement was granted as the ship was nowhere near ready to sail. Finally, on March 1, 1794, he sent Germaine what might well have been his last message, for in those days passengers could congratulate themselves on surviving an Atlantic crossing. Tearfully, she read: "This is my last letter from London; tomorrow I will be on my ship. As a parting request, dear friend, remember that your letters will be my sole pleasure." He asked her to find him a house near Coppet * where he could settle one day and be close to her. "Do everything possible, dear friend, to bring us together before a year passes. Good-bye; I love you with all my heart."

She searched in vain for such a refuge; events in Europe would not allow her to find it in one year or even two. But when he finally returned, his beloved Germaine had a better gift to offer: she opened Ali Baba's cave to him. We must be patient!

Monseigneur d'Autun Explores the Forests, Savannas, and Banking Houses of the New World

At the moment, Talleyrand was agonizingly seasick. The ship encountered a severe gale in the Channel; rather than risk being driven onto French shores—which would have doomed our hero either to a watery

* Mme de Staël's estate on Lake Geneva.

grave or to arrest and the scaffold—it put into the port of Falmouth. While the battered vessel was being caulked, Talleyrand went ashore and made the acquaintance of a rather odd individual, the former American general Benedict Arnold, branded a traitor for having disgraced himself during the War of Independence and forced into lonely exile in that Welsh village. Our voyager could reflect on the fate of a man who realized too late that there is a price for joining the enemy.[1]

The crossing took thirty-seven days, the first two weeks of which were a nightmare; afterwards, things looked up. So much so that the utter tranquility of infinite sky and sea filled him with intense serenity, an astounding discovery for someone with no literary feel for nature, whose experience was limited to a highly cultivated society. The sense of peace was so refreshing that he hated to see the voyage end as they sailed into Delaware Bay. A vessel bound for Calcutta crossed their path; he asked to transfer to it. Ah, an endless voyage to the South Seas! As long as he had to "wait," why not do it cradled in the arms of sea and sky instead of confronting strangers in a country that meant nothing to him? The longing was his passivity's revenge, its surrender to the pleasures of ocean life, to the lazy lapping of calm gulf waters. He never mentioned his æsthetic reactions and seems to have been unmoved by a tempest's tragic splendor, a turbulent sky, or a vast seething cauldron of green ocean.

Because no passage was to be had on the Calcutta-bound vessel, he docked at Philadelphia, to his complete indifference. Three years before, Chateaubriand had gazed on that city with his languishing sparrow-hawk's eye and strongly biased notions, "appalled to find that splendid carriages were commonplace, as were frivolous chatter, extremes of wealth and poverty, immoral establishments for banking and gambling, and noisy ballrooms and entertainment halls." Talleyrand's reaction was less pointed and probably more reliable. Without the slightest sign of enthusiasm, he observed the scene coldly and objectively. He was waiting. "I arrived full of hostility to the novelties that generally attract travelers. It was difficult for me to be at all curious about anything." [2] Talleyrand the anti-tourist.

In fact, the city had little to commend it. Brick everywhere; streets that met at right angles and looked alike; houses all seemingly from the same mold. What really interested this son of Montaigne, La Fontaine, and Voltaire, however, was humanity, society, laws, and money. America, for him, was what you read in the eyes of Americans. Writing to Madame to Staël, he said: "Here, among strangers, I am regarded with kindly concern such as I have not encountered for a long time." Talleyrand had finally reached a land free of hate.

But hatred soon made its appearance—from the French quarter. Lord Lansdowne had given him a letter of introduction to George Washington, not the usual hypocrisies, but a letter containing well-defined and measured eulogies. The bearer became friendly with distinguished citizens like Alexander Hamilton, secretary of the treasury, who offered to hand the letter to Washington. It appeared altogether certain that Talleyrand would be received by the President of the United States. Chateaubriand had enjoyed that privilege before he became famous. Alas, not Talleyrand; he was already too famous, his reputation having crossed the ocean ahead of him, thanks to Gouverneur Morris's letters. His episcopal activities were odd enough, but his private life had also come to Washington's attention and created a decidedly unfavorable opinion. In France, his mistresses were acceptable though not his financial undertakings; in America, people tended to admire his moneymaking genius while condemning his outrageously unconventional morals. Morality changes with the climate. In any event, Talleyrand was in disrepute in certain quarters; he was never invited to dine with the President.

At Hamilton's insistence, Washington might have changed his mind. But Talleyrand had more than the puritan sector to contend with. A Jacobin ambassador represented the French Republic in America and would not hear of an émigré setting foot in the presidential mansion. Joseph Fauchet, minister plenipotentiary, acted on orders from the Committee of Public Safety and would have been only too happy to open a branch office in New York with the head of Autun's former bishop nailed over the door. Talleyrand's arrival in America had created a great stir in diplomatic circles.

Fauchet was scared to death, and fear, we know, wreaks havoc on the human spirit. He reported to Paris on June 15, 1794:

> Some diabolical intrigue is afoot. What it is I do not know. But its authors are no mystery. . . . Try to imagine the foul deeds being plotted against the Republic. Beaumetz and Talleyrand are in Philadelphia on Lord Lansdowne's recommendation. . . . They have dined in all the best houses. . . . I realized what they were up to [?] and stated that they were shamelessly audacious, but I did not believe they would go so far as to call on the representative of a nation betrayed and doomed to despotism by their own efforts [as if Talleyrand had turned against France or even the Revolution, which he himself had brought to her

123

institutions, laws, and civil rights]. Mr. Hamilton desired that they be presented to the President of the United States. I saw that coming well in advance and managed to foil it. I held out persistently and finally received Washington's written pledge never to receive them either publicly or privately.

A glorious victory for the Committee of Public Safety over the combined forces of Talleyrand and George Washington. Still not satisfied, Fauchet was beginning to enjoy persecuting his countryman. "The conspiracy they have hatched is possibly the shrewdest and most ambitious ever launched against liberty, and, consequently, against human welfare. D'Autun and Beaumetz planned to subjugate Monroe, the new American ambassador to France. . . ." [3]

Enough of fantasies. Talleyrand had no such idea in mind. Having run out of money, his most pressing concern was to make some. We know him well enough by now to guess that this desperate need controlled his life.

The recent deportation from England had stifled his desire to mix in politics on alien shores. His associations with prominent families were not efforts to spin political intrigue but simply attempts to establish business connections. As usual, he did not complain at the President's disgraceful treatment of him—thereby corroborating Washington's statement to Lord Lansdowne in a letter defending his own conduct: "A man of his character, endowments, and merit is bound to surmount temporary difficulties arising in this age of revolution from political differences." A highly creditable assessment of a discredited visitor. On May 19, 1794, in observance of American law, he pledged "allegiance to the Republic of Pennsylvania and to the United States of America."

In no time he had found friends. One day, Moreau de Saint-Méry, Martinique's deputy to the Constituent Assembly and now a fellow émigré in Philadelphia, was in his bookshop when two men entered and proceeded to throw their arms around him. It was Talleyrand and Beaumetz, who took him out to dinner. Three other Frenchmen joined the group: the marquis de Blacons, a deputy from the Dauphiné region; the celebrated vicomte de Noailles; and Omer Talon, a deputy from Chartres. Also, the duc de La Rochefoucauld-Liancourt, of whom Talleyrand was very fond; a certain La Colombe, who had served as La Fayette's aide-de-camp; Volney, the world traveler whose books *Ruines* and *Voyage en Egypte* are classics; and a deadly bore named Demeunier, who never stopped babbling about himself, causing Talleyrand to remark that the man succeeded in making two distinct syllables out of the word "me." [4] Their subsequent meetings in Moreau's bookshop at 84 First

Street were outrageously boisterous and merry, all of them chattering like excited schoolboys, joking, shouting, and singing so loud that passers-by gathered in the streets. Moreau would bring out the Madeira, Talleyrand's favorite wine. Blacons teased the bishop, much to everyone's amusement, calling him "Monseigneur" and joking about his priestly past. Talleyrand had a singular way of getting even: he struck out with his fist—and his fists were like iron. Often Moreau was forced to quiet the group when the din threatened to drive away his customers. He and Talleyrand became fast friends and talked of settling in Louisiana, their version of dreaming. In London, Talleyrand had had his own circle of women, the salons, and an active social life—the *only* life as far as he was concerned. Philadelphia offered nothing of the sort. Little by little, however, the genuine warmth of the Moreau family won him over. He had a curious need to find a nest; perhaps it reminded him of his neglected childhood. Whenever he stayed for supper with the Moreaus in their apartment above the bookshop, he invariably lost track of the time. "He would leave, finally, after my wife reminded him: You can afford to sleep till noon tomorrow, but your friend here has to be up at seven to open the store." [5] Normally, he would not have come in contact with people like the Moreaus; he grew very attached to them and valued the evenings spent under their hospitable roof.

Unpretentious Philadelphians were eager for his company. He was extremely entertaining, a born raconteur who could be counted on to stimulate conversation. He also had a keen sense of the absurd and a barbed wit forever poised. Pontgibaud de Moré, a friend of his, reported, however, that "despite his great affability, Talleyrand never won the heart of Philadelphia society with his flippant attitude and manners. Their visitor's cynical contempt for the American notion of respectability shocked them beyond recall." Puritan and middle-class morality could not stomach the free thinking of an aristocrat whose flippancy passed for frivolity and further eroded his image.

Nobody and nothing could alter Talleyrand's personality; prudish Philadelphians were as powerless as the Jacobins on that score. Still, it came as a great shock to local businessmen, bankers, and shopkeepers, who carefully concealed their outrage, when the former bishop of Autun, descended from the counts of Périgord, casually walked the streets in the sight of Quakers and their wives with a beautiful black woman on his arm whose smile was as dazzling as the cheap trinkets she wore. A sight worth seeing on the main streets of Philadelphia in 1794.

Even his dog disgraced him. Talleyrand loved dogs and always had one around. We mentioned the one that tried to chew the hem of his episcopal robes. The dog he owned in Philadelphia was so well trained that on returning from his own private errands, he would thump at the door and be let in by Monseigneur or perhaps by the valet Courtiade. If no one opened the door, he went looking for his master at the home of his black mistress, and if no answer came from there either, he simply raised the latch, went in, and fell asleep on Doudou's bed, knowing that sooner or later his master would find him. It was a Philadelphia legend.

But the scandalous mistress and dog could not fill Talleyrand's life. "Undeterred by the present, and even less by the future, he speculated," Pontgibaud Moré tells us, "with no thought for anyone or anything." Moré misjudged him only about the future, for Talleyrand did think of it and of the friends who would share it but now were far away. The future meant returning to those friends and living a carefree life of ease. "I am interested only in ideas that can take me back to my friends," he wrote to Madame de Genlis, "and keep me there among them forever, no matter what happens to the rest of the world, free to shape with them a private universe all to ourselves, safe from the folly and malice plaguing Europe."

The rest of that letter reveals the writer's intimate side:

My advanced age [he was forty!] and a Revolution warrant the use of tender words that otherwise I would not dream of employing. My fondness for you is friendship unbounded by time, place, or circumstances. Please write to me; I shall not care if your letters are filled with proper names—mostly that of Madame de Valence [Madame de Genlis's daughter]. I would be happy if things worked out for you to live in Denmark rather than any other country. It is the one kingdom in Europe where I would probably settle. But I have no plans yet on that score. The only certainty is that as long as the war continues, I shall stay in America.[6]

To "shape a private universe all to ourselves" was going to take a lot of money. It called for châteaux, parks, stables, carriages, picture galleries, libraries, and an army of silent, flawless servants. To be free of stupidity and malice, one had to be rich. It was the same old refrain: money was the key to everything, including dreams, and Talleyrand knew it. "I am busy remaking my fortune with all the energy born of my plans for using it." His vision of a "private universe" peopled with friends, intellectual activity, luxury, and freedom gave him unbounded energy. He was resolved to "make dollars." How did he go about it? Let us watch.

Talleyrand queried an American from Maine: "If you were going to Philadelphia, would you plan to see General Washington?" "Of course," the man answered, "but I would make a point of seeing Mr. Bingham, who is supposed to be hugely wealthy." The idea that money conferred social position and honor stuck in his head. He had never needed money to climb the social ladder, having been born at the top. As to his honor, it was constantly in conflict with his need for money. He liked spending money. The richer one got, the more one spent. Americans used money to make more of it: the richer you are, the richer you get, was their attitude. He found that unseemly; toward the end of his life he told Barante: "Don't talk to me about a country where every single soul has put a price on his own dog."

Money was a means, not an end. His letter of May 12, 1794, to Madame de Staël dealt with the subject: "Reason prompts me to make money so as not to be perpetually dependent in later years; I am working on it. So far, however, I haven't found a good prospect. There is plenty of money to be made here—by people who already have it." [7]

His failure to make a fortune in America was due not to any lack of business instinct or professional conscience (he went surveying, as we shall see), but to a lack of capital. He was a bank agent, not a principal. Knowing that tremendous profits were to be made by investing in land and commodities, he did just that for wealthy men, but had to content himself with commissions. "Here there are more ways to make money than anywhere in the world. I am arranging to represent European establishments, and any order I receive will be welcome" (August 4, 1794). He was spelling it out to Madame de Staël, whose father, Necker, was one of Europe's richest men. The two of them and their friends might wish to buy land in America or to speculate in European-made merchandise that they could send Talleyrand for resale in the United States at 200 per cent profit. "It would make no sense to stay here and not cushion oneself against the vicissitudes of fortune by making a lot of money rapidly in commissions either on merchandise consigned to me, or on the purchase of public bond issues, or on the purchase of land." In the end, he devoted himself to land speculation in partnership with Cazenove, who represented a bank called the Holland Land Company and another group called the Pennsylvania Population Company. Cazenove introduced him to a fabulously rich and reckless American speculator, Robert Morris. Details of various transactions come to us through Fauchet, who spied on our dollar-hungry bishop for the Committee of Public Safety.

Acting as a broker, Talleyrand sold land to French émigrés wishing to settle in this country. American agents had an abominable reputation with English, Dutch, and French banks. He also planned to gain the confidence of overseas buyers by creating a European company to handle

127

publicity and sales. Fauchet branded that enterprise unpatriotic because émigrés would flee France taking along their gold and investing it in America. One such venture, "Asylum," was already in operation—the name itself appealed to émigrés—founded by the duc de Noailles and Omer Talon, and financed by Robert Morris. Talleyrand and Beaumetz arrived on the scene a bit late but managed to obtain for sale an immense virgin tract belonging to Henry Knox, secretary of war, who had carved himself a generous slice of Maine's untamed wilderness.

During the twenty-five months he spent in America then, Monsieur d'Autun blossomed into a real estate agent and land surveyor. In 1794 and 1795, you might have found him (if you were hardy enough to keep up with him as his valet Courtiade and Beaumetz did) at the age of forty, lame, once powdered and perfumed, indolent, and nocturnal, now plunging into virgin forests, wading through liana and underbrush past the rotting hulks of gigantic toppled trees, hacking a trail with his ax, or floundering about in treacherous swamps. What might Mesdames de Laval, de Brionne, and de Flahaut have said at the sight of their lover splattering about in some foul-smelling bog or shredding his clothes in briar patches? Gouverneur Morris would have been speechless for once, as he obviously could not have believed that a prelate who warmed Adelaide's bed could also hack his way through the wilds of Massachusetts. He had no idea that the Talleyrands were made of steel.

Why those exhausting expeditions? For what purpose? Simply to do business honestly. Before selling lots sight unseen to European buyers, he was determined to survey the sites and stake out boundaries, unlike a number of American brokers, who were selling inaccessible lots, or marshland, or previously sold acreage—or, still worse, nonexistent land.

Talleyrand was also paid for information he gave to the London banking firm of Chollet & Bourdin. He advised them of changing currency values, the rate of exchange, and conditions on the Philadelphia merchandise market. To Germaine (primarily for her father's benefit) he pointed out that financial dealings with America ought to be handled by the London bankers Maillard Seton & Co. through the agency of none other than the abbé Desrenaudes, his indispensable vicar-general and loyal friend, still in Paris in the shadow of the sinister, relentless guillotine. Desrenaudes acted as his eyes, ears—and hand on the future.

But business concerns did not shut his eyes to the singular grandeur of the American scene. During one of his trips he made the following notes for his *Memoirs:* "I discovered untamed nature, wilderness, forests as old as the earth; fragments of dead and rotted plants and timber strewn all over the ground where they had once grown uncultivated . . . vines so thick that sometimes they barred our way; riverbanks carpeted with fresh and hardy shoots; here and there a vast stretch of natural grassland. In other regions I saw flowers that were new to me."

He remarked an appalling lack of taste in American homes. Not their poverty but their ugliness offended him, their lack of harmony and comfort, their love of display. An utterly useless, out-of-place, and costly object or piece of furniture would dominate its shabby setting. On entering a log cabin in Ohio, he was stunned to see a magnificent grand piano covered with gilt-bronze decorations. Beaumetz asked to open and play it but was told that it was hopelessly out of tune; the tuner lived 250 miles away.

In September, one of his prospecting expeditions took him to Troy, near Albany, where he encountered a childhood friend, Miss Dillon, whose uncle was Archbishop Dillon of Narbonne. After marrying the marquis de La Tour du Pin-Gouvernet, she and her husband had emigrated to the Hudson region hoping to make their living as farmers. She was determined to make a success of her new career, and one day when Talleyrand came into her farmyard, he found her, hatchet in hand, trying to remove the bone from a leg of mutton that she planned to roast. She herself recorded the scene: "Suddenly a deep voice rang out behind me announcing, in French: 'No leg of mutton was ever spitted with greater dignity.' Turning quickly, I saw M. de Talleyrand and M. de Beaumetz. As M. de Talleyrand was highly amused by my leg of mutton, I invited him to come share it with us the next day. He accepted."

At twenty-four, this beautiful, elegant young woman raised at the French court was admired by all her untaught neighbors. Her ceaseless toil in kitchen and washhouse drew rapturous praise from the farmers' wives: "Happy husband! Happy husband!" Her delightful memoirs bear the title *Journal d'une femme de cinquante ans*. Though not intentionally malicious, she did not always approve of Talleyrand's ideas (those of his mother would have won her heart). Still we do not dismiss her; she measured Talleyrand with the yardstick of absolute virtue and was a good soul, not without wit:

M. de Talleyrand was kind to me, as indeed he has never failed to be, with his supreme gift of conversation. Having known me since childhood, he adopted a charmingly gracious and paternal attitude. Secretly I regretted that for many reasons I could not admire him, and that listening to him for an hour left unpleasant memories which later I was compelled to erase. He had no personal values, yet, oddly enough, deplored evil in others. If you heard him talking and did not know him, you would think he was a virtuous man. His delicate sense of propriety alone kept him from saying things that might have offended me; when that sometimes happened and the words were out, he would check himself immediately: "Ah, that's right, you don't approve of that." [8]

Talleyrand was extremely kind and generous to the La Tour du Pin couple. He sent the marquise a fine lady's saddle, a horse blanket, and other stable equipment; when she came down with a long siege of bronchitis, he dispatched messenger after messenger from his distant village to bring her quinine. He even saved the marquis from ruin by warning him that his banker Morris was about to go bankrupt.

His description of the marquise to Madame de Staël is a commentary on himself as well: "Her manners are simple and, a fact entirely to her credit here, she sleeps with her husband every night: they share a single room. Tell that to Mathieu and Narbonne; make them understand that it is essential to a good reputation in this country."

The information must have aroused a chorus of "What a country!" from Mathieu de Montmorency, Narbonne, and even Germaine, who was prone to tire of the same bedchamber—especially her husband's. Talleyrand was, to be sure, a man of vision in the political domain, but when it came to morals, manners, and style of life he was invariably "backward." Ah, Monseigneur, wait till the middle class takes over!

In Albany, he met his friend Hamilton's sister, Mrs. Van Rensselaer, who told him that her brother was resigning from the Treasury and returning to law practice in order to meet family needs. Talleyrand could hardly believe his ears; imagine a man turning his back on the post of secretary of the Treasury just to make a living! To an intimate friend of Calonne's and Mirabeau's, a former manipulator of government funds who had pocketed huge sums from foreign emissaries, it was unheard of. Even worse, he had heard that Hamilton was working to *feed his family*. Work was all right to pay off urgent debts before taking on new ones, or for gambling, a handsome carriage, women, fine furniture, wig-makers, or rare books and paintings. One could stoop to make money for such worthy purposes, even take it from a rogue like Simolin.

Upon hearing the bishop make those observations—though cautious, they were clear enough to anyone raised at the court of Versailles—Madame de La Tour du Pin noted: "Such an excuse struck M. de Talleyrand as altogether singular and, if you will, somewhat foolish."

The day after this pleasant visit in Albany, all of them, joined by a rich Englishman, John Law, called on General Shimpler, with whom Talleyrand had some business. The general was waiting for them on the front steps, waving a newspaper and shouting impatiently: "Hurry up! Hurry! There's great news from France." The paper reported events of the 9th Thermidor, Robespierre's fall and execution, the end of the Terror. Amid his joy, Talleyrand's first thought was for his sister-in-law Sabine de Sénozan, Archambaud's wife and a descendant of Sully's, who was still in France. Her noble-minded husband had seen fit to run off with Boson to safety in Germany leaving his wife behind to protect their property. She obeyed and, inevitably, was arrested. Cheered to think that she had been spared, Talleyrand continued reading the paper only to come across a list of the guillotine's last victims, those who rode in the tumbrils on the 8th Thermidor, with the name of the comtesse de Périgord among them. When sentence was passed, she was advised to plead pregnancy and thus postpone her execution. She refused to lie. She left three children whom we shall meet later on, a daughter who married into the Noailles family and became the princesse de Poix; a son, Louis, who died a soldier in Berlin; and finally the incredible Edmond, who inherited the title duc de Dino and married Dorothée of Courland. Talleyrand's sister-in-law deserves a passing salute; she, like the rest of his clan, despised "the bishop," but the bishop admired and respected her. Writing to Madame de Staël on September 8, 1795, he said: "In my last letter, which may well be at the bottom of the ocean, I told you about Madame de Périgord's children and asked you to help them in whatever way you can. The fact that my family and I do not see eye to eye is all the more reason for me to do what I can for them." Such were the "monster's" feelings about his kin.

Though he traveled as far north as Niagara Falls, his *Memoirs* have nothing to say about that riotous panorama of American nature. Enormity meant nothing to him. His only interest in the forests, prairies, rivers, and vast wilderness of this continent was their potential benefit to mankind. The splendid solitude was uninhabitable at the moment (at least for him), but speculation would introduce money and labor, and, ultimately, civilization. *That* was interesting. Chateaubriand's exalted paeans to untamed nature suggest the irreconcilable views of the two men.

Throughout his travels—and they were largely one long march— our limping bishop was accompanied by Beaumetz and his devoted, ceremonious servant Courtiade. When did he ever get paid in those days? Yet even when wading through the marshes, unshaven, his clothes in tatters, mud up to his ears, Talleyrand was always "Monseigneur" to Courtiade. Lost in the woods one evening, with little hope of finding their way out, Courtiade vanished. Amid the tall timbers, fading as night closed in, Talleyrand no longer could hear his valet's ax felling branches. Worried, he called out: "Courtiade, are you there?" From the dense undergrowth rose a desolate wail: "Alas, yes, Monseigneur, here I am." The familiar ring of that "Monseigneur" in the terrifying wilderness made him burst out laughing.

They encountered strangers; chance meetings in the wildwoods seldom turned out well. The three trappers made little distinction as to how they treated four-legged furry animals and two-legged furless ones with money in their pockets. But they did invite the Frenchmen into their warm hut with its oil lamp and three escaped convicts for company. Talleyrand chatted most entertainingly and sipped a horrid sort of brandy. He was so touched by the bearded strangers' hospitality that, under the spell of the conversation and the brandy, he made an incredibly rash promise to stay with the trappers and form a company. Courtiade had seen a few things in his day and was horrified. Just imagine how the servant of a prelate and nobleman must have felt on hearing his master accept a job trapping beavers and reducing himself to the company of convicts. It was enough to make anyone ill.

When sobriety returned with the morning sunlight, they realized how foolishly they had acted. To redeem their pledge of the night before cost them all the cash they had on them; the trappers grumbled, but took it. Talleyrand got off cheaply that time. It was just one small and successful transaction in a career of many.

He also made two trips to New York. In May, 1795, he was living on Stone Street where he stayed for several months. On July 4, standing on his balcony with compatriots Beaumetz, Cazenove, Moreau, and several others, he watched an Independence Day parade winding its way toward the governor's mansion. The French contingent included a group of newly arrived Jacobins singing revolutionary hymns. At the sight of Talleyrand and his friends, they stopped singing and cursed them roundly. A fine greeting from his homeland!

Also in New York, he renewed acquaintances with Blanc d'Hauterive, the former Oratorian he had met at Chanteloup when visiting Choiseul. The poor man was in dire need. The revolutionary government had sent him to New York as consul, but Jacobins in America wanted nothing to do with him. So he took up gardening and peddled in the streets the vegetables and flowers that he had raised where skyscrapers now stand.

Heat and pestilence drove Talleyrand and Beaumetz from New York on July 15; many Frenchmen found the city's unhealthy extremes of climate unbearable. They sailed north to Boston and cooler weather.

"Of all the cities I have seen thus far, I like Boston best. The surrounding countryside is pretty, and the way of life is simpler there," he wrote to Madame de Staël on August 4, 1796. He found Boston society more British and more refined; nearby Harvard College lent a cultivated atmosphere; its social life had traditions and an established elegance, which made that elegance more authentic. Such was Talleyrand's notion of "simplicity"; plainly, Boston was the most fashionable American city.

Talleyrand was not very content with his earnings in the land market. Dollars were hard to come by, so he hit on a scheme for going to India and making a fortune in no time. The steady, prosperous export-import trade between Philadelphia and Calcutta he knew to be yielding a profit of 500 per cent. He and Beaumetz outfitted a ship and obtained financing from Dutch and English banks whose confidence Talleyrand had won. Besides symbolizing a sudden windfall, India meant tremendous risk and endless exile. And all the while Talleyrand dreamed of returning to France, yearned for it, feared that he might never see his land again. In the end, he chose France over the prospect of becoming a nabob and turned his share of the enterprise over to his partner. Beaumetz, having just taken a wife, was doomed to exile and moneymaking. "He is not alone in considering this no mad venture," Talleyrand wrote. ". . . His wife, with an income of barely fifty louis, is a widow with three children." Worse than rounding the Cape of Good Hope.

With that singular sixth sense of his, had Talleyrand guessed that the scheme was headed for failure? Beaumetz died on reaching India. Blessed are they who never anchor weigh.

Talleyrand was avid for any scrap of news from France, preferably economic and financial news, which interested him even more than what went on in the government and politics. Never trusting paper money or inflation, he was relieved when the assignats were voided by the Directory, which governed after Robespierre's fall. In *Le Courrier de la France et des Colonies,* a small New York newspaper for French exiles in America which Moreau was barely able to finance, an unsigned article appeared on February 26, 1796: "It cannot be denied that the voiding of assignats is a blessing." The writer spoke most unflatteringly of Robespierre and painted an optimistic future for France as long as the Directory continued seeking peace, which was essential to the nation's recovery. "For how can you conceive of lasting tranquility in France without peace to restore order and abundance, sending many hands back to the plow, industrious men to the factories, and a flow of wise investments to expand commerce. Peace alone can bring prosperity back to France, making her once again a garden of delights where art and the pleasures of life combine with her gentle climate to draw visitors from all over the world." That idyllic vision bespoke the Enlightenment: peace brought stability, which in turn fostered domestic security, liberty, culture—and, of course, pleasures. All the blessings of civilization in one incomparable nation. It was *Candide*'s theme as well. The anonymous writer was, to be sure, Talleyrand.

The article suggests what was on his mind at that time. "The confining walls of my little room set my head to spinning out grand political designs and redrawing the map of the world." While his mistress was out walking, Talleyrand probably meditated on the future of his country. Now that Robespierre and his disciples were gone, France would revive, that is, produce and consume, sell and buy. No matter what type of government followed, Talleyrand was concerned only for the permanent interests of France, even if the new régime did not recall him from exile. Non-French historians and biographers have grasped Talleyrand's selfless patriotism more readily than a number of French authors, who might better be called pamphleteers (of genius, in some cases) than historians.

At that time, England was a barrier to Franco-American economic and financial cooperation. We can well imagine that Talleyrand felt it was useless to beat one's fist against the barrier; instead, he looked, listened, and derived from his own observations a rule of conduct applicable to future French governments. Though he left us no description of moonlit forests in the New World or Niagara Falls, he did tell us how the Paris government ought to treat a new and fabulously rich country. Writing to Lord Lansdowne on February 1, 1795, he reminded his friend that political ties between England and America had been severed irreparably and were a thing of the past: "Any implied or inferred optimism on that subject can only be regarded as the delirium of an ailing mind or else base and deceitful flattery." It would be interesting thus to watch developments between the mother country and the newly independent colonies. All this was said objectively, without hint of criticism or preference. There was a basis for future relations, for despite the schism, "America is English to the core, that is, England is still in a far better position than France to gain whatever ascendancy one nation can gain over another." Was that plain enough? That was how he felt in 1795. Despite their War of Independence which had ended twelve years earlier, "Americans are inclined to favor the English." Not that they had forgotten in the interval that "without France they would never have gained independence; but they are too sophisticated politically to believe in the so-called virtue of gratitude between nations."

Why should gratitude be involved here when it never was elsewhere? Self-interest, the most compelling motive, not sentiment is what attracted America to England. Talleyrand summed it up succinctly. In America, self-interest wears no disguise "because in that country everyone without exception is bent on making money. So money is the single universal cult; the amount one possesses is the measure of all distinctions."

Those observations were woven into the address he delivered before the Institut de France, which made him a member on April 4, 1797, on the theme of Anglo-American commercial relations. We mention it now because the ideas took shape during his stay in Philadelphia. Talleyrand stressed the potential benefit to be gained from a seemingly paradoxical situation, confusing to numerous French critics who felt that the American colonies had helped rather than hurt England by breaking away. England was intelligent enough to bury her resentment and think instead of her industry. The United States had none as yet, and would buy more readily from her after independence than before. Talleyrand firmly believed that peace had the power to subdue passions and to awaken man's constructive spirit. Speaking of Americans in the year 1795, he described them aptly as a "dispassionate" people. "Far be it from them to hate each other; they fought together, and together they are reaping the victory. Parties, factions, and hostilities have all vanished: like careful accountants, they saw nothing to gain there. Mercantile practices are harder to change than you think. Mutual interests weld together in one day, and perhaps forever, people who for years were raging enemies." That golden rule ought to govern future Anglo-Saxon politics, in fact, all politics. Talleyrand was the one to voice it, but did anyone listen? So much the worse for the deaf and the French.

His speech to the Institut undoubtedly reflected his convictions. He always felt that passions had a disastrous effect on politics, leading to civil or foreign wars, or both. They could paralyze the life of a nation and destroy everything it had built. The real victories were to be won in agriculture, commerce, and industry, victories for civilization, mankind's benefactor.

The 9th Thermidor: Exit Robespierre, Re-enter Talleyrand

"If I stay a year, I shall die here," Talleyrand announced somewhat dramatically to Madame de Staël. Dependable Germaine alerted everyone capable of "saving the bishop." Despite his yearning to return, however, his situation was not exactly desperate. Always resourceful, he found ways to compensate for rebuffs and his own impatience: the black mistress he paraded, the others not black and not paraded, the profit from investments which was substantial if not as abundant as anticipated, his friends, even his dog. Friends, both American and French, meant a great deal to him. Yet throughout his exile, he was his own best friend, never complaining or argumentative, responsive to his needs and his ego, the ideal partner for silent dialogues.

Leave America? Where would he go? France was his sole destination. On May 14, 1795, he wrote to Madame de Genlis: "I am not planning ahead [but that was all he was doing]; Europe will decide my future; nothing could make me reside in a country at war with France. I detest England, leaving only Switzerland or America, and so far I prefer America because she has the greatest love for our Republic to which I am bound, despite the affronts visited on me by one of the parties formerly in command of the Convention, by feelings and yearnings." [1]

Fine: if only Madame de Genlis had publicized the letter or given it a reading, as was the custom, some French spy surely would have reported the civic-mindedness of "Citizen Taillerand." It would have put a feather in his cap. In any event, he did not share the émigré mentality. He was no royalist, not because he opposed their cause but because Louis XVIII's party had no vision. If they began to look ahead, he would join them; if a king chose to rule according to constitutional principles with the support of an elected parliament, Talleyrand would back such a king.

Bewildering news reached him of an auction in Paris on March 31, 1795, of the property of "Talleran-Périgord, aristocrat, former bishop of Autun." Imagine them holding a public sale of his belongings while he was tramping the wilds of Massachusetts. The contents of that "posthumous" clearance sale of the personal effects and possessions of the "late" bishop are extremely amusing and revealing. Let us see what they were.

First, a purple cloth cassock priced at 60 livres and sold for 451—an astounding figure (400,000 old francs). A lace and batiste surplice started at 20 livres and reached 301. That lace must have been very rare! Who could have wanted to pay 300,000 francs for a clerical vestment in a bankrupt country where Catholic worship was banned? The entire wardrobe (extremely well supplied) fetched 13,377 livres, nearly 13 million francs. There were also paintings, drawings, and engravings that sold for very little; the collectors were elsewhere that day. The remainder of the sale was rather frivolous, for our bishop's closets contained some highly original items. An incredible assortment of ladies' apparel included outer and undergarments: an English tulle petticoat, a gown, a blue muslin underskirt banded with white chain stitching, great arrays of chintz and calico ruffles, piles of taffeta and cambric flounces . . . Where did they all come from? Who had left behind the profusion of camisoles, bloomers, and petticoats? Was he saving them for those special parties of his or as fetishes? The collection probably grew from his own indifference: visiting lady friends made themselves at home, dressing, undressing, or changing clothes at will; he never cared what they left behind or took with them, or what they ordered in his name and sent to his address. He was a supremely obliging host.

The sale inventory suggests a handsomely furnished house with dozens of beds, couches, and chairs of every description. But the best indication of his elegant and luxurious tastes was the quantity and quality of his household linens, the sale of which occupied one entire session and yielded 15,000 livres (nearly 15 million francs). The furniture fetched miserable prices: his magnificent mahogany piano went for 1,691 livres, a quarter of what it was worth. Twenty-two gilt armchairs with crimson and white carved lambrequins for 2,209 livres—worth five times more. They had even found two used lady's saddles in his old apartment in the rue Bellechasse, one covered with green cloth, the other with garnet, and an old yellow coach. A reminder of Harpagon's cellar storehouse. Several honest souls at once jumped to the conclusion (as malicious as it was unfounded) that the bishop was a pawnbroker on the side, an idea quite as amusing as the inventory of ladies' underwear. If usury could have opened the door to great wealth, he might have been a moneylender. Talleyrand operated at the top level, in government circles, not lending money on old saddles or rattletraps. As usual, when you aim too low you miss the target completely. So that was how the personal effects and property of "a certain Talleran-Périgor, rue Dominique, faubourg Germain, former Convent of Bellechasse" were dispersed. Yielding to "superstition," the auctioneer had removed the word "Saint" from his various addresses; the sale allowed him to pocket a little over 100 million old francs.

In Philadelphia, on June 16, 1795, Talleyrand wrote to the Convention pleading for permission to return to France and serve her. He sent the letter to Desrenaudes, relying on him to present it to the Assembly at the proper moment and through the proper channels. Desrenaudes, unfrocked now and teaching in the Ecoles Centrales in

Paris, managed to steer clear of political commitments while keeping an eagle eye on every shift in the Committee and supervising affairs for his superior and accomplice.

In August, 1795, Talleyrand met a Frenchman newly arrived in New York named Dupuy, who showed him a speech celebrating the 9th Thermidor given by Boissy d'Anglas the previous March, which "had restored to the people the exercise of their rights and to the Republic its independence." That such a speech could have been given and even applauded by the Convention was proof enough for our bishop that Jacobin rule had ended and that his petition might not fall on deaf ears. He was delighted to learn that "this day revived the reign of goodness and virtue in France." That was saying a lot, for Robespierre and the guillotine claimed to have enthroned the Lady Virtue, who, upon his death, lost much of her charm while humanity regained its own. As to goodness, Talleyrand's soul was bursting with beatitude in anticipation of the reign of goodness, his yearning for Paris more pressing than ever.

What else could he do to hasten matters? He had only his pen and his friends, the one forever pricking the others. To Germaine he wrote: "Either an earthquake will devastate all of Europe or else I shall return next May!" A curious incitement; he felt he must inspire enthusiasm for his homecoming. "Get the abbé Desrenaudes stirring," he added. Talleyrand continued to call Desrenaudes "l'abbé," just as Germaine always called her lover "the bishop."

Well, the abbé bestirred himself magnificently. Talleyrand's petition found its way into the proper official hands, was read in the Assembly on September 3 and published in *Le Moniteur*. Desrenaudes's efforts, his secret consultations, and backstairs manipulations finally paid off: rumor reported that Talleyrand desired to return, was a republican, had never emigrated, was victimized by that dreadful faction destroyed on the 9th Thermidor, had championed republican France abroad and was prepared to serve her in Paris—if she would open her arms to him.

As proof that he was a victim of tyranny, he claimed that the decree of banishment was founded "on so trivial a pretext that the officials responsible for collecting evidence against him never knew what to say."

Were the two letters to Louis XVI signed by the bishop of Autun and found among the king's official papers "so trivial a pretext"? His sister-in-law, along with countless others (republicans among them), had lost her head for less than that. He also reminded them of his services to the Constituent Assembly: the Declaration of the Rights of Man, confiscation of church property, public education, etc.

Boissy d'Anglas's speech had changed the climate favorably for people like Talleyrand. On August 11, 1795, Roederer's pamphlet *French Fugitives and Emigrés* appeared, presenting a clear distinction between persons who had fled France on the heels of the September, 1792, massacres and never borne arms against their country, and émigrés proper. Fugitives retained full rights as citizens, and he cited Talleyrand as an example. "Is not the conduct of Talleyrand and Beaumetz in London before the war and in America after its outbreak public knowledge? Did they for one moment cease to be Frenchmen?" The best possible propaganda for repatriation. The notoriety referred to by Roederer could be traced to Desrenaudes. By a fortunate coincidence having little to do with Autun's former vicar-general, Tallien, star performer of the 9th Thermidor (whose wife, the dusky Theresa, supplied the passion), rose before the Assembly in defense of French exiles, citing Talleyrand-Périgord, "who was listed as an émigré though he left the country on official government business." [2] The Republic was obligated to abolish that injustice and open its doors to a man possessed of a passport and written orders from Danton. The Assembly needed one more assenting voice to close the matter and issue a decree striking Talleyrand's name from the list of émigrés. Warmhearted and clever Germaine de Staël found that voice. She did better than that. She called the tune.

The whole maneuver resembled a vaudeville act with a cast of professionals. For the lead, Germaine chose Marie-Joseph Chénier, brother of the ill-fated poet who was guillotined. In her inimitable fashion, she entreated him to intervene and repeal the decree of banishment. Chénier had no use for Talleyrand and at first resisted the buxom siren's pleas; whereupon he found himself bewitched by another siren, half the size of the first and more melodious. On finding that her eloquence left him unmoved, Germaine, whose resourcefulness was inexhaustible where friends were concerned, had the bright idea of paralyzing Chénier's will so that he would have to aid the poor bishop exiled to the bogs of Massachusetts. The little siren who charmed Chénier was a friend of Germaine, Eugénie de la Bouchardie. This sweet, lovely damsel sang like an angel, accompanying herself on the harp. Each time Chénier threw himself at her feet—every evening, to be exact—Eugénie would start to sing (at Germaine's urgent request) a touching popular song called "Ballad of the Outlaw." [3] In the end, Chénier was so exhausted by Germaine's tirades and infatuated by Eugénie's warbling that one day he mounted the speaker's platform and championed the "outlaw" whose despair a cherished voice was currently pouring into his ear. Chénier was superb: "It is a matter of bestirring justice in defense of a man celebrated for his splendid service during the Constituent Assembly, in defense of a philosopher whose unswerving ideals and outstanding gifts rank him among the founders of French liberty. I speak of Talleyrand-Périgord, former bishop of Autun." Repeating the lesson Germaine had drummed into his ears, he stressed the "patriotic" nature of the outlaw's departure, his choice of exile in a friendly country, and his dedication to freedom's cause. Still under the spell of that bewitching voice, he finished dramatically: "I demand that you return Talleyrand, I demand him in the name of his many services, I demand him in the name of national justice, I demand him in the name of the Republic to which he may still dedicate his talents and energies, I demand him in the name of your glory, I demand him in the name of your hatred for the émigrés whose victim he, too, would be if cowards triumphed!"

Bravo Germaine! She had won. The Convention applauded and at once issued the following: "The National Convention decrees that Talleyrand-Périgord (former bishop of Autun) [the record of that bishopric would haunt him forever] may set foot once again on the soil of republican France and that his name shall be stricken from all émigré lists, thereby revoking the indictment against him."

That was September 4, 1795. The wonderful news did not reach Talleyrand in New York until November 2. He rushed to see Moreau and the two men fell into each other's arms.

Eager to reopen contact with the government, he got off a letter of thanks to the Directory's citizen minister of foreign relations, a certain Delacroix, who could not imagine how badly the signer of that congratulatory letter would disrupt his life several months later.

> Citizen Minister, after three years of exile, calumny, and persecution of every description, I was able at last to have an indictment quashed which even its authors could not take seriously. I acknowledge this redress of justice with clear and tranquil conscience. . . . When spring makes navigation possible once again, I shall return to the bosom of my country, dearer to me in its absence, whose honorable judgment imposes new tasks upon me. Kindly accept this expression of my respect, Citizen Minister, my gratitude, and my devotion, which I beg you to convey to the government of the Republic.[4]

The indispensable Germaine also received a grateful letter from New York dated November 14, 1795:

> Now, thanks to you, dear friend, the affair is ended. You did everything I asked. I wanted the same Convention which indicted me to rescind its decree. Next spring I shall leave here, bound for whatever port you

name, and spend the rest of my life near you, wherever you live [a sweeping promise, but his dream of a private little universe still beckoned]. I have many reasons for choosing to sail in May. Perhaps I shall return with a cargo of welcome necessities for the nation [welcome to his own pocket also], wouldn't you advise that? Will Monsieur de Staël have a small room for me? You are the one I should like to stay with when I arrive.

As might be expected, he wrote his own invitation. Germaine, too, was completely sold on the "private universe" over which she would preside, not by virtue of her beauty but of her glowing spirit, of that she was sure; also perhaps of the bishop's affections. Poor woman. Knowing her devotion to him, he demanded exactly that of her—plus the small service of convening for his benefit in her salon on the rue du Bac the most prominent and influential Parisians. Germaine's insatiable desire for knowledge was bound to attract new men rising from the ashes of the Terror as well as ghosts of the Ancien Régime emerging from their ratholes into her sunlit presence. "If you think I may run into trouble in any of our ports, I shall go to Holland and thence by land to the rue du Bac. Good-bye, dear friend, I love you with all my heart."

No longer speaking of what had been won by dint of such persistence and ingenuity, he was thinking ahead now of what had yet to be done—and asking for it. His *Memoirs* state that authorization for his return to France was unsolicited. That is not true. During the Directory, he himself related the series of maneuvers leading to his repatriation. Why the slip? Was it opportune during the Restoration to say that the Convention had welcomed him with open arms? Hardly. When he came to write those memoirs thirty years later, time had erased the memory of his friends' efforts, and he truly believed that his return from exile was a matter of course. Questioning his motives here will not get us very far, in any case. By his silence about the solicitations and the maneuvers, he avoided acknowledging his debt to Madame de Staël. Though he told her in 1795: "I love you with all my heart," by 1825 they had been quarreling for some time. That is why he avoided mentioning her inestimable help.

An even more telling reason for skipping that subject relates to Talleyrand's general outlook. For him, the past was pallid and lifeless; he looked ahead, interested in what tomorrow would bring. That he returned to France was the really meaningful fact, as well as what he did once he got there; but *how* he got there was pure anecdote. Germaine's hurt feelings were not anecdotal, however; he could forget so easily, she never forgot.

In early December he left New York for Philadelphia, planning to find a ship bound for France and to assemble a profitable cargo. Before leaving, he took one last walk around Manhattan with Beaumetz, who could think of nothing but his senseless impending marriage and the exciting expedition to India. They went to look at the ocean view from the ramparts of a fort at the foot of the island. The conversation was rather melancholy as they watched the waves breaking dizzily below. Talleyrand had just announced to his friend that he was not going to India. Beaumetz must have been stunned: having shared the best and worst of everything, an essential part of his life had come to a close. Perhaps the thought of death haunted him. Uncertain of the future, deeply hurt by his friend's desertion, Beaumetz may have been exasperated by the cool indifference with which Talleyrand switched tunes and jettisoned their plans. Or even more perhaps by the secret joy and expectation he sensed in Talleyrand, to whom he now meant nothing.[5] In any event, the bishop saw Beaumetz suddenly begin to tremble, his face contorted and wild with anger; staring deep into his eyes, he read there the awful thought that was making the wretched man quiver: "Beaumetz!" Talleyrand cried, "you want to kill me, you want to hurl me off this height into the sea! Deny it if you dare, you beast!" Beaumetz burst into tears, embraced his friend, and begged his pardon; he really had wanted to kill him. The incident illustrates one of the most enigmatic facets of Talleyrand. Beaumetz was not mistaken. Talleyrand's desertion meant that the enterprise was doomed, the same prophetic instinct that guided him a number of times later on. An odd proclivity for so logical and practical a man—yet fatalistic and willing to heed impulses more instinctive than cerebral. That is how he was; he knew it and knew enough to obey his inner promptings. Never did so unvindictive a man possess such a powerful weapon for vengeance: he could destroy men or their causes simply by scorning or ignoring them.

He soon forgot the Beaumetz incident. It was over and done with; Beaumetz was out of his life. Over the winter, Talleyrand collected stores of sugar, coffee, and spices destined to improve the diet of watery soup and moldy bread that Jacobin rule had imposed on the French. He applied for a new passport which Monsieur Adet, France's new consul in New York, did not cover with abuses, as had happened once before. They recorded his height this time as 5 *pieds* 5½ *pouces*, noted his blond hair and brows, blue eyes, and average nose (forgetting the snub this time). Nor did they mention his clubfoot. Before his departure, he was taken to visit a vast construction site where the Americans had decided to build their Federal City from the ground up. The name later became

Washington in honor of their founding President. That spectacle interested him far more than Niagara Falls.

One characteristic is worth mentioning which will surprise only those readers who trust Joseph Prud'homme's assessment of Talleyrand. We know how dearly he valued his friends. When the time came for him to part from Moreau and Beaumetz, he offered to take one son of each (they both had several) back to Paris and see that the lads were properly educated and launched on suitable careers. The fathers might have been willing, but the mothers would not hear of it, fearing that their sons would be forced to share Talleyrand's perilous existence. He would always face uncertainties, they felt; gambling and politics might destroy his fortune at any time. He heard their arguments with his usual calm, then, smiling, made this revealing statement: "No, I have nothing to fear at home, I know all the ins and outs of revolution." But the mothers were still fearful, so the sons bore the loss.

In a few months he would start to display some of his talents.

He waited until June 13 to sail aboard the Danish ship *Den Ny Proeve*, bound for Hamburg. Moreau and his son took him to the dock and waited for the vessel to move out to sea. They must have waved a hundred farewells, for not a breath of wind was stirring in Delaware Bay; the ship sat there for two days. On June 15, once again the sails were unfurled. Talleyrand sent a note to Moreau assuring him that all was well though they hadn't budged. Finally, on the eighteenth, they were at sea. Last message: "Here we are at sea, dear friend, with a faint but favorable wind. We have seen no privateers for two days. Farewell. In forty-five days I shall write you from the Elbe River. . . . We have a good captain but he sleeps fifteen hours at a stretch."

After a fine voyage, he arrived in Hamburg at the end of July, 1796, and immediately wrote to Moreau on the thirty-first: "Forty days from shore to shore, no privateers, a brief encounter fifty leagues out of Sorlingues with armed ships, rain every day. I don't know yet what the city is like. I have paid no calls. Cockades are the thing to wear. I put one on the moment I got here."

Everything was fine. He wore the tricolor badge of republican France to distinguish himself from émigrés. But before he even landed his past caught up with him in the person of Monsieur de Ricci, an émigré who came aboard at the urgent behest of Madame de Flahaut. She was now living in Hamburg and begged him not to come ashore, to sail with the next tide and make no effort to see her. Ricci's mission was indeed a surprise. It appeared that the dear lady, in her declining years, had embarked on the great love affair of her life: she was resolved to marry de Souza, the Portuguese ambassador to Denmark, and had good reason to think that the arrival of her former "soulmate," the father of her son, would upset her plans. Not the most placid soul, de Souza was likely to erupt at the sight of her former lover, especially as the restricted, rancorous atmosphere of émigré society bred an inordinately vicious strain of malice. Talleyrand had little interest in Adélaïde's Portuguese adventures; after four years of exile he was not about to turn and head out to sea again. In a few words, then, he dismissed the petty obstacle: "The whole thing is perfectly simple: a raging bout of jealousy. Women never die of it and it doesn't affect men." And off the ship he marched. That was how he broke with Madame de Flahaut: he could not forget her absurd demand, she could not forget his having rejected it.

He saw Madame de Genlis again, in her fifties now and as beautiful as ever. "Orléanism" bound them together, with one distinction: she was a fanatic, he a mere amateur. A constitutional monarchy under the prince d'Orléans was a serious possibility that warranted consideration, but there were other alternatives too. Madame de Genlis asked what Talleyrand's plans were. He swore that he would stay out of politics, having been well scalded in 1789, 1792, and in his years of exile; he felt obligated to Madame de Staël, with whom he thought he would like to spend the rest of his life. He and Madame de Genlis said good-bye, delighted with each other's company, each leaving a record of the meeting. He said of her: "The stability of self-possessed persons is due to their flexibility." A good maxim that applied even better to its author than to Madame de Genlis.

For her part, having listened skeptically to his solemn renunciation of politics, she observed that politicians and men of ambition were "like lovers who invariably take their own discontent and chagrin for rightful indifference." She was not wrong.

A delightful feature of this meeting of two survivors of another world was her request that Talleyrand send her from Paris a copy of Pierre Charron's *Traité de la sagesse*. To her astonishment, it reached her the next day—an Elzevir edition, elegantly printed and bound, which Talleyrand had saved from auction and kept with him always. It was his bible. This book by a friend of Montaigne's provided him with something of a talisman against the ills of mankind: ignorance, fanaticism, and tyranny. Madame de Genlis treasured it.

He saw some of his London friends again, like the fair Pamela *

---

* Pamela was said to be the daughter of the duc de Chartres and Madame de Genlis, who was governess to the Orléans children. Pamela was brought up with

who married Lord Fitz-James, and Mademoiselle de Sercey who became the wife of Conrad Mathiessen, a Hamburg banker. He must have encountered the whole Orléanist faction in Madame de Genlis's circle: Auguste and Charles de Lameth, the duc d'Aiguillon, Dumouriez, and Valence, his lady friend's son-in-law. The young duc d'Orléans, Louis-Philippe, was not in Hamburg at the time. The abbé Louis, Talleyrand's acolyte at the Festival of the Federation, was there. Did he meet him? Politics and money would bring them together later on. In a letter to Madame de Staël, Talleyrand unleashed his scorn at the incompetent gossips he met:

> I have no idea what to call the political views of French people in Hamburg and Altona. I gather that every one of them hates the English and wants to return to France. The property auctions are producing scores of republicans. There is talk of an Orléans party, the head of which, so my doctor told me the other day, cannot wait to visit America; of a Lameth party consisting of two members, one of whom is the incompetent Aiguillon; of a Dumouriez party comprising his valet Baptiste and his medical officer. If your Switzerland does not boast a more dangerous crowd than this, I can see how peaceful things in Paris will be this winter [August 19, 1796].

He also mentioned his health to her. Ill with fever for two weeks on his arrival in Hamburg, he saw very few people. He said he hoped to reach Paris by September 10 and asked her if she knew a young man named Benjamin Constant, author of a pamphlet he had just read, *De la Force du gouvernement,* which echoed, to his great delight, many of Narbonne's ideas. How could our poor "outlaw" guess that nobody was better informed about Benjamin Constant than Germaine, who had just embarked on an affair with him, too passionate and too publicized to turn out happily. Many a surprise awaits a returning exile. When you consider that Narbonne was Germaine's lover, the father of her child, and that her great heart was a melting pot for the feelings and ideas of all her loves, it is understandable why Talleyrand detected Narbonne's thoughts in Benjamin's pamphlet: they got there by the most direct route according to the theory of communicating vessels. There is no greater intelligence than love, provided, of course, that the lovers are exceptionally bright to begin with.

In the same letter he rebuked Madame de Staël for having spurned

---

the latter and Madame de Genlis called her her niece. This background explains her marriage to the duc de Fitz-James.

Mathieu de Montmorency and made him turn to religion, a shift which was likely to deprive Talleyrand of a friend: "It is bad for me."

Before leaving Hamburg, Talleyrand deposited his small fund of dollars (about 50 million old francs) in the Ricci bank. To Moreau, whose excellent Madeira he would no longer be sipping, he wrote: "I still have no plans for myself; I cannot tell much from here. I embrace you and love you."

He re-entered France via the Low Countries. Amsterdam was then the capital of the "Batavian Republic," a fiction invented by General Pichegru, and Brussels the chief town of a French department called the Dyle. Changes of that sort could only be expected to draw a cold stare and heavy silence from Talleyrand.

On reaching Paris he went to stay with Madame de Boufflers in Auteuil, then with General d'Arcon at "La Tuilerie" on the rue de l'Assomption. Why not with Germaine? She must have been at Coppet when he arrived. In its issue of September 25, 1796, the *Courrier République publicain* announced: "M. de Talleyrand-Périgord, former bishop of Autun, privileged émigré, has arrived in Paris." The "privileged émigré" must have gnashed his teeth.

Part Two
1796–1815

Paris Under the Directory

Expecting to return to his birthplace, Talleyrand found himself instead in surroundings far more unfamiliar than Massachusetts trapperdom: Paris under the Directory. Robespierre's death had released a great sigh of relief; prison gates sprang open and the populace trooped to public balls. Police tyranny gave way to every imaginable form of license totally unrelated to freedom. The wasteful extravagance of the new rich was no indication of prosperity, however, for France was bankrupt. Uncared for, unswept, buried under four years of litter, the streets of Paris were like open sewers. Henry Swinburne, an English diplomat, could not believe his eyes: grass framed the paving stones of the deserted faubourg Saint-Germain; through gaping windows the wind and rain buffeted the plundered mansions of once-privileged society. The Palais-Royal was a public dump, and the Comédie-Française, its filthy, rat-infested hall jammed with spectators, a place to avoid. Men did not remove their hats; women draped themselves in gauze: "the sight of their bare arms and legs made you shiver," our blushing Englishman observed. Surviving aristocrats who had managed to salvage any property at all were making fortunes: they opened salons which quickly became gambling dens or were hired out for public balls or assignations. Every breed of person came there. In one such salon Swinburne met society's current darling, Madame Tallien. Her face was barely visible under a black wig, but the rest of her was quite apparent beneath a gauze tunic.

The Elysée Palace, seized from the duchesse de Bourbon, had been converted into apartments, its vast, splendid rooms arbitrarily divided into rented plaster-and-gilt cubicles. The gardens became public fairgrounds dotted with lotteries, merry-go-rounds, swings, and hawkers. A son of the president of parliament in Toulouse was a tobacconist; a

149

captain in the French guard sold paper goods; a duchess married a notary; a priest worked as a printer's assistant, a bishop as an office messenger. What did it matter? They were lucky to be alive.

Every night Paris was host to two hundred balls of note. It was a mania of sorts. There were balls for the water carriers, for the colliers, even for aristocrats. Dancers trampled fear and death on paving stones still bloodstained, dancing for life.

Talleyrand observed and recorded it all:

> Balls, theatrical entertainments, and fireworks [which thrilled the crowd, so the Directory served them thrice weekly as a cheap substitute for bread] have replaced prisons and revolutionary committees. Ladies of the court have vanished; in their place are the mistresses of parvenus, waited upon by whores craving the same luxury and extravagance. In their wake hovers a swarm of featherbrains formerly known as "dandies," now called "merveilleux," who dance, talk politics, and sigh for royalty while nibbling ices or yawning at a display of fireworks.

First fanatics, now fools. Poor France. And behind those dregs of society said to be making history were twenty million betrayed, miserable Frenchmen, crushed by work and taxes, herded into the army, terrorized by robber bands plundering their villages, paid in worthless assignats that Paris workmen left lying in the gutter. Want was everywhere, or else corruption. Famine ruled the countryside.

Only politicians, royalist conspirators, or extremists took an interest in politics. The hopes of the French people were crushed. No one shouted "Vive la République!" except officials during public ceremonies. However, chroniclers of the period heard other mutterings from the crowd: "The Republic needs taking in hand by an able leader." A leader (able or not) in Italian is *Duce,* and in German, *Führer.* Two years later, the French pronounced it Bonaparte.

For the moment France was satisfied with Barras, her most prominent Director. No compromise was too great for him; intelligent and absolutely amoral, he might have stepped right out of *Les Liaisons dangereuses.* A man of taste and refinement, he had used the Revolution to shape his career and his fortune. A staunch advocate of Jacobin bloodbaths or of repression, whichever happened to serve his interests, he admitted frankly: "Years of civil strife are not years of morality." Undoubtedly that explains his fervent worship of the cult of virtue, along with his friends on the Committee of Public Safety. Barras was an aristocrat, related to the Pontevés and Castellanes, but had done more than his share to fill the tumbrils that fed the guillotine and later to bring down Robespierre. As a reward, he was elected Director, chief of state. The Luxembourg was his official residence, but he preferred his splendid mansion in Suresnes, sumptuously furnished with the nation's heirlooms, or his princely estate Grosbois, once the royal domain of the comte de Provence, the future Louis XVIII. A mixed crowd attended his receptions: former duchesses rubbed elbows with fashionable courtesans; Drouet, the postmaster general who had arrested Louis XVI at Varennes, went about congratulating dealers in national property; dukes out to make a fortune traded tips with pimps and gamblers. Joséphine de Beauharnais was a regular visitor; Madame Tallien acted as hostess. Barras was a poor administrator, as everyone knew, but a master of police spying, an unrivaled cheat at cards, dice, and elections, a king of panderers and debauchers. Thanks to the Revolution, he was also king of the Republic.

Benjamin Constant was fond enough of that strain of republicanism and displayed a certain appreciation for the Director. The two men had at least one vice in common: gambling. He credited Barras with sound practicality and a flair for nosing out threats to his power. At such times he prepared to strike, resolved to act, but, added Constant, "one never knew in which direction." A foreign diplomat said of him: "Barras would not hesitate to fling the Republic out the window if it did not maintain his dogs, his stables, his mistresses, his table, and his gambling losses."

From the woman's side Theresa Cabarrus, Madame Tallien, symbolized that glorious era as perfectly as Barras. "Our Lady of Thermidor," as she was known, had been snatched from the guillotine by Tallien. She married him and they lived in a "cottage" called "La Chaumière" at the foot of the allée des Veuves, which ran from the Champs-Elysées down to the Seine, a studiously rustic dwelling set amid trees with a large garden. It became a celebrated pleasure shrine. Citizeness Beauharnais was among its most admired attractions, but for eccentricity she could not compete with Fortunée Hamelin, who launched the fad for upswept hair "à la victime" and Athenian costumes.

The men, bored and disdainful, hair drooping like spaniels' ears, would appear in gray waistcoats and an apple-green cravat wound thirty-six times around the neck, wearing spectacles or carrying a lorgnette, with an enormous bludgeon passing for a cane in the other hand, and escorting their "vaporous" mistresses. The latter, equally audacious in buskins "purple as a fly's tail," advanced with the graceful tread of dancers toward such better times as the sages on the Committee of Public Safety had not foreseen.

151

One day Theresa and Fortunée Hamelin walked the Champs-Elysées wearing high-laced buskins and gauze tunics split up one side: neither modesty nor the cold prevented them from giving the sovereign masses a spectacle better than the guillotine.

Fortunée Hamelin was a Creole born in Haiti. Her licentious doings verged on scandal—and scandal under the Directory was the very pulse of life. She was known as "France's number one bawd." Her coloring, lips, and hair bespoke her West Indian blood and the fact that her parents were also natives who had interbred with dark-skinned persons. Her grace and charm were irresistible, and she knew how to display them; nor did she lack wit. She starred at Talleyrand's receptions, and it was there that she met the comte de Montrond, a friend of her host, who became her lover. At their first encounter, Montrond went straight to the point when the dusky Creole protested: "But you're married!" "Ah, so very little," he replied. "And I even less!" said she. They understood each other instantly. We shall meet the handsome Montrond many times, for from this point on he lived in Talleyrand's wake—and in Fortunée's petticoats, among dozens of others.

Amid this freakish carnival, Ignorance set out to defend Decency with measures quite as ridiculous as they were ineffectual. When Garnerin, the balloonist who had made a successful ascent and parachute landing in the parc Monceau, announced that he would repeat his feat, this time with a young woman who would be parachuted into the Elysée gardens, officials of the Republic banned "the immoral and indecent spectacle of two persons of opposite sexes rising into the air simultaneously." In deference to propriety, the young lady was replaced by a ewe. After that, who could accuse the government of forsaking virtue?

But Paris thrived on more than balls and fireworks: she went wild over proclamations of victory. At least one ray of splendor pierced the decadence. A young general of twenty-seven was leading the republican armies to victory after victory in northern Italy. Conquered Sardinia sued for peace; the news of Lodi set off celebrations all over Paris, and the French army's triumphant entry into Milan swelled even the mildest republican heads. The "merveilleuses" promoted antiquity and nudity more zealously than ever, while prostitutes deserted their alleys to market their charms and patriotism along the boulevards and the Champs-Elysées. Paris had repudiated committees, prisons, and public murder; she needed a hero to love and admire, a noble, handsome, young somebody, and a glorious cause. Bonaparte provided all that.

It was said that the Austrian army under Wurmser, beaten at Castiglione and Bassano and about to make its final stand in Mantua, was doomed. The sudden resurgence of patriotism and liberty was dizzying. France went slightly wild. Even more exciting than the victory bulletins and bundles of enemy banners were the enormous war indemnities and booty which the young man sent back from the front. The victories exalted the people and the gold kept the government running. All the while, idealistic republican-spirited proclamations were delivered to the plundered and liberated populations. Death to the vanquished! Long live General Bonaparte! Yes, that was how the French had distorted his name in order to make it more palatable. After all, how could anyone with a name like Napoleone Buonaparte expect to court fame?

Talleyrand was forty-two when he encountered the Paris of the Directory. Not easily offended or astonished, he decided to explore society methodically as he had done in the forests and fens of the New World. He waded up to his knees in the morass of the salons, the antechambers of power, the backrooms of the Assembly of Ancients and the Council of Five Hundred, the gambling dens and foul haunts of the Palais-Royal peopled by the most depraved yet well-informed persons. He knew "the ins and outs of revolution," but thought that Robespierre had changed the game. Actually, only the players, not the rules, were different, for politicians had lost interest in inventing new tactics. Talleyrand himself never changed, keeping his head powdered, wearing his silk suits, his exquisite linens and laces, his buckled shoes. Shunning all bias, he continued to uphold the virtues of common sense. Ambition, lust for money, insolence, and, of course, a clubfoot were his permanent trademarks. Thus did he reappear onstage.

By the time his dragging steps were raising creaks and groans from the ancient floorings of the faubourg Saint-Germain—abused as they had been under Jacobin heels—the Revolution, or what was left of it, was limping too. So badly that it took to its bed.

If You Don't Have What You Like, Learn to Like What You Have

Watching the scene around him, Talleyrand hesitated. He was cautious, yes, but also painfully broke. He borrowed 25,000 livres from Madame de Staël. On his scale of living, it was enough to scrape along for a few months. One of his contemporaries described meeting him in Madame de La Tour's house at Saint-Leu: "A most likable, good-tempered, and witty man in a circle of fashionable ladies with whom he was wagering a few louis in a friendly game of whist." Short of funds, he could not bet the way he used to. But be patient. The good old days may yet return. Relax and take strength for what lies ahead.

Madame de Staël sent him her latest work: *De la Littérature considérée dans ses rapports avec les institutions sociales*. Stunned with admiration, he wrote to her: "Your book is marvelous; if your reputation was not secure, it certainly is now." And he went on: "I spend my time here on financial enterprises initiated in America and Hamburg. I see a good deal of a very well-behaved woman named Madame de Brack and am always back in my own rooms by ten at night. I hope the Republic flourishes [so did Germaine and Benjamin]. I detest the aristocracy more than ever [the feeling was altogether mutual]. I long for your return and yearn to see you again; I love you with all my heart." [1] Germaine was at Coppet. The "private little universe" was never to materialize. Benjamin Constant had burst the dream bubble.

He was not handsome, with his reddish hair and long, snakelike body, nor gay; but he was brilliant, provocative, and spellbinding. Germaine succumbed permanently to his charm. She was literally captivated, and through ecstasy and heartbreak, hope and anguish, remained ever so.

Jealousy was alien to Talleyrand. He never experienced Germaine's passion for possessing a newcomer exclusively. He may even have been relieved, for now it was Benjamin on whom she unleashed the full tide of her amazon ardor, drowning him in the eloquence that Talleyrand had always found rather tiresome. Moreover, Germaine was kind enough to lend him the young man, thus providing him with a co-worker, assistant, spokesman, informant—whatever you will, but in any case an invaluable ally in his coming bid for ministerial power in the shadow of Madame de Staël.

With or without Benjamin, Talleyrand was dying to have Germaine back in Paris, out of self-interest as well as friendship. "In your opinion, is there a market in Switzerland for American real estate? If so, I could send someone there." Desrenaudes, for instance. It meant that he still held options on land in Massachusetts. He had hoped to sell it to French residents of Hamburg but had failed. Though stripped of their estates and titles and in dire want, the émigrés still chose to live and die in France if France would have them. Apparently he was not much more successful with Madame de Staël's friends, for which reason his career as a land broker came to a halt. Not his financial career, however, for Western bankers and businessmen had schooled him in some intricate and intrepid moneymaking tactics that he put to good use later on.

To test the pulse of things soon after his arrival, he took his seat in the political economy division of the Institut des Sciences Morales et

Politiques, the second level of the Institut des Sciences et des Arts, to which he had been elected on December 14, 1795, while still in America. He was made a founding member in recognition of his help in creating that institution. His reception as secretary of the Lycée des Arts, a learned society of high repute, took place on September 23, 1796.

The Institut met in the Salle des Caryatides of the Louvre. On two occasions he was asked to deliver oral reports in open session. The first, on April 4, 1797, was his "Memorandum on Anglo-American Commercial Relations," an outline of which appeared in his long letter to Lord Lansdowne. That speech had considerable impact; the entire diplomatic corps made a special point of attending. The ambassadors did well indeed to watch and listen to a fascinating personality expound political and economic principles which they would have to deal with sooner or later. They could not guess that the speaker was the future foreign minister, but they realized he was "somebody" who would amount to "something."

The second session took place on July 3, 1797, when he read to the Institut his "Essay on the Advantages to Be Derived from Colonies Under Present Conditions." A corollary of the first lecture, it contained ideas born of his experience in America. Talleyrand began by saying that the most sensible conduct for a nation fresh from revolution was to consign the whole nightmare to oblivion. And oblivion is to be found "in whatever offers man a glimpse of hope." The key to French recovery, as he saw it, was colonization, "which, after the turmoil is ended, may be the source of priceless benefits." He pointed out that France swarmed with bankrupt and disoriented citizens so accustomed to strife that they rebelled at the prospect of peace and a return to monotonous daily tasks; with adventurers who flourish in troubled times, as well as speculators, dream peddlers, and all breeds of social misfits, "those unable to relate to their peers, unable to acknowledge any degree of dependence." Colonies would provide an occupation for this large segment of society, besides bringing profit and hope to the nation. What about the colonial disasters of Louis XV? Talleyrand had foreseen the objection and blamed them on "total lack of planning." Only experienced colonial administrators should be responsible for organizing new colonies under a system guaranteeing liberty and justice for all. "Not domination, not monopoly, but force that is protective rather than aggressive." Colonial governors in the nineteenth and even the twentieth century could have learned something from Talleyrand's essay. Marshal Lyautey, for one, was familiar with it.

Talleyrand, whose name, influence, and suspected émigré status had made him a Jacobin target, threw caution to the winds in the interests of his country by boldly citing one of the great ministers of the Ancien Régime to reinforce his thesis. A startled audience heard him declare: "Monsieur le duc de Choiseul, one of the greatest visionaries of our century, predicted . . ." Not only did he mention a discredited aristocrat but gave the name full honors: "Monsieur le duc." Indeed, Choiseul had predicted that France and England would lose their American colonies and, to offset the loss, had already begun to "negotiate for the transfer of Egypt to France." Talleyrand's remark is apt on several accounts. It credits Choiseul with the same understanding and foresight that enabled Talleyrand, at the age of eighty-four, to forecast the course of twentieth-century European history which turned out to be far more reactionary than he had suggested. His reference to Egypt is also noteworthy and was to catch the imagination of young General Bonaparte, another visionary. This germ of an idea, then, was destined to take root and thrive.

Talleyrand's "prophecies" were staid and scholarly utterances. He lacked the imagination to invent things; he did not create events, he anticipated them, heralded them, and profited by them. Neither sage nor seer, he was simply a careful observer and dispassionate interpreter, far more intelligent than most of the talkers or hotheads around him. Now for the first time since the Terror, Talleyrand forgot the grim past and envisioned a France recommitted to life and to the greatness ahead of her. This he did by linking the new France to the old one. He began to emerge as the guardian of everything worth preserving in pre-revolutionary France. Repudiating the outworn feudal and monarchist philosophies, he inspired democratic France with the significance of her classical heritage. From the day he returned to his devastated homeland, this man, who had worked tirelessly to destroy, like so many dead branches on an ancient tree, the decadent and stifling institutions of the Ancien Régime, became the conscious instrument, the fearless voice of France's monarchist heritage. He would make the past enrich the present. He was truly "the man of France"—the same man of whom Chateaubriand said, in a moment of venomous spite: "His authority was weightless in matters concerning the future; he could not see ahead, only behind." Never was malice so blind.

His audience praised the conciseness, clarity, and pertinence of his "Memorandum." A great statesman seemed to have entered the stage.

But life was no easier for him. His presence was not altogether welcome; the same applied to his lengthy silences and alarming associations. He saw a great many Orléanists; though he had ridiculed their party, he still consorted with reputable members of it. Mentioning the fact to

Moreau, he spoke of ". . . this Orléans party everyone talks about and which, because it is invisible, is all the more dangerous. It is everywhere, yet unseen. I am credited with the leadership of this adroit faction. I think it must all be the handiwork of priests who are well occupied now [not in the churches, which were still closed], but don't worry, it is not serious." [2]

Despite the sarcasm, he was probably prevented from getting the hoped-for post of municipal adviser to the Paris region because of his suspicious activities.

He was being watched: Citizen Cochon, chief of police, had him under surveillance. In a report submitted to Barras and other Directory officials, we learn what was said during a dinner party attended by Talleyrand, General Brune, Desrenaudes, Maret, and Sémonville. Talleyrand's anti-émigré attitude was said to be the reason for police surveillance, but it was also claimed that he condemned Delacroix, the foreign minister, for his vulgarity and ignorance. Reubell, a Director known for his coarse tongue and brutality, excoriated Talleyrand, calling him a pillar of the Ancien Régime and an "insane liar." With fists punctuating his oaths on the nation's heirloom marquetry tabletops, he declared that the bishop was capable of the ultimate crime, that is, plotting against the pentarchs. It must be said that certain "words" concerning the government had escaped our hero's lips and reached the very sources apt to find them most objectionable. One day as he entered the Luxembourg leaning on his cane and on the arm of Colonel Lamothe, an attendant approached to impound the cane, following orders covering visitors to all public sessions of the government. He took it from Talleyrand, who commented loudly to the colonel on whose arm he now hung: "My dear man, it appears to me that your government is terribly afraid of being poked with a stick." From so illustrious a suspect as the spied-on lecturer at the Institut, the phrase did considerable damage in high places.

Citizen Cochon's agents also reported that Talleyrand attended a gathering of royalist conspirators at 16, rue de Provence in February, 1797; those present were Dumas, a member of the Council of Ancients; Montesquiou, a royalist; Roederer; Segier, former envoy to Russia, also a royalist; and the duchesse d'Aiguillon, Madame de Genlis's daughter. If not true, it is at least probable, for all of them were his friends and partisans of the duke.

Barras, the most prominent Director and an expert at conspiracy, took the whole matter lightly: "Let those gentlemen do what they wish and go on stirring up their trivial schemes." He saw little to fear in the Orléanists.

A month later, Cochon submitted another report on Talleyrand's activities, mentioning his association with La Vauguyon, reputed to be an agent of the comte de Provence. All this information cast him in a very dubious role. Talleyrand protested: "My clearly articulated desires have been and continue to be directed toward the welfare and the glory of the French Republic." A few people had the impertinence to laugh at the republican sentiments he proclaimed rather too sincerely to suit them.

One unsmiling republican was Chénier, principal architect of our "royalist" hero's repatriation. Indeed he rarely smiled at all, and with one and the same starched countenance managed to serve both the Republic that had guillotined his brother and his adorable Eugénie, who no longer sang her outlaw's ballad. He attacked Talleyrand: "The abbé Maurice's letter only proves that besides having been an Orléanist, and prevented from joining the Robespierrists because Maximilian wanted no part of him, he is turning into a Directorist so as to become whatever form of power is in the making. The rascal is like a sponge. . . ." Calling him "the abbé Maurice" was a joke, not an argument; calling him an anarchist was sheer idiocy. Being an Orléanist and advocating constitutional monarchy was something else, however: the single grain of truth in his statement. As for supporting Robespierre, Talleyrand never did. His frantic efforts to obtain a passport cannot be forgotten. A Directorist? He never had to become one; on hearing of the 9th Thermidor, he declared his loyalty to the Republic. The fact is that Talleyrand confused everyone; people feared him, so they attacked him.

In 1797, with tragedies and alexandrine meter still packing the theaters, it is understandable that a man like Chénier would vent his spleen in satiric verse. He did just that, our poetic tribune, and before demolishing Talleyrand in rhyme paid generous tribute to himself. Hark Modesty to thine own praise:

> My acts and speech sincere and true
> In the past, the present and the future too.
> [Now he lunges at the abbé Maurice]
> Impudent Maurice, glutton for shame and for gold,
> A lover of power, both the new and the old;
> Of every lost cause the greedy apostate
> Sells all his friends as he sold the state.

A glutton for shame? Never. Shame and remorse were strangers to Maurice. He betrayed only one lost political cause, if you consider it such: the church. Talleyrand never played a friend or his country false. When government fell into the hands of madmen, he fled. Chénier's poem may be an oddly interesting commentary on the times, but is certainly no factual record.

Hatred began to build. What caused it to gather like a wave, swelling and finally bursting in the nineteenth century in the sublime profusion of the *Mémoires d'outre-tombe*? Not Talleyrand's beliefs, opinions, inconsistencies, nor even his alleged betrayals, but the personality of the man. His manner, his tone of voice, his stare made some people's flesh crawl; yet those very objects of hate were a delight to Madame de Brionne, Germaine de Staël, Choiseul, Narbonne, and Montrond. Madame de Staël used to say: "If the art of conversation could be bought, I should go to the poorhouse to acquire his." Still other people would grit their teeth when he spoke, as though listening to Voltaire or Fontenelle. Every drop of blood in him bred that hostility: his elegant manners, his insolent smile, his flawless courtesy toward the depraved brutes running the government. Basically, they hated the aristocrat in him—and they were not mistaken, for in 1797 no Frenchman in Paris was more aristocratic than he. Diehard Jacobins squirmed to think that a head still sat on his shoulders, for Talleyrand's head was the type that should not have stayed there. Another antagonist was the Director Reubell, coarse and brutal, a former public prosecutor in Colmar. He had a physical loathing for Talleyrand; how he cultivated it will be seen.

Talleyrand got to know Paris society, but was too clever and cautious to commit himself to anyone. He went everywhere, gathering information, renewing old friendships or making new ones. His attitude was often amusing: in that mixed and ill-bred society, his gracious manners sometimes fooled the unsophisticated, who thought they had license to grab his arm or tug his sleeve or lapel. With a wilting look, he put them in their place—down, very low. "My politeness does not mean that I am listening to you or approve of you. My politeness does not mean that I like you." Of course, that was a bit too subtle for Reubell and his crew. When Talleyrand talked to his own breed of men, Reubell would complain: "They've put their heads together to murder us all!" And he proposed restoring the bishop's name to the émigré lists. The prospect of banishment and poverty was no laughing matter. Who would he see outside France? Emigrés? He headed the list of victims to be drawn and quartered! Barras quieted Reubell, whose venom continued to simmer: "Let Talleyrand remain in France," he said. "I was probably making too much fuss about him. Providing you don't plan to make him an important official one day. Why not appoint him to your cabinet?" Little did

Reubell know that his own clumsy sarcasm was the truth. A fool who thinks he is being entertaining usually comes closer to the truth than when he tries.

Though not as savage as the "purists," Larevellière-Lépeaux had private quirks that Talleyrand found absurdly pretentious. He dabbled in mysticism. His aim was to found a religion, or sect, to serve as his own political following, and he discussed his views with Talleyrand hoping that an ex-bishop would inject an aura of the true faith into this atheist-inspired dogma, Theophilanthropy. Talleyrand straightway baptized it "Thieves Incorporated," and decided that the only way to combat such a fraud was to stick pins in it. Having gone to great lengths to escape the church, Talleyrand was not about to be drawn into such patent mummery. The self-appointed high priest of the nation gave a lecture entitled "Considerations on Worship, Civil Ceremonies, and National Festivals," which our bishop was obliged to attend. He listened as one pontiff listens to another, then declared solemnly: "I have only one comment to make. To found his religion, Jesus Christ was crucified and reborn. Try to do as much." Another enemy was made.

Carnot, the great Carnot, had little love for him; he, too, could not stand Talleyrand's personality and accused him of having contaminated the new régime with the vices of the old one. Who knows what he took for vice in an era when virtue was decreed by Barras, the Talliens, and their set. If good manners, elegance, love of the arts, respect for individual liberty, the right to own property, and freedom of opinion are vices, then Talleyrand indeed was implanting them in the new society. With its first breath, the Directory had set a record for debauchery, prevarication, gambling, and all the rest, which subsequent French history could never match. Carnot said of Talleyrand: "He has no principles and changes them along with his linen." The statement is not only absurd (if he had no principles he could not change them) but false, for Talleyrand was always true to the principles of 1789 and to the Declaration of the Rights of Man. As for his linen, he changed it more frequently than Carnot and Reubell put together. Why the barrage of ill will when his two addresses to the Institut brought him only praise? Talleyrand's superior gifts provoked admiration in some quarters, but exasperation and fear in others where he was seen as a living rebuke, a constant reminder of the vulgar mediocrity of the Directors.

He began to be active politically and joined the Constitutional Club, loyal to the tenets of 1789 as opposed to the rightist Clichy Club, its rival. He declared publicly that it would be unwise to restore the monarchy under existing conditions and any attempt to do so would only revive hatreds, civil war, and the Terror. France needed a demo-cratic form of constitutional government, not a monarchy. That is what he advocated at a particular time and in a particular situation. His ideas changed with the changing scene.

In the club he met Bénjamin Constant (not by coincidence, as we shall see), Garret, Daunou, the abbé Sieyès, Generals Kléber and Jour-dan. Even Chénier was there, furious at having to associate with the infamous "abbé Maurice." Talleyrand, not Chénier, rose to leadership overnight. On learning that the bishop had assumed a powerful position in the club, Reubell observed, in prose as eloquent as Chénier's verse: "He is the eagle among birds of ill omen." Intending to pluck that eagle raw, he added: "May he be absorbed and neutralized." A simple-minded man. From time to time he and his cohorts would hurl abuse or strike out at him, but absorbing and neutralizing were Talleyrand's speciality.

Our hero had a cheerful word for everyone, anxious to show him-self in the best light. To one person he would rave about his friend Mirabeau; to another, he admitted owing his passport and his life to the indispensable Danton; for friends of Vergniaud and Gensonné he waved a Girondist banner; he even whispered confidentially to former members of the Committee of Public Safety that he had often been speechless with admiration at Robespierre's sublime virtue. Ah, the art of conversation . . . His literary talent, too, did not go unrewarded, for the new newspaper *Le Conservateur* put him in charge of its foreign affairs column.[3]

Still, he needed a position, a high position, which was what he meant by "entering affairs," in other words, state affairs that would make his fortune. Nearly successful, he was nominated to aid Letourneur de la Marche, a former Director, in the Anglo-French peace negotiations about to open in Lille. Barras favored it for two reasons: if everyone in Paris was talking about the brilliant and wicked Talleyrand, he ought to be given a chance to prove his worth. Furthermore, it was an ideal occasion to rid the capital of his disturbing presence. Barras was sure that once involved with government business, Talleyrand, like everyone else, would start making money and settle down. But Reubell was on his toes, and before the appointment could be made, he accused Talleyrand of selling France to foreign powers. Barras answered calmly: "Talleyrand, like countless others, serves his own ambition and his own interests." Reubell did not say a word. Who were the "countless others"? But just as Talleyrand was about to be appointed, Reubell protested: "If integrity and competence are what you seek, forget about Talleyrand. He is knav-ery incarnate, and starchy incompetence." As for the "knavery," he was no different from "countless others," Citizen Reubell. But calling him incompetent (with or without the starch) invalidates all other arguments. The nomination was withdrawn. The English were delighted; they could breathe again. Word of his appointment had already reached London: everyone pitied Lord Malmesbury, England's ambassador, who would have "to deal with a wretched scoundrel." In Bern, too, Virtue's apostles grew alarmed. That man Talleyrand was capable of making peace. What about business? A negotiator so dreaded by his adversaries surely must be a good one.

Madame de Staël Knocks on Doors and Fortune Opens Them

Bitterly disappointed, Talleyrand took his troubles to Madame de Staël. His touching description of the situation moved her to pledge that together they would win the highest office for him. He must put himself in the hands of his trusted friend. We always hear that Talleyrand was unprincipled, which is not true. One of his principles was this: "In critical situations, let women run things." Germaine did more than run things in her usual excited fashion; she launched an assault on the Directory. How did he ignite the inflammable Germaine? Let us watch.

Entering her house on the rue du Bac one day, silent, solemn, icy, he tossed his purse on the table in front of that stunned lady: "My dear child, I have twenty-five louis left, not enough to last me another month; you know I cannot walk and must have a carriage. If you don't find me a suitable position, I shall blow out my brains. Do something. If you love me, see what must be done."

Germaine's galloping imagination responded instantly: she heard the shot, saw the bishop's body crumple to the floor. Off she flew in a panic in search of a *position* to banish the fatal vision her lover had evoked. A ministerial post would be best, she decided, both for him and for the country. Obviously, he knew the right string to pull. In any case, women never reproached him for it and had a kinder opinion of him than men. Except for Madame de Montesson, Philippe-Egalité's widow. One day in her salon, a good friend of his, captivated by Talleyrand's brilliance, paid him this rather odd compliment: "If I were a woman, I could refuse you nothing." Before Talleyrand could reply, Madame de Montesson interjected: "Your favors, yes; your confidence, no." Why the slap? Because Talleyrand had not declared himself pro-Orléanist? Because after flirting with "the faction" he had pledged his energies to the Republic? Did the Orléanists feel they had the right to demand uncompromising loyalty? Indeed, every political group complained that he could not be pinned down. None would or could understand that he shunned any attachments that might restrict his advancement. Germaine de Staël, married to the Swedish ambassador, was his current attachment. She was hostess to republican politicians, émigrés, financiers, artists, and whatever oddities the wind scooped out of the Paris gutters and deposited on certain doorsteps. It all swept into her salon on the rue du Bac.

Talleyrand came there regularly only because of Germaine (and what she could do for him). The Neckers and the Staëls did not appeal to him either before 1789 or now in 1797. We know already what he thought of Necker; of Madame Necker, his wife, Talleyrand once said: "She has all the virtues and a single defect: she is insufferable." How was he to get a post in a government that credited him with "starchy incompetence" and his closest associate, Benjamin Constant, with "the candor and foolishness of a young mind"? The Directors shared that opinion of two of the most brilliant men of their time. The moral of the story is that incompetence and foolishness put to scorn the political aims of the men in the Luxembourg.

That "lazy" Talleyrand was up at six each morning conferring with Benjamin in his room and planning the day's maneuvers. From July, 1797, onward they worked closely together. His address to the Institut had boosted his credit in influential circles. There was considerable talk at the time of replacing the thoroughly unpopular foreign minister, who was ill to boot. Delacroix was dead and buried as far as the public was concerned, and Talleyrand was mentioned as a possible successor. He himself did most of the mentioning, discreetly, between parentheses, as it were. Barras was the one whose support they needed most; Germaine had already laid siege to him, vaunting the bishop's republican zeal, his extraordinary versatility, and—of all things—his virtue. Not content with that, she wanted Barras to meet her protégé and recognize his genius on the spot. So relentlessly did she press him that one day Barras grudgingly agreed to receive them both that same evening at nine in the Luxembourg. On seeing Talleyrand for the first time, Barras was sure the ghost of Robespierre had returned, so uncanny was the resemblance, he said. Taking Madame de Staël aside, he confessed his astonishment, and she seized the opportunity to assure him that Talleyrand was the better twin, warmhearted, loyal, and supremely trustworthy. Ardently she vowed that "He would walk through fire for you." Rushing to Talleyrand, who was waiting patiently, she seized his hand, assured him that he was highly regarded, and led him before Barras. With a sweeping bow, Talleyrand addressed him: "Your humble servant. Your grateful servant. My respect and gratitude are equaled only by my admiration." Barras, the recipient of many salutations in his lifetime, stared at his visitor in utter silence, his face just as impassive as Talleyrand's. Germaine was crestfallen, expecting some show of enthusiasm, a warm embrace or two. The next evening she was back at the same time, buttonholing Barras, pouring out more rapturous acclaim for her bishop and for the Director himself. "He thinks of you as something superhuman," she declared. What a scene that must have been, with Germaine distraught and gesticulating wildly, eyes brimming with tears, those black soulful eyes of hers ecstatically turned Heavenward, her plump hands kneading that mountainous bosom in an effort to coax out cavernous sighs, the flutter of her heavy, swarthy eyelids splashing tears or smiles over her theatrical features. Carried away, she outdid her previous performance; extolling Talleyrand's vices as well, she assured Barras: "He has every vice of the Ancien Régime and all those of the present one." Even a man of Barras's experience had to admit that was quite a record. Yet he stood there like an iceberg. She pressed on: "He will always have a foot in every party, so you could not have a more valuable agent." Was she alluding to an epigram that Chénier had fired off at the abbé Maurice?

> Into the party to which he is sold
> Stealthily he sneaks an unsteady foot.
> The other, planted in the opposite fold,
> Is tightly laced in a cripple's boot.

Finding Barras still unmoved, she launched a direct assault: "You must make him a minister, preferably of foreign affairs, for I have shown you his qualifications and fitness for such office." The Director condescended to take up the matter with his colleagues, knowing well enough how Reubell felt.

Two days later, Germaine was back again, ebullient as ever, only to be greeted by an icy blast: "The person you have sponsored is the object of near-universal dislike and distrust on the part of the Directors." Undaunted, she pressed on: "The better for you, Barras; your colleagues' distaste for Talleyrand will work to your advantage. He will guard you like a sheepdog, indeed he is the most faithful guardian you could have."

Barras cut short the interview and requested that she drop the question permanently.

While Germaine battled bravely in the front lines, Talleyrand was creeping around the flanks to encircle the target. He circumvented Barras by secretly wooing members of his family and friends with assurances that he, Talleyrand, was committed body and soul to the Director and would serve him through thick and thin. In the Luxembourg, in government circles, in the salons, even at the dinner table and in the privacy of his own rooms, some voice was always singing the bishop of Autun's virtues, vices, talents, and matchless devotion.

When the Constitutional Club's executive council was due to meet the Director, Talleyrand gave Benjamin Constant the limelight by having him declare to Barras that "the most powerful political group in Paris was at his feet." At those words, and a signal from Talleyrand, he, Benjamin, and all the others actually prostrated themselves before the Director. Though his face never lost its composure, he was thrilled: for a Jacobin, he was singularly vulnerable to idolatry.

Several days later, Germaine reopened her assault on the Luxembourg. There she loomed, wild-eyed, her turban askew and the curls tumbling out from under it, her neckerchief awry exposing her bosom, her enormous stature assuming monumental proportions. It was her big scene. Clutching Barras's arm, she sat him next to her on a couch, took his hands in hers, and began to speak. Her voice broke down, tears choked her, but her message was very plain: "Barras! Barras! Only you can help me, my friend; without you all is lost, lost. Do you know what he has said to me? What he just told me again? I was with him a few moments ago: maybe he is no longer alive; he threatened to jump into the Seine if you will not have him as foreign minister. He has but ten louis to his name."

An extraordinary scene. Germaine's petition was insane: He is penniless, so make him minister; otherwise he will commit suicide and you will have that on your conscience. Raving romanticism on behalf of the least romantic, most practical-minded of men. What a scene! Discounting the leading lady's originality and the theatrical atmosphere, what was left? Only an absurd proposal. Yet why condemn the drama? Drama is all-important; it does not mimic life, it creates it.

Inspired by the righteousness of her cause, Germaine engulfed Barras in a verbal torrent, assuring him that if Talleyrand had remained with the Convention he would have supported Barras every time (even in putting the king to death?). How could the Directory reject a man whom the émigrés wanted to draw and quarter? Or let a man drown, who, out of wounded civic pride, was ready to throw himself into the Seine? No, he has to be made minister. "Otherwise, my hope is gone and I myself shall die, for I can go on no longer." Seeing that she was about to faint, Barras cautiously maneuvered her into collapsing on the far end of the couch. From his account of the scene, he appears to have been deeply impressed by the quantity of flesh about to tumble into his arms. Fearing that posterity might think he took advantage of a swooning woman, he was careful to note in his Memoirs: "In similar circumstances never did I emerge purer and more innocent from such an ordeal."

Purity, on his pen, was nothing short of an insult to virtue. Germaine pulled herself together and left, still talking: "I will go see him. What can I say to comfort him? Could we ever forgive ourselves if he drowned?"

This time she received a reply: "Make your friend promise not to drown himself, for if he does there is nothing anyone can do for him." A truism, but he added: "We shall try to let his talents serve the Republic and his good will serve us." Hope still fluttered. Germaine flew out of there on wings.

She rushed into the carriage which had been waiting at the Luxembourg gates for the past hour; hidden in the back seat, a motionless, affable gentleman smiled at her. On hearing Germaine's story, no candidate for suicide appeared more willing than he to rejoin the living. Still, they wondered whether Barras's promises could be taken seriously. The next day Germaine rushed back to the Luxembourg to exploit her fragile gains. Buttonholing Barras once again, she plunged in boldly: "Just wait until you have a minister like him!" The Director cut her short and pushed her aside: "The subject of your friend is closed; I know it by heart. Good-bye, Madam."

Dumbfounded, but without an arm to fall on, she decided not to swoon, though there was good reason to do so. Should she make one last sally? Barras's humor did not appear to encourage it.

Then Talleyrand was invited to dine with the Director at his country estate in Suresnes. Arriving early, he found no one about and picked up a book to pass the time. Suddenly, in rushed a wild-eyed gardener shouting: "Monsieur Raymond has just drowned!" Who was he? A young secretary raised in Barras's household, of whom the Director had grown extremely fond. It was July, 1797; the weather was hot and Raymond had gone for a swim in the Seine which bordered the estate. He vanished. When Barras arrived and was told the story, he went berserk with grief, shrieking wildly and rushing off to lock himself in his room. Talleyrand, now rather upset by the mood of the evening, waited a bit, thinking his cause had expired along with the unfortunate young man. Barras sent his excuses, instructing his guest to dine without him; shortly afterwards he had him come upstairs. Another scene! His face contorted by grief, Barras clasped the hands of the proscribed aristocrat and bishop and, sobbing, embraced him. Talleyrand recorded the incident in his *Memoirs,* calling it his first meeting with Barras. Not so! He ignored their initial encounter for reasons we already know: he wished to avoid mentioning Madame de Staël and presenting himself in the posture of a petitioner, preferring to create the impression that Barras begged *him* to take a cabinet post. In any event, the evening was full of surprises for our hero. Let him recount the story himself; the ending is no less bizarre than the beginning. Talleyrand's plasticity is incredible: a sinner's tears upon his hands and cheeks awoke the priest in him. "I said all the comforting things that his condition and my own brought to mind [he knew indeed how to comfort sorrow]. He asked me to return to Paris with him [Barras was already under his spell]. Having known him less than two hours, I had reason to believe that he looked on me as his dearest friend!" [1]

So Talleyrand won the contest in that carriage returning them to Paris from Suresnes. Germaine had laid the groundwork, but her unbridled enthusiasm threatened to explode the whole affair. Ultimately, he had to fight and win on his own. A strange combination of events: the drowning that first seemed to have ruined everything turned out to be providential. Destiny had marked someone for drowning in the Seine but not Talleyrand, as Germaine feared and wanted others to believe. Fate took an innocent young man for its victim so that Talleyrand, by coddling the griefstricken Barras, extracted from him the promise of Delacroix's dismissal and his own nomination. It was simply a stroke of luck.

Barras then had to gain the consent of the other Directors, which was about as easy as halting the sun in its tracks. It did happen, however, on July 17, 1797.

A dreadful debate took place, with Carnot running true to form. When a seemingly intelligent man gives way to hate, envy, and fear, he invites disaster. "You mean that priestling [was he equating the bishop of Autun with some country cleric?], that rascal ready to sell every one of you just like that if it showed a profit?" "Whom has he sold?" Larevellière-Lépeaux inquired. The question was indeed judicious, for if Talleyrand was accused of selling, they had better specify the merchandise. Carnot's reason began to fail him: "God, to begin with," he declared. Someone pointed out that Talleyrand could not have betrayed God as he never believed in Him. "Why did he serve Him? Next, he sold his class." That is true and, in fact, is the only treason for which he could be condemned except by someone like Carnot. Only his own class and his family had grounds for complaint. Carnot's view was ultra-reactionary. To him, social castes were watertight. You were born in one, you stayed there, and for the rest of your life your mind was set against progress, against liberty, or for obscurantism. A fanatic's, not a statesman's way of thinking.

Someone, probably Barras, raised the point that Talleyrand's attitude in 1789 and 1790 reflected his convictions—"His ambition, you mean," was Carnot's rejoinder. "Afterwards he sold the king." A curious remark, altogether false, from the lips of a regicide. And the same judicious voice reminded him: "I do not think we are in a position to blame him." It is apparent that Talleyrand was treading on thin ice, the target of multiple hatreds: the clergy, his family, and the Bourbons on one hand, the Jacobins on the other. His foes, though bitterly divided, managed somehow, as if by some secret covenant, to speak the same language and voice the same accusations. Life in France after the era of artful living was very tricky.

Finally, the Directors took a vote. Of the five, four must have rejected Talleyrand. Then by making deals and pricking a few swollen heads, Barras, an expert at that sort of thing, got what he wanted: three out of five votes went to Talleyrand. Barras was as surprised as everyone else.

While those gentlemen were simultaneously raking him over the coals and electing him to office, Talleyrand was watching a play peacefully with one of his friends from court, Boniface de Castellane. In the middle of the performance, Benjamin Constant came running in, breathless. Throughout the historic meeting, he had stayed at his post behind Barras's chair. How could the poor squabbling Directors have guessed that Talleyrand was looking on and recording the scene through Benjamin's eyes? Actually, he had slipped into the room at Germaine's behest; as soon as he told her the outcome, she sent him off to the theater at a run. He cannot have regretted his mission. When Talleyrand heard the news of his appointment, he changed completely—Benjamin saw it happen—and became another person. For once his face, gestures, and words matched his thoughts. Joyfully he embraced Castellane and Benjamin Constant; the three hurried out of the theater into a coach, Talleyrand in the middle, the friends on either side. "Let's go thank Barras at once," he said. As they rode on, he squeezed the knees of his companions and, with each turn of the wheels, murmured over and over: "Now we have a chance to make an immense fortune, immense fortune, immense fortune . . ." He is supposed to have chanted that all the way to the gates of the Luxembourg, the chant of ambition and the drive for gold.

The decisive moment had come: at last he was engaged in affairs of state, momentous affairs, and until his death forty years later, all French and European "affairs" would bear his influence.

The High Cost of Opening Shop—
Bitter "Sweets" from America

His first official act as minister was that of a well-trained courtier: he prostrated himself before Barras and embraced him. The Director watched mutely. Talleyrand apologized for keeping him up past eleven, knowing that Barras always went to sleep early. He urged him to get ready for bed, promising to attend him. That is precisely what he did: attended the *petit-coucher* of his new sovereign. Everything went off smoothly, for Monseigneur was an old hand at turning down a bed, presenting a towel and nightshirt, and drawing curtains. Barras accepted those attentions, thinking that so versatile a man ought to be able to negotiate a superb treaty with all the essential clauses in the right place, as well as organize a *coup d'état* or a masked ball with equal flourish. As a sign of dismissal, Barras said: "Official notice of your appointment must have reached your house. Come tomorrow at noon and be presented to the Directory." Talleyrand bowed his way out—Barras must have felt a throne, not a bed, under him. Our hero had no delusions of grandeur, but was expert at provoking them in others.

Talleyrand's exit from the Luxembourg deserves mention. With the change in his status came a momentary change of behavior. Now that he was a minister of the Revolution, a Citizen Minister, he felt it incumbent on him to embrace first the Citizen Attendants, then the Citizen Torchbearers lighting his way along the Citizen Director's private stairs, and, once outside, he pumped the hand of the Citizen Doorkeeper. Then he went home. That outpouring of republican spirit had lasted about an hour and was never repeated. In a lifespan of eighty-four years, once is enough.

His appointment became official the next day, July 18, 1797: "The executive Directors invite you, Citizen, to appear tomorrow morning at ten in the Foreign Relations office when Citizen Delacroix, the incumbent minister, will transfer his functions to you." Carnot, president of the Directory, had signed the appointment, against his will no doubt, for in fact it was the Directory's death warrant. Here is what Madame de Staël had to say in 1814 about her part in the whole affair: "I am responsible and guilty in the eyes of God and men for having helped to

169

launch Talleyrand in affairs of state; it was a crime, a terrible crime." Later we will see what caused that hostility.

Our Citizen Minister was hardly elated to learn that his salary amounted to "37,000 myriagrams of wheat." It would have been simpler to say 100,000 livres, but the value of the livre was anyone's guess if indeed it really existed. All the same he was given 7,000 of them for living expenses. Peanuts! In three months he ran up debts of 55,000 livres for coaches and household furnishings, managing to spend money faster than the government doled it out. Soon his elegant white coach was seen whisking about the city. Unfortunately, it was not paid for; the coachmaker complained bitterly. Stationing himself in the porte-cochère of the rue du Bac, where the ministry of foreign relations was located, he buttonholed the new minister and handed him his bill: "Absolutely right, you ought to be paid whatever is owed you." "Ah, Citizen Minister, these are hard times and I'd appreciate it." "No need for appreciation; debts ought to be paid." Seeing the coach about to depart, the poor man clung to it, resolved to come off with something more substantial than good advice: "You will pay me, Citizen Minister, but when?" "When? What a nosy fellow you are." [1] Drive on, coachman! And off rolled the Citizen Minister. It might have been the scene between Don Juan and Monsieur Dimanche, and illustrates the cynical, brash side of Talleyrand. Because he was known to have treated not only coachmakers but also politicians in that manner, we can understand why certain accounts of his activities are less than flattering. His cynicism appears again in a biting comment he made one day to his friend Narbonne, whose finances were then as low as Talleyrand's once had been. Narbonne had come to see him and was cutting short the visit for fear he would not have enough money to pay the coach waiting for him outside. Talleyrand remarked blandly: "Why don't you have your own carriage?" "That's a bad joke," replied Narbonne, "you know I haven't a sou." "You miss the point: you must have a carriage to pay for one."

The salary was nothing compared to the "advantages," and Talleyrand's initial concern as foreign minister was to multiply these. Otherwise, his style of life would have made him a pauper. The Delacroix family had managed to get along with only a tenth of the money Talleyrand spent in the same house. After he left office, the good Reinhardt and his wife were content to live like Spartans, but there were no more receptions and official business was as dull as the trade in a tobacco shop.

Within a few weeks, by putting his new house in systematic order, Talleyrand was able to pocket between 500,000 and 600,000 livres. [2] A far cry from the 7,000 paid by the Directory. Word went round in diplomatic quarters that doing business with Talleyrand was extremely expensive. The Prussian ambassador reported to his sovereign: "The [French] foreign minister loves money and publicizes the fact that he does not wish to spend his retirement begging alms from his country." (At least he stated it openly, unlike other officials named in the report who also took money, but on the sly, which apparently was not offensive.) "His friends encourage that attitude." The Prussian diplomat went on to explain how to do business with the Frenchman once one's credentials were presented: "You can then make him some sort of gift, the amount of which I cannot presume to specify at the moment, but which ought not to be less than 300,000 francs."

Talleyrand was also making money unofficially. At his own expense, he hired agents to sell merchandise to Charles IV of Spain. Truguet, the French ambassador in Madrid, uncovered the enterprise and dismissed the agents from his own legation. But as Talleyrand observed, any diplomat who was that obtuse deserved to be fired.

A certain Madame Villars, who proffered her favors to one of the high priests of the régime, Merlin of Douai, and knew the "advantages" of republican dealings, had brought suit for damages against the ministry of war. She interested Talleyrand in her case, whereupon he amused himself collecting the lady's damages and keeping them. In fact, she had no more right to claim them than he, but he decided that having done all the work, he was entitled to the reward, especially as any woman consorting with a government official would be well provided for.

The French tend to forget that although foreign powers found Talleyrand costly to deal with, they respected his political aims, recognizing him for an expert negotiator determined to maintain peace. When he was nominated for Director, a number of governments supported him and backed that support with the sturdiest of arguments: money. Spain and Portugal contributed 1,500,000 livres (over a million old francs) to bribe the Directors, all of whom were for sale, none more so than Barras, who nevertheless kept detailed accounts in his Memoirs of every "transaction" Talleyrand made, forgetting his own more lucrative ones. Barras's source of information in the last years of the Directory was Madame de Staël. After falling out with the bishop, she turned into a gossipmonger, and because her rancor was as unbridled as her ardor, she exaggerated the "advantages." The record is clear on one question, however: Talleyrand drained off every sou he could get, and drainage facilities were abundant. It is said that during the two years of his ministry he siphoned off 13,500,000 livres—over 10 billion old francs. Fifteen foreign governments had helped erect the edifice of that "immense fortune." Even in the back of a cheap hired coach, Talleyrand never wasted his breath on idle chatter.

The corrupt Directors raised a howl on finding that the infamous ex-bishop was a better thief than they. Barras accused him of taking 500,000 francs from Portugal's ambassador to The Hague. Barras was right, but forgot that the affair went on record and that he himself was down in black and white as having received his own share, a smaller sum in keeping with his smaller service.

One affair caused considerable scandal during Talleyrand's tenure in the Foreign Office and was brought to light by three American envoys sent to collect indemnities from the Directory for American ships seized by French men-o'-war. The Americans had a number of callers: a woman, a banker, and two friends of Talleyrand, Montrond and Sainte-Foy. Knowing American business practices, Talleyrand instructed his agents to propose certain concessions in return for settling the claims. Talleyrand was to receive 50,000 louis, or a million livres, just for seeing that the negotiations took place in a friendly atmosphere. The money was not to be his alone; he intended to share it with the Citizen Directors, a portion for each of the five—even the ones who had opposed his appointment. A good chance to test whether Reubell would scorn money as he had scorned its procurer. Talleyrand also made it clear to the American delegation that the agents who so tactfully had proposed the "arrangement" expected to be paid off. Alas, the Americans were less aware of the tactful procedure than of the whole shady deal. They turned a deaf ear from October, 1797, until the following spring. Then, with no settlement forthcoming, they submitted a virulent report to their government on the revolting behavior of the French foreign minister. The report so outraged public opinion that it became the subject of a presidential message to Congress on April 3, 1798. An international scandal had broken.

Without batting an eyelash, Talleyrand defended his actions in an unsigned article in *Le Moniteur* of June 9, 1798, pointing out that a minister was not accountable for the indiscretions of irresponsible agents. His terse, breezy, and impersonal tone was pure insolence. Furious at Talleyrand's conduct, the American delegates packed up and went home. "This man to whom we have shown the warmest hospitality is the same minister we approached merely to obtain justice. And that ungrateful guest of ours, that renegade bishop, is not ashamed to charge us 50,000 pounds sterling for sweetness, 50,000 pounds for indulging his vices."

Out of the whole indignant tirade, Talleyrand remembered one word: "sweetness," meaning bribery. He adopted it, thinking that if

Americans could invent such an appropriate term they must know how to use it.

Madame de Staël was outraged by the capital's mounting hostility to Talleyrand. In her efforts to defend him, she encountered charges so unsettling that she resolved to call on the bishop in his study for a full explanation. Frantic as usual, she must have wept, pleaded, wrung her hands. She begged him to speak out and clear his name. He listened silently, then left the room. She never heard his version of the affair, which took its toll of their friendship.

His attitude defies understanding. Such "amorality" is indeed perplexing in a person of Talleyrand's gifts.

A Star Is Born

Talleyrand created two masterpieces, one unsigned, the other signed. The first, an artistic masterpiece conceived in strictest intimacy, bore the name Eugène Delacroix. The second took shape before the eyes of Europe while History applauded: the Congress of Vienna. It was also an offspring of Talleyrand, by Europe. But more about this later.

For the moment, let us peek at Eugène in his cradle, the son of a charming lady married to the foreign minister whom Talleyrand superseded through Madame de Staël's efforts.

Le Moniteur for the 24th Germinal of the Year VI (April 13, 1798) reported an astounding surgical operation—considering the period—compared to which a heart transplant is child's play. It was "The Removal of a Tumor Performed the 27th Fructidor of the Year V on Citizen Charles Delacroix, former Foreign Minister and Envoy Extraordinary of the French Republic to the Republic of Batavia." Under that heading followed a strange story.

Imbert Delonnes, a surgeon and public health officer—contrary to medical ethics and on specific orders from the Directory, which had it printed in the government printing office—published a detailed account for "all friends of humanity" of the operation he performed on the former diplomat. "The friends of humanity" were simply the citizens of France, who were informed officially that Minister Delacroix had suffered for fifteen years from "a monstrous tumor that had gradually invaded the most delicate male organs." Even Barras mentioned the monstrosity in his Memoirs: "the enormous growth covering the lower part of his abdomen, making him look like a pregnant woman in her ninth month at least." Barras also cited one of Madame de Staël's own arguments at the time she was hounding him to transfer Delacroix's post to her bishop and had said of the incumbent: "He is no minister, but a pregnant old woman." The "monstrosity" then, instead of remaining a private concern of the Delacroix household, became public knowledge (monstrous in itself) thanks to the surgeon's microscopic report: the ghastly thing weighed 32 pounds, measured 14.6 by 10.7 inches and, lest anyone forget it, was superbly engraved, wholly and sectionally, alongside the text.

The doctor proudly announced a surgical triumph: the patient not only had survived but had been returned to his wife feeling fifteen years younger. In other words, Delacroix allegedly regained the functions of "the most delicate male organs," though not, unfortunately, his ministerial ones.

Why the unseemly publicity and official interest: to glorify the surgeon's momentous achievement? To serve the interests of science? Were the latter true, an anonymous article would have had the same medical value.

The truth is that certain parties wanted Delacroix to receive wide publicity, thereby establishing a permanent record of the dates on which he underwent surgery and resumed his conjugal activities—and the triumphant results of same. For if Delacroix no longer resembled a pregnant woman, his wife surely did. The newspaper article and the surgeon's pamphlet proved beyond a doubt that Madame Delacroix's pregnancy was attributable to the doctor's competent scalpel. This indecent public exposure was intended to erase any blots from the ex-minister's history of marital felicity. To escape the disgrace of cuckoldry, he exhibited his repulsive affliction. But neither his honor nor the Directory's virtue could be saved, for Madame Delacroix's condition had already been explained differently. The *Moniteur* article came too late.

The facts and dates are these: Madame Delacroix gave birth to a son on April 26, 1798. The article had been scheduled to appear well ahead of the event, on April 2. As Delacroix had undergone his operation the previous September, had been seriously ill preceding it, and had convalesced for two months afterwards, making the end of November the earliest possible time at which "he recovered the benefits of virility," to quote *Le Moniteur,* it was impossible for any child born in April to be his. No infant would have survived delivery at six months.

We share the view of those close to Talleyrand and the Delacroix couple, and of reputable critics as well, that in matters of illegitimacy, circumstantial evidence corroborated by reliable witnesses provides adequate proof, especially when supported by subsequent events.

Madame Delacroix and Talleyrand were courting ardently and actively during the period Delacroix was residing in The Hague as ambassador to the Batavian Republic. At that distance, and with a tumor of that size, it would have been difficult to father his wife's son. What was Madame Delacroix like? In 1797 when Talleyrand knew her, she was thirty-eight, still fresh, attractive, and possessed of an ageless charm unrelated to time or good looks, but which all his mistresses had: skin like lilies and roses, tenderness, a subtle brilliance, an elegant way of gesturing and conversing. She had all those qualities. Though not of noble birth, she was an aristocrat nonetheless by virtue of her artistic sensibilities, culture, and refinement. Oeben, the royal cabinetmaker, was her father, and Riesener, another celebrated cabinetmaker, her uncle. As a girl, she had been presented to the queen at Versailles. She reminded Talleyrand of Mesdames de Flahaut, de Brionne, and de Laval, their soft voices, their comfortable way of life. Madame Delacroix, a firm believer in Voltaire and the monarchy, was not a conventional woman. In replacing her husband, Talleyrand had the courtesy to appoint him minister to The Hague, a small gesture of thanks to a poor fellow whose job and wife he had stolen. He kept the job, but as soon as Delacroix recovered his health, Talleyrand returned his wife—pregnant, it is true. What a memento of frail and transcendent love he bequeathed to that family and to France: the nineteenth century's greatest painter, Eugène Delacroix. If he had done nothing else but father such a son, it would have been feat enough.

Father and son kept silent about their kinship. They looked enough alike to avoid having to explain what informed society had known since 1798. Certain events in the career of Eugène Delacroix would go unexplained if the relationship did not exist. Would the young Delacroix, officially the son of a regicide in the National Convention, have gained access so readily to rightist salons in the faubourg Saint-Germain? The salons knew about it. The government did not know and refused to consider the son of a regicide for administrative office. His romantic, revolutionary, dazzling canvases, which official critics branded "daubery" and tried to keep the public from seeing, found a champion in 1822 when the painter exhibited his "Dante and Virgil." Then he received an overwhelming salute: "Monsieur Eugène Delacroix has had a stroke of genius." Just that. Who wrote it? Young Adolphe Thiers. Why? The young Rastignac from Marseille was courting Talleyrand, learning his habits, launching himself in his idol's footsteps. Having heard rumors of the young painter's parentage, he resolved to curry favor with the father by applauding the son's genius. Thiers was said later on to be a creature of Talleyrand; he already was. Not only that, but over the protests of critics and museum representatives, Delacroix's canvas and subsequent ones were purchased mysteriously by the government at astronomical prices, prices which no unknown young artist can attain without the influence of a powerful sponsor. After 1830, when Talleyrand was a star figure in the July Monarchy, the government commissioned a number of important works from Delacroix and became his patron—at least until Talleyrand's death.

Lastly, the facial resemblance and the haughty manner spoke for themselves. Delacroix and Talleyrand had the same arrogance. When Sosthène de La Rochefoucauld summoned the painter to change his style because the huge "Death of Sardanapolis," with all its nudes, shocked public taste, the answer was a categoric refusal—like Talleyrand's way of handling Larevellière-Lépeaux and the other Directors. Their style is alike, too, as seen in their letters and their way of life. Despite his revolutionary art, Delacroix never degenerated to a romantic dauber. With age, he came to resemble the prince more and more, his profile increasingly like Talleyrand's. And his ideas also: renouncing his barricades, he turned royalist and rejoined his class. His name was linked to society's smartest women, but in affairs, never in marriage. It was his severe and somewhat arrogant opinion that any formal union could spell trouble. Had not Saint-Simon warned that it is ill-advised "for bastards to perpetuate their race"?

Though no incontrovertible evidence of illegitimacy exists, one fact remains highly persuasive: when Eugène was born in April, 1798, no one took him for Delacroix's child, everyone for Talleyrand's. As a possible parent, only the bishop's name was suggested. For once, miraculously, all the malicious, invidious tongues found nothing to invent. We accept the opinion because coming events substantiated it. Besides producing a masterpiece, Talleyrand gave the world a creator of masterpieces.

Assigned a Uniform and an Address,
the Citizen Minister Manages a Coup d'Etat

During the Directory, special outfits were designed for the Directors and other high officials. The one earmarked for Talleyrand was not calculated to make him melt into the crowd. It included a cloak, breeches, and a coat with enormous lapels. Everything was solid black except for the flaming red lapels (the vest lapels were blue), the facings and linings, the vest and breeches. There was also a huge white silk sash. On the collar, the front of the coat, and along the cavernous cuffs were layers of colorful embroidery. A cascade of ribbons tumbled from his fine leather pumps. A sword and cross-belt, a hat with the brim tilted up in front and three great fiery plumes completed the outfit. It was in execrable taste. Instead of being dignified, the regalia was laughable. On seeing Talleyrand decked out like a cockatoo, Madame Sophie Gay remarked tartly: "His coat changed colors like a rainbow." The régime's colors, not his own.

His residence on the rue du Bac was the hôtel de Galliffet,* one of the handsomest buildings in the whole faubourg Saint-Germain. Constructed between 1776 and 1792, it was still unfinished at the start of the Revolution. The Galliffets never occupied it; they paid the builder and emigrated, whereupon the house was confiscated. It was brand new therefore in 1794 when the foreign minister moved in. One can still appreciate its simple, imposing classic lines. Over the years the spacious gardens have shrunk, marring the architectural beauty of the whole, for those soaring 30-foot columns were not designed to be hemmed in. Still, it is a handsome, noble edifice. Talleyrand's study is there today overlooking the main courtyard and a sweeping staircase worthy of a royal palace. On the second floor, the stairs are lined with columns and bas-reliefs lit from above by a cupolated skylight. Germaine de Staël's ghost still haunts the foot of the stairway where she stood when Bonaparte shattered her pride and Talleyrand ended their friendship.

The walls of this house are alive with the spirit of Talleyrand and his era. He lived there for several years, married, worked, and managed to couple France with a new Caesar. There he was host to society's darling of the season, Esseid Ali Effendi, the Turkish ambassador who had all the ladies swooning. He was an affable Moslem and never allowed duty to interfere with pleasure. Talleyrand gave him a sumptuous reception, producing the most beautiful women in Paris and a lavish buffet supper. Food was served on individual tables set in front of each chair. Talleyrand asked the guest of honor which lady he wished to sit next to during supper. His Excellency pointed to the loveliest, the most chaste and modest lady in the room: the marquise de La Tour du Pin—she who had spitted legs of mutton in the wilds of America.

The gossip sheets sneered at Talleyrand. One of them observed:

---

* The present Italian Cultural Service, just opposite the Italian embassy on the rue de Varenne where its entrance now is. Professor Giovanni Dalla Pozza, who directs the Service, allowed me to tour the building under his gracious guidance, for which I am most grateful to him.

"Where are you, Scarron? If ridicule, like honor, confers immortality, you will have recorded for posterity that majestic and absurd performance we have just witnessed. . . . The bishop of Autun all powdered and laced into his clothes as in the portrait depicting him as Alcibiades when he was the clergy's Alcibiades." His clerical past never failed to arouse hostility. Actually, as an official of the Directory he was no more disguised than he had been as a constitutional bishop.

Bent on destroying him, his rivals whispered it about that he was in league with England, France's foe, and eager for war. The police investigated the report. Talleyrand defended himself: "No one who knows me even slightly can find a word of truth or half-truth in all that." We can rely on his statement. A firm believer in peace, he considered war the easiest way out, the most savage, inhuman, uncivilized way out. War against England would be the height of absurdity as civilization had the most to lose from it.

Dealing with foreign governments was a problem. Lack of confidence in the Directors rendered them extremely wary and reluctant to make any commitments. Talleyrand's immediate concern was to restore that confidence.

He stirred optimism in the diplomatic community by circulating a letter furnishing arguments defending the situation in France in an effort to allay the doubts of foreign powers. His talent for composing religious or political "mandates" is already a matter of record. He now opened a campaign to persuade Europe that French unrest was not anarchy, that "slight differences of opinion in France [the differences were enormous and insoluble], all impulsive, are in a way the price demanded for the luxury of peace; yet upon these divisions, which perhaps are inevitable under a free Constitution, we dare to pin outrageous hopes. . . ." He was right to say that foreign powers were forging "outrageous hopes" if they thought political discord left France vulnerable. Less commendable, however, was his refusal to acknowledge the political decay tearing the country apart and inviting trouble from outside.

To bolster their authority, the Directors wanted it known that they were in complete accord with their generals. In reality, fear of the army made them reluctant to issue any orders. The generals sent back enemy banners and victory bulletins; the government gloried in them. Everything would be fine as long as there was a war to keep the generals and their troops off French soil.

Political dissent was also in evidence. To relieve its insecurity, the régime was constantly defending itself on domestic issues. Talleyrand called it "rousing public spirit." Various schemes were devised for doing that, none democratic. "The Executive Directory will do everything in its power to guarantee Frenchmen their liberty, their Constitution, their property, their peace of mind, their glorious destiny. . . . The Republic shall be preserved." (The same might be said at the bedside of a dying man.) Was the Republic in mortal danger? It would be amusing to know what Talleyrand thought of the campaign to rekindle civic-mindedness. He took part in one such initiative on the 18th Fructidor—September 4, 1797—and survived.

The Jacobin wing was causing trouble, ready on a moment's notice to reenact the violence of 1793. The Directors were all for exalting revolutionary virtue provided that they did not have to practice it. To cool the hotheads on the Committee of Public Safety, they began toying with the idea of a "purge" (it was exactly that). But in order not to play favorites, on the 18th Fructidor the government deported a handful of royalists to the Island of Cayenne. Talleyrand did not dispute the decision; as a matter of fact, it added fuel to his efforts to win over Madame de Staël and Benjamin Constant to the cause of "purging" the Jacobins. He was even asked to enlist support for the potentially brutal measure in intellectual circles. By flattering republican sentiments, he succeeded. Thus Germaine, who was opposed to violence, approved the violence of the 18th Fructidor on grounds that it would strike at both extremes of the political spectrum. All would-be members of the "private universe" were accomplices in the arrests, deportations, and disappearances that followed. They swallowed whatever Talleyrand served them from the Directory's kitchen. Dinner-table conversation at his house had a way of melting resistance.

He had given a large dinner party on August 18, barely a month after taking office. Benjamin Constant attended as an observer. There was another reception on September 2, with Madame de Staël, Madame Tallien, and a certain Madame Grand (remember her: she was beautiful, indifferent to purges or purity, born in India), Madame de Castellane, Generals Kléber, Bernadotte, Lannes, Augereau (it was he who finally agreed to use force), Berthier, Junot, and several others.[1] What a team they would have made ten years later! Their opinions varied, but when Bernadotte described the French army's triumphant entry into Milan on July 14 under Bonaparte, the room rang with applause. A toast to the Directory was raised, and Talleyrand managed to heap most of the honors on Barras as the one man whose authority warranted respect.

Two days later, the 18th of Fructidor, Carnot, Barthélemy, and a number of Jacobin deputies from the Five Hundred and from the Ancients were deported to Cayenne. The "reanimation" program was a huge success, thanks to the expert hand of Barras and the methodical mind of Talleyrand. Madame de Coigny summed it up: "Look what it means to have a man of breeding at the helm. We have Monsieur de Talleyrand issuing mandates to the whole country as if it were his diocese. A general, however, not a vicar-general, is proclaiming them." Augereau was the general.

While citizens were being shipped off to prison in Cayenne, Talleyrand was playing whist. Every so often a courier would appear and whisper a few words in his ear. A polite, inscrutable smile flitted across his lips as he went on playing. He was also following another game, for which he had determined the rules, being played out by five puppet Directors. His informants were simply confirming that the rules had been observed.

On the nineteenth, Madame de Staël was already protesting, trying desperately to help her royalist friends escape, telling everyone that Talleyrand was to blame. In one sentence, he put her in her place—as an accomplice: "Madame de Staël produced the 18th Fructidor, but not the 19th." Overbearing and voluble, she acted like a chief of state deciding the fate of men and institutions: "Bonaparte must exploit this. I want him made Director very soon. I want him there with Barras whom I keep. Sieyès, Talleyrand, Constant, and him: the government will be run superbly." What gall! "I want—I keep . . ." It was to be a Republic of Germaine's making. She sent word to Bonaparte that he had her favor and could count on her support. She wanted him to know "what I am doing for him, my interest in him; some nights I lie awake thinking of his victories; I know we would like each other." Bonaparte could not have cared less for a woman writer losing sleep on his account. Flattery and patronage were highly objectionable to a man of his character. He was not interested in the plans she had made for him; he would make his own.

The neatly executed purge did nothing for Talleyrand. Carnot's and Barthélemy's absence created two vacancies in the Executive Directory, neither of which he was asked to fill. Undismayed, he sent a new mandate to his ambassadors, explaining how foreign powers should interpret what has become commonly known as the *"coup d'état* of the 18th Fructidor." "By its courage and vision, by observing the strict secrecy required, the Directory proved its ability to govern in times of crisis." All of which was untrue. The Directors were cowards and totally blind.

The one true statement was that the policy of secrecy held fast, thanks to Talleyrand. He still had to "explain" the *coup d'état* and make it palatable outside France: anything unconstitutional aimed at establishing permanent constitutionality. What's a *coup d'état* if it works? Just another fact of life. But the best rhetoric was reserved for his letter to General Bonaparte in Italy.

The Iron Heel of the Directory

Already the régime seemed to reek of rotting flesh. At the very first council Talleyrand attended, the Executive Directors had turned in an execrable performance, with Carnot and Barras quarreling, each accusing the other of losing a dossier. Soon they were spitting out their mutual hate and contempt. Carnot suddenly raised his arm, announcing: "I swear on my word of honor that it is not true!" "Don't raise your hand," shouted his colleague, "there's blood dripping from it." They might have been two murderers reliving their crime and wiping each other's face in it.

They had another clash before the 18th Fructidor over Carnot's refusal to sign something. Once again Barras charged him with bloody hands. Carnot countered with "adventurer" and "idiot." Whereupon Barras jumped up: "Let's end this right now," and, tearing off their coats, they came at each other, fists raised. Yelling and screaming, the three other Directors intervened to separate the pair. Too bad they weren't wearing full regalia; the feathers would have flown. The hunchback Larevellière-Lépeaux shouted to the lame man for help. For once Talleyrand was petrified, but neither deaf nor blind.

He was from time to time the scapegoat of the Five Majesties whom the Revolution had saddled on France. To amuse themselves one day, they summoned him to appear behind closed doors and kept him standing, despite his lameness. Barras stared at him in silence, eyes laden with suspicion; finally he spoke in hostile tones: "Citizen, your intimacy with Citizen Lagarde, our secretary, is alarming; we await your explanation."

Talleyrand, if it must be known, had tried to win Lagarde's confidence, and by questioning him in a friendly, casual way managed to find out what was going on in some of the meetings from which he was excluded.

But to embarrass Talleyrand took more than five Citizen Directors with a greater talent for cursing than worming secrets out of the insolent Monseigneur d'Autun. Slowly, without a word, he picked up a sheet of paper and wrote his reply—wrote it because there were some words that Monseigneur d'Autun would not stoop to repeat, even to the persons who uttered them: "The trouble is that when you say f——, Lagarde only says d——." Being rather put out, they dismissed him.

Sometimes they made fun of him. He had it coming, for his adopted Jacobin attitude didn't suit him in the first place, and he overworked it anyway, harping on his "fervent patriotism," his ardent republicanism. "Why so, Monseigneur, when there's no need for it?" Barras asked him sarcastically. But even that could not dent his obsequious posture: the important thing was to hold his ground.

Reubell was the coarsest of the lot. He repaid Talleyrand's silent scorn a hundredfold. Knowing that his victim was helpless, he did everything he could to make the former aristocrat and prelate grovel.

When Reubell heard rumors that Spain had sanctioned English trade with her American colonies, he raised a storm of protest against the foreign minister for not advising the government of "that treason." In those days, treason was a household word. The Spanish sovereign was not obligated to ask Reubell's permission before signing a trade agreement with England. But it was a good excuse for a new war, which always delighted the Directors. Sensing trouble ahead, Talleyrand got off a memorandum at once. It was returned to him with this angry notation scrawled across the page: "Poor; redo in greater detail." Monseigneur obediently did his homework again and sent it on to the arrogant Reubell. The storm abated.

Then a new one broke. During a council meeting, Reubell pounced on all the papers submitted by the Foreign Office, crumpled them in a heap, and tossed them in the air, shouting in Talleyrand's direction: "Your style strikes me as pure bombast, without a trace of precision or discrimination. Stick to the facts! The facts! You always overlook them."

Worse than that: one day when Reubell sprang a question at him point-blank, Talleyrand insisted that the matter required some thought, and in self-defense, knowing Reubell would be furious, he made a point of flattering the irascible Director. Apologizing for his delay in answering, he said: "Even if I were thoroughly prepared, I would not trust myself to undertake a discussion with Citizen Reubell, whom everyone acknowledges to be Europe's expert in diplomacy and administration." Whereupon he excused himself to do some thinking. His persecutor hung on stubbornly: "If solitude is all it takes to fertilize your genius, I shall see to it that you have no distractions." He pushed him into an empty office, shut him up there for an hour, and then demanded his reply. Talleyrand had written nothing and complained of a headache.

Pointing to the door, Reubell said tauntingly: "Get thee to bed, Basil,* thy breath stinks of fever."

That is how France was governed in 1798: war on her borders, hunger at home, worthless currency, robber bands on every highway. Who cared? Reubell had just won a victory: "Now see your great hero for what he is . . ." he told the other Directors.

It is not hard to understand why Talleyrand and some of his friends were ready to bury the Directory's "corpse." But did he have to go on swallowing insults? He considered taking the post of ambassador to Constantinople. Then he had another idea: to Bonaparte he suggested dismissing Reubell. The general didn't quite understand; rather than cashier just one Director, he wanted to get rid of the lot of them. At the moment, Bonaparte had pyramids on his mind. Let it be said, however, that Talleyrand held his ground and did not suffer too badly from the shabby official treatment. No one could humiliate him. All he wanted was to live as he chose and ultimately to rid the country of its present governors. Neither vain nor conceited, he simply believed that by holding out long enough, he would prevail.

He even attempted to woo the hostile Reubell. Calling Talleyrand flexible is not an empty compliment. Perhaps he derived some private satisfaction from this little game, some distorted sense of pride or reverse humility. Patiently, he waited to trap his grizzly with honeyed words. In April, 1798, he finally got his chance. The Directors were planning for the approaching legislative elections, a crucial matter. Once before when the voting got out of hand and threatened to saddle them with a royalist majority, they had taken steps to weed out the offending deputies. Talleyrand tempted Reubell with a false hope, telling him that the same problem had been solved satisfactorily in England by allowing the government or the parties to buy votes. Infamy! The Directors shuddered. Better death than a corrupt Republic! They flung some (half-hearted) insults at Talleyrand and let it go at that. Afterwards the Citizen Directors put their heads together and decided to distribute bribes. In their generosity, they called on Talleyrand to allocate the money, which he did with an eye to the private desires of those honorable citizens—in short, he bought votes with government funds.

Virtue triumphed; that election showed a marked improvement over the previous one. It was a lot more amusing than having Reubell lock him up in an office.

* Character in Beaumarchais's *Marriage of Figaro* and *Barber of Seville;* a hypocrite and slanderer—Trans.

Talleyrand fared better with the Council of Ancients. The famous Dupont de Nemours had marked him for a brilliant career as early as 1788. His opinion is worth noting: "The present foreign minister has many genuine abilities. He combines sound judgment with ready intelligence, perseverance, and a great desire to win public approval through valid service."

A far cry from Reubell's estimate: "Talleyrand was the bane of existence, the prototype of treason and corruption. A powdered lackey of the Ancien Régime, he would have made a fine servant to parade publicly had his legs been better; but his legs are no better than his courage."

Talleyrand did not lose heart in that den of thieves, having pluck to spare, but his situation was becoming extremely uncomfortable. When openly threatened with dismissal, his only ally was Barras. The two of them had certain things in common: both were former aristocrats, both were shocked by the vulgar conduct of the other officials, and their initial meeting, after all, had been an emotional one, with the Citizen Director throwing himself into the former bishop's arms. Talleyrand often would wait for Barras at the gates of the Luxembourg, well hidden in the back of a coach. Barras would emerge from some irksome official meeting completely disgusted by the brutality and stupidity of the other Directors. After a warm greeting from Talleyrand, the two would talk confidentially. With his incomparable charm, Talleyrand thus enlisted the vicomte de Barras's continued support.

Talleyrand would have liked to become a Director, but with each vacancy another blank personality joined the Five. He clung to Barras: "You are the life of the Directory . . . you are the mind and strength of the Directory. If it were my good fortune to become your colleague, I should take pride in obeying you implicitly as a child obeys his father."

All the fine sentiments went unheard. First Neufchâteau, then Merlin of Douai were chosen; when the former stepped down on May 22, 1798, the post was grabbed from under his nose by Treilhard, a friend of the four other Directors. The Prussian minister expressed surprise that Talleyrand had managed to hang on so long: "Talleyrand's ministerial survival remains, as I have reported, precarious. If he succeeds in holding on, it will be a miracle of wits and endurance. Monsieur Barras is his only acknowledged friend in high circles; the other Directors, I am told, scarcely even address him." The diplomat went on to note that not everyone was convinced of Talleyrand's republican sympathies. Worse, his sole ally was as suspicious of him as Reubell: "Wit without character is good for nothing." A fine pronouncement coming from Barras! Later on, to his great sorrow, Barras discovered that the foreign minister was far from spineless, and that a "good-for-nothing" could boot a Director out the door.

For a moment, Talleyrand expected that it was his turn to be fired. Sottin, minister of police, had just been cashiered; even without having met the man, Talleyrand supposed him to be an imbecile. It should be said that apart from licking the boots of the Five with utmost servility—so fearful was he of being dismissed—he had no use for, and was not even acquainted with, the small fry of the régime, including those of cabinet rank. In the course of a dinner attended by persons of every political stripe, someone mentioned Sottin's dismissal to Talleyrand, who began at once to upbraid the poor ex-minister unmercifully: "He is one of those political wasps that never fails to foul the industrious hive of state. Anyway, what distinctions had this Sottin earned up till now? What had he done to deserve high office? They say he is a good dancer. That is a pitiable recommendation for a minister of the Republic."

Catching Talleyrand in an outright lie is a dismal experience; one cannot condone his impropriety and poor judgment. He was about to be soundly punished for it as he continued: "And what a name! There is not much to choose between Sottin and *sot*." * "You are right, sir," replied the gentleman on the opposite side of the table, "between a *sot* and Sottin there is sometimes no more than the width of a table." The gentleman was none other than Sottin himself.

He had been put in his place—and richly deserved it.

Talleyrand Nods to General Bonaparte

They had not met, but had exchanged letters. On July 26, 1797, shortly after taking office, Talleyrand wrote to General Bonaparte:

> I have the honor to inform you, General, that the Executive Directory has appointed me foreign minister. Awed by the crucial responsibilities ahead of me, I long to be certain that your glorious prestige will support and facilitate my negotiations. The very mention of the name Bonaparte has the effect of smoothing out difficulties.
>
> I shall not fail to advise you of the Directory's views as and when I am instructed to communicate them to you, but Renown, your herald, often will deprive me of the pleasure of reporting how you have fulfilled them.

Beguiling flattery, and a lesson in how to approach a new job and new associates when one has been schooled at Saint-Sulpice and has

* *Sot*: two-legged ass—Trans.

done one's apprenticeship in the Rheims diocese, the court at Versailles, and the boudoirs of fashionable ladies. It is the style of Racine, royal historiographer, also of Monseigneur d'Autun's mandates. Their impact on the religious community was no different from the impact of this message on Bonaparte: he realized that the writer was an extraordinary man. At last, he thought, someone of stature is in the government. Josephine joined the general in Italy bringing news from the capital. Arriving there on August 20, 1797, she spoke of Talleyrand, whose good and bad reputation was the talk of Paris. Bonaparte wrote to the Directors congratulating them on their choice, and to Talleyrand thanking him for his letter:

> Your appointment as foreign minister does credit to the government's good judgment. It proves your great abilities, your pure civic-mindedness, and your lack of sympathy for the deviations that dishonored the Revolution.
>
> I am flattered to be your steady correspondent and thus have the opportunity to express my high esteem for you. Fraternal greetings. Bonaparte.

With this exchange of letters began a prodigious adventure which committed France and all Europe unwittingly to a sublime and tragic course decreed by these two men, and which was to end one June night in 1815 in the mud and slaughter of Waterloo.

Each word was meaningful to contemporary readers: the "pure civic-mindedness" was the warranty of revolutionary sympathies in this constitutional bishop, ruling out any compromise with the royalists whose ranks had been decimated by Bonaparte's muskets in Toulon and later in front of the Church of Saint-Roch in Paris. A good point indeed. It is certain that Talleyrand, as Pasquier's Memoirs affirm, "was terrified of a Bourbon Restoration. He knew that his past made him totally alien to them." "Your lack of sympathy for the deviations that dishonored the Revolution" struck a balance: neither royalist nor terrorist. A second point in Talleyrand's favor.

In his *Memoirs,* Talleyrand confessed that he had discerned "in that young conqueror, in what he did, said, and wrote, something new enough, strong enough, clever and enterprising enough to justify pinning great hopes to his fortune."

They were only hopes. What might the facts have been?

As usual, Talleyrand expressed himself vaguely—it was easier for him, harder for others to fathom. What did he mean by "something new enough" in the young general? We know that Bonaparte was a brilliant soldier; but he fought brilliantly for himself. He won battles and then negotiated with the Italian states or with Austria on his own terms, never waiting for official instructions. Utterly insubordinate, he had signed the likes of a peace treaty in Bologna with the grand duke of Tuscany without bothering to consult the Directory, and had done the same with the Pope at Tolentino on February 19, 1797, with Austria's emperor at Leoben on April 18, and with Venice on May 16, 1797. All this before Talleyrand took office.

Delacroix had allowed Bonaparte to do as he pleased. History had no rebuke for that diplomatic nonentity who trod on nobody's toes, but whose ineptitude simply ruined France. Once Talleyrand came onstage, however, he was blamed for failing to impose authority. Yet we know the conditions under which he was forced to work and the Directors' tyranny. It is true that Talleyrand, as foreign minister, put no checks on Bonaparte. As a matter of fact, he went further and discreetly applauded the general's insubordination. But was that his fault or the fault of the régime in which he had barely managed to gain a toehold and was no more than tolerated?

Talleyrand wrote again to Bonaparte on the 18th Fructidor:

> Paris is calm; Augereau's conduct impeccable; it is plain that he has been to the right school. [Bonaparte's school, a highly flattering remark. The general had been unwilling to take on the purging operation. Having already bayoneted Parisians at Saint-Roch, he felt that another massacre after Vendémiaire might jeopardize his future plans. So he left to "Augereau's saber" the unpleasant task at hand.] A handful of terrorists tried to make trouble at one point. Augereau's firm stand sent them back to the faubourgs where they are now quiet. The Constitution was abandoned momentarily; we have returned to it once and for all, I trust.

The last sentence was sheer mockery, for he knew and Bonaparte knew that one day the Constitution would be tossed out the window forever. Together they would pick up the pieces. Clearly, they shared an almost magical understanding.

His letter of September 8 giving Napoleon a more or less free hand in Italy is even more enlightening: "If it allows us to hold the banks of the Rhine, if Venice does not go to the emperor, then it is a peace worthy of Bonaparte." Already bowing to Caesar! "In all other matters, act as you see fit; surely they will bear the seal of grandeur and stability you imprint on everything you do."

The last sentence is prophetic, indicating the pact already established between them. Talleyrand had nosed out the man who was to pull France out of the mire. Let it not be said that he acted out of self-interest at that particular moment. His interest—were he the greedy creature so commonly depicted—would have lain in making a fortune out of the Directory's corruption and in prolonging that pleasure by getting himself appointed Director. That would probably have happened if the Directory had not confronted two uncompromising foes of ignorance and inertia, Talleyrand and Bonaparte.

What other attitude toward the general could Talleyrand have had? From the beginning, he was most sympathetic to the brilliant young soldier whom he knew only through victory bulletins and the admirable treaties imposed on his enemies. Even if he had wanted to, how could he have opposed the general and the Directors? Under the existing régime, cabinet ministers never appeared before the two legislative chambers and were answerable only to the gilded and beplumed Pentarchs, who issued commands right and left which no one obeyed save the ministers as they could be dismissed at the drop of a hat. Our hero was not anxious to sacrifice his career; at the slightest sign of insubordination, Reubell would have cashiered him. On the other hand, Bonaparte did exactly as he pleased because the Directors were too scared to impose their authority, and also because he was swelling the nation's coffers with enormous war indemnities from conquered territories. Moreover, Talleyrand was willing to transmit official orders and play his role in the bureaucracy knowing that Bonaparte would act as he saw fit—and his judgment was infinitely superior to Reubell's. On two occasions Talleyrand informed the general that the government was opposed to abandoning the Venetian Republic to Austria (September 23, 1797). "We did not enter Italy to become traders of nations." A worthy principle, typical of how the Directory operated. Less than a month later, Bonaparte signed the Treaty of Campo Formio and handed over Venice to Austria. Flouted by its military commander, what did the government do? Recall him? Strip him of his command? Nothing of the sort: "Now there is peace, peace à la Bonaparte. My warmest compliments, General; words fail me. The Directory is pleased, the public overjoyed. Everything has worked out to perfection." No mention of Venice or insubordination. Then came the final paragraph: "The Italians may do some screaming, but that doesn't matter [what happened to the "traders of nations" idea?]." He concluded: "Farewell, General and peacemaker. Farewell! My regards, admiration, respect, gratitude—the list could go on forever."

After reading that letter, the general knew he had a formidable ally in Paris whose influence, if not official, was quite as powerful as that of the Directors. From afar the two men were drawn together, magnetized, linked by their secret complicity.

Napoleon was so conscious of it that he thought of becoming a Director along with Talleyrand and taking power after the 18th Fructidor. Neither of them was appointed. Whereupon Talleyrand wrote the general an important letter that has been lost. From Bonaparte's reply, we gather that he was disappointed and wanted to send Sieyès to confer with the commander in Italy. Sieyès, considered the most outstanding jurist of his day, would have been put to work drafting a constitution for the Cisalpine Republic. Bonaparte felt that political issues took precedence over military ones and was eager to expand his limited knowledge of them. After reading the letter, Talleyrand made this note: "Long letter, carefully written, in which he wanted me to see a different man from the one he has appeared to be thus far on the stage of history."

Talleyrand was not mistaken: Bonaparte was changing his image from soldier to legislator and statesman. He even had the notion of creating and presiding over a kind of proconsulship in Italy which would serve as a model for French institutions. Talleyrand did not care for the plan, and rightly so.

But still another and more fanciful project was preoccupying Napoleon. He dreamed of seizing Corfu and the Ionian Islands, delivering Greece from the Turks, conquering Constantinople, and marching across Turkey and Syria to Egypt, his real target and the seat of his projected Eastern Empire. Thus was his vision of the Orient born. He abandoned his plans for Greece and Turkey when the Italians showed lukewarm support for the venture. Talleyrand was no more enthusiastic than they and could not imagine why the Italian states would want to accept defeat and eventual enslavement by Bonaparte as against the Austrians. His defense of freedom, justice, and common sense elicited the following reply from the general: "I see from your letters that you persist in honoring a false assumption. You seem to think that liberty in a nation of indolent, superstitious Pantaloons and cowards sparks the will to achieve great things." So much for the Italians, whom he proceeded to label "degenerates." * In a letter dated October 7, 1797, he had already called them "a limp and spineless people." It would be interesting to know what kind of "liberty" Napoleon's army of occupation imposed. The dream of an Eastern Empire became a reality for him—but not for Talleyrand.

---

* The insult was redressed in 1812 when Napoleon publicly eulogized the Italian battalions he had dragged into Russia.

A year before, on May 10, 1796, our bishop had written: "What a man is our Bonaparte! Not yet twenty-eight, he has already savored the glories not only of war, but of peace, moderation, and mercy. The world is his." In a rare bout of enthusiasm, he was already crediting Napoleon with the moderation which he, Talleyrand, prized so highly. He praised it again as the mark of a superior mind when, on November 1, 1797, General Berthier and the brilliant mathematician Monge presented the government with the Treaty of Campo Formio signed by Napoleon. "Everlasting thanks to the Directory for knowing when to call a halt to his triumphs . . . for sensing that true greatness sets its own limits, true strength restrains itself, true glory arouses the nation's gratitude." [1]

It is a mistake to interpret those remarks as merely a crude attempt to feed the Directors' vanity. Though his main objective may have been to flatter his beplumed superiors, he was also expressing his political credo. Talleyrand commended the régime for qualities it did not possess and which he and Napoleon both did. (He may have attributed them a bit hastily to the general.) The praise therefore was intended for Bonaparte, himself, and the principles they shared: "true strength restrains itself"—"true greatness sets its own limits." Two golden rules.

How to Create the Illusion of Idleness

"I am lazy and take pleasure in being so" was Talleyrand's saying. No one denies it. This confirmed sensualist was able to take a subtle, profound, and immensely profitable pleasure in indolence. A particular type of indolence, in the tradition of Montaigne, La Fontaine, and several others. "Note that in their case the nonchalance is designed, the indolence deliberate, the ease supremely artful . . ." said Valéry. They were considered lazy because they chose to appear lazy. They thought idleness and leisure were desirable states of being, indicating the absence of compelling obligations or anxieties. That was Talleyrand's public face from 1774 to 1838 and it was what earned him the reputation for laziness.

As a matter of fact, he never overworked himself during his tenure as foreign minister. For one thing, he avoided physical exertion; for another, the Directors were afraid of him and gave him as little as possible to do. The five of them handled most matters themselves, behind closed doors, leaving only minor decisions to their appointed officials. Even Delacroix, for all his reliability, had no say in affairs and simply verbalized the Directors' wishes.

Referring to Talleyrand, the Prussian ambassador observed: "He is foreign minister in name only and does not enjoy the slightest influence." With so little to do, he did even less. His tortoise-like delay in executing orders became legendary. Oddly enough, the slow pace often proved a blessing. Whereas government policy (if you could call it that), with its sudden, violent decisions, sometimes resembled hysteria, Talleyrand was constantly applying the brakes. He waited, as he put it, for "the first Directorial volley" to go by. He knew the men he had to deal with: first shouts and fists pounding the table, followed by the silence of fear. The Directors would emerge from a meeting red-faced and breathless; they called it working. Familiar with the peculiarities behind their reasoning, Talleyrand used this knowledge to "cushion the recoil," as he put it blandly, and to let matters ride. Waiting was never a waste of time for it allowed ideas to mature, conflicts to fade, deadlines to recede, and op-posites to merge. Mazarin used to say: "Time and myself"; Talleyrand was not unlike the crafty cardinal and felt much the same way. Un-ripened by time, neither minor nor major endeavors endure. Talleyrand and France were shaped gradually, by patient, deliberate craftsmanship, not sudden strokes of genius. It took ten centuries for the French to produce a nation, and equally long to evolve a certain human species of which Talleyrand is the prototype.

Still, he complained of being kept in the background: "If you only knew how discouraging it is to be there." Did he miss being involved in important affairs of state? At first, yes, but after meeting Napoleon he realized that the important events lay ahead. Also, he was concerned lest his continued presence in the Directory's bear-garden jeopardize his future. The *Memoirs* claim that duty and self-sacrifice prompted him to serve that shabby régime in the hope of counteracting its most glaring and horrendous errors. "It should be remembered that in periods of up-heaval, the refusal to act gives aid and comfort to those bent on destruc-tion. Acquiescence does not signify endorsement of objectionable persons or causes; it is a way of mobilizing support for the future."

Written twenty-five years after the event, those excuses are amusing (not ludicrous) because the blend of truth and half-truth is so delicate that a false explanation from Talleyrand is always worth analyzing for the grain of truth it invariably contains. He need not insist on the self-sacrificing nature of his service to the government when we know that both he and Madame de Staël pounded long and hard at Barras's door. It is true, however, that once he took the stage—and helped himself to a generous slice of the pie—he curbed intemperance, mitigated violence, and prepared the way for a better government (in short, he helped to crush the Directory). When royalist accusers claimed that he discredited himself permanently under the régime, he had his chance to answer to those bitter and disruptive émigrés that the Directory was a transitional, waning, and therefore insignificant government. He felt that one should disregard the ephemeral side of politics and concentrate on enduring, contemporary trends that will determine future ones: "What is, almost invariably, is insignificant unless one bears in mind that what is produces what shall be, the point being that to get anywhere one has to start somewhere," he says in his *Memoirs*. He made his start under the Directory; not a very honorable start, but unimportant and short-lived. Somewhere along that muddy way, he met up with Bonaparte representing the outgrowth of the already-defunct government. He had only to bury the corpse and make way for the future. As he put it: "One must always put oneself in a position to choose between two alternatives." Once seated on the Directory's decaying throne, he began to prepare a more solid base for himself in the régime that was bound to supersede the dying one. And to wait. "After that, I had little to do but issue passports and sign visas."

A modest remark, for his efforts to bring peace to France and to Europe were much more than that. When he broached the possibility of ending hostilities with England to Reubell, the irate Director shouted: "What do you mean by suggesting peace with England? Only you would dare make such an absurd proposal. The only way to have peace is to humiliate and subjugate her." It is incredible that a head of state—a near-dictator—could be blind enough to encourage launching that impoverished, ungoverned, and divided nation into war with England.

Talleyrand recognized that his peace policy would come under attack because the men in power needed war to maintain their power. Such pragmatic notions had to be whispered in Paris. One day Talleyrand confided in the Prussian ambassador, casting an interesting light on public opinion and government practices in the year 1798: "You can see as well as I that France is a very young Republic; inexperienced and excitable, she makes mistakes and is blowing off steam; war will only perpetuate and augment them. Why? Because current education aims at war, because the triumphant republican armies have electrified the nation, and because the military profession offers faster and more honorable opportunities for advancement than any other. Peace will cast a pall on all that and revive old habits." An observation of cardinal importance, indicting the Jacobins for dooming France to war, gearing her people for war and thriving on war. It was in this sense, of course, that Napoleon looked upon himself as a "son of the Revolution."

Also to Talleyrand's credit during this unfortunate period were the negotiations he carried on for the peaceful and perfectly legal French annexation of Mulhouse and Geneva. The tiny republic of Mulhouse dispatched envoys, the treaty was concluded, and on March 1, 1798, union with France was unanimously approved.

That was the ideal pattern for annexations, if they had to occur. He did not in principle favor annexing territories and became increasingly opposed to it as France, or at least her rulers, annexed more and more of Europe. The Directory had created satellite republics under military occupation with all the unfortunate consequences attached: the Batavian, Roman, Swiss, and Parthenopean republics. Napoleon did not initiate the policy; he merely advanced it brilliantly, as history proves.

Replying to one of his colleagues in the Institut de France, who was preparing a statement on the desirable French attitude toward "liberated" nations (or "conquered," depending on which end of the sword one faced), Talleyrand said: "I maintain that the system of imposing liberty on one's neighbors by brute force is the best way to arouse hatred of it and make it fail." In one vivid phrase he summed up his feelings about conquest and military occupation: "One can do everything with bayonets except sit on them."

There we have Talleyrand at his best, his respect for individuals and nations totally opposed to Reubell's desire to "humiliate and subjugate" England and to the latter's attacks on Spanish "treason" as a pretext for "liberating" the people of Spain.

Talleyrand's reasonable and peaceful posture was no secret to foreign governments. On April 11, 1798, the Prussian minister advised his sovereign: "I have said it and I believe it: his appointment to this high office could put an end to future turmoil in Europe." As of 1798, Europe considered him a European, but that hope, as we know, was forever being frustrated by the Directory. The peace talks with England, begun in Lille in September, 1797, had collapsed.

Talleyrand felt that if France was doomed to make war on England, she was also obligated to make peace on the Continent. To that end he had Napoleon attend the Congress of Rastatt, the declared purpose of which was to end hostilities with Austria. The delegates were beating about the bush, and Talleyrand instructed the general thus: ". . . you will enable the French delegation to speed up the talks and overcome the delays of German diplomacy just as you have done with their armies" (February 21, 1798).

He often acted without the Directors' knowledge, or contrary to their orders, because it was in the interests of France. But two highly unpleasant affairs tarnished the nation's credit.

TALLEYRAND

In Rome, General Duphot, escorting the French ambassador Joseph Bonaparte (Napoleon's family had started to "infiltrate" Talleyrand's ministry), was murdered during a riot, proving how little the Romans cared for the ambassador. In retaliation, General Berthier occupied the city and, with fixed bayonets, proclaimed the Roman Republic.

On April 13, 1798, Bernadotte, France's ambassador in Vienna, was insulted by the citizens of that city. Returning to Paris, he demanded that hostilities with Austria, suspended during the Congress of Rastatt, be resumed. Talleyrand felt that Bernadotte should not have left his post and was duty-bound to extract an apology and signal reparations, warning that "wars would break out constantly if for every diplomatic insult we resorted to armed retaliation." As usual, his parting advice was politically sound and conciliatory: "My opinion is that here and now the Directory ought to set a lofty example of moderation in order to dispel whatever bad impressions of its practices and political principles may now exist."

Reubell, bellicose as ever, protested loudly. Talleyrand was an accomplished truckler except when it came to spelling out the truth on vital issues. The vital issues were peace and the nation's welfare. The Directory had no desire to hear the truth. Even today we find it hard to admit that France was not as universally admired as we like to think.

Meanwhile, the lazybones on the rue du Bac completed an enormous project. Ordered to compile a "General Survey of the Republic in Relation to All Other States," he was well equipped for the task and turned out a 100-page report packed with information and conclusions. A sample admonition went: "I repeat it because it is a fundamental truth: alliances, if they are to endure, require care, respect, and shared advantages." France was isolated and badly in need of allies, but no European nation was ready to join with her. The bitter truth was that with her 30 million well-knit, militarized citizens, France loomed as a threat to less populated and less cohesive Europe. The word "respect" here is meant to suggest that France aroused fear. Talleyrand was convinced that no nation could govern or keep the peace through fear. Fear led to war. Trust alone could ensure peace. France "must win trust in order to win true and useful allies."

Next, in his usual fashion, he went on to flatter the Directors for their most glaring faults—ironic perhaps, but it was his way of trying to make them act sensibly. "In times of crisis, the Republic has always displayed great, even astounding, moderation. In dealing with Prussia or Spain, with Naples or with the emperor, she has never abused her strength. Let her not parade it now on lesser occasions. Let her be consistent, resourceful, and intelligent; let her reputation as a great nation which was accorded out of admiration now be accorded out of trust."

The whole thrust of his message was: Let us make peace with Europe. Such was the thinking and the wisdom of that sphinx on the rue du Bac.

How could such a lazy fellow tackle so much work? The answer is simple: to cultivate his idleness, he built up a staff of assistants, all competent and hard-working friends of his.

The Confederates of His Idleness

Desrenaudes, Blanc d'Hauterive, Durand de Mareuil, and La Besnardière stood by him to the end of their lives or his. How was that for disloyalty. Why were they loyal? Because he was. They had plenty of opportunities to desert him. They were rewarded generously, but that is only part of the story. They stood by him during every phase of his checkered career. Was it purely out of self-interest? They were devoted to Talleyrand because in his service they could enjoy the prestige attached to high office at home and in foreign embassies. Many bribes must have been offered to them, which they never took. Madame de Chastenay observed savagely: "He kept friends, but, I daresay, almost the way one keeps dogs." Such cruelty simply denies the diabolic ex-bishop of Autun the right to friendships. Whether or not one grants him that right, the fact is that his closest aides were also remarkably devoted friends. Three of them were unfrocked priests, a common bond along with their work for Talleyrand. The following remark of his could not be more pointed: "In my office I always make others work harder than I do. Never bury yourself under a stack of papers. Find someone to sort them out. By making your subordinates work, you can stretch out your day beyond twenty-four hours."

There is an echo of Choiseul's advice at Chanteloup. But he fails to mention that an administrator must supervise each task he assigns, taking into consideration its importance and scope in order to get it done properly. He must also dominate his staff, and, infinitely more difficult, make them value his superior talents. Talleyrand's biographers have a hard time explaining his laziness: they fail to recognize his highly organized leisure. This is how the work got done: Desrenaudes was his favorite editor. Talleyrand would talk to him, after which Desrenaudes made a rough draft of his ideas. Then Talleyrand would look it over and edit it. Years of close collaboration enabled them to understand each other almost instinctively. Having shared the same background and the same books, it was natural for them to understand each other. Desrenaudes wrote rather well and was perfectly competent to draft the famous "mandates," instructions, and memoranda. Talleyrand provided the inspiration; Desrenaudes caught the theme and roughed in the melody, leaving only a few words to be corrected before the finished piece was ready for delivery. This method of collaboration gave rise to the story that Talleyrand simply put his stamp to whatever Desrenaudes set in front of him. Chateaubriand thought so, as we know. Talleyrand was never shy about scratching things out or rephrasing his ideas more ambiguously, so that his thoughts were at once crystal clear and evasive, not to be read inattentively, full of implications. Baron de Vitrolles said of those drafts: "When the rough text was handed to him, he would read it carefully. If it did not satisfy him, he would fold the sheet of paper and hand it back to its author, saying simply: 'That's not what I meant,' or 'That's not it,' or perhaps 'That's not quite it.' The piece was then reworked, aiming for the ultimate approval: 'That's it.' "

Talleyrand and Desrenaudes worked together in perfect harmony— except once during the Consulate when Talleyrand appointed him to the Tribunate, and the conscientious Desrenaudes, as his superior noticed, succumbed to "a mild bout of tribunitis" impelling him to oppose the very measure he had been urged to support. After Talleyrand pointed out that such capricious behavior was not appreciated, Desrenaudes still protested: "As tribune, I obey only my conscience." Obviously, public office had already soured his tongue. Talleyrand put him in his place: "Your conscience is indeed the issue: you were named to the Tribunate not for that but for your vote." The voice of reason spoke. Desrenaudes heard it and heeded it ever after.*

The foreign ministry was divided into North and South departments. The South had its offices on the main courtyard of the rue du Bac and was presided over by Blanc d'Hauterive, whose great tact and probity left his mark upon the service. His stern manner impressed people. Talleyrand could rely on him completely. The story went about that Hauterive entered the minister's bedroom as usual one morning. Talleyrand, awake but pretending to be half-asleep, was enjoying the scene. "Prince, a letter from the elector of . . ." "Well?" "It requires an an-

---

* Cf. Disraeli's stunning comment to a greenhorn M.P. who had chosen to support his conscience instead of his party: "Young man, you should have voted honorably with your party and not according to your conscience like an adventurer."

swer." "What! A personal one?" "Yes, of course, Prince, an elector after all . . ." "What a bore! How is one supposed to compose and write at the same time?" "Yes, Prince." "Come on, Hauterive, I'll write, you dictate."

The Northern division was headed by Durand de Mareuil, dapper, handsome, the kind of polished diplomat you might see on the stage and are less likely to find in the embassies. Madame de Rémusat, Talleyrand's mistress, amused herself watching his attempts to imitate the minister. They got along marvelously, and Talleyrand kept no secrets from him; he took him to Germany to work out the indemnification of mediatized princes. Talleyrand helped himself to a generous portion of those indemnities, as did his amiable assistant.

Like Desrenaudes, though to a lesser degree, Blanc d'Hauterive and Durand de Mareuil probably were so familiar with the thinking and mannerisms of their superior that a sentence or two, or a scribble of his sufficed for them to compose a text in his exact style. Durand's office was on the fourth floor of the rue du Bac; a private stairway led directly to the minister's private study on the ground floor and his apartment above it. The two small rooms on the main floor remain almost as they were in Talleyrand's day, elegant rather than impressive.

Others were close to him. Osmond, his staff supervisor and private secretary, took care of Talleyrand's personal affairs. Osmond's brother acted as tutor to Archambaud's children. Talleyrand had put Louis—the eldest nephew, the most gifted, and the family heir—in the care of Champagny, the French ambassador in Vienna. Talleyrand was fond of Louis; he wrote Champagny to train him in diplomacy and keep him far away "from Paris, which is about the worst thing he could encounter at eighteen." He knew what he was talking about. He added: "If he needs money, please give it to him and let me reimburse you." It is doubtful that Archambaud gave that much thought to his own son.

One day while reading an extraordinarily well-written memorandum, Talleyrand discovered the talents of La Besnardière, a young secretary who served him the rest of his life, faultless and indefatigable, a pillar of industry, tact, and devotion.

In a small room separate from the administrative offices was what might be called the "publicity department," where three editors, d'Arbelles, Lesur, and an English Jew named Goldsmith, issued press releases.

The accounting office, presided over by a Monsieur Bresson, was near the entrance. Whenever Talleyrand wanted to brighten the day for a member of his staff, he would suggest paying "a little visit to

M. Bresson," meaning that the man was due for a raise or a bonus of some sort.

Also assisting him in the ministry were Tony Roederer, son of the senator and Talleyrand's colleague in the Institut de France, and young Villemarest, who spent most of his time scribbling scurrilous tales which he published later under the title *Monsieur de Talleyrand*—a caricature rather than a portrait. He was the only disloyal one. An erudite librarian and valuable adviser, Lechevalier, and a humble fellow named Charpentier completed the staff. In 1809, as a mark of gratitude for his service, Charpentier was given the portrait of Talleyrand painted by Py.

Of course, the indispensable Courtiade was there, his valet and guardian angel of sorts, who served him during his bishopric, his London exile, his tramps through the bogs of Massachusetts, to the very end of his days. Behind the scenes and ever so tactfully, he actively cultivated Talleyrand's leisure. We should also mention the tall, stately Swiss whose post was under the archway. He would announce to visitors: "The minister is out," his authoritative tone discouraging any further queries. After 1802, with no less dignity, he proclaimed: "His Excellency is out." When Talleyrand became prince of Benevento, the Swiss would say: "His Serene Highness has stepped out." All over France, there was a marked tendency to revive traditional forms of address, so that Monsieur once more replaced Citizen. Talleyrand, who usually had ended his letters with "fraternal greetings," now reverted to the customary "I have the honor to greet you."

Last of the tenants was the little monkey, pride and joy of the mail room, who delighted anyone fortunate enough to watch her sealing letters. Josephine saw the performance one day and asked to have her, so Talleyrand sent the pet round to the Malmaison.

When Talleyrand reorganized the foreign ministry at the beginning of the Consulate, he wrote a highly informative memorandum on the nature of diplomacy and the training and necessary skills of a diplomat. Here are just a few key passages from this wholly interesting document: "In any well-run government, each administrative branch has a special mental attitude. This attitude lends unity, uniformity, and energy to its operations." He achieved that on the rue du Bac. During his absences, that special attitude kept the ministry functioning smoothly. One should aim for stability and cohesion among a select and responsible staff. As for diplomats: "There are two sets of attributes influencing the attitude and honor of the profession discussed herein: attributes of the heart and attributes of the mind." An amusing note, for the writer obviously credits himself with those assets, not to mention the unselfishness that he recommends to others. When he spoke of "every skill relative to the art of negotiating," he knew what he was talking about; perhaps it is something that cannot be taught.

As salary is an important consideration in any job, he lets us know that a novice in the ministry earned 600 francs (500,000 old francs), a secretary 3,000, a minister plenipotentiary 6,000, and an ambassador 10,000. When we find our hero receiving 100,000 in "sweets," we know the gift was no mean one, and that his 3 million francs on deposit in London and Hamburg could not possibly represent savings from his salary.

His ministry had not yet reclaimed its real name, foreign affairs, which had been dropped in 1794. When Talleyrand's request on that score was ignored by Napoleon, he did not press the matter. What was the hurry? He simply waited until 1814 to have his way.

Prince of diplomats, he was also unrivaled at collecting information singlehanded. His expertise in worming out secrets, in the art of suggestion, in imitating others in order to build their confidence and thus exert his influence on them alternately amazed and infuriated those who had dealings with him—and were sometimes the victims of it. Vitrolles, not the most indulgent of critics, tells us that Talleyrand did his real work outside the office, in society. "Wit and grace marked his conversation. He possessed the art of concealing his thoughts or his malice beneath a transparent veil of insinuations, words that imply something more than they express. It was the most savory conversation of an era when conversation was uniquely a function of intelligence. . . . Only when absolutely necessary did he inject his own personality."

At social gatherings, Talleyrand said very little. Many people who rhapsodized about his fascinating conversation never heard him say more than a syllable. Still, there were some memorable syllables. When he wanted to save himself the trouble of identifying the three newly appointed Consuls—Bonaparte, Cambacérès, and Lebrun—he called them *"Hic, Haec, Hoc,"* which in French was construed as *He* (Bonaparte), *She* (Cambacérès, who showed a marked appetite for the stronger sex), and *It* (the contemptible and neuter Lebrun). What more can one say in three syllables? His pronouncements on serious subjects rarely exceeded two or three sentences. Careful not to bore his listeners and to express himself lucidly, he questioned whether one could say very much on a profound subject. One should say little and think a great deal first. He never got into an argument, not even during council meetings under the Directory. When did anyone ever convince an adversary? Instead of listening and trying to understand, each party would grow more adamant, incensed, destructive, immoderate, hence stupid. He left the talking to the talkers. His words "never related to the crux of a matter, which concerned him not the least, but were prompted by some personal motive, some desire such as flattery." He had no use (unlike Napoleon) for "ideas" as the basis of a discussion: verbal jousting was a waste of time and boring, except if it served to evade a question.

He managed to create his own private court with certain foreign representatives whom he dominated completely, making them his creatures whether by his own or someone else's bribery. They would all get together for whist or charades, or simply for the kind of conversation at which he excelled. It was said that anyone who had never ridden in a coach with Talleyrand and his friends had no idea how captivating a conversationalist he was. These ambassadors represented an information system probably unmatched anywhere else in Europe. Gallo, the Neapolitan envoy, spied on other embassies for Talleyrand; Bunau, from Saxony, did the same; while the Spanish minister Azara had such contempt for European royalty—starting with the sovereign he represented—that he passed on to Talleyrand what he ought to have kept for Spanish ears. Lucchesini, the Prussian minister, was his confidant; Talleyrand gave him good advice, including the following: "Be bold, yes, bold; nothing else matters; if you want to rule Europe today, you must be bold" (he serenaded the First Consul with the same theme). The Prussian minister conveyed the message to his sovereign, who ignored it; Talleyrand's phrase finally struck home with Bismarck, who seized its meaning and had the courage to be bold.

From talking to women, he collected vast amounts of information which he stored away in his excellent memory. Once in a great while he used it, like a weapon or a secret bank account; never out of spite.

Of course, Talleyrand also relied on more vulgar methods of keeping abreast of the news. The postmaster general delivered stacks of letters to him, mostly addressed to other ministers and embassies. In Germany and Italy, he organized special police units dressed up like robbers and had them play stock bandit scenes attacking mail coaches and delivering dispatches to the French occupation authorities. All this would sift through to the rue du Bac. Next, he would be prophesying, in true sibylline fashion, the downfall of some German lord or a revolt in one of the Italian states which no one else had heard about. Naturally, he was taken for an oracle, but it was all a matter of savoir-faire.

He had a second staff—this one unofficial—of friends with inside information for sale. Talleyrand always enjoyed the shady side of affairs, the world of informers, agents, swindlers, and hustlers where he would never set foot yet managed to poke his finger via intermediaries. This spy system provided him with information as well as cash, and probably indulged his dubious taste for gambling and for manipulating a cast of unorthodox characters, all unscrupulous, but not untalented or un-attractive. About this aspect (which is not dubious at all) of his casual activities, he was totally silent. No trace of them exists, but we know who his associates were.

The most prominent, the most trusted, the most urbane, and prob-ably the greatest pirate of them all was Montrond, the beloved and indispensable comte de Montrond. He had married Aimée de Coigny after her divorce from the duc de Fleury. The marriage did not last; both husband and wife preferred their freedom. Montrond was an obvious aristocrat with the polish and poise of another era. He was also ex-tremely witty, and his good nature made one forget his total lack of principles. So delighted was Talleyrand with this consummate rogue that he called him "Hell's Christchild." A godsend if ever a bishop had one. The door was open day and night to Montrond, who was in on everything, for though he had no morals to start with, his tact and loyalty became virtues of a sort. One day when the vicomtesse de Laval asked Talleyrand the secret of his long friendship with Montrond, our hero replied: "You wonder why I am rather fond of Montrond? Because he has very few scruples." Montrond, perhaps piqued by the "rather" and the "very few," retorted: "And I, Madam, do you know why I am fond of Talleyrand? Because he has absolutely no scruples."

Talleyrand used him for confidential missions and private enter-tainments; they were both reckless gamblers. Still, their intimacy is surprising. Madame Hamelin, whom we met in her "merveilleuse" stage and who was Montrond's mistress for many years, disapproved of his close friendship with Talleyrand. Montrond reassured her with words that might have been borrowed from the pages of *Les Liaisons dangereuses*: "For God's sake, Madam, who could escape loving him? He is so unprincipled!" Not to be outdone, Talleyrand observed: "He is certainly the wittiest man I know." To prove it, he added: "Indeed, he doesn't have a sou, doesn't earn a thing, spends sixty thousand francs a year, and hasn't a debt in the world."

Other visitors, equally alarming but less good-natured, called at the rue du Bac. One was the former bishop of Orléans, whom Talley-rand had coaxed into supporting the Civil Constitution of the Clergy (using gold as a lure, Monsieur d'Autun managed to fish up a few such souls). Also Jarente de Senac d'Orgeval, an excitable fellow eager to do anything for 10 louis, having already indulged in every known vice.

Radix Sainte-Foy was no different from the others: as the comte d'Artois's treasurer prior to 1789, he had been convicted of fraud and condemned to hang; saved by the Revolution, he survived the Terror and now floated on the troubled waters of the Directory, his home port being Talleyrand's private office on the rue du Bac where he was welcomed with open arms. He ran errands. Another familiar face belonged to the fabulously rich Ouvrard, a banker if one must categorize him. He took up with Talleyrand during that twilight period between the latter's return from America and his appointment as foreign minister, years when people would do anything for money. In the race to make his fortune, Talleyrand, like an eel, swam upstream to reach the pot of gold: Ouvrard. Recognizing a fellow sufferer, the banker gave him sound advice on speculating. Later on, from the rue du Bac Talleyrand tipped him off to certain confidential information. Our hero never forgot past favors, especially when the current ones brought him cash. That is probably what Ouvrard's remark implies: "I saw him often socially; he was always extremely cordial and remained so after he took power." In 1798, a handful of gold no longer represented a fortune. After all, could one entertain Italy's conqueror in proper style on a beggarly "37,000 myriagrams of wheat"?

Equipped with men of such caliber, Talleyrand was able to perfect the art of leisure. "In affairs of state, everyone is content to grumble about delays," he observed sarcastically. The grumblers take on "an air of superiority," while those who must hear the complaints "appear prudent." Talleyrand regarded deliberation and prudence as fundamentals of diplomacy. Ambassadors would do well to read his advice to Andréossy as he was about to take up his duties in London: Find a good excuse to delay your reply, and never be decisive even if a particular decision seems inevitable. Louis XIV would often say, "I shall see." Such dilatory caution may appear intolerable; yet it proved beneficial during the Consulate and the Empire, the balmy period of their relationship, except when the emperor threw caution to the winds, as he did on several occasions. In his last years, Talleyrand noted: "The emperor, a man of action, was always grateful that I was in no hurry to execute his orders; it gave him a chance to reconsider decisions he had made too hastily."

Talleyrand's leisurely pace never represented neglect. He hated slovenliness, whether in his own attire, conduct, work, or even in his organized and disciplined indolence. Before criticizing that, one must remember that a particular failing goes by the same name for everyone, but can be interpreted a thousand different ways. We venture to suggest that Talleyrand managed to adapt leisure to diplomacy with salutary results. But if Chateaubriand once again takes issue, we will call this idleness on the part of the prince of diplomats a talent—of sorts. Will he forgive the concession?

Hopes and Fears Attending a Historic Encounter

Bonaparte arrived in Paris on December 5, 1797. He had just bought the house on the rue Chantereine where he and his wife, Joséphine de Beauharnais, had first met. Barras paid him a call that very evening. They were in a hurry; officialdom was anxious to pay court to the general. The next morning, however, it was Bonaparte who dispatched an aide to make an appointment with the citizen minister of foreign relations. The haste suited Talleyrand perfectly; he sent back word that the general was welcome day or night. Bonaparte came to the rue du Bac at eleven on the morning of December 7. Madame de Staël rushed over. The famous explorer Bougainville and several other persons were there. Napoleon entered. What a shock! A short, scrawny young man, deathly pale, with long, straight black hair plastered down the sides of his face, fine features that were rather sharp, severe, and marked by fatigue, a slightly aquiline nose, and lips like two wires squeezed together by a jutting jaw. Under narrow, well-defined brows were those eyes of his—those glowing, compelling eyes deep-set under swarthy lids, captivating, piercing, intimidating, brimming with willfulness, pride, and intelligence. His slender body was tense, his gestures curt; all his strength seemed concentrated in those commanding eyes. They startled and subdued everyone; Bonaparte's eyes had conquered persons far less sensitive to the fires of genius and ambition than Talleyrand and Germaine de Staël.

The meeting was momentous. Two worlds, two alien species conjoined—were married would be more exact—at a turning point in history. Like two magnets attracted by each other's brilliance, it was love at first sight. Cerebral love. Only money, his country, and now Bonaparte could inspire passion in Talleyrand. And like all passions, even the frigid sort, this one had a radiant beginning. What followed is another story.

That day Talleyrand allowed himself to be spellbound. These are his words, which read like the prelude to an idyll, but the finale of which would bring more grief to France and to Europe than Anthony and Cleopatra's ecstasy, for he was never to repeat them: "On seeing him for the first time, I was struck by his charming face. Twenty victories are so becoming to youth, to a bright glance, to pallor, to seeming exhaustion. . . ." It might have been the voice of Racine's Phaedra gazing on Hippolytus:

> But faithful, proud, a hint of wildness about him,
> Oh, charming youth enslaving hearts at every step
> As our gods are said to be, and as I behold you.

Talleyrand was an "old man" of forty-four, the "wild Hippolytus" only twenty-eight, with the "youth," "pallor," and "exhaustion" of a young hero overburdened with glory. Whereas his contemporaries found Bonaparte ugly, or at least odd-looking because of his small stature, his darting eyes, and nervousness, Talleyrand, himself a merciless critic, found him handsome: "Twenty victories are so becoming to youth . . ." Talleyrand ought to have poured out his eclogue in Greek. For him, the young general wore a halo of glory and was blessed with a gambler's greatest prize: luck. Bonaparte was always winning; he was Destiny's favored child. Our rational and optimistic hero had to admit that Bonaparte invariably turned up an ace. The divine breath of victory was in him. Talleyrand bowed low—and for once he meant it.

Bonaparte sensed that he had made a new conquest and was as proud of it as Talleyrand was pleased to surrender. What sort of triumph was it, anyway, for this Corsican upstart who, twenty years earlier, had been roaming the hills of his native island? He, too, had cause to be amazed by this singular minister who was so unlike the other officials or, as a matter of fact, his own countrymen in the year 1797.

Bonaparte discovered a man whose height, not personality, dominated him, a man of distinction, serene, and somewhat languid; who held himself very erect but appeared sinuous rather than stiff, the exact opposite of the small Corsican; whose rare gestures were unhurried and graceful, whose deep voice was soft and musical; whose poise was inbred. One could imagine him stepping out of Choiseul's private study or leaving Madame du Barry's toilette. His bright, glassy eyes expressed nothing in order to reveal nothing. Beardless and pale, with lips frozen in a vaguely polite smile, the face conveyed a sense of affable indolence. The turned-up nose could have looked inane on anyone else; on him, it was the most distinctive feature, indicative of his impudence. To greet his guest, Talleyrand had chosen not to ape the Directors by decking himself out like a circus performer. He dressed in his usual silk coat and breeches of gray, grayish-green, or mauve-gray, shoes with buckles, and white stockings. He moved about as little as possible. Walking was painful, but less painful than the conviction that he walked awkwardly; with the stubborn determination developed in childhood, he stiffened his posture so as not to appear twisted. Rather than drag his lame foot (as Chateaubriand claims he did), he had cultivated, not without ceaseless agony and effort, a sinuous walk likely to dismay strangers, as if he were gliding across the floor with odd, purposeful steps. Among his contemporaries, many early converts to "romanticism" regarded him as a terribly mysterious, peculiar, hence diabolic creature. Actually, he was altogether human. This aristocrat who knew how to live—in relation to society, that is, and preferably a level above it—belonged to a "breed" that Bonaparte had encountered occasionally but never really known, and that he admired and envied deeply: the old nobility. Watching the descendant of the counts of Périgord limping along, he realized that by some stroke of magic this aristocrat had managed to turn his infirmity into a distinction.

They withdrew for a brief chat. "We went into my study. Our first conversation was purely confidential on his part. [One may assume that Talleyrand employed his facile tongue to draw the general out.] He complimented me on my appointment to the foreign ministry and stressed how pleasant it had been to correspond with someone of a different sort from the Directors." Bonaparte had heard about the coarse insults Talleyrand had received from his superiors. The reference was therefore a tactful piece of flattery, which must have pleased our hero. The general obviously was making himself out to be a kindred spirit. He mentioned Talleyrand's uncle, the archbishop, whom our hero would have preferred to forget, simply to compare him to his own uncle, cardinal Fesch. It would be interesting to know how Talleyrand reacted to the implied parallel between a Corsican archdeacon and a Talleyrand-Périgord, archbishop and duke of Rheims, a peer of the realm. But that was of no consequence, for the romantic spell rendered everything rosy.

Certain obvious links bound them together. But were those links really meaningful? First, the Revolution, without which they would probably never have met; now its ashes brought them together. Moreover, each of them could trace his fortune to the same man, Barras, popularly known as "the king of corruption," to whom Talleyrand owed his office and Napoleon, his command and his wife. Having tired of Josephine, Barras had turned her over to Bonaparte and made her marry him. The wedding took place on March 9; on the third, his wife's former lover had conferred on Bonaparte the title of commander-in-chief of the Army of Italy—Barras's wedding present to his one-time mistress.

Another bond between them was their mutual disgust with the

Directory and political terrorism. Talleyrand looked on revolutionary violence as the height of absurdity, sheer romanticism, emotional chaos, the collapse of reason, in short, the antithesis of civilization. He asked: "What principles can men learn from impulsive acts, the spontaneous products of unleashed passions?" In Napoleon's eyes, revolution stood for disorder, the reign of demagogues, irresponsible leaders, and "ideologists." The last, of course, were the worst of the lot.

Both men felt that France deserved something better than the régime she was enduring currently and impatiently. As a Frenchman, an aristocrat, and an intellectual, Talleyrand could not bear to see the land of Enlightenment so degraded. His patriotism was neither bourgeois nationalism nor Jacobin chauvinism: he did not want France to dominate other nations, invade their borders, or intervene in their internal affairs. He loved the country his ancestors had shaped, the institutions her philosophers and her Revolution had perfected, because France symbolized civilization as he conceived the word. France should seek to dominate only through the achievements of her great men and her Bill of Rights, by radiating her spirit and her culture. He believed in respecting the sovereignty of other nations and, in the economic domain, he preached European solidarity: France ultimately must conduct her own affairs in concert, not in competition, with her neighbors in order to avoid the economic rivalries that lead to war. Through intelligent diplomacy, all parties could be made to see where their best interests lay. To him, Europe's community of interests was a factual reality obscured by mass emotions and clan warfare. As an objective observer with no ax to grind either for or against the Hapsburgs and Bourbons, he was able to see that Europe must have peace if prosperity, freedom, and culture were to flourish.

That foreign policy was alien to the Directory. Believing that Napoleon shared his ideas, Talleyrand bound himself to him as he had to no other man.

It was a sad misunderstanding. Bonaparte never became Talleyrand's—or anyone else's—disciple. He was Caesar. That Talleyrand could have nursed such an illusion in 1798 is understandable. He thought that his age and experience, his prestigious family background, his expert knowledge of European and overseas affairs, which Bonaparte lacked, would give him the necessary influence to conduct foreign policy and shape French economic recovery within the framework of law and order, prosperity, and peace—with the help of that young god of victory and good luck. But that vision, if you can call a common sense approach to government a vision, was of no more interest to the general than any other vision. Talleyrand was bewitched, not just by Napoleon's brilliant mind but by his ability to inspire confidence as well; and one further proof of his genius was the thorough job he made of taking Talleyrand in. Such an ambitious piece of deceit deserves a passing salute. He built up the foreign minister's confidence so that he would pass it on to the government. Talleyrand's successful record as propagandist was well known. When informed of the *coup d'état* of Fructidor, what did the butcher of Toulon do? Virtuously, and in the best republican spirit, he decried the violence: how shocking to use bayonets in defense of lawlessness! Here is Bonaparte's letter of October 19, 1797: "Let us have vigor without fanaticism, principles without demagogy, severity without cruelty. How tragic it is for a nation of 30 million in the eighteenth century to have recourse to bayonets in order to save their country. The tactics of violence condemn the lawmakers." The last sentence is pure Talleyrand. Hearing his own thoughts echoed by the brilliant young general, how could Talleyrand resist him?

To the Italian friends he used to establish his power, Napoleon sang quite a different tune about democracy in France. But for Frenchmen who saw him in Italy, he behaved like an ideal citizen general. When asked what he would do when victory had brought peace, he replied: "I shall retire to some quiet place and devote myself to studies worthy of the Institut de France." Talleyrand remembered the phrase, which was marvelous propaganda, and kept it for use in an address to the Luxembourg. The Institut at once made Bonaparte a member, and in thanking them, he had the audacity to observe with disarming candor: "I am honored by the votes of those distinguished men who comprise the Institut. I know all too well that before becoming their peer, I shall remain their pupil for a long time." Such modesty boosted the general's score for republican integrity. People said that he was really not like the others, that he would never make a grab for power. He even had to be prodded to take his seat in the Institut, and when he finally did, he was blushing violently. It was straight out of an Italian comedy. Why shouldn't Talleyrand have been spellbound, hearing echoes of his own ideas on peace and the futility and peril of military adventures? "The real conquests, the only unregretted ones, are those against ignorance. The worthiest and most meaningful occupation for nations is to extend the bounds of human knowledge." Such wisdom never hinted at a militaristic mind. The "ideologists" were wild about him, and Germaine enraptured: this general was a product not of the military academy but of the Encyclopedia. Garat, a spokesman for the régime, had this to say (Bonaparte's candor had infected him too): "Knowing his simple, modest tastes, his love of solitude, his passion for the arts and sciences, one would take him for a philosopher tearing himself away momentarily from cherished studies to go forth and conquer, then returning victorious to plunge back into them with fresh delight." [1]

Talleyrand was captivated by the notion that he and Bonaparte thought alike. At that time he had no way of knowing what an assimilative mind the young general had, enabling him to size up instantly Talleyrand's ideas and inclinations and to project a similar image for his own reasons. When Taine said of Bonaparte: "None of the then widely accepted political and social theories stirred him," he could have been talking about Talleyrand as well. It is the outlook of a Nietzschean Superman totally devoid of the beliefs that enslave his fellow men.

In his remarkable book *Napoléon et Talleyrand,* Emile Dard analyzes in detail their earliest relationship and, stressing the opening "misdeal" that involved those two extraordinary players in a game of false expectations, came up with this pithy observation: "It is unwise to fall in love without prior acquaintance." It was a rare and costly blunder on Talleyrand's part. They fell in love first, then got to know and judge each other. Too late Talleyrand saw the gulf between Napoleon and the young man he, as foreign minister, had known as Bonaparte. In fact, their ideas were worlds apart. Bonaparte trusted only his own instincts, relying on "illuminations" rather than reflection.

Bonaparte surpassed all Talleyrand's expectations. He was unique, a totally new breed of hero. Talleyrand, ruled by moderation and reason, was hopelessly duped by Bonaparte's immoderacy and unreasonableness. One of Talleyrand's weaknesses, or, shall we say, limitations was the notion that men of genius, like Descartes and Newton, were bound to be logical and systematic, that irrational behavior was unproductive and stupid. Bonaparte wreathed himself in shadows. In many ways he was a romantic hero; an avid reader of Ossian, he imagined himself on a prodigious, fateful mission. At times he talked like Ruy Blas or Lorenzaccio; at times he waxed Byronic: "What is the future? What is the past? What are we? What magic fluids surround us, concealing the most vital things from us? We are born, we live, and we die amid marvels." To Talleyrand, that was sheer delirium and a waste of breath, because such questions could never be answered. Popular metaphysics was mere idle talk.

So we find the two men spellbound with mutual admiration. Behind this strange romance of two minds, one superhuman and tyrannical, forcing the other to serve its ambition—momentarily—one can imagine the tensions and hostilities that would drive a wedge between the titans. With their first embrace, divorce was already on the way.

They acted as if there were no rift between them, each retaining his own character: Bonaparte was the young, fiery, exalted genius determined to stun the world with his own impact; and Talleyrand, in his middle years, a kind of ageless sphinx imparting wisdom and eyeing his fortune when all he was expected to do was perform small miracles at the card table or the ballot box, consigning the Republic to silence in the shadow of bayonets.

One cloud hung over the meeting. Bonaparte bowed to Madame de Staël, then abruptly turned his back to begin a long and animated conversation with Bougainville. Germaine was stunned and mortified, her head already brimming with plans for "her" general. She had said things about his wife, it is true, which Josephine must have heard and Bonaparte too. Madame Bonaparte considered Germaine ugly and pedantic; for her part, Germaine observed: "Anyone who thinks and acts like Josephine ought to be the housekeeper, not the wife of a hero. Imagine the fine conversations they must have. She talks of ruffles while he talks of battles."

In time the quarrel would grow bitter. Forced to make a choice, Talleyrand opted for the lucky side, but his lady friend did not take the betrayal lightly. The storm would be deafening.

How to Disguise Genius for the Government's Peace of Mind

It was incumbent on the Directors to give Italy's conqueror a fitting reception. They were not overjoyed, but recognized necessity, for the general's victories and spoils had kept them in office. They were afraid of him, yet popular acclaim demanded that he receive a hero's welcome. The Directors were at a loss to resolve public pressure and their own jitters.

When in doubt about handling a situation, call in a Talleyrand if you are fortunate enough to have one around. Barras did just that, putting our bishop (instead of the minister of war, whose province it was) in charge of organizing a celebration for the victorious general. His instructions to Talleyrand reveal the Directors' fears, their base motives, and their gross conceit: "It is not the military commander but the peacemaker, the citizen, whom we must celebrate and promote. I suggest you

209

look at it that way. You are tactful [a glimmer of approval at last]. Let your compliments reflect this; my colleagues are alarmed [what about himself?] by military glory, which, rather than being extinguished, ought to be illuminated and guided."

What could dim Bonaparte's glory: a political harangue? Nonsense. Or illuminate it? Sheer effrontery. Did its luster need such light as the dripping tapers of the Directory could provide? Gleaming in the bright Italian sun, it radiated all over Europe. Calmly and sympathetically, Talleyrand replied: "I know what military minds are like, Citizen Director." He was involved at the moment in one of his most ambitious schemes. Barras might have pondered the meaning of that reply, the smile accompanying it, and the deep obeisance that followed. Talleyrand bowed himself out of the room, pausing at the door to say with prayer-like solemnity: "I shall meditate upon the instructions I have been privileged to receive from you; they will be executed. I understood you, Citizen Director." The last phrase should have made the confirmed Jacobin shudder.

Everything would be executed: first the Director's orders, then the Directory.

In the Luxembourg's courtyard on the gloomy morning of December 10, 1797, Talleyrand held a reception not unworthy of the victor of Campo Formio. Whatever ridiculous touches the spectacle had were not the stage manager's fault and could be blamed on the gaudy regalia of the Directors and their retinue. Apparently they thought the one sure way to impress the crowd was by unfurling great splotches of color, thus creating a grotesque exhibition in the stately setting of that noble palace. Still, the mummery symbolized France. The Directors wore scarlet and gold mantles, from which their heads, buttressed by enormous embroidered white collars, emerged. They might have been embedded in plaster up to the ears. Beneath the scarlet was a blue frock coat (smothered with gold braid), a short white silk jacket (more gold), a sash, or rather a giant blue silk scarf tied at the waist (fringed with gold), white silk breeches, and a cross-belt over the jacket (trimmed with gold). Gold everywhere, yet the people had nothing. The cross-belts were bright red to set off the blue. Atop the whole outfit sat a hat sprouting tricolor ostrich plumes. To complete the effect, cascades of ribbons tumbled from every conceivable place, principally each shoe, which held clusters of blue bows. Robespierre's heirs waded in silk up to the ankles. Talleyrand was decked out in similar fashion. In his *Memoirs,* he refrained from boasting about his attire; after all, by now he was accustomed to disguises of every kind.

Portrait by J. S. Duplessis of Louis XVI.
Talleyrand was born just six months before the king
but managed to outlive him by 45 years; Montauban, Musée Ingres.

Charles-Daniel de Talleyrand;
Jean Morel collection, château de Valençay.

Marie-Victoire-Eléonore, Countess of Talleyrand-Périgord;
Jean Morel collection, château de Valençay.

Adélaïde, the Countess of
Flahaut, and heir, painted by
Mme A. Labille-Guyard.

La Dugazon pursued by
cupids, a gouache by C. J. B.
Hoin; private collection.

Girodet's portrait of Mlle Lange as a "Danae";
Paris, Wildenstein collection.

Mme de Talleyrand, in an engraving by Dickinson;
Paris, Bibliothèque Nationale.

Mme Vigée-Lebrun's
portrait of the same lady,
when she was Princess
of Benevento; château de
Valençay.

Mme Vigée-Lebrun's
portrait of Germaine de Staël
as Corinne; private
collection.

Madame Grand before she became Mme de Talleyrand,
by Antoine Vestier; Musée de Dijon.

Dorothée, Princess of Courland and Semgallen and Duchess of Sagan;
Jean Morel collection, château de Valençay.

Dorothée's mother, the Duchess of Courland, by Tischbein; Paris, collection of Count François de Castellane.

And her son, A.-E. de Talleyrand, in a miniature by Isabey; private collection.

Portrait of Madame de Staël by Gérard;
Musée de Versailles.

Talleyrand's watch, containing a miniature
of the Duchess of Dino; private collection.

Fête de la Fédération, July 14, 1790, by a folk painter;
Paris, Musée Carnavalet.

Portrait of Talleyrand by
J. F. Garneray. The letter
Talleyrand is writing is dated
1795. Garneray doubtless
met him after his return from
America, though; Versailles,
Musée Lambinet.

Eighteenth-century German
engraving of a Boston street
scene; Paris, Bibliothèque
Nationale.

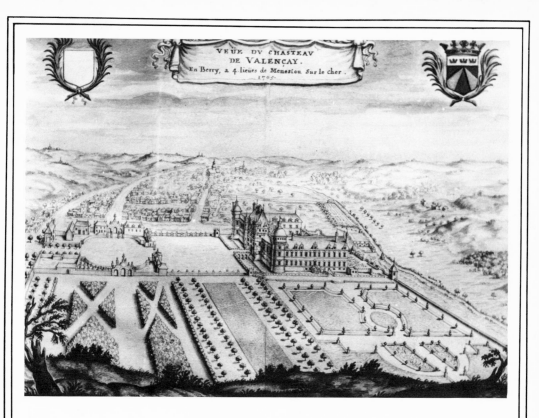

Above: a 1705 view of the château of Valençay; Paris, Bibliothèque Nationale.

And a modern photograph.

Talleyrand by Ingres;
private collection.

The five glittering Directors strutted across the courtyard to the rumble of cannonades. Two deafening salvos were the signal for them to halt, while a band played "songs dear to the hearts of republicans." The strains rose to the sky like some barbaric ode to death and destruction. Then the procession of plumes made its way to the altar of the nation. (Another altar! Talleyrand's career took him from one altar to the next, with or without God: Issy, Autun, the Altar of the Federation, and now this one. We shall catch a glimpse of others later on.) Behind this altar rose the sacred statues: Liberty, Equality, and Peace. As good a way as any of honoring invisible divinities. Wholly visible, on the other hand, were the piles of enemy standards captured by Bonaparte and clearly marked with the names of flesh-and-blood victories. The sight of them made the crowd lose interest in the official fuss and feathers. On this stage, Talleyrand, as organizer of the festivities, was about to introduce the star of the season in his most demanding role. As this star was also a political genius, not to mention a brilliant strategist and negotiator, he was assured of success and a throne in history's hall of fame. Still, this test performance was crucial. Left to his own devices, his arrogance and abruptness probably would have botched the performance. Just follow the stage directions and everything will work out; they have a way of revealing profound human truths.

While the Directors took their seats on gilded thrones facing the altar, the muted strains of a symphony descended on the public. Then a roar went up, an enormous clamor shut out the music, every voice crying: "Vive Bonaparte! Vive la République!" The good citizens were already blessing the union. Amid this wild excitement, the star made his entrance in the courtyard. Eyewitnesses said that Bonaparte appeared "calm and unassuming." He had been instructed to act that way. Into the tinseled spectacle with all its din, its gold and silks, its sabers and cannons, a small, solitary figure in gray advanced, without ribbons or feathers, his modest dress the focus of every eye. He became a giant. To the public, he stood for a simple, virtuous republican hero without glitter or ambition, a hard-working, down-to-earth servant of the state assigned to effectuate military successes and due for discharge when the job was done. What a talented actor he was to make the government and the public believe what they needed to believe. Under Talleyrand's direction, he fooled them into accepting him for his very opposite.

Escorting him was General Joubert at his side and Talleyrand behind, his impresario, who, by remaining unobtrusive, could best exhibit his young discovery and also conceal his management of the whole performance. Mixed with his fondness for Bonaparte was the desire to protect him, for a young hero blessed with good fortune was likely to run afoul of the jungles of the Directory. Some writers see the extraordinary relationship between the two men as purely a joint pursuit of profit and prestige, a high-level job of intrigue, thus reducing both to the proposition that self-interest is humanity's primary motive. But neither of them can be reduced to a single formula. Their ambition, their greed, their pride, their designing, like all their other imperfections, achieved monumental proportions. Let us say that selfish ambition eventually dominated the relationship, but on that particular day, a vision of the power and dignity of France stirred them both. Their encounter had kindled the vision; together, they could restore the nation's prestige. From that day onward, they shared a secret.

To Talleyrand fell the task of addressing the crowd, eulogizing a victorious general without mentioning his victories:

> Citizen Directors, I have the honor to present to the Executive Directory Citizen Bonaparte [no question of calling him General] who brings us the peace treaty ratified by the emperor. His presentation of this warranty of peace is bound to remind us of the marvelous exploits leading up to this great event [he avoids the unmentionable victories by circumlocution, but the allusion is still there]. May he rest assured, however, that for his sake I shall remain silent today about deeds that history will celebrate and posterity acclaim; in deference to his earnest desires, let me simply say that the glory redounding to the nation's credit belongs to the Revolution.

There it was: to allay official and public fears, Bonaparte became synonymous with the Revolution, and the campaigns that no one wanted to hear about symbolized Glory with a Jacobin label. The young man whom Talleyrand was introducing tactfully as a bashful soldier could never measure up to a conqueror. The small gray figure had all the earmarks of just another benign, self-effacing citizen. The performance was a total success, for officialdom suspected nothing, and the populace cheered for peace instead of war. Talleyrand had done a good job of launching Bonaparte on his career as peacemaker. The rest of the speech did not flatter the general's ego and could have provoked his ill will in the future. Actually, Talleyrand was acting very shrewdly, feeding the general's ambition, preparing a path for him indirectly but surely, and Bonaparte understood. The excitable young Corsican, who ought to have been referred to publicly by his impressive title of commander-in-chief of the Army of Italy, settled instead for the undistinguished designation of citizen. He held the winning ticket and knew it. Talleyrand addressed the audience: "And when I think of his tireless efforts to absolve himself of that glory . . ." Using the current vocabulary of republicanism, our bishop cited "the classic taste for simplicity that sets him apart." To put all fears to rest, he painted Bonaparte as a scholar, a bookworm, and, to make him totally acceptable, a mathematician and poet: ". . . his passion for the abstract sciences and for the sublime Ossian, who seems to lift him into the clouds."

The ultimate proof of his humble civic devotion was this: ". . . no one is ignorant of his profound distaste for ostentation, for luxury, for pomp and splendor, those wretched cravings of ordinary souls." (Rather ironic coming from Talleyrand; and considering the character of Josephine, the wife of this little man in gray, the renunciation of luxury was an even sharper irony which the public did not catch. What a great theatrical duo they made!) Going a step further to quash any doubts as to Bonaparte's potential military aspirations, Talleyrand declared: "Ah, far from fearing what some people call his ambition, I feel that one day we may have to entreat him to abandon the pleasures of a scholar's life. All of France will be free, but he perhaps never."

The last sentence is extraordinary. Chateaubriand found it prophetic, but then everything was tinged with mysticism for him. Not a prophecy, it is simply a serious reflection. If instead of insisting that Talleyrand was false, cunning, and rapacious, his critics would observe and listen to him calmly and intently as he observed and listened in order to understand the men and events of his day they might be able to figure him out. And insult him less.

He was not prophesying that day. Not one to have visions of the future, he was preparing it—and preparing the French for Bonaparte.

The phrase slipped by because it contained a password: "France will be free."

He was right . . . with one exception. France lost every shred of liberty. But the rest happened. Talleyrand was no crystal ball or star gazer; he read the minds and motives of leaders and nations, of generals and Citizen Directors.

Shy and motionless, Bonaparte listened, flattered nonetheless by the speaker's august manner. He then offered a brief acknowledgment, the last sentence of which was cleverly put: it is vague (did Talleyrand teach him the art of ambiguity?), optimistic, disquieting, and leaves one hanging in the air. "When the welfare of the French nation shall rest upon a firmer system of law, then shall the whole of Europe be free."

A roar of acclaim followed. Not interested in what he had to say, the crowd merely wanted to hear his voice, watch his face, and, if possible, touch the sleeve of the man who had signed the peace treaty. Jubilation swept into the streets and over the city.

Barras spoke next. He was long-winded and sententious, pouring out a flood of overworked, meaningless, colorless words. Bored to death, his listeners recognized the type of politician they didn't need. Barras climaxed his message by collapsing into Bonaparte's arms; his colleagues followed suit. The resulting confusion of silks, gold braid, and plumes apparently delighted the crowd, provoking another volley of cheers.

Chateaubriand observed the scene: "Monsieur de Talleyrand received the victor at the altar, reminded of having said Mass before another altar. A fugitive who returned from the United States to be appointed foreign minister through the patronage of Chénier and especially Madame de Staël, the bishop of Autun, sword at his side, was wearing a hat *à la Henri IV;* events decreed that such travesties be taken seriously." The truth is there, but badly interpreted. Monsieur de Talleyrand was no more taken in by his travesty than was the acid-tempered author of the *Mémoires d'outre-tombe.*

During the tumult greeting those effusive demonstrations, Talleyrand stood like a statue, his eyes little more than two blue slits beneath drooping eyelids. He smiled ever so faintly; the performance had been a success. Even the boredom injected by Barras had served to measure the new low to which the Directors' popularity had fallen. It would not take much to solidify the opposition, channel public scorn and antipathy into a conscious, explosive force. One day those feelings would prevail. He was thinking about it.

The celebration lacked something. As the Revolution was still unfinished (officially at least) the apathetic masses needed to be roused by anthems, a series of sublime choruses in which the people could hear and identify its own voice. The Conservatory students took up the *"Chant du retour,"* composed by Méhul to lyrics by Chénier. Talleyrand had commissioned the song, insisting that it be a masterpiece. It was. There were three parts: Warriors, Old Men, and Maidens, each offering the others his or her most prized possession. The Warriors pledged their glory, the Maidens their virginity, and the Old Men their wise counsel. Thus was France to be repeopled, and the three voices joined in unison:

> Long dreaded, now beloved of the earth
> Oh, French Republic
> May songs of pleasure replace the war cries
> Victory has conquered Peace.

The last line was the hopeful sob of a people bled white, overshadowed by want and uncertainty. Talleyrand shared the hope, believing that he had discovered the one man who could still "the war cries" and supplant them with "songs of pleasure," that providential man whose greatest conquest was peace.

No one guessed as yet that the little general, sober as a cricket, smothered by scarlet robes in the course of those Jacobin embraces, was in fact the Eagle.

Few people had paid much attention to that odd final phrase of Bonaparte's, yet someone was sufficiently puzzled by it to approach Talleyrand at the close of the ceremony and ask him what he made of it. Dreamy-eyed, Talleyrand pondered the question, then murmured absently: "There is a glimpse of the future in it." The sphinx had spoken.

The Citizen Minister Shows That He Is Talleyrand by Entertaining in the Grand Manner

The Directory had honored Bonaparte in its own fashion. Talleyrand had followed instructions. They had spoken and postured for the public and posterity. It was a rite, not a celebration. At that time no one in France knew how to celebrate—except Monsieur de Talleyrand, who wanted to be called simply Talleyrand and to forget for one evening that he was a "citizen." So on January 3, 1798 (14th Nivose, Year VI), he gave a ball worthy of the young god of victory, the likes of which had not been seen in years.

It was an act of courage for a discredited member of an unpopular government. His position was extremely unstable. Why did the Directors bother to keep him on? Out of superstition perhaps, for was it not said that his departure would be a bad omen? Or perhaps they thought he could do more damage at large than while subject to bureaucratic and police scrutiny.

Bold as he was, he took steps to lull the crude suspicions of the men he called "the iron heels of the Directory." By giving the ball for the general's wife, not the general, he made gallantry rather than politics the theme. The Jacobins mocked him all the more, but shrugged their shoulders and left him to his hopelessly aristocratic diversions. Imagine a former bishop—lame at that—inviting people to dance. It was enough to make one laugh. And the epitome of frivolity: you cut off people's heads and when you stop, they dance.

The ball took place in the hôtel de Galliffet on the rue du Bac.

That evening the gilt, the music, the lights, the scents transformed the splendid mansion into a magic crucible about to produce something new —probably to replace something else about to die. People are much too trustful in the midst of frivolity, laughter, glitter, and waltzes; indeed, there was waltzing for the first time in Paris on January 3, 1798. Talleyrand was far ahead of his times, even to the waltz.

With princely taste, he had arranged all the details; everything bore the invisible mark of his approval. It was said that he had gone to great trouble and expense only to curry favor with Josephine, and thus impress and ultimately win the general's loyalty. Not a bad guess, for Bonaparte was touched by the honors and courtesies shown to his wife. Josephine also, and that evening she caught a glimpse of what festivities had meant to another generation. Talleyrand treated her not just as queen of the ball, but as a queen, period. Never had he been so deferential to the Directors' wives. The general saw at once that Josephine was first lady of Paris for the occasion. Probably because Talleyrand took Bonaparte for the first man of France. In the eyes of everyone who was anyone, he had managed to surround Josephine with a halo of light. It was a sign, given by Monsieur de Talleyrand, and understood by Bonaparte.

The Directors paid scant attention to such things. But Bonaparte learned in the course of the evening that in casual conversation over a sumptuously laden table, or on a bench as one watched the dancers whirl by, a few words sufficed to say or do something momentous, or to have it done. Afterwards could he ever forget the sorcerer Talleyrand who had organized such a magnificent ball?

The sorcerer had gone to great lengths to make the evening unforgettable. First he hired Bellanger, the famous architect, and put him in charge. Soon an army of workmen swarming all over the house made it resemble backstage at the opera: carpenters, painters, candlemakers, plasterers, chandelier makers, florists, firework specialists, upholsterers, and a host of others whose mounting bills were to cost a fortune. Supplies and furnishings alone came to between 20 and 25 million old francs; on top of that were entertainers' and musicians' fees, and the food—always a lavish expense in Talleyrand's household. What the final figure was we do not know. All along the magnificent staircase were entwined sprigs of fragrant myrtle. A profusion of exotic aromatic plants decorated the various rooms, lit by immense crystal chandeliers sparkling like diamonds. The scent of amber was everywhere; Talleyrand adored perfumes. Upon entering the house, guests were enveloped in warmth, light, sweet odors, and soft music: the sorcerer's abode. They had just crossed the courtyard with its stately rows of Doric columns, which Talleyrand had converted into a military camp studded with tents and facsimiles of the weaponry that conquered Italy. What could be more decorative and inspiring than the martial splendor of those colorful, glittering uniforms, the arms, the banners, the trophies glowing in the light of campfires? What finer gift for the general's wife than this felicitous reminder of his conquests? The sorcerer had applied one further refinement of his courtier's art, having erected the likes of a Roman temple to house the bust of Brutus which Bonaparte had "found" on the Capitoline Hill and brought back to France. Brutus, idol of the Jacobins, was present, not because of any republican scruples but purely for flattery's sake—highly effective flattery at that. Bonaparte's pride swelled as he walked by. That was only the beginning, for along every inch of wall up and down the stairway stood or hung reproductions of the art treasures Bonaparte had brought back from Italy, priceless booty he had placed at the feet of the Republic. Talleyrand was expressing thanks for this, which the nation had neglected to do, in highly eloquent language.

A mere five hundred persons had been invited to gaze on the hero; few enough in view of the scramble for invitations, but too many in terms of quality. As it turned out, the mixture of guests was ideal. Art relies on proportion: "Something had to be done to alleviate the mediocrity of the Directors' wives, who naturally took the front seats." The solution was to fill the second and even third rows with less prominent but more elegant faces. Talleyrand invited the prettiest women in Paris —a few pretty heads had managed to survive atop pretty shoulders. No "incroyables" or "merveilleuses" appeared, but female fashions still bore witness to Madame Tallien's eccentricities. Thirteen-year-old Laure Permon, the future duchesse d'Abrantès, attended with her mother. She tells us that they dressed alike, each "in a white crepe gown trimmed with two wide bands of silver ribbon fringed in turn with an inch of pink gauze and silver lamé. In our hair we wore a garland of oak leaves with silvered veins." Oak, in that revolutionary, martial season, was all the rage. Ladies of fashion wore tulle, voile, gauze, and filmy pink and silver creations, the colors of the evening, so it seemed. All around were gowns *à la* Diana, tunics *à la* Ceres, veils *à la* Minerva, and buskins *à la* Omphale. Bare or veiled, breasts were freely displayed.

Besides government officials and the bureaucracy, the guests included all the big names in the business world (and a few nameless border districts) as well as those who possessed nothing but their names, having barely managed to survive exile and return home. The diplomatic corps turned out solidly, of course.

Two Directors were absent: Reubell, who could not abide "those people," and Larevellière-Lépeaux, still preaching his irreverent religion and deaf to our hero's sound advice on the necessity for crucifixion. The other three had condescended to bestir themselves. But with utter bad grace, and to show their contempt for Talleyrand, they did not dress for the occasion, appearing in everyday cloth coats and boots. They were taking revenge, parading their scorn for a man whose endowments, especially for political intrigue and extortion, far surpassed their own meager talents. Perhaps they thought they were playing a clever joke on the former aristocrat and bishop; if so, they were inordinately blind not to see something new taking shape that evening. The regal entrance of Bonaparte and Josephine upon Talleyrand's gleaming parquet floors should have warned them that such floors would prove fatal to Jacobin boots.

The general and his wife escorted fifteen-year-old Hortense de Beauharnais; mother and daughter radiated a serene beauty. Josephine wore a diadem of antique cameos, her husband's gift. Their entrance produced a curious effect on the mixed gathering in that magnificent setting: instead of cheers and applause, a hushed, prayer-like silence greeted Bonaparte, every eye fastened upon him as if entranced. In his high-buttoned gray frock coat, he remained obedient to the demands of modesty. Frail, holding himself very straight, his face set in a stern, commanding expression, he entered the hall like a visiting potentate. But Talleyrand's sorcery was so effective that the hero remained a citizen, causing no alarm. He was even lovable. Thus did he conquer the public; in France, that is, a far less awkward campaign than the Italian one.

Madame de Staël thought the time was ripe to make a conquest of her own: she was going to conquer the conqueror. At the foot of the stairs she waited impatiently. By throwing herself (literally) blindly against the delicate web Talleyrand had so artfully spun about the person of Bonaparte, she spread confusion and broke the spell in her efforts to win his attentions. Talleyrand could not prevent her from accosting his guest of honor. She pestered Arnauld, the general's escort, so mercilessly that he finally agreed to arrange a private talk. Arnauld tried to dissuade her from approaching Bonaparte, knowing that their first encounter had not been too pleasant. The second one was not likely to fare any better as Bonaparte had managed not to "see" Germaine, who was all too visible. But that fact seemed to escape her. She thought herself irresistible, to brilliant men above all. Relying on her great intellect to overwhelm him, she imagined herself and Bonaparte as the century's most celebrated couple, without understanding him in the least. She would win him over; he had only to nod his head and she would take

charge. Any number of things about her—her wealth, intellect, generosity, fidelity, love, disorganization, eloquence, and turbulence—could
have annoyed Bonaparte already and ruled out any further relationship.
But with her every fiber involved, the encounter was sheer disaster. She
rushed headlong into it. The badgered Arnauld relented and brought
them face to face. A head taller than her hero, she unleashed upon him
a stream of impassioned, pathetic, extravagant eulogy, which, if nothing
else, was in extremely poor taste. Sadly enough, her heart was in it. She
trusted her heart even when it made her do foolish things. Why didn't
she look at Bonaparte's face? It would have stopped her cold. She saw
nothing and no one except herself. She told him he was the prince of
men. Silence. Then she launched into a series of incredible questions:
"General, who represents your ideal of a wife?" With the coaching she
had just given him, he ought not to have hesitated in choosing her. He
answered curtly: "Mine!" She persisted: "That is simple enough, but
what kind of woman would you admire the most?" He replied: "She
who is the best housekeeper." Really, he was not very encouraging. Stubbornly, she returned to the question: "Granted, but whom would you
consider the first among women?" The unfailing adulation of "ideologist"
friends and/or lovers led her to expect the same tribute from Bonaparte.
Surely he would say that she was first among women, and she would be
his. But the glorious general countered rudely, cutting her to the quick:
"She who bears the most children." Turning on his heel, he walked
away, leaving her shocked and speechless.

Shortly afterwards she told Arnauld: "Your great man is indeed
odd."

Their interview resumed later. In the course of the evening, Bonaparte sat down on a chair near Madame de Staël. She struck at once:
"General! You! At my feet!"

"It is a mark of respect due your sex by mine."

Whereupon she plunged into an excited discussion of heroism,
which certainly got away from the subject of marriage. He responded
coolly; getting in deeper and deeper, she finally said: "General, don't
play dolls with me. Treat me like a man." With her build and Bonaparte's, dolls' play would have been rather awkward. Furthermore, in
Bonaparte's Mediterranean blood were certain fixed notions as to the
place of women. Even if he had wanted to, he could not have treated
her either as a man or a woman.

She was hopelessly dismayed, but not discouraged. For several more
years she continued to admire him.

What was Talleyrand's reaction to the incident? He stopped receiving Madame de Staël. In fact, she had burned her own bridges the first time she met Bonaparte. Talleyrand had a flair for nosing out failure as well as success before it happened; he was not one to row against the current. Bonaparte and Germaine were obviously incompatible. She had played her hand poorly and lost. Talleyrand did not like losers. Gradually he turned from her. What of their past tenderness, the favors she had done him, the "private little universe"? What were they worth? Today's victor, tomorrow's conqueror was Bonaparte. Victors are always right. Germaine was relegated to the ranks of the disgraced. During the Consulate, when Bonaparte asked him one day: "Who is Madame de Staël?", Talleyrand replied, with chilling cynicism: "An intriguer, to such a degree that I am here [in the foreign ministry] because of her." "Is she a good friend all the same?" "Friend?" he repeated, "she would toss her friends in the river in order to fish them out." A cruel remark? Cruelly true. Her compulsive do-goodism thrived on aiding victims of misfortune. That called for victims, however, and the misfortune of friends allowed Germaine to play God.

In any event, for some time now Talleyrand had found her and her way of expressing things offensive. She appeared ridiculous and annoying by continually asking questions involving herself; taking the limelight always, she forced other people to express their opinion of her. One day she confronted Talleyrand with this question: If she and Madame Récamier fell into the water, which of the two would he rescue? Talleyrand calmly replied: "I am certain, Madam, that you can swim like an angel." Bonaparte did not have that presence of mind or that wit. He was brutal.

She was forever exaggerating things, a capital sin in the bishop's eyes: "From an inch of fact, she embroiders stories by the yard. I know her so well that the only secrets I tell her are the ones I want everyone to know. Despite my caution, however, I find half the time that she has put all sorts of words in my mouth. Beware above all lest she meddle in Bonaparte's affairs; if ever he willingly became involved with her, Heaven and Hell would rock, not to mention the other planets and our own." He did not want Bonaparte and Germaine to be friends and secretly desired the rupture that occurred. Bonaparte never became "involved." Talleyrand made sure of that.

Feeling the wind change, she queried people more actively than ever, to put them "on the spot," one might say. She asked Talleyrand point-blank what he would do if the government issued a warrant for his arrest. He pretended not to hear her. It was quite clear. Turning to Benjamin Constant, she remarked all too brutally: "If he had me arrested, I would have to turn not to those whom I have helped but to those who have already served me. One must rely on one's record of help rendered and not of help received. You will go therefore," she instructed Benjamin, "to Chénier to whom we are obliged for Monsieur de Talleyrand's return to France." [1] She was recalling the past, but who cared about that?

Talleyrand's detractors attacked him for his highly debatable political "acts of treason," yet were far less critical when the treason involved friendship. Germaine had her own failings and peculiarities which he recognized and accepted. She had been a true and devoted friend. She would never have betrayed him. Suddenly he turned his back on her, admitting her to the company of the defeated and unwanted. One day exile would follow.

The incident between Bonaparte and Madame de Staël was significant, but could not spoil the festivities. All the results were not yet in. That evening, with the superb tact he invariably mustered in delicate situations, our illustrious aristocrat was bent on converting Jacobins to a style of life that had disappeared with the Ancien Régime—taking care to provide a familiar revolutionary façade which at once allowed them to deny their origins and their convictions and also shielded their host from criticism. Guests addressed each other as "Citizen" and listened to revolutionary songs (in the form of short arias). He had even thought to print this patriotic message on his invitations: "I trust that it will be found advisable to ban the wearing of any English-made article of attire." It was a period of seething hostility to England; Bonaparte wanted to turn the port of Boulogne into an armed camp from which to launch an invasion across the Channel. The government went wild over the scheme. Someone wrote a song about it and, as usual, the populace assumed that an invasion required no more effort than a few lines of doggerel:

> It's not as hard, believe me,
> As drinking up the sea,
> Drinking up the sea!

In Talleyrand's view, attacking England, like trying to drink up the sea, should not even be attempted. He knew also that it would be fatal to oppose the current wave of government-inspired hysteria calling for war with England. So he invited the honey-voiced Mademoiselle Dugazon to charm the warmongers, male and female, and lead the singing. And thereby put his own credentials in perfect order. A sudden, terrifying burst of notes electrified the guests: Marie-Joseph Chénier's *"Chant du départ."* Talleyrand was not exhorting his guests to live or die for the Republic, only to assemble for dinner. Five hundred persons proceeded into the dining hall where, as a novel touch, only the ladies were seated; the gentlemen remained standing, waiting upon them and taking refreshment as the dinner progressed. Talleyrand stood behind Citizeness Bonaparte's chair, attending her as only he knew how, that is, in the manner he wished to be served himself. An innocent little diversion to which our noble lord lent himself in behalf of the fair and gracious Josephine. His elegant, impeccable service at once made him the prince of hosts.

No less impeccable were the food and wines. Spartan diets faded to a memory, along with Spartan principles. Already dazzled by the splendid setting, the guests now raved about the dinner. Remember that France was emerging from a dreadful nightmare. For one night, people could forget it and contemplate the attractions of a more pleasurable life. No illusion, this was reality, a former society revived, a society which almost all of them had helped to destroy.

Talleyrand did not neglect the belle of the ball, Madame Bonaparte, in whose honor he had commissioned a song from the composer Despréaux which the noted singer Madame Lays performed: *"Il faut qu'on aime une fois."* Mars was forgotten while rose petals fluttered about the feet of Venus.

> Of the warrior, of the conquering hero
> Oh beloved companion!
> Possessing his heart
> Jointly with his country,
> Repay the boundless debt
> Of a great people to its defender;
> In providing for his happiness
> You discharge the nation's duty.

The song celebrating "him" as much as "her" moved the audience to tears. Bonaparte, impassive, felt the enchanting caress of renown.

Thus did a lame and sardonic sorcerer coax life out of ashes. He was right to think that his time and money were not wasted. The ball turned out to be one of Talleyrand's strokes of genius. For the first time since the monarchy's fall, Paris witnessed a celebration that was neither cult nor ritual, neither call to arms nor riot, but an homage to decorum, luxury, and the enjoyment of life. Tenants of the Ancien Régime instinctively recognized the familiar scene; all others, the majority, sons of the Revolution to which they were pledged, discovered a world of

enchantment. But more troubling than the enchantment was their realization that the seemingly hateful style of life to which they had just
given tacit approval was actually quite enviable.

Talleyrand, gliding or hobbling in and out among his guests, had
achieved one of the most significant and fruitful labors of his time by
providing the link between pre- and post-revolutionary France—
probably the most meaningful function of this revolutionary aristocrat's
career. From the eighteenth century into the nineteenth he went on un-
winding the bloodstained silk and gold thread joining the monarchy to
the new France. Combining the past with the future, he reflected both,
as did all the enlightened minds of his era; he pointed the way, he conveyed the appealing eloquence of an aristocratic culture to the world of
liberty, reason, and justice which his Declaration of the Rights of Man
helped to found. That evening, the crier could have shouted: "Gentlemen, Civilization is not dead!" But despite his precautions, the "purists"
were not to be fooled. Talleyrand had invited republicans and left the
Republic in the street. Why did he give such a ball at that particular
time? Six months earlier it would have been premature and dangerous;
six months later, it would not have caused a stir. Bonaparte's arrival was
the clue to political tempers in Paris. Talleyrand never tried to mold
opinion until he was sure of a following. He did not lead; he waited to
be pushed.

A minor incident illustrates the shift in popular sentiments that had
evolved during recent months. The dancers who performed at the ball
asked to eat with the guests. Talleyrand insisted on feeding them in the
pantry. They protested, but not one Jacobin took their part. So they ate
in the pantry, danced, and kept their mouths shut. Six months earlier,
they would have raised a storm. Talleyrand knew just how far to go and
when to stop—or start over again.

Bonaparte had learned the same thing. Writing in a rather cynical
vein to the Italian Count Melzi, he said: "Do you think I am conquering
Italy to bring fame and fortune to advocates of the Directory like Carnot
and Barras? And do you think I am doing it to establish a Republic?
What an idea! It is an illusion that infatuates the French, but it will pass
like all the others. They need glory, they need to satisfy their vanity; as
for liberty, however, they do not know its meaning." [2]

It is clear why Bonaparte felt the ball was such a success. He understood its every implication. Even on St. Helena he mentioned it. He
knew that Talleyrand was sounding out opinion; he heard the reply.
That night convinced him that France would soon be his. Then why not
pursue his destiny? So he took Esseid Ali by the arm, Turkey's genial

ambassador who was being stuffed with sweets and smothered with pretty women, and, under Talleyrand's benign eye, the two had a long talk. The turbaned guest had no idea that Talleyrand put him there for Bonaparte to "discover" and incorporate in his master plan for conquering Turkey's satellite, Egypt. Poor Esseid Ali ran up quite a bill for that hazardous conversation in which, unwittingly, he helped divest his country of its greatest prize.

What a ball! And to think that critics have railed at Talleyrand's pursuit of frivolous pleasures.

Bonaparte and Josephine left at one in the morning; the other guests stayed on. Exultant, the Directors' wives now saw themselves as queens of the ball. Bidding good-night to their host, the wives of two pillars of the Republic, Mesdames Merlin de Douai and François de Neufchâteau, let him know that they could appreciate the expense he must have incurred. "It must have cost a fortune, Citizen Minister," they said to Talleyrand. To which he replied just as innocently: "Not Peru, Citizenesses." All he had lost was money, which he could always get more of. The Jacobins had lost face, had wiped their bloodstained boots on Savonnerie carpets; they stood for Revolution no longer, but for Festivals. Bonaparte had pumped the Turkish ambassador. He was certain now that the weary French would do anything for the promise of order, prosperity, and glory . . . or vainglory. Everyone was content, including Talleyrand.

As *coups d'état* go, the ball on January 3 was perhaps more significant than the 18th Fructidor.

The Affair of January 21, 1798

Two weeks after the ball, the Directors put Talleyrand to work reeling General Bonaparte back into republican waters. Some whim or other seemed to be taking him in another direction. The cause was again a celebration, this time a rather sinister one, the anniversary of Louis XVI's death. Bonaparte had refused to take part in the ceremonies. True, he had been Robespierre's friend when it was politic to be one, and had even won himself something of a terrorist's reputation by butchering royalists in Toulon. But that was four years ago; now he no longer saw any reason to rejoice in the king's death—the king they had called a "tyrant" and whom Bonaparte had dismissed simply as a "pinhead," in Italian, to be accurate (*"Che coglione!"* he exclaimed on August 10 when Louis XVI forbade his guards to fire on the mob). Bonaparte's absence might discredit the revolutionary ceremony and its sponsors. The government saw danger ahead. The hero's attendance was essential if only to stamp his approval on the cult of the guillotine. Once again they dispatched Talleyrand to arrange matters. He must not antagonize the hotheaded Corsican by reminding him that participation in the rite was decreed by law. No, his approach would have to be more oblique. Off went Talleyrand to the rue Chantereine, and in his mellowest episcopal voice, offered Bonaparte a front seat next to the heads of government. The general refused bluntly. Unruffled, Talleyrand went on to express sympathy with Bonaparte's attitude and also to remind him that it might be politic to make a distinction between Bonaparte the soldier and Bonaparte member of the Institut. If the one persisted in refusing, the other might maintain the image of modesty so successful thus far and take a seat with his Institut colleagues in the third row—wearing his gray coat. He would be in the background, his tact would draw praise, and his presence would reassure the Jacobins without alarming the moderates. It was a rare occasion indeed when Bonaparte changed his mind under pressure from an adviser. Within the circle of prominent men who served him, few could claim to have influenced his decisions. For having managed to make the "hero" see reason several times during the rosy dawn of their romance, Talleyrand committed the monumental blunder of believing he would be able to sway him later on. In fact, Bonaparte was absolute master of Talleyrand and of every man in his army. For a time, of course.

For the moment, he took Talleyrand's advice; the Directors were satisfied with his concession. Representatives of the government and the organs of state filed into "the edifice formerly known as Saint-Sulpice." How many times since birth and baptism had Talleyrand stood beneath those vaults? What thoughts were churning in his powdered head on January 21, 1798? Did he muse on the fact that he was glorifying the death of Louis XVI? Did he think of his father bearing the Ampulla at the king's coronation? Of the Masses he attended with Dorothée, or the endless hours of prayer during which he had choked down his grief, his wasted youth, his ambitions and ideals? Hearing the *Te Deum* and *Tantum Ergo* had bored him then as much as the rhetoric of regicides did today, or the hymns of 1793 dotted with savage images:

> If some usurper would enslave France
> Swiftly let him feel the people's vengeance;
> Let him fall beneath the sword; let his bloody limbs
> Be cast upon the plains to devouring vultures.

Did Bonaparte reflect on the merciless fate of that "usurper"?

A tremendous ovation greeted the procession as it left the church. For whom was it intended? The most retiring, self-effacing dignitary. There could be no mistake: "Vive le général et l'Armée d'Italie!" The applause stunned him. On St. Helena he still had not forgotten it, or, for that matter, the disgust written on the Directors' faces. "With the result that this event only increased the displeasure of the men in power." Talleyrand was not displeased at all; everything was proceeding on course. The Directors had asked for the general and had got him through their own efforts. Through more of their own efforts, aided by strong public support, they were soon to have him constantly on their hands. And finally around their necks.

The Curriculum Vitae of a Beauty from India
Who Disrupted Monseigneur d'Autun's Career

The woman who was to become Madame de Talleyrand-Périgord, princess of Benevento, enters the story as the result of a police report. Why she came into Talleyrand's life in the first place is mystery enough.

Early in 1798, it was reported officially that a certain Madame Grand, of English descent, was carrying on a decidedly unpatriotic correspondence with one Lambertye, an émigré viscount living in England. The woman was probably an English spy—no worse suspicion could fall on anyone in those days. Her letters mentioned an important person to whom she attached great hopes and referred to as *"Pié-court."* * "The latter," her letters reported, "who appears destined for high office [a directorate], is thwarted by the Magician [Merlin de Douai] and his crew." The Directors identified limping Talleyrand with *Pié-court*; they might as well have charged him with espionage then and there. The woman was arrested. Gallant *Pié-court* obtained her release from prison. He wrote this eloquent plea to Barras: "Citizen Director, Madame Grand has just been arrested as a spy. She is the last person in the world, and the least likely, to become involved in such matters. She is from India, very beautiful and very indolent, the most idle woman I have ever met. I beg you to take an interest in her. Certainly there is not the slightest cause for pursuing this business, and I would be sorely vexed if it attracted attention."

The rest of the letter defies Talleyrand's customary reserve: "I love her, and I swear to you, man to man, that she has never, and could

* *Pié-court*: short foot—Trans.

never, cause trouble of this sort. She is Indian to the core, and you know how such women shun intrigue. Respectful greetings" (March 23, 1798).

More than a startling confession, that "I love her" marked an upheaval in his life.

The lady came from afar in every sense of the word. Catherine Noël Worlée was born on November 21, 1762, in Tranquebar, India, a Danish settlement ringed by French colonies. Her father was French, an official of the crown in the port of Pondichery, and a Chevalier de Saint-Louis. Her background therefore was not as humble as some malicious tongues suggest. An official record of her baptism exists, but other documents, especially those pertaining to her arrest—her numerous arrests—unfortunately are lost. Her future husband probably took pains to have those records expurgated, one of our hero's minor talents. Catherine Worlée married George Grand, an Englishman in the Indian civil service. Though she had nothing but the clothes on her back and a few modest pieces of jewelry, she was fifteen and inordinately pretty, with a slender, shapely figure and an alabaster complexion that became something of a legend. The nonchalance marking her a child of the tropics, coupled with her Nordic bloom, deep blue eyes, and stunning blond hair, made Madame Grand one of the great beauties of her day. Experts on the subject also declared that the black arch of her brows framed by those masses of blond curls made her eyes even more alluring. No one denies that she was beautiful. The fortunate Mr. Grand was drab and obtuse. Born in Surrey of French Huguenot émigré stock, he was taken for a Frenchman by the English, for an Englishman by the French. He was dull-witted though warm-hearted, neither of which qualities was appreciated by his spouse. When he took her to live in Calcutta, life began to unfold on a grand scale.

Sir Philip Francis, a prominent Englishman and something of a gay blade, was captivated by Madame Grand. He gave a ball for her, deluged her with attentions and gifts, and finally, on the night of December 8, 1778, gave "Cathy," as she was called, the surprise of her life when he climbed up a ladder and leaped through the window into her bed. Sir Philip noted in his Diary for that date: "Tonight the devil was loose in George Grand's house." George was dining out. When the visitor tried to exit the way he had come, he was pounced on by house servants waiting at the foot of the ladder, pummeled, and tied to a chair. Someone ran to fetch the outraged husband, who, it was reported, shed "a torrent of tears" in the arms of friends and went from house to house bemoaning his misfortune, collecting sympathy, and thereby apprising the whole community of his woe. Meanwhile Sir Philip, bored with waiting for the foolish husband to arrive and anxious to free himself, loosed a piercing whistle that brought a troop of men who scattered the Grand servants and carried Sir Philip to safety. Grand arrived, still in tears. After packing his guilty wife off to Chandernagor, he sent his seconds to her lover demanding satisfaction in a duel. When confronted with the matter, Sir Philip insolently replied that he had no idea what all the fuss was about. He even told his wife that he was the victim of a trumped-up quarrel because he had taken pity on a young girl married off to "an ugly, sordid old Frenchman." Lady Francis staunchly upheld her chivalrous husband. The court of Calcutta heard the case and ordered the infamous seducer to pay 50,000 rupees to George Grand, who declared promptly that he was "wholly satisfied." The simple-minded fellow had just discovered a gold mine.

But after reflecting that he had paid far too much for just a curtain-raiser, Sir Philip wanted to see the rest of the act. He went to Chandernagor and brought Cathy back to Calcutta; after several months, he put her on a ship bound for England. She did not stay there, and in 1783 we find her in Paris, according to a bill for 4,816 livres from a jeweler in the Palais-Royal. She was on the way up, not yet at the top but bent on getting there. Later she left the rue Sentier and rented a house on the rue d'Artois. Among her many lovers was the banker Valdec de Lessart, who served as foreign minister during the Legislative Assembly of 1791. Lessart and Talleyrand had been friends during the latter's diplomatic mission in London. Did Cathy know Talleyrand at the time? The record is silent, but in all likelihood she did. Lessart gave dinner parties in his mistress's rooms—the type of atmosphere Talleyrand found most relaxing. Did she play any part in his London mission? Again no record, but even if she were not involved, how could she have remained unknown to Talleyrand, Narbonne, and Lauzun? She went about a great deal, had a box in three different theaters, bought jewels, gold service, silverware, and furs. She was always beautifully dressed. When the spirit of economy happened to move her, she really triumphed, dining in nothing but her splendid tresses. None of her dinner partners could forget those masses of pale blond hair tumbling over her shoulders.

Vigée-Lebrun painted a portrait of Madame Grand in 1783, which tells us that the lady had arrived in society. Talleyrand could have met her in the painter's house. It is a fine portrait despite its rather affected sweetness. One could never tell from looking at the adorable, angelic face that its owner had cruised the seven seas and was destined to weather a good many more gales. Her fresh, pale beauty seemed un-

alterable. Oddly enough, Madame Grand and Talleyrand looked somewhat alike (Barras compared them both to Robespierre): the same
complexion, the same blond hair and blue eyes, the same indolence,
even the same upturned nose.

On August 10, 1792, a day of horrifying butchery, Madame Grand
realized that events in Paris could endanger her life. The truth dawned
on her only after the doorkeeper had been torn to pieces in front of her
eyes by a ragged, bloodstained mob of revolutionists. Though the reasoning process strained her mightily, it finally occurred to her that she
might be the next victim. She took flight. A few days later, on the dock
at Dover, she made a charming picture sitting mournfully atop her traveling case, still terrified, misty-eyed, and with only 6 louis sewn into her
petticoats. A young Englishman offered to help her; she sent him straight
to Paris to rescue her gold plate, her jewels, and her furs. He succeeded,
defying untold dangers, all for the beautiful, trusting eyes of the lady
from India. Her books stayed in France; she got them back later under
the Directory, when *Pié-court* arranged it.

The London atmosphere was not very amusing: though gentlemen
flocked to her, the ladies were hostile. She could not imagine why other
doors were shut when hers was always open. After Robespierre and his
guillotine went out of fashion, she applied for permission to return to
Paris. Alas, her name was on the list of proscribed émigrés. She went
back all the same, hoping to persuade some chivalrous Jacobin to strike
her name off the list—no more uncommon than sending another victim
to the guillotine.

She crossed the Channel with a gentleman named Spinola, whose
father-in-law, the duc de Lévis, had had the misfortune to lose his head
during the Terror. Spinola was returning to France to try to recover his
wife's property. Suspicious of these new arrivals from England, the
police arrested the couple. Spinola was deported; she stayed on. Whose
good graces protected her? Her own, no doubt: she must have found that
chivalrous Jacobin, and she took lodgings on the rue Saint-Nicaise. The
police kept her under surveillance and soon arrested her for the second
time. That was when Talleyrand intervened. How had he come to know
her so intimately?

Colmache, an English secretary of Talleyrand's, gives the following
account in his *Reminiscences of Prince Talleyrand*. During the Directory, in October or November, 1797, Foreign Minister Talleyrand returned home after a discouraging evening of whist, intending to go
straight to bed. A servant informed him that a lady with an introduction
from Montrond had been waiting to see him for hours about an urgent

matter. Tired and annoyed, Talleyrand decided to see her only as a courtesy to Montrond. He entered the room where the lady was waiting. All he could distinguish was a voluminous wrap and a hood blanketing his visitor's head; the gold tips of her buskins were barely visible, along with the gold gauze hem of her gown peeking out from beneath her cloak. She had fallen asleep by the fire. Startled by his entry, she jumped to her feet, her hood and cloak slipping to the floor: suddenly the flower bloomed, fresh, rosy, and dazzling. Talleyrand was speechless with delight, ready to move worlds for this charming, unknown visitor.

What did she want of him? Montrond had put panic in her heart—on her lovely face it was most becoming—making her believe that Bonaparte was on the verge of invading England, that banks would be looted and all her money lost, and that her one hope was to throw herself on Talleyrand's mercy. Talleyrand gathered that Montrond was sending him a present. His smile reassured her. Why leave in the dead of night? She had no objection to staying. So she remained under Talleyrand's roof, and would be there still if time and death had not dislodged her as ultimately they dislodge us all.

There are other versions of how she conquered his heart and hearth. Only the introduction varies; the conclusion is invariable: Madame Grand dug in. Some said that she was not introduced by Montrond but by the marquise de Sainte-Croix (Zoë Talon), a sister of the comtesse de Cayla, one of Louis XVIII's favorites, and that she was seeking protection from police harassment. This story is more reasonable than Bonaparte sacking London. In both versions, however, she came knocking at Talleyrand's door in the middle of the night. Another account reported that Talleyrand spent the evening with the duc de Laval and Sainte-Foy. After receiving his beauteous visitor and conducting her to her rooms, he rejoined his friends, a look of contentment on his face, and told them why. Delighted, they pressed him to display his treasure. Patience. They could see her tomorrow, the day after tomorrow—and every day thereafter for twenty-five years. But long before that, they had begun to find her unbearable.

In 1797 she was thirty-five and already starting to put on weight. Talleyrand used to count "three exquisitely sweet things about her: her skin, her breath, and her disposition." [1] As to intelligence, he said that hers was "like a rose." Commenting on the marriage in her Memoirs, Vigée-Lebrun noted that fortunately the husband had brains enough for both of them. Cathy's ignorance became a legend. Can it be true that when asked where she was born, she produced the painful pun: "Je suis d'Inde"? * It is a much-cited remark. And when Vivant Denon † returned from Egypt with an account of his trip, she confused it with Robinson Crusoe, asking why he had not come back with Friday. Talleyrand listened to that and a hundred other inane remarks with supreme indifference; he seemed delighted rather than annoyed. When Narbonne and Montrond wondered where he got his patience, he stunned them with this remark: "You must first have been Madame de Staël's lover before you can know the pleasure of loving an animal." Baron de Frenilly, one of Catherine's old flames, called her "Beauty and the Beast rolled up in one."

Such was the woman for whom Talleyrand, ex-bishop but bishop all the same, committed the most incomprehensible blunder of his whole career. To have loved her, lived with her, and made her mistress of his household is understandable in the light of all the joys she brought him; to have married her is something else.

Passion cannot explain it, for passion never entered Talleyrand's life: he was incapable of feeling it. Remember that Madame du Deffand placed her fingers over Fontenelle's heart, saying to him: "There, too, lies a brain." The same applies to Talleyrand.

Could this supposed love affair conceal some impulse quite alien to love? That would make our hero's ringing "I love her" a lie, suggesting that his infatuation was invented to hide something else. Behind the marriage lies a carefully guarded secret.

If not for love, why did he marry her? By the time he takes that leap we will know more about him and his circle of acquaintances. At the moment, we can only suspect some strange complicity linking them in the first place. It is hard to believe that her appearance at the ministry in the dead of night marked their first encounter. Is it not more likely that they were renewing then, in 1797, an existing relationship? A dangerous one perhaps? In a long, leisurely life interwoven with some of the most poignant, grandiose, or sordid events of modern history, his union with Madame Grand is the uniquely mysterious episode. The woman was a foreign element, unlike any other mistress of his. She was not his friend; though her name may have become Madame de Talleyrand, she never became part of his world.

Whereas most biographers seem content to define Madame Grand's

* *D'Inde*: from India; *dinde*: a foolish woman—Trans.
† Baron Dominique Vivant Denon (1747–1825), engraver and draftsman who joined the important artistic and scientific expedition organized in conjunction with Napoleon's Egyptian campaign; later director of the Louvre—Trans.

power as her "sensuality" (a point to which we will return later with shattering evidence), others have worked up a case for "sadism," which hardly seems relevant to the personality we know. Is it not possible that at the time she thrust herself into his life, Madame Grand aroused Talleyrand's fear of some unsuspected threat to him?

Let us leave him there, cozily attached to his rose without thorns—or without mystery, at any rate—and return to his dealings with the Directors.

Barras read Talleyrand's letter to the Executive Directory meeting in secret session, and unleashed an avalanche of insults on the head of his protégé. Hunchbacked Larevellière-Lépeaux led the attack this time, aiming his epithets at the bishop and the Catholic church. Talleyrand had confessed to a crime that only a priest of Rome could commit: the bishop's perversity stemmed from his religious training. Perversity, in that Director's eyes, consisted in loving a beautiful blonde unfortunate enough to have some English blood in her veins. What greater abomination was there?

Reubell silenced the hunchback's shrill complaints. Then Merlin spoke, injecting an ominous note. Merlin was a self-appointed expert in the law, unrivaled at distorting it beyond recognition. That reputation brought him into the government. He began by charging that a minister of the Republic had no business taking a mistress in England when there were plenty of fine ones at home, and that the "alleged love affair was in reality a political plot." Reviving old tenacious rumors about Talleyrand's illicit dealings with England, he called him: "A man sold to the English for whom Madame Grand can only be the ferryboat." The metaphor is clever enough, but not funny considering that it meant the death penalty for any lover of the ferryboat. His final words were full of menace. Let us not forget that four years earlier the same men had been denouncing and guillotining victims against whom they had no more evidence than Merlin against Talleyrand. He called for an investigation of Madame Grand in order to strike at the foreign minister: "If, as I hope, we succeed in exposing treachery, we will be doing an outstanding service to justice." Such a policy gave the police free rein. "After removing him from office as he deserves, we will transfer him to a military tribunal." The picture was perfectly clear: he was to die before a firing squad. Such were the arguments of Merlin the Magician of Douai.

Then Reubell snarled, his snarling less offensive than a serpent's hiss. He repeated a familiar list of accusations, unintentionally casting light on some otherwise obscure facets of our hero's character. Reubell's crude reactions explain some fairly common attitudes about Talleyrand

besides exposing (almost indecently) his bodily self. Reubell is speaking: "He could not find satisfaction in France, then, where there is no shortage of whores." So much for the future princesse de Talleyrand. Shifting his fire, he proceeded to attack Talleyrand personally, probing for one essential structural flaw. Reubell's hate, as if guided by animal instinct and visceral revulsion, approached the blemish, stripping it bare, down to the very odor and feel of the flesh. Among living creatures, consciously or unconsciously, relationships can be affected by a factor such as skin. A bristling hide registers one creature's hostility to another's intolerable physical presence. "He is a cripple, deprived of part of his limbs, barely able to stand up on two withered bones." What was he really saying? That Talleyrand's whole personality, not just his foot, was stunted. The animal, even bestial, side of his revulsion was irrepressible: in utter rejection, he disgorged him. Thus did Reubell express his disgust: "He is a living corpse with no excuse for indulging in things that provide other people with one." Yes, Talleyrand's sensuality definitely was tepid; he had no trouble controlling it, phlegmatic creature that he was. What right had he to stir up a storm over a mistress when carnal desire was not involved? Let him stay chaste, a monk. Castrated. Those were Reubell's thoughts: crude and shocking, but not inaccurate. Talleyrand's apathy, his pale, flaccid flesh, his tortoise-like deliberation, his sleek, beardless cheeks (he had hardly a hair on his face), suggest what was bothering Reubell: "He is a libertine without [sexual] need, without [sexual] means, invoking all the resources of debauchery according to Sade's precepts." The first part is tenable; the last, rubbish. In matters of the heart, Talleyrand was a gambler, but never out to break the bank.*
That does not mean he was sexless; as a matter of fact, he was a voluptuary, a languorous voluptuary, a tomcat gratified by his own caresses. What could he learn from Sade? A sadist is cruel, industrious, and inventive; Talleyrand yearned for tenderness, idleness, and fond embraces.

How strange that these subtle hints touching on Talleyrand's intimate habits should come from the mouth of such a lout.

The meeting continued. François de Neufchâteau had the courage to suggest that a man's privacy ought to be respected. "It is a sanctuary," he declared. The sanctuary resembled a carnival. During a lull, Barras turned the matter back to the chief of police (no longer Sottin) with

---

* A remark made by Madame de Flahaut, who was certainly in a better position than Reubell to pass judgment, supports the latter's invectives. On October 17, 1789, she wrote Gouverneur Morris that she was leaving Talleyrand because he lacked *"fortiter in re"* though abundantly provided with *"suaviter in modo,"* which alone was not enough.

instructions to settle it somehow. And settled it was, for the Indian beauty left prison and returned to her soft life in the foreign ministry. What a society! The spy, a prisoner only yesterday, crawled back into bed with the minister and presided over his household. The minister, lately threatened with a court-martial, retained his office, and things continued on their muddy course. As far as Talleyrand was concerned, nothing had happened.

The Orient Sets General Bonaparte Dreaming and Talleyrand Speculating

It will be recalled that on July 3, 1797, Talleyrand had delivered a remarkable paper before the Institut on the "Advantages to Be Derived from Colonies Under Present Conditions." Egypt served as illustration, an idea furnished by Choiseul. Volney's famous *Voyage en Egypte et en Syrie,* published in 1787, had popularized the subject. Talleyrand thought highly of the book, and relying on the combined knowledge of Choiseul and Volney, he had produced a plan for colonizing Egypt that sat there waiting for application. Talleyrand's paper reached Bonaparte in Italy and was a revelation. For some time the general had been gazing eastward; then and there he resolved to implement the plan. He often mentioned it to his military aides, as General Desaix's Diary confirms. Apparently, then, Talleyrand was unintentionally the spark behind the Eastern expedition. Later, quite intentionally, he urged Bonaparte to pursue it. His role warrants a definition at this point because he disclaimed any part in the adventure once it began to go badly.

Bonaparte addressed the government: "The time is approaching when we will feel that if we really wish to destroy England, we must seize control of Egypt." Talleyrand at once congratulated Bonaparte for his initiative. Sensing an ally at hand, the general wrote back: "Why don't we take the Island of Malta?" as well as Corfu, other Mediterranean islands, and the real target: Egypt. "We could sail from here with 25,000 troops and an escort of eight or ten men-o'-war or Venetian frigates and seize it. Egypt does not belong to the sultan" (September 13, 1797). The sultan could claim suzerainty but not sovereignty over Egypt. In any event, as Constantinople had every reason to be alarmed by such a scheme, it was politic to allay the sultan's fears. Hence the exquisite show of courtesy to Esseid Ali during Talleyrand's ball when he, of all the diplomats, had been earmarked for special treatment. That evening Bonaparte was bent on conquering him, not Germaine de Staël.

To Talleyrand fell the task of cajoling the sultan and finding out how he would react to the Egyptian project. Practical and provident as usual, Talleyrand reorganized the Ecole des Langues Orientales, increasing the number of students enrolled as Arabic interpreters. An odd coincidence.

On January 27, 1798, three weeks after the ball and after numerous conferences with the general, Talleyrand submitted a report on Egypt to the government on which the two of them had collaborated closely. Projecting the inevitable collapse of the Ottoman Empire, the report held that Russia and Austria should not be allowed to divide up the spoils without allotting France a share. "I give highest priority to Egypt, and the islands of Crete and Lemnos." A list of islands followed, stepping stones on the route to Egypt, and a wave of annexations. The report bears Talleyrand's signature. Yet he was philosophically opposed to an expansionist policy, and the terse, authoritarian tone is not the style of his directives. Why the violation of his principles? He put his stamp on a report dictated by Bonaparte. Why? Perhaps some casual remark he made later on will reveal the motive behind it. That was his habit: blandly worded, tucked between two commas, a parenthetical phrase of his sometimes discloses a monumental truth. Let us be patient.

Lest the government feel guilty about stabbing the sultan in the back, he wrote this into the report: "Why sacrifice ourselves any longer for a power that offers us dubious friendship and is also on the brink of collapse? Egypt means nothing to Turkey, who has no influence at all over her." Nevertheless, they continued cramming sweetmeats into Esseid Ali, who was not heard complaining about the "dubious friendship" lavished upon him.

The expedition was scheduled for the 1st Messidor (July, 1798), six months away. Neither the haste nor the submission of a wholly unsolicited report is typical of Talleyrand. He was more apt to forget to hand in one that had been requested of him. Still, the report exists; he signed and delivered it. In later years, that did not keep him from attributing the memorandum to Delacroix, saying it was found at the ministry after the latter's departure. Talleyrand's *Memoirs* are silent; one gathers that an Egyptian landing took place, but was he actually minister at the time? His benign penchant for "omission" crops up again. As evidence of his vital role in the affair, we know that he studied Magallon's records of his thirty-five years heading the French consulate in Cairo. There is still another report bearing Talleyrand's signature, the whiplash style and imperious reasoning of which point again to the same author. "Egypt was once a province of the Roman Republic; it must become one under the French Republic." Talleyrand would never have written such a sweeping statement in that peremptory tone. Yet he signed the statement and plenty of others along with it. The final honeyed phrases aimed at the government do identify at last the hand of Monsieur d'Autun: the monarchy was too frail to realize such a grandiose epic, the achievement of which was reserved for the Republic in order that it might astound the world. Amen. The overall plan is spelled out in detail, everything simple and easy, a series of projected invasions. A dream of sending a 15,000-man expeditionary force from Suez clear across to the Indies—with enormous booty: the timeworn fable of "Perette and the Pitcher of Milk." * How could a cautious soul like Talleyrand endorse such a project? The document never raised the possibility of storms or landing difficulties, the problem of supplying an army, or the danger of an epidemic; everything was idyllic—and cheap. Great stress was laid on the modest cost of the operation.

Fouché's opinion, expressed in his Memoirs, is worth noting. Though certainly not one to exonerate Talleyrand, why did he refuse to credit him with so much as a glimmer of intelligence? "The former bishop of Autun, so clever, so ingratiating, and whom Necker's scheming daughter had just lodged in the ministry of foreign affairs, conceived the brilliant idea of ostracism in Egypt." No, Bonaparte was the one with creative imagination; "clever and ingratiating" Talleyrand pressed him to act upon it. As for the word "ostracism," it could have occurred to Fouché only long afterwards. At the time of the Egyptian expedition, the Directors alone, in absolute secrecy, were wishing exile on the general and Talleyrand. The latter was playing simultaneously in two different theaters: courting Bonaparte by flattering his ambitions and currying favor with the Directory by encouraging the departure of the "ruthless and fearless general," as Fouché called him, adding observantly that the Corsican "put his back and all his ardor" into this expedition to the Orient, "which he already prided himself on ruling like a sultan and prophet." A vision which Talleyrand promoted but did little to help carry out. Once the adventure was under way, he washed his hands of it.

How do we know all this? Through Talleyrand's friend the Prussian ambassador in Paris, to whom he had whispered that the gathering of the fleet in Toulon Harbor was a prelude to the Egyptian operation. For a state secret, it was well kept. One of his confidential remarks throws

* La Fontaine's fable, the moral of which is Don't build castles in Spain (or, in the Aesop version, Don't count your eggs until they are hatched)—Trans.

236

light on the political designs behind the expedition: "It is meant to serve both a historic and a political purpose, the former by collecting monuments enabling us to trace the history of this part of the globe, the latter by turning official thoughts and acts away from revolutionary ideas which would have convulsed Europe; universal democracy is as great an illusion as universal monarchy once was."

That personal reflection wholly explains Talleyrand's bizarre position in the Egyptian affair. He was not interested in the East, the route to the Indies and Bonaparte's dream of carving an empire there. Let the fires of revolution spend themselves in the desert—and spare Europe. All that mattered to Talleyrand was venerable old Europe. If he seemed to encourage adventurism, it was only to reassure the European powers. If he confided secrets to the Prussian minister Sandoz-Rollin, it was not to preserve them but to make sure that Prussia and others heard about them. Word that France meant to curb her assault on Europe and bury her armies in the sands of Egypt would cheer the continent. Her neighbors could breathe again and hope for peace. Talleyrand and Bonaparte seemed to agree, when actually they were diametrically opposed, one bent on carving himself an empire, the other urging him to do his fighting somewhere else. "The sphinx on the rue du Bac" could see beyond the Pyramids and may well have foreseen that the government would disgrace itself further. As for the men in power, would they have protested the absence of their worst rival, Italy's conqueror? In short, all the parties had a stake in the adventure—which indeed it was—for different and even conflicting reasons.

Bonaparte was in such a hurry to get away that he did not attend the Congress of Rastatt to press for peace talks with Austria as Talleyrand had instructed. That act of disobedience left France at war with Austria and cost her dear. He chose instead to inspect military installations at Boulogne, hoping to throw England off the scent by making her think he was still planning to "drink up the sea." When Esseid Ali grew alarmed at talk of an Egyptian campaign, Talleyrand assured him that the Toulon fleet would not sail beyond Malta. Time would tell. . . .

The general's farewell to his ally on the rue du Bac is worth noting as it casts an odd light on the two men. Talleyrand had been ill in bed for several days when Bonaparte came by on his way to Toulon. About to go, he told the minister that he was out of funds and had no way of raising them before leaving Paris. Talleyrand could hardly believe his ears. The hero who had filled the Directory's coffers was penniless? To him that was probably the most disconcerting side of Bonaparte. Here is the account of it in his *Memoirs*. He said to the general—offering fresh evidence of his good will—

> "Well then, open the desk and you will find 100,000 francs of mine. They are yours now; you can repay me when you return." He hugged me, and it was pleasant to share his happiness. When he became Consul, he returned the money I had lent him. Sometime afterwards he asked me: "Why did you lend me that money? I have often wondered about it and could never understand your motive." "I had none," I told him. "I was feeling very ill and might never have seen you again; you were young and made such a vital, intense impression on me that I wanted to help you without any ulterior purpose."

(A truly warmhearted gesture on Talleyrand's part.) The icy shower was about to fall. " 'In that case,' Bonaparte went on, 'you acted deceitfully.' "

Words like that cut deep and can banish scruples in persons more inclined than Talleyrand to possess them. Thirty years later, he found that comment very interesting. We agree.

Before leaving, Bonaparte made Talleyrand promise to send a first-rate ambassador to allay fears in Constantinople. That ambassador extraordinary turned out to be none other than Talleyrand, who consented after the general had pressed him strenuously. Instead of rushing to pack his bags, however, he drafted instructions to an unnamed diplomat in Constantinople; the envoy slated to receive them was not even designated. The aim of the instructions was to persuade the sultan that the seizure of Egypt was not an assault on him but actually an effort to save him from his real foe, England. Any complaint on his part was thus ill-conceived.

On reaching Malta, Bonaparte sent one of his ships back to Toulon to take Talleyrand to Constantinople with all haste. As this ship, *La Badine,* was captured at sea by the English, Talleyrand never had to board it. In any event, he had already decided not to go to Turkey and never answered any of Bonaparte's notes from Egypt asking him if he had seen the sultan and how the latter had reacted. Talleyrand sat reading Bonaparte's dispatches in his office on the rue du Bac: "I do not know whether Talleyrand is in Constantinople; it is essential to send an ambassador to Constantinople; Talleyrand must go there and keep his word."

He did not go there or appoint a delegate of rank. A deputy named Boulouvard did the best he could in an extremely ticklish situation. He complained and was fearful—rightly so, for the whims of an offended sultan in the eighteenth century could prove disastrous to any hostage of his. Aware of that, Talleyrand, always the flower of courtesy, consoled the man: "I can appreciate how painful, delicate, and hazardous your position will become with respect to the Porte." To boost his courage: "Do not fear the Seven Towers." That was the notorious prison where the sultan's victims were tortured, usually by impalement. Talleyrand explained that the practice of torture, like the Ottoman Empire, was declining, becoming less common and less cruel. Anyway, Boulouvard could suffer and die in the knowledge that France would avenge him, as Esseid Ali would have to answer for it. We have no idea how Boulouvard responded to these comforting words.

By remaining at his post, Talleyrand frustrated the plans of two persons: Bonaparte (though Talleyrand's presence in Constantinople could not have affected the inevitable military fiasco) and François de Neufchâteau, ambitious to be foreign minister.

Talleyrand's position in this whole affair has had various interpretations. To some he was a traitor who broke his promise to Bonaparte by not going to Constantinople, a view reflecting hostility to Talleyrand and the conviction that Bonaparte could do no wrong. In an article by C. L. Lokke,[1] hostility and admiration bow to the facts: we see that Talleyrand and his staff were given almost nothing to do and that he was not permitted to exercise the slightest diplomatic initiative, not to speak of heading a mission to Constantinople which the Directors opposed. One valid reason for that opposition was the renewed threat of war with Austria. (General Bonaparte had flatly disregarded orders to negotiate peace at Rastatt as he had done so successfully at Campo Formio.) Moreover, a conflict was about to erupt with the United States.

It is quite evident that Talleyrand did not make any effort to arrange a mission to Constantinople, which struck him as neither judicious nor advantageous. Why promote an obvious failure? Coming events did not disprove him.

The Former Bishop Comes a Cropper at the Hands of Jacobins as Cunning as He

The expedition was ill-fated from the start. Everything went wrong. Paris turned out on September 18, 1798, to celebrate the French landing in Alexandria which in fact had occurred on July 1. The Aboukir fiasco took place on August 1, destroying the entire French fleet and marooning the army in the desert. Instead of toasting victory, they ought to have been mourning defeat. Chénier's glowing rhetoric subsided when reports from England told the truth. English ships controlled the Mediterranean and the transmittal of news from the East—disastrous news of Bonaparte's army. General exuberance turned to anger, and, as always, the public looked for a scapegoat, blaming the Directors for sending Bonaparte off to get rid of him. Talleyrand came off even worse, accused of diabolically masterminding an expedition that was bound to fail. We know better, yet Bonaparte, the real instigator bent on carving himself an empire, was taken for an innocent victim. Ignorant of his plans and ambitions, the public knew only the Citizen General, member of the Institut, heroic, brilliant, handsome, and betrayed by scheming politicians. An idol was in the making.

Bonaparte's absence was bitterly resented, especially now that war was breaking out disastrously all over an emboldened Europe.

At Rastatt, French plenipotentiaries were murdered by Austrian hussars. Faced with a European coalition and those brutal killings, Talleyrand grew bellicose in defense of the people's rights. The right to negotiate had been violated by the murder of the negotiators. For once he sided with the Jacobins against the imperial powers. "This crime must rouse all nations to indignation, especially free nations friendly to France, for it threatens them most. . . ." He urged all free peoples to unite with France so that "in this struggle of tyranny and crime against liberty, liberty shall triumph."

He preached war because everywhere French forces were under attack. The target was no longer the Jacobins; it was France. On all fronts her forces were retreating: Italy was lost, Holland and Switzerland evacuated, Alsace besieged. All this resulted from the Directory's senseless policy of alienating the whole of Europe. Talleyrand had warned the government to stop appointing former members of the National Convention to diplomatic posts abroad; they invariably behaved like strutting conquerors, their blundering ignorance earning them ridicule and hatred. The French representatives in New York when Talleyrand was there were a fair sample. With a crew like that, a foreign minister's hands were tied.

Yet the minister was held responsible. The press opened fire on Talleyrand, especially the Jacobin press, its organs *Le Républicain* and *Le Journal des Hommes Libres* carrying fierce headlines: "The Devil Visits the Directory" or "The Trial of an Adventuress Named Revolution." So virulent were the articles that the second paper came to be known as the *Journal des Tigres*. Posters attacking "The Devil" went up nightly along the streets. Leaflets came out, one of them, a century before Zola, with the title "Je vous accuse." Talleyrand was accused of attempting to revive the monarchy.

Among his fiercest assailants was Antonelle, a former marquis who had served on the Revolutionary Tribunal and gone on to become mayor of Arles. Plainly, he knew which strings to pull. In 1815, he campaigned ardently to restore the throne and church. July 2, 1799, marked his opening attack on Talleyrand. He blamed him for his noble birth. That was only an appetizer. He went on blaming him for his friendship with Choiseul-Gouffier, Louis XVIII's ambassador to Russia; for becoming a bishop and remaining one, reminding him that the sacrament is inviolable; for selling out to the English while sipping imperial Tokay with his crony Pitt (who had him deported from England). But the former marquis's wrath really exploded over the fact that Talleyrand had been appointed naval minister as well as foreign minister. "Yes, we repeat, the man who is ruining us is that eternal bishop of Autun, that great nobleman and charlatan who once knew everything and never learned anything. . . ." Next he accused him of conspiring to destroy the Revolution and, "like an Anglomaniac in the full treasonous sense of the word, to destroy France, starting with her fleet and her Constitution. . . . Thus one would have to exceed the stupidity of this vile, loathsome, and vicious schemer not to realize that the man sought ministerial power in Barthélemy's and Carnot's time solely to ruin the nation." [1]

What was Talleyrand to say? He never said a word. Close friends reported that he dozed off while reading a passage consigning him to the firing squad. We know that his motive in seeking high office was not to betray France to the English, but partly to make a fortune—which he succeeded in doing—and partly to make peace with Europe—which constant harassment and distrust prevented him from doing. Antonelle continued: "Your minister is an Anglo-émigré . . . a traitor, and his country's murderer." Finally, this saintly judge of the Revolutionary Tribunal unearthed something even worse than treason: adultery. In a tirade of outraged virtue, he blazed away at the lady from India: "Yes, at this very moment, like a favorite courtesan, she shares the couch of our émigré bishop." At this very moment—Oh, burning issue! Imagine avid readers snatching up newsprint that was barely dry. "It is our belief that now we have revealed the true and hidden cause of all our troubles."

Talleyrand's position was becoming untenable. In addition, two unsavory and rather dangerous affairs threatened him simultaneously, both instigated probably by the same people.

The first, and potentially more serious, resolved itself harmlessly. At the source of it was his London mission of 1792, the titular ambassador of which had been young Chauvelin. In 1798, that mission was branded an attempt to betray France. Chauvelin exonerated himself with a vigor born of fear and the guileless incompetence he had displayed at an earlier date. It was not difficult to prove his own innocence and Talleyrand's "guilt." Of what was he guilty? Securing England's neutrality. Instead of going down on their knees to him as they should, they charged him with high treason. Under the Directory, however, functionaries were not in the habit of losing jobs for such an offense. They lost them, it seems, for far more serious blunders—the foreign minister had been disrespectful to a future government agent, who, to make things worse, was his district's elector.

The second utterly disgraceful affair involved a certain Sébastien-Louis-Gabriel Jorry, a printer's son born in Paris in 1772, who joined the army of the Republic at age eighteen. Promotion was rapid in those times, and he became a second lieutenant. A wound he received at Jemappes turned out to be a blessing, advancing him to the rank of adjutant general. His conduct in battle left something to be desired. Now the one redeeming virtue of that makeshift army was its superb courage, but our Master Jorry managed to distinguish himself for cowardice. Demoted in 1794, he was dismissed from the ranks three years later on charges involving cravenness as well as his activities in the radical Babouvist movement. He was implicated in the trial of Babeuf and then cleared. By chance or circumstance, according to one's point of view, at the time he had dealings with Talleyrand the young man came up with a character witness in the person of Barras. Yes, Barras emerged as the arbiter of morality, championing the impeccable virtue of a twenty-five-year-old soldier discharged for unvalorous conduct, swearing him to be "an honorable soldier, courageous and upright, of uncommon excellence." But despite the lie, Barras was right on target, using Jorry to torpedo the insolent Anglo-émigré frigate "Talleyrand."

What had happened? The year before, toward the end of October, 1797, Talleyrand had had a visit at the ministry from two persons sent by the chief of police with this recommendation: "notoriously reckless and apt to be useful to our secret service in Italy." That they were two undesirables was quite clear—special gifts to the "liberated nations." Their absence would be a blessing to the Paris police, provide spies for the army of occupation, and keep two potential malefactors from starving. One was "General" Rossignol, the other Jorry. Talleyrand treated them courteously and offered them work in Rome, not bad for a start. "They asked to think it over and eat lunch," he reported. Having considered the offer at lunch, Rossignol rejected it. Jorry accepted, and pocketing an advance of 2,400 livres from the ministry coffers for his trip to Rome, he left, never returning to pick up his passport and orders. He had a good time at the government's expense.

Five months later there was an official investigation of the serious irregularity Talleyrand had committed. When asked about the incident, he was not very communicative as to who or what had been involved. He should have known better than to let the matter drop, never summoning Jorry or checking to see what had become of him. Still, with habitual caution, he omitted any mention of Jorry's name in the report he submitted. One would think he meant to shield him. Or did he suspect another trap? Maybe he simply forgot the man's name.

Not satisfied with the evasive reply, Merlin ordered the police to "institute criminal proceedings at once against Adjutant General Jorry."

Unknown to Talleyrand and against his will, the case was opened. On April 5, 1798, Jorry was taken into custody and immediately declared Talleyrand responsible for his arrest. Three days later he appeared in court, acknowledged having received a certain sum of money which he said he had not touched and was prepared to return, then stated under oath that he had never left France because the minister neglected to give him a passport and instructions. He prided himself on being the elector of his district and enjoying Barras's protection. Hearing that, the judge released him and quashed the indictment. A free man on April 8, Jorry began to exhibit his recklessness. The *Journal des Hommes Libres* offered him its pages. Posters vilifying the foreign minister went up on every street corner. As to where the funds came from for this concerted campaign, all Paris was seething with hate. And while Talleyrand paid scant attention, his friends grew alarmed; one came to warn him of the mounting danger. Scarcely listening, he said that he was expecting a visit from two large, uncommon personalities. Mystified, his friend tried to guess their identity. With Europe in flames, where could they be coming from? "Who are you talking about?" he asked Talleyrand. "Two bears from Bern," was the reply. He was wholly absorbed by the idea of two bears being shipped from Switzerland to the Paris Zoo, where a superb moat had just been dug to accommodate them. That is what preoccupied him at a time when he might have been set upon or even hanged for showing his face in the streets of Paris.

Jorry brought suit against the minister for arbitrary arrest and slander. Under the law, Talleyrand could not avoid arraignment, and because justice was rarely served in the courts of the Directory (even when government officials were concerned) he was on his guard. He published in *Le Moniteur* an impersonal, objective statement of the foreign minister's official position, describing what had happened between the minister and Jorry, and spelling out what no judge had chosen to recognize: that the action against Jorry had not been brought by the minister. Pointing to the absence of any dispute between the parties, he exposed a concerted effort to exploit the affair: "The whole thing would be pitiful and nothing more if behind the rage and slander of these disgusting posters one could ignore the ill-disguised purpose of an essentially destructive party bent on dishonoring the government."

More accurately, the purpose was to disgrace the foreign minister. With Bonaparte treading the desert sands and Talleyrand discredited, the Directors could breathe easier and feel free to carry out their private schemes.

They were so used to ignoring him that they did not even bother to inform him of administrative decisions, appointing and shifting ambassadors at will in total silence. Finding his funds frozen, he had to beg wages for his staff from the finance ministry while he himself went unpaid. They were dismissing him.

He continued to wear his mask of serenity, having already made his plans. His passport was in order; his fortune, about 2,500 million francs after two years in the government, was divided between Hamburg and London banks. Still, he played for time, doing everything he could to postpone the arraignment. He managed to delay it a year. Finally, on July 11, 1799, Antonelle's journal published a letter from Jorry demanding an explanation of the trial's deferment and of "the exceedingly criminal complaisance on behalf of the artisan of the Republic's woes." On July 12 the court issued its verdict in line with the position taken by the *Journal des Hommes Libres*, which, on July 13, could proclaim triumphantly that the innocent Jorry had been acquitted. The judges had openly condemned Talleyrand's conduct as unbefitting a minister. Surprisingly, he was not censured for his one and only mistake in handing over money without a receipt to an adventurer. Instead, he was indicted for and convicted of having the amateur spy arrested, though he had nothing to do with it.

The conviction Jorry won carried a fine of 100,000 francs (they tried their best to send Talleyrand to prison as well) and a printed notice of the verdict "in the number of two thousand copies, with damages payable by the accused." After hearing the decision, the accused sent in his resignation. That was on July 13, 1799. A week later, the Directors still had not acknowledged it. Talleyrand sent a second letter:

I shall never forgive myself for retaining an office in which, despite the knowledge that I did everything I could for the welfare of the Republic, I feel that my name alone, subjected as it is to flagrant daily abuse, could become an obstacle to government policies. And in any case, when a tribunal of the Seine has just condemned me without even summoning me for a hearing [good reason to distrust the legal system] and has labeled slanderous and unconstitutional an unwritten, unspoken accusation [he did not know that the denunciation bore Merlin's signature] which I never made or intended to make, then it is high time for me to resign. . . .

The date was July 20, 1799. This time his resignation was accepted with a small pat on the back "for his unflagging zeal, civic spirit, and understanding" [2] in performing official duties.

The *Journal des Hommes Libres* railed against praising a *traitor*. Talleyrand enjoyed at least the irony of the situation when he found out who was to succeed him, a man he himself had trained, a thoroughly honest, conscientious, punctilious, and self-effacing administrative assistant. Reinhardt had all the qualities his predecessor lacked, but none of the talents. Talleyrand and other pragmatic souls thought of him as a temporary substitute, a seat-warmer for his master. Reinhardt would have been the first to agree and was absolutely devoted to his superior. Talleyrand congratulated him warmly.

Instead of resenting it, he was pleased to have put ashore from a rotting vessel. Would he not be in a better position to scuttle it at the right moment? Now was the time to start building the new ship of state that would carry France forward. What did a creature like Jorry matter? Like a straw in the wind, he unwittingly steered Talleyrand—a bit sooner than expected—onto his true course: the advancement of his country.

His letter of resignation made a point of declaring his faith in the republican system. He was absenting himself, not deserting it. Actually, he was sorry to leave the rue du Bac and admitted so privately to the Prussian minister Sandoz-Rollin. Like the tightrope walker he was at heart, no sooner had he left the ministry than he began to apply his theory that one must always have an option to fall back on. Having lost his post, he needed another. Should it surprise us, then, to find that once the government had begun abusing him, he made overtures to an agent of Louis XVIII? Why, when to the Bourbons he was an anathema? He simply wanted to explore, to put out feelers, not knowing what lay ahead. The Directory was a rotting corpse; Bonaparte was in Egypt, but who knew if he would ever come back? Talleyrand's terms for bargaining with the king were that in the event of a Restoration, the ex-bishop of Autun would like to receive the title of duke and peer of the realm and to be wholly secularized. The king replied that he would grant him the duchy of Périgord if Rome would absolve him of his vows. An empty promise. Actually, Talleyrand was only testing the monarch's reactions as he preferred to see the House of Orléans take the throne. That was a vain wish, however, for the duc d'Orléans would have nothing more to do with politics. So Talleyrand, to enhance his republican credentials, conceived the diabolical scheme of using his Bourbon contacts to advance himself with Barras. The scheme's incredible treachery prompts us to mention that Barras alone recorded it.[3] It called for bringing all the Bourbon princes together in Wesel. "Nothing could be simpler," Talleyrand is supposed to have said, "than taking them into custody and transporting them to France for the Directory to deal with as it sees fit." Could he really have said that? Or was it Barras's underhanded attempt to sow permanent discord between Talleyrand and the Bourbons? According to Barras, Talleyrand is supposed to have added: "A fine haul that will net all the fish at once."

Talleyrand could only have come up with such an idea to ingratiate himself with the *Journal des Hommes Libres* and men like Reubell and Antonelle. It is highly implausible, not because the idea was so monstrous, but because Talleyrand had given up hope for the Directory. Barras probably went out of his way to take revenge in his Memoirs by blackening Talleyrand's reputation. He had his reasons, as we shall see.

Barras rejected the "haul" proposition, but as he was ill in bed at the time, Talleyrand hobbled over to pay him a visit. That was in July, 1799, after his first letter of resignation. He hoped to have as good results from comforting the sick man as once he had had from ministering to the bereft one. He tried to convince the ailing Director that the Jorry incident was aimed not at himself, Talleyrand, but at Barras, his letters to whom still ended with the phrase: "Eternal devotion." Barras, who secretly supported Jorry and knew what lay behind the whole affair, listened scornfully "to soothing, arid cajolery not unlike the purring of an Angora cat." How right he was to call Monsieur d'Autun an Angora cat!

Talleyrand decided to publish a pamphlet in his own defense. One instance does not mean a habit; he himself never boasted about it. Still, the printing cost did not bankrupt him, for once he had finished explaining that a minister, not an individual, was under attack, he charged the printer's bill to the ministry. Hitting back at his assailants, he called them paler revolutionaries than himself.

It was inevitable. Talleyrand, with his cassock and his noble blood, was doomed to go about protesting that he out-Jacobined the Jacobins, and always to be suspect in their camp. Such is the plight of turncoats. Magnifying his role between 1789 and 1791, he built himself up as the father of French liberty. In 1799 that was still highly acceptable; but in 1815, alas, his critics reprinted the pamphlet extolling the Revolution's blessings and his part in shaping them. For a time it made things very rough for him. Governments come and go but pamphlets are permanent. As sociologists say nowadays, the "conjuncture" had changed. Talleyrand would have liked that benign expression.

He was dodging other rebuffs well before 1815, the sharpest of which came from Delacroix, his nondescript predecessor, whom Talleyrand coolly and impudently had accused of fathering the Egyptian operation; but this time the paternity claim was hotly denied. Delacroix replied, easily proving that his attacker had played the decisive role. By persisting, Talleyrand simply cooked his own goose, for the only fact he could cite was a letter from Delacroix granting sick leave to Magallon, the French consul in Alexandria. Based on that evidence alone, he expected people to believe that the two men had conspired to conquer Egypt. On July 28, 1799, Delacroix published a scathing article to set the record straight. Talleyrand kept silent as he should have from the start. Never again would he respond to an attack or defend his position; he would be mute and inscrutable. His critics would rant and rave but not squeeze a word out of him.

Before leaving office, he gave the Republic one last gift: Fouché as minister of police—a far cry from Sottin, and one of the nightmarish personalities of a period which had more than its share of them. Fouché had been a subordinate attaché in the foreign ministry for a number of months. Talleyrand thought he deserved advancement though he scarcely knew him and had no desire to cultivate his friendship. He was acquainted with the man's bloody past. Actually, they had nothing in common; neither Fouché's former association with the Oratorians, his background, personality, manners, or his infamous career had any attraction for Talleyrand. When conversing with Fouché, our hero had the impression of gingerly fingering a filthy rag. Still, Talleyrand would have been the first to admit that a revolution may require dirty rags to wipe up dirty nooks and crannies. Knowing the Directors' fondness for programs aimed at "reanimating" civic spirit, he thought Fouché would be just their man. He was also taking his revenge. To get even with the Jacobins on the *Journal des Hommes Libres* who had treated him so vilely in the Jorry affair, he installed their worst enemy, leaving him behind to do them in: a fellow Jacobin of such impeccable standing that he could exterminate his own brethren and go unquestioned. Talleyrand told that to Sieyès, who now dominated the Directory, an able man, a lawyer, philosopher, and defender of the tenets of 1789 and the Rights of Man. He listened attentively to Talleyrand's parting advice before leaving the rue du Bac: "When Jacobins turn against us boldly and violently, only a Jacobin can combat them vigorously, struggle with them hand-to-hand, and hurl them down. Fouché, then, is your ideal man."

Sieyès agreed. Fouché took up his duties the day Talleyrand left office. The Jacobins rejoiced, foolishly, for the seed of their destruction was planted. What Fouché was like made little difference to Talleyrand. Their professional paths ran parallel, but they never became friends for they hated and distrusted each other—except once when they joined forces to gain a victory, and ended up hating each other more bitterly afterwards.

So Talleyrand left his splendid quarters on the rue du Bac and went to live on the rue Taitbout. The lady from India moved with him.

Conspiracy

What should he do next? Play whist all night, see a few people, dine with them, talk to them; see others to obtain information and to have them spread more or less fallacious tales calculated to hasten the régime's fall? Talleyrand was uneasy. Royalist activity was only creating problems. Another Chouan rising in the west. Jacobin demands for a new Terror posed a threat. Who could be counted on to bury the corpse?

During these few weeks of enforced idleness, Talleyrand conceived a plan for restoring the monarchy in France. Rejecting the Bourbons, he ventured to propose a Hohenzollern for the throne. The Prussian minister's dispatch covering this extravagant scheme is on record. Sainte-Foy acted as Talleyrand's intermediary. Berlin officials were stunned into silence. Such an initiative indicates the panic into which the Directory had plunged the French public. Talleyrand could not have made that unprecedented move without feeling that the country desperately needed a stable government.

On October 9, 1799, Bonaparte finally landed at Fréjus; he reached

Paris on the sixteenth. The crowds cheered him wildly. Never had a defeated general, liable for court-martial, received so exuberant a welcome. As Talleyrand had anticipated, public indifference to both Egypt and the French defeat there matched his own. The people welcomed Bonaparte as a saviour, and so did he. Why hesitate now that the future plainly belonged to Bonaparte?

The general received Talleyrand on the seventeenth, the morning after his arrival, greeting him with open arms despite his "defection" in Turkey.

The "conjuncture" was so favorable to their plans that they were able to plot and agree upon a strategy that same night. Talleyrand was to organize a vast intelligence network. He already had agents in the ministries, embassies, and salons, and in the very heart of the Directory he had Sieyès. Sieyès had one advantage over Talleyrand, a passion for words; he knew every accepted legal and philosophical doctrine plus a few of his own invention. It was said that he still had hopes of having his own Constitution adopted. That made a perfect arrangement, for Bonaparte would clear the way, Sieyès make the plans, and Talleyrand organize the reconstruction. Talleyrand was not a doer; he was a prodder who would appear after the spadework was done. In the maneuvers prefacing the 18th Brumaire, he was everywhere except in the front line. Bonaparte was delighted with the prospect of having Sieyès on his side as he meant to immobilize the government, not strangle it. Talleyrand proposed a compromise solution: "You want power, Sieyès wants a new Constitution. Unite and destroy what exists, for what exists is an obstacle to both of you."

Unfortunately, Sieyès and Bonaparte could not stand each other. And fortunately, Talleyrand was just the person to mediate their differences. He promised Bonaparte to bring Sieyès into line. Though Sieyès had declared that "no more dreadful or fiendish profession exists" than the office of Director, as a genuine republican he was bound to distrust Bonaparte's militarism. Talleyrand, donning his best clerical manner, went a-preaching to the ex-abbé Sieyès, assuring him of Bonaparte's republican sympathies and the modesty which had won him a seat in the Institut de France, not to mention the heart of Madame de Staël. On he crooned about Bonaparte being the one and only man capable of giving France the ideal Republic envisioned in the days of the Constituent Assembly; the Republic those barbarous Jacobins had never wanted and which Sieyès had been holding in reserve for eight years in the form of a superb Constitution inscribed deep in his heart, which now could benefit the nation and honor Sieyès, thanks to General Bonaparte. The abbé Sieyès thus agreed to meet with the general, seeing that he was a republican and a member of the Institut.

Talleyrand had told them the very things each hoped to hear about the other. The two of them were to schedule a meeting, which nearly fell through altogether because of a breach of etiquette on Bonaparte's side. The general sent one of his lieutenants to announce that he awaited Sieyès's visit. Director Sieyès had no intention of playing second fiddle and sent the fellow back where he came from. Once again Talleyrand had to intervene, hobbling back and forth between the Luxembourg and the rue Chantereine to salve blistered vanities and bring the parties together. It was as if he were representing the one true, though not yet official, government. In that spirit he congratulated General Brune for winning a victory against combined English and Russian forces and also published minutes of the meeting between Sieyès and Bonaparte. All of which was unusually presumptuous on his part, yet unquestionably expedient and sensible. Talleyrand always knew where victory, power, and profit lay.

On the domestic front, he enlisted the aid of Roederer, his eminent colleague in the Institut. Together they called at house after house, building the conspiracy which ultimately doomed the Directory. Sometimes he would leave Roederer huddled in the back of the carriage, go in alone, and explore the drawing room, angling for potential recruits. If things looked promising, he might call in Roederer for reinforcement and the two of them would work at enlisting support. If he ran into hostility, he simply headed back out the door and went exploring elsewhere. Sometimes it was not so easy, and Roederer might have to sit for hours in the back of the carriage, chilled to the bone—and perhaps spied on by the police, who kept the ex-minister under surveillance. All this took place after dark. Talleyrand's activities turned him into a night owl. He went to bed at three and rose at midday, a schedule that partly explains the pallor in his inscrutable face. At forty-five, he already looked like a ghost.

One evening, Bonaparte and other confederates had gathered in Talleyrand's rooms on the rue Taitbout to plan certain moves against the government. Talleyrand recorded in his *Memoirs* that about one o'clock in the morning, the sudden clatter of carriages and cavalry in the street made them all jump. Trembling, they stared at each other in silence, believing themselves denounced and about to be arrested. Snuffing the candles, they peered into the street. Heaving sighs of relief, they discovered nothing more than a damaged coach which was carrying receipts from a gambling house and had obtained a police escort. They laughed, but only to dispel the fear.

To Talleyrand fell another vital task, that of obtaining the indispensable cooperation of Barras. In a way, it was easier than converting Sieyès. The logic was very simple: for Barras to declare his support, one merely had to name a suitable figure in response to his question, "How much?" Bonaparte was prepared to pay providing it was handled discreetly; Talleyrand was only too delighted to comply. So he assured the chief Director that Bonaparte intended merely to make some slight reforms in the government, reducing five Directors to a single one—Barras, naturally (whom the "Angora cat" could manipulate with velvet caresses). Barras consented. Once the conspiracy was under way, he received another visit from Talleyrand, accompanied this time by the alarming Fouché and Lucien Bonaparte, president of the Council of Five Hundred. When they spoke of a single president for the new government and did not mention him, Barras saw that he had been duped. Too late. They had him by the neck. It was November 6, 1799, or 15th Brumaire in the civic jargon. Things ran smoothly with Bonaparte around—of necessity, considering he had only fifteen years to astound the world.

On the rue de la Victoire, formerly the rue Chantereine but renamed because of the final syllable (which, rather than meaning "queen" actually derived from *raine,* meaning "frog"), Citizeness Bonaparte was entertaining that evening. Imagine a wife giving a dinner party when her husband is about to overthrow the government! The police suspected nothing, especially as their chief was among the innocent guests, looking on as both spy and accomplice. To provide himself with an alibi, Talleyrand was home playing cards with Roederer, Régnault de Saint-Jean-d'Angély, and Lemaire. The latter made jokes to relieve the tension. Suddenly Arnault, one of the conspirators, appeared. Talleyrand was alarmed. What was happening? No one dared ask because others were present. Regnault flashed a questioning look at Arnault, who shook his head. Talleyrand read the same negative sign. The card game continued; while the ladies laughed at Lemaire's jokes, Talleyrand sidled over to Arnault, who whispered the news to him. Fresh from Josephine's party, he said that the coup planned for the next morning, 16th Brumaire, had been postponed, with Bonaparte's knowledge, until the 18th. The 16th Brumaire was not to be.

The whole business started anew. Josephine gave another dinner party on the 17th (the rules of the game forbade conspiracies during formal dinner parties). Saturday, November 9, 1799, marked the event. A century was drawing to a close, along with much else. History recorded

the *coup d'état* on the 18th Brumaire, Year VIII, according to the prevailing calendar.

Not tragic, it was tragi-comic at best, with a few laughs into the
bargain. The tragic overtones came later in the sublime and horrendous
aftermath that decimated Europe for fifteen years and left an imposing,
terrifying mask upon the face of France, at once exalting, ravaging, and
disfiguring her.

Let us sit next to Talleyrand in the prompter's box, for that was
really his role in the drama. The script was his own, however much the
actors liked to think they had written it. He accompanied Roederer and
General Macdonald to Bonaparte's house, where they all indulged in a
romantic little ceremony, swearing upon a crucifix not to reveal the conspiracy. Talleyrand was then to go to the Luxembourg and force Barras's
resignation. To hasten the matter, Talleyrand had on him a letter of
credit for 3 million francs. The important thing was to get rid of the Directors; since nobody wanted them arrested, they had to be removed tactfully.

Paris was perfectly calm, with troops all about. The Tuileries and
the Luxembourg were ringed by them. The Luxembourg was deserted.
It was lunchtime. In the dining room, where ordinarily the Directors
might have thirty or forty guests at table, Barras sat facing a single one,
Ouvrard, the banker.

Admiral Bruix accompanied Talleyrand. To help Barras make up
his mind, they took him to a window from which he could look out on
the encircled palace and see soldiers and citizens united in their hostility
to the government. The whole army took its orders from the general, the
people's idol. The Directory, including its officials, its lawmakers, clubs,
and press, could be wiped out at a signal from Bonaparte. Barras must
resign therefore, Talleyrand cajoled and entreated, appealing to the Director's sense of public duty. No need, for Barras had got the point; the
language of the street is always highly persuasive. Sitting down at a desk,
he penned a resignation which he handed to Talleyrand, a superb letter
puffed with sentiment and morality, dashed off in five minutes. As Barras
loved attention, this was the time to give it: Talleyrand kissed his hands,
calling him "France's leading patriot." It was the least he could do, for
Barras was soon to slip into obscurity. Beaming, Talleyrand left on the
admiral's arm. In one pocket was the marvelous letter of resignation; in
the other, the letter of credit intended to pay for it. As Barras had signed
without demanding payment, Talleyrand paid himself off instead. It
would compensate for the Director's insolence in furnishing bail to a
scoundrel named Jorry who had insulted the ex-minister in collusion

with the ex-Directory. Talleyrand, arch rogue in the grand manner, referred benignly to this type of enterprise as "an opportunity."

On to Saint-Cloud, then, for the final act. The Assemblies had been transferred there on the theory that they would be easier to control than in Paris, where mobs could suddenly turn violent. Montrond went along as Talleyrand's aide. Too bad that our hero was so reticent about this episode in his *Memoirs;* how delightful if he could have regaled us with the conversation between the "Angora cat" and "Hell's Christchild" as the coach sped them to the climax of all their efforts. Surely they discussed the possible outcome of this turmoil, an outcome that was far from certain. Just in case, Talleyrand had a berlin standing by, awaiting the results of the day.

Is there any reason for calling Talleyrand's involvement in the 18th Brumaire treason? It is best to ask what the nation was then demanding. Did Talleyrand and Bonaparte betray something or someone at that time —apart from Barras and his crew? We stress "at that time" because soon afterwards they did indeed sell freedom short. But on the eve of the 18th Brumaire, honest republicans saw eye to eye: Madame de Staël first and foremost, Benjamin Constant, Garat, Sieyès, Destutt de Tracy,* a truly dedicated and principled patriot, Cabanis,* and a host of others; Talleyrand and they were of one mind. The nation as a whole agreed with them. "You will beg him to return," he had predicted. Even Moreau, a staunch republican who had no use for militarists, wrote to Bonaparte: "Tired of being saddled with lawyers who are destroying the Republic, I offer you my support to save it." His support was the army. Joubert, another republican general, became so disgusted with Jacobin rule that one day he declared publicly: "Whenever you wish, I shall put an end to all this with twenty grenadiers." It can be said that if Bonaparte, Talleyrand, and their cohorts had not carried out the coup of 18th Brumaire, any number of generals would have done so. Bonaparte graphically described the Jacobins in the Directory as "people to piss on." Which didn't discourage them from extolling him as a "son of the Revolution." Poor mother, one might add.

The *coup d'état* was so timely that it operated, as Talleyrand had hoped, without bloodshed or retribution. In fact, it gave rise to a measure of clemency and appeasement by freeing prisoners and halting deportations. The guiding hand was skillful and firm, winning respect before it struck.

* Comte Destutt de Tracy and Georges Cabanis were influential theorists in the field of psychology—Trans.

To conclude these events: On the 19th Brumaire at Saint-Cloud when the Council of Five Hundred declared Bonaparte an outlaw, causing him to falter momentarily, it seemed as if the coup might fail. By sheer resolve, Lucien Bonaparte saved the day. Still, the proud general paled, disconcerted as never before by toga-draped politicians shouting insults that vexed him just as much as the shouters. Yes, the proud general was badly shaken. Standing nearby was Montrond, who saw him about to faint and whispered: "General Bonaparte, this will never do." Over the tumult and shouting suddenly rose an imperious drumroll. Exhorted by Murat and Leclerc, the grenadiers surged into the Orangerie. Out the windows fled the deputies, shouting "Liberty or death!" That same day three Consuls were appointed by decree: Sieyès, Roger Ducos, and Bonaparte. The Consulate was born. Talleyrand sighed with relief; he had wagered and won. Turning to Roederer, Roederer's son, and Montrond, he smiled benevolently: "My friends, it's time for dinner." So ended the prelude to one of history's greatest chapters.

Talleyrand Returns to the Foreign Office,
Letting Bygones Be Bygones

The casual dinner invitation on the 19th Brumaire took him and his friends to Madame Simons's house near Saint-Cloud. She was better known as Mademoiselle Lange, the celebrated actress who is still remembered today in the theater. Talleyrand had witnessed her marriage contract with François de Neufchâteau; afterwards she became the wife of a Belgian banker named Simons, but her heart, it was said, really belonged to Barras. At least until that evening. Barras, we may recall, had been forced to resign on the 17th Brumaire by Talleyrand, who not only deprived him of his job but of 3 million francs as well. And to complete the record, on the 19th he stole his mistress. Our limping hero was utterly victorious over the Directory.

No wonder, then, that Barras did not lean over backwards to speak kindly of Talleyrand in his Memoirs.

On November 14, having lost no time moving into Barras's apartments in the Luxembourg, Bonaparte received Roederer, his old and close friend Volney, and Talleyrand. He thanked them warmly for helping to bring the Consulate into being. Taking Talleyrand aside for a minute, he promised that very shortly he would be back in his old office on the rue du Bac. No surprise to our hero, who had always regarded loyal Reinhardt as simply an interim stand-in. On November 21, 1799,

Reinhardt took his wife and returned to his former embassy in Bern, and Talleyrand to the rue du Bac, his Indian household at heel. For purely political motives, Bonaparte was somewhat reluctant to return him to the ministry so soon. The Jorry affair had shaken public confidence, and the Jacobins were bound to resent Talleyrand's reinstatement. But in that post he was irreplaceable, so having been away from it for four months, he resumed it for seven years—years that carried greater weight than some centuries. Madame de Staël was delighted for him and told him so. He paid a call to thank her personally, shrugging off the whole matter as utterly inconsequential. Actually, he was happy as a lark, for now he could expect to make some real money.

The opposition attacked him as a former aristocrat, a bishop, a lackey of Pitt—familiar epithets that had lost their sting. For the first time, however, the press praised his efforts to bring peace and unity to Europe: "No choice could have been made that is more likely to realize the universal longing for peace. Talleyrand would have made peace long ago if he had had to contend solely with threats from abroad. But how could he prevail against the absurd policies and extravagant ambition of the majority of former Directors, who did all they could to perpetuate war by sowing revolution in every country we were able to enter?" [1]

Here is Bonaparte's opinion of Talleyrand at the time he restored him to office: "He has much of what it takes to be a diplomat: sophistication, first-hand knowledge of the courts of Europe, a shrewd tongue that says just enough and no more, an inscrutable countenance that never changes, and finally a great name." This great name appealed immensely to the young general. When informers came to report Talleyrand's latest piece of knavery, a bribe pocketed, a night in some gambling den, secret dealings, and amorous escapades, Bonaparte would listen, sullen and scowling, then shrug his shoulders and dismiss the taleteller with: "His great ancestry makes up for everything."

Bonaparte was not insensitive to public reactions, at least not at the beginning. He did not appreciate the bitter jibes aimed at his minister because of the colossal fortune Talleyrand had accumulated.* One day, with customary bluntness, he asked our hero how he had managed to

---

* It should be noted that the corruption of civil and military personnel reached epidemic proportions under the Directory, the Consulate, and the Empire. Individuals were rarely censured unless it served a political purpose. Bonaparte might have asked his brother Joseph, among countless others, how he rose from dire poverty along with his whole family, and after only five months as ambassador to Italy, managed to collect a fortune large enough to acquire the princely domain of Mortefontaine in Ermenonville where he entertained lavishly.

amass so much money. Like clockwork, Talleyrand shot back: "Oh, that's simple, I bought bonds on the 17th Brumaire and sold them three days later." Bonaparte had to admire Talleyrand's gift for parrying embarrassing questions with flattery. The remark is also interesting because it aptly conveys the near-miraculous confidence inspired by the new government. Peace and prosperity seemed just around the corner.

A few days after his return to office, Talleyrand conferred with Bonaparte in the Luxembourg. Bourrienne was also present and noted the minister's proposals: "Citizen Consul, you have put me in charge of the ministry of foreign affairs and I shall uphold your trust, but I must tell you that I wish to work exclusively with you. . . ." Not out of vanity, he went on to explain, but because the best interests of the nation called for concerted action. "You must become First Consul, and the First Consul must control whatever directly affects policy, that is, the ministry of the interior and the police for internal matters, my ministry for foreign matters, and finally the two principal organs of executive power, the army and navy."

In those important observations he introduced the title First Consul, which he gave to Bonaparte along with the notion of its jurisdictions. The First Consul was to have absolute authority over the four major ministries; executives would run the subordinate ministries of justice and finance. "It will amuse and occupy them while you, General, firmly in control of the vital reins of government, will be able to pursue your lofty purpose: the regeneration of France." [2]

Talleyrand had a knack for saying exactly the right thing. He had just expressed what Bonaparte intended to do but was reluctant to admit. Now that it was out in the open, the battle was half won.

Talleyrand left and Bonaparte turned to Bourrienne, saying: "You know, Bourrienne, Talleyrand gives sound advice; he is a very sensible man," adding: "He read my mind." No small feat, for Bonaparte was not exactly transparent. It was plain that the young and inexperienced chief of state found it exciting to have at his side such an agile mind, such a sensitive machine for predicting events, for detecting fissures and falsehood, for nosing out success. No one appreciated Talleyrand more than Napoleon Bonaparte, and this esteem on the part of an extraordinary genius is significant. After the 18th Brumaire they continued on the best of terms, the Turkish incident having disrupted that pattern only momentarily. It should be said that at first the Consulate did not boast a very brilliant court: "people of no account," according to Stendhal. It bothered Bonaparte, for this soldier, a child of the Revolution, much preferred the language and manners of the aristocracy. There was only one

Talleyrand in his retinue, whom he admired even when his "republican sense of virtue" balked at his minister's cheerful immorality.

The meeting left him under Talleyrand's spell. What better way was there to win friends abroad than with the beguiling tongue to which he, the invincible conqueror, had succumbed?

Talleyrand was aware of his power. He hoped to augment it and eventually to become indispensable. During the Consulate, Bonaparte never dispelled that illusion. A single frown from Bonaparte would have been sufficient warning. One can only surmise that the general must have been hopelessly entranced by Talleyrand's exquisite and unfailingly tactful flattery. Let no one imagine this was crude flunkeyism; it was, on the contrary, honest adulation aimed at a specific objective. His letters, full of respect and affectionate devotion, do not hint of falsity. Talleyrand, always in harmony with the most profound—and sometimes unconscious—national aspirations, welcomed Bonaparte, as did France, with love and admiration.

On May 22, 1800, having just recovered from some illness, he wrote to his idol while the general was crossing the Alps: "Now that I grow better and stronger each day, I feel ready to come join you if you think it advisable; I confess that the longer you are away, the greater is my desire —nay, even need—to be with you." [3]

Undoubtedly other ministers have been as devoted as he to their supreme commanders, but how many had the ability to express that devotion, that self-surrender not just to a cause but to the person embodying that cause?

After his victory at Marengo, Bonaparte received this salute, a superb demonstration of the art of flattery: "General, I have just come from the Tuileries. The audience of ambassadors could not have been more brilliant. I cannot attempt to describe the public acclaim, the admiration from abroad, and my own reactions to your letter to the Consuls. What a beginning and what a finale! Will posterity ever believe the wonders of that campaign? Under what happy auspices we await your return! There is some magic at the source of every empire; for us, the magic is reality" (June 21, 1800).

Who could resist such blandishments? Or the subtle, prophetic enchantment of the word "empire," like a flash of lightning in the hour of triumph, evoking the fabled past and linking it to the present. Talleyrand had just laid the cornerstone of an edifice which, in fact, had an element of magic: Napoleon's Empire. And how discreetly he abstained from personal sentiments in this letter celebrating a victory and the nation's glory.

At another time, when he was again in need of a rest and planned to take the waters at Bourbon-l'Archambault, Talleyrand mourned the prospect of separation from his idol. The romance was still on. In a letter altogether different from the preceding one, he confined himself to saying only what one might properly say to a chief (who had little use for tenderness). The prestige of his years and of his great name also gave him a certain leeway. In any event, it is a curious letter and throws some light on the subsequently unpredictable behavior of Napoleon Bonaparte and his minister.

General,

I depart with the single but painful regret of leaving you.

My attachment, my conviction that devoting my life to your destiny and to the great aspirations that fire you may help in some way to achieve them, have made me concerned about my health for the first time. But for that personal conviction, I should not hope to derive any benefit from the trip you permit me to take.

I leave you ailing also, possessed as always by that noble passion that denies rest to the body or relaxation to the mind. I fear that the human organism is not adapted to the pressures of that inexhaustible and truly sublime energy with which nature has endowed you.

When what you are thinking, what you are saying, and everything I see you doing becomes no more than a spectacle, then I shall know the utter deprivation that my prospective absence holds in store.

Allow me to repeat that I love you, that this parting grieves me, that I cannot wait to return to you, and that my devotion shall end only with my life.[4]

Another short letter giving his impressions of certain affairs concludes with the image of a soul pining for its mate: "I shall probably write some very poor stuff, but it is not my fault; I am not myself apart from you." A few sentences later, he ends with a compliment not even a saint could resist: "I do not like your library at all, you spend too much time there, I think it is damp; the ground floor is not for you, you were made for the heights."

Recalling Sully's words to Henri IV, Talleyrand served them up to Bonaparte: "Since binding myself to your destiny, I am yours in life as in death."

Needless to say, our hero's epistolary effusions convey the frills and flourish of a bygone era; but much more besides. Clearly, the intent is to dominate the general's thoughts, to be an obsessive, indispensable presence. This attempt to become something like Bonaparte's double carried him far afield. The courtship turned into servility. As the idol grew and lost touch with him, Talleyrand became increasingly ingratiating. He wrote this astounding letter on July 29, 1804, when "Napoleon was already showing beneath Bonaparte":

> Certainly I shall always be content with whatever befalls me as a result of Your Majesty's good will; yet I admit to a degree of jealousy, which Your Majesty will pardon, for expecting no other rewards than his, for serving him alone, and for not wishing his decisions concerning me to be expressed through mere intervention. Your Majesty knows, and I repeat it gladly, that as I am wearied and oppressed by political systems which for ten years have visited agony and grief on the French nation, any position I may hold in the institutions he has founded depends entirely on him. Therefore I ought not and cannot desire to enter any institution unless placed there by His Majesty and by him alone.

Why? He had just been elected to the Senate but did not relish the honor because it did not come from the Supreme One, directly from him. Yet according to reliable sources, he was still accepting "gifts" from clients of the Foreign Office which certainly did not emanate from the Supreme One. It was all a matter of custom, and custom decreed that the chief should close his eyes to corruption among his underlings.

Coupled with Talleyrand's exquisitely deferential and courtly manners was a streak of insolence that would have ruined the career of any other public servant. This is how he employed it with the First Consul.

When the Treaty of Amiens was signed, an important event ending the war with England and giving France the peace she expected from her military hero, Talleyrand indulged in an incredible display of impertinence. Bonaparte nervously and peevishly awaited the courier who was to bring him the parchment peace treaty. Talleyrand had already received it and was keeping it in his portfolio. The Council of Ministers began; Talleyrand let it run on despite the First Consul's restlessness. When all the routine matters were covered, Talleyrand announced with utter serenity: "I have good news for you. The treaty is signed; here it is." Bonaparte leaped up: "Why didn't you say so immediately?" The imperturbable minister replied: "Because you wouldn't have listened to anything after that. When you are happy, no one can come near you." [5]

His readiness to play such a trick, to retort that way and in turn receive something resembling a growl of thanks, amazed everyone. His impertinence went even further on occasion and was riskier, for it happened during the Empire when the idol had become a god. One summer day the Council of State met at Saint-Cloud. Everyone was waiting for Talleyrand to arrive. Pacing up and down in outraged impatience, the emperor grabbed a fistful of cherries and bit into them savagely. He was seething; it made him furious to waste time. Talleyrand arrived at last. Napoleon upbraided him: "You have kept me waiting, sir." Not deigning to answer, a vague smile on his lips, the latecomer walked over to the bowl of cherries and popped one into his mouth: "Sire, Your Majesty has the most delectable cherries in the Empire." Napoleon did not move a muscle. The meeting opened in frozen silence. Such was the extraordinary behavior of those two men. Bonaparte had bouts of incredible indulgence, patience, wrath, and forgiveness; his blistering tirades could give way to solemn vows of renewed trust, even affection. All the while Talleyrand, sure of himself and of his privileged status—irrational as it was and punctuated by stormy scenes—went his own way, said Amen, and never changed.

He enveloped Bonaparte. With the elegance, the grace, the refinements of another world, he habituated him to idolatry. By urging him always upward, he prepared his ultimate fall. Talleyrand never lost his love for Napoleon. Even during the Restoration, he noted in his *Memoirs:* "I loved Napoleon; I had even become personally attached to him despite his faults; at the start of his career I had felt drawn to him by the irresistible magnetism exerted by all great geniuses; I was truly grateful for his many kindnesses. Why conceal it? I had basked in his glory and in the rays it cast upon all those who furthered his noble endeavor."

People claim that Talleyrand repudiated everyone and everything, yet this disproves it. At the end of his life, he came round to feeling as he had long before: "I loved Napoleon." Loved him in the pursuit of their noble, common endeavor, the resurrection of France. Loved him in the beginning, one should add, for later on it was a different story.

Almost as a gift marking his return to the Foreign Office, Talleyrand had an opportunity to perform an act of clemency. Learning that the impetuous Jorry, together with thirty-seven impetuous fellows like him, had been arrested and was being held for deportation to French Guiana, Talleyrand at once interceded with the minister of police and obtained the young man's release. It was a charitable act. Talleyrand, as we know, did not hate or bear grudges; he was a stranger to those impulses. The proper thing to do, he believed, was to wipe the whole stupid affair out of his life, in which it had occupied thus far a minimum of space and time. He wrote this admirable letter in Jorry's behalf:

> I was grieved, Citizen Minister, to see Jorry's name on the list of persons condemned to exile. Jorry is a very young man whose errors deserve more indulgence than severity. He serves the Republic and is a soldier in the Army of Italy; perhaps enemy blows shall have punished him even before the law can exact its penalty; perhaps wounds or a

hero's death already honor his name. I must add that as Jorry, to my knowledge, has never given offense to anyone save myself, I feel it my duty to draw your attention to this matter; and because I desire strongly that the world forget my offense as I myself have forgotten it, I ask the personal favor that my petition be submitted forthwith to the Consuls of the Republic.[6]

So Talleyrand had no feelings and couldn't write! Yet in this instance, to all appearances, he went out of his way to forgive an injury, acting in a touching spirit of charity that suggests the enduring influence of his exposure to the priesthood.

Unable to resist blackening a man's every motive once they decide that his soul is tainted, some critics interpret Talleyrand's generous act as purely tactical. Because proscription had become a highly unpopular issue, they say, Talleyrand took this opportunity to alienate the minister of police who had imposed the sentence. There is no evidence to support that. In any event, his tactics proved impeccable, for not only did he save Jorry but everyone else on the list as well. Thanks to the broad impact of his letter, the proscription law was repealed. Just for pleasure, let us reread [in French] that admirable sentence which no one ever quotes and which might have come from Fénelon's pen: "Ayant le plus grand désir de voir mon offense oubliée de toute la terre comme elle l'est de moi." It may surprise some to learn that a few worthy creatures inhabit this populous world of ours.

In late December, 1799, an envoy from Louis XVIII arrived in Paris to sound out Bonaparte on what can only be called "the Bourbon illusions." They truly believed he would restore their throne, that one day Louis XVIII would re-enter and Bonaparte exit with a grand blue ribbon around his neck and an impressive title. After shipping him off somewhere, the monarchy could resume its cozy paternalistic role. Talleyrand presented the king's envoy Baron Hyde de Neuville to Consul Bonaparte. The meeting produced absolutely nothing. Highly skeptical, Talleyrand escorted Hyde de Neuville and his companion Andigné on their return home. Here he was, on the other side of the fence from those two men; yet they spoke the same language, they sat, bowed, opened and closed doors in a particular manner; it brought back memories. They talked, and what Talleyrand had to say astounded them. Of the First Consul, he observed: "If he gets through the first year, he will go far." When they asked if Bonaparte would be able to maintain his régime, Talleyrand told them Bonaparte *was* the régime, which existed only through him; that in itself was a problem. He was right. They also spoke of the royal princes. Talleyrand had not forgotten Monsieur and recalled the *"belle époque"* they had both known; he avowed that the crippled foot had changed his life completely, forcing him into the priesthood whereas he would have chosen an army career. Comparing his situation to what it could have been if he had followed his inclinations, he said slyly: "Who knows? I might have ended up an émigré like yourselves, or, like yourselves, the Bourbon envoy." [7]

Monsieur, to whom Talleyrand still felt friendly, sent La Tour du Pin to confer with the Consulate in 1800. This is what the Bourbons had in mind for Talleyrand if he could persuade the First Consul to step down in favor of Louis XVIII. Bonaparte would be given the rank of *connétable*. "But what would you do for Monsieur de Talleyrand?" La Tour du Pin had asked the future Charles X. "Of course I shall be glad to look after him . . . if we return to France. Truthfully, he cannot stay there, but I warrant him safe-conduct to go live in whatever foreign country he chooses." [8] Very kind! For restoring the monarchy they would spare his life and turn him at once into an exile. Their political ignorance bordered on fantasy.

Talleyrand Settles Down Comfortably with the New Régime

Nothing escaped the Eagle's sharp eyes. Bonaparte remembered vividly the impact of Talleyrand's ball on January 3, 1798. A great name is a great asset, and useful too. Bonaparte used Talleyrand like a billboard to welcome aristocracy. The First Consul wanted the support of nobles seeking repatriation. He needed them just as he needed popular favor. For his own part, Talleyrand knew that France missed her king. Elections confirmed that. Bonaparte also knew it. His comment concerning the 18th Brumaire and its aftermath, "I exorcised the dreadful spirit of innovation roaming the globe," acknowledged that his *coup d'état* was meant to end, not to perpetuate, the Revolution. He said so plainly on December 15, 1799, in proclaiming the new Constitution: "Citizens, the Revolution is made fast to the principles with which it began; it is ended." [1]

No one seriously doubted it. Talleyrand had given the ball to honor Josephine. Restoring a society of rank required first of all a nobility. "It is the one true pillar of the monarchy," Napoleon later asserted, "its regulator, its lever, its line of defense; without it the state is a rudderless ship, a drifting balloon."

Before creating a new nobility, he thought it best to use the old one, and Talleyrand was there to do recruiting. One of our hero's many assignments was to bring the old and new societies face to face at the dinner table or in the ballroom, and, hopefully, with their cooperation, in the bedroom.

Talleyrand bought himself a splendid villa in Neuilly, where he entertained for the first time on February 25, 1800. Bonaparte, who was bored by parties and attended them only for the sake of appearances, came to this one, which turned out to be a full-scale political operation. In addition to government officials, the guests included the first aristocrats willing to be seen with Bonaparte: the chevalier de Coigny, one of Louis XVI's intimates; the comte de Ségur, son of the marshal and ambassador to Russia; the duc de La Rochefoucauld-Liancourt, Louis XVI's master of the robes; Crillon, a deputy of the nobility; and Bernier, leader of the Vendée faction and a confirmed rebel. To the handful of proscripts from the 18th Fructidor, Bonaparte announced that their friends had been amnestied and would return shortly from exile in French Guiana. A number of the ladies bore illustrious names: Mesdames de Vergennes, de Castellane, d'Aiguillon, de Lameth, de Noailles, de Caumont, de Custine—even Madame de Flahaut, who eyed the lady from India with intense interest. A number of the other women were soon to open salons, breeding grounds of public opinion, where Talleyrand would come and go, setting the tone, dispensing and gathering information. What chief of state could boast such a prestigious director of propaganda? Only the most prestigious chief of state, Napoleon Bonaparte. The two reinforced each other.

A year later, to celebrate the peace with Austria signed at Lunéville (February 9, 1801) confirming France's new Rhenish frontier—Belgium had already been won along with the Palatinate and Aix-la-Chapelle— Talleyrand threw open his doors to all the factions. He was radiant; at last there was to be peace in Europe. And at home, too. The prosperous times he had yearned for ever since he entered politics were about to return. Science and the arts would bloom, luxuries abound. Once again Paris would be the heart of civilization, and Talleyrand its steward. He would be host not just to generals and ambassadors but also to learning and beauty from all over the world. People would flock there to display their creativity and wealth. That, thought Talleyrand, was the Consulate's gift to France, not the breathtaking victories but the peaceful spread of culture among all peoples.

He accomplished an undreamed-of feat for those times by entertaining the first two Bourbons to reappear in France, the duke and duchess of Tuscany, whose duchy Bonaparte had transformed into the kingdom of Etruria, a designation quite as "antique" as the chairs and tables of the 1800's. Talleyrand gave a splendid reception for the royal pair, turning his house into a model of the square in front of the Palazzo Vecchio in Florence to remind his guests of their homeland. Two famous prima donnas, Crescentini and Grassini, idols of the hour whom Bonaparte had brought back from Italy (along with other artistic treasures), sang in their native tongue. The king of Etruria opened the ball with General Leclerc's pretty wife Pauline, Bonaparte's sister. To many newcomers, the lavish supper revealed a whole world of enticements. Talleyrand taught the pleasures of life to a rising generation of military and administrative élites, a lesson which the Directors had never been able to grasp. In doing so, he enhanced Bonaparte's prestige and popularity.

Bonaparte did not overlook debts of this sort. In return, he had the names of Talleyrand and his brothers Archambaud and Boson stricken from the émigré lists and all their property returned to them. The two brothers were very handsome—and brainless, especially Archambaud, the elder, said to be "aussi bête que beau" and dubbed "Archi-beau archi-bête." To both of them Talleyrand was the soul of patience, kindness, and forgiveness. No sooner had they reached Paris than their blundering incompetence aroused Bonaparte's wrath. They made scandalous public confessions, which, luckily, no one took seriously. Two years earlier the Talleyrand family might have been hopelessly dishonored as English spies. For Archambaud and Boson were just that. On the eve of their repatriation, they were still waiting to collect from London's Foreign Office the current and back pay to which they were entitled as English soldiers. Their brother, the Consulate's minister of foreign relations, sent them a letter of introduction to Addington, his friend and English counterpart. Thanks to that, Archambaud and Boson collected their guineas, which they proceeded to jingle loudly the moment they set foot in France. Very poor judgment. Informed about this, Bonaparte ordered the two idiots to leave Paris and live elsewhere. Boson's supreme folly was to boast publicly of having had his retirement pay increased from 500 guineas to 900 "as a favor from Mr. Pitt."

Talleyrand kept silent about the whole ridiculous affair, but it returned unannounced to haunt him. As is well known, Bonaparte's brothers and sisters caused him serious embarrassments; still, he shielded them. Though Talleyrand helped his brothers repeatedly, he refused to do so when their monumental tactlessness banished them from the capital. The First Consul held that against him: "What can you expect from a man who hasn't a word to offer in defense of his family?" In this case, Talleyrand's silence appears to do him credit; Bonaparte would not forgive it. Such was the breach between two worlds, two species.

To put to rest the fear in certain quarters that his proposed Constitution "written with bayonets" would stifle civil liberties, the Consul, escorted by Talleyrand, paid a visit to Madame Helvétius in Auteuil. The philosopher's widow had not changed her ideas or her friends, who were the very "ideologists" Bonaparte detested, principally Madame de Staël. When the Consul observed pointedly to the old lady that her garden was rather small, she countered deftly: "General, you have no idea how much pleasure the tiniest patch of earth can give." By staying longer he might have learned something about respect for liberty, for the human rights, for the sovereignty of other nations.

Just across from the "philosophic" widow lived the marquise de Boufflers, who offered her house and grounds to Talleyrand for a picnic in the general's honor. Montrond arranged everything, including a hunt in the park. The day before the picnic he bought up thousands of half-tame rabbits from the Paris market and released them on the grounds that night. "The Consul arrived the next day with a glittering retinue. After lunch, they mounted up and rode into the park. Hearing horses and riders, and not having seen a single carrot or cabbage leaf all night, the rabbits ran out hoping to be fed. Without hesitating, Bonaparte solemnly opened fire, bringing down a dozen of the wretched creatures. Someone finally burst out laughing, followed by the entire party except the Consul, who bit his lip. Not expecting rabbits from the market place to act like pets, and anxious to curry favor, Talleyrand patched things up as best he could. . . ." [2]

Now that he was back in the government, Talleyrand had to deal with Fouché. On the surface their relationship was glacially polite; underneath, it was distinctly hostile. Fouché had been so steeped in the Terror that he was never able to wipe the blood of 1793 off his hands. Talleyrand preferred to consign all that to the past and forget about it. He put it thus: "Bonaparte may well be the Revolution's heir, but never its perpetuator."

He and Fouché also disagreed on the question of a divorce between Bonaparte and Josephine. Fouché was opposed; Talleyrand favored it, backed by the Consul's mother and brothers. How did they manage to agree for once? Because Monsieur d'Autun had quietly lectured them on the necessity for a son to inherit Bonaparte's power. France must have a monarchy, Talleyrand felt, and the only valid monarchy was a hereditary one. With the Bourbons disqualified, he was seriously considering what he called "the fourth dynasty." After the Merovingians, the Carolingians, and the Capetians would come the "Napoleonides"—our minister on the rue du Bac had a strong sense of continuity. As Josephine had borne Bonaparte no children, she threatened to interfere with the plans of Talleyrand as well as the Consul's brothers. Fouché had murdered so many partisans of hereditary monarchy, and the monarch along with them, that he felt they ought to wait at least seven years before investing a new one.

Talleyrand got little cooperation from Bonaparte's relatives. Lucien, the unruly brother whom Talleyrand dubbed "the big bully," issued a pamphlet entitled *Parallèle entre César, Cromwell, Monk et Bonaparte* with disastrous effects on our hero's designs. In the clumsiest terms, the author declared it imperative to establish hereditary power in the Bonaparte family, an announcement so ill-timed that if republicans had not still been cursing the corrupt Directory, they might have violently rejected the whole plan. Talleyrand approached this delicate matter quite differently; as combined priest and midwife, he brought the principle of heredity safely into the world. First he gained support for the notion that a society must not risk losing a great man, but that if he were to die, his son must carry on. Public acceptance of this principle subsequently created the demand for hereditary rule. When "the big bully" nearly ruined everything, his irate brother packed him off to the French embassy in Madrid. Poor Spain never had reason to bless the Bonapartes.

Josephine's anxiety concerned her marriage, not politics. She sensed the trouble ahead, and wrote: "I am sure Talleyrand has given Bonaparte a new Constitution stipulating hereditary government. Lucien is working for him in this affair, and Roederer for Lucien, but who Talleyrand works for is anybody's guess as one never knows what to expect of him."

He was working to create a solid and enduring government for France. Also, to provide Bonaparte with the magic words expressing his innermost desires, he told him: "You have no alternative but to stabilize the government, to dispel apprehension about the future, to give those who serve you peace of mind. . . . There is only one way: by designating your successor. Who can deny you the right to do this?" At this point the question of heredity was not raised, for it would have shocked certain sectors remaining to be wooed, notably Madame de Staël and her set. Time was working for this indefatigable idler; time, like an incubator, ripened his projects.

Shortly after Marengo, and despite the fine letter quoted earlier, Talleyrand's favor diminished somewhat. While Bonaparte was off in pursuit of glory, Talleyrand and Fouché declared a truce long enough to discuss certain matters. For instance: Suppose (God forbid!) Bonaparte did not return from Italy; suppose a stray bullet or cannonball were to defy all the rules of the game and kill a general instead of a foot soldier? Suppose he tumbled off some alpine cliff? Anyway, wasn't Paris as dangerous as the battlefield after that explosion on the rue Saint-Nicaise? What would happen if . . . ? And what would become of them in turn? Apparently they made certain arrangements to protect their current and future interests in the régime. Bonaparte learned about this on his return. From whom? From both of them, probably, one denouncing the other. Their confederate, the senator Clément de Ris, was arrested and simply vanished (the work of Citizen Fouché, no doubt). This story caused as much commotion as the explosion on the rue Saint-Nicaise and became known as "the shady affair." Balzac adopted it as the title of his novel *Une Ténébreuse Affaire.* Talleyrand kept his post, as did Fouché. Each in his own way was indispensable for keeping the cauldron boiling. But Bonaparte dressed them down severely for their intrigues.

The romance was losing its novelty or, if you wish, its warmth.

To rekindle it, Talleyrand decided to give a ball at the rue du Bac on July 14. It was another stunning performance. Madame de Staël implored her friend the bishop to invite her; he, in the name of that friendship, implored her to stay home. Knowing what Bonaparte thought of her and how she irritated him, he preferred to avoid a potentially disagreeable and even indecorous scene. With Bonaparte, it was best to expect the worst. She did not come, and the ball was a great success. The hero of Marengo had the cream of Paris society at his feet.

As Fouché was getting in the way, Talleyrand sought to discredit him. The incident on the rue Saint-Nicaise furnished the pretext. On December 24, 1800, Bonaparte miraculously escaped unharmed from an explosion that killed twenty-two persons and wounded fifty-six others. Talleyrand blamed the violence on Fouché's Jacobin friends; Fouché called it a royalist plot. Talleyrand was wrong. His aim was simply to demonstrate that the minister of police was incompetent to protect the First Consul's life. On the other hand, he was quite competent at trumping up conspiracies to gain credit for exposing them, and at arresting alleged criminals while would-be assassins of the nation's hero went scot free. Though he failed to disgrace Fouché, Talleyrand perfected a new technique in the repressive process, the cleverness of which was matched only by its illegality.

Instead of submitting a repressive law to the Tribunate, where it would be certain to arouse the opposition of "ideologist" deputies, he sent it to the Senate where the Consul was god, and it passed without a murmur. Talleyrand's only comment was: "Why have a Senate if you don't use it?" He used it so effectively that the procedure, known as *senatus consultum,* became a regular practice, permitting every conceivable abuse of power beneath the façade of legality. The Republic was dying. One hundred and thirty persons were deported without even a hearing.

As for Fouché, Talleyrand caught him in a compromising position and was able to get rid of him. A *senatus consultum* on August 4, 1802, put its stamp on the insertion of a heredity clause in the Constitution. Fouché criticized it. Talleyrand informed "the family"; they in turn delegated "the big bully" to discuss it with the First Consul, who ordered Fouché's dismissal. As compensation, he was made a senator. A few days later, he and Talleyrand met at the Vaudeville. They and the rest of society were amused by *Mme. Angot in the Sultan's Harem,* the harem Talleyrand never got to see in Constantinople.

In June, 1802, our hero received an unexpected visit from Calonne. Where had the brilliant Calonne been hiding? Did he perhaps relate the astounding saga of his tenure in the ministry of finance when he was squandering the monarchy's last funds? In any event, there he was, all powdered and dapper as if fresh from a tour of his estates. He brought with him yet another "plan." By now he had had plenty of time to rectify the one he used to ruin Louis XVI. Boldly, he announced his readiness to manage the Consulate's finances. Rumors told of his imminent appointment as minister. Fouché thought this was his chance to disgrace Talleyrand. Not that fast. A scornful critique of Calonne's proposals appeared in *Le Moniteur*. At whose behest? Bonaparte and Talleyrand both were probably behind it. Calonne was ruined. An order for his deportation followed. Bidding him good-bye most cheerfully, Talleyrand jibed: "Come now, Calonne, are you that eager to retire?" As ghosts go, this one was rather harmless and, for Talleyrand, no more than a false alarm.

The next one was not false. Again, it just missed its mark, and though not fatal, managed to leave an ugly scar. We may as well call the incident the "Affair of the Leaks" as a number of other sources have already done.

Letters and highly confidential documents were disappearing regularly from the rue du Bac. A series of inquiries and investigations led straight to the minister's door—and stopped there. Such a serious matter called for obtaining the First Consul's authorization to bypass that door. Someone suggested setting a trap: tell Talleyrand—and only Talleyrand—a secret, but make him think the same secret has been told to others. In the event of a leak, there would be only one possible culprit. At the last moment, Bonaparte rejected the scheme. Was he afraid of the truth? He ordered closer security measures but refused to take the crucial step for some unknown reason. . . . So nothing came to light. The romance flickered again, then brightened when Talleyrand produced a new delight for his master, who promptly forgot everything else. This occurred following the death in Santo Domingo of General Leclerc, Pauline Bonaparte's husband. The event caused no great emotion, merely creating a very attractive young widow. Still, the family went into mourning. Talleyrand instructed the entire diplomatic corps to wear black and pay condolences to the First Consul as if he were a reigning monarch. The effect of this was so magical, so touching to Bonaparte—it touched his most sensitive spot: his pride—that he embraced his minister. Our hero must have employed great finesse to talk someone like the emperor's ambassador into mourning a nobody named Leclerc, risen through the ranks of an army of sans-culottes. Talleyrand described his plan to someone, who warned him that he would have difficulty carrying it out. With customary insolence, he retorted: "The only difficulty will be preventing them from hiring mourners." After his expert handling of this matter, not a word was said about the leaks. He accompanied Bonaparte on a tour of Belgium. For the Consul, it was like having a first-hand guide to the courts and chancelleries of the Ancien Régime. Of course, Bonaparte knew many things his minister did not know: how to make war, for instance. Talleyrand, however, knew how to avoid it. He also knew the interests, vanities, traditions, and vulnerabilities of each government. For both of them, the experience was enjoyable and profitable.

On his return, Bonaparte restored to Talleyrand's cousin, the baron de Périgord, his confiscated estates. Seeing that he was in high favor, Talleyrand interceded on behalf of a young secretary in the Roman legation, attached to his ministry and serving the rising papal legate Fesch, Bonaparte's uncle, lately an army contractor. This irrepressible youth apparently had insulted Uncle Fesch in a number of sneering letters that were intercepted and shown to his nephew, the First Consul, who was outraged that anyone dared to scorn his illustrious Corsican relative. He ordered the man arrested. Vicomte René de Chateaubriand was writing those letters, which must have carried quite a sting, for Talleyrand had to intervene several times to win his pardon. Chateaubriand overlooked the favor and used the same pen later on to attack his benefactor viciously.

Chateaubriand's scathing assertion: "When he is not intriguing, M. de Talleyrand is engaged in traffic of some sort," undoubtedly reflects the fact that Chateaubriand knew nothing about traffic and was involved solely in intrigue, which, to his bitter grief, never added a penny to his fortune. In fact, Talleyrand did not seek out intrigue; it came to him. Some people exert that type of attraction.

It must have been operating when he attended a dinner party given by the duchesse de Luynes and found himself seated next to the abbé de Montesquiou, one of Louis XVIII's emissaries. The abbé wanted information. Was Bonaparte still opposed to a Bourbon Restoration? What were his views? Their hostess ushered them into a sitting room after dinner where they could talk freely. The lady from India wanted to join them; a royalist at heart, if she could not persuade Talleyrand to marry her, she was determined at least to make him wed the Bourbon cause. A good meal often lifted our hero's spirits and made him relatively talkative. He scoffed at the Bourbons's naïveté, their ignorance of reality, their lack of political judgment. In the end, he left Montesquiou with a ray of hope: the Bourbons must be patient; all was not lost, but nothing was definite. He counseled the abbé to give careful thought to who should represent the princes in future dealings with Bonaparte. Montesquiou saw at once that Talleyrand would do the mediating. Hope sprang into his heart: "Are we better off now than we were?" he queried. "For the future, yes; for the present, no," Talleyrand replied. "Bonaparte does not intend to abandon his position. [That was true.] He is not seeking to secure it." That part was false, and no one knew it better than Talleyrand, who had pressed the struggle for a hereditary monarchy.

Then why dangle pale and futile hopes in front of Louis XVIII's envoy? Because one has to plan ahead, to create choices for the future. It is never politic to discourage a loser, even if he doesn't appear to have one chance in a thousand. While there is breath in him, he can survive and even triumph. Time changes the color of a man's soul; why not the color of a flag as well?

Perhaps as a result of those whispered discussions, he disclosed to Lucchesini the plan he and Bonaparte had developed to win royalist support for the First Consul and his dynasty. They decided to approach Louis XVIII, who was living in utter poverty in Poland, and press him to renounce his own and his family's claims to the French throne. In return, he would receive a generous allowance and live handsomely in some distant corner of Europe. Warsaw was not distant enough; they toyed with the idea of Moscow, or even St. Helena, reputed to be a paradise for overthrown monarchs. Louis XVIII's reply settled the matter plainly: "I do not know what God has in store for me and my people, but I do know the duties he has imposed on me. As a Christian, I shall do my duty to the end; as a true son of St. Louis, and in his image, I shall command respect though I be in chains; as heir to Francis I, I want always to be able to say as he did: 'All is lost save honor.'"

Was Talleyrand amazed to discover an incorruptible man? No, nothing ever amazed him.

Talleyrand Nobly Executes Ignoble Policies

Talleyrand was concerned only for peace. He expected it from Bonaparte in view of the latter's professed ideal: "True primacy is to be master of one's own house and never to succumb to the ridiculous pretension of being master of another's." At first, Bonaparte gave him satisfactory assurances and, on December 25, 1799, promised there would be peace. On the twenty-sixth, he composed a superb letter to the English government which Talleyrand transmitted to his friend Lord Grenville, who in turn handed it to Prime Minister Pitt, also a friend of Talleyrand. And once again his hopes were dashed when Pitt rejected the proposals outright. Staggered, Talleyrand complained: "One would think that France had asked England to restore the Stuarts and give up India."

Austria ignored the peace offers and paid dearly, crushed at Marengo on June 24, 1800. Bonaparte imposed a harsh treaty, allowing her no voice in its terms. Neither Talleyrand nor anyone else was consulted. Madame Grand declared: "The First Consul did it all, wrote it all." That was the truth. Bonaparte treated his ministers the way they had been treated by the Directors. When Cobenzl, the Austrian minister, came to Paris for peace negotiations, Bonaparte at once made it clear that there would be no discussion. Talleyrand presented Cobenzl to the First Consul in one of the Tuileries drawing rooms. Bonaparte sat at a desk on which the only lighted lamp stood. There was no other chair in the room. As they entered, the Consul rose and sat down again abruptly without a word. They remained standing, the Austrian in front, Talleyrand behind. The First Consul rummaged through his papers, mumbling something about the terms of the treaty to be signed at Lunéville on February 9, 1801. Then he signaled that the interview was at an end. Austria signed.

Talleyrand would not have acted that way. He would have negotiated with Austria and signed a pact leading to a permanent alliance. The Treaty of Lunéville was a *diktat* inviting the Austrians to make a war of attrition, all the more as England was a ready ally hostile to France. Talleyrand would have found means to subvert such an alliance. He was deeply disturbed by the presence of French troops in Italy and

Germany, by the political reorganization of those countries dictated by France and backed up by her army. He confided to a friend: "I know what the First Consul ought to do, what his interests demand, as well as the interests of France and of Europe. He has two alternatives: the federal system which leaves each conquered ruler master of his own land under conditions favorable to the conqueror, just as today the First Consul could restore the king of Sardinia, the grand duke of Tuscany, etc. . . . On the other hand, what if he chooses to incorporate and unite? Then he faces an endless task." Bonaparte, as we know, chose the second path: annexation, military occupation, constant warfare, in short, the classic pattern of conquest with its inevitable consequences.

Having known all along what was right, during the next few years Talleyrand poured his best efforts into promoting the wrong things. He was under the spell as well as the tyranny of Bonaparte. In Berlin, Sandoz-Rollin observed: "The First Consul handles political matters the same way he handles military ones. Everything must yield to his will in the end. . . . Monsieur Talleyrand, who had been consulted at first on the question of appeasement [of Germany], has been replaced by Roederer and Regnaud. This minister has been called upon only for his signature, and that was in connection with his own appointment."

Madame de Cazenove d'Arlens noted in her Diary in 1803: "M. de Talleyrand has no influence over the First Consul. He needs infinite pliancy and tact to withstand the violent temper of his chief." She added: "M. de Périgord is exposed to crude and savage outbursts from the little Corsican." That, it seems, is what he had to put up with. And Talleyrand put up with it because it kept his position. An agent of the notorious comte d'Antraigues described the minister thus: "He perceives instantly, understands clearly, reasons boldly, but is fainthearted, for he so loves his position that the thought of causing offense renders him nearly frantic. . . ." Unfortunately, there is a good deal of sad truth in that observation: Talleyrand was behaving most obsequiously.

On December 14, 1799, while the treaty with Austria was being drafted, George Washington died. Talleyrand delivered a moving tribute to the man who had given his countrymen liberty, peace, prosperity, and enduring institutions. He spoke with authority, having come to appreciate America's genuine concern for democracy during his travels there. Forgetting his usual coldness, his voice rang out in praise of the man and his "nation, which one day will become a great nation, and which today is the wisest, most contented nation on earth." In describing Washington as "a man whose courage and genius did most to free his country from bondage and elevate it to the ranks of independent sovereign nations," could he have been wishing that Bonaparte would follow in those footsteps, that he would respect the rights of Frenchmen, the independence and sovereignty of others? His true thoughts always emerge obliquely.

He asked that a statue and a square in Paris be dedicated to the memory of Washington. Bonaparte ignored the request, just as he ignored appeals for moderation and respect for the law as well as for the sovereign rights and boundaries of nations. Talleyrand seemed to be adapting to the Consul's moody outbursts.

He set out cheerfully for Lyons on December 23, 1801, to confer with the Italian representatives of the Cisalpine Republic. The political gymnastics he performed there leave one breathless. En route, his carriage broke down—where else but in Autun! While it was under repair, he must have done some reminiscing. The thoughts that crossed his mind were hardly tender, though, for Autun meant only three weeks in his life, grumpy canons, and a fumbled Mass in the icy cathedral. Dust.

On reaching Lyons, he was greeted by deputies of the "sister republic," all carefully selected. "They will do your bidding before you have even expressed it," Talleyrand wrote to Bonaparte. Why bother with formalities? "What they think you wish will become law instantly." How wrong he was to steer Bonaparte toward Caesarism; it was probably his deadliest sin. At that time he was not betraying the régime, he was forging it; but he betrayed himself, or worse still, the wisdom, humanity, and justice he stood for.

Let us watch him in action. We can admire his remarkable poise while deploring the cause it serves. Roederer had drafted a very simple Constitution for this Republic, "very short, very clear," as he put it, apologizing for its brevity. Talleyrand interrupted: for a satellite country subject to intervention, it had to be "brief and obscure." After that he entertained the Cisalpine envoys at dinner. He rented a town house for thirty-four days at a cost of 32 million francs, added to which was 7 million livres for food and service, making a total of 5 billion francs for five weeks of negotiations—more than the entire city of Lyons spent in a year. He certainly "edited" the bills and collected rebates. Talleyrand must have pocketed some princely tips; after all, "he comes from a great family."

Having suffered cruelly during the Revolution (thanks largely to Fouché), the population of Lyons tried to make up for the years of famine and bloodshed by inflating prices. Two Italians found themselves being charged 130 livres (100,000 francs) for two chops and some ham. When they raised a furor, the authorities stepped in; by offering 3 livres, they worked the price down to 12. There were no bargains that month in Lyons.

The Cisalpine Republic addressed itself to electing a president. Oddly enough, the choice fell on Melzi, Bonaparte's confidant and spy during his Italian campaign. A perfectly reliable fellow. Still, Talleyrand felt there was room for improvement. In unctuous tones, he congratulated the delegates on the inspired decision of the electors (and the French intelligence service), adding: "You could make an even better choice and still keep Monsieur Melzi for the role he deserves." How exquisitely he chose his words; their own Cardinal Mazarini could not have expressed it better. The Italian deputies hesitated, looked at each other, whispered, and then asked to take a new vote. Monseigneur gazed benevolently upon his well-trained flock. General Bonaparte became president of the Cisalpine Republic.

Before leaving Lyons, Talleyrand also dealt with some serious matters, the plight of the silk industry for one. He repatriated all silk workers whom the Revolution had forced into exile. And in the treaty with Russia, he inserted a clause requiring her silk goods to be purchased in Lyons.

The real drama remained the war with England. He sent Montrond to London to feel out the situation before making any official pacifist overtures. The time was ripe, for Ireland was now a burning issue. Pitt had resigned; Addington, his successor, was willing to talk peace. At that point Talleyrand received a merciless snub from his chief. Imagine the foreign minister's dismay to hear the cannon booming from the Invalides and learn that it celebrated the signing of an armistice in London! He knew nothing about it.

People blushed for his sake. Why didn't he resign? Not only did he swallow the insult but sent fawning, unpardonably servile letters to his master. Still, it bred new discord, which, as one would expect with Talleyrand, developed very slowly, making the results that much more startling. Dining at the Malmaison that evening, he thought the occasion demanded an air of contempt. Not toward Bonaparte but toward the rest of the gathering; he had a right to be vexed and that was how he appeared.

He did not go to Amiens for the signing of the peace on March 25, 1802; he had not gone to Lunéville either. Joseph Bonaparte signed those treaties. Talleyrand congratulated him for taking his place.

This affront to his dignity failed to impair Talleyrand's judgment. He had the strength to put aside vanity and self-interest long enough to assess calmly and dispassionately the First Consul's achievement: "France enjoyed powerful influence and prestige abroad, more than enough to satisfy the most exacting patriotism. Her position was even miraculous because she had created it so rapidly. In less than two and a half years France had risen from the depths of degradation under the Directory to the front rank of European power." [1] Why, then, would he desert Bonaparte despite his coarse and ruthless tactics?

Talleyrand took to punning on occasion. Bonaparte was more amused than annoyed by it. He had appointed General Andréossy as ambassador to England without even informing his foreign minister (another major slight). The Consul was installing generals all over the map. Andréossy was incompetent. At the Malmaison, Bonaparte mentioned the need to name someone to the London post as if nothing had been done about it. He did not know that Talleyrand was already acquainted with the appointment. Feigning ignorance, Talleyrand suggested several persons; Bonaparte turned them all down of course, saying: "I shall handle it. Andréossy shall go."

Talleyrand, looking mystified: "Do you mean to appoint André also [*André aussi*]? Who is this André?"

Bonaparte, frowning: "I'm not talking about any André. I mean Andréossy. For heaven's sake, ANDRÉOSSY! The artillery general."

"Andréossy, oh yes, him. I didn't think of him. I was thinking of diplomats; no wonder I didn't think of him. Yes, of course, he's in artillery."

Another wound which in time could fester.

There were worse incidents. Talleyrand had advocated the restitution of conquered territories, and in particular, Piedmont, which belonged to the king of Sardinia. To do so would have been judicious as well as just. Without warning, Bonaparte annexed Piedmont on September 11, 1801, a seizure described in Talleyrand's *Memoirs* as "a monstrous violation of a nation's most sovereign right." All well and good, but no protest or comment came from his lips at the time it happened. England and a chorus of European powers sent up a howl. When called on to give up Malta as she was bound by treaty to do, England refused. Bonaparte's example thus gave his enemies the "right," so to speak, to flout their commitments. He was exasperated by Talleyrand's insistence that Malta was not worth a new war. Bonaparte considered war the only reliable means of communication.

England's new ambassador to France found his position untenable. Bonaparte and his circle were deliberately hostile, and he, Whitworth, avoided Talleyrand, the only person he could have talked to, having been warned that the foreign minister charged exorbitant prices for everything, including an audience. Actually, Talleyrand, saddled as he was with Madame Grand, rarely ventured into the English embassy for fear he and his lady friend would be denounced as English spies. Furthermore, the ambassador was dealing with Joseph Bonaparte, whose price he could afford. The mounting tension finally exploded. At a diplomatic reception given by Madame Bonaparte, the general vented his temper most rudely on Ambassador Whitworth. His crude and violent manner shocked the guests, whose governments soon heard about it, and won no prestige or friends for France. Europe's dream of peace dissolved when Bonaparte shouted: "Malta or war, and woe to those who violate treaties!"

Withworth demanded his passport and prepared to return home. A coach piled high with his luggage waited in the courtyard when Talleyrand arrived. He managed to calm Whitworth and persuade him not to leave.

Even Josephine chided her husband. "You made everyone tremble; they will think you ill-natured." Indeed, people were beginning to think just that, though no one had christened him "ogre" yet; he had not spilled enough blood. "It's true," he admitted, "I was wrong. I didn't want to come downstairs today. Talleyrand said things that put me in a bad mood, and then that stringbean of an ambassador had to stick his face right under my nose." So war was determined by Bonaparte's moods? Is a self-appointed Caesar entitled to be moody? Talleyrand had dared to suggest that he ought to curb his temper and control his nerves. Bonaparte would not brook the slightest hint of criticism. By offering sound advice, Talleyrand succeeded only in angering him. It was hopeless.

Two days later, an English ultimatum arrived. All was lost. In handing the note to the First Consul, Talleyrand called down a fresh storm of abuse and was informed that any minister daring to present such a note showed lack of respect. Megalomania was rearing its head. In the council that met to draft a reply, Talleyrand felt the full brunt of Bonaparte's anger. Only Joseph took his side to plead for peace. They were silenced. The ultimatum was rejected, making war inevitable. From then on the tragedy unfolded according to its own unalterable logic.

Talleyrand paid one last call on Whitworth to defend Bonaparte's contention that England was responsible for the breach. That might be true, but Bonaparte had given her every possible pretext for it. Still, a pretext is only a pretext. London knew perfectly well that waving an insolent note under the general's nose would make him strike. He struck, just as England expected. Talleyrand never would have gone to war again, not even over Malta. France's economic recovery had made remarkable strides in three years; agriculture, industry, commerce, and finance were flourishing. Whereas Talleyrand wanted to maintain and increase that prosperity, England was determined to halt it. In short, the peace through compromise advocated by Talleyrand threatened English interests more than Bonaparte's saber-rattling. Prudently, England elected war as the lesser risk. Talleyrand would not have left her the choice. The Warlord gave it to her.

Make Peace or Make War, but Keep On Making Money

The marquis de La Tour du Pin and his amiable wife returned to Paris after the 18th Brumaire. Talleyrand greeted them with open arms; expecting that they, like so many other friends, wished to serve the First Consul, he offered to help them. They refused, saying that they intended to live modestly off their estates. "Too bad," Talleyrand commented, "it doesn't make sense." The La Tour du Pin couple was not rich. "But, I explained," the marquise wrote, "we cannot afford to live in Paris." "Bah!" he retorted, "money can always be had when it's needed." Rather shocked, she concluded: "That's human nature for you." On the other hand, she was dazzled by Talleyrand's latest purchase, the Créqui mansion, which he had restored and furnished luxuriously with his unfailing good taste. This house on the rue d'Anjou later was demolished to make way for the boulevard Malesherbes. A magnificent property, its garden faced the rue de la Ville-l'Evêque. He no longer resided at the rue du Bac but continued to give dinners there for as many as a hundred guests, as well as formal receptions. The rue d'Anjou was his home. He summered in Auteuil or Neuilly, never staying very long in Auteuil, whereas Neuilly usually claimed several months of his year. He also bought Mademoiselle Lange's attractive house in which, on the 19th Brumaire, he had celebrated his triumph over the Directory and Barras. In addition he rented the château of Bry-sur-Marne, an exquisite villa built in Louis XV's reign by his finance minister Silhouette, whose expert money-raising techniques were less appreciated in his day than the paper cutouts bearing his name.

So Talleyrand lived in splendor, and to maintain that splendor he was willing to tolerate Bonaparte's insults, even to indulge his worst failings. The clink of gold, the rustle of silk, throngs of women in a perfumed haze—that was his life, the very breath that sustained him. For him, life was an endless process of acquiring and spending money without ever exceeding his means.

On the 18th Brumaire, his fortune was reputed to be 18 million livres (about 15 billion francs), a fabulous sum. Even more fabulous was his practice of sitting back and watching the money fall into his lap. His tactics amaze us not because they were devious but because they were simple, direct, and extraordinarily successful.

One day Bonaparte informed him that, as a gesture of good will, the monthly payments of 5 million livres which Spain was obligated to pay France under the Treaty of Basel would cease. Talleyrand observed that it would be wiser to start by cutting the remittances in half. The finance minister thus was advised to expect only 2.5 million livres. But Charles IV of Spain heard nothing about this from the rue du Bac and went on paying out 5 million every month. What happened to the balance? Talleyrand split it with Manuel Godoy, "the Prince of Peace," minister and court favorite in Madrid. This enterprise flourished for two and a half years. Bonaparte put an end to it in the Treaty of Lunéville by committing France to repay her entire debt to Spain.

Even before the 18th Brumaire we find Talleyrand mixed up in an affair which, though not the most brilliant deal he ever managed, generated tremors for years to come. Officially, it is known as the "Cohen-Bacri and Busnach Affair." Those two leaders of the Jewish community in Algiers had a monopoly of the grain market during the Regency. Earlier, when Talleyrand was serving the Directory, he had given the dealers written authorization to collect a debt which the French government owed the dey of Algiers. Now Messrs. Cohen-Bacri and Busnach had a devil of a time collecting the money because the amount indicated on the document signed by Talleyrand was infinitely greater than the amount of the dey's loan. Talleyrand, Cohen-Bacri, and Busnach undoubtedly planned to divide up the difference. To make sure their little fraud would succeed, Talleyrand wrote to the finance minister: "Our current relations with the Regency demand that we make every effort to show good will to the Jews." The finance minister felt that half the solicited amount was more than generous, and they received 7 million livres. The two dealers were ecstatic at such a windfall. But what about the rest of the money? Why give it up? One of them wrote: "If I didn't have the cripple in tow, I wouldn't count on anything more." [1] This is surely plain enough. Some thirty years later, King Charles X of France faced litigation involving the Cohen-Bacri incident as the focus of a dispute with the dey of Algiers. Then came the seizure of Algiers. The last chapter, a solution of sorts, was written in 1962.

In 1800 Talleyrand signed a commercial treaty with the United States. Briefly, he wanted the satisfaction of dumbfounding Robert Livingston, the American minister to France. When the latter turned up at the rue du Bac to sign the agreement, this is how the conversation went:

TALLEYRAND: "Have you money?"

LIVINGSTON: "Money? But Citizen Minister . . ." (sputtering)

TALLEYRAND: "Tell me frankly. Do you have money?"

LIVINGSTON: "Yes, but . . . I don't understand."

TALLEYRAND: "It's very simple though. The point is do you have a lot of money? You see, in my country it's very hard to do business. It takes a lot of money, but if you have it, there are no problems that can't be ironed out. Think about it. It's up to you to arrange things to satisfy the contracting parties." [2]

Livingston thought about it, Talleyrand pocketed 2 million livres, and the contracting parties got along fine.

While the Battle of Marengo was going on, he became involved with a high Austrian official, Saint-Julien, and by speculating in government bonds, made himself 7 million livres (about 5 billion francs).

Though Bonaparte would not allow him to sign the Treaty of Lunéville, Talleyrand managed nevertheless to extort 7 or 8 million livres in the course of negotiations with Austria. The figures are staggering when you consider that simultaneously he was getting 300,000 francs from the Austrian emperor (who still observed the ancient rite of sacrifice) and 400,000 from Bonaparte. But how did he get his hands on the 7 million? Because he knew that a clause in the treaty required the Austrian government to redeem at full value the bonds it had issued in the Lowlands (Belgium and Holland). The public had been advised— by whom? we wonder—that the bonds would be worthless once those countries came under French jurisdiction. Talleyrand bought up all the bonds he could locate through brokers desperate to get rid of them before the treaty was signed. After Lunéville, our hero cashed them at full value, thus acquiring sufficient money to maintain gracious living in the rue d'Anjou and the châteaux at Neuilly and Bry-sur-Marne.

He used a wide assortment of "gimmicks." What else can you call the performance he had Madame Grand put on to entice visitors to buy his favor? Bedecked with magnificent jewels, she would surround herself with ambassadors, bankers, and businessmen looking for good investments. The necklace of Siberian sapphires had been presented to her, she said, by the ambassador from St. Petersburg; the six strands of pearls came from the emperor's envoy; the diamond riviere from Prussia; the diadem from Rome. The whole act was meant to excite would-be buyers of influence—and influence was visibly for sale, though never at bargain prices.

Gamblers, even the lucky ones, have streaks of bad luck. At the time of the Treaty of Amiens, Talleyrand's calculations somehow missed their mark and he lost 2 million. However, Bonaparte maintained a constant flurry of wars, partitions, annexations, and spoliation, all of which could be minted. Talleyrand took his share, like everyone else. What bothered people, it seems, was that an open stream of gold flowed his way, whereas less stylish and meeker competitors hastily pocketed their loot, looking very embarrassed. As a matter of fact, his spending appeared to cause more offense than his extortions. Yet he had simply transposed his patrician habits to a new society, equally corrupted by money but invested by Rousseau and Robespierre with the language and trappings of "virtue."

His most lucrative undertaking was the reorganization of German principalities and the secularization of ecclesiastic properties owned by the prince-bishops. For several years, the bargaining among those virtually dispossessed German princes had enabled him, by playing one off against another, to collect sizable bribes. The really big ones started coming in after Lunéville in 1801 and reached a peak with the "Recess" of 1803, which, in effect, redistributed German territories to the highest bidders. To win this lottery, you had to buy the lucky number; Talleyrand did the drawing, or at least masterminded it from Paris while Durand de Mareuil worked on the spot, and was generously rewarded for his gallant efforts. Talleyrand made a practice of paying handsomely for the services of others, and charging handsomely for his own services, which he did not always perform but collected for in advance. For example, when the good prince of Weilburg set his heart on the presidency of the Batavian Republic, he paid our hero 5 million livres to arrange the matter. Bonaparte refused to cooperate, but Talleyrand pocketed the money anyway.

The game was so lucrative that he was able to play with an eye to Bonaparte's ambitions and contrary to his own better judgment. Bonaparte used Talleyrand to advance Prussian interests over those of the German princes and Austria, whereas Talleyrand feared Prussian ascendancy in Germany. He knew perfectly well what he was doing but could not resist so much money. He wrote the following to flatter his chief and the king of Prussia: "Prussia, of all the friendly powers [an outright lie, for France had no friends in 1801], is the one whose aggrandizement interests us most, whose affection we wish to retain, and upon whose strength and assistance we wish to rely in the future. The plans for your development thus are of concern to us: you must dominate northern Germany; the secularization policy will provide the tool. The First Consul is truly anxious to contribute to the rise of Prussia. . . ." Once again he played his own principles false in order to serve his master.

So conscious was he of his baneful role in Bonaparte's pernicious scheme that he never mentioned it to his friend Count Cobenzl, the Austrian minister who stayed with him in Neuilly. Cobenzl woke up to the truth after it was too late. He courted favor by entertaining Madame Grand's pugs; she in turn was supposed to promote Austria's cause with Talleyrand. And while Cobenzl wasted time over a silly woman and her dogs in Neuilly, Mareuil, Roux-Laborie, and the prince of Nassau-Siegen, a new gambling companion Talleyrand had adopted, were traveling all over Germany on business for our minister. The prince of Nassau-Siegen was reported to be "the biggest scoundrel on record." Montrond, of course, was part of the tour, sending on for Talleyrand's signature the decrees secularizing German bishoprics. For his efforts, "Hell's Christ-child" received pious "gifts" which he forwarded diligently to Talleyrand, keeping for himself only what he needed to gamble, to keep his mistresses and carriages, and to live the easy life of an amiable, licentious aristocrat. An ideal friend!

In Paris, with only a bird's-eye view of the situation, Talleyrand still knew exactly what to do. He often made marginal notes on letters from German princes desperate to retain their lands, such as the prince of Reuss, who wished to sign a peace treaty and alliance with France as between equals. He proposed: "Article I: the prince of Reuss recognizes the French Republic." In the margin, Talleyrand commented: "The French Republic is delighted to become acquainted with the prince of Reuss."

Apart from these civilities, the reshuffling of Germany netted our hero between 10 and 15 million livres.

On April 30, 1803, Bonaparte sold Louisiana to the United States. How are we ever to find out exactly what took place? Certainly not from Talleyrand, who barely mentions the subject. He did not trust himself to speak of something he knew intimately. The price was 80 million livres, reduced to 60 million. The government actually received 54 million after deduction of "negotiating expenses." Why the reductions? Who authorized them? And where did the balance go? Toward the up-keep of Valençay, perhaps?

Portugal dared to voice a timid complaint. Bonaparte had installed General Lannes in Lisbon as ambassador, with disastrous results. The Portuguese government asked to be relieved of this dashing officer.

Talleyrand met in Paris with the Portuguese minister, de Souza (Madame de Flahaut's husband, as we may recall, making it almost a family matter), and declared Lannes a featherbrain, urging de Souza to pass that opinion on to his superiors. Was it perhaps de Souza's domestic situation that inspired our hero to be so forthright? In any event, Lannes was recalled. The Portuguese government was relieved simultaneously of one undesirable and 4 million livres, which went into the French foreign minister's pocket. This last arrangement seems to have elicited murmurs from the Portuguese, thanks to which we know about the incident.[3]

Not all the moneymaking schemes went smoothly. One of them nearly backfired. A subsidy payable to the prince of Orange-Nassau, the king of Prussia's brother-in-law, was long overdue. When at last it was about to be settled, the funds were found to have all but melted away. Durand de Mareuil, Talleyrand's go-between, Duroc, president of the Batavian Republic, and Schimmelpenninck and Semonville, French representatives in The Hague, had jointly manipulated the money. The king of Prussia complained directly to the First Consul. As fate would have it, a letter from Mareuil turned up containing instructions for dividing up "the balance." This letter was given to Bonaparte, who, at the time, 1804, was in Aix-la-Chapelle. He summoned Talleyrand.

"Are you sure Durand issued no order from you?"

"No order, Sire, I am sure."

"Have him come here at once."

When Durand failed to appear, Bonaparte summoned Talleyrand once again: "Well, your Durand has not come; he is surely guilty. Are you positive that you gave him no orders?"

"Positive."

"Or that he has not written?"

"I am positive, unless Schimmelpenninck has misinterpreted his letter. I suspect Dutch bungling behind all this."

Furious, Bonaparte pointed to the door: "I don't need you in Mainz. Return to Paris and take a rest, which you need."

That closed the matter. Napoleon reportedly was outraged less by the theft than by the lie. "What a liar! I ought to send him back to Valençay, but then who could we put in the Foreign Office?"[4]

Talleyrand kept his position and went on extorting several million more from what he termed "the little marsh" (Holland). He told Cambacérès that as Napoleon neglected to reward his most loyal servitors, those servitors had to look out for themselves. Talleyrand was not deprived either of his duties or of Napoleon's confidence. Respect was something else, but Napoleon respected no one. As Talleyrand shared that view, the romance—or its semblance—still had a way to go.

France and Rome Are Reconciled—
Except Where Monsieur d'Autun Is Concerned

It seemed that every attempt of his to restore the former society sooner or later turned against him. The Directory stood for total permissiveness; the Consulate, for total change. In a sense, Talleyrand's fate was to create conditions most favorable to his country's prosperity and most unfavorable to his personal happiness. In order to live as he wished, he was forced to reconcile the irreconcilable. An orderly person by nature, he matured in an age of anarchy. Unfortunately, anarchy provided no money, no whist, no Madame de Flahaut or Madame de Brionne, no hôtel de Créqui, no Riesener furniture, no Mozart; in a word, it was suffocation. There lay the tragic secret of his hopeless suffering, for he did suffer, profoundly, all his life. He had no real joy; only compensations—large, spectacular ones, which invariably he paid for. But the true blessings of life are free: not being lame, for instance.

Once the Consulate had imposed its own standards of social conduct, the position of a minister, an ex-bishop, living in sin with a woman of the world, grew increasingly uncomfortable. It became no less than perilous in 1802 with the signing of the Concordat, whereby the Catholic church regained most of its former rights and privileges and the houses of worship were reopened. Talleyrand never gave the matter much thought; ambiguity being part of his nature, he saw nothing wrong with lodging his mistress in the ministry and having her preside over his official receptions and his household. Bonaparte, however, had strong— and loud—objections to the awkward situation of a high-born aristocrat who failed to "regularize" his status. As Talleyrand was already a bishop, he could become a cardinal once an understanding was reached with the church of Rome. Bonaparte felt that was the best way to reinstate Talleyrand among his peers and to tailor him to the orderly society Bonaparte so cherished: between the army, the church, and the police, France would be tamed. Talleyrand could still be a great minister, and no scarlet robe need prevent him from indulging his taste for luxury, for worldly pleasures, and for women. A touch of hypocrisy would do the trick.

Talleyrand refused the cardinalate, making it clear that his break with Rome had been final and he had no desire to play Tartuffe in scarlet robes. The proposal brought back sickening memories of his bitter youth.

That explains why he acted so perversely during negotiations with Rome over the terms of the Concordat; if his own fate had not hung upon that of the church, he would have thrown all his support behind the revival of Catholicism in France. His attitude toward the priesthood and Catholic doctrine remained steadfastly benevolent, as long as he did not have to be a part of it. Religion could help to unite the nation and to restore beliefs and traditions without affecting political institutions. Talleyrand considered the Declaration of the Rights of Man and the Revolution's achievements irreversible. "Those whom the Revolution has pardoned must also pardon the Revolution," a comment which represents him not only as conciliator but also as champion of the tenets of 1789. He worked hard for the Concordat therefore until the Pope refused to release him from the ecclesiastical vows of a consecrated bishop. The bishopric he had won with such effort was finally rising up to stifle him. On learning that Pius VII would not act to divest him of an unwanted and, as he and many others saw it, absurd distinction, he did his best to undermine the negotiations. Caselli, a papal representative in Paris, reported: "We have many enemies, but above all an implacable and all-powerful one in Autun."

Talleyrand stubbornly opposed any understanding with the Holy See that would not expressly release him from his vows. To cover his own circumstances as well as ecclesiastics who had renounced the priesthood and, in some cases, married, he won papal absolution for secularized priests. But, alas, that ruling excluded bishops.

He refused to admit defeat. Bonaparte supported him, for if he could not make him a cardinal, the only alternative was to secularize him. The legate Cardinal Caprara was summoned to the rue du Bac. Talleyrand informed him that he had just written to His Holiness— over Bonaparte's signature—asking to be absolved of his vows. To support his petition he cited precedents in church history that would allow Pius VII to grant the ex-bishop of Autun what former popes had granted other bishops. Cardinal Caprara knew of no precedent for the absolution of a bishop, although his interlocutor seemed well informed.

The letter to Pius VII contained this statement: "Now that France is becoming a Catholic nation once again, it is not fitting for a minister in whom great trust resides to be an object of uncertainty and controversy in respect to his former status."

"An object of uncertainty and controversy": surely that is perhaps the most accurate description of Talleyrand's personality, and he had to be the one to supply it. It coincides with another self-revealing comment he made: "I want people to go on for centuries discussing what I was like, what I believed, what I advocated." But instead of discussing this, let us try to depict it. In the letter Talleyrand admitted to having committed certain errors in the eyes of the church; he was vague, as he often chose to be, about what they were, and not the least repentant. Fearful lest the negotiations break down completely, the Pope ruled that this "penitent" and submissive son "might wear secular attire and serve the French Republic in an official capacity." Having combed the annals of the church, His Holiness was unhappy to say that no precedent could be found for secularizing a bishop. Talleyrand had been wearing civil dress since 1790 without anyone's permission. And why should duties assigned by the Republic need papal blessing? He wanted only one thing: release from ecclesiastical celibacy in order to marry Madame Grand, a fact so well known in Rome that they openly referred to Talleyrand's petition as "the Madame Grand clause."

The pontiff's response was so derisive and revealed such lack of understanding that Cardinal Caprara did not dare deliver it for fear of stirring up a storm of abuse.

Talleyrand had dispatched his letter to Rome in the care of a fellow named Cacault, a police spy lately turned diplomat in our minister's official employ, instructing him to deliver it and bring back the papal reply in absolute secrecy. Cacault left in early July but did not return to Paris until the end of the month, having been forced to cool his heels in the anterooms of the Holy See. Talleyrand was taking his annual cure at Bourbon-l'Archambault. The First Consul sent a terse message informing him that the Pope's answer had been received. The papal nuncio echoed this advice, only in more eloquent language. Talleyrand asked to see the pontifical brief, which came to him at Bourbon. He read it without a murmur. Nor did he show any emotion on his return to the capital. The legate assumed that the penitent sinner was humbled and reported this cheerful news to the Holy Father, a trifle prematurely.

The government equivocated, focusing solely on one sentence in the papal brief: "Citizen Maurice Talleyrand, minister of foreign relations, is returned to secular and laical life." That phrase was enacted into law by a council of state. As far as the general public was concerned, Talleyrand ceased to be either a priest or a bishop. No one paid the slightest attention to another sentence in the brief confirming the sacred and irrevocable nature of the episcopate: "No bishop has ever received a dispensation to marry."

The Concordat was signed on July 15, 1801, but failed to resolve the bishop of Autun's status.

The nation as a whole rejoiced in the event; only the Jacobins muttered, along with royalists who saw the usurper's power now firmly entrenched at the altar. Both Chateaubriand and his *Génie du christianisme* won a wide reputation at this time. The book advocated Bonaparte's own policy of thought control. Chateaubriand received personal compliments from the First Consul and even an embassy secretarial post.

On Easter Day, 1802, to celebrate the splendid reconciliation of Rome (merely a pawn in the dictator's plans) with France, whose troubles it allayed somewhat, a resounding *Te Deum* was sung in reopened and reconsecrated Notre Dame. With great pomp and ceremony, the Consuls arrived in state coaches drawn by eight horses, prominent persons by six or four. Thirty bishops lined the dais awaiting Bonaparte's arrival; at the entrance, the archbishop of Paris stood by the holy water font to bless him. Amid all the gold braid and bright colors representing the new régime, only two persons were able to follow the Mass with some degree of accuracy: the ex-bishop of Autun and the ex-Oratorian Fouché. Everyone looked to them for instruction as to when to kneel and cross himself. As both were government officials, protocol placed them side by side, thus allowing them to exchange occasional knowing winks beneath lowered lashes. The troops were restless, having been forced to attend by Berthier. Acting cautiously, General Augereau had asked Bonaparte to excuse veterans of the revolutionary army from participating in a ceremony which denied the Revolution, their beliefs, and their struggle. The Consul retorted that their duty was to obey. They obeyed, with apparent lack of enthusiasm. General Moreau alone refused to attend, pacing up and down in front of the Tuileries blowing smoke rings from his cigar. His defiance cost him dear.

In Talleyrand's *Memoirs*, both the Concordat and the "Madame Grand clause" are dismissed in short order: "Bonaparte obtained a papal brief covering my secularization dated June 29, 1802, from St. Peter's in Rome." The date at least is accurate.

Papal intransigence did not dissuade him from marrying Madame Grand.

Monsieur d'Autun Provides His Own Solution to the Celibacy Issue

In all her "glory," Madame Grand was about to enter the Périgord family and the bed of a prelate. She had left nothing to chance, no loose threads in her religious apparel. She showered favors on the papal legate and nuncio, who in turn danced attendance on her. If not on the Heavenward path, she was certainly headed for the most brilliant and talked-about marriage of the century. Having already obtained a divorce —and pardon for it from on high—there was no need for her to go wailing before any prince of the church. The title of princess would be her ultimate, and ample, reward. Her divorce had become official on April 7, 1798.

While Pius VII, Talleyrand, and Bonaparte were actively occupied with the "Madame Grand clause," three people gathered in Paris who once had chased the petticoats of Mademoiselle Worlée, the present Madame Grand. They were less prominent than the first three, but no less interested in the Roman affair. One was Sir Philip, dying to see his "Cathy" again, and preferably nude; to avoid a scandal, she left for the countryside. Next came Elijah, the Indian judge who had fined Sir Philip 50,000 rupees; and finally the recipient of those rupees, Mr. Grand, the husband, who had rented a flat on the rue de Richelieu. He was constantly heard from and constantly nosing about for a second 50,000 rupees. He received the equivalent of that amount and also the promise of a fine position—in some remote place. It seemed to satisfy him for the moment.

The marriage did take place. On September 9, 1802, the contract was signed at Neuilly. Talleyrand was exceedingly generous, giving his wife (who had come penniless to his door) the Créqui town house, the estate of Pont-de-Sains in the north, and part of his fortune. Nevertheless, he took care to appoint himself her sole heir in case she died before him. Bonaparte and Josephine witnessed the contract with their signatures, together with the two other Consuls, Talleyrand's two brothers Archambaud and Boson, and Maret, the secretary of state.

A civil ceremony was held on September 10 at the town hall on the rue de Verneuil in the tenth arrondissement. Madame Grand was thirty-nine. Though not furtive by any means, the wedding was quiet: open but deliberately inconspicuous. The public was informed without being invited.

287

The marriage contract contains an error, for it says that Charles Maurice is the son of Charles-Daniel Talleyrand-Périgord and Alexandrine-Victoire-Eléonore Damas d'Antigny, "both deceased." That is not true, for Talleyrand's mother was still alive; she died in 1809, aged eighty-one, at 34, rue d'Anjou. Why did he declare her dead, especially in the presence of his two brothers, who saw her regularly? He had not cut himself off from her; as a matter of fact, on her return from emigration in 1803, he found rooms for her near his own house on the rue d'Anjou. But would she have wanted to witness this insane marriage? Declaring her dead was more a token of respect than an insult.

Some sources claim that the civil ceremony was followed by a religious one supposedly held at Epinay, Madame Grand's legal residence. But that is most unlikely. What priest would have performed the marriage ceremony for a bishop? Of course, the famous decree issued by the council of state had fooled a great many people, even among the clergy. Monseigneur d'Aviau, archbishop of Bordeaux, wrote that the bishop of Autun had been "absolved of his priest's and bishop's vows." The lady, however, was a divorcée; in the eyes of the church, she remained the wife of the still extant Mr. Grand. How could any priest make that mistake? No evidence supports the rumor that a religious ceremony was performed.

Why did Talleyrand marry Madame Grand? For love of scandal, say those who prefer easy answers. Yet he looked upon scandal as a lack of good taste, ill-breeding, a violation of those very social strictures that contribute to human happiness. He himself lapsed into such failings from time to time, but unintentionally.

Various explanations of this "failing" have appeared, all rather improbable but interesting nonetheless. The most direct are usually the least convincing; for example, as Madame Grand was trustee of Talleyrand's fortune, he could not break off their relationship without impoverishing himself. Such lack of foresight on his part is highly dubious.

General Thiébauld's Memoirs contain a phrase alleged to have been uttered by Madame Grand in a fit of ill-humor: "If you don't marry me, I'll bring you down a foot." What mysterious complicity lurks behind that threat; what commerce or crime did they share? If some disgraceful incident chained them together, it must have involved spying for England, of which the Directory's police suspected her all along. We really don't know what it means. But could he not have married the woman to cause an irreparable breach with the church, to loose the final tie supposedly binding him to Rome, his celibacy? No, that kind of bravado was not his style. Furthermore, his chastity bothered him far less than the intolerable bondage he accepted by marrying this stupid, disreputable, even blacklisted woman. Did he give any reasons for this unheard-of marriage from his own pen? Of course not, except to his niece, Madame de Dino, but that was in 1836. After asking him about it many times, she extracted only this: he could not "find any reasonable explanation for the marriage. It was a time of general confusion. People didn't care much about anything, themselves or anyone else. You have no idea what follies men commit in periods of social decay."

The reply came too late. He was eighty-two in 1836. Thirty-four years had elapsed since the marriage. And what of the follies? In fact, 1802 was not a time of "social decay"; it was just the opposite, and Bonaparte had put his minister on notice either to get rid of his mistress or to marry her for the sake of decency and social convention. Of that much we are certain.

Chancellor Pasquier probably strikes the human side of the story in his Memoirs. His observations tally with our hero's indolent nature, which his mistress expertly exploited: "Talleyrand yielded to the ascendancy of importunity over weakness, to the longing for tranquility in a domestic setting to which he had grown accustomed, and finally to his complete indifference to the opinion of others."

In more prosaic terms, it was whispered about that Madame Grand badgered the life out of him on the subject of matrimony; rather than throw her out, he wed her to have peace. But he made her pay for it.

He probably would not have married her if Bonaparte had not interfered. Our illustrious general, a compulsive matchmaker, had his nose in everyone's affairs—and beds. Even Talleyrand could not escape.

Madame de Rémusat, Talleyrand's mistress and confidante during the Consulate and the Empire, tells us that several wives of foreign diplomats complained to the First Consul of having been received at the rue du Bac by the Grand woman, whose reputation they already knew. Rather than suffer such humiliation, they refused to attend any more receptions there. Bonaparte was furious with his minister. The new government needed prestige, not the disgrace of that Grand woman. Her doom was sealed. Bonaparte made it plain to Talleyrand that she must not live in the foreign ministry or any of his other residences. She thought the end had come. For once, this foolish woman acted very shrewdly: she went to Josephine for help. Who could have been more sympathetic to Madame Grand's plight, or forgiven so readily the same mistakes Josephine herself had made, or sensed the common bond uniting two very pretty, gregarious, luxury-loving fortune hunters?

Josephine promised to plead her cause. Grumbling, Bonaparte agreed to see her. She turned in a better performance than Germaine de Staël. Her weeping and moaning, her tear-drenched phrases, the hair tumbling about her face, her fluttering lashes did their work. Bonaparte weakened. He thundered: "There is only one answer. Let Talleyrand marry you and everything will be all right. But you must bear his name or never again set foot in his house."

It was exactly what she wanted.

She knew her bishop was incapable of saying No. If he could not bring himself even to fire a servant, how could he dismiss a woman he had loved, and probably still loved, someone he took for granted and did not have to listen to if he chose? In short, he accepted Madame Grand as he had accepted tonsure.

Napoleon judged him most unfairly: "Against my will, scandalizing the whole of Europe, he married his shameless mistress by whom he could not even have children." Fortunately, one might add. Talleyrand fathered such illustrious bastards that any legitimate offspring he and Madame Grand might have had would surely have proved disappointing. Let us say that he chose his mistresses better than his wife. But to return to Napoleon's words, it is significant that they were spoken in 1813. The emperor's mood had changed since 1802. The romance was long dead. He had forgotten his role in Talleyrand's marriage. What still persists is Napoleon's contempt for Madame Grand—and for Talleyrand in stooping to marry her. In this whole affair, Chateaubriand seems to have read Bonaparte's mind most accurately. The First Consul knew Talleyrand to be an invaluable servant; he expected far more important services from him. Bonaparte dreamed of a throne and needed his minister to make the dream come true. Talleyrand knew about thrones, monarchs, and court life. But Bonaparte knew what to expect from the strange, prodigious sorcerer who served him so disquietingly; that fluid, impenetrable, evasive minister of his might wriggle out of his grip. Could he ignore Talleyrand's flirtation with Hyde de Neuville? Or the abbé de Montesquiou? Or how many other agents of Louis XVIII? Talleyrand was a suspected royalist, not to say legitimist. People still suspect him of a million other things. Madame Grand and her senseless gossip fostered those suspicions, she, the frantic royalist and Catholic, who was unwelcome in the sight of either throne or altar. Bonaparte saw that the gulf between the Bourbons and Talleyrand could always be bridged by money, by skillful negotiation, by Talleyrand's yearning for the world to which he belonged, by his attraction to the paternalistic liberalism of the Bourbons, and their pacifism. All that he knew, for in

1802, what Bonaparte did not understand he could guess. Obsessive pride had not yet unhinged his genius. So in order to bind Talleyrand to him forever, to set him at loggerheads with both the Bourbons and the church, he demeaned him mercilessly. Neither Rome nor the Bourbons could ever pardon a bishop of noble blood for defying the Pope, the king, and his class in marrying an adventuress, a married woman, a suspected spy, and a notorious courtesan.

That is probably the most logical explanation of this strange marriage, and also the most Machiavellian. The credit goes entirely to the fortunate author of *Le Génie du christianisme,* who branded their union infamous by declaring that Bonaparte had attached the woman to Talleyrand "like a billboard." He waited thirty years to express that opinion. When, in his youth, he lunched at the rue du Bac in company with Madame Grand, he had nothing to say about "billboards," being more concerned with keeping his secretarial post in the French embassy in Rome and with admiring the poise and gracious manners of his host and patron. About the same time, a lady, commenting on Talleyrand's marriage, told him straight to his face: "You're wallowing in mud up to the neck, so why shouldn't it cover your head."

It was not the mud associated with this union that saddened Talleyrand; it was the boredom. Thinking he had cast off his ecclesiastic bonds, he found himself saddled instead with a new, far greater burden that did not even cancel out the other. This woman was his cross. He stopped loving her. Her vanity, ignorance, and indiscretions kept pace with her expanding waistline. She grew puffed and flabby, while her remarks took on a decidedly caustic edge. Her infidelity was the least of her husband's worries. Deep in his heart, why should he not have resented the man who had condemned him to this Calvary? And why should he have gone on serving forever the implacable master who, as Emile Dard puts it, "forced him to commit his greatest sin, an offense against good taste"?

At the rue du Bac, Citizeness Talleyrand (still the customary address in 1802) was deluged with visits from diplomatic wives who, two months earlier, had refused to see her. No longer was her past mentioned. Still, a shadow haunted her splendid success, the shadow of her one true husband, Mr. Grand. She was deathly afraid that, having spent what Talleyrand had given him, he would reappear some night in the midst of her guests and demand more or less amiably the support to which he was entitled for having been robbed of a beautiful, faithful wife—well a treasure, in any case, the proverbial hen with the golden eggs. She too undertook to find Mr. Grand a lucrative position in a remote corner of the globe. Talleyrand asked Van der Goes, secretary of foreign affairs in The Hague, to try to find a spot for this honorable fellow in some colonial outpost of the Batavian Republic, which, being merely an arm of the French one, had no objection. A post as privy councilor extraordinary (how accurate!) on the Cape of Good Hope was unearthed. The salary of 2,000 florins a year and the exotic locale made it altogether suitable.

Citizeness Talleyrand thanked Van der Goes in a letter dated September 23, 1802, to which she signed a name at once too new and too old for her. "You will note from the name which my marriage to M. de Talleyrand entitles me to bear, that this amiable gentleman's tender and sincere affection has made me the happiest of women." [1]

Three months passed and the honorable Mr. Grand was still around. Citizeness Talleyrand trembled. There was talk of another war with England, in the event of which, no ships would sail and she would be stuck with a husband on her hands. To remove this threat, Talleyrand began prodding Van der Goes with his pen: "It is thoroughly inconceivable how he [Mr. Grand] can remain in Amsterdam where, for over a month, he has been most unwelcome." At last, in March, 1803, he sailed, and after his safe arrival on the Cape was reported, his wife could sign herself triumphantly Madame de Talleyrand-Périgord.

Talleyrand's friends were appalled by the marriage; the duchesse de Luynes, the vicomtesse de Laval, Madame de Coigny, and Montrond all railed at him mercilessly. His icy composure prevailed, but he was hurt all the same, and the disgust he began to feel for the lady from India must have been embittered by the stinging reproaches of friends who meant more to him than his family. Surely the most painful rebuke was Courtiade's private lament: "Who would have thought we could commit such folly, we who have known all the most beautiful ladies at court, we who have known that charming comtesse de Brionne. To come to this end is almost unbelievable." Courtiade was heartbroken. Once again Talleyrand could measure his servant's loyal devotion.

Popular sentiment sided with the duchess and Courtiade, as evidenced by a contemporary ditty called "Blanchette" dedicated to Madame Grand. It went something like this:

> Blanchette is forty, pale and livid,
> Yet Blanchette weds a noble abbé;
> Why shouldn't a whore who's had her day
> Settle down and run an abbey?

The Married Bishop Bears a Striking Resemblance
to the Celibate Monsieur d'Autun

A lady of distinction arriving from Switzerland attended a reception at the rue du Bac shortly after the wedding. She commented: "The court-yard at the ministry of foreign affairs was so jammed with carriages that some had to leave before one could enter. Arriving inside, I mounted the staircase which was blazing with light and studded with flowers." [1] It was not a special occasion; you could drop in any day of the week and take in the same performance. The house was a miniature Versailles grafted onto the consular society. Having never laid eyes on Talleyrand, the visitor reveals her surprise in these rapidly noted impressions: "A figure pale as death dressed in red velvet embroidered with gold. Dress coat, sword, ruffled cuffs, formal hairdo. It was the minister himself, M. de Talleyrand. What an expression! Upon this ghostly frame lie the sensitive, lively features of the bishop of Autun." For the first time, someone compared his head to a death mask. It means that as he approached fifty, Talleyrand was beginning to look aged.

Enter Citizeness Talleyrand: "Then I passed through a large and splendid drawing room where Madame de Talleyrand was. She is tall, beautiful, well dressed, but her character is written on her face: stupidity and vanity. . . . The satisfaction of bearing a great name and occupying a high position has gone to her head. In leaning over backwards to avoid being too polite, she manages to be thoroughly impolite." Louis XIV was afraid of not being polite enough.

The visitor went on to note that the drawing rooms swarmed with a variety of ambassadors, bankers, traveling potentates and dignitaries, all bowing and scraping at the feet of Madame de Talleyrand. It was a parade of sorts. The Swiss lady also observed "lots of diamonds." If diamonds were being recalled from abroad or removed from cellar strongboxes, it was a sure sign of prosperity at home.

Talleyrand continued to frequent the salon of the duchesse de Luynes, whose town house was located on a strip of the rue Saint-Dominique that no longer exists, where the boulevards Raspail and Saint-Germain meet. He also saw the vicomtesse de Laval and the princesse de Vaudémont regularly, former mistresses of his. Their tightly knit and exclusive little circle usually gathered at the duchess's house. After the other dinner guests had left, they would draw their chairs up close and talk late into the night. Between midnight and two in the morning, the conversation flowed like streams of satin ribbon. Talleyrand was the only man in this female group consisting, for the most part, of former mistresses. The prolonged, mutual flirtation would give them all a chance to resavor the enchanting world of their youth. It was his favorite way to deceive his wife, the Grand woman.

Male friends were entertained on the rue d'Anjou, at which time our normally taciturn hero waxed loquacious in the presence of Narbonne, Choiseul, Montrond, Sainte-Foy, and his newest companion the prince of Nassau-Siegen. These were all-night affairs, with supper served at 2 A.M. His active night life accounts for the ghostly pallor in his cheeks.

One lady is conspicuously absent: Germaine de Staël. The to-do with Bonaparte had ruptured her friendship with Talleyrand and committed her to the "opposition," in whose camp she continued to speak her mind turbulently, sometimes emphatically, and often for reasons which Talleyrand preferred to ignore. Like others who must bow to strength, she tried to heal her wounds by writing a book. The result was her rapidly written novel *Delphine*. In it she pictured the woman she would have liked to be, a fragile, adorable creature. Readers could recognize not only herself but also the character of Talleyrand, who was depicted openly and maliciously in the person of Madame Vernon: "At heart she cared for nothing, believed in nothing, was troubled by nothing." Germaine drew this confession from Madame Vernon's (Talleyrand's) lips: "No one took care of me when I was a child. I bottled up my feelings, acquiring at an early age the art of dissimulation, stifling my natural sensitivity. . . . I grew up imbued with profound contempt for people, intensely distrustful of any form of virtue or affection."

No one was taken in. Some witty soul gave a copy of the book to Talleyrand. He read it and made no comment. A few people eagerly and slyly awaited his reaction; when it did not come, it was provoked. During a dinner party someone asked him what he thought of Madame de Staël's novel. He praised it warmly, calling her an extremely gifted writer: she succeeded "in representing the two of us, herself and me, in the guise of women."

Talleyrand watched over family interests, knowing the limitations of his brothers. He arranged a marriage between his niece Mélanie-Xavière de Périgord and Just de Noailles, who made his career at Napoleon's court as the emperor's chamberlain. The match was an honorable one for both families. Madame Grand did not agree, however; from her newly attained perch atop the Périgord genealogical tree, she expressed her disdain: "This match does us no honor, for what is the Noailles family next to the House of Périgord?"

After she had made a spectacle of herself, Bonaparte banished her forever from the Tuileries. On her first visit there after the wedding, the First Consul lectured her with customary severity, laying down certain rules of conduct to make up for her past laxity. The ordeal was unpardonably vulgar for the wife, insulting to the husband. Swallowing her pride, the lady from India responded with singular naïveté. How would she go about reshaping her reputation? "Citizen First Consul, I need only model myself after Citizeness Bonaparte." Was she really as dense as people said?

During a dinner at the English embassy, she raved about a diamond necklace the ambassadress was wearing, summing up her admiration thus: "It must have cost a fortune!" Her hostess replied that the price was not beyond Monsieur de Talleyrand's reach if he should wish to buy her one. Whereupon Madame Grand exclaimed: "Heavens, Madam, do you think I married the Pope?" No, she had been satisfied with a bishop. Still, worldly wisdom prompted her to invest in shady enterprises that brought her a little money to fall back on.

In the summer of 1803, her husband took her with him for the first time on his annual cure at Bourbon-l'Archambault where he had been going every August for the past thirty years. He observed the daily round of baths and showers scrupulously, convinced that it would prolong his good health. At the arrival of its illustrious visitor, the little town bubbled with activity. Everyone showered him with attentions; they even assigned him a private pool which to this day bears the name "Bains du Prince." A number of the houses in which he stayed, some previously host to famous persons, are now designated historic sites, as, for example, the Sévigné lodge. He always traveled with a retinue which, on arrival, began to expand from the nucleus of a few select persons. Even in the country, then, he had a pleasant, highly respectable social life. Though refined speech and manners were *de rigueur* there as in Paris, a more relaxed, gayer atmosphere prevailed. It makes one think of his great-grandmother's little court at Chalais; Talleyrand himself probably was reminded of it.

He spent hours playing whist and craps, a new dice game introduced from England, all the while receiving visitors. Local notables would come by, some to pay their respects, others to satisfy their curiosity or interest. A few asked him to transmit requests to the government. Half listening, he made mental notes of those requests and followed them up on his return to the capital. Simple, artless diversions gave him far more pleasure than his urbane Paris friends would have imagined. His physician, who traveled with him, had a passion for Latin quotations which not everyone, particularly the ladies, could understand. It amused Talleyrand to whet the curiosity of these ladies by making them think the doctor had made some improper remark in Latin too scandalous to translate. The good doctor spouted only trivia, the ladies eyed him suspiciously, and the resulting confusion tickled Talleyrand's sense of humor. He also had occasion to see a clergyman he had known ever since his own priesthood days. The abbé de la Romagère had a talent for composing songs that amused Talleyrand. Turning to Hauterive, who was listening but enjoying it less, Talleyrand said gravely: "Did you hear the abbé? We'll have to make him a bishop." [2] And it was done. The story seems right out of Voltaire.

He would listen patiently to his tiresome barber endlessly repeating the same old hunting tales and neighborhood gossip. An elderly gentleman from Limoges who had lived at court would harp on his memories of Versailles; Talleyrand listened and even invited him for a visit in Paris, during which he proved to be a most sympathetic host though the old courtier's stories all but put him to sleep. The sandman's name was baron de Saint-Etienne.

At Bourbon-l'Archambault, Talleyrand actually was talkative. He would tell stories, something he never did in Paris except in the privacy of his "magic circle." A young secretary remembered those pleasant times when the minister "would surrender to the delights of thinking aloud, like a grown-up child surrendering to the delights of recreation." Talleyrand, at the spa in Bourbon, invented holidays.

He enjoyed telling how he made a practice of breaking Don d'Azara's dishes. This distinguished gentleman, the Spanish ambassador, had committed an unpardonable faux pas, a rare occurrence in his circles, but such things do happen. Talleyrand had asked him for three pounds of chocolate, a Spanish specialty in those days. Azara had the chocolate delivered—alas, with the bill. It cried vengeance. After that, each time our hero dined with the Spanish ambassador he bribed the serving staff to drop all the chinaware possible during dinner. Talleyrand had the supreme satisfaction, he admitted, of "watching the venerable Spanish nobleman wince." [3]

While at the spa, a diminutive made her appearance in the household. They called her Charlotte; she was about five years old. She sprang up like a mushroom in the morning dew. One day the town suddenly discovered her standing between Monsieur and Madame de

Talleyrand. By unveiling her in that placid little watering place, they chose to surround her with provincial semi-obscurity before exposing her to the capital's glare. Her social launching—if you can call it that—was half-complete therefore when the Talleyrands returned to Paris, for neither he nor his tactless spouse would ever elaborate the child's pedigree. She remained simply "Charlotte" until her marriage in 1820 to a nephew of Talleyrand, baron Alexandre-Daniel de Périgord. One may be sure, however, that if Talleyrand married a penniless "foundling" to his nephew, she cannot have been "found" just anywhere. He was bountiful—not to say fatherly—in providing her dowry.

As no one seemed interested in explaining Charlotte's origin (Talleyrand's name was Charles, by the way), people advanced their own theories. They said she was the daughter of a French émigré in England. They said she was born to one of Madame de Brionne's daughters at the time Talleyrand was their lover (but that went back to 1785, and here Charlotte was five years old in 1805). They said she belonged to the comte de Beaujolais, Louis-Philippe d'Orléans's brother. They also took her for the offspring of Talleyrand's liaison with Madame Grand, which began in 1798. Though the dates reinforce that argument, still, it is only conjecture. What impressed everyone was the care and affection Talleyrand lavished on the little girl. He was fond of children and took a personal interest in her education and upbringing. Only his intimates could understand his readiness to indulge her mischief-making and her whims.

At the moment, Charlotte was crying a lot; she hated learning to read. Madame de Talleyrand was teaching her the alphabet and crying just as often. We might add that in addition to her blond hair and peaches-and-cream complexion, Madame Grand had a talent for weeping. Thus did Charlotte make her appearance, another enigma in Talleyrand's life.

When the watering season ended, Talleyrand asked Bonaparte's permission to stop off on the way home at Valençay, the estate he had purchased in May, 1803, and had never seen.

Valençay is more than a château, an estate, or a hunting lodge. It fulfilled a yearning, a political philosophy, a personal ambition; it symbolized a way of life and represented the very soul of Talleyrand. Bonaparte was the first to realize that for Talleyrand to function ideally, he needed to call himself statesman, diplomat, financier, political oracle, and, on top of all that, lord of a seat worthy of his name. In a way, Bonaparte forced Talleyrand to purchase Valençay, knowing what a marvelous tool this unique man represented, whose nobility and culture could enhance the image of his government. Instead of complaining about his minister's lavish spending, he exploited it. One day he told Talleyrand: "I want you to buy a fine estate, to give brilliant receptions for diplomats and foreign dignitaries; make people want to come there, make them feel that an invitation is a reward to the representatives of sovereigns with whom I am pleased." He was electing Talleyrand the steward of his imperial banquets. Not a bad choice, and not a bad way to show favor to compliant embassies. With Talleyrand already on hand, all they needed was the "fine estate."

Monsieur de Luçay, a prefect of the palace whose work kept him in close contact with the First Consul, owned the estate of Valençay in the département of Indre. Unable to maintain it, he looked for a buyer. His description of the property satisfied both Bonaparte and Talleyrand. The price, however, Talleyrand protested, was far beyond his modest means. This suddenly invented modesty stemmed from his knowledge that modesty is unfailingly rewarded by proud tyrants. After all, hadn't Bonaparte commanded him to buy . . . Whoever issues commands also incurs obligations—to pay, for instance. The Consul promised to pay part of the price. The deed of sale was registered in Paris in May, 1803, through two notaries, Maître Raguideau and Maître Chodron.

It was an impressive estate extending over 19,000 hectares, making it one of the several vast feudal holdings left in France. It embraced twenty-three communes, with Valençay the principal town and district seat. An extraordinary holdover from the Ancien Régime had tumbled into the lap of its prize survivor. In other words, the shipwreck's most illustrious victim claimed the best of the wreckage. As a result, the courtly and manorial traditions of former times lived on until 1838.

It was early September when Talleyrand first laid eyes on Valençay, 40 kilometers north of Chateauroux, bordering Berry and Touraine. The château rises above the narrow river Nahon, and is ringed by the two vast forests of Garseland and Gastine. (Without them, there would have been neither hunting nor splendid vistas.) The history of Valençay goes back far into the past. In the thirteenth century it belonged to Alix de Bourgogne, a descendant of Pierre de Courtenay. It passed to the d'Etampes dynasty of Touraine, remaining with them for three hundred years. These lords bore the title marquis d'Etampes et de Valençay. The greater part of the present château was built by them in the sixteenth century, including the distinctive, colossal keep. In the eighteenth century, John Law, the financier, contracted to buy Valençay; he never paid for it, however, and the sale was annulled. The next owner was

Chaumont de la Millière, whose daughter sold it in 1766 to the farmer-general of Villemorien. Being a rich man, the latter added the domain of Luçay and gave his son that title. The son was the Luçay from whom Talleyrand bought the property.

Everything was on a princely scale. The château had twenty-five master apartments. The first-floor gallery, fifty-six meters long, led to a chapel built over an angle of the courtyard. Talleyrand and his wife wandered through the maze of corridors and rooms; after three days they still had not seen the whole estate. The magnificent park stretched for 150 hectares; stately trees and gardens dotted the landscape. But they had to end their exhausting though enchanting tour, for Bonaparte wanted his minister back.

There was no dearth of gossip about Valençay or the sudden appearance of Charlotte. With regard to the former, one of Louis XVIII's agents reported: "It is said that he intends it for a little girl who has suddenly appeared in his house, no one knows from where." It was also rumored that "Charlotte X" would be known as Mademoiselle de Valençay. That honor, however, was destined for another.

From then on, Talleyrand made a habit of returning to Valençay every September. In 1804, his guest there for two weeks was Lucchesini, the Prussian minister; the next year it was the prince of Württemberg. The vast château came to life each fall, with its dazzling receptions, and created a legend for the whole region. A Chouan rebel seeking refuge at Valençay started the rumor that somewhere in the vast cellars Talleyrand had set up a printing press for counterfeit notes. The man obviously was not familiar with our hero's preference for genuine, ready-made cash. In time it struck Talleyrand that so much land ought to yield some income, not simply consume it. The Berry region was, as he put it, "naturally sluggish"; to shake off that torpor would take patience. In 1807 he wrote: "I am at Valençay attending to affairs that have been somewhat neglected for a while, and am trying to derive some gain from objects of general utility, merinos, a cotton-spinning machine, new crops." [4]

When agriculture proved unprofitable, he turned to industry. Valençay yielded him 180,000 francs in 1808, a very respectable income. In 1806 he added a bell-tower to the church. He set his wife to organizing a little school for twelve young girls. That prompted Madame de Staël to dub Citizeness Talleyrand a latter-day Maintenon, scarcely a compliment to either the new Sun King or his favorite!

When Valençay's lord returned to Paris, he had other problems to face.

TALLEYRAND

Never Stumbling, the Cripple Wades in Blood

At the close of 1803, Talleyrand was in great favor, ranking among the most influential men in France, perhaps the most influential one after Bonaparte. He had disposed of Fouché; Lucien was in disgrace, and Cambacérès too clever not to adapt to the winds of change. The time seemed ripe, as Talleyrand expressed it in the vernacular of the day, "for the First Consul's curule chair to be transformed into a throne."

No one did more than Talleyrand to set a crown on the First Consul's head. Napoleon never forgot it, even when he and his minister were at odds later on. In 1812 he told Caulaincourt: "He is one of the persons who helped to found my dynasty."

Talleyrand's help consisted in persuading the public to accept the coronation. But how was the distrust of all former regicide members of the Convention now peopling the assemblies and the administration to be overcome? By offering them a warranty that the future emperor and his court of former nobles would not turn upon them one day for their terrorist past. This warranty was the body of a murdered Bourbon prince. Louis XVI's murderers would feel safer if the new dynasty liquidated a prince of the same lineage; it would seal the bloody pact between the Terror and the Empire.

Who conceived the idea? Not Fouché, the sinister regicide, nor any of his henchmen, but the descendant of Adalbert de Périgord, our ex-bishop of Autun. Talleyrand was the one who proposed abducting and executing the duc d'Enghien. "When M. de Talleyrand, a priest and a gentleman, inspired and devised the crime by constantly igniting Bonaparte's fears, he was in dread of a possible Bourbon Restoration." This time Chateaubriand rightly castigates Talleyrand.

First he broached the idea, then subtly promoted it. With his talent for originating and justifying wholly unjustifiable events, he succeeded not only in selling the idea of this murder to the person who stood to benefit by it, but even in dulling the conscience of the murderers. Afterwards, safe from repercussions, he could stand back and indulge in some indignant name-calling.

What evidence is there of his guilt? Very little, for Talleyrand took pains to erase his bloody footprints. In 1814, during the agonizing defeat and occupation of Paris when he headed the provisional government, he managed to make off with all official documents related to the duke's murder. Every word he wrote about this frightful incident has vanished.

300

For indeed he wrote reports to the First Consul recommending the abduction and execution of the young duke; all of them disappeared except a letter in his own handwriting which apparently slipped down behind a drawer and thus escaped burning. At least two people read that letter: Méneval, Napoleon's secretary, and Chateaubriand. Though Chateaubriand, as we know, was perfectly capable of "inventing" such a letter or distorting its contents, this time he actually saw, handled, and read the document. Had he made a copy, he could have dealt his enemy a stunning blow. Méneval also saw the letter in the First Consul's possession on March 18, 1807; he saw it again in 1814 and summarized the contents thus: Reminding Bonaparte of their conversation the day before, Talleyrand continued to argue the need for committing some sensational act to persuade the nation (especially the Jacobins) that Bonaparte, unlike Monk in England, had no intention of restoring the Bourbons. Pointing out that the Cadoudal conspiracy, which had nearly claimed the First Consul's life, was a royalist plot devised by the princes, notably the duc d'Enghien, he called for punishment of all those involved. Chateaubriand was able to note one phrase in the letter: "If justice demands punishment, policy demands punishment without exception." The wording follows quite closely Méneval's version. Chateaubriand also quotes this sentence: "May I recommend M. de Caulaincourt to the First Consul, a man to whom he can give orders and who will execute them with as much discretion as fidelity." If Talleyrand did not write that, then an excellent parodist did. It has his ring. One can say that Méneval, Napoleon's devoted friend, would have moved Heaven and earth to exonerate the Consul, and that Chateaubriand's blind prejudice makes him a colorful but unreliable witness. Still, it is difficult to challenge them in this situation.

Unfortunately, it was only the beginning. Police agents had set a trap in Paris for the comte d'Artois. Warned, he managed to escape. Talleyrand then suggested that instead of the king's brother, his cousin, the duc d'Enghien, last of the Condés, would do for a victim. Talleyrand also was the one who drew Bonaparte's attention to the fact that the duke was in Ettenheim in the duchy of Baden-Baden, just over the border from Strasbourg. Having dropped the hint, he waited for it to germinate in the First Consul's head. It did. But for Talleyrand, Bonaparte would have remained ignorant of the duke's very existence and whereabouts. To make things even worse for the unfortunate grandson of the great Condé, a spy contributed a piece of misinformation. Talleyrand had implied that the prince's presence so close to the French border enabled him to direct royalist plots against the First Consul's life. Then came the false report that Dumouriez, the turncoat general, was with the duke at Ettenheim. Fearing the worst, Bonaparte is supposed to have exploded with anger: "Am I just a dog that anyone is free to beat?" Yet the man involved was not Dumouriez but Thumery, an inconsequential French émigré whose name on some German tongue had been taken for "Dumouriez."

On March 9, 1804, the rebel leader Cadoudal was arrested in Paris, dooming the royalist cause. The next day Bonaparte met with Fouché, Talleyrand, Cambacérès, and Murat. He was not interested in consulting them, only in obtaining their approval and support for the abduction and assassination of the duc d'Enghien. Cambacérès alone opposed the plan, thus inviting Bonaparte's scorn: "You have grown very sparing of Bourbon blood." He had decided to adopt the advice of Talleyrand, who, as Barras put it, "wanted to put a river of blood between the Bourbons and Napoleon." Perhaps the "river of blood" was our hero's answer to the "river of mud" which Bonaparte had placed between his minister and the Bourbons by forcing the bishop of Autun to marry Madame Grand. Talleyrand's gift for repartee was not exclusively verbal.

In his will, and rather magnanimously, Napoleon assumes full responsibility for the crime. When an English newspaper implicated Savary and Caulaincourt, the emperor, then in exile on St. Helena, protested angrily: "That's outrageous!" His will offered this explanation: "I had the duc d'Enghien arrested and convicted because the safety, the interests, and the honor of the French nation demanded it at a time when the comte d'Artois was the confessed leader of sixty assassins in Paris. In similar straits, I would again do just what I did."

He regretted nothing and blamed no one. Talleyrand must have felt relieved. In this case Napoleon's pride had spared our hero; but the truth came out on other occasions: "Talleyrand was the one who made me decide to arrest the duc d'Enghien, who was not even in the back of my mind. . . . I attached not the slightest importance to his presence on the banks of the Rhine and had no designs whatever on him."

In 1809, hearing that Talleyrand prided himself on having had no part in the deed and had washed his hands of it, the emperor thundered: "How amusing of him to play his tricks at my expense! Did I know the duc d'Enghien? Did I want to kill him?" No, of course not, but once having learned about him, he consented to put him to death. Napoleon never had trouble saying No when he wanted to.

Thiers [1] confirms that the First Consul issued and signed the orders delivered by Savary to Murat, which called for executing the duke at the fortress of Vincennes. The orders made it clear that the prisoner was to be sentenced to death rather than tried; they stated that immediately after sentencing (no doubt as to what the verdict would be), the prisoner was to be shot and buried in a courtyard of Vincennes. According to historians, Thiers's authority was a document in the possession of one of the Empire's ennobled families.

On the tenth and eleventh of March, 1804, Talleyrand sent notes to the baron of Edelsheim, Baden-Baden's minister in Paris, advising him that the duc d'Enghien was on Badenese soil and would be arrested and forcibly removed by French troops. No explanation, no excuse, no request for authorization, nothing remotely resembling due process of law. The law, in any event, had been violated, and for once Talleyrand even ignored "formalities." He was simply the instrument of a plan he had conceived but no longer controlled, which now was in the hands of executioners.

The duke was arrested on the night of March 14, 1804, by General Ordener, conducted to Strasbourg and then to Paris. Murat was in possession of Talleyrand's instructions. On March 20 the prisoner was taken before a military tribunal and sentenced to be shot. He had no legal counsel and no hearing. As we noted, his execution had been ordered before sentence was even pronounced. It was carried out immediately.

The only ray of hope, if there was one in the grim blackness of Vincennes, shone in the eyes of an innocent young soldier; the duc d'Enghien's courageous dignity turned a victim into a hero. They had suspended a lantern from his shoulder; its pale, flickering flame guided the musket fire straight to the target. At two-thirty in the morning the fateful deed was done.

Talleyrand was holding court at the duchesse de Luynes's, playing at dice. Knowing the execution was timed to the minute, at exactly two-thirty he lay down his cards and announced ominously: "The last Condé is no more." The guests froze. Uncomprehending, they stared at him, and for once he frightened them.

Josephine had tried to save the duke. On her knees she had begged her husband to spare the young prince. Her daughter Hortense was privy to those scenes. Josephine's entreaties might seem to incline the emperor to clemency, but his next encounter with Talleyrand invariably nullified the effect of her tears. She confided to Joseph Bonaparte: "The cripple makes me shiver. . . ." She was not the only one. In the ministry, Hauterive was speechless after reading the official version of the execution. Seeing his haggard face, Talleyrand asked: "What's the matter with you? Your eyes are popping out of your head!" [2]

"What's the matter with me is what ought to be the matter with you if you had read *Le Moniteur*. What a horrible thing!"

"Come now, are you mad?" the minister replied. "What's all the fuss about? A conspirator is captured near the frontier, taken to Paris and shot. What's so extraordinary about that?" [2]

He was already testing reactions to a carefully polished circular letter which he was preparing to dispatch to all the capitals in an effort to explain and justify. How many other horrible acts did he explain and justify in that fashion, such as the massacres of the tenth of August?

To the dismayed souls who persisted in regarding the execution as "extraordinary," he responded with a shrug: "Business is business."

Three days later, as a change of pace, Bonaparte ordered Talleyrand to give a ball. A little gaiety would make people forget. The entire diplomatic corps attended with barely a smile on any face. The assassination visibly had lowered Europe's morale. It was clear now that the French would stoop to anything. Why should anyone want to deal with or support a government that behaved so ignobly? Despite the general anxiety, our imperturbable host managed to conduct himself as the paragon of diplomacy.

On March 21, 1804, Chateaubriand sent him a letter of resignation. It was a courageous gesture. He had just been appointed minister to Valais, his sole source of income. He gave his wife's illness as an excuse for the shift. Talleyrand accepted the resignation without undue regret. The only real sufferer was Madame de Chateaubriand, who had some difficulty regaining not her health but her financial equilibrium. Having already spent money advanced by the ministry for their journey to Switzerland, they had to dip into Madame de Chateaubriand's dowry to settle the debt.

Foreign governments appeared much more accommodating than Chateaubriand in accepting Talleyrand's story. For once, his voice was forceful to match his unmitigated lies. Russia alone questioned his logic and asked for further details. This form of censure from a court in which assassination was the usual way to ascend the throne made Talleyrand reach for his pen. He parried the question with another one: France had not yet asked for an explanation of Czar Paul I's assassination in St. Petersburg and awaited it from Czar Alexander, his successor. A relative of Alexander's reported that this reply so wounded the czar that he never forgave Napoleon or his minister despite their amicable overtures later on.

Why then, contrary to personal and political inclinations, did Talleyrand steep himself in this murder? As always, he was looking ahead. If Bonaparte should be struck down, Talleyrand's own career and France's future would go down with him. By crowning Bonaparte, he thought France would have the two things she needed: a king and peace. The reckless determination of rebels like Cadoudal so filled him with dread that he saw no safety unless royalist terrorism were devitalized. That was his motive for wanting the duke killed. His solution was outrageous but it worked, for every Bourbon prince felt the guns of Vincennes trained on him.

At the same time, he had bound Bonaparte closer to him, for the two were now accomplices in a murder. Indissoluble, they could go on to build a new monarchy without shooting any more princes, simply by snuffing out liberty. The values Talleyrand had cherished and defended all along, liberty, human rights, justice, humanity, all the things that elevated him above his vices, were sacrificed to an assassination.

Try as he did to rid himself of it, the bloodstain stayed with him forever. Like episcopal unction, it was indelible.

Henceforth, bodily and spiritually he was a different man. The death mask someone observed around 1802 settled deeper upon his blanched features; the pitch-black night of Vincennes, the eerie glow of a lantern bringing death to an innocent man left their mark on a singular personality. The elegant, cynical aristocrat, the urbane cleric carried on, but with the advent of the new century our hero took on a new look. No longer quite so Voltairean or quite so manifestly enlightened, he was becoming a disturbing, shadowy figure. In the pursuit of worldly pleasures, one misstep has plunged us headlong into the shady sorcery of certain cellars in *La Comédie humaine*. One day Balzac will welcome Talleyrand as a brother. Voltaire turns away. And we turn the page on this shameful episode.

"The First to Become King Was a Contented Soldier"

Did Talleyrand remember this line from Voltaire as he thrust Italy's conqueror toward the throne? By 1804, France was ready to crown a ruler. The hereditary principle became law on April 23, 1804, in a council session attended by Talleyrand. On May 7 he sent off a tightly reasoned note to European embassies arguing the legitimacy of Napoleonic power: "It was a yearning that settled upon all our hearts once the troubled times were over." This yearning was for "Empire," though the word was never mentioned.

On May 18, 1804, a cannonade proclaimed the *senatus consultum*

305

transforming First Consul Bonaparte into an emperor. Though he did not attend the meeting, Talleyrand followed events closely and was among the first to intone "Your Majesty"—undoubtedly the only one to give it the proper inflection—to Emperor Napoleon I. He had not taken an especially active role in the last-minute dealings ushering in the Empire; he had laid its cornerstone, however, having advocated the need for a king ever since 1798. No one could match his success in instilling the desire for a Napoleonic monarchy in French society. He achieved his effects in an offhanded, almost cynical manner: a dream merchant with no use for his own products. Of Bonaparte, had he not said to Madame de Rémusat that "this combination of Roman Republic and Charlemagne is going to his head"?

He left the wording of the proclamation to the Assembly's clerks. Once you have a leader, a crown, and public acclaim, you simply sit back and record events. He left that to the experts.

Still, the proclamation was not wholly to his liking. He opposed the title of emperor, preferring king instead. "Empire" is a term denoting conquest, elastic boundaries, subjugation of remote territories, and, in short, uncertainty and war. Anyway, such a pompous title struck him as vulgar. "King of France" was noble, restrained, and reassuring even if it *was* illegitimate. Ultimately, peace and prosperity would confer certain rights on a régime that had none to begin with: the rights of success. Talleyrand was convinced that a benevolent, pacifist ruler would be highly popular. Bonaparte flatly refused a kingship, which, he felt, would reduce him to trailing slavishly after the Bourbons. He wanted to initiate history. "King" and "emperor" admittedly are only words, but how many divorces have sprung from words? One day, just for mischief's sake, Talleyrand sent General Berthier to cry up the advantages of kingship in Bonaparte's ear. Our hero stayed within earshot so as not to miss the storm. At the word "king," Bonaparte exploded: "Imbecile! Who sent you here to vex me this way? Next time, don't take on any such errand." [1]

On July 11, Talleyrand was made grand chamberlain to the emperor, his first imperial appointment. The Empire was less than two months old and a court was in the making. Talleyrand's position attached him personally to the emperor and gave him access to the imperial apartments; during meals he stood behind his sovereign's chair. His court attire was sumptuous: a bit showy, but nothing like the circus outfits worn by Barras and Reubell. Crimson velvet breeches and waistcoat, a matching cape faced with white silk, gold-braided collar, lapels and cuffs, lace neckband, white silk scarf worn crosswise, and a sword.

Six months later he received his first ribbon of the Legion of Honor.

Mere baubles. He was not satisfied, and rightly so. Cambacérès, for example, had been dignified with the new rank of arch-chancellor, a title Talleyrand should have received. He expected it and failed to get it; one of his close friends, Madame de Vaines, tells us why: "His wife is the cause of his not being arch-ed. They did not want her to become Her Most Serene Highness and, because of her husband's rank, on a par with the emperor's sisters. This awkward situation created a measure of domestic strife. But what can you expect? Sooner or later one's follies come home to roost." Talleyrand, who knew the value of titles, wrote to Stanislas de Girardin: "Highness, which is a title for those of royal blood, is meaningless for ordinary persons." Of course; but if the honor had been conferred on him, he certainly would not have turned it down. What really bothered him was seeing low-born politicians elevated to high distinctions. Having been severely lectured on the subject, Madame Grand waxed ecstatic about the new titles, claiming that her husband was delighted at the way they were being awarded. Such enthusiasm pricked Madame de Rémusat's curiosity, and she remarked: "She made such a point of repeating to me how happy her husband was, how satisfied, how cheerful, how well he got along with the emperor, that I was tempted to doubt her every word" (September 21, 1804).

Talleyrand enjoyed spinning Napoleon's head with flattery. It was he who fostered the vision of revived Carolingian glory. When the emperor halted his tour of the Rhenish provinces at Aix-la-Chapelle, Talleyrand wrote to him there: "It would seem both great and fitting that the city which for so long served as the seat of empire and Charlemagne's residence should blaze with the splendor of Your Majesty's presence, demonstrating the similarities which Europe has already recognized between the restorer of the Roman Empire and the founder of the French Empire." After such accolades, how could Napoleon possibly turn down Charlemagne's scepter, which was discovered (by a remarkable coincidence) just when he needed it? As fate would have it, the iron scepter they handed the emperor turned out to be a fake.

Talleyrand's flattery—which rapidly degenerated to pure servility —warrants further discussion. Napoleon was not always taken in by it. Talleyrand observed the traditional code, believing that by pleasing his sovereign he would win favor. But favor was no longer the game. Talleyrand imagined that he would be "the favorite," the nucleus of power in his revived monarchy. He was very wrong. Napoleon was the power, needing others only to execute his commands. Talleyrand considered this rigidity a breach of custom and of political practice. In fact, they were both wrong: Talleyrand in believing that he could attain the impossible; Napoleon in bypassing an invaluable councilor.

Talleyrand became disillusioned as he discovered that flattery, instead of winning him power, brought only certain material rewards and the dubious satisfaction of pleasing a master whom he gradually ceased to admire.

The birth of this glorious Empire called for a spectacular rite, a coronation. The idea was Napoleon's. People were stupefied by his announced intention of being consecrated and crowned in Notre Dame by the Pope, whom he would bring over for the occasion. Not that it was difficult to stupefy the public; the real task was persuading His Holiness to make the journey to Paris. It fell to Talleyrand, and he encountered resistance. Addressing Pius VII, he wrote: "His Majesty is pained to note some apparent feeling that he has not yet done everything possible to enable the sovereign pontiff to accept his invitation." Actually the "invitation" was nothing short of a command performance. Talleyrand proceeded to enumerate a long list of the First Consul's services to the Holy See, not forgetting to mention the two papal states he had restored to His Holiness, Pontecorvo and Benevento. How long they were to remain restored, and why and for whom they were to be reclaimed is another story we shall get to later on. In any event, the Pope yielded, whether out of gratitude or fear is not certain, and off went His Imperial Majesty's grand chamberlain to greet the Holy Father at Fontainebleau: an altogether unexpected encounter between a married, schismatic bishop and the bishop of Rome. We have no record of what was said or of the looks they exchanged.

Madame de Talleyrand (innocently enough) requested a papal audience. His Holiness refused to receive *"questa donna"* (that woman) under the name she currently bore. Talleyrand was said to have been deeply hurt by this rejection.

Talleyrand took part in the coronation as Périgords had always done. Once again he heard the *Te Deum* peal forth, bursting the vaults of Notre Dame, resounding all the way to Vienna, London, Berlin, St. Petersburg, Washington, Madrid, and wherever else the eyes of government were fixed in awe and trembling on this fateful anachronism in the making, a Western emperor. Talleyrand was now fifty; he had been twenty-one when Louis XVI was crowned. One more coronation awaited him in his seventy-first year, that of Charles X. On this December 2, 1804, was he thinking back to Louis XVI's anointment, the faces of his charming lady friends, or his father with sword unsheathed guarding the Sacred Ampulla? We have no idea. He skipped over it entirely in his

Memoirs. Coronations failed to inspire him. Anyway, this one was something of a circus, an impressive but slightly sham affair. He ought to have known, having had a hand in it. The ceremony, imposing of its kind, was planned by the comte de Ségur.

Notre Dame's interior was barely recognizable beneath all the painted cardboard. They had managed somehow to turn St. Louis's own cathedral into a sort of Greco-Egyptian paper temple, all pediments and pilasters, columns and obelisks in a profusion of trophies, banners, and Roman eagles. The eagle was everywhere, symbol of the times. Dignitaries and the military wore full regalia; the new court appeared in splendid silks, laces, and plumes. All the gold braid, all the jewels of France and Navarre (plus a few other sources) glittered on shoulders, sparkled on necks and foreheads. It was a truly imposing spectacle.

Etiquette, however, was not the hallmark of this new society, and things frequently got out of hand. Talleyrand noted this when, executing his duty as grand chamberlain, he went to fetch Napoleon from his apartment in the Tuileries: "But for the solemn occasion, I would have found it hard to contain myself. He [the emperor] had already put on his white velvet breeches dotted with gold bees, his lace ruff, and atop that his cavalry coat, the only dressing gown he ever owned."

Preparations dragged on for hours. The various processions had trouble forming outside the cathedral owing to the mass of carriages clogging the narrow streets. It was a cold December 2. Protocol having directed the Pope and high dignitaries to take their seats in the morning, His Holiness was left shivering for hours on his throne. No air of meditation filled the audience, only talk and laughter, people shuffling about and snorting to keep warm. The new highnesses and aspirants to that eminence clapped each other on the back as they munched away on meat pies.

The entrance of the imperial couple restored order; the nation sprang to attention and remained thus for ten years. You see this in David's masterful painting of the coronation.

Jacques-Louis David, having championed the Revolution, now surpassed himself in depicting imperial glory. How palettes change, along with everything else. In his enthusiasm, he even portrayed Letizia Bonaparte, absent as she was, having no desire to see her daughter-in-law Josephine, the widow Beauharnais, crowned empress. *"Questa donna,"* she probably muttered. Talleyrand stands near the altar between Berthier and Eugène de Beauharnais. He is larger than most of the figures around him and is wearing an amazing expression. One senses the irony, the biting sarcasm behind that haughty stare fixed on the vast audience of ordinary persons, mere characters in a fantastic opera of his own invention. Clearly, it is not the face of an idol-worshipper. Talleyrand seems to be an impassive, impartial witness to a ceremony of great significance to the public, but which he regards as the final ritual in a vast political epic.

The coronation was only a conclusion. The important question was how the new ruler would rule. Hopefully he would prove worthy of this venerable nation and her wise founders.

Six months later, Talleyrand attended still another coronation. In Milan, Napoleon placed the crown of Italy on his own head. That was the entire ceremony. He pronounced the traditional oath of kingship with all the assurance of a legitimate ruler of the Lombards: "Heaven bestowed it on me; woe to him who touches it!"

Recognizing this as blatant usurpation, Talleyrand made a pretense nevertheless of sanctioning the lamentable act. Just a few weeks earlier he had advised the empress that the emperor and his brother Lucien ought to be reconciled and Lucien made king of Italy as a reward. The proposal transmitted to Lucien demanded such subservience to the emperor that he rejected it outright, choosing to be free, as did Joseph when approached in turn. Thus Napoleon kept the crown for himself. Evidently the kingdom of Italy was not meant to become a dependency of the French Empire; it was simply swallowed up.

Talleyrand had the task of winning acceptance for this alarming annexation. His initial fear (subsequently justified) was of a rupture with Austria. Would she stand by and watch France expand her borders to the Tyrol, Venetia, and the very heart of the Italian peninsula? But in 1804 Talleyrand was not listening to his own conscience; he was courting favor. He groveled. Not by defying Napoleon's ambitions later on did he become a "traitor," but by serving them now. Someone familiar with his *modus operandi* said that Talleyrand's cleverness at the time consisted in "guessing what Bonaparte wants and giving it all his attention." To please his master, he even stooped to extolling his "moderation": "Your Majesty sought to give France a taste of order [which is true] and Europe a taste of peace [which is not true]." He seemed surprised that anyone dared compare the emperor to Alexander and Charlemagne; "idle and deceptive analogies," he called them. And he blazed up at this comment in the *Moniteur Universel* on March 19, 1805: "By constantly extending the frontiers of his empire, Alexander was merely preparing his own violent end." In this case, the critics were Madame de Staël's "ideologist" friends, Destutt de Tracy and Benjamin Constant among others, the watchdogs of liberty. In his fascination with the new crown, Talleyrand had forgotten all about them. Yet he was convinced that Napoleon's actions would lead inevitably to war.

In May, 1805, amid the distractions of the Milan coronation, Talleyrand received the Prussian orders of the Red Eagle and the Black Eagle. He did not refuse them, decorations being wholly appropriate to his style of life.

While Napoleon, king of the Lombards, and his court were being hailed in every corner of Italy, a rumor reached Paris that Talleyrand had died in Milan. Our hero's intimate friend Madame de Vaines, whose husband was in the coronation entourage, commented to General Thibaudeau in response to his assurance that the ex-bishop of Autun was no more: "Monsieur de Talleyrand dead in Milan? Well now, he certainly didn't ask for it. He led those Italian ladies a short and merry chase, especially a former mistress of Petiet's, the French minister in Milan, to whom he gave large sums of money. And heading the list was Madame Simons Lange [we met her earlier, the mistress stolen from Barras at whose house he dined on the 19th Brumaire], who either followed or preceded him in each city. Spiteful gossips who think he is no longer a great lover say that once again his desire to please made him act that way." The slanderous tidbit echoes Reubell's venomous jibe in the days of the Directory: "He lacked the means." Undoubtedly a man's fifties do not rouse him to feats of sexual prowess if he is not already a "great lover." Was he ever one? As for Madame de Lange, she is part of the decor, the "official" mistress perhaps so that the ex-lover may not appear to be "ex." Madame de Vaines continued: "He is presently taking the waters and resting in the company of his chaster half. When he returns, I intend to torment him about his love life during the trip to Italy."

If nothing else, the false report of his death serves to inform us of the health, movements, and rural pursuits of Talleyrand in his fiftieth year.

"While We Were Marching Through Germany"

In 1805, at the peak of his favor, Talleyrand was reaping the rewards of his docility. No one else spoke quite so freely to Napoleon. They had long conversations together almost daily, after which Talleyrand would submit reports to the emperor on certain points. Not one such memorandum has survived; Talleyrand destroyed them all. Napoleon found those private discussions intensely stimulating. One day he said to his chamberlain: "You are Europe's master of the art of conversation. What is your secret?" Talleyrand responded with another question: "In warfare, don't you always try to choose the field?" Yes, Napoleon preferred to do so but did not always have the option.

> Well, Sire, I select the field of conversation. I venture only where I have something to say. I ignore all the rest. Ordinarily I never allow myself to be questioned, except by you; if someone asks me something, it is because I myself have suggested the question. When I used to hunt, I would always fire at a distance of six paces and rarely bagged anything. Other hunters would shoot any time at anything. I never took chances. In a conversation, I let everything remote go by about which I can offer only banal comments; but when something crops up right under my nose, I never miss.

Rarely did Talleyrand expose himself at such length.

Evidence of his great favor was Napoleon's reaction when a special envoy of the czar proposed to hold private talks with the emperor. The slight was aimed at Talleyrand and came from Russian ambassador Markoff, whom our hero had dressed down at an earlier date. Napoleon sided with his minister. He defended him again when a letter from Markoff to Lucien Bonaparte containing some disparaging comments on Talleyrand was intercepted and handed to the emperor.

But war still threatened. Napoleon rattled his sabers at the English, who were in no mood to surrender Malta after the emperor had annexed Italy.

Then Cobenzl, Austria's ambassador, appeared; Talleyrand's schoolfellow at the Collège d'Harcourt, his houseguest in Paris and in Neuilly, and the faithful companion of Madame Grand and her pugs. An amiable if slightly ridiculous personality, he bore a message from Austria's Francis II that could have been an invitation to a ball. Instead, it was an ultimatum demanding French withdrawal from Italy. The curse called down on whoever dared touch the crown of Italy settled upon him who had seized it.

Napoleon could not negotiate, could not retreat. His acts were tragic because they were irreparable. He was driven to wage war and win, or lose everything. As a result, the naval base at Boulogne was abandoned and the army swarmed into Germany. France sent her full military might against Austria, leaving her coastline unguarded. So war was declared over the crown of Italy, a fantasy to begin with. The hostilities came as no surprise to Talleyrand, only the rapidity with which Austria had declared herself. "Talleyrand is in despair," Lucchesini reported to the king of Prussia, "and if he could have prevented or could

still prevent the clash or halt the course of events before success or defeat excites ambition or forces honor to continue, he would consider it
the most glorious opportunity of his career." [1]

He would have welcomed negotiations to try to stave off, or at least
interrupt, the fighting, but neither his vision nor his humanitarianism
could turn the tide. Still, in Europe's chancelleries Napoleon's minister
was acquiring a "pacifist" reputation. But in fact, at his master's demand,
Talleyrand was preparing a new note blaming all the trouble on Austria.

In 1805 he knew the full burden of serving Napoleon. Gone were
the delights of life on the rue du Bac or the rue d'Anjou or Neuilly, gone
the charming companionship of his admiring lady friends. Now, with
secretaries close at heel, he trudged all over Europe behind his master.
Our limping diplomat dragged his weary steps from bivouac to inn, from
mudhole to battlefield.

Joining Napoleon at Strasbourg on October 1, Talleyrand dined
with him and Rémusat that evening. The emperor planned to leave at
once and march his army day and night until they reached Austria.
After dinner, Talleyrand and Rémusat stepped into Napoleon's bedchamber for a moment. By so doing they witnessed an unforgettable
scene which Talleyrand recorded movingly and in detail many years
later in his *Memoirs*. The three of them were alone when Napoleon
suddenly crumpled to the floor. Motioning Talleyrand to shut the door,
he lost consciousness and began to moan, to foam at the mouth, to shake
convulsively. The seizure lasted a quarter of an hour. Talleyrand bathed
the emperor's temples with eau de Cologne. Napoleon finally regained
his senses, stood up, put on fresh clothes, and made the two men swear
never to divulge what they had seen—which has all the earmarks of an
epileptic fit. They were still trembling when Napoleon set off at the
head of his troops.

After that, Talleyrand began to fear Napoleon might die. What
would happen then? Anarchy? Better choose war. The thought of losing
him revived his fondness for the emperor, who was no less attached to
his minister. On October 1, 1805, bidding good-bye to Josephine and
Talleyrand, Napoleon declared in the presence of Rémusat: "It is indeed
distressing to leave the two persons we love best."

In the days ahead, Talleyrand's letters would bear witness to that
deep attachment. Some of the expressions hearken back to the budding
romance. "On learning from Her Majesty the empress that we shall have
no news of Your Majesty for four or five days, I was left with an indescribable feeling of distress."

In the same letter he spoke of the English fleet's "clandestine" departure for Cadiz. With his gift of prophecy, how is it that this maneuver of Nelson's did not also inspire him with "an indescribable feeling of distress"? Could he not guess that the secretly departed enemy fleet was heading for Trafalgar?

Shortly thereafter Napoleon bottled up the Austrian army in Ulm and forced its surrender. A stroke of genius. Another more modest one was his decision, purely whimsical, to marry Eugène de Beauharnais to the elector of Bavaria's daughter. Why? Just because the idea appealed to him. Instructions for negotiating the marriage warned "that the will and temper of Napoleon would brook no refusal." The marriage took place two months later, on January 16, 1806.

With little enough time ahead, Napoleon could not afford to waste a moment; Talleyrand moved more deliberately but with greater foresight. He advocated restraint, even in victory, a seemingly absurd policy which actually was judicious. After the capitulation of Ulm, he wrote to Napoleon urging him not to crush Austria or drive her to retaliate; through appeasement based upon moderate demands, he could recruit an ally for France. It was the same policy he had advanced in 1792 of securing peace in Europe by a strong alliance to maintain the balance of power.

This memorandum, written in Strasbourg and dispatched to Napoleon as he marched on Vienna, is a model of tact, political insight, temperance, and vision. No one can attribute it to the pen of Desrenaudes or Hauterive, for Talleyrand had only his secretaries with him in Strasbourg. He dictated, edited, redictated, and then reedited the text. The handwriting is the same as in all the previous notes, and this one we know to be his work.

To pacify Austria, he proposed removing the source of potential friction between her and France: their common boundaries. This called for creating between Italy and Austria a buffer state comprising Venetia, the Tyrol, and Trieste. To compensate Austria for her lost territories, they could offer her a block of the Balkans: Wallachia, Moldavia, Bessarabia, and northern Bulgaria.

Afterwards Talleyrand wrote to Hauterive describing his recommendations to the emperor, urging that peace replace incessant warfare, and concluding: "That is my dream for the evening." [2] And once again he was right: it was only a dream. Napoleon made no response to the memorandum, did not heed the warning—the summons even—behind Monsieur d'Autun's unctuous words. Talleyrand held out the choice of a conscious effort to make peace or open warfare carried to its inevitable consequences. The admonition deserved more attention than Napoleon gave it.

That memorandum reached the emperor when he was still ignorant of the fact that two days after the victory of Ulm, on October 21, 1805, the French fleet had been annihilated at Trafalgar. With his unfailing suavity Talleyrand broke the news of this terrible disaster: "I am deeply distressed to advise Your Majesty of the sad news I have received from Cadiz about the situation of the combined fleet." He ended the letter with a gallant flourish: "Genius and good luck were in Germany" (November 12, 1805). Ulm would deaden the pain of Trafalgar.

That same day he wrote to Hauterive, but on quite a different note. He seemed shaken, deeply moved, choosing words which, colorless as they are, were outside his normal vocabulary. He spoke of "horrible news"; he deplored the sufferings of wounded and captured prisoners fated to die in captivity. It "filled him with anguish." The "man of France" mourned defeat, was tormented by political uncertainties. A suspicion dawned that the Empire was stricken. Trafalgar opened the first rift. "What horrible news from Cadiz! May it not hinder any of the political operations which we would do well to undertake now. The first letters I have received are profoundly disturbing. I fear that further details will only compound the already heartrending picture. I am troubled by the wreckage of the fleet and the effect this disaster may have on the morale of our ports and crews." [3]

But it took more than that to dampen his courage. He went on to report that in Strasbourg they were celebrating the fall of Ulm, adding coolly: "We fired our cannon in Strasbourg just as you did; the bishop is cooking up a *Te Deum.*" Cooked-up *Te Deum*s were a familiar dish to Monseigneur d'Autun.

The end of October found him in Munich. The emperor planned to divide up Germany among the three major powers, France, Austria, and Prussia, the prelude to the Confederation of the Rhine. Napoleon dictated; Talleyrand, now merely the emperor's chief scribe for foreign matters, wrote. He took notes and stopped thinking. Napoleon was doing the thinking for everyone, carving, disjointing, and distributing. What became of those populations? They hardly counted. And their rulers? They trembled.

Constrained as he was, Talleyrand still managed to promote his policy of building national prestige. In 1802, during the Consulate, he stationed General Brune in Constantinople in an effort to maintain and enlarge the influence France had enjoyed in the Near East since the

Crusades. In 1805, he appointed a Turkish and a Persian specialist to the language faculty of the Collège de France in order to turn out trained personnel for diplomatic missions. One of those professors was the noted orientalist and statesman Silvestre de Sacy. But all such cultural efforts were bound to be dwarfed by the emperor's grandiose military designs.

We may recall the very patrician and very beautiful comtesse de Brionne, who became so enamored of the handsome abbé de Périgord that she sought to make him a cardinal. Still an exile, she was then living in Germany. She had never forgiven our hero's "perverse activities" on the eve of the Revolution. Upon his arrival in Linz where the countess now lived, Talleyrand sent a note (no doubt with that seductive pen of his) announcing his impending visit. He went to her house and was informed that she had just left town, probably to avoid him. He was handed a sealed envelope inscribed with his name and, underlined, the list of titles he had acquired during the Empire. The envelope was empty. Beneath his façade of indifference, he must have been deeply hurt by the rebuff of an old and eminent friend. It is the price one must pay, the thorn in one's flesh, for stepping out of line.

Another rumor of Talleyrand's death cheered the Paris aristocracy. Archambaud, whom Napoleon had allowed to return to the capital, rushed at once to inform "the widow." It was said that she turned in a splendid performance, shrieking, tearing her hair, and raving like a madwoman. Shortly thereafter a letter in Talleyrand's own hand announced that he was in excellent health. "The widow" dried her tears, the others stopped snickering, and Talleyrand made a pun. The privileged élite in the faubourg Saint-Germain, openly hostile to the Corsican usurper, delighted in issuing daily bulletins on the demise of this or that imperial retainer. The salons became virtual hecatombs, leading Talleyrand to observe: "Tongues in the faubourg Saint-Germain have slain more generals than Austrian cannons."

Talleyrand tells us that he walked the battlefield at dusk after Austerlitz. Yet on December 2 he dated his letters Vienna. What is one to believe? He described "the battlefield littered with corpses on which night was falling" and his grim tour on the arm of General Lannes. He noted: "I owe it to him and to the honor of the army to say that this man, who had just accomplished feats of valor, who had proved supremely courageous under fire, was nearly made ill by the sight of so many dead and maimed of all nations; he was so upset that while pointing out the various sites from which major attacks had been launched, he stopped and said to me: 'I cannot bear this any longer, unless you will help me split the skulls of these wretched Jews plundering the dead and dying.' "

Beneath the icy exterior was an awareness of the feelings of others; Talleyrand's moving and dignified tribute to General Lannes is also a tribute to his own sensibilities.

The courier from Paris brought Napoleon a letter from Madame de Genlis reporting the reactions of the aristocracy to Austerlitz. She quoted biting remarks of the blue bloods about "his so-called victory." Even in the flush of triumph, Napoleon could not tolerate scorn, and in Talleyrand's presence flew into a rage, shouting, stamping his feet, and roaring: "So they think they are better than I, those gentlemen of the faubourg Saint-Germain! We shall see, we shall see!"

Talleyrand watched him, unmoved. Years later he wrote: "When did it happen, that 'we shall see'? . . . just a few hours after the defeat of the Russians and Austrians." Napoleon's brilliant victory was totally unrelated to his angry, puerile threats. He was hypersensitive, especially to the nobility's jibes. It amused Talleyrand to watch the small, frail man lose control of himself and stamp on his hat because a few haughty remnants of the Bourbon court were foolish enough to sneer at him. Talleyrand also commented, with a knowing smile, that Napoleon claimed a second victory on his return to Paris when he learned that three ladies of rank, Mesdames de Montmorency, de Mortemart, and de Chevreuse, had consented to attend Josephine in the Tuileries.

After Austerlitz he launched another effort to make an honorable peace with Austria. La Besnardière had to trail along, never knowing from one day to the next where he would lodge his papers or his secretaries. "La Besnardière is well," Talleyrand reported to Hauterive, "though the trip was long and uncomfortable; lack of food and horses, or finding dead bodies on the road was not part of our professional training. . . . This routine does not exactly appeal to La Besnardière. He doesn't mind working late, but not till midnight or two in the morning."

Talleyrand did not speak for himself. Chances are, however, that the routine did not appeal to him either, as he had to put up with the same discomforts and long hours. He was unwilling to acknowledge feelings that he attributed to a subordinate.

Three days after Austerlitz, he wrote to Napoleon: "I rejoice in Your Majesty's success as one whose thoughts and affections are closely concerned with Your Majesty's happiness and renown. . . . Your Majesty may now crush the Austrian monarchy or raise it up. Once crushed, it will be beyond even Your Majesty's power to reassemble the fragments and re-create a single body. Yet the existence of this single body is essential. It is indispensable to the future security of civilized nations." [4]

The final words of that letter warned prophetically that the Austrian monarchy was absolutely indispensable to European security.*

The letter's only effect was to provoke displeasure. Napoleon had his own peace plan; Talleyrand bowed once again to the emperor's will. The terms imposed on the Austrians by the Treaty of Pressburg went entirely against his grain.

Napoleon's decision to give Hanover (a dependency of the English crown) to Prussia, who deserved no such windfall, drew praise from Talleyrand. Strengthening Prussia was a risk, he knew, yet he wrote to Napoleon: "Once the treaty has been ratified in Berlin, Your Majesty will control North Germany as well as the South through his alliance with the three electors. . . . But while he is negotiating as skillfully as he directs battles, I am left in an extremely awkward position."

On December 17, 1805, he was writing from Brno, the Moravian capital: "Brno is a horrible place; there are four to five thousand wounded here. Great numbers of them die every day. Yesterday the stench was unbearable."

The stench in victory's wake. With infection rampant, the slightest wound proved fatal. That was the other face of glory, the military glory whose parade face even he failed to appreciate.

To cheer himself up, he added: "Today it is freezing, which is good for everyone," and asked that they be sure to send him some Malaga wine, "very dry and the least liqueur-like possible." After all, one might as well grin in the face of adversity.

He was in Pressburg for the signing of the peace on December 26, 1805. Clearly, Napoleon was not one to let negotiations drag. Austria signed everything. Talleyrand wrote to the emperor: "I have the honor to submit to Your Majesty the treaty we have just executed. Never has France dictated or Austria signed such a document. . . ."

Napoleon was still not satisfied. Talleyrand had taken it upon himself (a habit of his) to grant certain concessions. For example, he had deferred the payment of war indemnities, whereas Napoleon demanded immediate settlement. To be perfectly honest, he had also reduced their figure by 10 per cent, which sent the emperor into a fury. Surely our

* The prophecy was still not understood in 1918. Subsequent history has shown that the fundamental error of the Versailles Treaty was to have done what Talleyrand begged Napoleon not to do. Where are the fragments of the Hapsburg Empire today? Half of Europe has crumbled away. Can anyone put it together again?

hero collected a commission on the discount? Half, they say. Estimating that his minister had furnished his own reward, Napoleon withheld the compliments and wrote this instead: "You made a treaty for me in Pressburg which annoys me considerably." If the choice had been his, Talleyrand would have made a treaty infinitely more advantageous in the long run to the emperor and his Empire.

When a monument commemorating the Peace of Pressburg was to be raised in 1812, Talleyrand, in a note dated March 12, refused to be represented in the sculpture. That was his way of disclaiming any liability for a pact which he had been forced to sign.

Talleyrand's contacts with Austrian diplomats in Pressburg were significant. Metternich observed later that France was divided into two parties, the militarists who pledged to sink or swim with the emperor, and those who had begun to measure the destructive impact of Napoleon's "restless genius." This last point of view was shared, he said, by the minister of foreign relations and the minister of police, Talleyrand and Fouché. Metternich was even more specific: "During the campaign of 1805, M. de Talleyrand determined to bring all his influence to bear against Napoleon's ruinous projects. . . . We are indebted to him for the slight, more or less favorable modifications in the Pressburg negotiations."

If Talleyrand meekly defended the emperor's plans in public, he looked out for his own interests in private. His eyes were on the future. Trafalgar and Austerlitz, a stunning defeat, a brilliant victory, taught him that both events had one thing in common: they were bound to start other wars. His sympathies had shifted.

Experience told Talleyrand that the business of state and the business of one's own pocket were closely related. He was an expert at combining the two for the betterment of both. At this time he owed 600,000 francs to his friend Choiseul, then ambassador to Turkey, and fancied that he could get the Austrian government to pay his debt.

The idea came to him in 1804. All he needed was an excuse for requesting the money. He found one, and a very dignified memorandum reached Vienna asking for reimbursement of the 600,000 francs advanced by Choiseul to care for Austrian prisoners in Turkey. Cobenzl commented that "the Austrian government was always prepared to pay its debts, but 60,000 florins for nothing was rather hard to swallow." Talleyrand reported to Choiseul: "They wouldn't do what I asked for you, but rest assured that I'll avenge you when they're least expecting it and in a way they won't forget."

He managed somehow to obtain 100,000 francs on April 26 with help from the prince of Liechtenstein. By pressing his suit, he came up with a second installment of 100,000 francs on November 27. At that point they asked him to sign a receipt so as not to have to make a third payment. They were very simple-minded to imagine that a single draft would settle anything, or that two, backed up by a receipt, would end the affair. Alas, it did not.

Talleyrand resumed his campaign after the Treaty of Pressburg. Was he not responsible for slipping in some slight changes in Austria's favor? Had not Metternich recognized him as "a friend"? He was in a much better position now to cajole them into pouring out the whole sum instead of waiting for the driblets. At the conclusion of a peace treaty, it was customary for sovereigns to make gifts to the signatory ministers. Talleyrand thus received from Francis II a coffer of diamonds, on the cover of which was a painted portrait of the donor. Stadion, the minister presenting the gift, reported that Talleyrand was deeply touched. "He was eager to know whether the portrait represented a good likeness; I hastened to assure him that it did." A cozy scene! Was Francis II's countenance more fascinating on that coffer or imprinted on the 60,000 florins secretly paid that day "to a person whose name is known only to His Majesty"—the exact amount Talleyrand had sworn to make Austria pay Choiseul.

Before leaving Vienna, he called on the prince de Ligne, one of Europe's ornaments, who was living there. They had never met and would meet again later at the Congress of Vienna. The prince de Ligne lived rather shabbily. The Revolution had ruined him; all his property in France and Belgium had been confiscated. He had entered Austria's service, but despite great competence and courage (more likely because of his courage) he lost favor and was disgraced. Seventy years old at the time, he seemed the incarnation of the old Europe, a composite Voltaire, Richelieu, Frederick II, Louis XV, and Beaumarchais, a supremely cultured man. The most brilliant minds in Vienna and throughout Europe flocked to his door. When Talleyrand met him he was already afflicted with failing vision, with curtailed activity, with the burdens of age and poverty; yet he radiated his gladness to be alive, to have friends and a keen sense of humor. Being cheerful and witty were his luxuries. Countess Potocka said of him: "One would have thought he had chosen poverty in order to be happy." After Talleyrand's visit, the prince wrote to an old and equally blue-blooded friend of his, the prince d'Arenberg: "You can imagine how pleased he was to call on me, for there are no more Frenchmen in the world apart from him and you and me, who are not even that." Pure Voltaire.

That encounter made up for the comtesse de Brionne's stinging rebuff.

How to Become a Reigning Prince and a Serene Highness
for the Benefit of One's Subjects and Madame Grand

During the emperor's absence, Paris suffered a grave monetary crisis. Talleyrand, as we recall, had launched a brilliant career for himself in finance, and his experiences in England and America prepared him to deal with fiscal problems. In a government more concerned with economic issues than with war and foreign diplomacy as Napoleon's was, our ex-deputy of the clergy might have made his mark in public finance. Instead, he devoted his energies during the Empire to improving his personal finance. All the same, he wrote to the emperor proposing a reorganization of the Bank of France, which had shown itself incapable of averting the recent crisis. "In principle," Talleyrand asserted, "the Bank ought to be operated for the benefit of the public rather than of the stockholders and ought to furnish official currency." In modern terms, we would say that the Bank of France should act as a public service agency, not a private operation serving private interests. It is an English idea postulating that whatever serves the public interest also benefits the private sector. The letter was never acknowledged.

The Treaty of Pressburg was ratified on January 1, 1806, which Talleyrand identified as "the day the French reverted to the Gregorian calendar and seemed to embark on a new era." The new era in fact had begun on the 19th Brumaire. Six years passed before it was decided to shelve Pluviôse, Ventôse, Vendémiaire, Fructidor, and the rest of that overworked crew. Our hero was due for a laurel or two. The 5 million francs said to have vanished into one of his frilly cuffs at the peace table (or under it) were merely a secret "offering." Such a glorious occasion warranted a glorious reward; Napoleon made him prince of Benevento, at once elevating him—and Madame Grand—to a Serene Highness.

Like all Talleyrand's dealings, this one had its element of knavery, but what stylish knavery! We may recall that in listing Bonaparte's services to the Vatican, Talleyrand had not neglected to remind His Holiness that the principalities of Pontecorvo and Benevento had been restored to him. A short-term favor it turned out to be, for the two states, part of the Kingdom of Naples, were soon reincorporated into the French Empire. With Talleyrand's blessing. That particular annexation apparently did not offend him. Joseph Bonaparte became the new king of Naples;

the Bourbons were driven out of Italy, except in Sicily, where English ships and English guns on Malta protected their throne. In an effort to dispossess the Pope courteously, Talleyrand came forth with some amusing sophistries. The French desired to "relieve" His Holiness of the problems of managing two enclaves in alien territory. Were not the problems great, and was not the "alien" territory French? Our minister's caution knew no bounds: "Under a new government and in so inflammable a country, one must snuff out any sparks." Florid language. In short, the two princedoms were stolen. An imperial decree issued at Saint-Cloud on June 5, 1806, settled the matter: "Napoleon, by the grace of God and the Constitutions emperor of the French and king of Italy, hereby greets you. Desiring to bestow upon our great chamberlain and minister of foreign affairs Talleyrand a token of our esteem for his service to the crown, we are resolved to transfer and do hereby transfer the princedom of Benevento with the title of prince and duke of Benevento to his possession and sovereignty as a direct fief of the crown."

The duchy of Pontecorvo was given to Bernadotte.

European leaders learned of the new boundaries only through diplomatic news dispatches. No one bothered to inform them.

In Vienna, Madame Reinhardt wrote that "a French news dispatch announces a new king [Louis of Holland] . . . and princes of Benevento and Pontecorvo. It seems like a dream; one wonders whether all this can actually be happening in a civilized universe ordered by God. Here [in Vienna] no one talks about it, or rather they keep silent, crushed by a sense of helplessness." [1]

Who or what rules the earth is hard to say, but under Napoleon it certainly was not the law. "Orders" were issued, illegal, arbitrary, and autocratic. As for the helpless victims, it is comforting to think that their distress, like the dictates of an individual, was ephemeral. Such was Talleyrand's approximate view of Napoleon's rule. Yet he instructed Alquié, France's ambassador to the Vatican, to press the Pope to accept the imperial decree, going so far as to demand the pontiff's "total renunciation of his claims to Benevento." His Holiness, like everyone else, had to read Le Moniteur to learn that he was dispossessed. Though he was courageous enough to protest, if only for the record, that the two duchies had belonged for centuries to the Holy See, his argument made no impression on the bishop of Autun who, in 1789, had nationalized abbeys founded in Merovingian times.

In Paris, the new princess of Benevento was deluged with callers eager to congratulate the minister. Talleyrand would direct them to the mistress of the house, saying: "She is the one to be complimented; wives are always delighted to become princesses." His wife most of all. The duchesse d'Abrantès had this to say about the princess of Benevento: "I became involved then in a painful friendship, for friendship with Madame de Talleyrand was invariably disastrous. As a result, she would appear regularly twice a week, once in the morning for an informal visit, once in the evening for the sake of appearances, she said, which was always an annoyance though I could not tell her so and she was incapable of discerning it. I escaped her by seeking the company of Monsieur de Talleyrand, knowing she would not disturb me as she feared and no longer loved him."

Her Serene Highness was euphoric. She held court seated in an armchair, her feet resting on a cushion embroidered with the arms of Périgord. She signed herself "Sovereign princesse de Talleyrand"; when the spirit moved her, she specified "Reigning Princess."

To her husband, the Neapolitan title was merely a bauble. He used to say that being addressed as Highness was as pleasant a practice as receiving a standard 3 francs for legal consultations. The dig was aimed at Cambacérès. Talleyrand's single bias, it seems, touched upon his noble ancestry. He never discussed it but was deeply conscious of it nonetheless. Only once did this pride of blood rather than vanity come to the surface. It was during a trip to Poland when his friend Baron von Gagern often addressed him publicly as Highness, and Talleyrand finally said: "Do not call me Highness; I am less and perhaps better than that; call me plain Monsieur de Talleyrand."

Cautious as a cat, Talleyrand was determined to avoid any unpleasantness in occupying his princedom. When it came time to expel the papal troops, he enjoined his deputies to act "discreetly, lawfully [a little late for that], peacefully, and without fanfare." Keep it quiet, in other words; *Te Deums* would not do for a papal expulsion. He added glibly: "Persuasive methods would be preferable and also would correspond to my policy and my nature."

The occupation preceded those instructions and turned into a noisy affair conducted by a French general heading a detachment of Joseph's army. The general at once proclaimed himself governor. Talleyrand was exceedingly put out by these developments. He hastily dispatched a deputy with orders to dismiss the general and his troops and to remove any signs of military occupation. "Assure the inhabitants," he directed, "that I am concerned for their welfare. If I value this sovereignty at all, it is because I hope and desire that my authority shall be esteemed."

It was true, for he had nothing to gain from a poor and rather insignificant princedom with a population of 40,000, 18,000 of whom lived in the capital. The annual income of 40,000 francs was only one-fifth of what he received from Valençay, which could have yielded far more.

Talleyrand never set foot in Benevento, ruling it by proxy. Being an imperial fief, the principality had its agency in Paris under the direction of Roux and Rochette.

Talleyrand's deputy in Benevento was an Alsatian named Louis de Beer, an able and firm administrator. His job was not enviable as both natives and clergy regarded him as an occupying authority and an intruder. Furthermore, he was only the prince's lieutenant. Despite these difficulties, he served the people well and earned his prince's esteem.

When trouble broke out, it was usually because of Joseph Bonaparte's autocratic rule. One day a nephew of his from the Clary clan charged into the peaceful princedom with three hundred horsemen. Napoleon's relatives ran riot everywhere. De Beer took a firm stand against Frenchmen invading a French possession, and Talleyrand, being on good terms with Joseph, straightened the matter out.

The military incursions resumed when Murat became king of Naples. His wife, Caroline Bonaparte, as well as the emperor had to intervene and curb that power-hungry general. In addition, there were robber bands—and Calabrian robbers were no Robin Hoods—who claimed to be resisting the French intruders but in reality were simply preying on travelers, farmers, and villagers.

Despite the cares of state and long trips in the emperor's entourage, Talleyrand never lost touch with Benevento. He continued to write de Beer, complimenting him for his loyal service, and to govern from afar. He introduced the Napoleonic Code, required all official acts to be published in French as well as Italian, and made French the official language. His sovereignty ended before the language could take hold, though the groundwork for it had been laid in organized primary education for all children.

He did not neglect the precepts contained in his monumental report on public instruction of 1790. The princedom of Benevento was the only European state to provide free public education. Against the current of contemporary thinking, he promoted intellectual opportunities for women, asserting that "educating women is one of the best ways to refine and uplift morals."

Monuments were not forsaken in Benevento. Talleyrand was responsible for restoring the magnificent Arch of Trajan and for building a public fountain. The following inscription was carved on a second fountain which he restored to use: "Naids exiled in the years of turbulence returned in the reign of Carlo-Maurizio." And indeed the fountains filled, the waters splashed, for where Talleyrand reigned, abundance followed. His benevolent rule won him popular favor.

But it could not last. When the system collapsed in 1814, Murat, king of Naples and Napoleon's brother-in-law, seized Benevento and annexed it, thus ending the reign of Carlo-Maurizio. But Benevento brought our hero at least one satisfaction: in 1808 during the Congress of Erfurt, at a state dinner for reigning sovereigns, Berthier, reigning prince of Neuchâtel, and Talleyrand, reigning prince of Benevento, sat in company with the crowned heads of Europe.

It also brought him a little money. The Congress of Vienna restored Benevento to the Holy See, but after Monseigneur d'Autun had proved such a good sport about returning the stolen property, His Holiness directed that Talleyrand was to be paid a small income for life out of Benevento's receipts. Not very much, but a bonus is a bonus. Anyway, when Napoleon was defeated in 1814, Talleyrand found time to send Montor, an embassy secretary in Rome, to Benevento with orders to empty the cash drawers of the realm and relay the loot to Paris. Our dispossessed prince thus made more money from surrendering his princedom than from ruling it. For Talleyrand, every affair, ill-fated or not, ultimately had to show a profit.

The Catacombs of the Rue du Bac, or the Sublime Art of the Double Cross

Talleyrand had hopes of peace at the outset of negotiations with England. The opportunity to reopen talks with London arrived in a letter from an English friend he had met in 1792, informing him that George III's police had uncovered a plot to assassinate Napoleon. This extraordinary news came from Prime Minister Charles James Fox. Talleyrand wrote back, and the two began to explore possible peace terms. England wanted to be enticed by the return of Hanover, which the French had ceded rather hastily to Prussia. As Napoleon was then giving Berlin the cold shoulder, he ought not to have refused that condition. England also wanted Malta, however, and Sicily in return for having secured it for the Neapolitan Bourbons. Then what would they have done about the king of Naples? Returned his kingdom over which Joseph Bonaparte now reigned? A hopeless dilemma.

Napoleon's decision to take Hanover back from the Prussians was followed up by remarks no less than scathing on the lips of a chief of state: "Prussia received Hanover out of fear and shall return it out of fear, and with respect to any equivalents she may have given [the poisonous gift had cost her money], I shall repay them with promises sufficient to gratify the vanity of a cabinet that will have to satisfy this country." [1] Such unqualified cynicism would be hard to match. We should remember those words; Prussia found them impossible to forget when it came time to settle accounts in 1815, in 1870, and perhaps even afterwards.

The negotiations took place in Paris, conducted by Lord Lauderdale, and were a failure. Lauderdale called for his passport and, for some unknown reason, presented a sword to the French representative, Champagny, who refused it. Talleyrand dressed him down, saying that he should have accepted it and made a gift in return. Napoleon was indifferent to the parley or its outcome, knowing that even if England were prepared to conciliate the issues of Hanover and Sicily, his own acts would breach the peace very shortly. He was in the process of reorganizing Germany into the Confederation of the Rhine, a new French satellite. Furthermore, his yet undisclosed plan for a continental blockade was bound to bring on war with England. As the whole map of Germany changed, numerous small states melted into larger ones in the name of cohesion. The new kingdoms of Bavaria and Württemberg made their appearance. Talleyrand suffered a setback when Louis Bonaparte took the throne of Holland: our hero promoted his brother Boson for the post of grand chamberlain, but Louis would not have him. Murat was given the grand duchy of Berg, after the duke of Nassau had been dispossessed by some fancy maneuvers contrived by Beurnonville. The French did as they pleased because Europe feared Napoleon; he cultivated that fear and reaped its rewards.

The prince of Benevento took part in the dismantling and reassembling processes. Summoned to Paris, the German princes never knew what to expect from him. Talleyrand received them one by one, charming or threatening them by turns, luring them with promises that Napoleon's invincible army would protect them from their suzerain lord the Austrian emperor. Having sold them the idea of unity, he brought them all together on July 12, 1806, at the rue du Bac to hear the terms establishing the Confederation of the Rhine. They had no choice but to sign. Francis II thus learned that his sacrosanct Empire had collapsed. The act of confederation was ratified in Munich on July 26, 1806. Berthier, the French signatory, was accompanied by Louis de Périgord, Archambaud's eldest son and Talleyrand's favorite nephew, who took the treaty back to Paris. Another Talleyrand had entered public affairs.

Clearly, Talleyrand's visible (as well as invisible) role in dismembering the Holy Roman Empire was a major one—and highly profitable.

Woe to the princes who arrived empty-handed! Their lands were handed out to others who could pay. Baron von Gagern, a close German observer, had this to say about the prince of Benevento: "He looked upon his high position as a gold mine. His favors had to be paid for not with the customary snuffbox or diamonds, but in hard cash." That explains why so few of the "sugarplums" can be traced. After all, what is less cumbersome than cash, or more practical? And why, in 1806, should he oppose Napoleon's ambitions? It would have been sheer madness. The machine was grinding along full speed; nothing could stop it. Talleyrand recognized its errors and defects, but France seemed content. She was paying in money and in blood for her glory, her domestic tranquility, and the fascination of her military might. Still enthralled by captured enemy standards, she was not yet bled white. Talleyrand asked no questions and concentrated on filling his pockets.

Were it not for his associates, Talleyrand's dealings with the Germans would be difficult to trace. He did not operate alone, and, as we know, never had trouble recruiting loyal helpers. Besides the ministerial staff working more or less openly, he had a subsidiary, unofficial staff, no less efficient or well connected than the other, yet not always pursuing the same objectives. The two Dalbergs,[2] uncle and nephew, occupied this twilight zone. Whereas some authors seem to consider the Dalbergs mere episodic figures in Talleyrand's life, in fact the nephew was extremely close to our hero and associated with all the important events of his career during the Consulate, the Empire, and the dawn of the Restoration. Without Dalberg, Talleyrand could not have manipulated the German princes so successfully. Without Dalberg, he could not have carried out so spectacularly what his biographers call "the Betrayal," meaning the one involving Napoleon (as if there were but one genuine betrayal). Without Dalberg, treason would be reduced to a formula and Talleyrand to the stereotyped traitor who plunges a knife into his benefactor. The image is insulting. If there was treachery, it went on backstage, out of the public eye. So let us trail the two of them, Dalberg and Talleyrand, through the twists and turns of backstairs politics.

Dalberg, like Talleyrand, came of ancient noble stock. The Dalbergs claimed descent from a Roman knight settled in the Palatinate. Since the time of Charlemagne, they had acknowledged no lesser rank than baron. They had princes for relatives, and great wealth. In 1800, uncle Karl-Theodor and nephew Emmerich were the family heirs.

The uncle was a bishop, feudal-style, with vast landholdings, some of which were inherited, some obtained from the church. Prior to 1789

327

he was much the same sort of prelate as Monseigneur d'Autun, an urbane, free-thinking libertine who longed for Rome not because the Pope was there but because the girls were—and he made no bones about it. His sumptuous palace was host to Wieland, Goethe, Herder, Schiller, and Johannes von Müller, the Swiss historian who won Voltaire's sympathies at Ferney. He corresponded with Joseph II and with Catherine II, for whom he composed bold, innovative political treatises. Despite his miter, he belonged to the philosophical sect of Bavarian Illuminati; Mirabeau had been a member and had recruited Talleyrand. This mutual interest in Freemasonry probably was the source of Talleyrand's friendship with the Rhenish prelate, though of course they shared a taste for other things. Their outlook, background, and appetites coincided.

Driven from the left bank of the Rhine and dispossessed by the Revolution, the Dalbergs settled in Austria. Their hatred of the Revolution, and, by extension, of France, is understandable. They hated in their own peculiar fashion, however, with a silent, invisible hatred that Talleyrand could appreciate and even utilize. So perfect was their duplicity that the French took them for allies, and during the Recess of 1803 the only lands which escaped secularization belonged to the Dalbergs, to the prior of the Order of Malta, and to the grand master of the Teutonic Knights. A signal favor indeed considering that Talleyrand had charge of the affair. The elder Dalberg began courting Napoleon when he was First Consul, employing, oddly enough, the same flatteries as Talleyrand. He urged him to become emperor and even wrote a book for his edification, *Remarques sur le règne de Charlemagne*. At the same time, he was sending out anonymous letters to all the German princes urging rebellion against the French Empire. Plainly, this Dalberg bears close watching.

In 1804, as a reward for their loyalty, uncle and nephew were invited to the coronation. Napoleon even granted a private audience to Karl-Theodor "because of his high birth." The emperor was delighted to have this illustrious personage serve France and the future Confederation of the Rhine. What form would this service take? No one asked him. Talleyrand was close to the younger Dalberg, Baden-Baden's minister to Paris, much closer to him than to his day-to-day associates. Emmerich de Dalberg shared his uncle's attitude toward the French Revolution and the Corsican usurper. He was a small, intense man, rather sickly, and markedly spiteful. Of that spite, his friend baron de Vitrolles, Louis XVIII's political agent, commented that "there was enough of it in his face to discourage trust and put people on guard." Talleyrand never relaxed his guard or disclosed secrets; he gave out information for a purpose. When Dalberg came to Paris in 1802, he generously offered to facilitate our minister's task of secularizing church lands in Germany. He hated the First Consul enough to consider assassinating him. And Talleyrand was his confidant. In 1814 we find him implicated in the alarming Maubreuil affair; but as early as 1804 he was bent on killing Napoleon—in a less brutal fashion. Markoff, Russia's insufferably arrogant ambassador to Paris, was forced to resign when Napoleon's agents discovered a hotbed of espionage in the Russian embassy which was in contact with the notorious comte d'Antraigues. As one might expect, Markoff's departure did not stop the spying. He was not replaced immediately, and during the vacancy the embassy's confidential dispatches to St. Petersburg were entrusted to no less a personage than Dalberg. The Russians trusted him, and so he would collect and transmit intelligence personally to the czar, who in turn passed it on to London. The "Affair of the Leaks" comes to mind, which so mystified First Consul Bonaparte when suspicion pointed to his minister of foreign relations. Talleyrand was in fact the bosom friend of the most highly organized and officially blessed spy in Paris, cunningly planted in the heart of the imperial system.

One piece of information thus smuggled from Paris to St. Petersburg and on to London was vital enough to warrant mention, and even if no evidence exists to implicate Talleyrand, the fact remains that his dear friend Dalberg transmitted it. How did he get his hands on such information, an order directing the French fleet anchored at Brest, La Rochelle, and Toulon to join the Spanish fleet, sail for the Antilles, then return at full speed to attack England? Secrecy would guarantee them several days' head start, and with the Channel clear, Napoleon could attempt his invasion. But the order leaked out and Nelson was forewarned; he caught up with the French ships at Trafalgar. This information bore the signature of someone calling himself "Son of the Friend" whose identity remains a mystery. A minor agent named Michel was arrested and shot for stealing documents from the ministry of war, which explains nothing. That Dalberg transmitted the dispatch is beyond question, also that Talleyrand was using Dalberg; but whether Dalberg was also using Talleyrand we do not know. Besides the return of his estates, Dalberg received "compensations," one of which was rather alarming: the privilege of including his dispatches among those of the Foreign Ministry. Thanks to Talleyrand and the safe-conduct warranted by the Imperial Eagles, Dalberg's messages were speeded to his uncle, Frankfurt's administrator, and thence to St. Petersburg. Our hero, Napoleon's minister, was providing postal service for an espionage network. There is evidence of one case at least in which Talleyrand employed Dalberg to arrange a matter of considerable significance to his future career. When the duc d'Enghien was abducted from Baden-Baden and executed, Dalberg, Baden's minister to Paris, was in a position to know all the facts of that sordid affair. He concocted an alibi for Talleyrand, and the two of them composed a letter to the czar, signed "the Friend," depicting Talleyrand as the victim of a plot to murder the young duke. He was guiltless, the victim of false accusations; indeed, he had turned white on hearing of the prince's death. No one in Paris had seen Talleyrand blanch on that occasion—or any other, as a matter of fact. The letter went on to assert that immediately after learning of the plot, Talleyrand sent a messenger to warn the duke to "leave at once." The warning was supposed to have arrived early enough for him to save himself. Despite what others said, the czar's confidence in Dalberg, "the Friend," was unshakable. He was convinced of Talleyrand's innocence, in this instance at least. For us, the question is which of them, Dalberg or Talleyrand, was "the Friend" and which the "Son of the Friend"?

After the Battle of Friedland, Talleyrand saw to it that his helper became a naturalized citizen and obtained a post worth 200,000 francs annually as state councilor. Uncle Dalberg became prince-primate of Frankfurt, a virtual sovereign. He resigned after Leipzig, however, realizing that the time was fast approaching when it would be unhealthy to owe the French any favors. He managed to preserve his fortune and his good name by passing for a solid German citizen when the French Empire collapsed.

Meanwhile, with "strokes of genius" Napoleon pursued his dazzling schemes, unaware of these patient and ultimately successful efforts to shatter his dreams.

Prussia came under attack for daring to mobilize. She could count on support from Russia and England. Talleyrand had to report her insolent conduct to the emperor in August, 1806. Off to Germany again and more discomfort, late hours, not to mention the company of insufferable boors in the imperial entourage. Too bad, as just before leaving Paris Talleyrand had met Victor de Broglie at Madame de Laval's, the brilliant young duke who was to become Louis-Philippe's minister. His conversation alone revealed a man of great promise. On the eve of his departure for Mainz where the emperor was organizing his assault on Prussia, Talleyrand found time to wind up an interesting and agreeable transaction, the purchase of Marie-Joseph Chénier's library containing some very fine editions. Chénier had been dismissed as inspector general of the University of Paris for his liberal ideas and was forced to sell his books. Talleyrand bought them to rebuild his own library. Once again our bibliophile made an excellent investment for the days ahead.

To trusted friends in Mainz—the Dalbergs and Metternich, who recorded his statements—Talleyrand admitted dislike for this latest aggression. Though he had no sympathy for Prussia, at the same time he saw no justification for Napoleon's wanting to make her the dominant German state at Austria's expense in 1805, and a year later threatening to wipe her off the map.

It was September, 1806, and as the waters of Bourbon-l'Archambault were denied him, he settled instead for those of Wiesbaden. Our hero was not one to let a war disrupt his style of life. In Wiesbaden he met Hortense de Beauharnais, Louis Bonaparte's wife and Holland's new queen. Talleyrand was a discovery to her. "For years," she wrote, "I had watched him enter the salons of Malmaison with a haughty air, limping, reaching for the nearest chair to lean on, bowing perfunctorily." In the relaxed atmosphere of a foreign spa, the real Talleyrand was revealed to her: "He looked for me and really put himself out. I was surprised, even flattered, for the attentions of a man who seldom pays them are all the more precious, and I am convinced that his reputation as a great wit rests on the little he says and says well rather than on anything remarkable he has done. . . ." Surely good Queen Hortense did not know half the "remarkable" things Talleyrand was doing. Her comments are interesting, and she is not the first to say that the prince of Benevento husbanded his wit. "He is remarkable chiefly for his impeccable manners, for his ability to read men's minds and to elude them [what follows is astute], combined with an indolence which makes him so gentle and pliable that it resembles kindness." What use would he have for kindness? He had something better, the fascination of abandoned virtue, a natural fascination that enveloped and disarmed. Yet the seeming gentleness could produce a totally opposite effect on tense, highstrung, and emotional persons—Chateaubriand, for one. He and others like him were exasperated by Talleyrand's nonchalant, lackadaisical manner, the pleasant mask concealing a ruthless intelligence which delighted in assessing impudently the havoc it wrought. Hortense also observed that he was "indulgent toward vice." Yes, because he abhorred slander and denied anyone the right to judge another's conduct. Anyway, he was worldly wise enough to know that trying to disentangle vice from virtue is a waste of effort. He lived in strange times, when morals changed along with the calendar, the clubs, the salons, the gambling houses. He was far too intelligent to accept generalizations, except as applied to vulgarity. Hortense noticed that he listened a great deal and never argued, never contradicted; a wry smile conveyed his disapproval. Clearly he was a superior man, for in the course of his long life, only Napoleon (who regretted it) and a mad adventurer named Maubreuil told him what they thought of him, whereas his contemporaries slandered him mercilessly in their journals and memoirs. Hortense aptly described the prince's intriguing charm: "The fascination he exerts, which is considerable, depends chiefly on the vanity of others. I myself was prey to it. The mere fact of his deigning to address you at once makes him endearing, and you are on the brink of falling in love if he inquires after your health." [3] Madame de Sévigné said as much of Louis XIV.

Throughout this entire year of 1806 Talleyrand idolized Napoleon. We should make a note of this before the mood passes. Hearing rumors of plots to assassinate the emperor, Talleyrand wrote to him on October 20, 1806: "All these tales are frightful. But Your Majesty must know everything, and who dares to tell him if not those who venerate him?"

He showered the emperor with flattery knowing that disaster was in store. He waited for others to find it out, waited to read the same understanding in other faces. That was yet to come. As it would have been futile, he made no attempt this time to counsel a reasonable peace. Napoleon expected obedience, not advice.

An exhausting interlude began for our prince when the French army marched into Berlin. Victory brought a flood of entreaties as the Prussians desperately sought promises of the same support he had given Austria. The illusion was a vain one. Talleyrand had no more sympathy for Prussia than for Russia. No country denying popular rights and liberties was civilized, he felt. His Europe consisted of Vienna, Paris, and London, whereas Prussia was a menace to the other German states. Then, at the pinnacle of his glory, enraptured by his own ambition, Napoleon signed the famous decree in Berlin on November 21, 1806, establishing the continental blockade. Who fostered megalomania by producing historic and legal precedents to justify shutting off Europe to English trade? Talleyrand, to our everlasting dismay. His memorandum bore the date November 20; the imperial decree of the twenty-first virtually recapitulated his text, a model of clarity and restraint, a masterpiece of good sense in defense of folly.

Talleyrand's *Memoirs* relate an incident that took place while he was in Berlin. Later on it proved to be of great significance. In Berlin Napoleon received a note from the Spanish prime minister Manuel Godoy, "the Prince of Peace," advising that his country wanted no part in a blockade which would ruin her economy, and that she preferred to maintain free trade with England. This defection threatened to topple the whole insane edifice, which demanded constant shoring up by force of arms. Europe was unwilling to starve and go bankrupt. Therefore Spain had to be crushed. In his wrath, Napoleon "swore then and there to destroy the Spanish branch of the House of Bourbon utterly." To which Talleyrand added: "and I, secretly, swore at any cost to cease acting as his minister as soon as we returned to France."

That was the origin of the lunatic war with Spain, and, according to him, of the decision to "divorce" Napoleon. But divorce in the life of a Talleyrand, like marriage, is not arrived at hastily, casually, or without secret arrangements.

Perhaps we ought to question whether his resolve really dated from the time Napoleon determined to crush the Spanish Bourbons. The *Memoirs* were written in 1816, during the Restoration, when it was politic to link Napoleon's curse on the Bourbons with his own refusal to serve the emperor. More likely his decision followed the Peace of Pressburg. In any event, we are forewarned that Talleyrand wears a mask. Napoleon's minister is his enemy.

Having conquered Prussia, the emperor moved on to Poland. Reluctantly, Talleyrand joined him there.

Mud and Vexations on the Eastern Front

In Posen, Talleyrand met the king of Saxony, Frederick Augustus, who, upon joining the Confederation of the Rhine, had become Napoleon's ally. A treaty signed on December 11, 1806, bound his fate to the emperor's. He was an affable man with the courtly manners of another era, and took an immediate liking to Talleyrand to whom he presented a portrait of himself painted by Gérard, saying: "I chose that which least resembled a gift and most represented a token of friendship." Such gracious gestures were foreign to the "mess hall" mentality of the imperial train. The king of Saxony was so affable that even Napoleon took to him. When several French generals expressed interest in removing certain prize objects from the splendid royal art collection which the new ally and his predecessors had formed, Frederick Augustus grew visibly distressed, declaring that he himself was not entitled to national treasures. Talleyrand could appreciate such scruples; he sympathized with the good monarch and obtained Napoleon's pledge to leave the Dresden Gallery intact. And as the prince of Benevento always managed to wind up his affairs in the black, he became a million richer in parting from the good king of Saxony. A shining example of savoir-vivre.

The journey to Warsaw was horrendous, for Poland in December was a sea of mud. Talleyrand's carriage sank in to the wheel hubs, requiring twelve soldiers to free it; the wretched fellows labored in waist-high mud, grumbling aloud: "Why does he have to come to this God-forsaken country to work his diplomacy?" How right they were.

Warsaw cheered their arrival. Prussia's defeat had rung out like the trumpet of the Resurrection. Marching eastward, Napoleon had made promising statements: "It is in the interest of France, in the interest of Europe, that Poland exist." Remember that in 1772, Poland had been partitioned among three autocrats, the czar, the king of Prussia, and the emperor of Austria. Talleyrand always felt that the Ancien Régime had made a great mistake in sanctioning that partition. His objective judgment was simply that the dismemberment of Poland threatened peace on the continent. Europe's traditional power structure had shifted at the expense of France, the only great power to gain nothing from it. Moreover, he was extremely apprehensive of Russia's westward expansion; that, undoubtedly, was his chief fear. He warned Austria that by sharing a frontier with Russia she stood to lose more than her part of Poland and advised her to set up a buffer state as a shield against the Slavs. In Vienna, Ambassador Andréossy transmitted Talleyrand's arguments to the Austrian government, appealing to them to renounce their share of Poland in exchange for Silesia. Dalberg, serving as Talleyrand's eyes and ears among the Polish aristocrats, collected 4 million florins for our hero's benefit. The zealous champion of martyred Poland grew even more zealous.

In princely splendor befitting his rank, the prince of Benevento was lodged in the Radziwill mansion. As the Polish winter was too severe for fighting, Napoleon decided they should dance. Cripple that he was, our hero had to arrange it. Balls were Talleyrand's specialty, and the one that he gave now kindled hopes of Poland's liberation. In any event, the Poles put more spirit into their dancing than the French. In her lively Memoirs, the eminent Countess Potocka recorded the Franco-Polish social season of 1806–7. Talleyrand sounded the call to arms, rounding up a roomful of elegant ladies to present to the emperor. After putting them through "basic training," he could be sure that all Poland would fall in behind a squadron of beauties waltzing to the beat of a magician's wand. "We waited a long time," the countess wrote, "on the evening of the presentation, and admittedly our curiosity was mixed with apprehension. Suddenly a rush of sound broke the silence, the doors burst open, and M. de Talleyrand advanced declaiming in a loud, clear voice that magic word which causes everyone to tremble: the emperor!" [1]

When the first flurry of excitement had passed, the countess found herself less interested in the idol than in his grand chamberlain; her aunt (whom we shall meet shortly) Countess Tyszkiewicz, née Poniatowska, was Talleyrand's friend and a privileged member of his inner circle along with Mesdames de Laval, de Luynes, etc. Her niece claimed that she was less his friend than his slave. Subsequent events suggest that she was not exaggerating. Countess Potocka had fashioned her own private image of the supreme male embodiment of wisdom, chivalry, kindness, and all the rest. But what did she find? "If I were to judge him according to his effect on me, I would say that he seemed blasé and bored with everything, eager for money, anxious for the favors of a master whom he despised, spineless and unprincipled, in a word, morally and physically unfit."

She described the prince in full dress, limping, haughty, sour-faced, visibly disgusted by the constant traveling, the country, the people, the war, and the master. Here was the emperor's grand chamberlain, rigged out with a Calabrian princedom, performing his duties, as it were; she watched him "advancing painfully to the center of the ballroom with a napkin folded over one arm, holding a silver platter as he comes to offer a glass of lemonade to the monarch he treated like a parvenu." Besides playing butler, Talleyrand performed another role by introducing to Napoleon the dainty, doll-like Countess Maria Walewska,* whom he had invited for just that purpose. He served her up to his master along with the lemonade—and the napkin draped over one arm. Why did he do it? Because he thought Napoleon, like every other king and emperor of the French, ought to take a mistress. His master lacked refinement, Talleyrand felt; never idle, never tempted by frivolous pleasures, perhaps he could be humanized by a woman. His obsession with glory and conquest might be corrected—if not cured—by love. Years later Napoleon told Baron Gourgaud: "Talleyrand is the one who procured[!] her for me; she offered no struggle." Maria was not the first. Talleyrand was determined to make his master fall in love. The emperor said that his grand chamberlain "always had his pockets full of women." Even privately, Napoleon treated Talleyrand like a lackey. He would summon him in the middle of the night, a practice scarcely calculated to diminish the

* Maria Walewska and Napoleon first met on January 1, 1807, on the road to Warsaw. She was in simple country dress. Napoleon wanted to see her again, so Talleyrand arranged an official presentation at the ball described by Countess Potocka.

latter's growing store of ill-disguised resentment. One night the emperor dozed off over some papers he was discussing with his minister. Soon Talleyrand did the same. Napoleon awoke with a start: "What's this? I think he's asleep!" he exclaimed. "Hey there, you rascal, what do you mean by falling asleep in my presence!" The work went on until five in the morning, the hour at which our hero would have been leaving the whist table in Paris.

On another occasion in Finkenstein, where Talleyrand had joined the emperor on the way to Friedland and Tilsit, His Majesty, an insomniac, woke him in the middle of the night to have him read aloud. Tyrants about to fall often indulge in whims for which they pay dearly when those they have humiliated have a chance to settle accounts. The book he read from that night was *Corinne*, Madame de Staël's second novel. Napoleon muttered grumpily: "You are fond of this woman; let's see if she makes any sense." He was aware of the breach between Talleyrand and baroness de Staël. Palace gossip kept him abreast of her every utterance against "the bishop." Germaine's first novel had portrayed him disguised as a woman, but *Corinne* baldly presented him as "M. de Maltigues," whose remarks called to mind the prince of Benevento: "The only worthwhile thing in life is riches or power or both." It reminds us of the vow he once took, as his coach rolled away from the Luxembourg, to make "an immense fortune." Germaine's character also voiced this opinion: "Friendships are tools to be used or abandoned according to circumstances." Was she not the victim of that precept? Another hair-raising observation: "The only significant distinction we need make in this world is between birds in cages and birds at liberty." Or this, which might apply better to Montrond or Narbonne: "Virtue is a language for common folk, which the augurs cannot converse in without laughing."

Her caricature only points to a resemblance. If she sought revenge by hurting him, she missed her target. Talleyrand never questioned her right to think as she did; but to come out and say so was ingenuous, ill-bred, and unnecessary. Discussing oneself or others indicated lack of good taste.

Napoleon listened for a few minutes, then, without so much as a compliment to either reader or author, gave them both a surly dismissal: "There's no feeling in it, only a hodge-podge of words. Go to bed; this is a waste of time." [2]

The grand chamberlain withdrew ceremoniously and limped off to bed.

The months in Warsaw between December, 1806, and May, 1807, involved our hero in duties other than supplying lemonade and women.

Napoleon made impossible demands on him, all of which he carried out flawlessly, a unique record of supposed idleness. Many of these duties were unofficial, independent of the Foreign Office. Officially, he dealt with ambassadors, one of whom was baron de Vincent, a native of Lorraine employed by the Austrian chancellery. Napoleon treated him most cordially, even too cordially, suggesting the distinct possibility of an alliance with Austria to the astonished baron. Vincent was unprepared for that in the face of Napoleon's known preference for a Russian alliance which would seal Austria's fate. The very purpose of his visit to Warsaw was to see how the wind was blowing. Napoleon's plans were a mystery from one day to the next. Talleyrand took the initiative through Dalberg, pressing Vienna urgently to reconsider his standing offer of Silesia in exchange for Austria's share of Poland. Baron de Vincent might have accepted. However, the prospect of a war with Russia fired the hopes of captive nations after Napoleon came near to defeat at Eylau. Europe might still survive. Vienna preferred to wait and see. Talleyrand urged Vincent to accept the barter for Europe's sake, knowing that Napoleon would march to further triumphs—temporarily. But if Russia fell, the emperor would be inflexible. By rejecting Talleyrand's advice, Austria gambled and lost. The whole picture changed after Friedland when victory smiled once more on Napoleon, leaving him in no mood to explore an Austrian alliance. Talleyrand lamented the turn of events but saw that nothing could be done after Friedland to offset Russian influence on Napoleon. As always, our hero yielded to the political facts of life. He set out for Tilsit to woo the czar.

Before there could be any talk of victory or peace treaties, the war had to be organized from Warsaw and occupied Poland administered. Napoleon left those tasks to his foreign minister. His army was all that mattered; his Empire rested on cannon and bayonets. Talleyrand had to wring provisions for the French forces out of destitute Poland. The miracle is that he did it, though quartermastering was not precisely to his liking. He preferred handling money and words, both odorless, colorless substances. In addition, as Warsaw's governor he was expected to run the capital. He reported the following tender scene to the emperor in the field: "This morning I made the rounds of every hospital in Warsaw. To the wounded of Ostrolenka I distributed the bonuses which Your Majesty chose to award [a napoleon to all infantrymen, 5 to officers]. I stood at their bedsides listening to petty personal requests and I comforted them." No doubt he did. Madame de Staël would have enjoyed disguising our prince as a sister of charity.

Talleyrand made friends in Poland whose help enabled him to do what he had to do, prominent persons such as Prince (later Marshal) Poniatowski, Countess Tyszkiewicz's brother.

The war was becoming arduous. Never had Napoleon confronted fiercer foes than the climate and the Russian army. February 8, 1807, saw the savage, useless slaughter of Eylau. Napoleon almost lost that battle, which Talleyrand described as "barely won"—so barely that winds of defeat seemed to be gathering somewhere in the East. Dalberg, invisible but active all the same, was convinced that bloody Eylau marked a critical stage in the Empire. And in Talleyrand's conduct.

Not just Talleyrand's, for Napoleon's generals were also growing weary. The glittering adventure might be their last if the Empire foundered. They looked to peace to solidify the régime and their own positions. After returning to Warsaw, our prince assailed the emperor with fervent protests of devotion. He was sorely distressed by his master's prolonged absence, he wrote, and wished to report good news from Warsaw, having officiated at the blessing of the Polish flag, which, united with the Imperial Eagle, would revive Poland according to the emperor's promise. "I leave Warsaw highly confident and tranquil," he said on May 3, 1807. On June 18, when word reached him in Danzig of the triumph at Friedland, he hastened to dispatch his compliments. Napoleon could have read the prickly message between the lines, but he was too blind:

> It [the victory] will go down as one of history's great events. But I see it not in terms of glory alone; I like to imagine it as a harbinger, a pledge of peace, the security which Your Majesty, after ceaseless effort, privations, and perils, has wrested for his subjects; I like to think of it as the final victory Your Majesty need win. That is why I cherish it, for despite its splendor, I must confess that its value would shrink immeasurably if Your Majesty were to march on to fresh battles exposing himself to fresh perils, the thought of which alarms me the more readily in view of Your Majesty's known scorn for them.[3]

The final flourish cannot disguise the gravity of this latest admonition. The first came after Pressburg and was rejected. This was the second. There would be no third. Napoleon would not make peace. He would sign a truce with Russia only to facilitate an attack on England. But Talleyrand was never in a hurry.

On June 23, 1807, the emperor left for Königsberg near the Russian border. Talleyrand redoubled his flattery, strangely enough, as if to mute his recent warning: "Your Majesty has now brought his affairs to a point which I would not have dreamed possible. I am lost in admiration. Yet Your Majesty has accustomed me for some time to marvels." [4]

Already Dalberg and he were uneasy about the imperial succession. "What would we do if Napoleon were killed?" Their plan was to salvage the Empire by placing Joseph Bonaparte on the throne; they counted on support from all the régime's creditors. Simple-minded Joseph would need a good government, meaning a government chosen and presided over by Talleyrand. He would turn out to be one of those nondescript rulers whom Napoleon generously compared to "pigs fattening in their palaces." To pacify Europe, France would withdraw to the Alps and the Rhine. The scheme was even proposed to foreign governments "in case of an accident." Metternich heard about it from Talleyrand's busiest agent. Dalberg, of course. The two of them planned it jointly.

For the time being, Napoleon was very much alive and about to cross the Niemen. Talleyrand grew anxious: Was the emperor about to plunge into Russia? Talleyrand guessed the sheer folly of a war with the czar. The risks were so great—and Napoleon was rash enough to take them—that he came to think it would be wisest to withdraw to western Europe and abandon all plans, including the revival of Poland. When negotiations for peace and an alliance with the czar opened shortly afterwards at Tilsit, Talleyrand did not raise a finger in Poland's behalf despite his promises and the 4 million florins he had received. Our hero's failure to deliver his part of a prepaid bargain should not surprise us. The only surprise is the fact that he returned those 4 million florins to the Poles and promptly washed his hands of them. It was one of the rare impulses to which our cautious hero yielded. "We must make the emperor abandon the notion of a Polish state. These people are hopeless. With Poles you cannot organize anything but disorder."

Talleyrand had little to say about the Treaty of Tilsit. Napoleon called on him merely to sign an alliance with Russia's emissary General Kourakine. The czar had been promised (but not in writing) the remains of the Ottoman Empire plus Moldavia and Wallachia. Talleyrand opposed any such concessions permitting Russian penetration of Central Europe. He wanted those provinces to go to Austria and form a bulwark against the peoples of the steppes.

Talleyrand at least had the satisfaction of seeing Murat's demands denied for an all-out war on Russia. That came later, unfortunately, along with the Empire's collapse. For the sake of wearing Poland's crown, ambitious Murat would have invaded Russia.

One day as Murat was leaving Napoleon's study, Talleyrand encountered him, saying: "Your Highness, you have forced us to make war, but you shall not prevent us from making peace."

He found life on the banks of the Niemen even more unbearable than in Warsaw. Although the camp was host to French, Prussian, and Russian generals and diplomats, it was still a camp. Talleyrand was not about to accept the rigors of military life without his accustomed comforts and luxuries, his silver service, his cooks, his musicians . . . Unfortunately, such refinements were not to be found in eastern Prussia or along the Russian border, and were not in keeping with current standards. There was no wine on the prince of Benevento's table. Even in wartime, on barbarian soil, he insisted on full wine decanters. To Daru (Stendhal's cousin), the quartermaster general, he wrote: "My dear Daru, of one thing I am certain: when you were translating Horace and came to that delightful ode beginning *Nunc est bibendum* [Now let us drink] you never thought Horace was recommending water; yet that is just what I am reduced to unless you send me some of the provisions furnished to the emperor." [5] Wine thus appeared on two tables, Napoleon's and Talleyrand's.

At Tilsit he met Queen Louise of Prussia, known for her beauty, her brains, and her dignity. She came to beg the conqueror to spare Prussia. On July 6, 1807, Napoleon received her coldly and scornfully. Her proud reply was worthy of Frederick the Great. Talleyrand enjoyed quoting her rejoinder with just a hint of complacency. Napoleon finally silenced him: "I don't know what you find so irresistible about the queen of Prussia's remarks. I advise you to speak of something else."

Indeed, Queen Louise's plight fairly melted the heart of our prince: "I was indignant at what I saw and what I heard, but I was obliged to conceal my indignation." (Brave prince: How indignant were you after the revolutionist butchery of August 10? Or the duc d'Enghien's murder? But let him finish his tear-laden tale.) "I have very pleasant memories of the things she told me and the confidences she murmured: 'Monsieur de Bénévent,' she said the last time I had the privilege of escorting her to her carriage, 'only two persons regret my coming here: I and you. You are not angry, are you, that I should leave in this frame of mind?' Tears of compassion and pride filling my eyes were my only reply." [6]

A touching scene. The queen treated him as true comte de Périgord: "You and I alone matter." That is what really impressed our hero. As for the weeping, he never wept after that fateful night preceding his ordainment. So we may simply overlook the tears which he invented to enhance the scene.

His eagerness to quit Poland, Russia, and camp life grew more acute because off in another corner of the continent "an affair" was brewing that required immediate attention. He mentioned it obliquely to Savary, who had no idea what was afoot. "Haste is essential," he declared, "as the emperor has more pressing business elsewhere which may enter into a peace treaty. If he does not attend to it while the mood is upon him, he will have to face new difficulties here." [7]

What was this secret affair which called for abandoning Poland and pacifying the czar? Talleyrand knew because he and Napoleon were contriving it privately. Let us bear in mind his acknowledged involvement. The affair he was so eager to settle concerned Spain. His prayers were answered, for on July 9, 1807, Napoleon and the French army broke camp.

The Prince of Benevento Leaves the Ministry to Save Face and His Official Income

Talleyrand stopped off in Dresden to visit good King Frederick Augustus of Saxony and was warmly welcomed back into his natural habitat, the aristocracy. Balls and receptions honored him; the French minister's house where he stayed was besieged by processions of callers. There Talleyrand held court in a small drawing room to which only select visitors were admitted. He busied himself with matters of major and minor significance, including a shopping trip with the minister's wife and her maidservant for fine linens to take back to Paris. He also took back a million florins with the compliments of Frederick Augustus.

The journey east had resolved certain questions in his mind. The fate of the Empire and of Europe was clear, though not very comforting. As historian Albert Sorel has said, Talleyrand realized that post-revolutionary France would have to maintain her traditional boundaries if she meant to have peace. But if she was bent on conquest, then "conquest would annihilate liberty." Talleyrand had discerned "traversing the epic of the Republic and the Empire the long, disastrous dislocation in French history inclining the Republic toward military dictatorship, military dictatorship toward world rule, and world rule toward the tragedy of Moscow."

What happened in August, 1807? Talleyrand left the ministry of foreign relations. The reasons given in his *Memoirs* coincide with what we already know: he disapproved of the emperor's policies, recognized the frailty of his Empire, and was tired of having his own advice ignored or rejected. "As soon as I saw him embark on those revolutionary enterprises which ruined him, I left the ministry, for which he never forgave me." In reality Napoleon's anti-European "revolutionary enterprises" had been operating for some time with Talleyrand's cooperation. Did he really leave voluntarily as he said: "I left the ministry of my own free will"? Napoleon told Las Cases that after hearing so many complaints about Talleyrand's rapacity he had been obliged to dismiss him. Was he cashiered? No one even suggested it at the time he left the rue du Bac. Metternich, Austria's ambassador to France, who was well acquainted with Talleyrand's affairs, claimed that Talleyrand chose to leave through indolence. That argument supports our hero's preference for idleness but not his overwhelming ambition and cupidity.

His actions, as always, are shrouded in mist. Savary asserts that Napoleon admitted having been vexed by Talleyrand's resignation. In 1813, referring to Talleyrand's inexplicable behavior, the emperor said to Caulaincourt: "Why did he want to leave the ministry? He would still be there if he had wished it." The fact is that in 1807 Napoleon had come to find Talleyrand intolerable, indispensable, and irreplaceable. He had every reason to dismiss him and did not do it. So Talleyrand did what he did on many other occasions: found himself a replacement and slipped quietly from power without anyone really knowing whether he had resigned or been dismissed. Even more confusing was his continued attendance at the emperor's councils. What advice did he give there? The only kind Napoleon would tolerate: support for his own follies. Later, Talleyrand disclaimed any responsibility for the emperor's mistakes on grounds that he had left office. The main thing was to remove himself from the scene. As Emile Dard, one of his most reliable biographers, puts it: "No one can accuse him of having forsaken the emperor on the brink of his downfall; he parted from him at the height of his glory." That is perfectly true.

On his return from Saxony in the summer of 1807, Talleyrand brooded over the humiliation he had suffered at Napoleon's hands by having been denied a voice in the peace negotiations when the entire diplomatic community, the queen of Prussia, and even the French generals had counted on him to halt the Warlord's advance.

Furthermore, he felt that he deserved higher rewards for his services. He still ached from the secret hurt inflicted in 1804 with the elevation of Cambacérès and Lebrun to Serene Highnesses. The moment had come for him to win a high dignitary's title. Napoleon would not allow his officials to accumulate offices and was angered by Talleyrand's solicitation as it left him, the emperor, in the position of either having to refuse it or else grant it on condition that the new high dignitary renounce his portfolio.

Talleyrand was too worldly wise and too tactful to have blundered into confronting Napoleon with that choice. He did it deliberately. Napoleon took him at his word and gave him the rank of vice-grand elector. Wily Fouché could not resist jeering: "It is the only vice he lacked." Surely a compliment to our hero's many talents.

That was Talleyrand's device for extricating himself from the rue du Bac without anyone knowing whether he had left by the front door or through the window. Once again he managed to make himself "an object of controversy" and coiner of apt phrases. "I do not wish to be Europe's executioner" were his parting words.

The assertion in his *Memoirs* that he served Napoleon "loyally and zealously" is true. Indeed, to feed his hunger for imperial favor he supported endeavors contrary to his own principles. His claim to have kept "the sovereign's authority within bounds" is not true, however, because his very flexibility and zeal were concessions to tyranny. When he credits himself for having "dealt tactfully with Europe to win pardon for the joy and glory of the French," he is also inventing. Not once did he oppose the seizure of a territory, much less the fragmentation of Germany. It would be more accurate to say that that was his intention but that he did not try to carry it out because the damage was already irreversible. He deserves credit for his sound political insights and censure for blessing the failures of the man he served.

According to the rules, our hero escorted his successor, Champagny (the future duc de Cadore), on a tour of the ministry. Of the new minister, he had this to say: "The only difference between Champagny and me is that if the emperor commands him to cut off someone's head, he does it within the hour, whereas it would take me a month to carry out the order."

Surely there were other differences, if only in their respective manners of appointing and dismissing staff. As minister, Talleyrand had observed the conscientious efforts of a rather shy employee, whom he rewarded with a consulship. Never expecting such recognition, the man thanked him profusely, confessing astonishment at his own promotion because not once in his whole life had he enjoyed a lucky break. "You have been unlucky?" Talleyrand asked him. "Then I shall not appoint you." And he removed his name from the list of new consuls. Mazarin and Napoleon felt the same way.

Talleyrand amused himself by shocking Champagny in the course of introducing him to the ministry staff when, as parting advice, he strongly recommended a leisurely and casual pace for executing state affairs. "Sir, these are worthy persons of whom you may be satisfied. You will find them loyal, competent, punctilious, but, due to my influence, less than zealous." Seeing Champagny's mouth drop, Talleyrand was encouraged to continue somewhat condescendingly: "Yes, sir, except for a few petty clerks who cannot wait to close their envelopes, everyone here is extremely calm and unaccustomed to haste. After you have handled the emperor's European affairs for a while, you will appreciate the importance of not sealing and dispatching his orders too promptly."

Napoleon produced one of his rare smiles on hearing about Champagny's amazed reactions. So strongly did he approve of Talleyrand's advice that he personally counseled the new minister: "You ought to keep my letters under your pillow for three or four days before sending them." In later years, Talleyrand recalled the advantages of conducting foreign affairs at a snail's pace: "The emperor exposed himself to danger the moment he was able to do a quarter of an hour sooner what I obliged him to do a quarter of an hour later." "The moment" of course referred to the day he left office, August 10, 1807. Champagny took over on the ninth, leaving Talleyrand to sign the mail for the last time on August 10. He did so with his own inimitable flourish: "The dispatch which I have the honor of sending Your Majesty today will be my last official act. First and last, gratitude and devotion guide me always." [1]

That remained to be seen. In any event, he exited gracefully. But what advantage was there in this self-imposed semi-disgrace? He became vice-grand elector, the grand elector being Joseph, king of Italy. Flippantly, he dismissed such eminent titles as "honorable and lucrative sinecures." Indeed, his own was worth 330,000 francs. As grand chamberlain he received 40,000, with an additional 120,000 from his princedom and from Valençay, not to mention 5,000 for wearing a ribbon of the Legion of Honor, making a total annual income of half a million (about 300 million old francs).

Plus a few other trifles. As a Serene Highness and the Empire's third (alas!) most prominent dignitary, he ranked after Cambacérès and Lebrun in claiming the best seats for Te Deums in Notre Dame.

Another of his duties placed him at the bedside of Queen Hortense when, on April 20, 1808, she gave birth in Paris to her first son, Napoléon-Louis Charles. He complimented the new mother with this casual but apt comment: "It is Your Majesty's business to give us princes. Upon her rests our future security." Changing the subject, he sat down by her bed.

The queen, in labor, never forgot his visit. Talleyrand's excessive partiality to powder, ointments, and scents is an old story. He was so heavily perfumed that the poor mother-to-be had visions of choking. No matter how you look at it, our hero left an indelible impression wherever he went.

The child born that day breathing the fragrant air supplied by Talleyrand made his mark in history as Napoleon III.*

The promotion entitled him to a more elegant, starchier suit of clothes than he had worn as grand chamberlain. Prud-hon's portrait in the Carnavalet Museum depicts him thus. His expression could hardly be less inviting, perhaps reflecting his stiff and imposing new clothes. Or did the painter sense the hidden self which had begun to emerge during the Consulate? Whatever the explanation, the figure presented is majestic and disquieting, still haughty but no longer sardonic. The century had changed him.

He also earned the right to new armorial bearings, among which, to be sure, one could distinguish the three rampant lions of the House of Périgord, disguised as they were (like their owner), wedded (like their owner) to other heraldic beasts: a boar representing Benevento (Calabria) and an eagle, which, being the ubiquitous imperial symbol, might have represented almost anything—"an eagle clutching a bolt of lightning." As if a Talleyrand-Périgord bearing a name eminent for nine centuries needed to upgrade his coat of arms!

But despite his finery, his boar, his eagle, and his sinecure, Talleyrand soon longed to be back in the ministry. He was fifty-three.

At Leisure, the Prince of Benevento Causes More Anxiety Than in Office

He returned to the rue d'Anjou and the card tables. Montrond and Narbonne were still around; the "young bucks" of his court days at Versailles became once more his constant companions. They would gamble

---

* Queen Hortense's second son, an illegitimate child by Flahaut de la Billarderie, son of our bishop of Autun, also became famous as the duc de Morny. He engineered the *coup d'état* of December 2 which brought his half brother to the throne and installed himself as minister of the interior until 1862. Upon his death, Count Walewski, Napoleon's son by Maria Walewska, took his place, prompting Napoleon III to remark: "Drive out the natural. . . ."

or attend demonstrations by the celebrated German phrenologist Gall, half physician, half quack, who had the social élite running to him to find out who they were and the probable course of their lives which he could diagnose, apparently, just by feeling the bumps on their skulls. But none of these activities could compensate for Talleyrand's lost rein on "the affairs of Europe." He told Madame de Rémusat: "Rest assured that with all his faults the emperor is still very necessary to France today as he knows how to maintain her, and we ought to help in every possible way." Evidently he was sorry to have "departed" a bit prematurely. For other ears he had other words. He and Metternich were good friends, having reached a perfect understanding. The two had similar backgrounds and education; Metternich was less complex yet utterly faithless; both were monuments to the Ancien Régime transplanted to the new one. Compared to the Austrian statesman, Talleyrand had far more penetrating insight and broader vision, but for versatility and artful dissimulation the two were rivals. To Metternich, Talleyrand freely confided his anxieties and regrets for the fate of the Empire. Metternich believed that Talleyrand's political career had come to an end.

Still our hero insisted on dropping intriguing remarks which set the salons buzzing. "My poor little mind," he began owlishly, "fails to comprehend that what we are doing beyond the Rhine will last any longer than the great man who is ordering it. After him, no nation will willingly submit to another nation. The emperor's vigilant and vigorous hand will preserve us, but what will come after him? Nature does not produce two men of his stature."

Apart from any flattery, the point he wanted to make was that Napoleon's achievements would not survive him, as frustrated nationalism was bound to bring down the edifice he had shored up with bayonets alone; the days of the Empire were numbered. Sheer common sense.

How is it that the ubiquitous imperial police (with one or two spies in every family, every salon, every café, every coach) did not relay the wily and insinuating remarks of a man of such caliber to Napoleon? It is incredible. Were intelligence reports being screened? Napoleon continued to see Talleyrand, listen to him, and inform him of current affairs in order to bask in his flattery and to allow himself to be propelled to his own perdition. There was no need to "betray" him; he would do it himself if left alone. Every tragedy has its fatality.

Napoleon thus threw himself recklessly into the fateful Spanish adventure. To hear Talleyrand speaking of it to Madame de Rémusat, one would think he believed Napoleon's projected move against Spain was utter madness:

> If he takes the kind of advice he gets these days, I shall not answer for the consequences. He is caught in a noose. Murat wants to be king of Spain, so they woo the Prince of Peace [that wretch Manuel Godoy] in hopes of winning his favor, as if he had any credit at the Spanish court. A fine plan of the emperor's indeed to arrive in a country where he has the reputation of being in league with one of its hated ministers. I know he is playing the minister false and will reject him when he sees his uselessness, but he might have spared himself the cost of this despicable treachery.

Sad but true. Still, judging from his pointed criticism of the emperor's latest schemes, one would never guess that a month after leaving the ministry, in September, 1807, Talleyrand himself had conferred at Fontainebleau with Izquierdo, Godoy's emissary, with an eye to liquidating the Spanish Bourbons. Formally, he backed Napoleon's policy; informally, he condemned it. To the above he added this perceptive comment: "But ambition, anger, pride, and a few imbeciles he listens to often blind him. He distrusts me the moment I mention moderation, and once he stops believing in me, just watch how he will involve himself and us in any number of foolish blunders. . . ."

Because Talleyrand was never rash, he hastened to muffle that ugly admission with an oath of loyalty, strictly formal, to be sure: "Yet I shall stand by him to the end [was he tending a patient on the brink of death?]. Having associated myself with the creation of his Empire, I wish it to stand as my final achievement, and as long as I live, however successful my plan, I shall not give it up." [1]

His loyalty was not to the emperor but to the Empire. Words, on the lips of our hero, have meaning. His loyalty was conditional; he made it clear that it required "success" in order to endure. Now we know what to expect.

Judging from his *Memoirs,* one would think Talleyrand had had nothing to do with the "Spanish intrigue." He dismisses the whole affair and his involvement with a few vague comments. "I fought the plan forcefully by exposing the immorality and the perils of such an undertaking." Where, when, in what form? Did he submit any report or memorandum? He assailed "the most memorable of all Napoleon's outrages," but that assault came during the Restoration, whereas in 1808 he gave no sign of opposition. As a matter of fact, at a dinner party Pasquier heard him advocate usurpation thus: "Since Louis XIV, the crown of Spain has belonged to France's reigning family. . . . It is one of the richest shares of our great king's bequest, and the emperor ought to re-assemble this entire heritage; he must not, he cannot afford to give up a single part of it."

Talleyrand probably drummed that message into Napoleon's ear by way of encouragement. Ever since 1792 he had nursed a profound distaste for the Bourbons, and not just the French branch but the Spanish and Neapolitan branches as well. When Napoleon drove the Bourbons from Naples and put his brother Joseph on their throne, Madame de Rémusat had complained bitterly. She got little sympathy from her friend Talleyrand: "Madam, we will not see the end of this until no Bourbon sits upon a throne in Europe." This time his meaning was crystal clear. The reason we cannot trace his participation is that in 1814 he destroyed official records of the Spanish and duc d'Enghien affairs.

Learning of the low blow dealt at Bayonne on May 8, 1808, Talley-rand hastened to compliment the emperor for having lured Spain's infante, the prince of Asturia, along with his brother and uncle, into a trap and then arrested them after forcing them to renounce their rights to the Spanish throne. Had Talleyrand forgotten his role in creating the Declaration of the Rights of Man? How could he write: "Everyone here marvels at the turn of events, a turn so fortunate that one could not ask for better"? That single, incriminating letter escaped the fire. The baiting and trapping of three royal captives without firing a shot is seen as a glorious exploit. The victor of Austerlitz had stooped to rat-catching. Talleyrand continued to pour out flattery. Never had the voice of doom spoken more explicitly, more persuasively. The worst of it was that he involved the French people in the disgraceful act: "Even the public is satisfied." He had "the public" saying whatever he chose. Another treachery of Talleyrand's which his detractors fail to mention is the fact that in betraying freedom and justice, he forswore himself.

Let it be said that though he flattered Napoleon, he did not en-courage him to make war. As a matter of fact, he had made him pledge not to cross the Pyrenees, just as he had pledged earlier not to trespass beyond the Niemen: "Your Majesty would allow me to hope that matters will be settled in Bayonne so that he will not be forced to venture beyond French boundaries, which I wholeheartedly desire."

Napoleon was not interested in Talleyrand's desires and had already invaded Spain. Discouraged, our hero congratulated him all the same, comparing Marshal Bessières's victory at Medina del Rio Seco to Almanza's, which had secured the Spanish throne for Louis XIV's grand-son, Philip V. This time the crown went to Joseph Bonaparte. Talleyrand vainly insists (for Bourbon ears primarily) in his *Memoirs* that in August, 1808, in Nantes, Napoleon dressed him down severely for opposing the attack on Spain. One cannot believe that story. In Nantes, where he was summoned by imperial order, he may have managed to influence Napoleon, not morally or ethically as he would like us to think, but by stressing the impact of recent bad news from Spain. The time of reversals had begun. The imperial tide was turning. General Dupont had surrendered at Bailén on July 20. Dreadful as it was, the event called for comment. Talleyrand made no effort to discomfit his master, and ob-servers who saw him after the Nantes meeting said that his favor had never been greater. At Talleyrand's house in Paris, Pasquier met the duke of San Carlos, escort to the Spanish princes, and the abbé de Pradt, later archbishop of Malines. Pasquier was amazed to hear the prince of Benevento congratulate himself on being the emperor's choice for custodian of the Spanish royal prisoners. We may well share his amaze-ment when we see the manner in which the vice-grand elector was promoted to the rank of jailer. Why the playacting? Why grovel and then publicize it to boot? The façade was necessary to cover up another one: the emperor must not doubt his unswerving loyalty. Imperial trust would enable Talleyrand to remain party to secret dealings among Aus-tria, Russia, and Germany. Later on, he was the only person capable of negotiating with Europe's monarchs. Talleyrand continued to negotiate in his own fashion; Napoleon was on his way to exile when it finally dawned on him what lay behind his adviser's zeal.

Despite Talleyrand's efforts to remain aloof (officially) from the Spanish affair, Napoleon probably suspected his duplicity and resolved to weaken his position and humiliate him. On May 9, 1808, we may recall, the emperor arrested the Spanish princes in Bayonne; he found it both convenient and agreeable to hand them over to the prince of Benevento for custody at the château de Valençay. It was also a reminder that having helped pay for it, he had certain rights there. Talleyrand received his orders in a letter from the emperor announcing the prisoners' arrival "on Tuesday at Valençay. Get there beforehand on Monday evening. . . .

"I wish the princes to be received without ceremony, but decently; do your best to entertain them. If Valençay has a theater, you might bring in some comedians." Besides the comedy, he had other diversions in mind. "You could have Madame de Talleyrand come with four or five ladies." (Are we to imagine His Serene Highness, napkin draped over his arm, presenting his wife and her ladies to the captive princes? How contemptible!) The emperor went on:

> If the prince of Asturia should become attached to some pretty and re-liable woman, no harm would be done; it would be another way of keeping track of him. [His Imperial Majesty's lofty mind managed to think of everything.] As for your mission, it is honorable enough. Re-ceiving three illustrious persons and entertaining them is quite in keep-ing with the character of the nation [hear the intruder scorning the nation which opened its arms to him] and your position [so much for the French nobility crawling on all fours in the Tuileries]. In the week or ten days you spend with them, you will find out what they are thinking, which will help me decide what to do.[2]

This letter, more of a whiplash than a compliment, elicited the smile we noted when the prince announced his new jailer's role to Pasquier. The smile should not be taken too seriously; the lash left no visible mark, but the pain it brought was deep inside. Talleyrand's dissimulation and inscrutability amazed everyone. General Lannes observed, in his crude soldier's tongue: "Talleyrand can be booted in the a— and not show it on his face." Stendhal said the same thing more elegantly: "Never was a face less of a barometer." Had there been a "barometer" to consult, it would have registered hatred from then on.

Serenely, submissively, in measured phrases, the prince of Bene-vento acknowledged His Majesty's whiplash:

> I shall respond with exceeding care to the confidence with which Your Majesty honors me. Madame de Talleyrand left yesterday evening to give preliminary orders at Valençay. The château is amply furnished with cooks, linen, and china of all kinds. The princes will enjoy every diversion permitted by the presently inclement weather. I shall provide them with daily Masses, a park to walk in, woods for riding though poorly stocked with game, horses, meals at all hours, and music. There is no theater, but it would be practically impossible anyway to find actors. We will have enough young people so that the princes may dance if they wish.
> I am requesting the police inspector to prepare his Valençay brigade for service, to set up several posts in the neighborhood, and to order his men to stand watch inconspicuously [May 13, 1808].

All went smoothly. Madame de Talleyrand faced her "duties" cheer-fully and succumbed rapidly when the infantes' escort, the duke of San Carlos, took a fancy to the fading charms of this stout lady, who unleashed upon her lover the ardor rejected by Talleyrand since their marriage. As host, to royalty this time, Talleyrand was unrivaled. The Spanish flag, with its gold and crimson stripes, flew atop Valençay's enormous keep. It continued to flutter there many years after the princes had left. Talleyrand did his best to make their captivity pleasurable. He had no trouble discovering what they were thinking because they did not think. One look at Goya's portraits of them will confirm this. Foolish playthings amused them; they liked making miniature gardens in their rooms and irrigating them with streams of water. Talleyrand's parquet floors bear witness to this. The princes were innocuous, but the police could not appreciate this; preferring to imagine them as bellicose and scheming, they followed the infantes everywhere. Talleyrand finally laid down the law: he, not the emperor or the police, was master of the château and its park. His servility had limits. He put up a wall around the park so that his guests could amuse themselves safe from peering eyes. They had brought along a guitarist who would perch in the trees and strum boleros in the evening. Madame de Talleyrand played the piano. Daytime was for hunting. On rainy days, no amount of urging could keep the royal youngsters in the library; they fled from books or reading. Evenings were whiled away in the company of some young lady.

In his *Memoirs,* Talleyrand writes: "In addition to these distractions in which everyone took a hand, the princes also had the consolations of religion; great misfortune inspires faith and stirs the heart." A touching note, followed by this edifying one: "The day ended in public prayers to which anyone visiting the château was invited: the local officers of the guard and even police from headquarters." A comforting sight, those police on bended knee taking guidance from Monseigneur d'Autun.

In August he was torn from his pious retreat for a command appearance at Nantes. From Nantes he swung over to Paris, then returned to Valençay for just a few days. Napoleon was already waiting to take him to Erfurt, in Germany, to meet the czar and various other sovereigns.

During that brief trip Talleyrand heard the dreadful news that his nephew Louis de Périgord had died of typhoid in Berlin on June 18, 1808. Louis had been easily his favorite relative; the family and he had invested all their hopes in him. Everyone who knew Louis de Périgord agreed that he was a fine officer, an honorable and courageous gentleman, an ideal friend. Talleyrand had made him his heir and left him the princedom of Benevento.

Louis's death produced no tearful scenes. Talleyrand's grief found expression instead in brief messages to intimate friends of the family such as the marquis d'Osmond:

I haven't written lately, my dear Osmond, knowing that you practically live amongst my kin. You are so much a part of us that you too have suffered the terrible loss we bear.

Please see Forel and, however cruel the facts may be, find out everything that happened from the time poor Louis arrived in Berlin.

Farewell. I am utterly miserable, I can assure you. I thought of him as the head of my family after I am gone, a universally admired and respected head. Now there is none. Farewell. Warmest regards.[3]

It was the naked truth. On his lips, "I am utterly miserable" becomes a poignant cry, and the next sentence conveys his despair at the prospect of a leaderless, insecure family. Edmond, the younger nephew, was incapable of holding his relatives together.

When Talleyrand arrived in Paris, his inalterable countenance was visibly altered. So was his conversation, his behavior, even the way he treated guests. He was griefstricken. Madame de Rémusat and Madame de Vaines were much affected by the impenetrable sorrow of their friend.

Far more lachrymose was his farewell to the prisoners of Valençay. The three princes came before him, eyes glistening with tears, to present a gift and their compliments to the host who had turned their "captivity" into a garden of pleasures. To the former bishop of Autun they gave their Spanish prayer books, and he, whose chief asset was not precisely piety, professed astonishment at their gesture. Referring to the pious offerings, he said: "I accepted them with awe and with an emotion so compelling that I would not have the temerity to express it." Nor we the naïveté to believe it.

What we may safely believe, however, is that the princes, shocked by the crude trap sprung on them at Bayonne, found a luxurious sanctuary in which to revive their spirits in the custody, or rather under the protection, of a kindly grand seigneur who provided for their every comfort and even attempted to institute court ceremonial. Liberty they were denied, but not the deference due their rank or the pleasures of the idle rich. Our hero was always at his best when called on to demonstrate his social gifts, his respect for others, in short, the unique cultural heritage of the Enlightenment.

It was natural for his prisoners to become fond of him. If the letter they composed and sent round to him does small credit to their tutors, at least it conveys their good will and appreciation for their "jailer":

Prince, dear cousin, and dear friend:

The many kindnesses shown us by Your Serene Highness since it has been our good fortune to know him, the gracious hospitality we owe him, and a thousand reasons for our heartfelt gratitude added to the high esteem which his noble character has inspired, make it our pleasant duty to assure the prince through the intermediary of the duke of San Carlos and Canon Escoiquiz, bearers of this letter, of our undying friendship, unable as we are to express it more than imperfectly as well as the regret inspired by your absence though we hope it will advance our affairs and that we will have the pleasure of seeing him again.

Give heed, Prince, to this outpouring of our hearts. It is too genuine not to be felt by you.

Your affectionate cousins and friends,

Ferdinand, Charles, Antonio
August 30, 1808[4]

Unknown to them, the farewell was final. Their sojourn at Valençay was only an accident of history. Talleyrand had gone on to prepare the emperor's business at Erfurt. Since leaving the ministry, he was beginning to resemble a glorified butler—his duties as grand chamberlain called for it. The fuse he lit at Erfurt produced such an explosion that not until 1816 was he free to return to Valençay. Eight years later the world had changed completely. Thanks to the explosion, his royal prisoners regained their freedom and returned to Madrid. Did they ever think back on the delights of captivity *à la* Talleyrand? Nothing suggests that they did. San Carlos alone retained his affinity for the well-cushioned flanks of his "jaileress," the (reigning) princess of Benevento.

"Perfidy Is Noble Against Tyranny"
—*Corneille,* Cinna

On September 24, 1808, during the conference at Erfurt, Metternich advised his government: "Talleyrand has not yet defected; he rails, and wishes to manage things." Indeed, Talleyrand was providing Metternich, whom he dubbed the "Pale One," with information of special interest to Austria. Emperor Francis was on very poor terms with Napoleon. The Franco-Russian alliance had left Austria in a highly vulnerable position, waiting to be torn to shreds by the czar and the emperor of the French after the latter had subdued Spain. She was arming secretly in fear and trembling. To Talleyrand's regret, she had not been invited to the talks at Erfurt.

He favored an Austrian alliance and, expert conciliator that he was, came up with a plan, which he described to Metternich, for thawing relations between Vienna and Paris: "Do you know what I would do if I were your government? I would offer to exchange decorations. The emperor prizes any gesture of your court as coming from established nobility." Talleyrand was proposing that the rulers and supreme dignitaries of each country exchange their highest decorations in the Order of the Golden Fleece and the Legion of Honor. Metternich pointed out that only individuals with five hundred years of recognized nobility were eligible for the Golden Fleece, adding: "You alone, then, could receive it, and it will be interesting to see how the emperor proves his noble ancestry." The two men smiled understandingly and dropped the question of the Golden Fleece.

Talleyrand was determined to pacify Austria; Napoleon would not hear of it. Yet the war in Spain had weakened his prestige, and he was anxious to keep Germany at bay as long as French forces were tied up behind the Pyrenees. Furthermore, as he was beginning to doubt the reliability of his Russian ally, he saw a pressing need to strengthen the Tilsit agreements.

Napoleon gambled with destiny at Erfurt just as on the battlefield. If Russia and Austria were to join forces at that moment, they could destroy him. The solution was to keep them apart, and to cajole and hoodwink the czar. For that, Napoleon had the distinct advantage of his skill as both actor and inveigler. Alexander was impressionable, highly vulnerable to enticing visions of eastward expansion, of a defunct Ottoman Empire, of possessing the Dardanelles. And as he was known to chase petticoats, they would procure him some. The Comédie Française also joined the campaign, with Corneille called into service. Napoleon chose to present *Cinna* because of its many allusions to his imperial glory. His greatest asset in a game of this kind was, of course, the prince of Benevento. But he never suspected that this ace was a fraud or that Talleyrand had a long-range view of the proceedings. Meanwhile, what Talleyrand saw at much closer range was the correspondence exchanged by Caulaincourt, ambassador to St. Petersburg, with the czar and the emperor. Caulaincourt kept no secrets from Talleyrand, whom he liked and admired. Even outside the ministry, then, our hero had access to letters passing among those three personages and thus kept abreast of Napoleon's plans, his arguments, his deficiencies. Napoleon was unaware of the ties between Caulaincourt and his former minister. Knowing that Talleyrand was liked by the czar, he would use him to outwit Alexander while Caulaincourt kept a sharp eye on what this enigmatic diplomat was up to.

Napoleon asked Talleyrand to draft a pact with the czar. In essence, the emperor wanted to take everything and give nothing, except a series of promises based on conditions which, if ever applied, would invalidate the promises. Talleyrand produced the draft. Napoleon complimented him for invoking principles wherever possible to avoid granting concessions. "Principles are fine; they entail no commitment." But that applies to the other party, too, and Napoleon needed the czar's commitment. Once again they promised him Moldavia and Wallachia, "but with the mediation of France." "That clause is good," said Napoleon, thinking that he could always refuse to mediate. By pledging these Danubian provinces to Russia, the emperor was also menacing Austria; he enjoyed alarming or threatening nations and individuals. "Only when alarmed do they obey," he declared. A clause conspicuously absent from Talleyrand's draft was the vital one committing Russia to join France in a war against Austria. It was not there because Talleyrand opposed it.

"It is the crucial clause, how could you forget it? Are you still an Austrian?" demanded Napoleon.

"A little, Sire, but I think it would be more accurate to say that I am never Russian and always French."

The witty remark fell on deaf ears. Napoleon had these recommendations to impart:

> During the trip, you will seek frequent opportunities to be with Emperor Alexander. You know him well; you speak his language. Tell him that in the service to mankind which our alliance can render is revealed one of the grand designs of providence [as if the designs of providence would interest an ambitious, mystical czar]. Together we are destined to reorder Europe [what kind of order was that? The Spanish variety, assuredly]. We are both young; there is no call for haste. Tell him that nothing will be done without public approval, and that Europe, unafraid of our power, ultimately will rejoice to see our great enterprise achieved [sheer insanity to imagine Europe rejoicing at having been torn up and enslaved by two tyrants]. The security of neighboring powers, continental interests, to be sure, seven million Greeks liberated, etc. . . . . Great opportunities for philanthropy. I leave the details to you; my only requirement is that it be philanthropy at a distance. Farewell.[1]

Pure cynicism, especially the "philanthropy at a distance." One wonders how Talleyrand reacted.

To talk with Alexander, he had no need of philanthropic themes supplied by Napoleon; his own private themes stood ready. The one piece of advice he followed, probably with tongue in cheek, was: "See Emperor Alexander often." He used and abused that permission, as we shall see. Talleyrand had been in touch with the czar since 1801 and had received a diamond-framed portrait of him as well as a gracious letter. He knew him primarily through Caulaincourt, whose admiration for Alexander was as enthusiastic as for Talleyrand, and who transmitted confidential, but always laudatory, remarks about each to the other. The czar knew that Talleyrand's feelings for Napoleon had changed radically since 1804 and that he now opposed imperial policy.

If Napoleon had negotiated privately with Alexander, he would have prevailed. The czar was weak and indecisive; the brilliant, charming emperor would have had his way. By calling in Talleyrand, he defeated his own purpose. Talleyrand destroyed Napoleon's influence over the czar and turned the latter against his ally.

Because he told Metternich everything and advised him what his government must do for its own survival, by the end of the conference Talleyrand had managed to unite Austria and Russia against Napoleon, who, for the sake of his own security, had whetted their hostility. Such was the outcome of Talleyrand's frequent conversations with the czar in compliance with Napoleon's orders.

Let us examine the maneuvers he employed to achieve what some historians call "the betrayal at Erfurt," which, in reality, was little more than a realignment of arbitrarily dislocated powers. To Napoleon, it was treachery; to France and the rest of Europe, wisdom.

Caulaincourt was the first person Talleyrand saw after his arrival at Erfurt on September 21, 1808. They discussed the situation and agreed on their objective; how to accomplish it was the next step. Talleyrand liked and respected Caulaincourt, and assigned him a leading role at Erfurt in his *Memoirs,* not in an effort to compromise him (Talleyrand did not feel compromised himself) but to tout his competence: "M. de Caulaincourt's merits ultimately must be duly recognized." Neither of them dreamed he would be branded "traitor" one day for trying to halt a rampaging tyrant. They believed—correctly at the time—that they reflected the overwhelming desire of the French and European community. The bloodbath had lasted since 1792; it was time to end it. Talleyrand's *Memoirs* do not deny his role in this; in fact, he was rather proud of it. During the Restoration, when he grew impatient with extremist orators whose every speech was a boast that they were saving the monarchy, he remarked to Vitrolles: "Day after day they claim to be saving the monarchy; well, at Erfurt I saved Europe."

All was in order for Napoleon's arrival at Erfurt on September 27. He made a shattering entrance; everything trembled. The horde of fawning German princes bettered their past record of servility. Even Talleyrand was disgusted: "Never has there been seen such a genius for slavishness. . . . At Erfurt I did not see a single hand proudly stroking the lion's mane." [2]

The czar's face lit up at the sight of Talleyrand standing beside Napoleon: "He is an old acquaintance; I am delighted to see him; I was hoping he would be along." This air of friendly concern and complicity led Talleyrand to write: "M. de Caulaincourt had met with him and told him that I was fully informed of everything going on." As Talleyrand held the door of the czar's carriage, Alexander said softly: "We shall see each other." Exactly as Napoleon had wished. So now his affairs were under way; two different affairs: the Russian alliance and, surprisingly, a matrimonial project. Talleyrand was instructed to obtain the hand of one of the czar's sisters for Napoleon, who had decided to divorce Josephine and remarry. Napoleon was in no hurry for the negotiations to open; he wanted time to impress the czar. It would take several days to condition Alexander: "Before we begin, I wish the czar to be dazzled by the spectacle of my power; this always facilitates negotiations."

This was all to the best for Talleyrand, as the treaty only interfered with his plans. He put it aside and concentrated on intrigues aimed at undermining Napoleon's cause.

Talleyrand operated as usual, in the company of socially prominent women. Central Europe's nobility had gathered at Erfurt. The princess of Thurn-Taxis could boast the most brilliant salon. There one evening, as Talleyrand was radiating his charm upon a circle of princesses and duchesses, the czar entered unannounced and casually called for a cup of tea. Offhandedly he informed his hostess that he would come there every evening after the theater. As he spoke, he stared at Talleyrand. Alexander and our hero thus parleyed nightly over the teacups, from midnight until two, Talleyrand's prime working hours.

During the day there were parties, receptions, and plays. Talma captivated Napoleon; the actor might have been his mouthpiece. When Talma played Cinna, the emperor gazed out at the audience of princes and kings and seemed to say: "Listen carefully, it is I who speak." He would have done better to listen to his grand chamberlain's conversations with the czar in the princess of Thurn-Taxis's salon following each performance: "Sire, what did you come here to do? It is up to you to save Europe, and you will only succeed by resisting Napoleon. The French are a civilized nation, their ruler is not; Russia's ruler is civilized, his people are not. Therefore Russia's ruler must be the French people's ally." [3]

Was it treachery to champion the French nation against a tyrant destroying and bleeding her to death? Napoleon no longer represented France. France needed help.

The czar was thrilled to hear such talk. Russia's new ambassador, Count Tolstoy, had already reported that Talleyrand headed the silent opposition in Paris; little did he think our hero would offer to lead a crusade for liberation. Talleyrand's temerity now had public support; he no longer stood alone as in 1804. Joseph de Maistre recounts what three familiar Frenchmen said to Tolstoy at Erfurt: "Talleyrand, Berthier, and Lannes told Marshal Count Tolstoy that they were pretty well fed up with their beloved master, and if ever they decided to execute an about-face, they would be flattered to serve Alexander."

Two French marshals ready to desert with the bishop of Autun? What were Fouché's agents doing?

Talleyrand told the czar: "The Rhine, the Alps, the Pyrenees are conquests of France; the rest is the emperor's conquest, and France makes no claim to it." Alexander was struck by the truth of this. He knew that silent France no longer stood behind Napoleon and that among all the high officials and generals, one voice dared to utter those secret thoughts. He assumed therefore that the French would gladly hand back Napoleon's plunder—a new imperial district centered in Hamburg, another in Rome—so that Europe's peace and stability could be restored.

Suddenly Alexander saw things differently and was induced to adopt a more favorable attitude toward Austria, just as Metternich had been won over to sympathy for Russia. The Austrian diplomat explained it: "Because, according to Talleyrand, French interests demand unity of the powers capable of withstanding Napoleon in order to stem the tide of his insatiable ambition; because Napoleon's cause is no longer that of France [with the two causes dissociated, the nation's interests held precedence]; and because Europe can be saved only if Austria and Russia stand firmly united."

Trusting Talleyrand completely, the czar let him read the treaty which Napoleon had given him in strictest secrecy, pledging him not to show it to another soul, not even his foreign minister. Napoleon had copied out Talleyrand's draft in his own hand. Talleyrand smiled when he saw it, being well acquainted with the text, its flaws, and the clauses open to various interpretations. His *Memoirs* tell us so.

He gained one advantage for his Viennese friends. Napoleon refused to have Austria represented at the conference, but allowed baron de Vincent to come to Erfurt. Dalberg took charge of him, with the result that voiceless Austria gained at least an ear. Every conversation with the czar, every proposal, every shift of Napoleonic humor was reported to

Vincent. Austria found Talleyrand a more effective champion than her own ambassadors. He would rehearse Vincent and then send him to the czar, who found himself besieged by the "Talleyrand organization"; Caulaincourt, Tolstoy, Vincent, the princess of Thurn-Taxis, and Talleyrand were drumming in the same message. The czar thus learned that his supposed enemies in Vienna were prepared to make common cause with him against Napoleon. "What is Monsieur de Vincent telling me?" Alexander suddenly asked Talleyrand one night.

> "Some very reasonable things, Sire, for he hopes Your Majesty will not let Emperor Napoleon induce him to adopt measures hostile or at least offensive to Austria, and if Your Majesty will allow me to say so, I share the same hopes."
> "I, too, desire it," said the puzzled czar, "but it is very difficult as Emperor Napoleon appears to be adamant."
> "But, Sire, you wish to make certain observations. Would it not be possible for Your Majesty to consider superfluous the clauses involving Austria, saying that they are implied by the Treaty of Tilsit . . . ?"[4]

He drilled the czar on effective ways to nullify the treaty: "I noticed that Emperor Alexander was pleased by me," noted Talleyrand; "he took pencil notes of everything I told him."

The next day, like a diligent pupil, the czar showed him what he had written. "He said graciously: 'You will recognize yourself here and there.'" After his mentor had allowed that "these observations would do," Alexander presented them to Napoleon. The emperor of the French was dumbfounded. Assuming that the czar had been reduced to an obliging pawn, Napoleon discovered instead an immovable rook. "In a conference lasting three hours, the czar did not yield an inch to the emperor." Talleyrand had the satisfaction of seeing his lessons bear fruit.

Alexander was no longer interested in an alliance with a ruler whose prestige was crumbling in Spain and already damaged in France. Alarmed by the czar's sudden about-face during their conference, Napoleon told his secretly elated adviser: "I got nowhere with Emperor Alexander; I rejected everything he said, but he is stubborn. I made absolutely no headway."

Talleyrand deftly soothed his master's pride. "Sire," said Renard,

> "I think Your Majesty has made a great deal [of progress] since arriving here, for Emperor Alexander is wholly in your spell."
> "If that's what you see, then you have been taken in," Napoleon snorted scornfully [the idea of being "taken in" must have amused our hero in this situation]. "If he likes me so much, why doesn't he sign?"

"Sire, his knightly code of honor is such that he is offended by excessive caution [very shrewd]. He feels bound to you more strongly by his word and his affection than by any treaty. His letters, which you gave me to read, reveal this."

"Utter nonsense!" exclaimed the master.[5]

Talleyrand went on cajoling; Napoleon ordered him to talk to the czar further and persuade him that his real interest lay in a unilateral alliance with France. Talleyrand promised to devote his nights to this noble endeavor.

Talleyrand invited Goethe and Wieland to dinner after Napoleon had summoned them for a lengthy talk. In describing that meeting, they reported that the emperor had assailed Tacitus, whom Goethe defended, and extolled Corneille. Our hero saw the two writers again in Weimar where the talks shifted for a day. That evening he was closeted once more with the czar, who had decided to approach the emperor of Austria by letter and attempt to patch up their differences. Talleyrand was delighted to find Alexander progressing in the desired direction.

"Emperor Francis needs reassurance," Talleyrand observed benignly, "and I do not doubt that Your Majesty's letter will have that effect."

"At least that is my intention," replied the czar.

Talleyrand considered it a victory.

Now all he had to do was win for his master the hand of Grand Duchess Catherine, Alexander's sister. To crown the alliance, so Napoleon thought. Talleyrand disapproved of the match and did everything he could to discourage it short of courting an outright refusal. Rather than broach the question, he sent Caulaincourt ahead to sound out the czar, who was not opposed. Our hero then stepped in to speak his piece: "He understood exactly what I had in mind, precisely what I wanted him to understand." That meant no refusal and no marriage. "I confess that for Europe's sake I dreaded one more alliance between France and Russia." The remark throws some light on Talleyrand's reservations about Russia. A pact with the czar definitely would help to overthrow the tyrant, but what then? The matrimonial project succeeded only in dulling Napoleon's caution. Three months later, the prospective bride married the duke of Oldenburg. A younger sister was only fourteen; the emperor was given to understand that he could wait for her. How could a distrustful man be so credulous?

The marriage, like the alliance, had failed. The two sovereigns parted on October 14, 1808, exchanging warm embraces. They had signed a document which was not a pact, which committed neither party to do anything, and which called on Russia to consult England before seizing Moldavia and Wallachia—as if England would condone a Russian approach to Constantinople via the Balkans.

Napoleon, his fate already sealed, was in the grip of:

> That spirit of imprudence and error
> Inevitably proclaiming the fall of kings.

But the emperor was not listening to Racine. Talleyrand, on the other hand, listened to everything, and during a performance of *Cinna* was struck by one line which Corneille seemed to have written just for him: "Perfidy is noble against tyranny."

So ended the hopes Napoleon had invested in this conference; so began the downfall of his Empire. In the autumn air lingered the scent of burned-out lanterns and chilled festivities. The time of reversals had come.

Talleyrand's hand can often be discerned in events which he was absent from but helped to shape. Five years after Erfurt, during the terrible retreat from Moscow, Napoleon hastened homeward wrapped in his own gloomy thoughts. As the sled bore him along, he recalled the conference and tried to reason out the czar's perplexing about-face which had scuttled the alliance. Sitting next to him was Caulaincourt, friend and accomplice of Talleyrand, Alexander, and Vincent. Napoleon suddenly declared that he suspected someone of having "betrayed" him. In that frigid wasteland of despair, the reminder of Erfurt sent a shiver icier than the Moscow winter along Caulaincourt's spine. With tremendous relief he heard that Napoleon suspected General Lannes. Recalling that Lannes had been sent ahead to escort the czar to Erfurt, the emperor reasoned that the general had probably yielded once again to his lowest instincts and used those private conversations with the czar to persuade him "that Napoleon sought to deceive him, that his ambition was boundless, that only war could achieve results, and that he must distrust him utterly." [6]

Caulaincourt does not say whether or not he betrayed his master. It hardly matters. Lannes was dead in 1813, but Talleyrand was very much alive.

Grounds for Divorce

The relationship between Napoleon and Talleyrand was so extraordinary, so significant to the course of history, that here on the brink of their fatal rupture we must try to understand it from our vantage point in time, free of the passions of their contemporaries.

Napoleon was twice divorced, first from Talleyrand at Erfurt, then from Josephine in 1809. The first divorce was unspoken. Talleyrand was never replaced.

Public pressure ultimately reinforced Talleyrand's personal motives, which had been accumulating since 1802. If private grievances alone had been at issue, probably he would not have looked for revenge. He yielded at last to a compelling urge, saying: "There is someone more intelligent than Voltaire, more powerful than the emperor: the people."

The voice of "the people" was a voice of silence during the Empire; Talleyrand could recognize it almost immediately. If it raised a cry, he pretended not to hear. As, for instance, when Madame de Staël wrote: "Fifty leagues from her borders, France is studded with citadels, houses of detention, cities serving as prisons for a multitude of individuals confined by the will of one man, conscripts of despair. . . ."

A strange state of affairs, for "sweet France" to be dotted with detention camps and subjecting persons to house arrest: "in Dijon, Spanish refugees who refuse to swear allegiance . . . in Auxonne, English prisoners," and in Besançon, "more Spaniards." In the Jura, the dungeons of Fort-de-Joux swarmed with French political prisoners; Toussaint L'Ouverture, Santo Domingo's black liberator, perished there from the cold along with many others.

Despite his silence, how is it that Talleyrand did not condemn such flagrant abuse of authority? How could he ignore the terrible truths uttered by Madame de Staël, frantic at being hunted like a common thief: "Like a criminal, then, I was forced to flee two countries, Switzerland and France, at the command of a man less French than I, I who was born on the banks of the Seine where his tyranny naturalized him. Where is his country? The lands which bow to him. His fellow countrymen? They are the slaves who obey his commands."[1] Even if he had broken with her, Talleyrand knew Germaine was right.

He was well aware that Napoleon had made war his unique industry, sacrificing economic and social needs, not to mention public education. The emperor was more Caesar than modern chief of state. That also discredited him for Talleyrand, who had seen Anglo-Saxon "moneymaking" at close range and regarded prosperity as the path to national security.

At Erfurt, he had felt the pulse of France; his own heart throbbed in unison. France, behind her wall of police spies and silence, shared his thoughts. Never before had the world's most loquacious people remained mute for fifteen years. In 1808, they began at last to make signs, fearful ones: 300,000 rebellious conscripts took to the woods and refused to serve in the ranks. An unheard-of departure from Gallic tradition. Resisting military service gained public acceptance, reflecting neither cowardice nor lack of patriotism, but simply a national instinct for survival. France needed to look ahead, and Talleyrand had his eyes on France. His anti-Napoleonic campaign relied heavily on the deep-rooted nationalism of the French and other European peoples.

The chain reaction driving governments and whole populations to rise against the imperial armies began in Spain. "Make war on the king of Spain, not on the Spanish people," Talleyrand had advised Napoleon. Other warnings followed. "Your glory, Sire, shall come to grief in Spain," was the message Napoleon received from his brother Joseph, installed as puppet ruler of that unfortunate kingdom. Joseph was prepared to defy the emperor and come to terms with the Spanish, but they wanted no part of him. He said: "I am not appalled by my situation, though it is unique in history. I do not have a single follower." Unfortunately, he had just one, Napoleon, whose credentials were singularly distasteful to the Spanish. Their catechism went thus:

"What threatens our security?"

"The emperor of the French."

"What kind of man is he?"

"Another grandee and receptacle of all vices."

"Is it a sin to kill a Frenchman?"

"No, killing one of those heretic dogs is the way to Heaven."

That was the European image of France under Napoleon. French prestige had never been greater than when Voltaire, Diderot, d'Alembert, and Maupertuis traveled about or exported a literary ideal of their nation.

It is easy to understand why Talleyrand, a product of that same cultural tradition, resented the distorted national image cast by Napoleon's war-making. How could a reasonable, practical man listen to certain romantic ravings of Napoleon without feeling his flesh crawl? "I am helpless if a wave of power sweeps me on to conquer the world. . . ." The thought that the future of France and all Europe hung on the visions and irresponsible utterances of one man was enough to make anyone tremble. On another level, Napoleon's remark to Fouché, which Talleyrand heard about, was no less alarming: "Europe is no more than a rotten old whore whom I shall use as I please with 800,000 men." [2]

That is why Talleyrand and Napoleon were divorced. Napoleon looked upon France as a conquered nation, an ideal springboard to further conquests. Hers was the language of European culture, hers the prestige of philosophic exploration. She was but a stage in the glorious epic which Napoleon had ordained for himself. To Talleyrand, France was flesh and blood, the roots of his being, a familiar, cherished face. In his mind, her physical image occupied fixed geographical and historical boundaries. Her prosperity was as significant to him as the well-being of his own kin. All this was totally alien to lawless ambition, to violence, to imperialist predatoriness. Talleyrand's weapons were tradition, knowledge, law, and time. He alone dared to challenge Europe's invincible ruler. He went about it fearlessly, confident that it was his duty to intervene in defense of his country. A cripple commanding a squadron of elegant ladies in the faubourg Saint-Germain calmly began to rock the colossus off its pedestal. This is what has come to be known as "treason."

The Prince of Benevento Changes Residence and Marries Off His Nephew: Two Lucrative Affairs

On his return to Paris on about October 15, 1808, Talleyrand admittedly reverted to "the petty habits of a great dignitary." To occupy himself more seriously, he sat for a portrait by Gérard. It is one of the best portraits of him; less sinister and formal than Prud'hon's, it conveys the spirit of Monsieur d'Autun. Abbé Sieyès, who never forgave him for leaping straight out of the Directory into the Empire with the agility and courage of a trapezist, mocked this portrait, saying: "He resembles an old woman who has just removed her rouge and beauty marks." [1] The remark itself suggests an old woman. Goethe's reaction is of greater interest:

> We see the foremost statesman of his age perfectly at ease, seated, calmly awaiting whatever fortune is about to dispense, wearing ordinary court dress, sword at his side, his plumed hat out of reach on the couch; in this tastefully elegant room [Talleyrand's natural habitat], he seems to be waiting for word that his coach is ready to take him to a conference. We could not help thinking of the gods of Epicurus, who "live where there is no rain or snow, where never tempest blows." Our seated figure seems to emanate that perfect tranquility; the storms raging around him never touch him. One can conceive of him possessing such an expression and not conceive how he retains it. His gaze is utterly impenetrable; he looks straight ahead, but the spectator cannot tell whether he is looking at him. . . . Our penetration is too shallow, our experience too spare, our imagination too narrow to comprehend this human

being. This is the effect he will have one day on the historian turning to this portrait for instruction.[2]

Goethe's comments are indeed instructive, reflecting the lofty vision and the humility of one category of genius in the presence of another. Such a thoughtful, incisive tribute cannot be compared to the flippant gibes of abbé Sieyès.

Talleyrand liked painting and painters. He often visited Gérard's studio. One day that winter, Gérard sent round to him as a gift his own portrait of Canova which Talleyrand had seen and admired there. The artist received this note, dated February 21, 1809, by return: "Your kindness, my dear Gérard, in giving me the portrait of Canova forces me to renounce my own principles and adds to my gratitude. You make it very difficult to visit your studio, as there one cannot say, without risk, what one likes and admires." [3]

Why do some biographers imply that he liked paintings only as investments? Was it because he sold his pictures as well as his books? Surely that is no evidence of lacking appreciation of either art or literature. He was so fond of pictures that when visiting Madame de Souza (whom we knew as Madame de Flahaut when our hero was still bishop of Autun), he spent all his time admiring his favorite works of art in her husband's collection. Talleyrand's son, Eugène Delacroix, also liked paintings.

In 1809, at the age of fifty-five, he sold his house on the rue d'Anjou and bought the hôtel de Monaco on the rue de Varenne, which, of course, he remodeled and refurnished. He added a wing to the mansion, better known today as the hôtel Matignon. It became one of the great centers of Parisian social life. Later, the Austrian embassy was located there, until 1914. It became government property in 1918. Now it is the premier's residence and one of the handsomest buildings in the faubourg Saint-Germain. Talleyrand had a chef named Boucher, the finest chef in Paris, perhaps the finest ever. History records that some of his dinners included forty-eight different dishes. Boucher's salary was no less than that of an ambassador, and indeed, he carried the glory of French *haute cuisine* to every embassy and capital in Europe.

Flattered by the stunning effects obtained whenever the grand chamberlain and vice-grand elector exercised his court functions, Napoleon ordered Talleyrand to give four dinners weekly, each for thirty-six guests. The emperor personally drew up the guest list: members of the legislature, state councilors, government officials who were refusing to tow the line. Napoleon thought that his grand chamberlain's sumptuous table could serve the imperial cause. He wrote to him that these dinners had no other purpose than "to bring them all together [councilors and ministers] so that you may get to know the principal ones and mold their frame of mind." He was instructing Talleyrand to bring them gently to heel. If Napoleon had been able to read the prince of Benevento's mind, he would have guessed that those dinners might become a school for insubordination. However, Talleyrand was too cautious to try such tactics. So the emperor was satisfied and the guests he sent to the hôtel Matignon well indoctrinated and well fed. Still, Talleyrand took the opportunity to point out certain governmental shortcomings to Napoleon, saying that the ideas had come to him from listening to legislative deputies. He told the emperor that this body's lack of deliberative powers conflicted with the nation's character: "Frenchmen of any class whatever cannot remain assembled in silence. . . ." Well, Napoleon preferred a silent Assembly, deprived of lawmaking powers despite its legislative function. Another suggestion from Talleyrand generated equal enthusiasm: "We must have representation in France in order to levy taxes. . . ." That grievance had appeared long before in the revolutionary *Cahiers*. The sound advice was of course drowned in a flood of flattery; Napoleon made no effort to salvage it.

For the moment, Napoleon had worse problems than the mutterings of presumptuous, would-be lawmakers. He was in Spain, where the situation was rapidly deteriorating. He had gone there fully expecting his august presence to paralyze the Spanish nation with fear and admiration. Instead, he won the Battle of Somosierra by a hair. Talleyrand responded with ardent flattery, as if Erfurt had changed nothing. He hoped the emperor would "rally everyone to the welcome prospect of a noble and blissful reign [with Joseph on the Spanish throne]. Weary and routed, alienated by discord, appalled by the spectacle of anarchy, Spaniards in all walks of life must seek a rallying point. And who is better equipped than Your Majesty to shape budding national inclinations to conform to the realization of his aims?" (December 8, 1808)

He was lying deliberately, knowing that the "budding inclinations" of the Spanish people were fiercely hostile to Napoleon's aims. The flattery cost him nothing and did not interfere with his current talks in Paris with Metternich, who relayed them faithfully to Vienna. Their subject was simply Napoleon's downfall and various ways to maintain his dynasty. They also discussed how much of an "offering" the Austrian government was prepared to pay him. For does anyone imagine that his superb services to Vienna and to the czar were free? The prince of Benevento's household swallowed up money. The purchase and remodeling of the hôtel Matignon plus the cost of entertaining Spain's princes at Valençay were ruining Talleyrand. He deserved some thanks. From the Austrian end, things took their normal course: Dalberg and bankers in Bremen and Hamburg managed the affair so neatly that not a trace of those payments exists. Barras's Memoirs assert that Austria paid him 17 million, a sum so gigantic as to appear incredible. One-quarter of that figure, 3 billion old francs, is more plausible.

Dealing with Russia was harder. Moscow never paid—or paid next to nothing. As Czar Alexander could not seem to master the crystalline language of arithmetic, Talleyrand adopted another tongue.

He resorted to the language of the heart; more precisely, he discussed engagement and marriage. Since the death of his nephew Louis, Talleyrand had been worrying about the future of Louis's younger brother, Edmond de Périgord, that is to say, about the prospects of his own family, to whom Talleyrand remained devoted. Over the years, this attachment, once merely conventional, deepened and became meaningful; his grief over the loss of Louis showed this. His brother Archambaud grew increasingly withdrawn, leaving Talleyrand the burdens as well as the prestige of family leadership. For this reason, the prince of Benevento was resolved to open up a brilliant career for his nephew and heir, Edmond. Even in the midst of Europe's crisis, the problem haunted him. At Erfurt, while negotiating with the czar for Napoleon's marriage to one of the grand duchesses, he submitted a second matrimonial request in behalf of his nephew. He asked Alexander for the hand of Dorothée of Courland, whose mother, the duchess of Courland, was a Russian subject.

"Sire," he addressed Alexander, "as Your Majesty is so felicitously disposed to speak of marriage, I should like to ask a favor. I have had the misfortune to lose my elder nephew, a young man of promise. I have another for whom I would like to arrange a suitable match; but in France, I cannot hope for this. The emperor bespeaks the wealthy heiresses for his generals. Among Your Majesty's subjects is a family to which I earnestly desire to be linked through marriage. In behalf of my nephew, I seek the hand of Princess Dorothée of Courland." His request fared better than Napoleon's; the czar promptly granted it as it cost him nothing.

Talleyrand was telling the truth. There was little hope of Edmond making a brilliant match. As he was not one of Napoleon's officers, how could he marry a woman of noble birth even half as rich as his uncle planned?

Talleyrand combed the continent for a rich heiress. In the process, he discovered Dorothée. Judging from his *Memoirs,* one would think that this match was a pleasant idyll, a series of happy coincidences. Actually, he had made an exhaustive study of Europe's available heiresses, while Dalberg, aided by a Pole named Batowski, investigated their prospects. Batowski, whom he first met in Warsaw, narrowed the choice to Dorothée. He alone, as we shall see, was in a unique position to provide full details on the mother and daughter, not to mention their fortune.

Talleyrand put it this way:

> In Germany and in Poland, I had often heard of the duchess of Courland. I knew of her singularly lofty sentiments, her elegance, her sterling and gracious character. [Not a word about the duchess's unusual living arrangements, her ailments, or her colossal wealth.] Her youngest daughter was marriageable. The choice could only have pleased Napoleon. It did not rob him of a match for one of his generals, who would have been rejected; in fact, it must have flattered his vain hopes of attracting foreign aristocrats to France. I resolved then to solicit Princess Dorothée's hand for my nephew; and in order to prevent Emperor Napoleon from changing his mind or mood and withdrawing his consent, I asked Emperor Alexander, a close friend of the duchess of Courland's, to solicit her daughter's hand personally for my nephew.[4]

He implies that he first approached Napoleon about his plans, whereas in fact he waited to do so until the whole question was settled with the czar.

Who was Dorothée of Courland?[5] Her future role is vital, for Talleyrand's later years are permeated with the presence of this strange niece. By getting acquainted with her before marriage, we can best understand the years that followed. She was a daughter of Pierre, duke of Courland; her mother, countess of Medem, was the duke's third wife. Named Biren after his father (whose own father had served the old dukes of Courland as a groom), Pierre became the favorite of Czarina Anna Ivanovna.[6] He was extremely handsome and the czarina made him duke of Courland. Upon the death of his protectress, he was exiled to Siberia, later to be reprieved by Catherine II, who restored his duchy to him. There he retired, holding court like a sovereign at Mittau, his capital. He died in 1800.

These Birens were known for their good looks, their irascible tempers, their idiosyncrasies, and their cruelty. Lust and ribaldry attracted them far more than pleasure. Dorothée's mother, however, came of noble stock and was highly educated. Though not ideally pretty (her nose, they said, was a little too long), she was charming and spirited. Because of her fondness for art and artists, she turned Mittau into a haven of refined elegance in remote eastern Europe. What really singled her out as an eccentric in East Prussia was her admiration for Napoleon and everything French. It ruined her reputation, but people overlooked this owing to the immense fortune she possessed. She was mistress of the duchy of Courland, the princedom of Sagan, Prince Piccolomini's vast Bohemian holdings, and the palace of Unter den Linden in Berlin. She hated Sagan, a gloomy barracks furnished in the taste of Wallenstein, its former owner. The estate of Löbikau was to her liking, more intimate and cheerful. There she lived with her lover Batowski, who spoke of her to Talleyrand in Warsaw, after Iena. Batowski had had his heyday, but age, the political misfortunes of his country, and his position of kept lover combined to sour his innately trying temperament. Romanticism claimed him. He took a fancy to forests and prevailed on the duchess to build him, at considerable expense, a fantastic, lavish woodland abode. He worshipped the night, the moon, the mist, nightmares, and graveyards. He became Shakespearean, that is, impossible to live with. But before reaching that extremity, he fathered one of the duchess's daughters, our Dorothée. Apparently no one cared to have her bear her father's name.

The duchess paid little attention to her daughters, least of all her youngest one. Dorothée was a melancholy child, strong-willed, and secretive. She was not close to her mother, whose frivolity she found unbearable. (The duchess's frivolity was real enough, but whatever the child thought, it was quite bearable.) Dorothée was taught by an intelligent, cultivated tutor, who instilled in her a love of literature. He was an Italian, a former abbé named Piattoli, veteran intriguer and companion of Prince Adam Czartoryski, with whom he was forever concocting new schemes to further complicate the already hopeless imbroglio of Polish politics. By extolling Czartoryski's merits to his pupil, Piattoli succeeded in making her fall in love, at fourteen, with a forty-year-old prince whom she had never seen but whose gray temples and melancholy eyes had won her heart from the tales told by her tutor. Dorothée had sworn to marry no one but Czartoryski—and she was stubborn.

Her three older sisters were married, one to a prince of the Rohan family, one to a Hohenzollern, and the third to a Neapolitan nobleman, the duke of Acerenza. All three were beautiful, rich, loose-living, and hostile to Napoleon and to France.

Dorothée shared this hatred, if only to antagonize her mother. She has left a wholly credible portrait of herself during this period; her tongue was sharp but honest. Moreover, her contemporaries bear out the description. "Small, olive-skinned, painfully thin, perpetually sick as a child, I had deep, dark eyes so large that they set my other features in disproportion. I would have been plainly ugly but for the apparent strength of character in my face."

Where did she get the jet-black hair, the gypsy complexion, the skeletal figure? People wondered. The one thing she did not claim—out of pride, not modesty—was to have possessed the world's most captivating eyes. Rather than black, they were deep violet, intensely mobile and expressive, reflecting the smoldering life within that fragile, disease-wasted body. But try to gaze at those eyes! She rarely allowed it, quickly assuming an icy stare of contempt. No, Mademoiselle Batowski was not what you might call a dependable investment.

Mother and daughter had separate households. Dorothée possessed her own fortune and string of private residences. She lived at Tannenfeld, the wilderness abode built for Batowski. It conformed to her natural reserve. A train of suitors for her hand and fortune, princes of Hohenlohe, Solms, Reuss, and Mecklenburg, beat a path to her mother's door at Löbikau. Dorothée received their proposals coldly, but discouraged no one from hoping that he might prove a serious rival to the indifferent Czartoryski. The flurry of activity around her mother did not alter her somber hopes.

Hearing of the siege in progress, Talleyrand resolved to beat all the suitors at their own game. Less than a month after Erfurt, the duchess of Courland received a message from the czar summoning her to dine on October 16, 1808. About five o'clock that same evening, four persons appeared at the gates of Löbikau: Alexander I, Prince Troubetskoy, Caulaincourt, and Edmond. The duchess had her two eldest daughters with her, Princess Hohenlohe and the duchess of Acerenza, and having managed to entice Dorothée out of her forest, she too was present. The other unsuspecting wooers paid court to the czar. It became evident that Alexander, who normally displayed his famous Slavic charm quite readily, reserved it now exclusively for Dorothée. He teased her about her train of suitors. Then, suddenly, he asked her if she had not noticed the striking resemblance between Prince Czartoryski and Lieutenant de Périgord at the far end of the table.

"To whom does Your Majesty refer?" she asked.

"Why, the young man sitting over there, the prince of Benevento's nephew who is accompanying the duke of Vicenza [Caulaincourt] to St. Petersburg."

"Forgive me, Sire, I had not noticed the duke of Vicenza's aide; I am so near-sighted that I cannot see his features from here."

She was indeed near-sighted, and also clever enough to convey her lack of interest in the lieutenant whose features she was not eager to examine at close or long range.

Caulaincourt spoke highly of the lieutenant. Dorothée paid no attention. The dinner was not very cheerful. As they rose from the table, the czar asked to speak privately with the duchess. She was upset, though she had warned Dorothée to be nice, or at least polite, to the duke of Vicenza. "You know the czar treats him as a friend. I have not asked your sisters to speak to him. I wish you to pay attention to M. de Caulaincourt as I would not have him go away offended." Dorothée did just as she pleased, however. It was Caulaincourt who paid considerable attention to her, a great deal more than she desired, to the extent of arranging her future life. He noted in his Memoirs: "Emperor Alexander and I set out for Weimar and Löbikau to see the duchess of Courland. During that visit I arranged a match between her daughter and M. Edmond de Périgord, thanks to the eminent intervention of that prince."

The next step was to advise the mother of the decision taken at Erfurt and to obtain her consent. The czar was engaged in doing just that in the adjoining room.

He had no difficulty, as the duchess did not care for Czartoryski, whereas the Périgord match would fulfill her ambition to live in Paris. Of course, she also approved of an alliance with the prestigious Périgords, especially a nephew of the prince of Benevento, the Empire's third ranking dignitary.

Now only Dorothée's consent was needed. The duchess made it plain to Alexander that this was more than she could manage: her daughter was anti-French, in love with Czartoryski, deaf to her mother's wishes, and stubborn as a goat. The czar interrupted, saying that Czartoryski had no desire to marry Dorothée, and that the girl's feelings about France did not matter a bit. The political leanings of any fifteen-year-old could be ignored. The duchess must bring her daughter around to accept the lieutenant, for he, Alexander, had so promised the prince of Benevento, who would not take No for an answer. It was a command. The duchess, a subject of the czar, to whom she was beholden for most of her estates, needed no further explanation. She curtseyed very low.

They returned to the drawing room. After a brief display of his legendary charm, the czar left with his escorts.

Dorothée now had to be informed. The next day, when her mother asked her what she thought of the lieutenant, the girl said that she had not even glanced at him. Whereupon she left for Berlin and stayed there three months, until January, 1809, still dreaming of Czartoryski.

Caulaincourt made notes of the Löbikau episode which Edmond took to his uncle in Paris. Talleyrand was satisfied. The young lady's frame of mind did not worry him. "Edmond has arrived, my dear Caulaincourt. I shall ask the emperor to send him to you. You have looked after uncle and nephew very well; he has told me all you did in his behalf" (October 26, 1808).

Talleyrand helped matters along in silence; also in haste. Three days later he obtained imperial consent to the union, just before Napoleon left to settle (so he thought) the Spanish situation. Edmond was in less of a hurry than anyone, having no desire to return to St. Petersburg or to visit his "fiancée" on the way. Talleyrand prodded him gently, arranging a three-month leave from Edmond's commander, General Berthier, so that he could visit Löbikau. That, as Talleyrand explained to Caulaincourt, was "more than enough time to begin and end a very interesting affair for himself which I undertook with your help." Having no confidence in his nephew's brains or resourcefulness, he sent Batowski along with him, saying: "He knows how to do business, and knows all there is to know about the duchess of Courland"—blunt and to the point. He added: "After spending a week with her, he will write me exactly what we should and can do. At the end of that week, Edmond will place himself at your command in St. Petersburg and remain there until we have a definite answer."

If everything went smoothly, Talleyrand would then press Archambaud into service. "Archambaud will leave for Löbikau to draw up the contracts with the advice of his business agent. Then Edmond can arrive at the same time as his father and everything will proceed rapidly. . . ."

Edmond left with Batowski on November 15, 1808. On arrival at the duchess of Courland's, he delivered a thoughtful letter from his uncle. She was touched. Edmond did not see Dorothée, who was still in Berlin. He went on to St. Petersburg. Batowski remained behind; as a favor to Talleyrand, he managed to regain the duchess's good will and spent the winter with her. In replying to Talleyrand, the duchess acknowledged her daughter's obdurate character. She did not like to press her, she said. It was clear to Talleyrand that she would not object to having pressure applied from on high. So he called on Caulaincourt to ask the czar to intervene again in such a manner that neither mother nor daughter could refuse. He wrote thus on December 26:

> I am writing the emperor today to thank him for the letter with which he honored me. I wish Edmond to leave for Löbikau so as to arrive there on February 3. That will suit the duchess, who is expecting a houseful of company that day [Talleyrand did not overlook social obligations as a means of furthering his own affairs]. They will stay as long as Batowski and he think desirable, after which he will come to Paris. . . . If he happened to bear a letter from Emperor Alexander for the duchess and if that letter were to express the czar's interest in him, I think this would be very useful. The duchess seems much inclined to cooperate with us. I am sending Edmond a letter for the duchess in reply to the one I have received from her.

He arranged thus to have the czar intervene anew. Dorothée returned from Berlin for her mother's birthday, stopping on the way to visit Piattoli, whom she found at death's door. She looked to him for solace and some cheerful news of her aging Prince Charming. But the ailing man, well rehearsed by now, told her that he had nothing further to say about Czartoryski and that she must forget him. Dorothée was uncertain what to do. Her mother welcomed her with unwonted tenderness: "My mother greeted me with more joy and warmth than I had ever seen her display before." It made her anxious, and Batowski's return to the fold seemed to augur ill. She was allowed to relax for four days. On the evening of the fourth, the hunting horn wailed, announcing visitors. In walked Edmond de Périgord, just as his uncle had ordered. Dorothée instantly grasped the whole scenario and fled to her room, weeping in the arms of her governess Mademoiselle Hoffmann. She knew that her mother's motive for wanting her to marry the lieutenant was that she found Frenchmen the most amusing people on earth. Drying her tears, Dorothée made her way into the drawing room where jubilation reigned. Even the morose Batowski was beaming. Her mother had never looked more radiant; tension obviously enhanced her natural charms. In her hands were letters which she carried around all evening. She introduced Edmond to Dorothée. Knowing what was in the wind, this time the young girl took a close look at the privileged suitor. Edmond, like his father Archambaud and his brother Louis, was handsome. Rather tall, robust, and well built, he carried himself proudly. His somewhat elongated face with its symmetrical features, thin, straight nose, dark eyes which were tepid rather than warm, glassy rather than lively, and pleasant, boyish smile all combined to give him the appearance of an attractive young man not overly endowed with either brains or character. He neither impressed nor depressed Dorothée.

The next morning, Dorothée called on her mother while she was still in bed. Scattered over the covers were the letters she had carried about all evening. The duchess told her daughter to read them. One, dated January 10, 1809, had come from the czar at Talleyrand's request and made plain just what His Imperial Highness expected of both mother and daughter: "M. de Périgord . . . is a charming young man of excellent character, who could make any woman happy. I strongly hope that Your Highness and the young princess share my views and that this highly desirable union will take place."

Though only fifteen, Dorothée knew the meaning of an imperial "I strongly hope." To make sure she did, her mother told her: "You know that in Russia a sovereign's bounty is not to be relied on; that everything depends on his mood, and that my greatest interest lies in cultivating his good will. I have promised to prevail on you to make the marriage he desires, so I beg you not to reject it before considering the advantages to our family which can result from this union."

Having digested the czar's fiat, Dorothée went on to read Talleyrand's madrigals, which had nothing more comforting to offer her. Surprisingly, the ex-bishop of Autun sought to promote his design by citing his own mother's earnest desire for this union. How curious for him to conjure up the venerable comtesse de Périgord in connection with this marriage, only a few weeks before her death. Having pronounced her dead on the occasion of his own wedding, he was now reviving her for his nephew's. The reason was that Dorothée of Courland was not Madame Grand, nor was Edmond de Périgord a bishop. In fact, Talleyrand had visited his aging mother to consult her about the projected marriage.[7] Her approval delighted him. At least one trace exists of the respectful relations between son and mother, his letter of November 14, 1808, to the duchess of Courland informing her that he had approached his mother. "He asked her consent [to this project] the moment he devised it."

Talleyrand proceeded to use his mother's blessing to melt Dorothée's unrelenting heart. Having defied the czar's edict, she was now swayed by the imprecations of a dying woman. Not all at once, however. Deploring the young girl's pigheadedness, her mother gave her three more days to think it over, entreating her to behave civilly to the lieutenant; also to Batowski, who was then lecturing her on the illustrious Périgords and the prince of Benevento's sterling virtues.

Dorothée looked in vain to her governess for help; Mademoiselle Hoffmann plainly stood for surrender. Batowski lavished such praise on the prince of Benevento, the flower of French nobility, that one would have taken him for the aspiring bridegroom. Which reminds us of the rather delicate matter Batowski had to deal with: the former bishop's marriage to the Grand woman, whose existence could not be denied. Batowski skirted the issue by describing the princess of Benevento as a person "so undistinguished and insignificant as to amount to no hindrance," thus blunting the only aspersion anyone might cast on this brilliant match.

Dorothée still would not yield. Her mother became frantic. Batowski had an idea: if Dorothée's sole defense was her absurd love for Czartoryski, then they must prove to her that she loved in vain. He rushed to Piattoli's bedside and cajoled the dying man into writing his pupil a fanciful letter announcing that Prince Czartoryski had just taken Miss Matuschewitz for his bride in Warsaw, with the blessing of his mother and the whole city. Speechless, Dorothée in turn rushed to her tutor's bedside only to hear him confirm, ever so faintly, Batowski's advice to give up her fancies and obey her mother.

Back at Löbikau, as chance would have it, the miserable girl encountered Countess Oguinska fresh from Warsaw and bubbling with news of Prince Czartoryski's wedding. Dorothée fled. Bursting into tears of anger and humiliation, she announced to her mother that she was ready to marry Edmond de Périgord. Overjoyed, her mother joined her in abusing the Polish prince, praised her choice of husbands, and rushed off to tell the aspirant. "I had an impulse to stop her . . ." Dorothée confessed in her Memoirs.

Throughout this turbulent episode, Edmond sat idly by, a model of placidity. His fiancée, despite her own acute distress, assessed him quite accurately: "It was impossible to predict his temperament or his thoughts, for no one has ever relied so heavily . . . on silence."

How could she tell what he was like? His sole assets were immediately visible: a handsome face and elegant figure. Plus, of course, his uncle, whose presence no one forgot.

The duchess left the young couple alone. The affair was settled as far as she was concerned. They stood there in silence, ill at ease, strangers to the adventure foisted upon them. Taking the initiative, Dorothée gravely uttered this little speech: "I hope, sir, that you will find happiness in the marriage arranged for us. But I must confess something which you undoubtedly know already, that I am yielding to my mother's wishes, without dislike for you, truly, and with only indifference. Perhaps I shall be happy; I like to think so, but surely you can understand my reluctance to abandon my homeland and my friends, and will not be offended, at least in the beginning, to find me sad." If the words were not Dorothée's own, one might question whether a confused and rebellious girl of fifteen could produce such a perceptive analysis.

Edmond agreed with her. He deserves credit for his candor and spontaneity: "Heavens, I understand you perfectly. As a matter of fact, I am only marrying at my uncle's insistence, for at my age a bachelor's life is far more agreeable. . . ."

In short, they concurred on the central issue that neither one wanted to marry the other. After the wedding, they would simply spend a minimum of time together.

Edmond returned to Paris the next day, February 24, 1809.

The reader who imagines that we have neglected Talleyrand during this German episode is ignoring his omnipresence. In reality, all the persons we have seen rushing to and from the neighborhood of Löbikau, including the czar and Batowski, were pieces in a chess game masterminded by the prince of Benevento. Neither castle, king, knight, nor bishop, Edmond was a mere pawn, the lowliest of pieces. Birth was his only asset, and obedience the only virtue demanded of him. The brains, the will, and the power were Talleyrand's.

On hearing the news, our hero wrote to the duchess: "I trust that Princess Dorothée will welcome the marks of affection I wish to show her, the unfailing solicitude with which I and my entire family would surround her" (March 7, 1809).

He informed the czar in court idiom far more elusive than its florid simplicity suggests: "All has succeeded, Sire, as one might expect after two such mighty powers as yours and Love have deigned to intercede."

Success indeed, for Alexander had siphoned a colossal fortune into the Périgord family, a fact that went unmentioned. Talleyrand preferred to speak only of a gracious sovereign allied to the power of Love. He made a practice of cajoling and flattering the czar, anticipating the time when His Majesty would be needed to perform a service quite different from that of marriage broker. "Each day I have ever-increasing gratitude to lay at Your Majesty's feet. I would be his devoted servant if he had done nothing for me; I shall be because he is the symbol of perfect goodness and the qualities that continue to ennoble the world's greatest throne. It is comforting to think that upon you, Sire, now rests the fate of the world and the progress of civilization."

The reference to Erfurt combined with the avalanche of flattery called for certain precautions lest the letter be intercepted, copied, and shown to the "other" emperor, whose subject, until the next change of régime, Talleyrand continued to be. So he smoothed over the situation by declaring: "My unfailing attachment to Emperor Napoleon, whose boundless genius I admire, whose trust has often been placed in me, whose generous benefactions have won my heart forever . . ." So saying, he wished for peace between "the two colossi" but avoided mentioning an alliance.[8]

Politics had produced this union, which in turn fostered more politics. Had not Talleyrand promised Alexander that if Dorothée married his nephew, the duchess of Courland would serve as an excellent liaison between the daughter's uncle and her "Little Father the Czar"? Spies at no charge! The czar saw endless possibilities in the marriage. A regular correspondence thus opened between Talleyrand and the duchess, friendly at first, then very friendly, until, when they came to know each other well, it became infinitely tender.

Edmond and Dorothée were married in Frankfurt on April 22, 1809. By coincidence, no doubt, the ceremony was performed by Prince-Primate Theodor de Dalberg. The Dalbergs never missed out on a lucrative affair.

The young comtesse Edmond de Périgord and her husband came to live with the prince of Benevento in Paris. The duchess of Courland joined the household. She was the happiest by far. Rather than to look after the newlyweds, she came there to make a pleasant life for herself —and succeeded better than they. When we return to them later on, they will still be under the benign tutelage of Talleyrand, master of their destinies.

The Prince of Benevento's Shady Associates

How can we imagine the activities of a man like Talleyrand, even when out of power, as being "insignificant"? During the London interval in 1792, when he took up fishing, Pitt became suspicious enough of those piscatory expeditions to deport our angler hero. And what of his tea-drinking in the princess of Thurn-Taxis's salon at Erfurt? During the winter of 1809, his dinner parties, his social engagements, his whist-playing, the very expression in his eyes boded ill for his rejected master, now absent. In one breath he promised Napoleon fame and glory in Spain; in the next, he was sowing venomous anti-war sentiments in the salons of Paris. "Crowns are being crudely seized, not slyly filched." Sometimes he expressed himself so bluntly that friends trembled for his safety. In Madame de Rémusat's salon he calmly predicted the fall of the Empire. He was exploiting the unpopularity of the Spanish adventure: ". . . to declare oneself an enemy of the people is an irreparable error."

It took courage to defy the ubiquitous imperial police. How did Talleyrand's verbal sallies escape them? Who censored or watered down his flippant remarks for presentation to the emperor? And if the emperor knew about them, why didn't he retaliate? We simply do not know.

The witty comments were mere artifices, bait to attract fellow dissenters. The régime had to be undermined and replaced, a task beyond the powers of any one man, especially a man of ideas, not action, like Talleyrand, who organized others to act for him. The situation called for a conspiracy, but with whom? Allies are permanent risks, each a potential traitor awaiting his hour. Who should know this better than our hero?

Whichever guardian spirit presides over conspiracy and intrigue chose to send him a man, defiled from head to toe, wholly committed to the Revolution's worst savagery, a master of deceit, treachery, "spontaneous" massacres, mysterious disappearances, timely suicides, deadly explosions claiming the lives of innocent bystanders, a man who knew everything about everyone in France, not to mention the rest of Europe, and whose name was Fouché, minister of police. Fouché happened to be available just when Talleyrand needed someone.

Up to that moment they were worlds apart. They detested each other. Their hostility amused the public. Talleyrand would jibe: "A minister of police is a man who starts out minding his own business and gradually minds everyone's business."

When someone claimed that the minister of police held all humanity in utter contempt, the prince of Benevento remarked that it was "because he has examined himself very thoroughly." But contempt was not what set them at odds; it was their education, their tastes and background, their epidermis, if you will. Talleyrand, the wealthy, affable, dissolute, utterly detached aristocrat who went about calmly advertising his vices and his debts, was an anathema to this ill-favored, struggling, dour, ugly ex-priest with his freckles, his unruly mop of red hair, and his bloodshot eyes at once repulsive and terrifying. Like an indigent shopkeeper, Fouché lived on a shoestring with his wretched wife and a sickly daughter whom he pampered and shrouded like a vice. This man, steeped in the blood of thousands of innocent victims massacred by his order in Lyons and elsewhere, was a model husband and father. As he never spent what he stole, people took him for an honest man. He simply put it away in the cellar. Apart from his crimes, his hands were immaculate. He made Talleyrand ill.

This repulsion remained impregnable until the day ambition seemed to overcome it, the day calling for a "bold stroke." That is just what happened.

They would never have bridged the gap if Blanc d'Hauterive had not brought them face to face and produced a reconciliation. Hauterive, we may recall, was Talleyrand's right-hand man in the Foreign Ministry. A former Oratorian like Fouché, he had remained on good terms with the minister of police and could see no reason why the two men persisted in their hostility. Knowing Talleyrand's opinion of Napoleonic policies, and finding Fouché's was the same, he set about persuading them that they were natural allies.

Their first meeting occurred (of all places) at the princesse de Vaudémont's, born a Montmorency. She had a reputation for insurgency. Hers, they said, was "the spirit of a Holy Leaguer, the temperament of a Frondist." Her salon was a gathering place for individuals of every rank and politics. No single personality dominated; her own was forceful enough. "She claimed the right for her lapdogs to nip ministers and ambassadors." Friends found a warm welcome and absolute freedom. Aimée de Coigny said of her: "One may regard her house as the gentle refuge of friendship and a risky place for tottering governments [a clear warning]. There one can conspire in perfect safety, and life is so pleasant and innocent that spies drop all caution." Talleyrand was certainly an expert at choosing ideal nests in which to hatch the Empire's doom. His meeting with the regicide went smoothly and they shook hands. Talleyrand courted his favor, and if Fouché came out with some commonplace, our bishop, looking impressed, would murmur solemnly: "Careful, Fouché, that is the province of high diplomacy." When the teasing was done, they prepared to take up a highly dangerous game: they would either overthrow Napoleon or die in the attempt.

Letizia Bonaparte, the emperor's mother, came to one of those gatherings and was surprised to see Fouché there. She was even more surprised to find him talking to Talleyrand. Edging up to listen, she caught enough of the conversation to understand what they thought of her "Nabulio." Too bad she didn't hear more, for on that day and others, they were likely to have been saying:

> FOUCHÉ (*sinister and intense*): I am always amazed that some Jacques Clément has not cropped up to rid us of the Corsican just as that monk rid France of Henri III.

TALLEYRAND

TALLEYRAND (*unctuous, sighing*): What can we expect? Religion is
dying.

Madame Letizia was so intrigued that she wrote to the emperor in Spain.

Nor was she the first to have uncovered the plot. Metternich knew
far more about it and informed his government: "At present two men
lead opinion and influence in France, Messieurs de Talleyrand and
Fouché; formerly opposed as to views and interests, they have been
united by circumstances independent of themselves." He knew perfectly
well (because Talleyrand kept no secrets from him) that the purpose of
their alliance was to overthrow Napoleon. His description of the mood of
France is particularly arresting: ". . . a nation exhausted by a long
series of efforts, dismayed by the endless journey its present master
would still have it undertake. . . ." A nation no longer disposed "to
support, at the price of its own blood and fortune, schemes which are
the private concern of this master."

Echoes of Talleyrand himself. The conflict of emperor *versus* nation
is clearly exposed in these two lines of Metternich's: "France has not
waged war since the Peace of Lunéville. Napoleon is the one who wages
war using the French as resources." That was why Talleyrand sided with
France.

Metternich also described the two conspirators as "firmly resolved
to seize the opportunity if the opportunity arises, lacking courage to
provoke it." [1] We have to read between the lines: "occasion" means an
eventual assassination, already implied by Fouché's reference to Jacques
Clément. Metternich adds that the two conspirators are prepared to take
the rudder of a ship whose captain has lost touch with reality. Translate
this as Talleyrand and Fouché planning ahead for a provisional government. Whom would it include? Themselves to begin with, naturally.
Who else? They would need a man who was also a symbol. A Bourbon?
Out of the question. Our two friends would have gone straight to the
gallows. Napoleon's brothers? Pygmies. The choice narrowed to Murat.
Being Napoleon's brother-in-law, he would rally the Bonapartists. He
was a big, brave, dashing fellow, not too shrewd at that—the perfect
choice. They wrote to him in Naples where he ruled (if you can call it
that) over a kingdom comprising just as many soldiers bent on maintaining order as subjects bent on overthrowing him. With astonishing boldness, they asked him to be ready at a moment's notice to return to Paris
if Napoleon should die. They were counting on the daggers of Spanish
patriots.

On December 20, 1808, Talleyrand and his friend gave an unforgettable demonstration of political propaganda for the edification of prominent public figures. That evening the prince of Benevento hosted one of his magnificent receptions for the cream of French society, the entire diplomatic corps, dignitaries, government officials, the banking world, and a scattering of internationally known adventurers. He alone could have drawn such an attendance. On this public stage the two confederates gave a silent performance the echoes of which resounded from St. Petersburg to Valladolid and threw Napoleon into a rage. Talleyrand's salons were swarming with guests when, suddenly, with proper pause for effect, a man was announced whose name rang out like a danger signal in those marble halls. Fouché was seen crossing a threshold which destiny had enjoined him from crossing. He stepped forward, wearing the first smile ever seen on his face, and entered the house of his arch enemy as if it were his own, stopping for a moment as if to announce to the astonished guests: "Yes, indeed, it is I; you are not dreaming," and waiting for his limping host to approach, take his arm, and lean upon it confidently. Without a word, the pair made the rounds of all the rooms at a hobble, the picture of cordiality.

The promenade served as a proclamation. No one could fail to grasp their collusion and its purpose. For just an instant Napoleon's throne tottered. Then, having produced the desired reaction, the two went off in a corner and plotted in earnest, surrounded by three hundred persons, most of whom were now mentally wording the dispatches they would send off at dawn to announce this revelation to every nook and cranny of the continent.

Europe thus learned that Napoleon was in trouble not only in Spain but in Paris as well. The arm-in-arm cordiality of the two men was also a banner rallying other dissenters. The best part of the act was the complete silence.

At Valladolid, Napoleon received Talleyrand's letter to Murat, which had been intercepted by Eugène de Beauharnais, along with word of the Talleyrand-Fouché conspiracy. The emperor was stunned. He left Spain instantly and reached Paris in five days, a feat considering the condition of Spanish roads at that time, the general disorder, and the weather. At eight o'clock on the morning of January 23, he entered the Tuileries. The brunt of his wrath fell on Talleyrand, not Fouché. He was seething. Yet he took time to have his agents verify the reports sent to him in Spain. Meanwhile, he toured the construction site of the Louvre and received ambassadors. On January 28, he called a restricted meeting of his council. Talleyrand attended in his capacity of vice-grand elector. Cambacérès, Fouché, Lebrun, and Decrès were present also; the others were away. This was Napoleon's turn to make a "scene," but unlike the other, it was not silent.

The Scene on January 28, or the Wrath of Augustus

It was not the first time Napoleon had flared up at Talleyrand, who suffered less abuse than the other dignitaries and ministers. The emperor was forever unleashing his anger on handy objects, his hat, for instance, which he stamped on regularly. He might have heeded Talleyrand's advice: "Never rail at objects because they could not care less." In the presence of the grand chamberlain, Napoleon avoided rudeness or vulgarity; in his absence, he said what he pleased. He had warned General Clarke not to get mixed up with Talleyrand: "He is a s—t; he will befoul you." He also declared that Talleyrand "was the man who had stolen most." Beg pardon, Sire, but it was less than your brothers, your sisters, and your generals. Were you forgetting that your court existed on plunder? "What a liar!" Napoleon was known to exclaim. But, Sire, the Pope could say the same of you and not be far wrong. Did you not lie to the Spanish princes to entice them into your trap at Bayonne? We ought to bear such facts in mind as we watch the famous scene that left everyone trembling, yet did no harm except to the image of Your Imperial Majesty.

In the hands of Caesar, a thunderbolt could be lethal: the thunder rumbled, but no lightning flashed. Napoleon paced back and forth, hands clasped behind his back, engrossed in his thoughts, a perturbing figure. He warmed up to his subject by making some generalizations about what had gone on in the capital during his absence. The legislature had dared to vote down certain provisions of the new Code; speculators had brought the Stock Exchange to the brink of ruin; in short, "they" were banking on his death. "They" had doubted him, "they" had acted independently. "Those whom I have made great dignitaries or ministers cease to be free in thought or word and must remain my instruments." An excellent definition of tyranny and, by the same token, of slavery. Unable to sit in the emperor's presence, or stand because of his infirmity, Talleyrand was leaning on the mantel, facing the others, with the emperor in between. Suddenly Napoleon turned on Talleyrand, unleashing the full tide of his wrath: "For them, treason has begun when they permit themselves to doubt; it is complete if they go from doubt to dissent." [1]

At the word "treason," Talleyrand must have felt his head falling.

He was sure that he was exposed. And he was. His conduct warranted the death penalty. The others, pale as ghosts, were certain that he would get it. Talleyrand stood watching, cold and disdainful, as the little man in a snug-fitting frock coat waved and shouted. He had grown fleshy, his skin was sallow, his head balding; how different from the young god of victory. Anger stripped him of his dignity, making him appear like some ancestral avenger, perhaps merely grotesque if he had not held the power of death over all of them.

The prince of Benevento gave the impression that he was listening to something which really did not interest him in the least. Nothing could exasperate a boiling temper more than this elusive arrogance. Napoleon raged, without naming the object of his wrath. The harder he stared at the guilty party, the plainer was that disdain written all over Talleyrand's face. It was too much; the emperor lost control of himself. Rushing over to Talleyrand, as if about to start a street-corner brawl, he screamed at him:

> Thief! Thief! You are a thief! You are a coward, a man of no faith, you do not believe in God. [Let's get to the point. Is he a traitor or not?] All your life you have failed in your duties, you have deceived and betrayed everyone. Nothing is sacred to you. You would sell your father. I have showered you with riches and there is nothing you would not do to hurt me. So for ten months now, because you took it into your head [wrong; Talleyrand gambled his head and his fortune only on certainties] that my business in Spain was faring badly, you have had the effrontery to tell anyone who would listen that you always opposed my encroachment on that kingdom, whereas you were the one who first gave me the idea, who constantly pushed me into it. [Wrong, Sire, for no one was ever able to influence you. Talleyrand helped you, perfidiously in all probability, to rationalize your ambition to rule Spain. He also proposed any number of peaceful endeavors during the Directory which you would never listen to.] And that man, that wretched man, who told me where he was residing? Who urged me to strike at him?

He was speaking of the duc d'Enghien. The reproach was warranted, but if Napoleon had not wanted to kill Enghien, no amount of advice from Talleyrand could have made him do it. Talleyrand facilitated matters for him, of that we can be sure, but for an emperor to berate his closest adviser was a great mistake. Still shouting, he went on: "So what are your plans? What are you after? Come out and say it! ["It" was in the letter to Murat.] You deserve to be broken like glass." The rest of the storm faded into vain and senseless threats: "I have the power to do it, but I have too much contempt for you to bother. Why didn't I have you

hanged from the gates of the Tuileries? But there is still time for that."
Pausing long enough to catch his breath, he flung out the much-repeated
phrase: "You, by the way, are s—t in a silk stocking." The victor of
Austerlitz had just slipped on something he never should have named.[2]

"Justice" and vengeance were now out of the question. For a tyrant
to make such a slip was, in Talleyrand's words, "the beginning of the
end." Rather than clemency, it was the first sign of abdication.

Our abused prince withstood the foul blast without a murmur.
Stony-eyed, with his ghostly white, immobile face and pale, pursed lips,
he looked like a mummy. In his rage, Napoleon may have had the urge
to slap him, but was put off by the cold disdain on that face. He delivered a different kind of blow, an outrageous insult. "What about your
wife? You never told me that San Carlos was your wife's lover."

Stung to the quick, Talleyrand looked this emperor in the eye and,
always the perfect courtier, replied: "Indeed, Sire, it did not occur to me
that this information had any bearing on Your Majesty's glory or my
own."

Napoleon was outdone; he had lost face. Talleyrand had taken the
field. Now each had to make his exit as gracefully as possible. Moving
toward the door, the emperor stopped and, wheeling around, launched a
final thunderbolt at Talleyrand and Fouché: "Bear in mind that if a
revolution comes, no matter what part you have played in it, it will crush
you both." A sterile threat. The two confederates were not revolutionists;
one revolution had been enough for them.

The prince of Benevento took his time, then slowly limped across
the room in the sight of his pale and trembling colleagues, all with visions of the mummy dangling from the gates of the Tuileries. He knew
that they had missed the point; they thought that Jupiter had been there
when it was only a second-rate, ill-bred actor. About to leave the room,
he turned to them, saying: "What a pity, gentlemen, that so great a man
should be so ill-mannered."

The remark was extremely clever as it minimized the whole incident. Treason and hangings were out; rudeness was the issue. Surely he
thought of Fénelon's aphorism, which he cited on other occasions: "Insults serve as arguments for those who are in the wrong." But rather than
waste this pearl on swine, he saved it for the lovely ladies waiting for
him at the comtesse de Laval's.

He poured out the whole story to them, and to them alone. There is not
a word of it in his *Memoirs*. Outraged after hearing his cold and cynical
account of the painful scene, Madame de Laval cried: "What! He said

that to you? Right to your face?" "Yes, that and a few more insults . . ." which he calmly named.

She blazed up. "What? you listened to him? You were right next to him and didn't pick up a chair, a pair of tongs, a poker—anything! You didn't go at him?"

"Oh, I thought of it all right, but I'm too lazy." [3]

The phrase depicts him perfectly. Should he allow an upstart's abusive tongue to jeopardize his career? It would be sheer madness. Still, audacity has its limits. That night he felt ill. The next day, January 29, he stayed in bed, expecting to be arrested. Instead, he received a letter informing him that he was relieved of his post of grand chamberlain and must return the symbolic key. He much preferred rendering up the key than his soul to an execution squad at Vincennes. Now he was deprived of the right to enter the imperial apartments as well as the salary of 40,000 francs that went with it. As he was taking in 500,000 a year, the loss did not ruin him, but he wasted no time looking about for other sources of income. He returned the key to the emperor with a note in his own inimitable style: "My consolation is that I belong to Your Majesty, strengthened as I am by two feelings which no sorrow can overcome or lessen, gratitude and devotion, which shall end only with my life."

Less than twenty-four hours after enduring that abusive broadside! When will he cease to amaze us?

He felt well enough by the evening of the twenty-ninth to leave his bed and attend the court circle. Mute and impenetrable, as if carved out of stone, his sphinxlike countenance defied the darting glances. The emperor entered, walked about speaking to one person or another, took snuff; he talked to the neighbor on Talleyrand's right, walked in front of the prince without looking at him, spoke to the neighbor on his left. Talleyrand had come for no other purpose than finding that out: Napoleon had ignored him but had not barred him from the Tuileries. Success! His wife did not fare so well. She was commanded never to set foot again in the palace and to withdraw to her estate at Pont-de-Sains. As for San Carlos, whose liaison with the princess had been publicized so awkwardly the day before, he was banished to Bourg-en-Bresse. Madame Grand thus was deprived of her only consolation.

Everyone in Paris was talking about "the scene." They assumed that Talleyrand's career was finished; anyone in his frightful situation would have dug in at Valençay. Well, he was not anyone, and he made this plain two days later by advertising his presence at a palace diplomatic reception. All eyes followed him, but the emperor walked right by as if his ex-grand chamberlain were invisible. Then Talleyrand really outdid himself. When a diplomat standing next to him was asked a question by Napoleon, Talleyrand provided the answer instead. Astounded, Napoleon paused long enough for our hero to bow very low and kiss the emperor's hand. There was a stunned silence. Diplomats agreed that it was an act of genius. An Arab proverb says: "Kiss the hand that you cannot bite." Perhaps it applies here. Roumiantsof, a Russian diplomat beaten at his own game, reported having witnessed a stroke of genius.

Talleyrand hoped for even better results. To this end, he "put the ladies to work," in this case, Madame de Rémusat, whom he despatched in tears to throw herself at Queen Hortense's feet, sobbing her heart out at the incomprehensible disgrace visited upon the prince of Benevento. Was he not the emperor's most devoted servant? Hortense's chief remembrance of him was the heavy perfume he wore. She agreed to see him, hear his grievances, and plead his cause with Napoleon. With wide-open windows she received the prince of Benevento. He shed no tears and was not contrite; he was Talleyrand, a self-possessed, dignified courtier, doling out compliments and hardly mentioning his own affairs. The queen of Holland had the impression that a visiting potentate was allowing her the privilege of carrying a message to the emperor. She couldn't get over it. "Queen or not, get to work, Madam!" And indeed, Hortense did what she could to help the disgraced but unbowed prince. She recorded her visit with the emperor and her assurances to him that his grand chamberlain's despair was as bottomless as his devotion. "I lied so hard," she says, "that I could barely keep a straight face." Napoleon was the one to burst out laughing. Knowing what to expect of Talleyrand's sincerity or despair or devotion, he chided her for being hopelessly naïve. Then she tried to defend the prince by saying that he never opened his mouth in public, so how could he attack the emperor? "If he says nothing in your presence, daughter, he unburdens himself about two in the morning in the houses of lady friends like Madame de Laval. Actually, I am not harming him. I simply do not want him mixing in my affairs any longer." [4]

Napoleon was not mistaken about the gossiping that went on at two in the morning at Madame de Laval's; it made him furious. As to his attitude toward Talleyrand, it was exactly as he had expressed it. A few weeks later, on March 6, 1809, he told Roederer: "I shall do him no harm; I shall let him keep his other positions." What curious tolerance, reminiscent of the Directorate and the era of their romance. Talleyrand was never treated like other people. This very "clemency" of Napoleon's, because it is a weakness, makes him a more humane and engaging personality. He himself said: "I still have the same feeling for him that I once had; but I have deprived him of the right to enter my study at any hour. Thus he can never have a private talk with me or be able to say that he did or did not advise me to do something." [5]

He wanted to wash his hands of Talleyrand but could not get along without him. In scoffing at Hortense, he was dismissing a greater threat to his dynasty than the Bailén fiasco. "His capacity for inconsistencies is limitless," Talleyrand said of Napoleon in his last years. The situation clearly called for him either to shoot Talleyrand or bind him fast to the imperial cause. Why the empty public threats, the unatonable humiliation? Hortense put it plainly: "The emperor humiliates too much and punishes too little." Talleyrand dreaded disgrace more than the punishment that never arrived. Two days after the blowup, only Metternich, writing to Vienna, knew the true feelings of the prince of Benevento, "who had unmasked himself fully." He had told Metternich that he had made a cold-blooded decision to place himself in the service of Austria against Napoleon. "He believed that it was his duty to enter into direct relations with Austria, that in the past he had rejected offers tendered by Count Cobenzl which now he would accept." He added: "I am now free and our cause is a common one."

That was how he used the freedom Napoleon left him. He rode the inevitable tide of events. Napoleon was doomed, so why not hasten his downfall?

And because politics, even the politics of inevitability, must nourish its honorable practitioners, always from silver dishes, he did not neglect the subject of money. "He [Talleyrand] led me to anticipate that he needed several hundred thousand francs." Metternich had assured him that Austria would pay "whatever he might reasonably ask." [6] Talleyrand received 100,000 francs on the spot. In two days he more than made up for the income lost at court. The future promised to be even more lucrative.

But what a price to pay! Life on a tightrope; no ties to anything. His sense of inner freedom was extraordinary, almost abnormal. Did his master think he could buy loyalty with sinecures or a Calabrian principedom? The church could not buy him with miter, crosier, and solemn, inviolable oaths. Talleyrand served others to serve himself. When he stooped, it was to conquer money or power, crude passions but for the fact that they went hand in hand with higher aspirations: to serve civilization and its embodiment, France. The vision he pursued across the years and the régimes was to enjoy life in a country which placed the highest value on its humanity. Napoleon had betrayed that ideal. So much the worse for him. Openly or secretly, Talleyrand served France, even as he worked against her current master.

The Repudiated Prince Regains His Freedom and Nurses His Wounds

Talleyrand wasted no time adjusting to the shift in his fortunes. "I had to make my way of life appear detached and lethargic so as not to arouse Napoleon's suspicions." The police, he knew, were spying on him. Not for a moment did he curtail his contacts with Metternich, who was far more apprehensive than he. Fear was alien to Talleyrand. Shrewdness, not the cowardice some claim, prompted his extreme caution. "Fear never entered my soul," he wrote; "I can almost say that the hatred he [Napoleon] showed me did more harm to him than to me." [1]

He played his double game with utter composure, never letting up the barrage of flattery he leveled at the emperor. When hostilities broke out with Germany and Napoleon was wounded slightly, Talleyrand wrote to him: "Your glory, Sire, is our pride, but your life is our existence."

Whatever we may think of it, the spell of a veteran sorcerer still operated. Confiding his regrets to Caulaincourt four years later, Napoleon recalled what Talleyrand had had to say about the Spanish campaign. "I have no intention of criticizing him for it. He is a good judge of events, the most competent minister I ever had."

Yes, Talleyrand was a good judge of events. Speaking of Napoleon in his *Memoirs,* he said: "He attacked Spain shamelessly, without the slightest pretext; no nation can accept such dishonor." He also criticized Napoleon's tactical blunders in that disastrous war: "At that crucial period in his career, one is almost led to believe that he was swept on by some irresistible force blinding his powers of reason. His Spanish enterprise was sheer madness." Talleyrand also deplored the fact that Napoleon had been in a position to restore the balance of power and unity in Europe, but failed to do so: "A genuine balance of power could have made war impossible. Proper organization would have brought the highest degree of civilization to all nations." It was the same vision embraced by the *philosophes* of the eighteenth century. Talleyrand went on sadly: "Napoleon could have done all those things and failed to do them. . . . Instead, he laid the groundwork for what we now see [unfortunately, we see it straight through the nineteenth century, we see it in 1914, in 1940; and even today Europe is fragmented]. He is responsible for the perils threatening Europe in the East. He must and will be judged by these results."

That prophecy, unfortunately, is tainted with illusion. Talleyrand believed that history would condemn Napoleon, but Napoleon escaped into legend. Talleyrand's verdict ultimately explains both the courtship and the divorce: "Posterity will say that this man was endowed with great intellectual powers but did not understand the true nature of glory. . . ." Glory that comes from building, not invading, the security of nations.

As of 1809, everything was finished between the two men. But whereas Talleyrand, an implacable, silent foe, protested loyalty to the enemy of France and the whole continent, Napoleon, having reviled him, still felt, and always would, an attachment to this amoral aristocrat, this astute statesman who had given him a glimpse of the future, of the meaning of peace, the pleasures of life, of the paradise forbidden by inexorable destiny to this fading Caesar.

On June 24, 1809, Talleyrand's mother died. Not a word of this in his *Memoirs*. We know merely that he applied for permission to bury her in the Picpus cemetery next to Archambaud's wife, who had gone to the guillotine following the 9th Thermidor. Permission was denied on grounds that "the former nobility was seeking to turn Picpus into its own exclusive cemetery." His silence does not mean that he was insensitive to this loss. Michel Missoffe has written very aptly on this point.[2]

Talleyrand never cut himself off from his relatives. If he chose not to speak of them, it is best to interpret facts, not his silence. As Missoffe has shown, Talleyrand's various addresses throw light on the subject. He always lived close to his parents. Upon leaving his father's house at 1, rue Saint-Dominique, he moved to the rue de Bellechasse, which corresponded to 9, rue Saint-Dominique. After his father's death, his mother, with the help of the archbishop of Rheims, Talleyrand's uncle, bought a town house on the rue de Lille. Talleyrand then moved to the rue de l'Université, where it intersects the rue de Beaune, in order to be nearer her. And when his mother returned from emigration in 1803, he installed her at 36, rue d'Anjou because he was then living at 35, the Créqui mansion. What can explain this intentional proximity unless it was the mutual wish to see one another easily?

He did not really miss Napoleon's court. He had always found it boring because it *was* boring. Never a traditional court, it was always something of an affected, rigid, and frequently ostentatious imitation. He said so himself, providing a self-portrait into the bargain: "Luxury at the courts established by Napoleon was a mockery. Bonapartist luxury was neither German nor French, it was a mixture, a studied luxury acquired from all over. . . . The most salient feature of this type of luxury was its absolute lack of decorum, and in France, any serious departure from decorum invites ridicule." He might have added that no target of ridicule can expect to endure. Then came a cruel jibe: "The Bonapartes deluded themselves into thinking that their feeble imitation of the monarchs whose thrones they usurped amounted to succession." Temporarily perhaps.

His duties as grand chamberlain frequently had obliged him to bear with palace receptions. Napoleon himself finally tired of the starchy self-importance displayed by his courtiers and thought Talleyrand could make them relax. Our hero went about it in his own way. One can imagine the grand chamberlain advancing "with solemn countenance to indicate the august desire: 'Gentlemen, the emperor does not jest, but he expects *you* to.' The remark went round the court and produced some cheerful faces." [3]

Observers recorded occasional volleys of wit. One day Napoleon, with customary bluntness, rudely addressed the duchesse de Fleury:

"Well, Madam, do you still love men?"

"Yes, Sire, especially polite ones."

Another sally, this time from Talleyrand. He was greeting a lady who had just received a court appointment requiring her to swear an oath of office in the presence of the grand chamberlain. The highly seductive outfit she chose to appear in elicited the comment: "Indeed, Madam, these are rather short skirts for an oath of fidelity."

Once, the emperor came out with a pungent remark. He believed in palmistry and, as Josephine's Memoirs tell us, often had his hand read. Ultimately, a smattering of this pseudo-science rubbed off on him, and one day he took Talleyrand's hand, examined it, and cried: "My astonished genius trembles before yours." Little did he guess the truth of that.

A number of the emperor's remarks came to Talleyrand's ears while he was in disgrace and pleased him no end. The war with Austria had ended; they were negotiating a new treaty with Vienna. Champagny, Talleyrand's successor in the foreign ministry, seemed to be dragging his feet. The emperor, who thought obsessively of Talleyrand, grew impatient, saying to poor Champagny: "You stipulated one hundred million in indemnity for France; it will all go to the treasury, I know. In Talleyrand's time we might have been lucky enough to receive sixty of it. And there would have been ten for him. But the business would have been finished two weeks ago. Finish it." [4]

One can only infer that time lost through incompetence was less costly than the bribes Talleyrand took, and that there is no worse minister than an honest one.

It was clear in many ways that Napoleon regretted Talleyrand's absence; still, he had not forgiven him. This was evident when an English newspaper came out in praise of Talleyrand and Fouché, saying that the French situation had worsened steadily since their disgrace. The remark only rekindled Napoleon's wrath and caused trouble for both men.

In the haze of autumn, on November 13, 1809, a faint sign of spring came his way from the Tuileries. The emperor summoned him to receive the king of Saxony and conduct him to Meaux. Talleyrand hastened to comply, partly out of fondness for King Frederick Augustus, partly out of the hope that this signaled his return to favor. The hope was a vain one.

The Disgraced Prince Does Not Forsake His Pleasures
or His Gallery of "Antiques"

During his disgrace, "his women" clustered about him. Even some new recruits applied for admission to the dazzling gallery of personalities comprising the court of this fallen monarch biding his time. How does one describe that bevy of fading beauties, steadfastly gracious, charming, and loyal? Nowadays someone is bound to label them "the syndicate of former mistresses." During the Restoration, one insulting journalist made his fortune by describing the prince surrounded by his ladies as "the old satrap in his seraglio." All of them played at reviving their vanished youth and the gilded life they had known in 1785; a comradeship bound them together more tender than friendship, less fragile than the love it had supplanted. In Talleyrand's life, nothing is purposeless, pleasure least of all.

Every evening he would visit either at Madame de Luynes's or Madame de Laval's to learn what was being said in the salons: financial news, the latest love affair, backstairs diplomatic gossip, and the common gossip reported by household servants. Around two in the morning, every morning, the discredited minister received a briefing on the day's events. His "seraglio" was his intelligence network and probably operated far more effectively than the imperial police. Let us see who were the ornaments of this harem.

The vicomtesse de Laval had beautiful dark eyes—"eyes in velvet

breeches," the duc de Laval-Montmorency, her brother-in-law, innocently observed. Aimée de Coigny appraised her less innocently: "She is
the most piquant, the gayest, the most autocratic, and the least congenial
of women. Mistress to M. de Talleyrand when she was pretty and now
his very demanding companion, she is really the only woman who can
influence him." One can imagine her working away, or seeming to, at a
large piece of knitting as they talked, weaving their own magic spell.
Madame de Coigny added rather observantly: "The privacy of Madame
de Laval's inner sanctum assured M. de Talleyrand that he was among
friends, and set his mind at ease. Having no crimes to confess, his mis-
behaviors appeared less significant when he could see that they had not
alienated the only persons who might have been shocked." So he had a
conscience and feelings after all, and reserved them for persons he considered fit to judge him!

Talleyrand enjoyed teasing the simple-minded duc de Laval. This
well-intentioned gentleman had a passion for buying pictures impulsively. One day Talleyrand engaged him in this conversation:

"I wager that you have bought still another bad picture!"

"Well, yes," admitted the duke, "it's one of those things you
wouldn't mind hanging in your library. It represents two famous people."

"And who are these people?"

"Someone named Laura. The man's name sounds like 'Patraque.'"

"Once and for all you ought to get the hero's name straight. My
dear fellow, surely you mean Laura and Plutarch?"

"Yes, that's it," said the duke, falling into the trap. "I always forget
that devilish Plutarch. Some people at the auction were saying 'Petrarch'
but they didn't know any more than I the right name of Laura's sweet-
heart." [1]

The "seraglio" rocked with laughter.

We come next to the duchesse de Luynes, his other devotee. "Built
like a gendarme, dressed like a common housewife, she had a passion
for gaming, a stentorian voice, a shattering laugh, a rare gift for contra-
dicting rudely, all of which passed for 'originality.' " [2] This portrait is by
Countess Potocka, whose prime virtue was not charity. The duchess "née
Montmorency" could afford to say just what she thought. In public she
called Napoleon a drunken stableman, which was why "he came round
to admire the nobility with its strength of character and its steadfast attitudes." She and Talleyrand shared a wealth of memories both secret and
public. She was the one who had worked with her bare hands to terrace
the Champ de Mars for the Festival of the Federation, trundling her
mahogany wheelbarrow along the sacred slope where her sacred bishop

had conducted a singular Mass. How could anyone forget such patriotic memories?

Countess Tyszkiewicz née Poniatowska was a fervent idolatress. She was forty-seven or forty-eight at the time, not very attractive, with one glass eye, though the other one sparkled more than enough to make up for it. For twenty-five years she had been madly in love with Talleyrand, going back to before the Revolution. When he left the hôtel Matignon for the rue Saint-Florentin, she moved to a house opposite his. To be near him, she took up whist with a passion and spent nights shuffling cards at her idol's side. Whether because she was a poor player or because her one good eye was not up to following the game while admiring her partner, she would lose heavily every night, and yet every night she was happy. She also spent a fortune piling gifts at the feet of her idol, who accepted her worship with typical indifference. In his own way he was deeply attached to this homely, devoted, and loving woman. One of the apartments at Valençay was hers permanently, and in order to extend the cohabitation indefinitely, he carried out her wish to be buried next to him in Valençay's chapel. When she died in 1834, Montrond was stunned to see Talleyrand weep, "for the first time," he said. We questioned his tears for the queen of Prussia, but those he shed for the Polish countess were surely real.

A newcomer—stranger to the seraglio—made several appearances, the countess of Kielmannsegge. She was German, the daughter of a marshal at the Saxon court, remarkably intelligent and well educated. She did not get along with her Prussian, anti-French husband. They separated. In Berlin she met the duchess of Courland, who shared her admiration for Napoleon. The duchess brought her to Paris and introduced her to Talleyrand. This was his reward for inviting her to dinner: "As M. de Talleyrand approached with awkward, wobbly steps, his twinkling eyes set in a head with serpentine jaws, a hypnotic smile on his lips, and the most outrageous flattery pouring out of him, I said to myself: 'Nature seems to have left you a choice between tiger and serpent. You chose the anaconda.' And that impression has stayed with me. . . . His high forehead twitched restlessly. . . . His morals and habits were deplorable, his wit cruel . . . he admitted himself that he 'needed vice to practice virtue.' " [3]

One might expect that if so virtuous a lady were offended by the sight of this monstrous anaconda, she would remove herself from its presence. Nothing of the sort. The countess wormed her way into his circle of admiring ladies, smiling and fawning her way to acceptance, mortified if the "serpent" neglected to compliment her or invite her out.

Napoleon accepted her even more readily; she probably spied for him in Talleyrand's entourage. Why didn't she have our hero arrested? Though he distrusted her, he would have found it impossible to prevent her from reporting compromising conversations or letters. He tried to get rid of her, calling her "la grande haquenée" * because she clung to the duchess and to him. Countess Kielmannsegge remained forever loyal to Napoleon, serving him in Germany during his trials of 1813. The emperor still wrote to her from St. Helena; when he died, she wore mourning. On her tombstone were the words: "Alone and obedient."

One day Talleyrand tried to embarrass her by asking: "What do you think posterity's opinion of me will be?" This elicited one of the strangest and most penetrating comments ever made about Talleyrand, and one with which he agreed. "That you set out to stir up controversy about yourself." Staring at her in amazement, he said: "You are right, you are absolutely right. I want people to go on for centuries debating what I was like, what I believed, what I stood for."

He got what he wanted, for we are still arguing.

Madame de Rémusat belonged to the gallery of female admirers but not to the seraglio. A niece of Vergennes, Louis XVI's able foreign minister, she had married François de Rémusat, who was much older than she. Through Josephine, he became the emperor's first chamberlain and his wife the empress's lady-in-waiting. Talleyrand was twenty-six years older than she—when he met her in 1809, she was thirty and he fifty-six. The youngest of his worshippers, she was rather charming and pretty, honest about her thoughts and feelings; unfortunately, intrigue seemed to fascinate her, as an observer rather than participant. Her affection for Talleyrand was perfectly platonic; she did not hide it from her husband, who, knowing her nature, was not upset. She would also talk about him to her son Charles—they called him "le Curé." One day during a tedious session of the Senate, "le Curé" composed, as was customary in those times, a word portrait of her, calling her Clari. Highly flattering, it ended thus: "A wealth of ideas, vivid perception, an active imagination, acute sensitivity, and unfailing kindness are expressed in her countenance. . . . Clari's mind is broad and cultivated. No one converses better than she."

We are not surprised therefore, as some of their contemporaries were that an eminent personality should choose to spend many an evening chatting with Madame de Rémusat before going off to join his seraglio.

* Or: "that gawky mare"—Trans.

His oldest friends were also friends of the ladies. Narbonne was the official lover of Madame de Laval, who shared her favors with Talleyrand. To avoid problems of precedence, it was decided that Narbonne would act as husband and Talleyrand as lover. Everything worked smoothly. He saw a good deal of Choiseul-Gouffier, Jaucourt, Prince Poniatowski (the countess's brother), Adrien de Montmorency, and Mesdames de La Tour du Pin, de Jaucourt, de Baufremont, de Coigny, Balbi, and de Souza (Adélaïde de Flahaut): one big family. When Countess Potocka came to Paris the following year, 1810, she was invited to Madame de Laval's where she met Talleyrand. She prized that invitation, knowing that in Paris society it represented "a hallmark of gracious hospitality and good taste," and adding waspishly: "Madame de Talleyrand never came there. She was right."

The closest of Talleyrand's close friends was still Montrond, his companion of the London period and the "wild years" of the Directory. Nothing could alter that friendship. On January 13, 1810, Talleyrand wrote to him: "Get it into your head and your heart that whatever affects you is and will always be of paramount interest to me. I tell you this once and for all. No one loves you more tenderly than I."

Our knowledge of Montrond also casts light on Talleyrand. He made a living by gambling and cheating. He was launched on that career in the army, when a young lieutenant caught him red-handed. They fought a duel; the cheater killed his challenger. After that, a good portion of Montrond's income came from cheating, which led Talleyrand to comment cruelly: "He lives off his own death." Montrond resided in London during the Revolution; Aimée de Coigny joined him there. She had married the duc de Fleury and taken Biron and a certain actor as lovers, but the handsome Montrond was her real passion. Foolishly they returned to France, only to be locked up in Saint-Lazare Prison where they came to know André Chénier, who was inspired to write *La Jeune Captive,* as well as a verse drama, *Blanche et Pure Colombe, aimable prisonnière* (pure white dove, gentle prisoner), for Aimée de Coigny. The poet had not bothered to count the feathers she had already lost. By promising a jailer 100 louis which he did not possess, Montrond saved Aimée and himself. Once free, they were rash enough to marry. Montrond practically bankrupted his wife and divorced her. Aimée then married her actor, who devoured the remainder of her fortune. Later on, she ran into Montrond once again in the prince of Benevento's house. He was the first of the "muscadins." * The gilded youth aped his clothes,

* Royalist dandies who appeared in 1793—Trans.

his neckbands, his mannerisms. When his hair began to thin, his devotees tore out their own locks to supply a curly toupee for the middle of his forehead. Montrond's wit was not easy to imitate; Talleyrand adored his sayings. "The world's worst crime is an ass," Montrond declared. Speaking of the bailli de Fenelle, commander of the Order of Malta, a short, wiry, diaphanous man, Montrond called him the boldest fellow in France because he stepped out in a high wind. One day one of his gambling partners arrived weeping and wearing mourning: "I have lost my wife," he moaned. "To lansquenet?" * inquired Montrond. And when a lady asked him to donate to the cause of repentant girls, he answered: "If they are repentant, I shall give them nothing. If they are not, I'll do my own charity work."

His retort to an English admiral who took him prisoner during the war became a national treasure. A gallant English officer raised a toast to the French. Touched by the gesture, Montrond rose to acknowledge it. At which point the admiral grumbled: "They are all scoundrels and I make no exception." Montrond sat down, filled his glass, raised it to the admiral, and said to his face: "I drink to the English; they are all gentlemen, but I make exceptions."

The list of his mistresses was unending: the notorious Madame Hamelin; the duchesse d'Abrantès; Lady Yarmouth, with whom he fathered a famous son, Lord Seymour, better known as "milord d'Arsouille"; and, of course, Pauline Bonaparte. He nearly conquered the unassailable Juliette Récamier by sweeping her off in a coach to an appointed rendezvous, when Madame Hamelin, who was following them, blocked the street with her carriage and roused the neighborhood, screaming: "Help! Help! This coach is carrying a poor woman who has stolen my husband!" When people ran up to open the coach door, out stepped the goddess Juliette, slightly mussed and greatly incensed. The perfidious Hamelin woman said she had made a mistake, that her husband was not on the scene, and off she ran to spread the story.

Montrond amused Talleyrand; he also served him. With his perfect English and excellent connections in London, he was just the man for Talleyrand to employ for both private and official missions. By tipping him off to a speculative bonanza, Talleyrand put two million in Montrond's pockets, which vanished just as quickly.

Montrond was really upset by the marriage to Madame Grand. He never showed it, but neither did he kneel at the princess of Benevento's feet. On the other hand, he was extremely fond of Flahaut, Talleyrand's

---

* A card game; also a sixteenth-century foot soldier—Trans.

son, and formed the link between father and son. Montrond was fifteen years younger than Talleyrand and fifteen years older than Flahaut, who was then twenty-five. When Montrond came into imperial disfavor in the wake of Talleyrand's disgrace, Charles de Flahaut, who was well thought of at court, spoke up for him. Because he liked Charles, Napoleon made allowances for his lively candor.

If it is true that friends tend to look alike, then Montrond's personality reveals something about Talleyrand.

Someone new had come into our prince's life, the duchess of Courland. Occasionally she stepped into "the little universe" at Madame de Laval's, not as an acknowledged member, but as a probationary one. The others had twenty years or more of seniority in the seraglio. They made her wait her turn. She spent summers at the château de Rosny, Edmond de Périgord's estate, which he inherited from his mother, a descendant of Sully. Her winter home was Talleyrand's house in Paris. His marked attentions to her made the others a bit jealous, though jealousy was actually beyond their range of sentiments. There were petty rivalries perhaps, each idolatress eager to walk upstairs with "the satrap" and receive his good-night. The duchess was delightful; she spoke perfect French with just a slight, charming accent. And she spoke a great deal —too much, the others said. Talleyrand alone did not seem bothered by it. Very soon the relationship had gone beyond friendship. He sent warm and tender letters to her almost daily; time did not cool their love. On January 20, 1814, he wrote: "Good-bye, you with the good head and perfect heart. I love you deeply. See that Dorothée hears what I have told you. Good-bye my angel. This message should be burned." Obedience was not among the angel's virtues, for the letter still exists. On January 25: "I can bear anything when I am with you. You! You! You! You are the dearest thing to me."

That sounds like passion. In Talleyrand's case, one never knows. In the presence of women and in conversation he was reserved and even cold. But he could scorch the paper with his pen. Or was it only the paper?

In writing about Talleyrand and the duchess of Courland, Lady Yarmouth, Montrond's mistress, said: "He seems to be captivated by age, for all his conquests are virtual antiques." There is truth in this. The duchess was forty-seven; none of her rivals would forgive her age, her fortune, or Talleyrand's favors. Their liaison rested upon something other than her charm. A staunch admirer of Napoleon before coming to France, she turned gradually, with Talleyrand's help, into his fiercest enemy. During visits to the Château-neuf de Saint-Germain, she was in contact with Count Nesselrode, the czar's envoy, and a man named Tchernychev, who, in today's rough terms, would be called a spy. She was the eyes, ears, and voice of Talleyrand among these gentlemen. Obedient to the czar, in love with Talleyrand, she followed the latter's instructions and gave Nesselrode information that went into his dispatches to St. Petersburg. In good weather Talleyrand would ride out to Saint-Germain. He must have been a rather absurd picture on horseback; one can imagine him astride too small a mount, his dangling legs almost grazing the ground between his horse's hooves.

An invitation from Talleyrand was as sought after as a summons from the palace. Nowhere else was there finer food and wine. Giving elegant, lavish dinners was in his blood, an important facet of his worldly attitude. He ate only one meal a day, dinner at six o'clock. It warmed him up, and by the end of the meal, left him unexpectedly talkative. The *bon vivant* in him was part of his inheritance from the old aristocracy. He had a witty, caustic tongue when he loosened it under the exciting spell of those splendid dinner receptions. It was one of his rare diplomatic failings, Napoleon recollected on St. Helena in 1817. "You can never make him talk when you want to," said Mademoiselle Raucourt, the actress, "but after dinner, surrounded by five or six friends, you should hear him gossiping like an old crone." He liked his guests to feel at ease during dinner, to talk freely and spontaneously. "In private life he was the essence of sincerity, having no need to deceive anyone," one of his contemporaries observed. After dinner there would be a reception and sometimes dancing. The reception did not begin until eleven, followed by a midnight supper and conversation until one in the morning. Then the sacred hour struck as the gaming tables were brought out. Talleyrand sat down with his companions; the other guests either followed suit or talked. From that moment on, he shut himself off in his own cocoon-like world of calculations. Nothing penetrated that solitude. It must have been very strange to see a man so active politically and socially disappear into himself in the midst of a reception. Paul Valéry has said: "The reality of games lies solely with the player." Blanketed in his own secret silence, every player is an enigma. On some evenings no one heard a sound from him until it was time to announce his cards. Guests who came there expecting to be dazzled by his presence often went home grumbling. A German princess traveled for miles and pulled all sorts of strings to obtain an invitation to one of his dinners so that she could see and hear the prince. She even ended up sitting next to him. Not a word did he utter. The unhappy princess complained to her hostess that she would have been content "with two or three words for my own ears"; the reply she got was: "That is out of the question, princess; he has not said Low Mass for years."

When he chose, however, he could be expansive and seem to say what was on everyone's mind. At other times he was laconic, dropping remarks taken for maxims. People said he prepared them in advance, like Rivarol, who used to write his own on a cardboard which he propped up on the mirror so as to memorize them while shaving before going out to dinner. Talleyrand must have done that on occasion. But there were also times when some impish spirit inspired the perfect retort, like the comment he dropped about Chateaubriand when *Les Martyrs* made such a stir. The book had everyone ecstatic save Talleyrand, who rejected the general enthusiasm for rhetoric and religious exhibitionism. One evening at the hôtel Matignon, Fontanes was raving about the beauty of the passage in *Les Martyrs* in which the ill-fated Eudore and Cymodocée are devoured by wild beasts.* "Just like the book," Talleyrand observed. Chateaubriand made him pay for that pun and others; his *Mémoires d'outre-tombe* invented a new type of martyrdom for the prince of sarcasm.

Talleyrand was fond of chamber music. In his household he employed a Czech pianist named Dussek, a violinist, and a harpist. He liked extremely severe music and found even Mozart a bit too romantic and pleasant. So while the hours devoted to conversation resembled pure diversion, the musical interludes were sober, the silence religious, the immobility absolute. This presents a new feature of the prince.

From time to time he was seen dining with the two Bellegarde sisters, good-looking women, full of the spirited wit common to the aristocracy in 1785, and totally immoral. Or, if you prefer, let us say they were gracious and had few scruples. Talleyrand would see Mesdames de Laval and de Coigny there, and a poet named Népomucène Lemercier, more famous for his name than his verses, and a few other writers just as unknown to posterity as to their own times. Also the painter Gérard, whom he liked. The main attractions at these Bellegarde dinners were Talleyrand and Aimée de Coigny. One of the guests had the cheek to say: "The clicking of those two tongues delighted us no end." We might add at this point that one of the Bellegarde sisters had a child by the actor Garat and put it out to nurse with the same foster mother who raised Talleyrand's grandson the duc de Morny,† offspring of Charles

---

* *"Bêtes"* also means "dumb creatures"—Trans.

† During the autumn of 1811, unnoticed and unsung, a child was born whose birth certificate stated that he entered this world on October 21, 1811, in Paris, though actually this occurred in Switzerland. His parents were not named. Mon-

de Flahaut's liaison with Queen Hortense. Unforeseen ties thus joined these mothers, fathers, sons, and grandfathers of bastards.

That was how Talleyrand spent the period of his disgrace. Deprived of his ministry and of his grand chamberlain's gold key, he still maintained the essential part of himself, his social life. On the fringe of power, it enabled him to exert a parasitic hold. His influence reached its zenith when, relieved of his offices, he was free to mold opinion. Needless to say, his image still haunted the imperial council chamber and Napoleon's head.

Sorrows, Rebuffs, and Financial Headaches

At the beginning of 1810, Talleyrand had momentary hopes that a breach was about to open which would restore him to favor. It involved the emperor's divorce from Josephine and his remarriage.

Talleyrand had favored the divorce as far back as the Consulate. He felt the emperor ought to wed a princess of one of Europe's ancient royal houses. In his terms, only two such houses, the Hapsburgs and the Bourbons, were worthy of wearing the imperial crown. A Bourbon marriage was utterly impossible, leaving only a Hapsburg match, which seemed doubly enticing to our prince as it would entail an Austrian alliance. That would have meant the end of the war, perpetuation of the imperial

---

sieur Demorny, whose name he bore, at once disappeared from the picture. The unnamed parents are familiar enough: his mother, Queen Hortense, his father, General de Flahaut, Talleyrand's son. Because of them, the child, who made himself a brilliant career during the Second Empire as the duc de Morny, enters our story. He was raised openly and without stigma by his grandmother, Madame de Souza. Later on, Morny felt so comfortable about his bastardy that he paraded it casually, in typical Talleyrand fashion: "In my ancestry we have been bastards from mother to son for three generations." That was no exaggeration. Nor was this comment of his: "I am the great-grandson of a king, grandson of a bishop, son of a queen, and brother of an emperor." The fact that his half brother Napoléon-Louis became emperor was due more to Morny than anyone else. With consummate skill, he organized and executed the December 2 *coup d'état* ushering in the Second Empire. An extraordinary repetition: Talleyrand contrived the 18th Brumaire, his grandson the upheaval of December 2. Morny was a conspicuous, ambitious, and intelligent man, an affable Don Juan and worldly wise, obviously "one of the family." He was minister of the interior until his death in 1862, after which the Empire crumbled. Was this a coincidence? We find that Talleyrand had considerable impact on the history of nineteenth-century France.

dynasty, and prosperity. He imagined himself nonchalantly showered with glory, riches, and honor. France at the pinnacle.

It was essential for Josephine to disappear quietly. When she consented, what do we find but the prince of Benevento writing to her children Eugène and Hortense the equivalent of a letter of condolence full of hypocrisy and flattery.

A new empress had to be found. Napoleon revived his suit for the hand of Grand Duchess Anna, the czar's younger sister. Caulaincourt took charge of the affair. At that moment, out of the blue, the court of Vienna took fright at the prospect of a Franco-Russian match, seeing itself crushed between these two empires. As the price of survival, Austria offered the hand of Archduchess Marie Louise to the "ogre." The fairy-tale dimension of a marriage uniting a descendant of Charles V and General Bonaparte is lost upon our modern minds.

The news caused high excitement in Paris. Napoleon found the offer flattering: a niece of Marie Antoinette! And his son would be able to say: "We of the nobility . . ." into the bargain. He called a council on January 28, 1810, to decide between a Russian or an Austrian marriage. Talleyrand attended as one of the dignitaries of the realm, and when it was his turn to speak, he did so with customary tact and relevance. In promoting the Austrian match against heated opposition, he employed arguments prepared long in advance, and seasoned with a certain tinge of complacent flattery, knowing that Napoleon's pride made him favor "the daughter of the Caesars."

Talleyrand was interested in peace and the welfare of France. In this instance, wisdom and imperial pride lay along the same route, so he flattered the pride. It was daring and clever of him to evoke Louis XVI's death and to maintain that by marrying the niece of those murdered sovereigns, the emperor could clear France of a crime attributable to some base faction. The nation could then re-enter the family of reigning dynasties. Talleyrand's much-cherished notion of continuity would be consummated by this miraculous marriage: the new and the old France would slip into bed together, the Revolution and monarchist Europe would be reconciled.

The House of Austria alone would provide continuity, for her policies were not those of one man but of a dynasty which had fought for its own interests for centuries. His argument gained the emperor's support.

Talleyrand's reward was an invitation to the wedding of Napoleon and Marie Louise in the Louvre on April 2. It was not his return to favor. He could not resist dispatching a flattering letter to the emperor after the ceremony. He also arranged for "his captives" at Valençay to celebrate the occasion with fireworks in honor of the man who had stolen their throne and sent them into exile. The sound of the fireworks reached all the way to the Tuileries and was credited to Talleyrand; Napoleon was not deaf to a handful of skyrockets.

But for safety's sake, as one never knows how things may turn out, shortly after the wedding the prince of Benevento took the duchess of Courland to visit the tearful Josephine at Malmaison. The two referred to her privately as "the legalized sultana."

The fair weather did not last; a new imperial storm blew up. In May, 1810, Napoleon suffered a setback both as to his pride and his plans over the issue of his cherished continental blockade. Hardly anyone else believed the "system" would work, and as silent resistance to this absurd project grew, so did his own stubbornness. The first defector was his own brother Louis, king of Holland, who turned to the English for help in protecting Dutch shores from the blockade.

The second attempt to break the blockade was led by the banker Ouvrard,* Talleyrand's pretentious friend, and probably in league with Louis of Holland, for Ouvrard happened to be returning from a mysterious trip to Amsterdam. Though Talleyrand may not have been behind it, he objected so little that he even furnished Ouvrard with a list of London addresses, introductions to important persons, and arguments that could be used to encourage the routing of trade around the blockade. No sooner had Ouvrard returned from Amsterdam than he was arrested in the house of Madame Hamelin, Montrond's former mistress, by the sinister Savary. The same old addresses. Unfortunately, Talleyrand happened to be there also. He was not arrested, but Napoleon demanded a written explanation of his presence under Madame Hamelin's roof and of his relationship with Ouvrard. Apparently the explanation was not very clear, as the emperor said he found it "painful" to read. He also expressed regrets that the vice-grand elector had been surprised at such a place and such a time. Fouché was cashiered that very day, June 3, 1810; Savary replaced him as minister of police. Talleyrand took courage and was the first to call on the ousted official. After leaving Fouché, he toured all the salons spreading the news that Napoleon had committed another blunder: "Undoubtedly M. Fouché made a serious

---

* Gabriel Ouvrard, born near Clisson in 1770, was imprisoned three times, in 1800, then on February 17, 1810, and finally on June 3, 1810. Napoleon hated and feared him, yet needed his money. When threatened by the First Consul following the 18th Brumaire, Ouvrard provided funds for the naval base at Boulogne and, later on, for equipping the Grand Army. He paid out 2 million francs a day to Napoleon after his return from Elba.

mistake; I would find a substitute for him, a particular one: Fouché himself."

He did not visit Ouvrard, who spent two years in Sainte-Pélagie Prison, but he missed this friend who seemed to have a knack for discovering gold mines. When the emperor told him: "With 500,000 men you can do what you want," Ouvrard countered: "With fifty millions you can do far more."

Talleyrand had not seen the last of Napoleon's anger. A new storm struck over another shady affair.

In his zest for shuffling and reshuffling the map of Europe, Napoleon currently was engaged in creating a new French (!) département to be known as "Bouches de l'Elbe," with Hamburg its central seat. The rich burghers in this most prosperous of Hansa communities, hoping to stave off outright annexation and the loss of long-established commercial autonomy, implored aid from Talleyrand for which they advanced him 4 million (2 billion old francs). So great was his reputation for selling influence that the good citizens of Hamburg thought they could buy their freedom if they paid him enough. But Talleyrand's influence had ended; he did nothing except take their offering. Hamburg asked Napoleon to return the money. There was no trace of it. Vanished, it had been eaten up by the remodeling of the hôtel de Monaco (today's hôtel Matignon), Valençay, banquets, gambling . . .

Napoleon summoned him and raised a fresh storm. The prince of Benevento weathered it in silence. No sanctions were invoked.

At that moment, Mademoiselle de Lange's millionaire husband, the Belgian banker Simons, fell into utter bankruptcy. Talleyrand had placed 4 million with the affable Simons, which now were lost; a catastrophe. Where was he to turn? Then he recalled that the czar, principal beneficiary of Talleyrand's intrigues at Erfurt, had never paid him. Alexander felt he had acquitted himself by marrying off Dorothée to Edmond. Talleyrand would have preferred something more "fluid." He went to work on the czar in a long and curious letter, like some beguiling dance of the veils, ripe with the promise of gratitude and devotion, submission, even worship, and ending on this note: "I need 1,500,000 francs; next November is when I must have them. Though it is a simple matter [the most natural thing in the world to him], I must take care how I go about obtaining them at present and returning them once my situation improves."

Returning them? Fancy that! Things have changed: the idea did not occur to him before. He continued anxiously: "I must wind up the matter just as inconspicuously and therefore must address myself to

403

someone discreet enough, if he really would help me, to take the absolutely essential precaution I will indicate."

The ogre was watching him—at least Savary was—and that meant danger. Next came detailed instructions for transmitting the czar's money to its appointed destination without leaving a trace. One slip would give Savary all he needed. After outlining this highly honorable and, to be sure, ethical transaction, he concludes: "The active spite of those unacquainted with trust, or good will, or purity of purpose [oh, purity of purpose that inspired thee to take money from foreign powers!] compels me to beseech Your Majesty to burn this letter." [1]

Another disobedient soul! The letter is here before our eyes. Alexander even kept the draft of his reply to Talleyrand. His tactics were simply Talleyrand's own, the old dialogue between the ferret and the weasel. Alexander wrote back that he did not doubt for a moment our hero's financial need, that he was moved by the prince's confident appeal to imperial largesse. Then came the refusal. His reason for not sending the money, he explained with comic hypocrisy, was to avoid compromising his correspondent. Out of affection he kept him holding his breath: "regretfully, therefore, dear prince, do I deny myself the pleasure it always gives me to oblige you."

The ferret had outsmarted the weasel.

It was a severe blow to Talleyrand, who, for the third time, put his library up for auction. The sale took place on April 30, 1811, and included a fine edition of Voltaire's *Henriade,* the complete, fully illustrated Diderot *Encyclopédie,* and other collector's items. The whole sale fetched a relatively modest price. He sighed and shrugged his shoulders: "One must adjust to the times and bend to each situation." That maxim, which slipped from his pen spontaneously, expresses him perfectly. We must allow events to shape us, avoid rigidity so as not to be broken. Adaptability means survival.

He did not give up with the czar. How could he give up, anyway, when it was his practice never to give battle? He took a new tack, through Count Nesselrode, the Russian envoy in Paris. A curious situation because Kourakine was the official ambassador, a voluminous, peculiar, diamond-studded, dull-witted personality. No one paid him any attention except Champagny, the minister of foreign affairs. They were the only two people in Europe who still respected the Tilsit agreements. Metternich, now Austria's foreign minister, had been replaced in the Paris embassy by Prince Schwarzenberg, another nonentity. Talleyrand did not even bother to see him. Under these circumstances, how could Russia and Austria accomplish any serious business in Paris? By sending an ambassador extraordinary responsible only to his own sovereign, the czar in Nesselrode's case, Emperor Francis in Count Floret's. The strangest thing about their mission was that they were accredited not to Napoleon's government but to Talleyrand. To explain this, we might recall that Dalberg had originally introduced Talleyrand and Nesselrode. In their secret correspondence, Talleyrand was referred to as "Cousin Henry." Nesselrode now informed his sovereign of "Cousin Henry's" latest request. Instead of cash Talleyrand said that he wanted import licenses enabling the holder to skirt the blockade, using Russian ports, and bring scarce items into France. "If these were granted to me right now, it would represent a tremendous advantage which I should be more than happy to receive from His Majesty Emperor Alexander" (March 17, 1811). It is perfectly clear that the sale of such merchandise would result in colossal profits. Talleyrand liked to do things on a grand scale.

Somehow, people just didn't seem to understand. The residents of Hamburg wanted their money back and told Napoleon so. Valençay, too, had its share of troubles: princely treatment for the Spanish princes had cost him 700,000 francs, only 40,000 of which had come from the government. What is more, the estate, which had yielded an income of 150,000 before the royal captives arrived, was not producing a sou and falling into neglect. He took a desperate step—and a risky one—by asking Napoleon to buy Benevento from him. The reply came back like a whiplash: the emperor did not care to buy things. He desired only to take back the princedom and incorporate it into the Empire.

Whereupon Talleyrand wrote to Montrond: "I believe you will find me very much changed. Concern for oneself and anxiety over others necessarily alters one's personality." [2]

The blows rained down. He thought relief was in sight on February 11, 1811, when the finance ministry sent him 150,000 francs for the rent at Valençay, only to have that same ministry demand immediate return of the 650,000 francs which he had collected improperly from cities in the Hanseatic League. "Make it clear to him," Napoleon personally instructed Mollien, the finance minister, "that if he does not return the money, you will have to have him arrested, unless he settles the matter satisfactorily with me." [3]

Disgrace continued to haunt him. Still, he let no occasion pass that might restore him to favor. The birth of Napoleon's son, the king of Rome, was an excuse to re-enter "the apartments" from which he had been barred since the scene of January 28, 1809. He had been in no hurry to do so, fearing a rebuff. What made him do it now was his disgust at the way Arch-Chancellor Cambacérès was behaving: the wretch had already made two visits to the palace. "He has the advantage of one visit over me," Talleyrand said scornfully. So he went there once and, before Napoleon left for Holland, called a second time, on October 21, 1811. If he really said what he is presumed to have said, then he must have had double vision as well as supernatural powers, for tradition has him leaning over the infant king of Rome in his cradle and murmuring: "All this will end in a Bourbon."

The Prince Remains Cool in the Face of Imperial Caprice

We never mention the princess of Benevento because she was rarely seen and never heard. She had returned from the marshlands of Pont-de-Sains and now, like a phantom, haunted the hôtel Matignon where "she managed to survive only by virtue of an incredible combination of guile and stupidity." Actually, Talleyrand left her to her own devices; during the summer he lived with the duchess of Courland at the Château-neuf de Saint-Germain, which she had rented. When it came time for his annual cure at Bourbon-l'Archambault, his wife joined him for three weeks.

Having passed her novitiate, the duchess of Courland was now a full-fledged member of the seraglio, and so well thought of that the vicomtesse de Laval joined the couple at Saint-Germain, turning the romantic duo into a conspiratorial trio. It was idyllic; he did the talking, they walked on air.

One summer evening in 1811 their "little universe" was thrown into panic by the arrival of an officer bearing a letter from Savary, duke of Rovigo, the minister of police. Once again Talleyrand had the disagreeable experience of being notified that his wife was deceiving him with the duke of San Carlos and that the emperor would not stand for it. Did Talleyrand really care? It was rumored that his wife had gone dressed as a man to Valençay to meet her lover. The emperor banished her again to her estate at Pont-de-Sains and decreed that her negligent husband must accompany her. Being forced to live in that dreary marsh-infested district with his wife was a fate worse than death. The thought of leaving Paris was more than he could bear. He wrote to Savary. It was not easy to phrase what he had to say; after ten trial drafts, he handed the final text to the officer who waited until one in the morning for the reply.

Talleyrand in turn left for Paris at five o'clock. Savary did not keep him waiting. He listened; the game was won. The sorcerer obtained a new verdict: his unfaithful wife would go to the marshes alone. Thus he and his ladies were free to carry on their secret dealings. Napoleon's attitude was strange. He believed that humiliating and bankrupting Talleyrand would bring him to his knees. Eventually, he hoped, when the prince of Benevento could take no more insults, when he was ruined and repudiated by the buyers of influence, he would come crawling back to his master: "I want Talleyrand, who has often been disloyal to me and has provided so many examples of immorality, to be forced to rely exclusively on my bounty." But Talleyrand no longer trusted the emperor's "bounty." The Empire was doomed. He urged Metternich to have the czar make peace with Turkey so that Russia could give her undivided attention to the war Napoleon was about to unleash for the restoration of Poland. He pressed for a Russo-Austrian alliance and for both countries to arm. Talleyrand predicted that 1812 would be the crucial year of this new war in the East; he was not mistaken. In 1812, for the first time, Napoleon's military preparations were behind schedule. The overconfident czar wanted to declare war, a potential blunder which Talleyrand averted, pointing out that it was advisable to wait until more imperial troops were committed to Spain along with the key officers needed to command the Grand Army. Also, Napoleon must appear once again the aggressor, ready to put Europe to the torch. Nothing was more damaging to Napoleon than this secret guidance exerted by Talleyrand on the enemies of the French Empire. Nesselrode had this impression of Talleyrand and Fouché: "These men believed that instead of betraying their master they were shielding him from the folly of his passions by preventing him from continuing these perpetual wars which were depopulating France, impoverishing her, and threatening to culminate in tragedy."

They were perfectly aware of their own treachery, but believed they were serving the cause of their war-weary nation. They also believed that the czar wanted peace; on that score, they had something to learn. There is no doubt that they intended to crush Napoleon. Someone overheard Talleyrand telling his exultant lady friends in the privacy of Saint-Germain: "That's how we will destroy him!" Gleefully clapping their hands, they repeated after him: "We will destroy him! We will destroy him!"

At the close of an interview at the Trianon Palace in 1812, Napoleon told Talleyrand: "What a devil you are! I cannot avoid discussing my affairs with you or stop myself from liking you." What an admission!

Talleyrand merely reiterated prudent advice that fell on deaf ears: give up the idea of restoring Poland, pacify Austria and Russia, get out of Spain. It was too late.

Nesselrode said: "There never had been a clear reconciliation between the two men." Or an explicit rupture. This ambiguity worked to Talleyrand's advantage. He could have returned to the imperial fold if he wanted, for Napoleon's "inconsistency" provided several opportunities which his dangerous vice-grand elector did not fail to note. On January 31, 1812, the emperor paid him 1,280,000 francs for the hôtel Matignon. And when he ordered Mollien, his finance minister, not to garnish Talleyrand's salary, this was equivalent to a gift of the 650,000 francs which Talleyrand had been commanded to return. Why, then, just a few months earlier, had he imposed mortgage payments on Talleyrand's properties? The inconsistency was all the more glaring in view of the fact that when others like Marshal Brune were ordered to liquidate their debts, they were forced to pay them off. Only Talleyrand was exempted.

Selling the hôtel Matignon was painful; seeing the emperor eye him more favorably was heartening. In fact, he was so sure that his stranded ship was about to make harbor that he went out and bought the hôtel de l'Infantado on the corner of the rue Saint-Florentin and the rue de Rivoli, as well as a country house at Saint-Brice, north of Paris. The hôtel de l'Infantado is truly a princely residence; the name derived from its former occupant, the duke of the Infantado, a Spanish grandee who had owned it until 1789.

Talleyrand's financial recovery in 1812 cannot be attributed solely to Napoleon's unexpected largesse—unless, as Michel Missoffe suggests, the emperor gave him funds obtained from the "special domain," that is, the spoils of war. Napoleon, who had a habit of making that sort of gift, said of Talleyrand: "He was not the only one, for Ney, Oudinot, and many others would never begin or end a battle without asking me for money" [1]—an edifying comment on imperial largesse. The surprise is that as late as 1812 Talleyrand was still benefiting from it. It had not kept him from complaining for a year that he was penniless. He had even auctioned his books once again; the sale brought little money but good publicity. In short, the economic depression of 1810, inevitable companion of the blockade, had victimized him and many others; but whereas they saw their fortunes engulfed, his managed to stay afloat with the help of the emperor, who harassed and delivered him by turns, receiving for such incongruous behavior the usual objections to harassment, but no gratitude for his clemency and generosity.

The "reconciliation" was serious enough for Napoleon to ask Talleyrand to come with him to organize the new Polish state he planned to establish. Talleyrand seemed agreeable. The emperor demanded secrecy. Why then did this utterly impenetrable man, the paragon of discretion, tell everyone in Paris about the project if not to ensure that nothing would come of it? Napoleon was so angered by Talleyrand's conduct that he shouted to Caulaincourt: "I shall order him banished from Paris. I forbid you to go to his house or talk to him about that." Once again, however, the emperor never lifted a finger against Talleyrand.

Why cling to a ruler bound for his own destruction? Talleyrand knew that the Russians had armed, that Napoleon's vast international military machine was no longer the reliable instrument it had once been when the regiments were exclusively French and commanded by highly trained officers. The tragic outcome of the approaching war with Russia seemed so evident that in the salons he did not even bother to disguise his thoughts. At this time he is supposed to have coined the phrase: "This is the beginning of the end."

In February, 1812, Napoleon made one more gesture. He named Talleyrand to a court-martial convened to decide the fate of Generals Dupont and Vedel, who had surrendered at Bailén. It was an honor our hero would have cheerfully declined. Throughout the sessions he wore his sphinxlike mask, and when asked his opinion, he laid the blame on "a disgraceful act." Nothing more. He added, however, that as there had been no treason, the emperor ought to forgive and forget. It was just like Talleyrand to recommend "blotting out" the whole matter.

When Napoleon set out to invade Russia in the spring of 1812, Talleyrand's miniature "Europe galante" broke up. The duchess of Courland, dubbed the "sultana" of the hôtel Matignon, returned to her estates in the face of impending war; Countess Tyszkiewicz wanted to be in Warsaw to witness Poland's rebirth; others returned to their country seats. The exodus might have saddened him had he not possessed a knack for adjusting to and finding diversion in new situations. "I have arranged the departures of these ladies," he wrote, "in such a manner that every afternoon for a whole week, I shall see one of them to her carriage at half past one. That is really very entertaining." [2]

A single new recruit sufficed to replace all the lost ones: that, too, was very entertaining.

The Emperor Thwarts Talleyrand, Even in the Privacy of His Own Home

She was the wisp of a girl we met a while back, Dorothée, comtesse Edmond de Périgord, Talleyrand's niece. She had not left. She remained at her uncle's side—indeed, for the rest of his life.[1]

Her husband, on the other hand, was almost never at home. He was a colonel in the Eighth Light Cavalry of Murat's army. Dorothée and the duchess of Courland resided in the hôtel Matignon. Profoundly Germanic, or rather Prussian, the comtesse de Périgord had a difficult time adjusting to Parisian society, of whose tastes, morals, customs, and ideas she disapproved. She remained an outsider, a disdainful observer; society made her suffer for it. Her keen and cultivated mind lifted her far above many of the peacocks who snubbed her; so did her proud will and ambition. Youth counted against her at first, for at the tender age of sixteen she was obliged to make her way at court and in Paris society. Youth, however, did not enhance her looks. Summing up the various opinions about her, Lacour-Gayet reported that she was "what women commonly call a prune." Even Talleyrand, who compelled respect for her, did not find her attractive. He was polite, but as she was extremely stiff and withdrawn, he made no effort to coax her out of her shell. The young exile wrapped herself in bitter solitude.

Yet with those deep violet eyes of hers, those piercing eyes, she observed Talleyrand carefully, knowing instinctively that he, not her scatter-brained husband, ruled her destiny. She looked for, and found, the real man behind the mask, a man unknown to his contemporaries; what she discovered thrilled her and won her esteem.

She surmised that her uncle's most impressive quality was not his influence, or wealth, or even his brilliant mind; it was the special courage he possessed, an indomitable courage. "A kind of courage marked by coolness and presence of mind, a bold temperament, an instinctive bravery which instills an irresistible craving for danger in all its forms, which makes peril alluring and hazards inviting." True enough, Talleyrand had always lived dangerously. Jeopardy and insecurity acted like strong stimulants upon his phlegmatic nature to gear it for action. And in this year of 1812, knowing that a police spy could denounce him, or that one of his letters to Metternich or the czar could be intercepted, Talleyrand existed in what commonly passes for a trancelike state. For him, however, it was more akin to the mild euphoria of a gambler living out the tense expectancy of a double-or-nothing bet. "Beneath his noble features, his slow movements, his sybaritic way of life, a core of fearless audacity shone through from time to time, revealing a whole new set of faculties and making him, simply because of the contrast, one of the most original and engaging human beings." [2]

Dorothée's extraordinary discovery contained only one error: what she termed "a whole new set of faculties" was actually ingrained in him, instinctive, his inheritance from the ancient lords of Périgord. Ancestral Archambaults and Hélies in coats of mail shaped that wily, uncompromising audacity, to which eight or ten centuries of civilization added polish and refinement. That is what surprised and attracted Dorothée. She was able to perceive it because she lacked the prejudices, the jealousies, the obsessions of Talleyrand's French associates. She was not easy to know. Stendhal saw her at Mass at the Tuileries on January 1, 1811. Struck by her expression, he noted the following in his diary: "An impressive crowd. During Mass, I enjoyed watching the face of Madame la comtesse de Périgord; she had such a pure expression. If I did not fear being carried away by my present taste for German women, I would attribute these qualities to her German birth. . . ." [3]

Her Protestant upbringing and lonely, protected childhood had made her rather ingenuous and lent her a puritanical air which Napoleon paid her credit for in his own fashion: "As for you, you are respectable," he told her, "you are not like Madame So-and-so" who was standing right there as he pointed an accusing finger.

Dorothée's first son was born on March 12, 1811. The emperor and empress stood as godparents. As for her husband, Edmond was as shallow as his father, as passionate a gambler as his uncle, and an irresponsible rake besides. He squandered his wife's money, not to mention his own inheritance. Glittering uniforms were his great weakness. One day he appeared before Berthier, his chief, with such an array of gold braid, spangles, and gems that the general ordered him to remove the outfit, saying that it was no uniform. This little folly had cost him a fortune; gambling and women completely bankrupted him. His wife grew contemptuous, he became bored with her, and soon they hated each other. In the meantime, however, several years and one easy pregnancy had ripened the "prune." The skinny, sour young girl had filled out gracefully. Narbonne was the first to notice that she had turned quite pretty. Madame de Staël's former lover at once resolved to take the young lady in hand. In the fashion of the times, he began courting her with a barrage

411

of innuendoes and ironies which left Dorothée totally bewildered. Talleyrand saw what Narbonne was up to and quickly put a stop to it: "Hold your tongue, Narbonne, Madame de Périgord is too young to understand what you're saying and too German to appreciate you." For just that reason, her uncle gained her affections. But he took his time. He looked her over carefully and—being a less observant person than she was—found nothing particularly attractive there. The fact is that Dorothée was a melancholy soul and her mournful aloofness was not apt to win the sympathy of a man who found sadness tiresome and even foolish. Dorothée was appointed lady-in-waiting to the empress but performed her duties with the greatest reluctance. The court treated her like an intruder. Napoleon thought highly of her, yet managed to insult her publicly. On August 14, 1811, with the court gathered at Saint-Cloud, the emperor addressed the young comtesse de Périgord: "Your husband really behaves too foolishly. How can he have bought 10,000 francs worth of cameos?"

"Sire," Dorothée replied, "Your Majesty has been misinformed. My husband has not done such a foolish thing."

But he had. Napoleon turned to say something to Berthier, then addressed Dorothée again: "In any event, as you know, those wretched Périgords ceased to be of any concern to me a long while ago."

Hurt and blushing, Dorothée's eyes filled with tears as she defended the Périgords: "Sire, my husband and my uncle have always served Your Majesty zealously and will continue to do so as long as it pleases Your Majesty. In any case, their past services merit at least that Your Majesty should not mock them." [4]

Napoleon did one of his about-faces several days later, inviting her to dine at the palace and treating her with marked courtesy. Too late, for the damage was done. Once he heard about the incident, Talleyrand was only further embittered against the emperor. Napoleon's cutting remarks had turned the ladies of the court from Dorothée; his attentions when she came to dinner restored her credit with them. As a result, Dorothée despised the emperor as well as his court. It was an extremely painful year for her. She sought refuge in religion and became a convert to Catholicism. Bossuet's writings are said to have brought her to that faith. The ceremony was quiet and dignified; an ordinary parish priest performed the baptism and gave her communion. Ever afterwards she practiced her religion faithfully. During the early years of an unhappy marriage, her virtue never wavered. Considering her husband's character and the moral climate of the times, she had every reason to follow the trend. Her virtue held fast until the Empire fell, then it too collapsed.

. . .

Before rejoining his troops in Dresden in May, 1812, Napoleon placed several incomparably petty and tactless restrictions on Talleyrand. He forbade him to dispose of imperial endowments for the benefit of Charlotte. At a time when war-torn Spain was hurling back his regiments, when he was about to send to its destruction in Russia the greatest army ever assembled, the emperor of the French concerned himself with the fiscal affairs of an illegitimate child just to vex his ex-grand chamberlain. He should have taken Talleyrand along and had him watched instead of leaving him idle and rancorous in Paris. There was a further insult: he informed Talleyrand that any failure to show respect for his wife would be punished by exile. This was a new twist: Napoleon championing the Grand woman. What prompted the emperor to behave so peevishly? What was to prevent Talleyrand from forgetting the "benefits" and remembering only the vexations? As political adviser in Poland, Napoleon took along the abbé de Pradt, a less than brilliant recruit. Napoleon realized his mistake and said so to Caulaincourt in the course of the confession made to his master of the horse while a sleigh sped them from Moscow to Warsaw.[5] "That choice is what cost me my campaign. . . . Talleyrand would have accomplished more through Mme Tyszkiewicz's salon than Maret and Pradt with all their talking. . . . I have often wished that Talleyrand were here." Too late; he should have taken him along and not meddled with his wife and Charlotte. In high society, nothing is more dangerous than petty acts of spite.

In the capital, Talleyrand appeared to ignore the vexatious measures. Family concerns preoccupied him: he was anxious for Edmond to distinguish himself on the battlefield instead of earning a reputation for extravagance and record gambling debts. If Edmond could manage to be cited in a victory bulletin, Talleyrand would share his glory. His ambition was to adopt his nephew and Dorothée and make them his heirs; also to provide Charlotte with a suitable dowry and arrange a match for her. This meant waiting for the emperor to return, along with a better frame of mind—or not return at all, which would have suited Talleyrand even better.

Knowing that the police were reading his letters, he said all the right things: rejoiced over the victory of Moscow, hoped for a glorious peace and the rebirth of Poland. When speaking of himself, he dismissed any cause for alarm: "I shall stay off in my corner leading the unvaried, almost monotonous life I have adopted." Savary's police should not lose sleep over him.

During that summer of 1812 he went to take the waters as usual at Bourbon-l'Archambault. His brother Boson went with him. Scant company. Boson was no genius; besides which he was deaf. All day long he soaked his head and still could not cure his deafness. The princesse de Talleyrand was there too, this being the conjugal season. She read aloud to him in the evenings. During the day he worked on an essay about Choiseul's statesmanship, which he probably intended for the *Memoirs* he was now planning to write.

At the end of August, instead of returning to Paris they went on to Saint-Brice. The little tribe resumed the tempo of life at Bourbon. Boson brought along his deafness and his daughter Georgine, who went riding with Charlotte. Sometimes Talleyrand rode with them. He would give them simple little history lessons which interested him far more than his young charges. Tutoring young girls was indeed a strange occupation for a confirmed libertine. He traced for them on the map the route of Napoleon's army as it plunged deeper into Russia's vast reaches. With what comments, one wonders?

He made a brief trip to Paris to hear a *Te Deum* sung in Notre Dame in celebration of the victory of Moscow. In October, they all returned to the rue Saint-Florentin. In November, he attended a dinner honoring the eighty-eighth birthday of abbé Morellet, Voltaire's friend, whom the sage of Ferney had dubbed "abbé Mords-les" *—vestige of the era which had taught our abbé de Périgord the art of living.

The Bourbon Name Makes Talleyrand Think Ahead

As the seraglio had disbanded, Talleyrand fell back on the company of Aimée de Coigny, a harem unto herself. She came to see him every day and spent two hours in his library. They spoke freely. She was then mistress to comte de Boisgelin, Louis XVIII's agent, who anticipated Napoleon's downfall and the return of the Bourbons. Knowing that Aimée de Coigny saw the prince of Benevento regularly, Boisgelin urged her to draw him into their camp. It was a delicate subject. Madame de Coigny and Talleyrand were agreed that Napoleon must be overthrown, but not as to what should replace him. Talleyrand wanted civil rights restored and spoke of forming a government with veteran liberals who supported the Empire but were opposed to tyranny, liberals such as Garat and Sieyès, whom he called the loyal servants of liberty. "We must

---

* *"Mordre"* means "to bite or snap at"; hence, a snappish abbé—Trans.

rekindle in their minds the ideals of their youth." Such was his political doctrine at the moment; he was ready to participate in an interim government. "And as the emperor is retreating from Moscow, he is far away." He felt safe because of the distance between him and Napoleon. Just a few days before, General Malet had nearly succeeded in overthrowing the government. Malet's plans named Talleyrand and Fouché as two of the "Consuls of the Republic." It was extremely dangerous for the two confederates to be mixed up in Malet's harebrained scheme. At once he sent off a letter to the duchess of Courland—for the eyes of the police—dismissing the Malet conspiracy as "a slight stir instigated by that good-for-nothing General Malet who was not kept under close enough surveillance." [1] This prudent letter disarmed the minister of police. Actually, the Malet affair was much more serious. The public suddenly became aware that the imperial throne was unstable. This conspiracy had much the same effect as the fall of Bailén, which revealed that the Grand Army was no longer invincible. Up and down the social ladder, people were beginning to realize that Napoleon's throne was as wobbly as a rickety old chair. This awareness grew, undermining public confidence. The colossus whose invulnerability had been disproved was capable of collapsing.

Aimée de Coigny failed to convert Talleyrand to the Bourbon cause. Still, he had not closed the door. When the post was vacant, one would see.

News of the disastrous retreat across the Beresina reached Paris on December 16, 1812. France suddenly was confronted with the reality of total failure in the Russian campaign. Talleyrand took it as confirmation of all the things he had tried to tell Napoleon ever since Austerlitz.

On December 18, 1812, Dorothée was attending the empress at the Tuileries. She heard sounds at the door of Marie Louise's apartment and saw two sinister figures bundled up in thick furs. One she recognized as the emperor, the other, Caulaincourt. Everyone thought *he* was in Poland, but *he* was here. She sent a message at once to her uncle. A servant woke Talleyrand to deliver it. Thus he was among the first in the capital to know of Napoleon's return.

He took immediate precautions. The Malet affair had disturbed the emperor far more than crossing the Beresina. Police spies became doubly vigilant. No more visits from Aimée de Coigny. But that did not rule out conspiracy; times had never been so ripe for it. They decided to hold tea parties at the princesse de Vaudémont's house; Dalberg came, bringing his friend Vitrolles, another royalist agent. Aimée de Coigny encouraged the conspiracy. Before long, these Dalberg-Vitrolles-Talleyrand talks began to develop, with no apparent effort on the part of any one of them, the color of Bourbon and the fragrance of lilies. That was a house to remember: "The armchairs were so comfortable and life so pleasant and uneventful that the spies would doze off." [2]

Then Napoleon and Talleyrand played another round. The emperor held council at the Tuileries and asked for the opinion of his advisers. When it was Talleyrand's turn to speak, he recommended immediate negotiations for peace—and peace at any price. A return to the boundaries recognized by the Treaty of Lunéville. Prussia had just signed an alliance with the czar, meaning that the remnants of the Grand Army would never be able to hold Germany. With the authority, the courage, and the lucidity derived from undeniable facts and long experience, Talleyrand told Napoleon: "Negotiate. You now hold pledges in your hands which you can afford to abandon. Tomorrow you may have lost them, and then your ability to negotiate is also lost." [3]

Is this the man they call a traitor? None of the emperor's brothers, or generals, or fervent admirers ever offered him better advice. If Napoleon had listened, he might have saved his throne; at least he would have preserved the borders which the monarchy and the Revolution had given France.

Napoleon did not listen to him. Later, on Elba, he said that if he had hanged Talleyrand and Fouché he could have saved his throne. He was wrong about that. But he preferred to take counsel from Maret, duke of Bassano. Watching this brainless sycophant run the ministry he himself had administered, Talleyrand attacked him mercilessly: "I know of only one man on earth more stupid than M. Maret." "Who would that be, Monseigneur?" "The duke of Bassano." When Maret returned from Poland, Talleyrand was at the Tuileries and, on hearing the duke of Bassano announced, said: "See how people exaggerate. Weren't we told that all the baggage was lost? But here Maret is back again!" [4] Napoleon wanted to get rid of this useless "baggage" and offered Talleyrand his former ministry. Why? Though he rejected Talleyrand's policies, he still wanted to continue exploiting his prestige and ability.

The era of Napoleonic decrees had ended. In the waning years of the Empire, Napoleon's whims and rages caused considerable alarm. People close to him had the impression that his mind was unbalanced. Foreign diplomats reported as much to their governments; it seems that the word "inconsistency" was a popular euphemism. And so Talleyrand refused the post, saying icily: "I am not acquainted with your affairs."

"You know all about them," shouted the emperor in a rage, "but you want to betray me."

"No, Sire," Talleyrand continued calmly, "but I do not wish to take charge of them because I believe they conflict with my vision of the glory and welfare of my country." [5]

Talleyrand had been thinking this since 1805; he waited seven years to say it. In fact, he had remained staunchly faithful to the ideals contained in his memorandum of 1792, in his speech on Bonaparte's return from Italy, and in his memorandum on the Peace of Pressburg. Continuity and fidelity are two qualities of Talleyrand's which people are apt to overlook. His ideas changed less frequently than the régimes he served.

So Napoleon's régime already belonged to the past. The question now was not whether it could continue but what would replace it. Why did Talleyrand listen to—but not commit himself to—the Bourbon agents? He would not seek them out; he wanted them to make the advances. Then he would wait and see.

It just so happened that at the time Vitrolles was discussing with Talleyrand the future of crown and church, our bishop of Autun wrote to his uncle the archbishop of Rheims, who was attached to the dreary little court of Louis XVIII in Hartwell, England. The letter cannot have displeased the archbishop as he hastened to read it to Louis XVIII. This stout, astute gentleman smiled to think that a lost sheep remembered the fold. An excellent omen. "God be praised!" he declared. "Bonaparte must be near his end, for I wager that when the Directory was about to fall your nephew wrote in the same vein to the conqueror of Italy. If you reply, tell him that I accept the augury of his good remembrance." Louis XVIII understood better than Napoleon that to be forsaken by Talleyrand was to be lost.

Rages and Reconciliations Merely Destroy Imperial Prestige

During the ominous year 1813, Talleyrand wrote frequently to his dear duchess. They were affable messages devoid of politics or mention of the war. The minister of police had no cause for alarm. They appeared to be the writings of a decent, law-abiding citizen, a loyal subject of the emperor, more preoccupied with family affairs than with what was happening in Germany where Napoleon was going down to defeat. Dresden was a hollow victory; Leipzig tolled the knell of Napoleon's occupation of Germany. The French were forced to fall back—if there was time—to save the remains of their battered and disorganized army.

Talleyrand lavished compliments on Marie Louise, making it appear that she was the ruler he would have liked to serve. After she had presided over a council of ministers, he commented: "She listens admirably and poses questions that prove how attentive she has been." She sounds like a star pupil.

After attending Mass at Notre Dame, he reported that everything was fine and rosy. Paris was bursting into bloom, the ladies were elegantly dressed, it was the month of the Virgin. Who would guess from his letter that tragedy was gathering? There was only one small blot on the otherwise cheerful scene: all went off perfectly "except for Cardinal Maury, who officiated with dignity." The bishop of Autun could have put him right. On May 24, he closed his letter to the duchess with these words: "My only happiness is at your side; that is where I long to be. All ambition has left me." Excellent news! He appeared to have no other care in the world than Charlotte, who had just turned fourteen and "is developing rapidly." His *Memoirs* were also developing; one of his letters mentions that he spent "time correcting what I wrote at the spa on several periods I know well that preceded the Revolution. . . ." He spoke of his poor handwriting, and will continue to complain about it regularly because everyone else does; his secretaries had such difficulty deciphering his scrawl that he was obliged to recopy it himself or dictate.

Not a word about Napoleon in all this correspondence, although a new bout of imperial anger had produced another confrontation. The countess of Kielmannsegge's Memoirs relate that some of Talleyrand's letters were intercepted and handed to the emperor. Rage, hat-stomping, dire threats against the traitor; again, no steps taken. Talleyrand emerged from the emperor's study as fresh and serene as if he had just stepped out of Madame de Laval's boudoir. To the pale and trembling courtiers lined up in the antechamber who had heard the thunderclaps from within, Talleyrand announced coolly: "The emperor is charming this morning."

In a conversation with Molé,[1] Napoleon denied the merits and ability of the man he had sought just a few days before—this was March 29—to put in charge of foreign affairs. The abrupt shifts and sudden moods of the despot on the eve of his downfall simply cannot be explained.

Napoleon told Molé that "his [Talleyrand's] reputation is due partly to chance. . . . Upon my oath, I cannot truly say that it has helped me very much, or that he has provided me with expedients which would indicate a genuinely resourceful mind . . . or great ability. . . . I do not think he is, as you said, a highly intelligent man; you have only to look at his life." Then the subject of "his disgraceful mistress" came up again, the same old story. That sorry woman Madame Grand had no impact at all either on the Empire or on her husband's career. Stunned at this utter demolition of the man, Molé offered politely: "At least the emperor will admit that his conversation is extremely pleasing, witty, and charming."

"Oh, that is his crowning glory, and he knows it." Napoleon conceded grudgingly that he made an art of conversation. An art sufficient to destroy a despot who had lost touch with reality.

Still, this good-for-nothing Talleyrand managed to perform one more service for the emperor. After the defeat at Leipzig, Napoleon's forces found themselves nearly walled up in Germany. If the Bavarians cut off his avenue of retreat to France, it would mean another Bailén. Talleyrand was so well informed by his agents that he was able to warn Napoleon of the danger. Thus, in the nick of time, he got his army through to Hanau and reached the Rhine. Talleyrand saved it from encirclement. The only encouragement from the emperor was the comment that he had acted only to show up Maret's incompetence. One would call that discouragement.

The encouragements came from elsewhere. We learn of them through Madame de La Tour du Pin's *Mémoires d'une femme de cinquante ans*. Talleyrand had great respect for her; she admired but did not respect him. They were very fond of each other. She went to see him in Paris in November, 1813. He had just returned from Saint-Brice. Reports of the disastrous German campaign had upset her, for France might be next in line for disaster. She inquired whether he had seen Napoleon and what the emperor was saying.

" 'Don't talk to me about your emperor. He is finished.'

" 'Why finished? What do you mean?' I asked him.

" 'I mean,' he replied, 'that he is a man who will hide himself under the bed.' "

She was shocked to hear such bitter words from Talleyrand. He added: " 'He has lost all his supplies, he is through.' " It was true.

Afterwards, very casually, he gave her an article to read from an English newspaper describing a dinner given by the Prince Regent in honor of the duchesse d'Angoulême, daughter of Louis XVI and Marie Antoinette. The walls of the banquet hall had blue hangings decorated with lilies, and the table too. No comment was needed. The wind had shifted in London; lilies were coming into bloom again. Talleyrand kept an eye on the wind. As a matter of fact, it was blowing in the direction he had secretly selected. When Madame de La Tour du Pin stared at him in disbelief, he said, as she described it, "with that faint, knowing sneer that he alone possessed: 'Ah, how foolish you are. Go now and don't catch cold.'"

Talleyrand's business with the court at Hartwell was well under way by now. Madame de Coigny, playing the game, had won a marvelous new recruit for the cause of the monarchy: Blacas, Louis XVIII's adviser, wanted certain information from Talleyrand for the exiled monarch. Hopes ran high.

Perhaps Talleyrand never explained to Madame de La Tour du Pin why he felt so bitter toward "her emperor." He ought to have told her Napoleon's insulting greeting at his levee at Saint-Cloud on November 9, 1813:

> "What are you doing here? ["Seeing you for the last time," Talleyrand might have replied with proper dramatic inflection.] I know that you fancy yourself heading the regency council if I should fall. Take care, sir, there is nothing to gain by contesting my power. I tell you that if I were dangerously ill, you would die first."
>
> "Sire, I did not need such a warning to pray Heaven fervently for the preservation of Your Majesty." [2]

That was the third time His Majesty had threatened the life of one of his dignitaries, who shrugged it off, publicly. A few days later, Napoleon learned of his defeat at Vitoria, which allowed the combined English and Spanish forces to march straight through to the Bidassoa River, thus threatening France with an invasion from the southwest. At Saint-Cloud he saw the prince of Benevento, who, though consigned to the firing squad, was neither intimidated nor any less courtly. Napoleon went up to his former minister as if nothing had happened, described the Spanish situation, and asked his advice. With his nose in the air, Talleyrand replied: "Well, now, you consult me as if we had not quarreled."

"Circumstances dictate," replied Napoleon. "Let's forget the past and the future and hear what you have to say about the present moment." [3]

Talleyrand was prompt to oblige, expressing total disapproval of the emperor's Spanish policy. "Issue a proclamation freeing King Ferdinand and withdraw your troops." A harsh lesson for this man who had never listened to anyone and refused to make concessions. Accordingly, by the so-called Treaty of Valençay signed on December 11, 1813, Napoleon restored the Spanish princes to freedom and their throne. On March 3,

1814, they left Valençay. Good timing, as Napoleon himself left a few months later—after abdicating. Talleyrand recovered his château with its park and forests, but never went there. Paris was moving, exciting, even for a man who "had no further ambitions."

Once again the emperor offered Talleyrand his old portfolio, provided he gave up the office of vice-grand elector. Was he bargaining? How blind. Napoleon should have been glad that anyone would still serve him.

"If the emperor trusts me," Talleyrand said, "he should not degrade me; and if he does not trust me, why employ me?" Thus Talleyrand rejected an unacceptable proposal. His *Memoirs* justly assert that "the peculiar thing about Napoleon's behavior toward me is that even when his suspicions about me were greatest, he tried to win me back. Thus, in December, 1813, he asked me to return to the ministry of foreign affairs, which I refused outright, knowing that we could never agree on the only way out of the maze into which his follies had thrust him."

His ultimate folly was to threaten his minister, while at the same time clinging to him. Napoleon was in a quandary.

By imperial decree Talleyrand was appointed to a committee including high dignitaries such as Fontanes. It met at the end of December, at which time Fontanes, observing the practice of every other committee, read a plethoric statement larded with rhetorical bombast congratulating His Majesty upon his will to fight on until he "could sign a peace with all nations"—from his political graveyard. Talleyrand sat listening, a faint smile on his lips. Exhibitions of this kind no longer made any sense. He was not looking around him; he looked straight ahead. It was not yet time to act, so he let Fontanes go on talking. In a letter to the duchess of Courland he commented: "There is no cause yet for anxiety; we must prepare ourselves calmly for events so as not to act imprudently" (December 28, 1813). We may rest assured that Talleyrand would not act imprudently. With the caution and agility of a tightrope walker he managed to slip past the firing squad, and on January 1, 1814, paid an unexpected visit to former Empress Joséphine. They exchanged New Year's greetings and a few memories.

The first of January was not so pleasant in Paris. Napoleon saluted the New Year by leveling a violent tirade at the legislature. The emperor's waning power was now concentrated, unfortunately, in his temper. Talleyrand had been well acquainted with the fact for some time, but others were appalled by the scene. Talleyrand had one source of great contentment, however, the duchess of Courland's arrival in Paris. His daily message for January 2 read thus: "At dinner, dear friend, we shall see each other at last. I embrace you and love you with all my heart."

Dine in peace; the rest would work itself out. Not right away, though, for on January 16, Napoleon stirred up another storm, which took a nasty turn. He had no specific criticism of Talleyrand to offer, but others had reported certain remarks which the vice-grand elector had made concerning the future of the régime. Talleyrand confronted the emperor with the quiet courage already observed by his niece. Exposed to so violent a rage, his life was in danger. Yet, when Mass was over, the emperor proposed sending him as a plenipotentiary to treat with the allies. Of course Talleyrand refused.

"Whoever now refuses to serve me is of necessity my enemy," shouted Napoleon. Evidently. Cambacérès, Caulaincourt, and Savary were present and assumed that Talleyrand's end had come. Napoleon raged: "We shall see. Bring Monsieur de Bassano here." That meant arrest and whatever was to follow. By some miracle, the duke of Bassano was nowhere to be found; Napoleon's anger abated and Talleyrand left. What is one to think of a ruler who offers "his enemy" plenary powers or the firing squad?

Several days later, there was another alert: Napoleon accused Talleyrand of spreading misinformation which led to panic selling of government bonds. The ensuing investigation proved nothing. But each incident only increased Talleyrand's sense of peril and he had Courtiade burn a great many papers which might have compromised him.[4]

When Caulaincourt courageously took on the task of foreign minister and left for Châtillon to try to make peace with the coalition, Talleyrand had the audacity to suggest that it was in Caulaincourt's interest to serve the cause of Napoleon's successors. Caulaincourt was stunned to hear him speak in favor of the Bourbons. Without answering, he walked out of the room and never told anyone what Talleyrand had just said. In fact, a short while before, the imperial vice-grand elector had become the highly discreet, highly respected political adviser of Louis XVIII. It was even rumored that a certain royal proclamation circulating throughout France on January 2 was inspired by the former bishop of Autun.

Certain edifying remarks in Queen Hortense's Memoirs are invoked frequently to establish Talleyrand's amorality: "Long humiliated, the prince of Benevento saw how precarious the situation was and tried to take advantage of it. He had the means to do harm. He used them. Rarely does hatred devoid of courage [did it not take courage to be the lone dissenter in Napoleon's court?] let slip an opportunity that it has waited furtively to seize." When was Talleyrand furtive? Nobody was more open than he. The whole of Paris and every crown in Europe knew what he thought of the declining emperor. As to the moralistic judgments of this lady, whose opinion was shared by many of her contemporaries, it is interesting to note that Hortense de Beauharnais was beholden to Napoleon for everything she had: riches, husband, crown, the very clothes she wore; yet in 1814, after he abdicated, she rushed to throw herself at the feet of Louis XVIII, who recounted with just a tinge of irony her act of prostration, her protestations of loyalty, and her request for the title of duchess. Louis XVIII, with an enigmatic smile, made her duchess of Saint-Leu. After Napoleon returned from Elba, Saint-Leu reverted to Bonapartism and worked against the king who had made her duchess. She was not exactly the most reliable judge of morality.

On January 25 Napoleon left to rejoin his troops. The die was cast: Talleyrand and the emperor never came face to face again. As Talleyrand had wished, the empress remained in Paris. Her presence was reassuring. She presided over the regency council on which Talleyrand served. He wrote to the duchess of Courland: "As long as she [the empress] is here, Paris is more livable than any other place; if she were to leave, it would be best to have arranged the removal of all obstacles to your immediate departure. That is my advice, dear friend. I love you with all my heart."

In the daily messages that followed we read of the mounting anguish of the situation, the approaching allied forces, and the encirclement of Paris. Heavy defeats wiped out yesterday's victories. Sixteen-year-old boys, brave as veterans, died in droves. They died fighting the only justifiable battle of the Empire, the defense of France. And France was routed. Far from immune to the heartbreak of the French campaign, Talleyrand wrote: "No one with a drop of French blood can avoid suffering the dreadful agonies and humiliation that our wretched country suffers."

The situation was tragic. If a man like Talleyrand felt relieved by the tyrant's defeat, at the same time he was griefstricken because the defeat was also his country's. He had seen it coming and had wanted to spare the nation. Now it was fatal; one must get it over with as soon as possible.

Even in the heat of battle Napoleon still thought about the conduct of his vice-grand elector. He had him closely watched. He wrote to his brother Joseph, who was residing in the Luxembourg palace, that the empress should leave Paris if the capital were threatened, though Talleyrand wanted to keep her there. "Beware of that man. I have associated with him for sixteen years; I have even shown him favor. But surely he is the greatest enemy of our House now that fortune has abandoned him" (Nogent, February 8, 1814).

Savary had him followed and spied on his visitors. One day he was informed that the former abbé de Pradt (now archbishop of Malines), Dalberg, and Baron Louis were meeting at Talleyrand's house, all of whom were suspect. Savary decided to surprise them. Talleyrand related the incident in his *Memoirs;* so did Savary, and the two versions are very close. Savary entered the house unannounced, and burst in upon the four conspirators. "I entered so suddenly that they looked as if I had come in through the window." The conversation, so animated a moment before, broke off sharply and no one knew what to say. Savary did not put them at ease: "This time, make no excuses, I have caught you in the act of conspiring." The face of the archbishop of Malines was distorted by fear; Talleyrand's, as usual, like marble. His account claims that Savary had spoken jokingly. However, Talleyrand had a habit of sweetening unpleasant things. Stendhal knew about the incident and wrote: "But for the duke of Rovigo's lack of resolve, Talleyrand would have been arrested in 1814 before the fall of Paris." Talleyrand summed up the incident with a moralistic sigh: "Being minister of police is a decidedly ugly profession." [5]

A Flick of Talleyrand's Wrist Precipitates Napoleon's Downfall

Abbé Louis was an old acquaintance who had served at the Mass of the Federation. After flirting with theology, he moved up to high finance and, being a clever fellow, became an expert swindler. The title of baron and a high treasury post still did not satsify him, for his heart was set on heading a ministry. While waiting for the Empire to fall, he became friendly with the bishop of Autun. Each of the former clerics had high hopes of landing himself a glossy portfolio.

Talleyrand also won the support of Bourrienne, Napoleon's secretary, who had been dismissed for dishonesty. Later he was recalled, but instead of serving the emperor, he served Talleyrand, who could offer him a stake in the future. The service he performed was relaying all the information he could glean from Napoleon's correspondence. One should add that Bourrienne was the best of friends with Lavalette, the postmaster general, who opened all the mail. So if Napoleon read Talleyrand's letters, Talleyrand knew the contents of the emperor's correspondence.

Two other members of the confederacy were the charming Aimée de Coigny and the abbé de Montesquiou. The abbé, another old acquaintance of Talleyrand, had remained true to king and church. He was penniless and totally dependent on the princesse de Poix's hospitality. Unflagging confidence in the imminent return of the monarchy buoyed his spirits. He plotted in utter serenity, with a sense of detachment and objectivity which his more animated accomplices may not have shared. He was only a dreamer, whereas the others had already paved the way for a provisional government and a Constitution. The legitimate throne awaited. As soon as the "ogre" was gone, they would seat the king upon it.

Catastrophe approached by leaps and bounds. Talleyrand wrote to the duchess: "I shall come to see you this morning. We are on the brink of a terrible crisis. God will protect us. Farewell. I embrace you with all . . ." The letter breaks off. It deserves comment just for the mention of God. Was it a sign of genuine anxiety or contemporary rhetoric? He experienced a sudden rush of feeling for Charlotte, commending her, in the event of something unforeseen, to the duchess's care: ". . . we are four days away from who knows what. I commend Charlotte to you. See that she receives a good education; mold her character after your own." [1]

Were his fears imaginary? Hardly, for up to the very end Napoleon was capable of ordering a few trusted aides to shoot those who had disavowed him. Talleyrand headed the list. What may have saved him was the company of so many traitors. No one had more worshippers or more betrayers than Napoleon. In his final hour, the disloyalty of his closest followers—brothers, generals, dignitaries—lent stature to the emperor. For Dalberg, abbé Louis etched this savage picture of perfidy: "The man is a corpse, not stinking as yet." An appropriate caption for one of Goya's macabre etchings.

The following lines from Pasquier's Memoirs aptly describe Talleyrand's attitude during those agonizing days: "Observe everything; make a point of knowing everything; without taking unnecessary risks, try to exploit whatever difficulties arise from one moment to the next and be prepared to strike the fatal blow if a safe opportunity arises."

Prudence, boldness, patience—familiar qualities all. With a clear conscience he reads aloud in private to Aimée de Coigny and a group of friends from *Les Entretiens du maréchal d'Hocquincourt et du père Canaye,* a masterpiece of liberal mischief-making. They must have been delightful reading sessions; and did they not conceal some less commendable occupation? The house on the rue Saint-Florentin had a constant stream of visitors. Everyone who was anyone came there looking for advice as to how to save his fortune, his position, his titles. The parade of callers was in itself a plebiscite, spontaneously identifying the government of the future. But what form of government was it to be? Talleyrand remained silent. Someone must take a stand. Aimée de Coigny finally was delegated by her lover Bruno de Boisgelin to entreat the prince of Benevento to utter a single, brief, meaningful word: "king." Talleyrand knew why she had come, with her simpering, her insidious questions and feigned innocence, but he was content to wait. He waited for a certain attitude toward kingship to take hold of the public. A king was on hand. If whispered often enough, the name of the king would create the desire, then the necessity for him, and finally the monarchy would be restored. Talleyrand rejected the regency council established by Napoleon. "But what are we to do?" Madame de Coigny asked him. "Don't we have his son?" Talleyrand replied. That was no help to the Bourbon cause. She pressed him further: "Nothing else?" He evaded the question. When she brought him back to it, he suggested the duc d'Orléans, saying that he had always been sympathetic to the Orléans branch. This would have dashed the hopes of the main Bourbon branch. Aimée de Coigny said: "No, the duc d'Orléans is a usurper, of better family than another, but still a usurper. Why not the brother of Louis XVI?"

She got nothing for her pains. Talleyrand remained silent. A few days later they were talking confidentially and she heard him whisper: "Madame de Coigny, I am willing to accept a king, but . . ." She was elated, certain that with Talleyrand's consent, the monarchy would return. He would stop at nothing, even crowning the murdered king's brother. Her reply was prudent and less than enthusiastic: "Well, Monsieur de Talleyrand, you are preserving the freedom of our wretched nation by granting her the sole instrument of her security, a fat, feeble king who will be forced to legislate wisely."

She forgot the "but." Talleyrand provided it: "I stand ready," he said with a smile, "but I must warn you how I stand with that family. My relations with Monsieur le comte d'Artois can be ironed out because we have had dealings already which in good part explain my conduct. His brother, however, does not know me at all. I must tell you that I do not relish the prospect of receiving no gratitude and having instead to seek pardon or justify my actions. I have no way of reaching his ear." [2]

He was naming the various obstacles bound to arise sooner or later between the legitimists and the bishop of Autun. Still, for the sake of peace and to allow France to recover from her ordeal, he had decided to accept "the fat, feeble king" who was wise and witty. By telling Madame

de Coigny that he had "no way to reach his ear," Talleyrand was dropping a broad hint for her to find the way.

That ingenious fellow Dalberg came up with the link, a royalist
agent friend of his, Vitrolles. No one wanted a new government built
around Bonaparte's brothers and generals, but a Bourbon Restoration
would require allied consent. Dalberg left Paris on March 6 with Vitrolles
and on the tenth they were consulting the allied chiefs of state. He told
them that Paris was awaiting their arrival and that a provisional government was ready to function if they approved. Such an initiative may
appear monstrous when France was repelling an invasion. Its utility,
however, was to spare the country from foreign occupation. Talleyrand
pushed negotiations to the limit of what the wartime situation permitted.
He gave Vitrolles a three-line message on a tiny, crumpled piece of paper.
It was handed to Nesselrode, who recognized the writing as Dalberg's.
The message read: "The bearer of this note is completely trustworthy;
listen to him and recognize my voice. It is time to talk more plainly. You
are walking with crutches; use your legs and do what is in your power."

It was the cue to march on the capital, that Paris was an open city.
Vitrolles was received by the czar, Metternich, and Lord Castlereagh, all
of whom were elated by the note. One can understand Talleyrand's
eagerness to avoid the horrors of foreign occupation, to put an end to the
bloodshed, to "deliver the nation from a madman," but not his open
invitation to besiege Paris. We found motives for his acts of apostasy and
excuses for his cupidity, we condemned (but not in anger) his flattery
that was more insolent than servile; but we have to draw the line at this
"little scrap of paper." If only for the sake of those sixteen-year-old boys
thrust into uniform and sent into battle, who were blown to bits so that
their country could claim one final victory at Montmirail. Had Talleyrand forgotten them? To the Russians and Prussians, his message was
plain: "Crush them, they are at the wall." How can one look upon the
author of this scrap of paper without blushing? He never blushed. He
had not written the message; it was dictated by him. The ineffable Dalberg did the writing—not too willingly, either. At first he refused, feeling
that Nesselrode ought to be able to identify "Cousin Henry's" writing.
In the end, Dalberg yielded, but was furious and went about saying:
"You don't know that monkey, he would not risk singeing the tip of his
paw even if all the chestnuts were his." [3]

Nesselrode noted that the message "determined the march on
Paris." We said before that a word from Talleyrand occasionally had an
incredible impact; never was this impact so tragic.

At this time he also wrote to his dear duchess complaining about the slow pace of the allied advance: "Prince Schwarzenberg with his 100,000 men faces only Marmont's and Mortier's forces which can offer no resistance, yet he does not budge. It is really incredible. Never before has Austrian slowness so richly deserved to become proverbial. Emperor Francis must be surprised indeed at his son-in-law's activity" (March 24, 1814).

For once Talleyrand was in a hurry. In the meantime, life went on, offering its small comforts: "Farewell, my angel, we dine together, but I shall see you before dinner—How I love you!" [4]

Charlotte took her breakfast sitting on the prince's bed; a note from the duchess brightened his day; the allies were encircling Paris, and Talleyrand wrote to his dear duchess: "I could not wish for a better start to the morning" (March 25, 1814).

"In 1814, That Rascal Talleyrand Was There; I Was Not" (Fouché); Well, You Should Have Been

Vitrolles was at Nancy with the comte d'Artois. Before the princes were even on the throne they started making trouble. News that Talleyrand had joined the legitimist cause failed to excite the future Charles X, foolish fellow, who was of the opinion that such support could be highly compromising. Back in Paris, however, Talleyrand was playing whist with the empress and Queen Hortense. Molé made the fourth. They joked about the victory claims of the allies, who boasted that they were at the gates of Paris. With approving smiles, the prince of Benevento fostered the remarkable unconcern of the two ladies. But with the end fast approaching, it was time now to deal with the empress. No more whist.

On March 28, at a dinner given by Madame de Rémusat, he rebuked Pasquier, prefect of police, for opposing the departure of the empress, saying that for safety's sake she and her son must leave the city. Pasquier stoutly upheld the opposite view, then left. Whereupon Talleyrand said something that revealed his plans to everyone present: "I did not know that Monsieur Pasquier was so hostile to the House of Bourbon; the advice he gave could affect it most adversely." [1]

Now that she knew where Talleyrand stood, Madame de Rémusat informed Pasquier. The mere fact of declaring himself was sure to attract a flood of sympathy for the Bourbon cause. Did he not have an infallible eye for success?

The Council of Regents met that same day. As the gravity of the situation was at last apparent to all, the councilors had to decide whether the empress and her son should leave the capital or remain. Napoleon had written to his brother Joseph that under no circumstances were his wife and son to be allowed to fall into enemy hands, so they must leave while the roads were open. The council resolved that she must stay; Talleyrand supported their position. In the end, however, the emperor's command prevailed, and Marie Louise made ready to leave.

Talleyrand's reversal on this issue drew considerable comment, to which he offered this explanation: "I knew that the empress distrusted me and that if I favored departure, she would stay. I advocated her remaining so that she would leave."

A lesson in the art of handling regents.

The empress and the king of Rome left for Blois on March 29. They also left a void. There was only a halfhearted attempt to defend the gates of Paris. In his *Mémoires d'outre-tombe,* Chateaubriand shook a rancorous fist at Talleyrand: "All M. de Talleyrand had to do now was hobble around at the feet of the colossus he could not overthrow." But the colossus was already felled. And the limping Talleyrand was the man about to restore legitimacy—not Chateaubriand. After the council meeting, Talleyrand said to Savary: "Instead of insulting me, the emperor would have done better to rid himself of the men who fed his suspicions. He would have realized that friends like that were a greater menace than his enemies." [2] True enough, and at that very time Napoleon was sighing: "Ah, if Talleyrand were here, he would get me out of this."

The prince of Benevento had succeeded in evicting the empress, but had it occurred to him that as vice-grand elector of the Empire it was his duty to escort her? The fact was brought to his attention. What? Chase after the remnants of a fallen régime? Let others do it. He would not commit himself: "Maybe tomorrow, maybe never," as the saying goes; it turned out to be never. This is how it happened. Instead of refusing to depart, our wily hero packed his bags; he went even one step further: he left. That morning Paris trembled as the cannon roared at Pantin and Romainville, the gunfire clattered at Montmartre and La Villette. What was Talleyrand waiting for that day, March 30, 1814? For Paris to be surrounded. This note to the duchess is revealing: "I will come to see you early. I am waiting to hear the news. I love you with all my heart and the thought that you are troubled, and anxious, and perhaps rightfully troubled, grieves me. My angel, I love you, I love you." While the empress was trotting off into exile.

By midday the city was lost. Fighting was still going on at the porte du Trône, but the allies were ready to enter Paris. Talleyrand chose that moment to play-act at joining the empress. His presence in Paris was vital, for he was the bridge between the rising power and the dying one, enabling the country to function. And according to his own maxim, "Politics are made by women," on that desperate evening, March 30, he and Madame de Rémusat, whom he had coached thoroughly, went to call on Pasquier. One can imagine him half-hidden behind the lady, pushing her forward to speak to the prefect of police: "Go ahead, Madam, you are destiny's instrument." Madame de Rémusat, who was Pasquier's cousin, recited her lesson: Monsieur de Talleyrand was torn between two duties, feeling compelled to join the empress; but, on the other hand, if he left Paris, who would speak for the city and for the rights of the nation to the allied authorities? Who else but Talleyrand was so at ease with foreign rulers, their ambassadors and generals? Who better equipped than he to negotiate with the victors? Pasquier could not deny the truth of this but wondered how he could possibly help. Madame de Rémusat replied simply: "He is here to ask your advice." Talleyrand pretended to grope for words, his inner turmoil causing him to stammer. Madame de Rémusat took pity on her inarticulate friend and spoke for him: she suggested that her cousin arrange some sort of incident at the gates of Paris for it to appear that the prince of Benevento had left to meet the empress at Rambouillet. Pasquier could stir up a handful of brawlers to scream and yell that no one had the right to leave the city and that officials ought to be there to protect the rights of the citizens. Wide-eyed, Pasquier protested that his function was to maintain order, not organize riots. But he had another idea: "Monsieur de Rémusat holds a command in the national guard which is responsible for protecting one of the gates of the city. Let Monsieur de Talleyrand appear there and attempt to leave; then Monsieur de Rémusat can do with his national guards what you have asked me to do with the populace." [3] An even better scheme than their own.

Without delay, the vice-grand elector (for how much longer?) set out in his carriage with his secretary Perrey. Rémusat had been informed of the proceedings and awaited them at the Passy gate. When Talleyrand's carriage drew up, it was ordered to turn around and go back. He protested vigorously, and loudly enough to be heard. He even took the precaution of approaching a second gate and denouncing the flagrant abuse of authority. He chose the wrong gate, for its commander happened to be a conscientious soul who immediately took it upon himself to redress the grievance and offered him an escort to Rambouillet. Devil of a fellow! Talleyrand managed to wriggle out of the offer and returned home. At least he could rely on Rémusat's eyewitness account; that was all he needed. He had departed without ever arriving. Everything was fine.

How did so many people hear the news? On his return to the rue Saint-Florentin he found the courtyard, the stairway, the front hall swarming with visitors, like a beehive in spring. Dozens of persons wanted to shake his hand. Bourrienne was among the first to greet him. They sensed that here was their future leader. Later on, at two in the morning, Marshal Marmont, duke of Ragusa, signed articles of surrender in the presence of Colonel Orloff, the czar's envoy. Talleyrand called at Marmont's house and asked to speak to him. He questioned him first as to whether any exit from Paris was still open—hardly a confidential matter—and went on to deplore the country's wretched condition— scarcely a state secret—after which he suggested a number of remedies, but emphasized no particular one. Without mentioning the Bourbons, he spoke so convincingly of legitimacy that fifteen minutes later, after he had gone, Marmont found himself an ardent advocate of Louis XVIII. The bishop of Autun's "sermons" had that effect on people. Before leaving, Talleyrand asked Orloff to "kindly present to His Majesty the emperor of Russia the profound and humble respect of the prince of Benevento." "Prince," replied Orloff, "rest assured that this submission will be brought to His Majesty's attention." [4]

The house was silent on his return; Courtiade had stayed up to prepare him for bed, waiting with nightclothes and the usual unguents and perfumes. Then did His Serene Highness really know serenity. It had been a busy day. What had he actually accomplished? Nothing. He had been present. He had stepped in to fill a void because someone had to represent and speak for the nation. The czar knew that that someone eagerly awaited his arrival in Paris and could be counted on to reorganize France in the wake of Napoleon's downfall. At that moment, defeated and abandoned, Napoleon reached Fontainebleau. It was his final hour.

Early the next morning, March 31, something of a miracle occurred at the hôtel de Talleyrand: the master of the house was up at six, dressed, powdered, and ready for the fray. This unprecedented effort to be out of bed before eleven illustrated the gravity of the situation. Despite the haste, he was still at his toilette, draped in his peignoir with a scarf around his neck while Courtiade powdered and arranged his hair, when Nesselrode arrived. In a rare fit of emotion, Talleyrand stood up and, trailing towels and his clubfoot, threw himself into Nesselrode's arms, smothering him in clouds of powder. The great day of capitulation dawned, fragrant with the scent of bergamot.

Nesselrode had been sent ahead by the czar to help draft a proclamation that was to be made when the allied armies and their sovereigns entered Paris. Talleyrand had expected just that. He sent for his confidants, Dalberg, abbé Louis, and the abbé de Pradt, and broke the good news to them. All were prepared to collaborate with the coalition forces. To prevent civil strife, it was essential to assure the public that order was about to be restored. Talleyrand, Dalberg, and Nesselrode took charge of drafting a declaration, with Roux de Laborie writing from dictation. Talleyrand had other things to do and left them to complete the single page of writing. In no time they were finished. Incredible speed! Not really, for Dalberg had already drawn up a draft the night before which they had all approved. Talleyrand had written it. Only the czar's signature was lacking. When Alexander arrived shortly thereafter, he read the document and signed it after adding one sentence, the gesture of a generous victor. Frenchmen should not forget that they owe thanks to Talleyrand for suggesting it to the czar. The allied proclamation was conciliatory, demanding that Bonaparte abdicate and promising to deal leniently with France providing she established a stable and moderate government. The allies would respect her natural boundaries, and, the czar added, at Talleyrand's prompting, speaking for the allied sovereigns collectively: "They can do even more because they will always profess the principle that France must be great and strong for the sake of European security." That sentence saved France from destruction and dismemberment.

Talleyrand's critics say that he settled for too little. What was he to do? Ask them to go back home and reinstate the defeated emperor or his son, or one of his brothers, or Marie Louise, who was most probably Metternich's puppet? Does anyone believe that the allies were his to command? That they would have allowed France to keep the "Bouches d'Elbe," Holland, and Italy just because the czar was smiled at by Talleyrand? Or England the "Bouches de l'Escaut" and Antwerp? Talleyrand was no miracle worker; he exercised his superb intelligence and ability with triumphant results, which, come to think of it, *is* something of a miracle.

Let him explain his own conduct during that period of his life: "The routed Napoleon had to disappear from the world stage; such is the fate of vanquished usurpers. But France, once overrun, how heavy were the odds against her." Yes, after the "usurper" had run his lightning course and then plunged to his destruction, France had to pick up the pieces. What would happen to the country? Talleyrand had foreseen the dénouement a long while back and had planned for the future. "I felt it was my right to do this a number of years before. . . . This was neither betraying Napoleon nor conspiring against him, although he declared more than once that it was." What follows has an extraordinary flavor of historic truth and sincerity; it is the key to this enigmatic political career: "The only conspiring I have ever done was when I had the majority of France as an accomplice and was seeking hand in hand with her the salvation of my country." [5]

It is evident that the vice-grand elector's "conspiracy" never would have succeeded if the emperor's closest associates had not disavowed him and the people besides. The legend came later. But in 1814, France had taken all she could take; Napoleon's wars and conquests and annexations sickened her with disgust. When Talleyrand said: "The only dangerous conspirator he [Napoleon] ever had was himself," he spoke the truth. To the endless controversy Talleyrand has incited, why add an unjustified criticism of his valuable service to France and her people in 1814?

The Vacant Throne Needs an Occupant: Talleyrand Has One in Reserve

On March 31 the allied armies and their rulers marched into Paris along the boulevards converging onto the place Louis XV (now the place de la Concorde). Talleyrand watched them from his windows overlooking the rue de Rivoli. The czar was in the center, flanked by the king of Prussia on his left and Schwarzenberg, Austria's plenipotentiary, on his right. Meanwhile, they had combed the city for a printer to turn out the declaration in a hurry. The one they found changed the title of the document to "Proclamation." Alexander and Talleyrand gave their approval, and by the day's end the proclamation was in print. Before that, a minor and rather original incident served to push Alexander into the arms of Talleyrand—all to the good of France. Alexander received warning that his intended lodgings, the Elysée Palace, had been mined. Talleyrand appeared skeptical, but decided to exploit the rumor. Instead of refuting the tale, he invited the czar to stay with him, which Alexander did. How like Talleyrand to have launched that rumor. It has the flavor of his imagination. He would never have laid a mine, but would not have failed to exploit an invented one. No damage, no noise, no bloodshed: pure profit. Thus did Talleyrand end up host, major-domo, chamberlain, adviser, and confidant of the czar. His ambition to be the "favorite" was fulfilled unexpectedly. He played the part brilliantly, cajoling, entertaining, and informing the czar, strewing laurels at the feet of the deserving conqueror. Nor was the czar always aware that he served Talleyrand's designs. Those "working conditions" were thus ideal for the prince of diplomats. And he worked constantly, even at the dinner table. At that time, Talleyrand employed Carême, one of the most celebrated chefs in French gastronomic history, to do his cooking, and could boast the finest table in Europe.

Many persons sat at it. Even the abbé de Pradt, archbishop of Malines, an ambitious scoundrel who took himself very seriously. They called him the "scullion of the political kitchen." One day he came to the rue Saint-Florentin complaining bitterly that no one ever gave him anything important to do. After hearing him out, Talleyrand replied, with an artful smile: "Who would want to push you aside? Right this instant you can perform an important service. Have you a white handkerchief?"

"Yes," answered the abbé, mystified.

"Very white?"

"I suppose so."

"Show it to me."

The dialogue was pure farce and getting rather confusing. Talleyrand played his part in dead seriousness. Neither of them knew what was coming next. Talleyrand took the handkerchief, unfurled it, waved it, raised it like a banner, and cried: "Long live the king!" A fine performance to put on in the Salon of the Eagle, as it was known, where the fate of France was being decided.

"See what I just did? Now go out, take the boulevard de la Madeleine as far as the faubourg Saint-Antoine, and keep waving your handkerchief and shouting: 'Long live the king!' "

Visibly alarmed at this odd mission, the thimble-sized archbishop protested: "But, Prince, you are not being sensible. Look at my clothes, my clerical hat, my cross, my Order of the Legion of Honor."

"That's just the point. If you weren't dressed that way, you would have to go home and change. Your episcopal cross, your forelock, your ring of powdered hair, they will create a scandal. And scandal is exactly what we need." Whereupon he propelled the archbishop out the door. For a just cause, someone had to go into the streets shouting: Long live the king! Also, this pint-size meddler had to look like a fool. Both objectives were met. The archbishop went into his act the moment he set foot in the rue Royale, where throngs waited to see the parade of victors. People stared at him. Once he reached the poor districts, the farce turned sour when the gawkers and beggars at his heels attracted a gang of roaming urchins who set up a rowdy counterdemonstration. Hastily stuffing the banner into his pocket, the archbishop fled, but not soon enough to avoid being roughly handled and spattered with mud. He made his way

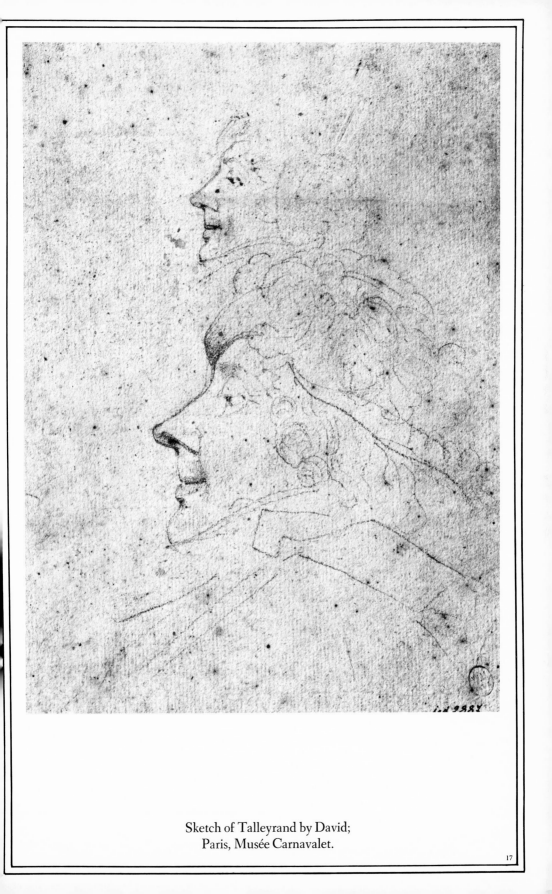

Sketch of Talleyrand by David;
Paris, Musée Carnavalet.

Detail of David's painting of Napoleon's coronation, 1804;
Paris, Musée du Louvre.

Talleyrand is in the right foreground
behind the man with the orb.

The Duke of Wellington by Goya; London, The British Museum.

The Duke d'Enghien, a prisoner in the moats at Vincennes.
Painting by Jean Paul Laurens; Chantilly, Musée Condé.

Eighteenth-century illustration of the entrance
and court of the Collège d'Harcourt;
Paris, Bibliothèque des Arts Décoratifs.

Detail from Gérard's painting
of Charles X's coronation, 1825;
Chartres, Musée des Beaux Arts.

"Le Petit Coblentz," the boulevard de Gand under the Directory.
Some of those caricatured are identified left to right as Isabey, Vestris,
Jᵐ Murat, Garat, Mme Récamier, Bonaparte, and, tipping his hat, Talleyrand.
Engraving by E. Loizelet; Paris, Bibliothèque Nationale.

Cartoon of the Congress of Vienna (May 13, 1815);
Paris, Bibliothèque Nationale.

Engraving by Blanchard of "A Parisian Seraglio or le Bon Ton de 1802."
Parisian life under the Consulate;
Paris, Bibliothèque Nationale.

A society ball under the Empire, engraving after Bosio;
Paris, Bibliothèque Nationale.

"The Man with Six Heads," a political cartoon from the April 1815 issue of *Le Nain Fou*. Talleyrand is shown wearing, simultaneously, the costumes of a bishop, a chamberlain of the Empire and a minister of Louis XVIII. The heads also show his various roles; and one hand carries a bishop's miter while the other holds a rocket with three pinwheels. The signature is Exxxxx (perhaps Eugène Delacroix); Paris, Bibliothèque Nationale.

Eugène Delacroix self-portrait;
Paris, Musée du Louvre.

French eighteenth-century portrait of Talleyrand
at sixteen; private collection.

Talleyrand by P. P. Prud'hon;
château de Valençay.

Painted by Prud'hon again in 1809, as vice-grand elector of the Empire;
Paris, collection of Count François de Castellane.

Again by Prud'hon;
Chevrier Marcille collection.

As the elder statesman by Ary Scheffer;
Chantilly, Musée Condé.

back to the rue Saint-Florentin along side streets, muddied, tattered, and panting for breath. His return to the drawing room was not precisely unnoticed. He reported his harrowing mission. Talleyrand listened, then replied coldly: "I warned you that dressed as you are presently, you would cause a sensation." [1] That was his only reward for insisting on a choice mission. The mission itself was not futile, for by nightfall many a household knew that "Long live the king!" had been shouted along the boulevards, meaning perhaps that the king would return.

Chateaubriand relates that even the princess of Benevento was mobilized for the propaganda effort. She had no reason to protest, having always been a staunch Bourbonite. She rode about Paris in her coach, he tells us, exalting the pious House of Bourbon. If what he says is true, then Madame Grand must have performed remarkably. Who knows? According to Chateaubriand, all royalists had to be either émigrés, or headless, or approved by him.

But royalism called for royalty. Where was this king? Talleyrand had brought one out of oblivion.

The czar did not look kindly on a Bourbon Restoration, preferring a Council of Regents to govern until Napoleon II, the king of Rome, attained majority. Austria agreed; Archduchess Marie Louise, the French regent, would not have opposed the wishes of her Hapsburg father, the emperor. England was pro-Bourbon, her regent committed to return Louis XVIII to his throne. England refused to deal with Napoleon, or Marie Louise, or his brothers, or any of their representatives. Fifteen years of war and a blockade had made up their minds. The Bourbons symbolized peace, reason, respect for law. As for Napoleon, he would rather have seen his wife and son dead than puppet rulers manipulated by Talleyrand, Fouché, and Metternich. He told Las Cases that he had ordered Marie Louise to leave Paris in order to "thwart all those who hoped that a regency would allow them to rule." Always cautious, Talleyrand would have accepted a regency council if Napoleon were not alive. But as long as he lived, the risks were too great. His existence would sow corruption in government, his agents would incite dissension among the people, leaving the country permanently on the brink of civil war.

About this time a rumor circulated that Talleyrand had tried to have the emperor assassinated. As Dalberg was constantly saying that Napoleon's sudden disappearance would simplify the political situation, the notion of assassination was just beyond. People even identified the assassin as someone brought to Talleyrand by Laborie on April 2, 1814, and ordered to dispatch Napoleon. He was an adventurer of noble

435

blood, who had fought briefly with the Chouans and then become somewhat warped. His name: the marquis de Maubreuil. Talleyrand always insisted that he never said anything of significance to the man. Yet some of Talleyrand's most innocent remarks are known to have been highly significant. Shortly afterwards, Maubreuil was arrested for attacking the queen of Westphalia's carriage and stealing her jewels and money—several million at the time. In self-defense, Maubreuil accused Talleyrand of supplying the men and funds to assassinate the emperor. But the charge makes no sense. Who would have benefited from the murder? Talleyrand? He was far too clever. The czar would not have condoned the crime, nor would England. Furthermore, such tactics were alien to our hero, who would not have risked his whole future just for a temporary gain.

His future was bound up with the Bourbons, though as a last resort. So the czar and Austria had to be won over. His *Memoirs* describe the arguments he employed. Could the throne be preserved for the family of the man "who had pushed France and Europe into the abyss" while that man still lived? "He would always be listening behind the door," as he put it. The Bourbons alone could provide what France desired because they represented *legitimacy*. Talleyrand did not coin the word, as some would claim; it was first uttered by Louis XVIII at the time of Napoleon's coronation. "Europe's prime need and greatest interest," Talleyrand wrote, "thus lay in banishing all doctrines of usurpation and reviving the principle of legitimacy, sole remedy for all the ills plaguing her, sole means of preventing their return." [2]

Here we see Talleyrand returning to a principle and sticking to it. In his eyes, a legitimate ruler is synonymous with the law. The law attains utmost force when incarnated by a ruler whose power is indisputable. He was not defending Louis XVIII or the House of Bourbon, he was defending France. This admirable sentence came from his pen: "Under the House of Bourbon, France ceased to be gigantic and became grand once again." Napoleon's remark was an echo: "If the nation seeks peace on the basis of its old boundaries, I shall say: 'Go look for another ruler, I am too great for you.'"

It involved a clash between two principles, or ideals: Empire *versus* Monarchy. Talleyrand wanted a monarchy because it represented moderation, stability, and endurance. He even quotes "an authority" who supported his view: Napoleon himself. Faced with defeat, Napoleon derived a sense of bitter satisfaction from the thought that only a Bourbon could rule France. His farewell address at Fontainebleau contained this surprising advice to his followers: "You must serve the Bourbons, gentlemen, as faithfully as you served me; if they are well advised, they will show you preferment." He was saying that Talleyrand would give them counsel. "It is to the interest of all of you that he [Talleyrand] remain with the government, for he will not share the bias of émigrés and persons who will return with the king. He may even teach him something about men and events." Too bad Napoleon himself had been unwilling to learn.

The words of the emperor at Fontainebleau on the eve of his attempted suicide conveyed a serenity and grandeur which vanished whenever his temper grew stormy.

> I forgive Talleyrand, for I mistreated him. He would not have remained in France if I had triumphed. The Bourbons will do well to employ him; he loves money and intrigue, but he is capable. I have always had a liking for him. I don't know how I allowed myself to quarrel with him over Maret, for both men were useful to me. . . . My affairs went well as long as Talleyrand handled them. It was his fault if he fell into my disfavor. Why did he want to leave the ministry? He knew France and Europe better than anyone. He will win over the émigrés without alienating the new men or yourselves. It is to your interest that he stays.

Talleyrand pleaded the cause of legitimacy so persuasively that the czar yielded. What were Russia's demands? That France remain at peace within her natural boundaries, and that she be strong enough to achieve a balance of power with Austria and England. Talleyrand argued that a Bourbon régime alone could keep France peaceful as well as strong: "To institute something durable and have it accepted without protest calls for action based on a principle. A principle makes us strong, minimizes resistance and, in any case, causes opposition to fade rapidly. And there is only one principle: Louis XVIII is a principle. He is the legitimate king of France." [3]

The czar asked him: "How do I know that France desires the House of Bourbon?"

"By a vote, Sire, that I shall have taken in the Senate, the result of which Your Majesty will see immediately."

"Are you sure?"

"I will answer for it, Sire." [4]

Everything was arranged during the night of March 31. No one slept in Paris. Allied soldiers and citizens roamed the streets. There was activity everywhere. Propriety and patriotism had collapsed simultaneously. Cossacks, Prussians, and Austrians could not complain about Parisian hospitality.

TALLEYRAND

Talleyrand held a dinner for the allied rulers and then took them to the opera. The glittering audience of prominent personalities behaved quite as improperly as the street mobs. In truth, Napoleon's fall did not induce national mourning. The victors were looked upon as liberators. In time, myths arose to mask these indignities.

The house on the rue Saint-Florentin blazed with light when they returned from the opera. Crowds of distinguished visitors lined the staircase and filled the reception rooms. Like a sovereign, Talleyrand received the sovereign heads of Europe.

During the night, his faithful band, including Jaucourt, Dalberg, Louis, and Pradt, sent messengers all over Paris to waken senators and deliver a summons for the next day while urging them to attend and give France a provisional government, a government free to express its will, a Constitution, a chamber with real legal and fiscal powers. Nothing definite was said about the nature of the régime or who would replace the "usurper," the name everyone used for Napoleon since the day before. Senators with republican fiber and a faint remembrance of Jacobin sentiment felt a stir of emotion; they rose from their beds and attended the meeting. Not all of them: only 63 out of 140. Those truly nostalgic for the Republic came. Like cavalry horses retired to pasture, peacefully growing old and fat but whinnying suddenly when the bugler in the village brass band strikes up *"Sambre et Meuse,"* the former Jacobins decked out in their splendid imperial harnesses executed a parade charge on hearing Talleyrand speak of constitutional liberties. They came and voted. Ailing senators sent their excuses and voted in bed. Talleyrand had the subtle pleasure of restoring the monarchy with the consent of Jacobin and regicide senators.

On April 1 he submitted the results of the voting and the list of senators' signatures to the czar. This prime organ of state called for deposing Napoleon, restoring the House of Bourbon, and readopting a Constitution. The czar yielded to what was termed in all seriousness "the popular will." Austria followed suit. England rejoiced, for Talleyrand had fulfilled her secret desires. While our diplomat was on the best of terms with Alexander, he was actually a far better friend of the English. When the time came, he needed only to nod in the direction of London in order to renew their thwarted but persistent courtship.

Later, the royalists tried to minimize Talleyrand's part in the Restoration. Nothing infuriated them more than hearing him tell distinguished visitors, as he showed them the Salon of the Eagle on the rue Saint-Florentin and pointed to the table at which Alexander I, the king of Prussia, Schwarzenberg, and Castlereagh had sat, "Yes, gentlemen, in this very room we restored the Bourbon throne and a monarchy fourteen centuries old." Yet Vitrolles, who knew better than anyone that without Talleyrand Russia, Austria, and the French themselves never would have recalled Louis XVIII, wrote that "he endured the Restoration as a necessity and confronted it with all his courage." He did not endure it, he created it; he did not confront it, he imposed it.

The Jacobins were committed by their vote. Now the royalists began to strut about, thinking that once "the renegade" had done his work, they would send him flying. Talleyrand taught them and the king a lesson in humility. Two visitors came to him. First, the comte de Sémallé, the comte d'Artois's emissary, wanted an audience with the czar. Talleyrand politely informed him that the czar was not available and made it clear that he, not the czar, was handling the affairs of France. All spoken very gently and with a moist eye attesting to the tender secrets he and the comte d'Artois shared as a result of their memorable conversation on the night of July 17, 1789. Despite the flowers and honey, Sémallé found himself playing second fiddle to Talleyrand who, the next day, was elected president of the provisional government, hence master of France. He advised Sémallé to see that the Bourbons entered Paris bearing the tricolor flag, not the flag of truce. When Sémallé protested, Talleyrand replied: "Do you think, sir, that the interests of a nation can be sacrificed to the vanity of one family?" The whiplike remark covered eight centuries of history, all the way back to the year 987. The Périgord of 1814 was plainly acting as king-maker to his Capetian contemporary, just as his ancestor Adalbert de Périgord had crowned the first Capetian. Talleyrand assumed what amounted to a hereditary right to mold his nation's history. No one had better credentials than he to represent France and turn her face to the future.

The second visitor, Caulaincourt, caused more excitement. Caulaincourt, still loyal to Napoleon, arrived from Fontainebleau with messages from the vanquished emperor whom he supported more strongly than ever. Twice he knocked at the door of the hôtel de Talleyrand and twice was turned away. Such loyalty on the part of the imperial master of the horse was now unseemly. His fine sentiments were irksome and totally useless. Caulaincourt made a third attempt, approaching the czar at the close of a council session. Talleyrand could only watch and worry, for Alexander was very fond of Caulaincourt. What would happen? Would he grant him an audience, or listen to him? Would the impressionable czar weaken and change his mind? Talleyrand heard Caulaincourt tell the czar that Napoleon accepted all his conditions. Alexander replied: "Too late." Caulaincourt withdrew, leaving Talleyrand to sigh with relief: "Caulaincourt has been definitely refused." He did not conceal his pleasure.

At Fontainebleau, the usurper had no choice but to abdicate and release his "faithful" followers, who could not wait to offer their services to the new masters of Paris.

The Senate-appointed provisional government headed by Talleyrand included such names as Jaucourt, Dalberg, Beurnonville, and the abbé de Montesquiou. Chateaubriand said that Talleyrand had peopled the government with his "whist partners." Indeed, the similarities were striking.

On April 2, Talleyrand had the Senate vote the acknowledgment of Napoleon's abdication and the authorization for an address to the French army, some sections of which had not heard about the recent events and were still fighting, absolving them of allegiance to Napoleon, "a man who is not even French." The phrase came from Fontanes, an official of the Empire whom Napoleon had showered with favors. After surrendering his troops, Marmont arrived wan and harried at the rue Saint-Florentin; much to his amazement, he was greeted like a hero. Talleyrand said: "Let him eat first and talk later." A sumptuous meal was set before Marmont, while his host, with a certain sense of satisfaction, observed this marshal of the Empire who had yielded so readily to pressure.

Talleyrand took Dupont de Nemours as adviser, a brilliant man whom he had known since the Directory. Roux de Laborie remained his private secretary; he knew everything and could do what had to be done at any and all hours.

A sure sign of success was the arrival of a flattering letter dated April 3, 1814, from Benjamin Constant, a discriminating man. He was surfacing again, the 18th Brumaire and his close ties with Madame de Staël having forced him to lie low. "It is pleasant to express admiration for a man who is at once the saviour of France and the most amiable of Frenchmen. I write this after reading the basic tenets of the projected Constitution."

Disregarding the customary blandishments, that opinion is worth noting as it indicates that the Constitution which Talleyrand was drafting and hoping to have the king sign before royalist opposition could solidify was regarded by a discerning liberal as a return to liberty and legality. "Forgive me if I do not list your titles. Europe and history will gladly do so, but the proudest title will always be that of president of the Senate." [5]

Not all the reaction was quite so complimentary. Journalists began finding their voices again, and using them. Contemporary cartoonists depicted Talleyrand as a weathervane, dubbing him "the six-headed man," "Mr. Sail-with-the-wind," "Mr. Fair Wind," or "Mr. Whirligig." Those who sneered at the "weathervane" would have realized, had they looked around, that the great majority of Frenchmen were also turning in the wind. The only difference was that Talleyrand whirled so that others would copy him.

Some spoke of a rash of "betrayals," others of an effort to "change," or "adapt," or simply to "survive." When desertion is widespread, the loyal few stand out like sore thumbs. Like poor Caulaincourt. Everyone rushed into line at the rue Saint-Florentin hoping for a fine position in the new government; generals who had wept crocodile tears yesterday in the courtyard at Fontainebleau; magistrates who had consigned to the galleys all those who refused to serve in Napoleon's army. Merlin of Thionville, the extremist responsible for the butchery of August 10, became the monarchy's noisiest adherent in his desperate efforts to win a niche in the new régime. He even offered to organize volunteers for restoring the monarchy, this man who had murdered persons suspected of harboring Louis XVI. Why did Talleyrand refuse his services? The sight of so many fortune-hunters gave him an idea: he sent one of his aides to find out whether Josephine would support the Bourbons. Her refusal proved that at least one loyal soul remained. By now the deserters were common and flagrant; no need to coddle them. Furthermore, our prince was toying with two of them. He told Marmont, Napoleon's once trusted confidant, that Jourdan had made his troops raise the royal cockade. It was a lie. Then he told Jourdan that Marmont and his troops had defected. As neither general cared to be caught napping, they and their armies hastily donned the royalist cockade.[6] All this stage play afforded his Serene Highness a certain satisfaction.

From his window he followed the *Te Deum* in the place Louis XV honoring the allied rulers or their deputies, the very spot where Louis XVI and his queen had been beheaded.

Talleyrand sent his brother Archambaud into the streets on the same flag-waving mission that he had assigned to the abbé de Pradt. After all, what could he do with a brother "so handsome and so stupid" except to make him into a flag? On the rue du faubourg Saint-Honoré, members of the national guard were cocking their rifles at the sight of this agitator with a screaming mob at his heels, when just in time they recognized the prince's brother.

We know that every great man is something of an actor. Fresh proof of the fact is seen here. Talleyrand decided to present to the czar and the king of Prussia the senators whose vote had determined the recent events. Despite their known flexibility, some of these senators refused to bow to the victors. Undiscouraged, our resourceful prince put out a call for about forty toadies to fill the seats at a lavish supper created by Carême and served upon silver dishes, who, at a given signal would lift their glasses to toast the king. Being a senator was unnecessary; looking like one was enough. So Talleyrand dressed his forty actors like senators of the Empire, rehearsed them, and their lusty "Long live Louis XVIII!" rang with greater than senatorial conviction. The czar was well satisfied with this royalist demonstration. Talleyrand too.

The King Presents Himself, Crown and All; Talleyrand Presents Him with a Constitution

Time was running out. The Constitution had to be ready for the king's arrival. On April 3 a committee met at the rue Saint-Florentin and presented the draft of a document which was nothing other than a carbon copy of the Constitution of 1791. Talleyrand recognized it at once from having served in the Constituent Assembly. He rejected it, telling the senators that Louis XVIII would not accept a hollow Constitution. "The prince who must accept and implement it is best equipped to judge it," he said somewhat anxiously. Louis XVIII, unlike the Spanish Bourbons, had eyes in his head and used them. Talleyrand sent the committee back to work and by April 10 they had prepared a text known as the Constitutional Charter. Talleyrand accepted it. That same day he wrote to the duchess of Courland: "The family dinner will not be until Monday. . . . Come for dinner and bring Dorothée. I embrace you. Read the first twenty lines of Le Moniteur. Everything is done and well done." [1]

In fact Le Moniteur proclaimed that "Louis-Stanislas-Xavier of France was recalled by the will of the French people according to a constitutional charter." [2]

The Empire became history; the Restoration dawned.

Besides affairs of state, Talleyrand thought of his own pressing affairs. On April 7 he sent a certain Villers to the Tuileries to round up all the files which our hero had kept on the duc d'Enghien episode and the outbreak of the war with Spain. The keeper of records refused to turn them over. A second instance of loyalty to the emperor! He was fired at once and replaced—momentarily—by Villers. The temporary appointment lasted just long enough for him to carry off those particular files and burn them. Everything except that one letter from Talleyrand to Napoleon which slipped down behind a drawer, only to be found later and used by Chateaubriand to incriminate Talleyrand in the duc d'Enghien's death. Aimée de Coigny observed mischievously: "M. de Talleyrand burns very efficiently." Afterwards, Villers turned his job back to the obstinate Bonapartist, leaving him to reign over empty file boxes.

As our hero needed money and was in a good position to get it, he sold his country house at Saint-Brice for a tidy sum. All he had to do was brazenly intimidate the license-holder of all the gambling houses in the capital. He gave him a choice of buying Saint-Brice for 800,000 francs or having the license to his livelihood revoked. (Saint-Brice, incidentally, was worth 200,000 francs.) The transaction was concluded. Talleyrand may have taken the attitude that after so many years of gaming losses, he was due at last for a rebate.

On Easter Day he gave a dinner worth noting. Rather than a diplomatic affair, it was a "family" dinner notwithstanding the presence of the czar. Talleyrand wrote: "I am inviting Archambaud and would like Dorothée to preside because Archambaud is dining with us. She is to receive him in my house." A new note. And what of the duchess, her mother? Edmond is out of the picture, an allied prisoner. This appears to be the first dinner at which Dorothée presided, the start of a prestigious career as hostess. The Treaty of Fontainebleau was signed the next day, April 11. Stripped of authority in France and Italy, Bonaparte was granted sovereign title for life to the Island of Elba and retained the right to be addressed as emperor.

In imposing those terms, Alexander knowingly irritated Talleyrand and the English, who had both hoped to send Napoleon farther away, to the Azores. He was too big to keep so close at hand. As Talleyrand put it, he could "listen at the door." It amused the czar to dangle this sword of Damocles over western Europe.

On April 12, Talleyrand and members of the provisional government went to meet the comte d'Artois at the gates of Paris. The comte d'Artois had taken the title "Lieutenant General of the Realm." Talleyrand tells us in his *Memoirs*: "He was as kind to me then as on the night of July 17, 1789, when we each went our separate ways, he to exile, I plunging into the whirlwind that left me ultimately head of the provisional government."

A convenient linking of those two dates. And in fact, the whirlwind had brought Talleyrand round to placing the murdered king's brother on the throne. If the comte d'Artois was gracious, Talleyrand was a paragon of courtly deference. "Sire, the joy we feel on this day of regeneration is beyond expression. . . ." And this was the man who told Madame de Staël: "For France, the House of Bourbon is finished." Calling him a liar is too simple. Instead, note that while our hero is pouring out his florid message, he leans casually against the king's brother's leg as the latter sits astride his horse. And with the same impudence he had once displayed during Mass at the Feast of the Federation, he now places himself on a familiar footing with the erstwhile king of royal dandies. With a word, Talleyrand made it clear to the notables surrounding the count that a Périgord was totally at ease with princes of the blood. For his part, Monsieur, the king's brother, murmured some gracious comment for Talleyrand's ears alone.

That night, April 12, Monsieur slept in the Tuileries and Talleyrand under his own roof, where quiet now reigned. The czar had moved into the Elysée Palace and the bed of Caroline Bonaparte, Madame Murat, queen of Naples. Talleyrand went to sleep at his usual hour, about three o'clock, after editing a description of the comte d'Artois's return to Paris. The real event was immaterial; it had to be blown up into something momentous. Patrons of Le Moniteur would read the definitive account of a royal prince's entry into the capital founded by Saint Louis. Beugnot was in charge of sketching out the article. When Dupont de Nemours asked to help, Talleyrand objected, saying: "No, not you. You would turn it into a poem, I know you. Beugnot will do for this. . . ." Beugnot's Memoirs relate the incident. Nobody could remember what Monsieur had said, including Talleyrand, who urged: "Make up a little speech for him." Beugnot hesitated to put words in the prince's mouth. Talleyrand reassured him: "After two days he will believe he said it, and he will have said it. You won't have had anything to do with it." Beugnot's first draft was rather stiff and bombastic. Talleyrand told him: "Make it short and simple." Beugnot came back with his second effort, which was also rejected. "I made it too long, too affected," he admitted. Then the third attempt:

> Finally I came up with the version in Le Moniteur which has the prince saying: "No more divisions! Peace and France! At last I see my country again. Nothing has changed except there is one more Frenchman."
> "You've done it at last," said Talleyrand. "That was indeed what Monsieur said; I warrant those were his very words. Now you can relax." [3]

Just as Talleyrand had anticipated, the newspapers joyously pounced on Beugnot's final phrase. Every speaker somehow wove it into his text. "There is one more Frenchman" made an instant hit. And proudest of all was the comte d'Artois, its author; he imagined himself uttering the words to a wildly cheering throng; he quoted himself, interpreted himself, reveled in his own genius. Talleyrand had no trouble convincing him that he was indispensable to the realm.

Fouché had returned from Naples on April 8. Heading for the rue Saint-Florentin, he dined there and came back often. The two men renewed their alliance. For the moment, Fouché had no influence. Talleyrand brought him to the Senate for a meeting of the provisional government. At once he realized that Fouché sided with him on two issues involving a clash with the royalists, typical clashes revealing the gulf between new men like Talleyrand and diehards of the Ancien Régime who had "learned nothing and forgotten nothing."

The first eruption came on April 13. Sémallé incited it by referring to the crown jewels, worth 8 or 10 million, which the empress had taken with her and which were later recovered at Orléans. Sémallé had turned them over to the comte d'Artois. Talleyrand objected to such a fortune being handed over to a royal prince as if it were his personal property. He and Fouché maintained that Marie Louise's coffers were national property and belonged to the treasury. Sémallé and Montesquiou protested that only the king could dispose of them. It was decided to await the king's arrival. Though he appeared to yield, Talleyrand did not forget that the Constitution superseded the "acts of princes."

The comte d'Artois's title "Lieutenant General of the Realm" was another issue. Who gave it to him? Sémallé and Montesquiou claimed that it came "from his brother, the king." Talleyrand reminded them that there was a government, a Senate, a Constitution, and that any political title assumed by Monsieur required Senate approval. Monsieur must appear before that body, address it formally, and be duly confirmed in his office by an official organ of state. Monsieur was ill-advised, after listening to Vitrolles, to suggest that his brother would have objections to the Constitution. Already, only two days after Monsieur's return! That was the first rift.

Talleyrand had sent an emissary, a friend, to greet the comte d'Artois on his approach to Paris. He was Ouvrard, whom we already know. How can any government exist without one or more Ouvrards to lean on? A banker coming between Talleyrand and the new régime's representative could mean only one thing: money. And plenty of it. Where from, and in what form? Barras, an inveterate meddler, assured posterity that after heading the provisional government for a week, Talleyrand cleared 28 million. The outlandish figure at once discredits the story. It is quite probable that England rewarded him for protecting her interests. The czar did not give him money. The Bourbons probably were the most generous of all, as with Nesselrode, on whom they bestowed lavish gifts "far greater than those customarily received by diplomats." Talleyrand's venality was not exceptional, only his ability to make and spend money.

But Barras's estimates of Talleyrand's fortune cannot be taken seriously. He is too dishonest to speak honestly of anyone, especially Talleyrand, whom he hated. Chateaubriand's censure is quite as venomous, but at least does not name any figures. "When M. de Talleyrand is not conspiring he is involved in some sort of swindle." Not quite accurate, for our hero was able to do both simultaneously. A journalist remarked that the prince's wealth was no great surprise as "he had sold out everyone who had bought him." And while the arrows fly, let us quote one more observer with a rather different viewpoint: "M. de Talleyrand is a man of infinite wit who is constantly in need of money." Stendhal said that.

Madame de Staël returned to Paris as promptly as the Bourbons. Talleyrand called on her; the meeting was not a brilliant success.

A Caustic Encounter Between the Descendants of Hugh Capet and of Adalbert

Since the capitulation, nothing had been done to end the existing state of war between France and the allies. On April 19, 1814, Metternich proposed that Talleyrand sign an armistice. Talleyrand accepted the terms it imposed. France was reduced to the borders of 1792, not those of the Treaty of Lunéville, as Talleyrand had hoped. Napoleon had refused to make peace after the Russian campaign. "Negotiate while you have pledges," the prince had warned him. Today, every army in Europe was occupying France; the pledges were gone. France was deprived even of the conquests of the Revolution, sanctioned at Lunéville. Such was the outcome of Napoleon's glorious wars.

Many of Talleyrand's enemies blamed him for the harsh terms. However painful a blow to national pride was struck by the loss of territorial gains from the Revolution, which rounded out so neatly the frontiers won by the kings of France, one has to admit in all fairness that the loss of Napoleon's exorbitant conquests was inevitable. Talleyrand had to accept it. In the first place, far worse terms could have been imposed if someone else had been heading the provisional government. He was criticized for giving up French military strongholds such as Antwerp

446

and Hamburg which had never surrendered. But what could he do with them: tell their French defenders to fight to the last and never give up? Did anyone think those bastions could have held out against all of Europe? Did they forget that France stood alone, without a single ally, that universal reprobation deprived her even of the hope of winning friends? These firebrands bent on preserving the boundaries of the Empire, had they forgotten as they sat comfortably in Paris offices or smoke-filled coffeehouses that all of northern and eastern France, almost to the gates of Paris, was in the hands of Uhlans and Cossacks? And that from the Pyrenees to Bordeaux, England and Spain were in control? Once again Talleyrand was branded "traitor" for not defending that which was indefensible. In reality, during 1814 and 1815, grim years, he was truly "the man of France" as Dr. Lafforgue calls him, using a phrase from the *Memoirs*. Talleyrand won Europe's trust and quelled her desire for revenge, having none himself.

Talleyrand's common sense and consistent policies are familiar to us. This is how he justified his attitude in 1814: "The armistice was both necessary and politic. There was a need to replace the allies' force with confidence, but first to inspire them with it." [1]

Wisely, he chose to present France as peace-seeking, and indeed the country needed peace, needed to re-enter the community of nations, to erase the distrust and hatred that Napoleon's armies instilled in the peoples of conquered nations. That hatred still persists, especially in Spain.

The armistice agreement was signed on April 23, 1814. His critics complain, for once, that he moved too fast; he should have talked some more, they say, dragged out the discussions. How can anyone forget that the armistice was indispensable? France, at war with Europe since 1792, was exhausted, economically ruined. Of course, some people may feel that he adopted a rather frivolous attitude toward "his armistice" in a letter to the duchess on April 23: "I have finished my armistice. Even as it stands, it's a good piece of work. Later on, a month from now, we shall have the peace treaty." The bantering tone reflects his urbanity, not his true feelings. Elsewhere he spoke of the "grievous and humiliating" terms of this armistice. At least "This convention dealt with the most urgent matters, which were the freeing of territories, release of prisoners, repatriation of French troops beyond the Rhine, and the cessation of impoverishing requisitions." [2]

Quite an achievement. Two months after Napoleon's defeat, Talleyrand had ended the occupation and brought French prisoners home. Having to give up Nice, Savoy, and the Rhine was indeed mortifying, but whose fault was it: Talleyrand's, forced to endure a despot's rule, or Napoleon's, the cause of it all?

Interestingly enough, most non-French historians point out how lucky France was in her crisis to have had Talleyrand shielding the defeated nation against the wrath of her vengeful conquerors, whereas certain French authors blame him for bargaining less effectively than if Napoleon had been victorious.

All this was going on minus the king. When would His Majesty make an appearance? Perhaps Talleyrand had come up with a singularly unhurried ruler. Finally, on April 24, His Unhurried and Ungainly Majesty touched shore at Calais. Talleyrand sent his brother Boson (the deaf one) to meet the king. In the interim, he bombarded His Majesty with a series of diplomatic notes recommending, not unwisely, among other things, that the Constitution be adopted even if it appeared somewhat too liberal. Those tactless comments dropped by the comte d'Artois on his arrival boded no good.

There were also private notes: "M. de Talleyrand willingly devotes his whole life to serving the king and asks nothing in return." And in the same breath: "He deems his presence necessary at the ministry of foreign relations and asks to head that office." Hardly a request as far as he was concerned; he took the matter for granted. Next, "he entreats the king's gracious consent to grant to M. Edmond de Périgord the title of first aide-de-camp of his royal person and to Madame Edmond de Périgord the title of lady-in-waiting to the queen, a privilege of which her conduct and piety render her worthy." It was true that her conduct and austere piety had gained even Napoleon's attention; Louis XVIII would remember the remark. "He also recommends M. Edmond de Périgord to His Majesty's attention when the first dukes and peers are created." [3] As merit (surely the uncle's) deserved recognition, Edmond de Périgord was promoted to the rank of brigadier general.

Talleyrand proceeded to Compiègne where, on April 29, 1814, he was received for the first time by Louis XVIII. It was not the most convivial encounter for either one. They did not know each other. Both men were nearly sixty years old. One dragged a foot, the other both feet. They had many reasons to detest each other and, as a matter of fact, had already proclaimed them all. Neither had any illusions about their mutual good will, or, for that matter, the good will of humanity. Talleyrand had a keen mind, the king also. Talleyrand knew the old society as intimately as the new one; the king was less familiar with the new one but capable of applying his first-hand experience of old world politics to the current situation and seeing what went on—which he knew about anyway, but only second-hand, whereas Talleyrand was in the thick of it. They both knew what they were talking about. Talleyrand would have preferred to find the king more nimble physically and less so mentally. But he took him as he was, though none too readily at that. From the start, Louis XVIII wanted this renegade bishop and husband of the Grand woman to know that he, the king, was dealing with him only out of necessity. To make that perfectly plain, he kept Talleyrand waiting for three hours. Old wives' revenge. Instead of thanks, he offered humiliation, the kind that produces only bitterness, with sometimes shocking results. When Talleyrand was finally admitted, the king held out his hand cordially and delivered this little speech to the son of the counts of Périgord: "I am glad to see you. Our houses date back to the same period. My ancestors were more clever. If yours had been cleverer than mine, you would now be telling me: draw up a chair, sit by me, and let us discuss our business. But it is I who say to you: sit down and let us talk." [4]

Very shrewdly, the king ignored the Revolution and everything since that might be termed the bone of contention. At the same time, he touched upon the one source of Talleyrand's pride, his noble ancestry, and also put him in his place—"sit down and let us talk"—in case Talleyrand had built up any illusions of self-importance because of his role in the Restoration. Yet that much recognition from the sovereign was not to be scoffed at. Louis adopted a more bantering tone as the audience progressed. With apparent irony, he confessed wide-eyed admiration for the ease with which Talleyrand, after serving the Directory and the Empire, had overthrown the former to install the latter, and then the latter to return to common sense. With serene self-confidence, Talleyrand replied softly yet ominously: "Good heavens, Sire, I really had nothing to do with all that; it is something mysterious inside of me that brings misfortune to governments which neglect me." [5]

Like an alert player, Louis must have countered the warning with a smile not calculated to gladden his subject's heart. Talleyrand's remembrance of this episode was none too pleasant. As he came from the audience chamber, he told Beugnot: "We have parted content with each other." But later on, Colmache, his secretary in London, was privy to quite another version: "Louis XVIII was the world's most arrant liar. I cannot tell you how disappointed I was after meeting with him for the first time in 1814 . . . I could tell the man's character by the way he greeted me. Egotistical, insensitive, epicurean, ungrateful, that is how I have always found Louis XVIII." Strange; it sounds more like Chateaubriand describing the bishop of Autun.

The king and the prince met again at Saint-Ouen, where the full Senate awaited Louis XVIII. Talleyrand presented this body to its sovereign. His speech, of course, was a torrent of flattery. Still, one would prefer not to think of the prince of Benevento saying: "In returning to the throne, you are succeeding twenty years of ruin and misfortune." For a certain period of time had he not helped to administer that "ruin and misfortune"? In any event, he had the tact to remove from the declaration signed at Saint-Ouen, forerunner of the new Charter, this needlessly provocative phrase accompanying the date: "of the year 1814 and the nineteenth of our reign." [6] Foolishly, the phrase was restored later on.

On May 11, our hero attended another solemn Mass in Notre Dame, this time for the repose of Louis XVI's soul. He attended as minister for foreign affairs. The king had granted his request to change the name from "foreign relations." Now Talleyrand proudly bore the title of his illustrious predecessors Choiseul and Vergennes.

At the close of Mass, he remarked lightly but typically: "That cleanses the soil of France. After such a ceremony, everything ought to be forgotten." If only the émigrés and Jacobins had listened.

The Problems of Treaty-Making, of Serving a Legitimate Monarch, and of Remaining Friends with a Czar

For the third time in its history—and in the history of France—Talleyrand reoccupied the foreign ministry. With utter composure he took his oath of allegiance to Louis XVIII. Oaths never disturbed him; they were a hobby of sorts, judging by the number he had made since his seminary days. The unusual quantity of them prompted his remark to the king: "Sire, it is my thirteenth; I hope it will be the last." Being kept waiting three hours for an audience was not something to be taken lightly.

Now only business took him to the rue du Bac, where he would tour the various offices and maintain personal contact with his staff. He continued to live in high style on the rue Saint-Florentin. The cream of European society gathered there. Wellington and he struck up a friendship, linking him once more to England. Madame de Staël appeared regularly. "I am vexed that you did not come to my house yesterday evening. Wellington came; he stayed for ages. Madame de Staël was here. That made for a lively evening," he wrote to the duchess on June 10, 1814.[1]

450

Madame Grand was still there, much more voluminous and much less voluble than in the days of the Directory and smugly enthroned on something resembling a cathedra, with her feet resting on a cushion the size of a breastplate on which she had embroidered the arms of the Périgords. Like Napoleon, and like other women of easy virtue, she might have said: "My life is an adventure story." Though dazzled by this unhoped-for benevolence of fortune, she was under orders from her husband to keep silent.

As for him, he remained indifferent to criticism, slander, caricature, or insult, openly frequenting the fashionable public houses. He ate ices at Tortoni's; like an expert he appraised the feminine fashions worn by exquisite "ladies" who regularly visited those places. He was seen there with Blacas, Louis XVIII's favorite, the mere approach of whom made Talleyrand ill. Still, Blacas had free access to the king, Blacas had the king's ear, and the king listened to Blacas. Now there was a man to watch.

Occasionally he was a target of ridicule. An English cartoonist depicted him, flanked by his wife, facing the king in Notre Dame. The caption read: "Paris, May 6: Yesterday after Mass, Mgr the bishop of Autun had the honor of presenting his wife to the son of Saint Louis." Nowadays people hardly smile at that, but in 1814 the three lines must have enraged many a royalist.

A more important matter was the post of prime minister, which he had sought but which the king would not give him. So adamant was his insistence that Louis XVIII, knowing the office rightly belonged to the man who had restored the monarchy, refused to fill it rather than consign it to Talleyrand.

The Treaty of Paris was signed on May 31. It spelled out the relations between France and Europe, but did not settle outstanding differences between various European states. The treaty repeated the terms of the armistice. It provided for ending the occupation of France, returning French prisoners, and eliminating the requisitions imposed by the occupying forces. In his *Memoirs*, Talleyrand said: "When I think of the date of those treaties of 1814, of the many difficulties I encountered, of the spirit of revenge I found in some of the negotiators with whom I dealt and which I was obliged to combat, I await with confidence posterity's judgment." And he added: "In the end, we kept all the marvelous art objects taken by force from museums all over Europe." That, too, was important. In 1815, alas, the allies remembered how Napoleon had plundered their treasure houses, and they plundered the French ones.

This treaty, like everything Talleyrand did, was hotly debated in

451

the years ahead. We who are removed from the antagonisms and rivalries of those times can better weigh its merits. Diplomats, historians, and foreigners in particular speak of it more kindly than politicians. Lyautey, a great patriot and humanitarian whose stature is beyond question, said of the treaty: "After a war so hopelessly lost, could a better peace be won?" We must remember that Talleyrand, who loved his country intensely, was a product of the eighteenth century and therefore more of a European than a "Jacobin patriot." He firmly believed that the nations of Europe had common interests. Boundaries seemed to him an outworn concept; like Voltaire and the prince de Ligne, he considered them purely conventional divisions between civilized nations, whereas the one valid boundary separated Enlightened Europe—England, Austria, Germany, and France—from eastern Europe. That was why he pleaded desperately with Napoleon not to overrun Austria, for the Hapsburg Empire was Europe's sentinel on the threshold of Asia. When Napoleon's Empire collapsed, Talleyrand did the best he could to salvage what he could of France. His own efforts did not dissatisfy him: "I have finished my treaty with the four great powers. . . . It is a very good one, based on perfect equality, and even noble. . . . My friends, and especially you, ought to be pleased with me," he wrote to the duchess. His friends may have been pleased; but what about others? [2]

For two months he went at an exhausting pace, working tirelessly round the clock for weeks on end. The multitude of budding intrigues, subterfuges, betrayals, reversals, defeats, and even successes was wearing him out. "A few more weeks and I hope to return to a work schedule free of pressure," he wrote. Peace, he thought, was meant for him too.

Not so. Louis XVIII gave him more headaches than inflexible diplomats. By incessant tampering with the Constitution, the king and his cohorts reduced it to an instrument of absolute power, or nearly so. Talleyrand and his friends were no paragons of virtue and austerity, but they possessed a keen sense of reality and knew that France without a liberal Constitution was ungovernable. France and the monarchy could prosper only by respecting this national aspiration. Talleyrand told this to the king. But Louis XVIII, who listened only to his brother, to Blacas, to Vitrolles and his ultra-royalist friends, did just the opposite. Talleyrand was shocked and upset that the free press abolished by Napoleon was not restored. He had campaigned in good faith for the king, thinking that a stable monarchy would revive civil liberties. He went a step further by publicly condemning the reinstitution of Catholicism as the state religion. It was one of the reasons for those fierce attacks by the author of *Le Génie du christianisme* and *Les Martyrs* against this un-frocked official who dared to demand freedom of conscience.

Another issue further widened the breach. Royalists, with the king's support, wanted deputies to serve without pay. It would guarantee that such posts went to the rich. "The service of deputies will be that much more honorable because it is given for nothing," declared the king. "Yes, Sire," Talleyrand replied, without conviction, "but what is given for nothing will cost us dear." [3] He knew that people who line their own pockets can be a drain.

On June 3, the czar left Paris. Talleyrand was stunned. Alexander refused an audience and left without seeing him again. What had caused the rift? Talleyrand wrote a long letter to the czar several days later protesting that he had taken no part in weakening the Constitution. We know that he openly blamed this on the king and his party. But Alexander was convinced that Talleyrand had made a hollow promise to adopt a liberal Constitution only to win Russia's support for the Bourbons, and that he really wanted to revive an absolute monarchy. The czar obviously was mistaken; this readiness on the part of St. Petersburg's autocrat to blame Talleyrand for not being liberal enough is a curious twist. In 1814, serfdom in Russia was more rigorous than in thirteenth-century France. In any event, away from home the Little Father felt free to indulge his Jacobin fancies—provided the Jacobins stayed in Paris where they belonged. Talleyrand's superb letter absolving himself, flattering the czar, and reminding him of their past friendly relations in an effort to regain his favor went unanswered. The rift was serious—and inevitable. Misinformation and czarist whimsy provoked it but do not explain the deeper causes. The czar supported Talleyrand's aims as long as Napoleon was disrupting Europe, but once Napoleon went down to defeat, Alexander was clearly an obstacle to the reconstruction of western Europe. Talleyrand had ceased to be useful to the czar. Thus the temporary friends went their separate ways, the czar to Moscow, seat of greedy ambitions to overrun Europe, and Talleyrand to Europe, intent on opposing the thrust from the East.*

---

* To indicate the way in which certain French historians overly fascinated with Napoleon have depicted Talleyrand, we quote this alarming sentence of Louis Madelin's (*Talleyrand*, p. 220): "It is probable that the Russian ruler, who was more French than some Frenchmen, did not limit his disapproval to the prince's domestic policies and extended his severity to his complacent attitude in settling the problem of boundaries." "It is probable," as this historian puts it, that Talleyrand had to be discredited at any cost.

In time of need, Louis XVIII could forget his scruples long enough to entrust Talleyrand with the responsibilities—but not the title—of a prime minister. He called on him to present the appropriations bill developed by baron Louis. Talleyrand thus revived his talent for high finance and the memory of his experience as the clergy's representative and recorder to the Constituent Assembly. He made an excellent speech before the Chamber of Peers, which inspired confidence in baron Louis's fiscal program. And indeed, baron Louis was a remarkable finance minister. France enjoyed a period of great fiscal stability during the Restoration.

Talleyrand's position at court was most uncomfortable. After the duchesse d'Angoulême gave him a surly reception, he had no reason to expect any different attitude from the royal family. The comte d'Artois and his clique scorned everyone connected however slightly with the Revolution and the Empire. It was foolish, for those "repentant" revolutionists would have stooped to anything to redeem themselves. In the army, officers of the Empire were removed and their places given to officers of the Condé or Vendée regiments. In short, the new monarch created enemies right and left after the nation had welcomed him so trustfully.

Talleyrand was kept out of sight. Blacas alone had any influence on the king: "The prince of Benevento has none at the moment," a foreign ambassador reported. "And he complains of it. Well-informed persons seem to think that he will keep his position and that the king, while sharply curtailing his sphere of activity, values his ability too much to part with it for good."

This was well observed. Louis XVIII was keeping his dangerous minister in reserve to send to the Congress of Vienna. The king was too shrewd to overlook the fact that he had Europe's most artful diplomat at hand. Sending him to Vienna would rid Paris of his disturbing presence. Let him intrigue against other nations; here in the capital he was likely to intrigue against the throne. In short, Louis XVIII and his circle cheered the departure of Talleyrand, whom they could not stand.

Preparations for the Great Parade of Vienna

It had been decided that two months after the Treaty of Paris was signed, a Congress would take place in Vienna to discuss the application of the treaty and to rebuild Europe on the ruins of the Empire. France had retained merely the right of representation at the Congress, but had no vote. She could listen but had no deliberative power. The four victors, England, Austria, Prussia, and Russia, had the power. France sat on the sidelines, along with Sweden, Spain, Denmark, Portugal, and the German states. That made for a large silent company. The "small powers," as they were known, were expected to behave themselves and wait hopefully for scraps to come their way—or be taken from them if they proved uncooperative, too weak, or lacked effective representation. Europe thus would establish "a real and durable stability," said the Big Four. The stability they had in mind involved dividing up the spoils of the Empire.

Before leaving for Vienna, Talleyrand had long conversations with the king. Together they drew up a detailed set of instructions for Talleyrand to take with him. On a one-to-one basis, the king and his minister got along very well. Away from his court and, in particular, from his brother, Louis showed himself to be amazingly astute, discerning, and deeply concerned for his country. "I think that when these Instructions are known, France will be proud of the sovereign who has signed them," Talleyrand wrote to the duchess. Unfortunately, the pleasant interlude was not repeated. People have said that the Instructions, a model of their kind as to style, clarity, and vision, were written by La Besnardière. They have the unmistakable ring of Talleyrand.

The king charged him to pursue four objectives vital to French security: to prevent Austria or any prince of her House from ever ruling over states belonging to the king of Sardinia; to restore Naples to its legitimate Bourbon sovereign Ferdinand IV; to keep Poland forever out of Russian hands; and to see that Prussia did not acquire either Saxony or the Rhineland.

There were several reasons for the last. Louis XVIII felt friendly toward King Frederick Augustus, who, as an ally of France, was a target of the coalition powers. Also, political reasoning dictated that Prussian expansion must be blocked in eastern Europe as well as along the Rhine where she had no right to be. The objectives perhaps were irreconcilable; future history would show their frightful consequences.

Talleyrand did not set out single-handed to press his case. The eternal Dalberg went with him, as well as Alexis de Noailles and the marquis de La Tour du Pin-Gouvernet. Talleyrand said slyly that Dalberg was there to leak the secrets they wanted spread, Noailles to spy on him for Louis XVIII, and La Tour du Pin to validate passports. La Besnardière was there to do the serious work. Talleyrand added: "It is essential to make the French embassy a pleasant place." He brought Dorothée with him. His niece had developed into a splendid young woman, who had come to terms not only with society but also with herself. Because of her important role at the Congress, her new personality warrants an admiring glance.

By accompanying her uncle to Vienna and becoming the official hostess of Europe's greatest diplomat, she broke with her past and with her husband. At the age of twenty-two, she came to realize that she would never find the "conventional happiness that only certain women find," as she wrote. So she sampled another kind of happiness. As fate had brought her into the house of her husband's uncle—the most unconventional of men—her affections reached out to him. He became a father figure (he was sixty), friend, lover, and teacher. When she lost a baby daughter in 1814 during that frantically busy period when Talleyrand was housing the czar and his retinue, her uncle showered her with tenderness. Who could imagine this busy statesman taking a few moments out of each day to console the young mother? He alone shared her grief. She never forgot it. When she set aside her mourning and followed her uncle to Vienna, Dorothée was a changed woman, having channeled her grief into a spiritual revolt. In place of her customary austerity was a new urbanity, a readiness for adventure. It also meant the end of her marriage. When her husband became a general, she took her children to live on the rue Saint-Florentin. Edmond stayed at the rue d'Anjou. Dorothée's arrival took Madame Grand's breath away. She hated her niece and also feared her. She kept silent and brooded. And because Talleyrand's love life was no less complicated than his political life, there was the added problem of the duchess, the "official sultana," Dorothée's mother. When the duchess of Courland saw her daughter leave her husband's house and go off to Vienna, she herself not having been invited to follow "the satrap," her imagination began to wander. She repaired to the seraglio, where Madame de Laval tried to comfort her. The sultana of title had had her title withdrawn. Now she was on a par with the others. The cause of her disgrace was not yet clear to her, but she had not failed to notice the mysterious charm and attraction of her daughter. By accompanying the prince of Benevento to Vienna, Dorothée provided him with a major advantage that the Treaty of Paris had neglected to deny France.

Talleyrand left Jaucourt in charge of the ministry during his absence: Jaucourt, the epitome of integrity and honor, a close friend of his and of Dorothée.

Everything was ready, and on September 16, 1814, Talleyrand and his retinue set out for the great international parade of Vienna. Louis XVIII had just conferred on him the title prince de Talleyrand, which he brought along for added luster. He did not give up his old title, prince of Benevento, until several months later. He also wore the Order of the Golden Fleece, a recent decoration from Emperor Francis II during his brief stay in Paris the month before. Armed with his new princedom and Austria's prestigious decoration, he prepared to plunge headlong into that sensational vanity fair known as the Congress of Vienna; but no title, decoration, ribbon, or diamond could match the comtesse de Périgord.

The Prince de Talleyrand Peacefully Disrupts the Coalition

Talleyrand arrived in Vienna on September 23, 1814, where he and Dalberg installed themselves in the Kaunitz Palace. Moths had chewed their way into everything; bedding, carpets, and drapes all needed repair. Despite this delay in getting settled, he began paying diplomatic calls the very next day. And on that day any illusions he might have nursed as to allied benevolence were promptly shattered. He said so himself: "There was far more than distrust to obliterate, far more than distrust to combat, far more than ambition to repress; there was the need to nullify everything done without the knowledge of France." [1] The great powers had carved up Europe even before the arrival of France's representatives, who, theoretically, had nothing to say about it anyway. Our prince displayed his usual impeccable manners on these diplomatic visits. Pozzo di Borgo, the czar's adviser and, like his master, hostile to Talleyrand, told everyone that "even his civilities are usurious investments which must be paid for by the end of the day." He added: "But you know the rascal better than I." [2]

Talleyrand's initial efforts were not very encouraging. Another obstacle—perhaps unknown to him but which the diplomatic archives reveal—was that Louis XVIII, who distrusted him, was in secret collusion with Metternich through the agency of the comte de Bombelles, Austria's minister to Paris, and was acting contrary to some of his own instructions to Talleyrand. Metternich had this to say to Bombelles: "Talleyrand is feared at court more than he is trusted. I would say that the king has nothing resembling complete confidence in his minister. After swearing me to secrecy, comte de Blacas told me that the king has no intention of demanding that Austria declare war against Naples [Murat] and would be satisfied if we maintain order with the troops we have in our Italian territories. Comte de Blacas begs Your Excellency to communicate this confidential information to no one but His Imperial

Majesty." ³ In this way the king was undercutting his own representative. After instructing Talleyrand to urge that Naples be handed over to Ferdinand IV, Louis XVIII secretly reversed himself.

Talleyrand wrote regularly to his royal master. He described the resistance he was encountering: "Defeat and the Treaty of Paris have not destroyed the spirit of the coalition." France was still isolated—and Talleyrand with her. If diplomacy is not warfare, it is a form of it, the only form Talleyrand ever waged. But with Europe in league against him, he was unable to negotiate simply because the great powers would not admit him to their parleys. He was up against a wall. The thing to do was find a crevice, enlarge it, and slip through.

If the allies had been united, they would have dismembered France. Their fearful greed saved France because it kept them divided. Also, someone had come along to whet their appetites instead of appeasing them, to sharpen their rivalries, to accentuate their disagreements. But that was only half the battle. After setting them hopelessly at odds with one another, someone would have to resolve the discord into a degree of harmony if Europe was to have peace and France a voice.

The feat of skill that enabled France to regain her position among the great nations of the world and her voice in the concert of Europe was accomplished by Talleyrand. He showed astounding dignity and tact in the face of insults. He wrote to the duchess: "I will not relinquish the policy of moderation and calm which the king in his lofty position can promote." Who then could make him relinquish that policy? Napoleon with his hot temper never succeeded.

In a spirit of friendliness and geniality attesting to their former good relations, Nesselrode and Metternich invited him to attend a conference of the great powers. It was a major blunder. He listened in silence, withdrawn. At one point, the expression "allied powers" slipped off the tongue of one of the four. He pricked up his ears; with an air of hurt pride, like a disappointed parent, he chided them: "Have I understood correctly? Allies? Against whom? No longer against Napoleon: he is on the Island of Elba. No longer against France; we are at peace. Or against the king of France, for he is a guarantor of the peace. Gentlemen, let us speak frankly. If there are still allied powers, then I do not belong here. . . ." ⁴

Actually, his colleagues agreed with him, but when confronted with such audacity none of them could utter a word. They listened in astonishment. He stayed and took advantage of their bewilderment. Representing a defeated power, he adopted a pose of superiority: "And yet," he added, "if I were not here, you would miss me. I am perhaps the only one who is asking for nothing [this had impact]. All I ask for France is respect. I want nothing, I repeat, and I have much to contribute. . . ." [5]

He had made them listen. From then on, everything hinged on the magic of his shining intelligence and exquisite civility. The first word from this silent onlooker, whom all would have preferred to remain speechless and blind, was addressed to the conquerors who were dividing up Europe like a plucked chicken, and it was the word "law." He invoked the law in this jungle ruled by tigers and leopards, not to mention a few snakes. His listeners were dumbfounded. Europe had not heard that word for twenty years. It had even greater impact because it took everyone by surprise, and also because Talleyrand invoked the law not in his own behalf but in behalf of the small nations, the marginal nations, Napoleon's victims, now due to be victimized in turn by Napoleon's conquerors. These "small nations" included Spain, Württemberg, Portugal, Sweden, and Denmark. Having made the mistake of being weak, they were being treated like captives. Such is the barbarous law of the jungle, except when a Talleyrand tries his hand at making the jungle less barbarous. He wished to serve the law, yes, but he also chose that honorable way to serve the interests of France and Louis XVIII, which, in 1814, were equivalent. As for his own interests, one may be sure that the cause of law served them handsomely.

He championed the small nations. His weapons were his words, his dinner parties, his niece, his sphinxlike expression, and his exquisite polish. It was no easy task, for his antagonists were adamant. He wrote to the duchess of Courland: "Your Prussians are passionately fond of Bonaparte's doctrine of usurpation; they detest only its successful applications [an apt analysis]. They are dreadful, especially M. de Humboldt. . . . They intend to destroy Saxony as if it were their right, as if conquest alone conferred sovereignty. I protest all such notions." [6]

With utmost dignity and restraint, a vanquished power eloquently addressed its powerful neighbors. Amid the slightly mad atmosphere of the Congress, the sumptuous, gossiping, thoroughly debauched, and shamelessly rapacious confusion of Vienna, a degree of discipline attached itself to the French representative. Thanks to him, suddenly and without any great commotion, France regained her voice and justice found a champion. "I shall be gentle and conciliatory, yet positive," he wrote to Louis XVIII, "speaking only of principles and sticking to them." The principles he dealt with had nothing to do with conventional morality. The only kind of morality he recognized was that which permitted men to live freely in a society sufficiently organized, prosperous, and stratified to resist individual fancies termed vices when they conflicted too severely with the vices of others. Such was the attitude of the prince de Talleyrand, defender of international law and justice at the Congress of Vienna.

On hearing Talleyrand enunciate those principles in his calm, aloof, authoritative manner, Spain's deputy, the chevalier de Labrador, hailed his action and sent all the small, ignored nations scurrying to the side of France's representative. Our prince prudently advised them to insist on their right to participate in the main conference, which right was theirs as signatories to the Treaty of Paris. The Big Four thus were forced to open up their discussions to the "small nations." The conference expanded, and because Talleyrand had discovered a crevice, he simply slipped in with the others. Had he not signed the Treaty of Paris as well? "Talleyrand's and Labrador's intervention seriously thwarted our plans," wrote Gentz, secretary general of the Congress and Metternich's confidant. The great powers were so discouraged that they burned the minutes of their previous sessions; the newcomers would not have enjoyed reading them. As of that moment, unfortunately, nothing of significance was dealt with in the meetings. The "small nations" grew bored and stayed away. Only Talleyrand, for whom nothing was a waste of time, remained, turning the foursome into a fivesome. Having slipped in the back way, he was soon in command.

Russia and Prussia were causing the most serious problems. The czar wanted all of Poland, wanted it with a fury. He was making common cause with the Prussians, who wanted Saxony not to mention many other things, but principally Saxony. Alexander had promised to support Prussia's Saxon ambitions in return for the Prussian part of Poland. Louis XVIII and Talleyrand were strongly opposed to both demands. Talleyrand wrote to the duchess on November 17: "He [the czar] is not the same man that he was in Paris. His philanthropy has become exceedingly aggressive. . . . Emperor Alexander has converted his philanthropy into bald Jacobinism."

Then came the showdown. Talleyrand had his scene with this despot as with "the other." He relates a private conversation with Alexander I in his *Memoirs*:

> "I shall keep what I occupy," said the czar.
> "Your Majesty surely cannot wish to keep that which is not yours."
> "I am in agreement with the great powers."
> "I do not know whether Your Majesty considers France one of those powers."

"Yes, of course I do. But if you would not have each one pursue his own expedients, then what are you after?"

"I rank legality before expedients."

"Europe's expedients are legal."

"This is not your language, Sire; it is unlike you and denies your true feelings."

This confrontation with the czar, leader of the coalition, temporarily the most powerful ruler on the Continent, unreliable and headstrong, was extremely significant to the course of European history. Knowing the Russian emperor's temperament, Talleyrand tried to needle him. Imagine the comedy: "Then I turned toward the wall near which I was, I leaned my head against it, and, pounding the paneling, I moaned: 'Europe! Europe! Poor Europe!' Then turning back to the emperor: 'Shall it be said,' I asked him, 'that you destroyed her?'

" 'There will be war before I give up what I occupy,' the barbarian thundered." How could he remain unmoved by the unheard-of spectacle of the prince of impassivity banging his head against the wall? In a fury, the czar strode past the bowing Talleyrand. Imperial boots stamped across the floor, the door slammed. Talleyrand had gone to a lot of trouble for nothing. He went out in turn, unruffled. It was not the first scene he had lived through.

Three days later he had a long talk with Metternich. No shouts, no slammed doors, no stamping of feet; their dealings were far more refined and subtle. The whole spectrum of European reconstruction came under discussion. Though the interests they represented were in conflict on a good many points, they both came from the same mold, had the same education, shared the same values. Talleyrand was infinitely more broad-minded and visionary than the Austrian statesman, still firmly wedded to the old régime he served, but the two were equally glib-tongued and crafty. Talleyrand had no difficulty pointing out that by seizing Poland, Russia would acquire a common border with Austria, a border reaching into the very heart of Europe. Metternich had already considered this, but Talleyrand's description of the situation was sufficiently graphic to make the Hapsburg envoy's flesh crawl. And by taking Saxony, Prussia would border on the Austrian Empire. The heirs of Frederick II were greedy; if their power in Germany were not offset by Austria's, the whole of Germany would fall under the Prussian thumb. Metternich came to realize that the real threat to Austria was from Berlin and St. Petersburg, not Paris. Prussia was already aware of this. When Prussia's minister, listening to the minutes of the previous meeting, heard it said that henceforth the negotiations would be carried on in accordance with the public right, he was shocked by the use of such words: "What is the public right doing here?" he demanded. Talleyrand retorted: "It brings you here."

The council sensed that it had a leader.

As he walked out, Alexander shrugged his shoulders in irritation and uttered what was probably the greatest compliment he could pay to defeated France: "Talleyrand is acting like Louis XIV's minister." This opinion, not offered in friendship, was enough to clear Talleyrand of charges that he failed to look out for his country's interests. As a matter of fact, Talleyrand was not the Sun King's minister, he was no minister to any king or any government, not Louis XIV any more than Napoleon or the Directory. But he was invariably the minister of France, whether under the monarchy or the Revolution. He can be blamed for almost anything except having failed to serve his country. At this time in Vienna, he was Louis XVIII's loyal servant, a task for which he deserves credit; the king had to be supported at all costs if the country was to regain its strength, rebuild its prosperity, its armies, and its institutions.

It was difficult to accept Austrian backing. Louis XVIII had instructed him to have Murat removed from the throne of Naples. It was unthinkable that Austria, after defeating Napoleon, should permit a brother-in-law of the tyrant to retain an Italian crown which he had stolen from a legitimate monarch. Yet it happened. Austria was involved in all sorts of intrigue in Italy where she had serious ambitions, so she supported the usurper. The czar advised Talleyrand that he would rid Naples of Murat by bringing pressure on Austria, but only if France would yield on the subject of Saxony. Tit for tat. The Russian diplomat was treated to an admirable lesson in morality and integrity: "You talk of a bargain and I cannot make one. Fortunately I am not as free as you are. Your wishes and interests determine your actions, but I am obliged to obey principles, and principles do not compromise." [7]

Imagine! Yet he managed to strike an incredible bargain. Two months after the Congress opened, he had aroused such distrust in Austria and England against the aggressive East that on January 3, 1815, in great secrecy, the three western powers, England, France, and Austria, signed a treaty of alliance against Prussia and Russia. Here was France, lately an outcast, now an ally of the most respectable of the civilized nations. Talleyrand had every reason to write thus to his sovereign on the day after the treaty was signed, January 4, 1815: "Now, Sire, the coalition is dissolved, and forever [the "forever" lasted three months while Napoleon prepared to return]. Not only is France no longer isolated in Europe, but Your Majesty has a federal system such as fifty years of negotiations are not likely to have yielded him. . . ." [8] The result was that Prussia acquired only one part of Saxony and Russia a part of Poland.

We know the fate of secrets. The czar soon found out about the treaty and knew that Talleyrand had inspired it. He turned against his former accomplice. By and large, the hatred did Talleyrand more credit than the so-called friendship with which Alexander had honored him at Erfurt.

Still, he permitted—or was obliged to permit—one disastrous change to take place: Prussian occupation of the Rhineland. Historically and politically it was a disgrace. Peaceful Catholic provinces oriented toward work, study, and artistic creation came under the domination of Protestant, militaristic, aggressive Prussia. Napoleon had been crushed in the name of European security; with the Rhineland awarded to Prussia, European security was destroyed for a century and a half. How could Talleyrand close his eyes to such a scandal? Louis XVIII's instructions specifically urged him not to yield on this point. The demand came not from Russia or Prussia but from England, however, and Talleyrand could refuse her nothing. He was unwilling to alienate his staunchest ally. England bears the responsibility for this shameless act which she willfully fostered. The situation was this: because Louis XVIII refused to allow Prussia to dispossess his relative the king of Saxony, and because Prussia was greedily bent on swallowing up Saxony, the Rhineland, Luxembourg, and Belgium, England supported one claim, the Rhineland. She did it mainly to install a war machine on the French border. She reasoned that what Napoleon had succeeded in doing once, other Napoleons might try to repeat. France thus found herself under constant, threatening surveillance by an army permanently camped only 220 kilometers from Paris on an open frontier. A nation mad for revenge ever since Iena was installed on France's doorstep. England came out very well, having established at no cost to herself a terrible watchman on the Rhine. The rest is history: Bismarck, Sadowa, Sedan, the annexation of Alsace-Lorraine, the First World War, Hitler—Europe's murder. Like his friend Voltaire, Talleyrand might have said: "Lord, protect me from my friends; I can take care of my enemies."

Saxony's poor king, a prisoner in Berlin, wept at his fate and that of his captive land. He appealed for help to Talleyrand. Knowing what language to use in order to be heard, he sent him 6 million francs. Murat, seeing his throne tottering and threatened by Talleyrand, tried to appease him with 800,000 francs. Ferdinand IV, Naples's legitimate king, knowing that Louis XVIII had instructed Talleyrand to back his cause, sent our hero 3,700,000 francs; the affable margrave of Baden-Baden one million; and so on. There must have been other insignificant offerings that escape our knowledge because no one bothered to record them. The total comes to a few billion francs in our time. Some insolent soul remarked: "To this ex-bishop, the holiest vessels are the *pots-de-vin* [bribes]." Rather, let us say that the immensity of those "douceurs" matched the importance of the services he rendered.

He used every possible device to impose his own presence and that of his country, to attract the chorus, however discordant, of nations. Thus on January 21 he organized a solemn funeral service in memory of Louis XVI. The heads of Europe were present. Prince de Talleyrand sat in the front row representing the French king: "The ceremony was in no way lacking," he reported to Louis XVIII, "or the pomp befitting the occasion, or the choice of spectators, or the pain which the event commemorated must always arouse."

Did he recall the January 21 of 1798 when, during the Directory, Citizen Talleyrand engaged Bonaparte to join with the Jacobins and celebrate the happy anniversary of the monarch's death? What do memories matter anyway; times change . . .

With Talleyrand's Help the Congress Is Entertained, and His Niece as Well

What are the tedious sessions of a Congress gathered in a city gone mad? Sheer boredom, which has to be relieved. The members of the Congress did just that.

During the autumn and winter of 1814–15, Vienna assembled everyone in Europe with a great name and a great fortune—or crafty enough to acquire one. Assembled is hardly the word; packed in would be more accurate. Palaces and hovels were jammed, rented out for astronomic prices. The work of the Congress was nothing compared to the incredible intrigue and espionage running abreast of official activities, and which could cancel them out, orient or disorient them. The receptions teemed with secret agents. Everyone was a spy and was spied upon. The walls had ears as well as the beds; coachmen turned out to be police agents, duchesses were apprentice spies. For a few months Vienna was in a whirl, host to the high and mighty who had come to shape Europe's future and also to forget twenty years of fear, war, suffering, the horrors of revolution, of invasion, desolation, and death, which had been daily threats to all. For the heads of Europe, for the powerful, the bankers, the diplomats, the ladies of the court—and sometimes of the street—the Congress of Vienna meant the end of all their woes. It was primarily a celebration of peace. Debauchery and politics were everywhere. The licentiousness of prominent persons is pitilessly recorded in reports both reliable and astounding. Metternich's crowning glory was not the Congress but the policing of it. Talleyrand survived the whirl of events without damage. His reserve and dignified bearing caused a stir. Looking down his nose at the carryings-on of Europe's nobility, he jested: "In Vienna, the cooking is done in the bedroom." His niece Dorothée was all he needed.

Of all the women he had known, Dorothée best fulfilled his wants. Not only was she extremely intelligent, but she possessed a different kind of intelligence from her uncle's. She was rigor, force, profundity; he, intuition and finesse. She gave him energy. Her mind was like a man's. She subdued him; he enjoyed it. He gave her more than his house and his heart; he shared his work and his secrets with her; she became his confidante, his anchor, often his adviser. To this sixty-one-year-old man without illusions, she promised a new life. For the first time, probably, he was in love. To prove it, for the first time he suffered.

Once before in his lifetime he had experienced an emotional upheaval, a strange unsettling of his normal composure. Rather than love, it was something like an inner tremor followed by the sense of attachment to someone, of belonging to a fascinating personality. One cannot call it enthusiasm because enthusiasm is always indiscreet, whereas the warmth he felt remained discreet, though no less intense and sincere, as we know, for his encounter with the genius of young Bonaparte was the event which first impelled him to become attached, devoted, admiring. He had crossed paths with the most extraordinary embodiment of intelligence.

The second emotional shock of his life came when he discovered right in his own house and in his nephew's bed Dorothée of Courland, his niece. Before her intelligence and her will could be known, the "prune" first had to reveal her beauty. In each case, his head rather than his heart was stirred. But the progress of his liaison with Dorothée shows that cerebral loves, like other loves, have their labyrinth, their tragedies —and even their offspring.

The aging satrap and his dazzling, mysterious Dorothée must have been quite a sight as they sat side by side on a sofa receiving guests in the Kaunitz Palace. Around them clustered the greatest titles in Europe; the most elegant and clever men and women stood fascinated. When Archduke John asked Talleyrand what he was doing in Paris during the attack on France, the prince replied: "I limped." Imperious Dorothée found the relationship deeply satisfying to her social and intellectual ambitions.

In Vienna, all her austere principles were swept aside. She yielded to the general folly. In later years she confessed: "Vienna! My whole destiny is in that word." Everyone who experienced that delightful truce between two catastrophes was unable to forget it. No one returned from Vienna unchanged. Especially Dorothée.

The pattern of dissipation was handed down from on high. On October 8, after ten days of talks, the weary Congress declared a recess until November 1 so that it could dance.

Political rivalries became entwined with amorous ones. The czar vied with Metternich for the favors of the duchess of Sagan, Dorothée's sister. She had had three husbands. She wore them out fast enough to be able to claim: "I am ruining myself with husbands," or at least with divorces. Lovers being less costly, she consumed them even more readily. At one point Talleyrand used her to find out what her two rival lovers thought of Louis XVIII's minister.

From the moment he arrived, Talleyrand became an object of acute concern to the Austrian police. Not because he intrigued, but because he did not. That was unforgivable. His diplomatic and household staffs were incorruptible; the police could not slip a single agent into the Kaunitz Palace. They were convinced that sinister plots were being hatched behind those high windows where the lights stayed on all night. Talleyrand enjoyed worrying the agents of his friend Metternich.

Austria's spies lost sleep over one particularly mysterious member of Talleyrand's household. This person's existence was known, but no one had ever laid eyes on him. All their schemes failed. Still, the reports noted one detail: he took his meals at a small table in Talleyrand's rooms. At night, agents creeping along the palace walls heard a piano playing until dawn. The music, they assumed, had no other purpose than muffling conspirators' voices. Two weeks later, with the help of a sarcastic comment from Talleyrand, Metternich finally discovered that the person was Neukomm, an Austrian, thirty-six years of age, a pianist in Talleyrand's service for the past six years, who lived under the prince's roof. Talleyrand had asked him to compose a *Te Deum* in honor of Louis XVIII's return. He had brought him to Vienna along with the rest of his princely retinue, much like a Kapellmeister attached to some traveling nobleman.

Despite this explanation, the entire Congress was convinced that

Talleyrand's pianist was a spy. Actually, he was a perfectly respectable and innocuous musician, but his employer's gift for attracting attention from the police discredited him. Talleyrand always surrounded himself with such mild and utterly devoted persons. This private side of his life, deliberately maintained—like his feelings for his family—has escaped the notice of critics and certain biographers. The brilliance of his social position tends to hide the truth: we think we know all about him because we know his political activities and his social image. Our hero displayed his vices more readily than his virtues or his sensitivity. He knew the jungle. During the Congress, he would spend many a night alone, re-gathering his forces through reading and especially through music. He found it necessary to nourish this secret sensitivity of his; music gave him strength and repose. To compensate for the cynicism, coldness, and cupidity of the day, he had the joys of the night. La Tour du Pin had placed a deep armchair in his study. There he ensconced himself voluptuously, and there, motionless and silent for hours, he meditated. Slipping in like a ghost, Neukomm would play in muted tones, filling the wondrous silence with Haydn and Mozart.

On a table, Dalberg kept a row of files which the prince needed to consult. He leafed through them while Neukomm played softly; the lively, graceful strains of *Il Seraglio* inspired our prince. Meditation was a pleasure. He could conjure up the chessboard of world affairs, society, the nations of Europe and their frontiers, all of it reduced to an ideal diagram from which the power structure clearly emerged; he prepared what he would talk about the next day, shaped his plans, set his traps, perfected his *bons mots*. Thus, in the world of his imagination he created and rehearsed the role he would play next day on the stage of history.

All this time Metternich's agents were at their wit's end to know the identity of "Talleyrand's spy." Gossip and his own cynical manner denied that "the limping Mephistopheles" could be a music lover. He was.

In Vienna, to enhance the image he wished to create, he added even more starch to his already celebrated collar. The term "stiff-necked" has no better illustration.

He lived there as he did in Paris, rising late and enjoying a royal levee. In Vienna, he refined the protocol of this ceremony, which later became one of the famous sights of Paris. Just by drawing on his shirt he created legends about himself, like a star performer. The comments, sarcastic or admiring, but always impassioned, added fire to the debate.

His dinners were no less celebrated. His chef Carême had come with him to Vienna. But if there was great attention given to the cooking, the master of the house gave twice that attention to conducting conversation. He wanted it to be relaxed and even whimsical. It was generally understood that even in discussing politics, one could talk freely, not being bound by what was said. The remarks he made or inspired, the clever phrases he would reshape into even wittier ones, were brilliant as well as instructive. His urbane elegance never detracted from his affable delivery. Like the splendid actor he was, he never forgot that he was there to represent France. One evening his dinner guests were extolling the cheeses of their respective homelands: Lord Castlereagh, English Stilton; a Swiss, Emmenthal; Falk, Holland's Edam; Alvino, Italian Strachino. Talleyrand listened. He lacked arguments, that is, French cheeses. A valet entered and announced the arrival of a courier from Paris.

"What is he bringing?" asked Talleyrand.

"Dispatches from the court and a case of Brie cheese."

"Very good. Put the dispatches in the chancellery and the cheese on the table," said the prince. Turning to his guests: "I refrained from taking part in the discussion and, as your host, crying up a product of French soil, but it is here. Judge for yourself, gentlemen." [1] The Brie rendered its cream to the knife. It was a feast, and no one argued the point. No diplomatic victory was too small for Talleyrand.

He had also brought the painter Isabey to Vienna. In despair over the fall of Napoleon, whose court painter he was, Isabey had come to Talleyrand on the rue Saint-Florentin to relate his woes and seek help. Talleyrand contemplated him in silence. He already had thought how to remedy the artist's disgrace. Pointing to a large canvas on the wall in front of them representing "The Congress of Münster" painted by Terborch, he said to Isabey: "Why not come to Vienna? You will be the Terborch of a Congress where great things will be achieved." [2] Isabey took his advice. The prince introduced him to the eminent personalities of the Congress and Isabey painted the famous picture of Vienna's notables grouped around the table on which Europe was dissected. It is a fine painting and a valuable document. Talleyrand has a prominent place there and deserves it.

The least talkative and most unruffled of those celebrities drew the greatest throng of curious, admiring, ambitious, spiteful, or loyal spectators. In the magnificent receptions which took place in imperial Vienna's splendid baroque palaces, Talleyrand's entrance never failed to cause a stir. People lined up to watch his slow, dramatic steps, a procession of admirers at his heels. Dorothée was now used to this and, with her natural elegance, did credit to the Paris fashions she had once scorned. Her mother had given her splendid jewels. Under her uncle's guidance, she succeeded in becoming one of the reigning beauties of the Congress. They were the most talked of pair in Vienna. A faint aura of scandal—not to say incest—was part of their success.

Talleyrand always dressed well. His thick hair, carefully curled and powdered by Courtiade, was knotted at the neck in a ribbon. His dress coat might be lilac or purple—a reminder of his episcopate?—or perhaps dove-gray silk brocade; around his neck hung the Order of the Golden Fleece. He wore black silk stockings with gold clocks; his pumps had red heels and diamond buckles. Sixty years had not added girth to him, only wrinkles. Through various régimes and circumstances, Talleyrand had held a steady course from 1780 to 1815. Fire did not burn or scar him; time scarcely touched him. This aura of enigmatic permanence raised Talleyrand, the most human of men, above ordinary humanity. The manners, the style, the unreal power he possessed transcended the common experience. His mission among nations and among men was to maintain and pass on certain forms of happiness which others were bent on destroying. In the shattered world of 1815 he stood as a symbol, a symbol lame as the society of the previous century which was headed for oblivion, yet survived in him. No one ever surprised him in public—I should say on the stage—without his sphinxlike mask. The mask which Nietzsche called a sign of greatness and of depth. Even as a child Talleyrand realized that life required one to wear a mask in order to survive and to pass clear, as he did, of history's dark alleys.

In Vienna he met one of his peers, a "son of kings," as Gobineau would have said, the prince de Ligne. They are as one in the mirror of their times, each serving to explain the other. Destiny had cut them from the same cloth, for the prince de Ligne could claim sixty quarterings of nobility. Like Talleyrand, he never crowed about his ancestry. As he put it: "Deeds of title are food for rats and fools, titles that one picks up in court antechambers." Like Talleyrand, he had no trace of chauvinism and was the most European of Europeans. Here was a man on whom life had heaped bitterness which he turned into joy. His greatest asset was the courage to live a full life. He trained for this in pre-revolutionary France, the period which he called the "date of Europe's great happiness," a view shared by Talleyrand. Both of them had numerous love affairs but never allowed their passions to enslave or grieve them. "In matters of the heart," said the prince de Ligne, "only the beginning is a delight. No wonder people are eager to begin again so often." His own marriage was a fiasco, not a tragedy. No tears or tirades, only this jest: "My wife's heart departed; mine remained."

The conversation between these two illustrious noblemen, while invariably courteous, was not always mild. They crossed swords and were known to draw blood over a point of wit.

Ligne told Talleyrand: "Here you are something of a king of France. Louis XVIII is forced to obey you." A dangerous remark if it should come to the king's ears. And it did. Talleyrand countered by saying that he was no stranger to slander and that certain people in Paris charged him with betraying Napoleon for seven years. "What?" cried the prince de Ligne in surprise, "Only seven years? And I suspected you all along of twenty!" He recalled the famous Mass during the Festival of the Federation when, according to Ligne, the bishop of Autun "amused himself by setting a Phrygian cap on the head of God." The prince de Ligne acknowledged the extraordinary influence which Talleyrand exercised over Europe's rulers and diplomats. When Louis XVIII's minister entered the council, he wrote, "Alexander turns silent, Francis makes for the nearest door, and Frederick stares at his boots."

The Congress of Vienna was the last spectacle enjoyed, surely with mixed emotions, by the prince de Ligne. It brought down the curtain on the world he had known, culminating in a Congress which, to say the least, did not appear to take life very seriously. "It does not walk," Ligne said, "it dances." The Congress outlasted him. In the funeral oration after his death, Talleyrand returned the gibe: "And the Congress shall inter him dancing all the while."

Louis XVIII anxiously inquired whether Talleyrand needed additional staff from the embassy. The prince thanked the king: "Sire, I need cooks more than diplomats."

As a matter of fact, his aides left much to be desired. Noailles and La Tour du Pin were of no help whatever. The comte de Noailles was ambassador to Vienna; after deserting Napoleon at the proper time, he threw himself into the arms of the Bourbons and the church. Talleyrand was aware that Noailles's job was to spy on him for Blacas and the king. What he thought of Noailles was no secret. On one fast day, a roast was brought to Talleyrand's table. Noailles, having recently overhauled his religious notions, was shocked to see the meat and refused to touch it. "Under Bonaparte, sir, a roast never frightened you," Talleyrand flung at him across the table. Nor titles and pensions either.

Certain women were elated by his frank and coquettish manner of parading the very vices held against him. The hypocrisy of his censors never failed to amuse our prince. Calmly and deliberately, he provoked hypocrisy until it grew savage. He enjoyed talking to the duchess of Sagan, who was anything but a hypocrite. She would relate hair-raising scenes she caused between the czar and Metternich. At one point they were ready to fight a duel. The duchess thought it was great sport to watch two empires fighting over her. Talleyrand was grateful to her for telling him about it. He could speak freely to her: "This morning again," he reported, "I am blamed for changing my mind. But is there better proof of my constancy than remaining faithful to my inconstancy?" She who had had three husbands in a short period, and a flock of lovers, could appreciate his position.

In discussing his political career with close friends and attempting to evaluate it, he would repeat a phrase which Goethe had quoted to him at Erfurt, originally from Martin Luther: "My good works cause me greater fear than my sins." A probing remark which Talleyrand applied to himself. What was his "good work" and where was his "sin" as a statesman? Was it unswerving loyalty or deliberate and purposeful neglect? "Régimes pass, France remains. Sometimes by serving a régime zealously, one can betray all the interests of one's country, but by serving the latter, one is sure to betray no more than intermittencies."

A marvelous expression: political régimes are simply "intermittencies." Like foundation make-up on the face of a nation. The flick of a cloth—a riot, a defeat—and the make-up is gone. The nation is still there, puts on a new face according to the fashion of the day, and carries on. Must one be loyal to a coat of make-up?

Talleyrand was bored on occasion during sessions of the Congress. He scribbled. If someone made a remark involving him, he would raise an eyebrow and take it in. In due course he would produce a rebuttal. Meanwhile, he went on scribbling. The police triumphantly laid hands on one such sheet of his, thinking they had discovered state secrets. To their amazement, it was a dissertation in flawless Latin on the rotation of heavenly bodies. What was diplomacy coming to? The final sentence also was surprising: "Veneris revolutione perpetua." Then followed several tender epithets addressed to a certain Isabella. Was he being unfaithful to Dorothée? So while the great powers dismembered Saxony and Poland, prince de Talleyrand was wandering through infinite space and encountering love, whose cyclical occurrence in life is as perpetual as the movements of the stars. It was one way of avoiding the tiresome company of Prussians and Russians.

Of all his enemies, Princess Bagration was the most outspoken and vulgar. She was one of the czar's mistresses and spies. A thorough libertine, she turned her Cossack charms on Talleyrand, who was not at all interested. In revenge, she told people that he disgusted her, "with his fishy eyes and heavy lids which he kept lowered like shutters over a shop window." He got back at the princess, a secret agent between the sheets:

"Her way of casually overhearing secrets must present certain draw-backs."

A favorite trick of his to stir people up was by deliberately "putting his foot in it." He would invent a secret, let it out, and then pretend to catch himself. The facial reactions were most revealing. Baron von Stetten discovered this game of Talleyrand's and described it aptly: "M. de Talleyrand fires a pistol into the air to see who will jump out the window."

Nothing ever upset him, even being caught outright in a lie. If he happened to be talking about someone and the person walked in, he would greet him warmly: "Ah, my dear fellow, we were just saying the nastiest things about you!" The other fellow was invariably delighted while the rest of his audience marveled at Talleyrand's utter composure. If he were expounding an idea and a known opponent of it came in, he switched to the opposite argument and carried it far enough to draw applause from the newcomer. If a listener happened to protest, the prince fixed him in a stony stare that strangled further comment.

If the results were those he wanted, nothing else interested him. Approval meant nothing to him, and was not even pleasurable. Who cared about praise? It always came from below. Flattery was something he knew all about.

Like a veteran cardplayer, his greatest satisfaction was forcing his opponents to show their hands. One first had to disconcert them, stop them short with some withering statement. By tripping them up you revealed their true colors. One day he was heard enunciating the following excellent principle in his unctuous prelate's voice: "In business one ought to show one's hand." The fact that he kept plenty of cards up his sleeve was public knowledge. There he sat watching through half-closed eyes the effect he had produced: one person was trying to keep from laughing, another was dying to protest but did not dare, another looked contemptuous, while still another seemed to have missed the point.

All of them knew about Talleyrand's dealings with the German princes at the time Napoleon established the Confederation of the Rhine. That did not stop him from proclaiming: "France has never been involved in German affairs." Such statements baffled his listeners.

He kept other ministers in awe by the witty sayings he strewed about like nails under their feet. To throw off the yoke of French occupation, Prussia had established Leagues called *Tugendbund* ("Leagues of Virtue"). These Leagues had no purpose after the signing of the peace, yet Prussia decided to use them in Italy to liberate Italian states occupied by Austria. The same old story of licensed Virtue arrogating the right to invade someone else's affairs. Why didn't Prussian Virtue crusade for Poland's deliverance? Or Saxony's? Or the Rhineland's? Talleyrand launched this barb: "You can add virtue to every sauce but it still smells like rotting dog flesh."

No other setting so encouraged his intrigues or his gift for manipulating and captivating as that European ferment known as the Congress of Vienna. Still, above all the feverish gaiety hovered a cloud.

A Shadow Falls on the Congress, Ending the Gaiety

At the Council table, Europe's mighty rulers sensed an invisible, dreadful presence creeping into their midst. Not Talleyrand, whose insolence they could readily define. "The other" was merely a vague suspicion, which Talleyrand was quietly cultivating. Indeed, Napoleon's ghost occasionally cast a pall over the festivities. Heedless Europe danced in the Eagle's piercing gaze. He was too close for comfort. Talleyrand managed to get that idea across from time to time. "As long as Napoleon remains so close to the French coast," he warned repeatedly, "he will be a danger." England, too, was concerned about the danger. Metternich agreed, but Francis II wanted to bury the subject. As for Alexander, he worried Talleyrand greatly, this czar, at once so headstrong and so apathetic, at the mercy of a look, a flower, a fit of rage. When denied a part of Poland, he shouted: "Beware, I shall loose the monster!" He used Napoleon like a scarecrow to frighten others. Then the storm passed and everyone rushed to the ballroom.

One episode disturbed the merrymaking: the plague. An epidemic had broken out in Silesia; slowly and surely it advanced on Vienna. There it could find choice victims. At the very mention of it, a kind of hurricane gripped the city. Pestilence made no allowances for silks or pearls, quarterings of nobility, youth, or beauty. Was the plague awed by this elegant society or surfeited with humbler victims? It stopped short at the gates of Vienna. It did not approve of waltzes.

That left "the other," the "usurper," the "ogre," the "monster," in other words, Bonaparte. Word reaching Vienna of his escape touched off a panic as if an explosion had shattered every window. Europe's ballroom emptied. The hysteria was a spontaneous tribute to the imperial fugitive.

How had he managed to escape? Had the czarist summons reached his ears and tempted him to try? It was more involved than that. Talleyrand in league with his English friends was probably responsible.

We have no documentary proof of the daring plot which enabled

Napoleon to go free; a perfect plot leaves no trace. Talleyrand and the English government, shielded by Metternich, could have put their heads together and pulled off such a stunt.

To make up for the lack of written evidence, assumptions have arisen based on attitudes, relationships, phrases purposely dropped by the accomplices, services performed for no apparent reason—in short, the flight from Elba can only be explained by the "cooperation" which should have cost the heads of persons responsible for guarding the emperor and who aided his escape.[1]

Prior to the escapade, there had been an attempted conspiracy. That earlier one was never executed, but some details are known. Sir Sydney Smith was to sail from Sardinia and abduct Napoleon. Sir Colin Campbell, high commissioner for the emperor on the Island of Elba, sent a report to Talleyrand (why Talleyrand?) advising that the enterprise presented insurmountable difficulties. Emperor Francis is said to have opposed a violent abduction for he was, in spite of everything, the "monster's" father-in-law. The organizers had intended to treat Napoleon just as he had treated the duc d'Enghien: a former Chouan rebel named Brulart, embittered since the Vendée had been put to the torch in the name of "pacification," was supposed to dispatch the usurper. Austria's emperor was unwilling to embark on such an adventure. In view of these various obstacles, Talleyrand and his friend Lord Charles Stewart, England's minister in Vienna, worked out a subtler plan. Their idea was to inveigle Napoleon into escaping from his island, to persuade him that such an insane project could really succeed. Castlereagh is said to have thought up the plan while Talleyrand filled in the details and Metternich sanctioned it. He also provided the services of Austria's General Koller who was sent to Elba.

In Vienna, Talleyrand dropped hints: "Yes, we removed him from the battlefields, but he is right on the tip of our spyglass," he said one evening in Prince Schwarzenberg's palace. Castlereagh remarked to that same Austrian prince: "It is Alexander's fault that Napoleon is on the Island of Elba. If they had listened to Talleyrand and me, he would have been deported 16,000 leagues away, to the Azores or even farther." It is a fact that Talleyrand had proposed the Azores or St. Helena. The fitting up of Elba with its simulated court and army was both ridiculous and dangerous. Such restraint, Talleyrand warned, "is so mild that it resembles a gesture of politeness." What was to be done? As we know, opinions change only when new developments occur. Napoleon had to put himself in the wrong, prove himself incorrigible, forswear himself, and, ultimately, bring down a new sentence on his head. That was the essence of Castlereagh's and Talleyrand's plan. Talleyrand knew Napoleon's restless, imaginative nature, that he could not stand confinement and idleness. His former minister was aware that if carefully screened, respectful, and admiring visitors whispered false assurances of popularity in the emperor's ear, of revival, escape, fervor, and glory, he would not resist. Koller played the tempter successfully, assuring Napoleon of the aid and comfort he would encounter, suggesting that his return to France was not impossible, that the allies were already tired of the Bourbons, that the French people missed their emperor. Why should Napoleon not have trusted Koller? He spoke for Francis II, his own father-in-law, whom Napoleon knew to be still loyal. Did Napoleon have any reason to suspect that Koller spoke for his former minister Talleyrand? As destiny would have it, the voice from Vienna echoed exactly what his loyal worshippers were telling him. Friends and foes alike pushed him into this fatal venture.

His enemies did more to hasten his escape than his supporters. In Vienna, Castlereagh and Talleyrand received daily bulletins on events at Elba and knew exactly what preparations Napoleon and his followers were making. Actually, Napoleon made little effort to conceal them, having been assured that discretion was unnecessary. On February 21, a spy known as "Oil Merchant" reported the following: "I myself watched as they hoisted aboard the *Inconstant* sixty cases of cartridges, bales of equipment and provisions." Where did the ammunition come from? And where was it bound? This report came to the attention of Castlereagh and Talleyrand. No reaction. Everything was proceeding according to plan.

In the meanwhile, it was politic in Vienna to ridicule the Island of Elba, a ferruginous pebble where rust and boredom were corroding the one-time emperor of the West. People snickered at the absurd court and its ruler, whose "household" consisted of a cook, a wardrobe mistress, and a pianist. Princess Bagration was particularly scornful. Let it be said that Talleyrand never spoke ill of Napoleon and paid no attention to the insulting remarks of others. In February, 1815, false rumors of an escape had sent the birdhouse into a panic. Then came the reassurances. How could he escape? It was impossible. The island was ringed with British ships, their cannon trained on the tiny port barring any exit. On February 26, the rumors were even more precise—in an extraordinary audience, Napoleon personally announced his departure to the island's notables: "Gentlemen, I leave you; France summons me, the Bourbons have ruined her." The rest was even more significant: "Several nations will be glad to see me return."

Who gave him "the green light," so to speak? The best evidence that his departure had been arranged was the manner in which he departed. It was quite incredible. On the one hand, the French fleet out of Toulon, under orders to keep Elba under surveillance, failed to do so. As for the British navy, its conduct was even more startling. Campbell, its commander, knew all about the departure, as did everyone on the island; just at that time he was given leave to go to Florence and visit his mistress, which he did, leaving the ring of English ships leaderless. He returned to Elba two days after Napoleon had left, his leave coinciding with the date of the escape. England's admiralty never called for an explanation, nor gave one.

But the crowning fact was that the vessels at anchor in the harbor were ordered not to fire on the imperial convoy or even challenge it.

Contemporary reactions were less naïve than the historians writing at the close of the nineteenth century. An English cartoon of the time represents Napoleon ("Boney") unlocking his cell door to escape while his English guards pretend to be asleep, and one of them says: "Don't make so much noise, Boney, or we'll have to wake up."

So the trap that claimed Napoleon in 1815 was an open secret. On February 26, according to plan, he set sail for France. And lest anyone imagine that the prisoner slipped into a rowboat concealed by rocks and mist, we hasten to add that he embarked in broad daylight, in the harbor, aboard the *Inconstant* with nine hundred men. Yes, nine hundred! Never was an expedition less secret. From their ships, the English could train their field glasses on him; they could train their cannons too, but field glasses were all they used. Once the imperial convoy had reached the open sea, the English vessels pretended to give chase. "A chase so half-hearted," reported one observer, "that it surprised the sailors."

Nothing surprised Talleyrand. On the morning of February 28, he had not yet risen. Seated on his bed, Dorothée chatted with him as she breakfasted with "her intimate uncle." She was looking forward to the evening's entertainment, a play in which she would star.

A servant brought a letter from Metternich. "He is probably informing me what time the Congress will hold its conference," the prince observed. Dorothée opened the message: "Bonaparte has left the isle of Elba!" she cried. "Oh, Uncle, what about my rehearsal?"

"It will take place, Madam," he assured her with his customary calm.

People wondered where the fugitive would try to land. In Italy, or perhaps America? Surely not in France. Russia's ambassador to France,

Pozzo di Borgo, had warned: "If he sets foot there, he will be seized the moment he lands and hanged from the nearest tree."

Talleyrand listened politely. He knew the Eagle's habits, and was waiting for him to swoop down on Paris.

In Vienna, the Congress was breaking up. Europe had been cooked and now, like a cold soufflé, was caving in. Violins played to deaf ears, candles poured out wax, then expired in a trail of smoke. The party was over. And in any event this elegant carnival was external to the history of this period—not part of the drama, but simply an interlude which Napoleon, history's most accomplished tragedian, had just ended. His return to France opened the fifth, conclusive act: slaughter and final destruction.

In the beginning, however, some greeted his escape as a blessing. The English, the Austrians, the Bourbons felt that by seizing him promptly, they could deal with the troublemaker once and for all. He had broken his word; all the nations had outlawed him, and this time they would put him away.

Talleyrand calculated the high risks that he and Castlereagh had taken. A gambler knows when to take risks. Talleyrand always did so deliberately. France was in a pitiable state. Her army had been dismantled; her administrative cadres, thinned out and renewed after a royalist purge, were still green; her financial situation after twenty-five years of Revolution and Empire, was desperate. Napoleon would return to find in office only a handful of the "traitors" who had betrayed him the previous April and would now swear loyalty for the time he remained in power. With all his genius, even Napoleon could not mobilize the resources which Talleyrand had salvaged. Perhaps he could still win a battle, two at most, but the success would be born of despair. He was doomed. It was written thus, not in the stars as romantic legends have insisted, but on the books of the Bank of France, on the administrative rolls, in the statistics of the gendarmerie, in every report from the prefects. France would not and could not fight any longer, except for the newest ranks of the military, who might take arms but could not conquer a Europe united in the determination to end hostilities.

Talleyrand and Castlereagh must have turned a cold and scornful eye on Bonaparte's fanatic admirers rushing to greet their idol, thinking they were giving him a triumph when in fact they were propelling him to his doom. Unperturbed, Talleyrand predicted: "It is a matter of weeks, he will not last long."

Vienna's residents deserted the ballrooms for the churches. While the Eagle "soared from one parish to the next," reorganizing his army and approaching Paris, a lot of praying went on. Talleyrand remained impassive, so serene that he was suspected of having a hand in Napoleon's game. In Vienna people said: "He has set the house ablaze in order to save it from the plague."

At this time Talleyrand came in contact with one Ruffo, a Neapolitan in charge of his affairs in Naples and Benevento. Ruffo was not blind. On March 8, 1815, after talking with the prince for four hours he came away amazed, as were the Viennese, by "the utter beatitude of the illustrious diplomat." Ruffo expressed surprise: "Should he not be the first to lose countenance as the emperor's return must strike him, of all people, as the overwhelming catastrophe of his life?" Unquestionably Napoleon's return was neither a catastrophe to him nor a surprise. "And oddly enough," the shrewd Neapolitan went on, "this time the serenity is not an attitude. It has no trace of the tension he sometimes displays and which is his feigned tranquility."

Surely these observations are proof of the matter. Other people in Vienna had remarked that Talleyrand walked with a lighter step since the day Napoleon escaped. When an Eagle flies, a cripple has wings.

When assailed with questions, he would calm people's fears with the same phrase: "It is a matter of weeks; he will not last long." His manner rather than his words had a reassuring effect.

There had been a hitch in his plans for the escape. A police report of March 18 noted that when Talleyrand read the news that all obstacles had been removed between Paris and Napoleon and that the latter could look forward to a homecoming in the capital, the prince was observed to have "scratched his head with both hands." An extraordinary gesture for him, which confounded his secretaries, the police noted. If his head-scratching had involved a single finger, the situation would have been serious; with one hand, it would have been grave; but with both hands, they could expect the worst.

In this case, the worst, as Talleyrand saw it, was Louis XVIII's cowardice in leaving the country for the second time. On the night of March 20, 1815, Napoleon slept in the royal bed. Talleyrand informed his embassy staff that the government to which they owed their livelihood was at that moment bumping along in a coach between Paris and the Low Countries in the shape of a fat old man without money or honor. At this depressing news, the staff dispersed. Talleyrand kept only Courtiade and a houseman.

The king's flight—not part of the original escape plan—bankrupted Talleyrand. Gaymuller, the banker who had been transmitting funds to him from the capital, refused to do so now. One of Napoleon's first acts on re-entering Paris was to dispossess Talleyrand. He was penniless—and a moment later, affluent. Some mysterious person informed the banks that he would cover any and all debts that our prince might care to run up. Quite a commitment. Who was this generous, anonymous guarantor? Castlereagh, acting on behalf of the English government. And what linked these two personalities so intimately? Castlereagh and our prince had put together the scheme to promote Napoleon's escape in order to lock him up more securely. Thus we realize that though the conspiracy left no trace, it did have certain felicitous results.

Schulmeister,* well known in European circles as a spy for Napoleon, was reported to be in Vienna. We know that he and his patron Fouché had refused to support Napoleon. They knew what was coming. Was Schulmeister involved in the escape plot? We do not know. Was he the bearer of a strange letter meant only for Talleyrand's eyes which the police managed to steal? Unsigned, it was a warning, a death threat; Metternich read it for Talleyrand. The threat came from "scoundrels who are aware that you have inspired all the great and noble acts aimed at destroying them." The so-called scoundrels referred to persons who had risked everything on the emperor's return, only to find out that Talleyrand devised the escape for a totally different purpose. More and more questions began to be asked in Vienna about this odd flight. Lord Stewart, England's ambassador and Talleyrand's close friend, took to drinking heavily. Roaring with laughter at the dinner table, he shouted: "I have that crazy Bonaparte on the tip of my fork." Rather indiscreet; Talleyrand pretended not to hear. Sometimes, late at night, if you pressed him hard enough he would relax and admit that European hysteria in the face of threatened rearmament was not such a bad thing: it was, he said, "a bout of fever attacking nations which had ceased trembling too soon." Less discreet on another occasion, he had the audacity to remark that Napoleon's boisterous return was an excellent opportunity to "catch the tapeworm by its head." And to keep us guessing about his

---

* Karl Ludwig Schulmeister, native of New-Freistett, a Strasbourg grocer. He was an agent of Fouché's, utterly devoted to Napoleon whom he served with cleverness and efficiency. He crops up in Germany, Prussia, Austria, and at Erfurt. Present yet invisible in Vienna during the Congress, he probably served Talleyrand whom he took to be the outstanding statesman of the post-Napoleonic era. He burned all his papers, but may have been involved in the escape from Elba. There is evidence that he went to see Napoleon several days before the latter left the island. Schulmeister died in 1853. He revealed nothing about his activities but received a visit in 1850 from Louis-Napoléon (i.e., Napoléon-Louis) Bonaparte.

part in the plot, Talleyrand sent armloads of letters and files roaring up the chimney. When asked if Napoleon had many followers in Paris, he replied: "I don't know; I only know that he has too many in Vienna." And indeed Napoleon's admirers were springing up all over since his return to the capital. Women and young romantics went wild over him, along with those eager for novelty at any price, for noise, bombs, cavalry charges. After twenty-five years of slaughter they cried: "More!" Princess Bagration joined the throng. She swore she would throw herself in the emperor's arms if she ever met him. Napoleon did not deserve such an outrage. Talleyrand made this scathing remark when Jérôme Bonaparte joined his brother in Paris: "Now I recognize that man who dotes too much on women. He loses his head for nothing. . . ." What scorn lies in that "for nothing"! Talleyrand looked upon the "Eagle's flight," which enraptured so many people, as merely a trap. Waterloo was "for nothing." Sadly enough, Talleyrand was right.

The Congress Ends and Dorothée Flees

Talleyrand's position *vis-à-vis* the coalition had become impossible. Fear of Napoleon had rekindled the fierce anti-French sentiments which Talleyrand tried so hard to dispel. What could he say to the people who blamed France for failing to hang Napoleon and then for rallying anew to his banner? Vienna charged France as an accomplice of the "monster" and declared war upon this incorrigible nation. Once Napoleon was out of the way, France would pay dearly for him. Talleyrand was shocked to hear Prussia, Austria, and Russia call for carving up his country.

In the end, Napoleon's flight turned out very badly. Talleyrand cloaked himself in silence, watching for a chance to parry. He knew that the prestige of France would prevent her from being destroyed or even partitioned. At worst—and it would involve serious risk for the future—her foes might attempt to pare her down. He was determined to stand fast: "Failure to yield can mean self-destruction," he said, "but to yield is to weaken." No minister of a defeated power was ever in such desperate need to defend an indefensible nation. He had to dissociate the cause of Napoleon from that of the French people and to plead for them. It meant going against the evidence, but such a task was not beyond our hero's gifts.

The Congress met several more times in March. Talleyrand wasted no opportunity to urge his views on every minister he could buttonhole; he entertained and was entertained, encouraging his niece to do the same, as well as the duchess of Courland after Napoleon's return had forced her to leave the capital and come to Vienna. Talleyrand would indoctrinate the ladies whom the duchess and Dorothée brought to him and in whose houses he poured out his message. In turn he would dispatch his flying squadron to preach in the homes of influential men. At dinner parties, at balls, in bed, everyone must pass on the word that of all Napoleon's victims, France deserved the most pity, and that it was unjust—as well as dangerous—to link the tyrant's name with the nation he had bled and ruined. This is what the politicians must be made to believe. The ladies had their weapons, let them use them. Were they not defending a sacred cause? What would happen to civilized society if France came under Prussian and Russian rule?

He prepared a statement, known as the Declaration of March 13, 1815, by which the Congress acknowledged that the conflict about to resume in Europe was the fault not of France but of one man's ambition, that Europe was not at war with France or her legitimate government, but only with Napoleon. By exonerating the French nation and the king, Talleyrand laid the groundwork for the future peace treaty and the restoration of Bourbon power, and saved his country from dismemberment.

But would the irate Congress endorse the Declaration? On the morning of the thirteenth he was still in doubt. Only his secretaries knew his fear. The council was to meet that day in Metternich's house. Talleyrand set forth on his mission to preserve his nation's integrity. The statement was in his pocket, a scrap of paper on which he and his aides had worked the whole night. They saw him into his carriage, all of them pale and anxious. Leaning through the window, he told them: "Wait for me; to stave off impatience, watch for my return from the palace windows. If I succeed, you will see me in the carriage window holding up the treaty on which hangs the fate of France and Europe."

They awaited the return of the champion gone out to do single combat for their beleaguered country. Would France be wiped off the map as Princess Bagration and the Prussian officers had predicted? At last the carriage reappeared, and in the window was a hand waving a sheet of paper. Success! France was not to be torn to shreds. His aides embraced each other joyfully.

Among the great events were small incidents, one of which is touching. He met Madame de Brionne once again. We recall her unwillingness to receive him at the time of the Treaty of Pressburg. The snub had wounded him. Madame de Brionne forgave him in 1815, seeing what he had done for the Bourbons and for France. "Here you are at last!" she greeted him. "I always knew that I would see you once more. I may have been displeased with you, but I have never stopped loving you. My interest has followed you everywhere."

Since 1785: a truly gigantic "everywhere." Talleyrand writes: "I could not say a word. I was crying." Tears that we can believe in. " 'Your position is admirable,' she told me. 'Oh, yes, I find it admirable.' " Madame de Brionne did not have long to live. Talleyrand was overwhelmed by the beauty and grace of their injured yet vital friendship, and by the abysmal grief and affliction separating them. "Tears were choking me, I felt faint and went for a breath of air on the banks of the Danube."

Shortly thereafter, she died.

Then another sorrow tore at Talleyrand's heart: Dorothée. His niece had lovers. Most of them remain anonymous because Dorothée knew them only casually, if at all, and never saw them again. A few of her liaisons are on record. She had an affair with Count Trauttmansdorff, imperial master of the horse, a handsome, fickle rake, the image of Edmond. She soon left him for the count of Clam. This affair was more serious. Though jealousy was not part of Talleyrand's makeup, it is certain that he was anxious and, in all probability, fearful of losing her. He knew that with him she had everything a beautiful, ambitious young woman could desire—except the one thing she sought from her lovers. He then realized that Dorothée took after her mother and her three sisters, the princess of Sagan, the duchess of Acerenza, and Princess Hohenzollern. The four Courland ladies left a solid trail of affairs all over Europe. The fifth, Dorothée, joined the family procession in Vienna.

The duchess moved into the Kaunitz Palace on March 24. Alas, her place had been filled—entirely—by her own daughter. We have no knowledge of how the trio felt or what sort of vague explanation must have been offered to the returning duchess.

Talleyrand had still another visitor, his old friend the indispensable Montrond. He came from Paris, fresh and in good spirits. It was possible to go from one enemy country to the other in the middle of a war, for war had broken out afresh. Europe's armies were on the march, converging on France. Florid-lipped Montrond had come as Napoleon's special secret envoy to win Talleyrand back to the emperor's service. Saint-Leon, an acolyte whom Talleyrand knew, was with Montrond. The two coaxed him with every argument they could think of to bring him round. Not that Montrond had suddenly been converted to emperor-worship; in reality he was eager to get his hands on the reward Napoleon had promised for bringing Talleyrand back to him, an annual allowance for life of 200,000 francs (20 million old francs). Montrond, who could never hang onto money, tried desperately to recruit Talleyrand. He was talking to a wall. Some persons in Vienna and in Louis XVIII's entourage at Ghent believed Talleyrand was playing a double game and was about to rejoin Napoleon. But their distrust was very ill-founded. Napoleon was a rotten plank and Montrond a fool to waste his time chasing after an income for life—a life of only ninety days.

On June 9 Talleyrand signed the final acts of the Congress of Vienna. On the tenth, he climbed into his coach, announcing that he was going to Belgium at the summons of his impatient sovereign. It was a sad parting. Talleyrand had thought that Dorothée's affair with Clam, although more durable than the others, would end with the Congress. He stayed on in vain past the dates set by Louis XVIII, despite several reminders from the monarch; but Dorothée's passion only grew, and her "intimate uncle" was forced to recognize the galling fact that she could not tear herself away from her lover. Rather than follow Talleyrand to Belgium, she chose to return to Sagan, hoping to see Clam in Germany where his regiment was stationed. On June 3 she left.

That was Talleyrand's private reason, reinforced by several other less private ones, for being in no haste to obey Louis XVIII's summonses. He felt that he could be more useful to the king and to his country in Vienna than at the court in Ghent, where the émigré coterie led by Blacas now dominated. There he would have to put up with rancor, stupidity, and ignorance of political realities, plus the withering scorn of those who still looked upon him as the former bishop of Autun, husband of the Grand woman. They would never forgive that sacrilege.

Admittedly, his delay in leaving Vienna carried a hint of insolence. He would have to pay for it.

On June 19, in passing through Aix-la-Chapelle he heard that a great battle had taken place the day before, that Napoleon had been routed by the conjunction of Wellington's and Blücher's armies. Waterloo. Up to that point he had traveled at a leisurely pace, having been nine days out of Vienna. He took four more days getting to Brussels. Finally, on June 23, he reached Mons where Louis XVIII, tired of waiting, acted as if he no longer expected him. The king's ill-humor was to grow far worse.

From that time Talleyrand had unstinted praise "for our great, our admirable duke"—Wellington, of course, the victor of Waterloo. Was he not a friend? A friend who was to become a valuable connection. Ultimately, France would benefit from this.

TALLEYRAND

Vanity Is an Ugly Trait and a Serious Blunder

Talleyrand collected a small court as soon as he arrived at Mons. First Jaucourt, who had taken his place in the ministry of foreign affairs, and baron Louis, both of whom offered friendship, devotion, and business. Had not Talleyrand been treated like a king in Vienna? Why not also at Mons? He came there expecting praise and rewards. But, under the influence of Blacas and his faction, Louis XVIII seemed in a mood to send him packing. Any European monarch would have emptied his coffers to have Talleyrand as minister. Metternich had ordered the Austrian minister in Brussels to "consult Talleyrand on all occasions and be guided by his advice." But incompetent rulers ought to let themselves be ruled by the saviours of their country. Of course, one must admit that a minister's impertinence can offend kingly dignity, as for example when summoned to appear forthwith before his sovereign, Talleyrand insolently replied: "I am never in a hurry. Tomorrow is time enough."

Chateaubriand paid him a visit. Talleyrand received him kindly, and noted that the viscount "complained about everything and everybody." There was cause for complaint a week after Waterloo. Chateaubriand managed to find a new subject for lament in the way he was greeted by the prince—too amicably, it seems. How unbearable! "He presented me with all the blandishments with which normally he cajoled petty upstarts and important fools." We do not associate him with the petty breed; he was a man of great ambition, anxious to reach the heights. The viscount nobly refused to be cajoled and invited the prince to go see the king. The poor king was on the rack, his greatest torment not the aftermath of Waterloo, but a court faction demanding that he dismiss his great favorite Blacas. He was also furious at Talleyrand for boasting publicly "of having set the crown on Louis XVIII's head a second time." It was true, but he didn't have to say so. Once was bad enough; twice, unthinkable. Someone warned him of the king's ill temper. Talleyrand smiled. He was indispensable and invulnerable. Chateaubriand tried to smooth things out and told Talleyrand to seek an immediate audience as His Majesty was leaving Mons. What madness seized Talleyrand? With unnatural bravado, he blustered: "He wouldn't dare." Not exactly his wittiest remark. It suggests something new, a sign of old age; he is losing his coolness, becoming touchy and vain. In Vienna, observers already noticed the growing arrogance which he would find occasion to display in the years ahead. Was he disillusioned on Dorothée's account? Or had his triumph in Vienna gone to his head?

Chateaubriand reported back to the king, who commented laconically: "As he wishes," then added: "I shall leave at three o'clock." And he did, at three in the morning.

They wakened Talleyrand: "The king is leaving." "Foiled!" he shouted. "Betrayed!" A slight exaggeration. Rushing into his clothes, taking Ricé's arm, he hobbled as fast as possible to the king. None too soon, for the royal coach was passing through the gates. They managed to halt it. When the king asked who had stopped his coach, a postilion informed him: "Sire, it is Monsieur de Talleyrand." "He is asleep," replied the monarch. No, the prince was actually there, and on foot. Ordering his coachman to turn back, Louis XVIII deigned to meet with his minister. After allowing the prince to speak, he addressed him coldly, as if he had not heard a word: "Prince, you are leaving us. The waters will do you good. Let us hear from you."

Talleyrand was stunned. He had been dismissed. The king re-entered his coach. This kind of dismissal was far more humiliating than Bonaparte's wrath.

Still, we have no reason to believe that "he foamed at the mouth with rage," as Chateaubriand puts it. The expression betrays the viscount's perverse pleasure in seeing Talleyrand humiliated rather than Talleyrand's reaction. The bitterness contained in these few lines he wrote to the duc de Levis-Mirepoix in the royal entourage probably conveyed his true feelings: "Just look, Monsieur le Duc, how they treat me. I put back a crown on the king's head. I am going to Germany to start a new emigration." [1] A piece of nonsense—as far as we know, it was the first he had ever uttered.

The only mention he ever made of this episode was a line to the duchess of Courland: "I was not pleased with my first audience."

In his *Mémoires d'outre-tombe,* Chateaubriand insists that he made every effort to reconcile the king and his minister. He visited Talleyrand and offered to intervene. The suave viscount used—just as Talleyrand did—the services of a woman, the duchess of Duras, whom he referred to as "my sister." Shortly thereafter a note came from the duke, her husband, announcing that everything was patched up. In reality, these quarrels and reconciliations, these insolent quips and resulting snubs were like the bickerings of two old dowagers. It was perfectly evident that Louis XVIII could not get along without Talleyrand and that Talleyrand could not exist without power any more than without light or air.

The Capetian and the Périgord hated each other as peers, the worst kind of enmity. But as fate had harnessed them to one chariot temporarily, pull they must together.

While marking time at Mons, Talleyrand recalled that the king of Naples had promised him 6 million francs. He sent Perrey, one of his secretaries, to Naples to collect the money. Alas, the deal was off. Perrey was soundly reminded that Talleyrand had done nothing, and that he had not promised to restore Ferdinand's throne to him until the Congress had decided to get rid of Murat. Under those conditions, Ferdinand owed him nothing. After much parleying and explaining, Perrey won his demands and brought back a draft for the 6 million. Talleyrand was willing to embrace Perrey to show his pleasure, "but would not allow him to wear a Neapolitan decoration as a token of the trip and his efforts, the memory of which was to remain in the bank and nowhere else." [2]

On arriving at Cambrai, Louis XVIII summoned Talleyrand, who came full speed.

During the short audience at Mons, he had handed the king a memorandum recommending what should be done during this critical period. Paris was occupied by Napoleon, who might still put up a desperate fight, invite a siege of the capital and destroy it. That whole question remained to be seen. What should the king do? Chateaubriand and Talleyrand agreed on one point: that Louis XVIII must not return to his capital behind foreign armies. He must remain independent. It was suggested that he proceed to unoccupied Lyons, set up his government, and deal with the victors from there, but not re-enter Paris until its liberation. Even Metternich wrote to Talleyrand urging him to remind the king that he must represent all Frenchmen—even regicides—must reconcile the factions and eschew foreign influence. Europe's rulers were beginning to fear that extremist demands would revive revolutionary fervor. Even a lamppost could not remain deaf to Chateaubriand's burning cry: "Legitimacy would re-enter Paris behind scarlet uniforms freshly dyed in the crimson blood of Frenchmen. . . ."

The ultra-royalists and the king were not impressed. They would not heed Talleyrand or Chateaubriand. But fearing that he might be disgraced, and eager to regain his ministry, Talleyrand ignored his own good advice and, to win favor, adopted the view of the king and his coterie. He makes no secret of it and no apology either: "I renounced my own convictions and followed the king to Cambrai to bring up the rear, he and I, of the English army."

The king's return was even more painful than his flight.

Talleyrand's Preparations for Returning the King to His Throne

Napoleon helped the Restoration by leaving Paris on June 29 and retiring to the Malmaison. To facilitate his return, Louis XVIII issued a declaration from Cateau-Cambrésis. He would have been better off without it as it offended many Frenchmen, though not the ultra-royalists. It also offended other governments. Talleyrand and Beugnot drafted a second declaration. As we know, Talleyrand had a flair for turning out public proclamations. It was a moderate statement, acknowledging the errors committed at the start of the Restoration and promising that they would not be repeated: "There is no substitute for experience; it was not wasted." It promised to forget the past except for those who had served Bonaparte during the Hundred Days. When the document was read in council, the passages in which the king admitted his errors aroused violent protests from the comte d'Artois. As author of the document, Talleyrand answered:

"Monsieur will forgive me for differing with him. I find these expressions necessary and therefore appropriate. The king has made mistakes; his affections have led him astray. There is nothing terrible about that."

"Am I, sir, the person implied here?" demanded the comte d'Artois.

"Yes, since Monsieur has put the discussion on this level. Monsieur has done a great deal of harm."

"The prince de Talleyrand forgets himself!" shouted Monsieur.

"I fear so," countered Talleyrand, "but the truth carries me away." [1]

That day he was not currying favor. If the Bourbons had listened to him, they might have saved the monarchy in France.

The duc de Berry, Monsieur's son, also flew at Talleyrand. Louis XVIII silenced his nephew: "Enough, nephew, it is my responsibility alone to deal with what is said in my presence and in my council." [2]

The declaration was published practically intact. Talleyrand was satisfied, but from then on, the comte d'Artois, the duc de Berry, their coterie, and the ultra-royalists were determined to have his head. Right now, however, he was the man of the hour. The army of courtiers—excepting ultra-royalists—besieged Talleyrand, not Monsieur. He was tomorrow's power. The favor-seekers swarmed all over him, practically under his bed. He listened and dispensed his false benedictions. One officeseeker, when asked by Talleyrand on what grounds he claimed the king's gratitude, replied: "But, Prince, I was in Ghent." Admittedly it was something of an honor to have accepted uncertainty and discomfort in the shadow of a shadowy king during the Hundred Days. Talleyrand expressed surprise: "You say you went to Ghent? There are those who went to Ghent and those who came back from Ghent. The number of those who stayed with His Majesty was perhaps seven or eight hundred. But the number returning from Ghent was, as far as I know, over fifty thousand."[3] The petitioner abandoned his suit.

On July 3, the king, the court, and all the baggage came to a halt behind the English supply wagons at Roye; Talleyrand sent off a note to the duchess still in Baden-Baden: ". . . the king is admirable, and when not diverted by Monsieur's influence, is excellent . . . Wellington . . . is an admirable man. He has great character, simplicity, and is something of a god on the battlefield. . . . Bonaparte is at Cherbourg and will set sail. I hope the English capture him. He is taking a lot of money. . . . They say he will go to America. . . ."[4]

There was yet another council at Roye. Talleyrand threw out a feeler, proposing that government positions be offered to anyone capable of filling them, including the regicides. The king gasped, then, pounding the arms of his chair, solemnly declared: "Never!" Chateaubriand relates the incident in his *Mémoires d'outre-tombe* with the brief commentary: "Never in twenty-four hours." The harsh truth of this soon was apparent. Talleyrand had not been talking abstractly; he had a specific regicide in mind, Fouché. With incredible shrewdness, Fouché had made himself indispensable. He had Paris in the palm of his hand, the nobility, even the comte d'Artois, at his feet.

Talleyrand had no desire to form a cabinet with Fouché, also known as the duke of Otranto. But Fouché's presence would guarantee peace and order in the capital on the king's return.

He and Fouché met at Neuilly in Wellington's presence. In fact, the victor of Waterloo and his friend Talleyrand were planning a viable cabinet which would allow the second Restoration to get off to a start. Pozzo di Borgo, Alexander's eyes and ears, was also there. The discussion was more sensible since the comte d'Artois had not been invited to participate. The situation was critical; there were threats of rioting in Paris. If, because of untimely scruples, Fouché had been rejected and had joined the opposition, a civil war might have broken out while foreign troops occupied the capital. For if Fouché was capable of quelling a riot, he was also capable of fomenting one. Talleyrand left the meeting convinced that order would prevail with Fouché as minister of police. The ministry would be in safe hands and the venerable machinery of government would start up again.

Talleyrand returned to Saint-Denis where Louis XVIII waited until all was in readiness for his return to Paris. He explained the situation; the king understood: "Do what you think necessary to serve me." It had already been done.

The royalists were frantic. Vitrolles searched everywhere for Talleyrand, even broke into his bedchamber at four in the morning. Now that he was back in Paris, our prince had resumed his nocturnal activity. Vitrolles thought Talleyrand was being dressed for his levee when actually he had just been undressed and was having his nightclothes put on, cocoon-like layers of flannel and wool and bonnets that encased him like some oversize baby grown old, pale, and listless. Jaucourt and baron Louis watched the scene in their shirtsleeves. Vitrolles was dying for the prince to tell him the results of his talk with Fouché. Yawning, Talleyrand replied: "Your duke of Otranto had nothing to say." "He is your duke of Otranto much more than mine," Vitrolles snapped back at this laconic woolen bundle.

Talleyrand could have told him that Fouché had already accepted the post of minister of police.

The rest of the tale is best told by Chateaubriand. Deals of this sort were part and parcel of the shady politics of Balzac's time. The new minister of Louis XVI's brother, the man who had massacred royalists at Lyons, appeared before the king at Saint-Denis on July 7 to take his oath to the crown. Chateaubriand happened to be there also, having come to pay his respects to the king. His Majesty was stopping temporarily at the ancient abbey of the Capetian kings. Chateaubriand sat waiting in a dark corner of a dimly lit room outside the royal chamber: "Suddenly," he writes, "the door opened: Vice entered leaning on Crime, M. de Talleyrand on the arm of M. Fouché; the infernal vision passed slowly before me, entered the king's chamber, and vanished." Did Chateaubriand really witness that scene from the shadows? Whether or not it ever happened is irrelevant, for his description is now history. The protagonists of it are perpetually associated with words that forever degrade them: "Vice . . . leaning on Crime." Chateaubriand goes on: "Fouché had just sworn fealty and homage to his lord. The trusty regicide, going down on his knees, laid the hands which had caused Louis XVI's head to fall between the hands of the royal martyr's brother. The apostate bishop went surety for the oath."

Seeing the ex-bishop and ex-terrorist drive off together in the same carriage, Pozzo di Borgo remarked: "I should like to hear what those two lambs are saying." [4] Rastignac might have made that comment.

Protected by such an efficient chief of police, Louis XVIII was able to install himself in the Tuileries without being bombed, stoned, or spat upon. The only insults were timorous Bonapartist murmurs. On July 8, Louis XVIII slept in Napoleon's bed in the Tuileries Palace.

The king made his official entrance, as French kings had done for centuries, along the rue Saint-Denis. Talleyrand saw no necessity for taking part in the ceremony so he took the road through the Batignolles district. One would almost think that he shunned the royal procession. He huddled in the back of an ordinary gray barouche which the Prussians had lent him. Thus he entered the city in the king of Prussia's baggage train, unknown to anyone. On the other hand, Louis XVIII followed the English supply wagons into Paris and everyone knew it. Talleyrand rode down the faubourg Saint-Honoré to the rue Saint-Florentin, his valet Courtiade on the footboard.

What had happened since Bonaparte's return? Nothing at all. One hundred days of vacation from legitimate power.

One of the happier consequences of the occupation was his having sent Madame Grand to London. She stayed there. His sumptuous mansion was intact. The seals affixed by Napoleon's order had been removed and some of the dust. Our prince could simply slip between fresh sheets in his cozy flannel nightclothes and muse on the one-time emperor of the West who was now prisoner on an English ship. He himself had just been appointed prime minister to Louis XVIII. He was about to resume the lavish style of life he had known as minister to the "usurper." Thus certain earthly splendors pass, while others remain.

For the First Time Talleyrand Mixes Politics and Passion

Prince de Talleyrand's cabinet was far from mediocre. There was baron Louis in finance, Fouché in the police, the eminent Gouvion Saint-Cyr in war, conscientious and competent Pasquier in the justice and interior departments, and Jaucourt in maritime affairs. It was in fact a government aimed at national recovery. Only the counterrevolutionists complained. Talleyrand regretted the desertion of the duc de Richelieu, who had made his reputation justly as governor of Odessa by regenerating that city and the Crimea. His refusal to accept the ministry of the king's household was couched in seemingly modest language; Richelieu said that having been away from France for twenty-two years, he felt inadequate to the responsibilities of a cabinet post. It was merely an excuse, for the duke was loath to work with any government that included Fouché.

In his stead, Talleyrand maliciously proposed the duc de La Vauguyon, whom the king could not stand. His Majesty heard the name and grew sullen. Talleyrand was insistent. The king's lip continued to drop. Then, judging the time ripe, Talleyrand named the man he really wanted, Alexis de Noailles, whom he had taken to Vienna and trained— indeed that is the word—to lace his shoes. He was reliable. The king hastily consented.

One important post remained untenanted, the prefect of police. All the qualified candidates had declined it. In 1815, it was an impossible job. Imagine Paris occupied by four foreign armies seething with revenge, indulging in every variety of extortion, theft, rape, and violence. Imagine a suffering, ill-fed, confused population unemployed, exploited by political factions, and, of course, plagued by crime. Baron Louis had come up with a potential candidate, a young lawyer from Libourne, "goodlooking," tactful, devoid of timidity as well as distinction, but unknown. Louis presented him to Talleyrand. Unable even to recall the name of the applicant for this untenable post, Talleyrand referred to him thus: "You know, the one who looks like a rather handsome hairdresser." [1] The young man's name was Decazes. Baron Louis took Decazes by the arm and said in front of Talleyrand: "Decazes, you are the prefect of police." Talleyrand said nothing. Thus began one of the finest political careers in history. Talleyrand did nothing to further it; he did not like this lawyer whose sudden, unwarranted favor irritated him, and he did not hide his feelings. It was the surest way to lose what little confidence Louis XVIII still bestowed on him grudgingly.

"What do people have against him?" Louis XVIII asked Talleyrand. "He works hard and loves me dearly. No one likes him here; they consider him a bit vain." "Yes, Sire," Talleyrand agreed, "vain and incompetent." [2]

The friction did not make his task any easier. At home he had to contend with ultra-royalists and the comte d'Artois, Bonapartists, and republicans. Abroad, the czar and Prussia, who could not forgive his defense of right and principle at the Congress of Vienna. His support came from England and Austria, who felt that as long as Talleyrand was in power, France would have a stable government. The czar, on the other hand, would not have frowned on some republican adventure.

Talleyrand attempted to muzzle the most articulate royalists to keep them from influencing the king. He had the courage to exclude the comte d'Artois and his son from the Council of Ministers. "We owe you

no thanks," Monsieur told him, "you have barred us from the council."
"Monsieur will thank me for it when he is king," replied Périgord to the
future Charles X.[3]

In the departments of the Midi, the Ultras behaved abominably,
fomenting anarchy, the "White Terror," openly insulting the crown.
Talleyrand branded these counterrevolutionist émigrés, "domestic foreigners." He was the one who coined the famous phrase: "Those people
have learned nothing and forgotten nothing." He had a special facility
for forgetting. They insisted on reminding him that he had taken holy
vows and also a wife. He kept his composure, but was hurt nonetheless.
One evening he was attempting to convert some of these diehards: "Gentlemen, you are trying to revive the Ancien Régime and that is impossible." One of them replied: "But, Monseigneur, who could imagine
making you bishop of Autun again? It would be madness. . . ."

Madness also to try to convince them that they were destroying the
monarchy faster than the republicans. Talleyrand suggested to the king
that the tricolor flag be adopted in an effort to reconcile the crown and
the people. Though only a gesture, at least it would have been visible.
Louis XVIII understood and was ready to consent, but Artois and his
coterie threatened to leave France if the monarchy did not retain the
white flag.

The prime minister also had to deal with the savagery of the occupying armies. The allied troops caused incredible suffering. Tales
from the occupied regions were terrifying. Whole villages pillaged and
burned, their occupants slaughtered. France's poor were made to pay for
Napoleon's conquests. The Prussians were especially brutal. "Prussian
insincerity can only be compared to Prussian barbarism," Talleyrand
wrote on August 29. Blücher was inciting his own troops to violence.
Then he got the idea of blowing up the Pont d'Iéna, which had the misfortune of commemorating one of Napoleon's victories over the Prussians.
A victory indeed if it brought Blücher and his hordes to Paris. Talleyrand
protested in an effort to save the bridge. Blücher's reply came back: "At
that moment [when the bridge blows up] I should like M. de Talleyrand
to be standing on it." In this instance, Louis XVIII acted like a king. To
Blücher he sent word that he, not Talleyrand, would blow up with the
bridge, and ordered his coach. The other allies intervened so that neither
the bridge nor the king went up in smoke. The Prussian general took his
revenge instead on the population. The bridge was rebaptized "Pont de
l'Ecole Militaire" in order, as Talleyrand put it, to satisfy "the savage
vanity of the Prussians."

What was Talleyrand doing amid all these worries? He says that he was working. Yet the king, the other cabinet members, and his con-temporaries blame him for doing nothing. He never decided anything on time. Papers piled up; complaints poured in to the king. But on August 20 Talleyrand wrote to the duchess: "The ministry's daily output sur-prises me. The complaint that we are slow stems from the excited temper of our country"—and from the minister's nonchalance, no doubt. Had this nonchalance grown worse? Perhaps. This failing of his appeared more pronounced because of his responsibilities as prime minister. He was holding that position for the first time in his life. Was it too much for him?

He was not cardinal Richelieu or even Mazarin, although he re-sembled the latter in certain respects. Despite his prodigious talents, however, he still was not competent to be chief minister of state. He possessed all the versatility which enabled his two illustrious predecessors to attain the heights of power, but he lacked the strength of character to exercise and maintain it. It was beyond him. His obsequious manner was not a mask, it was a profound inner need. His cleverness led him to exploit what was essentially a weakness. Despite his arrogance and his impertinence, he felt compelled to act as intermediary, to serve, to kneel to the power that kept him from ruling yet urged him to act like a ruler.

When Louis XVIII took the saddle after Napoleon, Talleyrand felt as if the reins suddenly went slack. He lost his way. He returned to old habits (his sybaritic life, as Dorothée put it), indulging his fondness for women and his woman's fondness for social gatherings.

And if, in this period, he grew laxer than ever, he had fresh cause to be discouraged. "Everything is so difficult, so onerous," he wrote to the duchess on August 26, 1815, "that one can only hope it will not last. Out of all this trouble some good must come." Moreover, he had lost the ability to split his energies in two and to dominate the political stage. He was tired. The duchess returned to the capital, and he welcomed the peace and quiet she offered him and which he longed for. Still, he missed Dorothée. Where was she off to with her Clam? It tormented him. The summer of 1815 was sad indeed. He was at the pinnacle of his ambition, and he was extremely unhappy. This temporary depression left him testy. His dear friend Countess Tyszkiewicz felt the rough edge of his temper. She had only one good eye, poor woman, and when his worried look began to alarm her, she would inquire, perhaps too persistently, how he was. He answered: "As you see, Madam."

Dorothée returned to Paris on July 20, 1815, bringing her lover with her. It was hardly a triumphant homecoming for her, for Talleyrand, or for her husband Edmond de Périgord. The affair gave neither of the lovers a sense of peace. Dorothée invested too much passion and pride in it, while Clam contributed little passion and much conceit. The duchess was troubled by the harmful effects of this liaison, not so much the upset Clam was causing in her daughter's life but what Dorothée was doing to Talleyrand. The more passionate his niece's attachment to Clam, the more Talleyrand loved her. Meanwhile, the duchess of Courland's tender affection concealed her jealous torment. Rarely does a friendship that succeeds love turn out to be as trusting as theirs.

Suddenly Edmond came to life. He decided, for reasons known only to himself, to treat Dorothée as his wife. There was a duel. The records do not identify Edmond's adversary, calling him simply "an Austrian major." Some highly influential person erased all traces of the episode, but we are told that the four Courland ladies, the duchess and her daughters, were delighted that "Périgord received a large saber cut across his face."

Talleyrand anxiously followed the course of Dorothée's affair. Did she not wish to live in Vienna? He felt that the loss of her would be irreparable. The cares of state were nothing in the face of such agony.

Chancellor Pasquier's Memoirs point out that the time when the greatest burden of political responsibility fell on Talleyrand's shoulders "was also the time when he was past sixty and chose to yield to an all-consuming passion that completely dominated his mind." When Talleyrand thought that Dorothée was going to leave him, "he fell into a state of physical and moral prostration impossible to describe."

In her Memoirs, Madame de Boigne remarked that "M. de Talleyrand is out of his mind." And Charles de Rémusat, his good friend, wrote that it was "the torments of desire and jealousy that made M. de Talleyrand appear, these past months, so unlike his usual self."

Our minister's excessive nonchalance and the king's displeasure are understandable.

Talleyrand had stayed on in the ministry of foreign affairs. The department had not changed in fifteen years: Hauterive, La Besnardière, and the same old staff were still there. So great was his influence over them—they might have been models of him—that in his absence they spoke, reasoned, and wrote for him and like him. As for the other ministries, he didn't care what happened there, or rather, prevented anything from happening.

Now for a close look at him in August, 1815. He is sixty-one. He rises between eleven and noon. Charles de Rémusat describes his levee, the ritual of which never varied until his death:

The prince entered a private drawing room or dressing room. He was tall, with broad shoulders and hips, and always wore loose-fitting clothes. At this moment all one saw was a vast assembly of flannel, cotton, fustian, cambric, a whitish mass advancing with a limp, lounging along, casually greeting those present, sitting down in front of the fireplace where three valets waited, one tall, powdered, dressed like his master except for black silk stockings, supervising his toilet rather than performing it [that was Courtiade]; the two others, wearing aprons over barber's gray livery, were employed principally as hairdressers. They began at once to strip the stockings and flannel wrappers off his legs, which were then placed in a small bucket of eau de Cologne. He was served a cup of camomile tea during the course of the ceremony, which was all he took for breakfast. The rest of him was enveloped in drawers, vests, dressing gowns, with all sorts of odds and ends flopping about, and on his head was a kind of tight-fitting cambric bonnet tied under the chin with a pale ribbon; it had earflaps and a headband reaching down to the eyebrows, surmounting a pale, expressionless face with rush-colored eyes, the underpart of which was bounded by thick neckcloths covering a rather short neck.

Uncombed and unset, his thick, fine hair, which must have been blond at one time, had whitened probably owing to powder more than age. He was rather vain about his fine head of hair, which he kept until the end of his life. The two valets then set about combing, curling, pommading, and powdering him; in the meanwhile, a servant brought him a silver bowl and washcloth for his face. Of all the details of his toilet, which was interesting and therefore not too distasteful to watch, one of the most noteworthy was his consumption of one or two large glasses of warm water which he sucked in through the nose and spit out, much the way the elephant uses his trunk. By the time his hair was done, his feet usually had been dried and his valets had slipped on wool stockings, white silk stockings, black silk breeches, and his large shoes with buckles. Then he would rise to his feet rather painfully, slipping off his two or three dressing gowns while someone dexterously passed a shirt over his head. Then the first valet wound several white satin cravats about his neck; at that moment his hat was put on because in former times it was not considered good taste for the hair to look freshly set. Instead of being tucked into his black silk breeches, his shirt usually hung outside, like an overblouse, and often he would remain in this state, chatting with his audience, which sometimes included women. It was said that he received the emperor of Russia in that outfit. By that time it was about one in the afternoon, and as he did not like to hurry or to change his habits, there were very few occasions during the Republic, the Empire, or the Restoration when he considered the situation grave enough to disturb any part of this ritual.

495

Throughout this exhibition, "there was a steady stream of callers." Women would come, but their presence never made him uneasy, and he did not even bother to turn his back when his shirt was being changed. A pile of French and English newspapers were "on a table; they were picked up, read, discussed. In the midst of his ablutions, Talleyrand would drop a maxim or a jibe." Those present scooped them up and carried them elsewhere.

We have a different portrait and a different description of the levee dating from about the same period. It is by Molé, supposedly Talleyrand's "friend"; in any event, he never missed a reception on the rue Saint-Florentin. The description is interesting not only for what it tells us about our hero but for its insistence on the ravages time inflicted on him. Molé brings out "the wan, lifeless, sagging skin" on his face, "his arrogant look and glassy eyes." Age had a good deal to do with it—but so did malice. When Molé writes: "his mouth, perhaps the only one of its kind, at once conveys debauchery, surfeit, disdain," it seems a great deal for one mouth to convey; might he not have settled for lassitude and disdain? That same mouth also conveyed wit, urbanity, tenderness. There is nothing surprising about the pale skin: the preponderantly nocturnal life of our prince and his lymphatic constitution denied him a rosy complexion. Molé goes on to tell of "a monster, half man, half serpent." Such menageries were all the rage at the beginning of the century. Though the picture is composite, the details are correct: "He is a combination of grand seigneur, woman, priest, and cat; the grand seigneur and the priest dominate." If one is to believe Molé and the Rémusats, who, like Madame de Staël, always referred to Talleyrand as "le Curé," it would seem that the ecclesiastical character of our hero persisted throughout his career.

Molé was highly impressed by the levee. He noted a number of details which had escaped Charles de Rémusat. The bed was so constructed that Talleyrand slept sitting up instead of prone. His reason for wearing so many layers of clothing was not to keep warm but to cushion an infantile and slightly morbid fear of falling out of bed in his sleep. Molé observes certain repugnant facets of Talleyrand's toilet, especially his habit of sniffling water up into his nose and ejecting it through the nostrils and mouth: "His ablutions and his cascades lasted for over a quarter of an hour, during which time his private drawing room became filled with prominent personalities. . . . The first washing was followed by a footbath during which his hair was done; he displayed for all to see the talons serving as his feet with a shameless indifference that always surprised me." If the "monster's" shamelessness was a surprise, so was the complacency of all those faithful, obsequious spectators contemplating its "monstrosities."

In the afternoon, he went over to the rue du Bac. He stayed no more than two hours, for dinner was set for five o'clock. It was his only meal and the great event of the day. The climax of work and pleasure. Could these contacts and conversations, often so useful and of such capital importance, take the place of office work for a premier? He thought so. Metternich, Wellington, Nesselrode, and Castlereagh dined with him, a real council of Europe. Essential to the task of a foreign minister. But it did not take care of all the paper work piling up on the king's table. When he really concentrated on something, it was usually between two and three in the morning—a rather late start to a prime minister's day. That is what he termed "working all morning long."

Family affairs were expedited just as promptly; he arranged Charlotte's marriage after one hour's discussion with his brothers. Boson's son, Alexandre de Périgord, was to be her husband. Undoubtedly, Talleyrand gave a cheerful account of the charming young lady's background and of the dowry with which he provided her. How easy it was to arrange things! He gave nameless Charlotte her rightful name, for she was in all probability his own daughter; and the money would remain in the family. Périgord plus Périgord, the circle closed, allowing nothing to escape.

Later, Alexandre was prefect of Arras. In 1830, the press published some biting remarks about "his bastard administration," recalling his wife's parentage, and said that "he was both the son-in-law and the nephew of prince de Talleyrand." The prince had a knack for getting himself into awkward situations; but somehow they never bothered him.

Talleyrand Believes He Is Indispensable; the King Disagrees

Talleyrand had to step in once again to protest the inordinate demands of the occupying powers, which, this time, were acting mercilessly. To prevent him from repeating the maneuvers he had used in Vienna, they barred him from their conferences. He raised all sorts of arguments against treating France like an enemy nation. Had they not signed a peace treaty with her? The treaty was still valid since the legitimate government which had signed it was in Ghent during the recent hostilities; therefore the peace entered into by the European coalition and the king of France remained unbroken. Talleyrand further reminded the allies of the Declaration they had signed in Vienna affirming that their enemy was Napoleon, the usurper, and not France. Unfortunately, the allies saw things differently. France had welcomed the "usurper," participated in his crime, and must pay the penalty. "The Flight of the Eagle"—that spectacular performance turned out to be a costly one.

Talleyrand had to face still another assault. This time the allies were demanding the return of art treasures gathered by Napoleon from museums, palaces, and churches in all the countries on which he had showered his glories. In 1814, Talleyrand had been able to save those works of art. Now it was out of the question. Even his friend Wellington took a hand in dismantling the Louvre. The Pope sent the sculptor Canova to recover objects which Napoleon had taken from the Vatican. Looking down his nose, Canova complained to Talleyrand that a man who was, as he declared pompously, "The ambassador of our Holy Father" ought to be treated more respectfully. "Packing agent would be more accurate," Talleyrand replied sweetly.

The loss of these treasures occasioned a pun of his comparing the state of French museums to that of her army: "The army is like the Louvre. Both contain only old frames."

He was shocked by the allied note containing the peace terms they planned to "impose": "I was highly indignant at the note I received, the form of which was even more insolent than the terms it contained. The council unanimously approved the reply I proposed to make." [1]

He protested, invoking every possible argument. On September 22, 1815, the allies informed him that they would not ease their demands. What should he do to combat a wall of hostility reinforced by cannon and bayonets? Cut his own throat? Self-sacrifice is not in the credo of a man who wears six flannel vests, keeps a harem of duchesses and a chef called Carême. He resigned himself to signing the treaty, a hard blow to his pride.

There was another problem, domestic this time. The elections of 1815 gave France a Chamber of Deputies sarcastically dubbed "the vanishing Chamber" because its membership was almost exclusively ultra-royalist. Not only were the allies crushing France, but now the country was becoming ungovernable, this reactionary majority posing a serious threat to the monarchy. Talleyrand felt his position jeopardized, and to keep his cabinet afloat, decided to jettison Fouché, his most compromising colleague. But the court forgot that this undesirable had made it possible for the king to re-enter Paris. Talleyrand was hoping that His Majesty would assign Fouché to some very distant embassy. Vitrolles had a hand in the matter and noted the details in his Memoirs. The Council of Ministers met one evening on the rue Saint-Florentin, and just as they were dispersing, Talleyrand began speaking in very general terms about foreign travels, embassies, and the prestige of French diplomats abroad, especially in America—America the beautiful! And he began extolling her forests and plains, his voice rising. No one knew what lay behind the rhapsody. Some of the ministers left. Fouché lingered, sorting his papers, listening. "It is a beautiful country, I know it well, I have traveled across it, have lived in it; yes, a superb country," Talleyrand sang on. Vitrolles, standing next to him, knew what he was up to, and was fascinated by the performance. "They have rivers unlike any we know," Talleyrand chanted on, "and none more beautiful than the Potomac." Fouché remained insensitive to the lure of the Potomac. "And magnificent forests of trees that we grow here in tubs. I can't remember their name. . . ." "Daturas," Vitrolles murmured. "Yes, that's it, whole forests of daturas," Talleyrand nodded delightedly. Fouché shot him a pale glance; he had understood. The minister of police was forewarned. As soon as Fouché left, Talleyrand turned to Vitrolles: "This time I definitely twisted his neck." In a matter of days the plan was executed. On September 19, His Majesty appointed Joseph Fouché ambassador to Saxony and sent him to Dresden. They were hoping he would refuse, but he took the bone they tossed him. Soon afterwards, the bone was withdrawn; he lost his embassy and was banished. No country offered him refuge. Austria allowed him to stay, under police surveillance. He died a miserable exile in Trieste, upon a heap of gold wrung from his crimes.

If Talleyrand thought he could protect himself by getting rid of Fouché, the illusion was short-lived. He heard that the following conversation had taken place among Ultra deputies:

> "The king was right to dismiss Fouché, but when will he dismiss the other?"
> "The other? Which other?"
> "Monsieur de Talleyrand himself."
> "Well, they will probably take into account his services in getting rid of the regicide minister."
> "Possibly, but the king still would be well advised to remove this minister of the Revolution." [2]

Perhaps this recalls that odd unfinished business of a credit, known as the Bacri-Busnach credit, which had been pending on the books of the foreign ministry since the Directory. It was a subject of discord between the French government and the dey of Algiers. We find Talleyrand once again involved as he sent Consul Duval to Algiers. Duval probably offered an unsatisfactory settlement and provoked an insult from the dey, which, as we know, led Charles X to close the matter once and for all in 1830 by seizing Algiers.

That was the least of our minister's worries. His cabinet was tottering. Only the king's active support could have kept it from falling. Talleyrand himself remarked: "A cabinet in need of support is a cabinet about to fall." His own fell without any support. He recalled one stinging remark that Louis XVIII had addressed to his minister. Though Talleyrand dubbed him "the prankster king," His Majesty's "pranks" could be insulting: "Talleyrand calls himself 'de' Périgord; he is off by only one letter: he is 'du' Périgord." * Pure spite: had not Louis XVIII remarked on first meeting Talleyrand that their two houses were equally ancient? He stung Talleyrand where it hurt most. Actually, the king was trying to convey that if Talleyrand wished to leave office, no one would stop him. Talleyrand realized that but was not ready to leave. The king insisted, urging him to return to Valençay, assuring him that his health would benefit from a prolonged rest in that lovely spot. An old, familiar tune: the song of the daturas. As Talleyrand persisted in missing the point, the king pressed him more pointedly: "Is Valençay so far from Paris?" The reply caught him off balance: "Sire, twenty leagues farther than from Paris to Ghent."

With the king unable to provide leadership, the government grew steadily weaker. According to his *Memoirs,* Talleyrand refused to accept the conditions imposed by the coalition and, for that reason, handed in his resignation. He adds: "The king accepted it with apparent relief." A rather neat way of explaining the situation. His resignation undoubtedly was a relief to the king. But Talleyrand did not want to leave office; he was dismissed. Louis XVIII played his hand like an expert. On September 24, Talleyrand, with baron Louis and Dalberg for support, went to see the king. The trio tried to blackmail Louis XVIII in order to strengthen Talleyrand's position as prime minister. Talleyrand asked for unconditional support from His Majesty in the Chamber of Deputies; otherwise, he would resign. He thought the king would fall all over him, that nobody else would be able to form a cabinet. Unmoved, the king sat staring at the ceiling. He had already decided what to do. Coolly, in our hero's best style, he replied: "Well then, I shall take a new minister." [3]

Talleyrand, beaten at his own game, found himself quietly dismissed. He wrote to the duchess the next day: "We leave without a

* The king was deriding his nobility, implying that Talleyrand was just a native of Périgord—Trans.

single compliment. The notice in the official journal is absolutely matter-of-fact; not a single word about us, as if we had never existed."

What did he expect? A fond farewell, eulogies, gratitude? The Bourbons were never very grateful to anyone. Talleyrand made no mistake when he said: "The ingratitude is barely disguised." Yet it is surprising that a man of such keen insights should have expected anything different.

His attitude toward the duc de Richelieu, who succeeded him, betrays contempt which also might have been better disguised. In the past, he was cleverer at dissimulating, but his wit had not lost its edge. Richelieu had served the czar for twenty years as governor of Odessa. Hearing of Richelieu's appointment, Talleyrand commented: "A fine choice indeed; he knows the Crimea better than anyone in France."

He shared his thoughts with the duchess, counting on her to disseminate them through "the seraglio": "We now have a cabinet to end all cabinets: the president is Russian; Corvetto, the minister of finance, is Genoese; all this for the purpose of defending the interests of France. It will be interesting to write about when I write."

When he tells us in the *Memoirs*: "I can say therefore that I retired from public affairs without regret, determined never again to assume a position of leadership," we find it hard to believe. He probably would have gone back to the Foreign Office at the drop of a hat—Louis XVIII's or any of his successors'. Though the king may have failed to praise him, he did not deny him a token of esteem, the office of grand chamberlain, conferred on September 28. Once again Talleyrand found himself attached to the royal person. He could enter the king's apartments at will and stood behind his sovereign's chair at state dinners. He was not indifferent to this honor, or to Richelieu's visit and congratulations, or to the letter of notification in His Majesty's own hand. "It has all been handled decorously," he had to admit. The office of chamberlain provided an additional yearly income of 100,000 francs, a great comfort to a man facing retirement.

Part Three
1815–1838

Retirement from Politics and from Matrimony

He adopted the habits of a hermit. For the daily political whirl he had only contempt. We can imagine how convincing was his life of renunciation: society continued to flock to his levees and dinners. Yet for Charles de Rémusat's ears he extolled the merits of country living, said he was thinking of retiring to his "cottage" at Valençay and cultivating his garden. On October 18, 1815, a few weeks after his dismissal, he wrote to the duchess of Courland: "I have spent thirty years of my life thinking of nothing but my country's welfare. Now I am looking after my own affairs, which I have totally neglected. That is my present outlook, a real revolution over my normal frame of mind." One cannot deny that he thought of his country and served it well; but as for having completely neglected his own interests, that is sheer hypocrisy.

In reality, our hermit had direct contact with the outside world. In addition to his duties as grand chamberlain, he was a life member of the Chamber of Peers. This carried the privilege of attending government sessions, speaking his mind, and continuing thus to exercise a political function. He used this privilege exclusively to assail his successor, Richelieu. Talleyrand prided himself on not having signed the Treaty of Paris. "I am still relieved, as you must be too, that my name is not among the signatories of this fine deed," he wrote on November 24, 1815. Why take credit for it? He had been dismissed before the treaty was signed. And we know anyway that he would have signed it just as he signed the armistice of 1814 and the Treaty of Paris of 1814.

When Marshal Ney was brought to trial, Talleyrand found an excuse for not participating in the proceedings. That did not stop him from attacking Richelieu: "It is a sad occasion for those who signed the Treaty of Pressburg and crossed the Niemen. What shameful times!"

This hypocritical appeal to Bonapartist sentiment marked the depths of his discontent. In return, Richelieu had only kind words for Talleyrand. On Christmas Day, 1815, he informed our hero that his hereditary peerage and his title prince de Talleyrand had been declared transferable by royal decree to his brother Archambaud and to the latter's male heirs. Great news to the family and a great satisfaction to Talleyrand.

He was also made a member of the Academy of Humanities. Lady Morgan first laid eyes on him at the time of his reception and was impressed by "his remarkably calm expression, the face of a sleeping child." Molé had called him a "monster."

In the spring of 1816, following Louis XVIII's sarcastic advice, he visited Valençay. He had not seen it since the departure of the Spanish princes in 1808. Traces of their innocent indoor horticultural experiments were still visible. Parquet floors damaged by their irrigation projects had to be repaired. He ought to have sent the bill to St. Helena!

Despite the remoteness of the capital, the redecoration of Valençay, and the delights of the countryside, he was obsessed by the bitter humiliation of his dismissal. It came out in his letters: "The Richelieu cabinet is heartily detested. This is constantly evident. M. de Richelieu is detested more than anyone else because he is the most prominent. . . . No one knows the names of the other members. An influential gentleman from Chateauroux was saying yesterday at dinner that Decazes is the power behind this cabinet."[1]

Richelieu and Decazes, the latter minister of police, became his favorite victims. He battered away at the régime with his biting wit, which carried strong currents of all too apparent spite and rancor. Sir Henry Bulwer attributes this remark to him: "Nature placed eyes in the foreheads of human beings so that they could look ahead, but the Bourbons have them in the rear and look backward." Even his colleagues in the Chamber of Peers became targets of his sarcasm. In an effort to mollify him, someone said: "In spite of everything, they are not without consciences." He replied: "Yes, I know, my friend Sémonville has several of them." And another time, when someone mentioned that this Sémonville had grown very stout: "I don't understand," said Talleyrand innocently. "What don't you understand, Monseigneur?" "What possible interest he has in putting on weight."

Exasperation made him savage. Ruhlière, a friend of his, was talking to him and others: "I have committed only one spiteful act in my whole life." "When will it be over?" retorted Talleyrand.

Hearing of his peevish humor, Louis XVIII said philosophically: "The wounded vanity, the frustrated ambition dominating his letters make them extremely curious." Curious perhaps, but disgrace did not enhance Talleyrand's temperament.

While with bitter vigilance he observed every move of the government's, the government was no less attentive to the activities and opinions of its too illustrious ex-member. He had a visit—purely a courtesy call, he was told—from the prefect of the Indre and his secretary. Actually, they came by for a chat in order to measure the extent of the prince's hostility toward the régime. The investigation stemmed from some nonsense reported by one of the townspeople in Valençay, who came regularly to the château and claimed that "Prince Taillerang" was plotting to restore Napoleon II and become regent; that Napoleon was not on St. Helena but hiding somewhere in the neighborhood; and that all his information came from the prince's own lips. Expecting to confront the conspirators, the prefect tumbled instead on the most charming of tableaux: the prince in his library sorting a shipment of books from Paris aided by two very pretty, elegant ladies, the duchess of Courland and Dorothée. The books were unsold items from the third auction of his library in London in May, 1816. The sale, which fetched him 210,000 francs, was by far the most lucrative yet.

His great comfort at that time was the presence of the duchess and Dorothée. A month before, while the duchess was still in Silesia, Talleyrand had written asking her to come to stay at Valençay. "I shall have your rooms put in order, the carpet removed and everything tidied so that in October you will be fairly comfortable . . . dear friend, we will spend our lives in the same places, the same occupations, the very same way of life. I know no happiness comparable to spending the days with you . . ." (May 21, 1816).

The duchess did not wait for autumn; she came at a gallop. Dorothée was already at Valençay. Where did she come from and how long had she been back? In November, 1815, she had left for Italy and Vienna. Talleyrand tried to keep her from going, but the affair with Clam appealed more strongly to her. Her uncle wrote to her in Venice thinking she was there. On December 21 she was in Vienna with her two sisters. Talleyrand sent Gentz to implore her to return to the rue Saint-Florentin. The effort was successful; Dorothée was breaking up with Clam. After a series of ups and downs, the two lovers finally separated for good in February. She emerged mutilated and humiliated, almost hating her lover. Before leaving Vienna, she saw Gentz on February 21. In his diary he described her thus: "As remarkable for the subtlety of her mind as for her depravity of heart, this woman has been an object of study and amusement for me."

Dorothée returned to her uncle and never left him again. Theirs was an extraordinary kinship of the mind. He wrote to her: "With you one can skip right over intermediate ideas. Your mind never gets in a rut, and in that respect you have ceased to be German. You have remained so in all your habits except those of the mind; that has no more of an accent than your speech." A simple, sincere expression of intense admiration, the admiration of one mind for another. "You must admit that it would be a great mistake to deprive ourselves of one another as I would lose my movement and you your repose."

She responded with mutual admiration, as noted in her Memoirs: "My long acquaintance with M. de Talleyrand has made me more critical of others. The minds I encounter now seem slow, diffuse, caught up in petty distractions."

The prince soon had to tear himself away from the delights of rediscovery because as grand chamberlain he was required to attend the wedding of the duc de Berry, heir to the throne after the duc d'Angoulême. Berry was marrying Caroline of Bourbon-Sicily, daughter of King Ferdinand of Naples. This union was in part Talleyrand's doing. First they had thought of marrying the duke to the czar's younger sister, Grand Duchess Anna, on whom Napoleon had set his sights. Talleyrand had advised against the alliance in Napoleon's case and later in the duke's, citing the differences of religion and birth, the House of Holstein-Romanof being far inferior to the blood of Saint Louis and Louis XIV. He proposed a marriage with Caroline of Bourbon-Sicily, the choice finally adopted by the royal family.

Louis XVIII invited Talleyrand to ride in his coach to Fontainebleau to meet the young princess. Talleyrand was delighted to share the state coach, delighted to join in the splendid pageant of a union he favored, delighted to resume the courtier's role so natural to him, delighted to be cajoled by royalty, and most assuredly delighted to hear His Majesty relate the latest court scandals, a favorite occupation which he performed brilliantly. The world had been sunny ever since Dorothée and the duchess returned.

He found the royal princess charming and noted her attractive features. One, however, seemed to be missing: "She is well provided with a place for an ample bosom, but it has yet to appear." The duc de Berry must be patient. Talleyrand added: "Her eyes seem to wander off into space, but," he hastened to explain, "she is not cross-eyed." Who else would have the impertinence to say that about a royal highness? And he ends the panegyric: "She is gay, alert, and nimble, although decidedly pigeon-toed." In short, a perfect princess, with one or two flaws.

The opulent marriage ceremony took place in the Tuileries, a far cry from the full-dress parades reviewed by Napoleon which used to pass for gala festivities in the days of the Empire. Talleyrand cut a splendid figure and was universally admired. His uncle the archbishop, Monseigneur de Talleyrand-Périgord, the king's chaplain, said Mass. The family was in prominence. Our hero had one criticism to offer about the ball that followed, which, like those at Versailles, included waltzes. He felt that court dress was not appropriate to the whirling motion of the waltz. Charles de Rémusat and many others noticed the prince's lively and genial disposition. Rémusat wrote to his mother that Talleyrand was "as charming as he can be, smiling, amusing the king, telling one story after another, totally at ease, nothing ministerial about him, and certainly nothing suggesting a disgraced minister. . . . His cheerfulness makes a lot of people uneasy" (June 17–19, 1816).

But the spiteful had no cause for alarm. Talleyrand was happy not because he planned to overturn the cabinet but because "his women" were waiting for him at Valençay. They, too, were happy to be back. Dorothée had always preferred out-of-the-way châteaux to life in Paris. There was even a secret reason behind the prince's smile: he was in the process of negotiating an amicable end to his own marriage. He was just glimpsing that delicious moment when the hateful yoke of his bondage to Madame Grand would be undone.

We may recall that on his return to Paris in a Prussian barouche, he found his house empty, his wife gone. Why did the princesse de Talleyrand run off to London while he was in Vienna and Ghent? Because cohabitating with Dorothée was so painful an experience that she could not bear the thought of the niece's return. The triangle—or quadrangle, when the duchess of Courland came to share the prince with her own daughter—was so distressing to Madame de Talleyrand that she fled. It was a harebrained decision. Instead of seeking out her husband, she went to London, then to Brussels, and finally settled at Pont-de-Sains, an estate north of Paris. She then realized her mistake, but upon returning to Paris, found her place taken. Talleyrand did not want to see or hear from her again.

His wife's return left him in a rather embarrassing position which Louis XVIII found extremely spicy. A married bishop involved with three women, his wife, his niece, and his niece's mother, was indeed an uncommon spectacle. "The prankster king" mocked him: "Is it true that Madame de Talleyrand has come back? Now there's something you can't ignore." Even a king, as he quickly found out, should not have raised the subject. The retort came flying back: "I, too, had to endure my twentieth of March" (the day Napoleon marched back to Paris). The king turned on his heel and left.

Talleyrand wrote to the duchess on June 1, 1816, that he would act handsomely toward his wife if he could be sure of getting rid of her. He would not have been capable of cruelty to her: "But I must get it over with. I am not afraid to make financial sacrifices."

Fortunately, energetic Dorothée took charge of the matter. Talleyrand lacked the courage to turn his wife out. Dorothée provided a plan "to get it over with"; all he had to do was pay out the money. "As money is the real motive behind all of Madame de Talleyrand's actions," Dorothée wrote to him on June 14, 1816,

> one must always start from that premise in dealing with her, and accordingly I venture to offer this word of advice to spare you a distressing correspondence which you would find distasteful. Here it is. Send someone to her at once, not devious like M. Roux, but have M. Perrey go with some kind of letter of credit; let him inform Mme de Talleyrand on your orders that she will not get her hands on a single penny of the allowance you are giving her until she is back in England, and that she gets nothing if she leaves there. Let M. Perrey escort her as far as Calais or Ostend and not leave until he has taken her aboard ship. This is very good advice I can assure you, and you would be wrong not to heed it.[2]

Dorothée stood firm. If Madame de Talleyrand refused to set sail for London and were to return to her husband's house, Dorothée had ample means to make her regret every moment under his roof. But as predicted, the princesse de Talleyrand yielded, accepting an allowance and banishment.

By an amusing coincidence which elated Louis XVIII, Chateaubriand was afflicted simultaneously with domestic problems. The court had made it known discreetly—more or less—to Chateaubriand, who had also cast aside his spouse, that the throne would prefer to see the author of Le Génie du christianisme living in Christian fashion with his wife. Just as the pious viscount was recovering his spouse, Talleyrand was shipping his own to London. Wagging tongues in the capital invented this quatrain immortalizing the viscount's chagrin and the prince's relief:

> "The Devil take convention!" said Chateaubriand,
> "My wife has to come back home."
> "Thank heavens for convention," countered Talleyrand,
> "At last I'll get rid of my own."[3]

Having settled that matter, he returned at once to Valençay. The ladies repacked their luggage in preparation for taking the waters at

Bourbon-l'Archambault. Countess Tyszkiewicz was coming with them. Before leaving, Talleyrand had the staircase of Valençay remodeled and encountered problems finding the proper stone.

The ultra-royalist mayor of Bourbon-l'Archambault had heard about Talleyrand's disgrace, and to win favor at court, decided to snub his oldest and most illustrious client. Talleyrand brought a complaint. As a result, Decazes, the minister of police, personally delivered a stern dressing down to that overzealous mayor, reminding him of "the unfailing respect due Monsieur de Talleyrand's rank in whatever situation he may happen to be." Decazes, his *bête noire,* was not as ill-natured as Talleyrand made him out to be.

Spiteful Ambition

He was not about to disarm himself purely on that account. When the king dissolved "the undiscoverable Chamber" on September 5, 1816, Talleyrand should have been the first to rejoice. Instead, he assailed the action just because Richelieu had promoted it. Back in Paris once again with his little harem, the house on the rue Saint-Florentin became opposition headquarters. During the height of Talleyrand's favor, the stream of callers had never been so steady. Those who had insulted him as minister flattered him in his disfavor. The most ardent royalists swore by him. His levee drew crowds. Even Madame de Staël attended, not to give heart to the Ultras but to remain informed. Declaiming eloquently, with curls bobbing, she appealed only to a limited following owing to "all the flying sparks that stir her imagination and her mind," as Talleyrand put it. During the autumn of 1816, he was insufferably rancorous. The qualities he valued most, and normally possessed—moderation, tact, and self-possession—suddenly failed him. In her impulsive, frequently tactless way, Madame de Staël asked him one day if he had joined the Ultras, a remark which ordinarily he would have dismissed with some flippant retort. Instead, he treated it seriously: "If you mean that I am opposed to the administration, yes, I am against the administration in general and Decazes in particular." Wednesday became his reception day because Decazes had the same day; he hoped to empty the minister's rooms. He gave a dinner party the same night Decazes gave one and invited the other cabinet members, who did not dare cancel the one or refuse the other. Bitterness made him unrecognizable, robbed him of all restraint. One evening he caused a scene unworthy of himself. As we know, his single meal of the day was dinner, but that dinner made up for three other meals. The profusion of rich dishes, the abundance of wines, the exciting company and conversation often went to his head. He would leave the table and, normally the soul of discretion, would start to talk, too much at times, and not always in a seemly fashion. "Like a woman, he succumbs to the need to talk about what is on his mind. . . . After dinner now, regularly since he left the government, he launches into assaults on Decazes and M. de Richelieu." [1] He did exactly that on the night of November 18, 1816, at the close of a formal dinner at the English embassy. A number of important guests were there, including George Canning and several French cabinet officials, one of whom was baron Pasquier, president of the Chamber.

Talleyrand's violent diatribe against the government was even more shocking because it exploded in a foreign embassy. A circle gathered around him. He raged bitterly at having been spied on at Valençay and at Bourbon-l'Archambault. He blamed the foreign minister for signing the Treaty of Paris. His crude language made Pasquier decide to leave. Seeing him move toward the door, Talleyrand tried to bring Pasquier back with assurances that his criticism was aimed solely at the minister of police, Decazes, whom he called a pimp, according to Molé. "A Chamber cannot have relations with him without degrading itself."

Pasquier replied that cabinet officials were jointly responsible and he would not tolerate such an affront to all of them. He turned and left. That ended the evening. The next day the whole capital heard about it.

As the party had ended abruptly, Talleyrand went on to Madame de Laval's. His seraglio heard all about the incident. The version they heard, however, was highly innocuous, amusing, and fallacious. So naturally the loyal sultanas flew to the defense of their satrap when anyone dared confront them with the actual facts.

The Council of Ministers discussed the grand chamberlain's offensive conduct. There were demands for his recall and exile. Richelieu and Decazes, who had taken the brunt of his wrath, suggested the most lenient punishment: banning him from the Tuileries. They could not forget that Louis XVIII owed his throne, and they their posts, to Talleyrand. Besides, they might need him again. Thus La Châtre, first gentleman of the king's chamber, handed our hero a note from His Majesty advising him not to appear at court until further notice. Talleyrand wrote back that the king's most loyal subject respectfully submitted to the punishment inflicted on him. He would obey, and bear the wounds of suffering innocence; but as a reminder of his true temper, he ended the letter with this parting shot: "I would ask His Majesty's pardon for my poor handwriting were I not aware that His Majesty has long been acquainted with it and finds it perfectly legible."

He was better at ending letters than dinners. Lord Stewart, the English ambassador, reported the incident to London. Talleyrand thought it politic to write his own version at once to his friend Wellington. Judging from that letter, one would assume that the dinner party had been a great success and that only troublemakers were likely to criticize him.

For the duchess of Courland, this whole incident was reduced to the few lines he wrote to her on November 29, not to deplore what had happened but to pride himself on his fine letter to the king and on the increasing attendance at his levees. "I am complaining about one minister. Just that and no more." He had a talent for drawing the line at whatever put him in a bad light.

And the incident did tarnish his image, even in the eyes of those who cared for him. In Toulouse, Madame de Rémusat heard unpleasant reports of the Lord Stewart affair. She did not conceal her disapproval and wished she had been with him. "If I had been able to regain some of my former credit, I might have stopped him. I have done so two or three times in the past. Women have much greater influence on him than men, and those now around him lack vigor and conviction [so much for the duchess, for Dorothée, and for the seraglio to which Madame de Rémusat did not belong]. A mixture of praise and blame goes a long way with him." Obviously she knew him well; she also knew exactly how much she could get away with. "I would not be able to keep from speaking to him seriously; that might displease him and we would quarrel."

He had at least one advocate, Chateaubriand, who commended him publicly in the Chamber of Peers. Though there was no call for congratulations, for once they had something in common: resentment.

Madame de Staël knew that his disgrace would not last. She compared Talleyrand to a popular child's toy shaped like a little figure, with a hollow upper part and lead base; when knocked about, it rolled and pitched, but always recovered its balance.

Talleyrand saw his chance to stand upright when the king ordered a solemn ceremony held on January 21, 1817, in the basilica of Saint-Denis to commemorate Louis XVI's death. Talleyrand appeared in his grand chamberlain's robes and prepared to take his place among the highest officials of the crown. After all, he had been banned from the Tuileries but not from Saint-Denis. The marquis de Dreux-Brézé, grand master of ceremonies, approached and asked him, on orders from the king, to sit instead with the Chamber of Peers. He did so. It was clear that restoration of his privileges must await the royal pleasure. Anyway, he tried . . .

Finally, in February, Richelieu himself proposed ending the prince's disgrace. He had no difficulty convincing his colleagues that barring Talleyrand from the court was the best way to make his salons the core of anti-government activity. On February 28, he was invited to the palace and received cordially by the king. They spoke privately for a minute, chatting about this and that; everything went smoothly. Talleyrand wrote to the duchess: "So it went off well enough. We ought to content ourselves and say nothing." Louis XVIII hoped his grand chamberlain would do just that. But the grand chamberlain expected more from his sovereign: a cabinet post. He did not get it. Resentment can act like an absurd ailment to plague a man whose self-control denies his anger an outlet.

Minor Affairs Do Not Enhance Talleyrand's Stature

The royalists had succeeded in dampening Talleyrand's fire. Only his burning resentment glowed. At this time Rostopchin, Moscow's notorious incendiary, visited the French capital to see three Parisian landmarks: Talleyrand, Fouché, and an actor named Potier. After seeing all three, he decided that Potier alone deserved his reputation. Talleyrand did not put himself out for the Muscovite.

When the prince was working, his detractors said that he was twiddling his thumbs. Now that he was idle, they blamed him for doing certain things. Thus Decazes's agents, who kept Talleyrand under constant surveillance, noticed that an emissary of his old friend Metternich was paying him secret visits and receiving documents, which in turn were handed to the Austrian embassy and forwarded to Vienna. And there was another heinous activity: whenever he condescended to attend a session of the Chamber of Peers, it was only to launch gleeful attacks on the electoral law introduced by "his friend" Molé, minister of the interior. It must be said that Talleyrand's liberal and enlightened arguments made far more sense than the royalist position. On another occasion, January 23, 1817, when he took the floor in defense of personal liberty, his sense of justice and skillful handling of the subject won him the debate. He demonstrated that personal freedom was inseparable from freedom of the press. When the same debate came up again several years later over the issue of censorship, he used the same arguments to champion freedom of the press. These were only skirmishes, but over major issues, a vexation to the government, a pleasure to the liberals.

Did bitter frustration drive him into the unspeakable bargain referred to in his letter of January 17, 1817?[1] This letter, addressed to Metternich, reached the latter through Madame de Souza via a Portuguese courier. Long after they had fallen from his favor, Talleyrand's ladies continued to serve him.

> . . . Today I mean to tell you about a matter of some interest. A Russian has tried to extract from the archives of the foreign ministry Bonaparte's correspondence with me following his return from Egypt. He was unable to do so. It was believed that I had taken it with me [which is true] and I was approached as to whether I would consider giving it up to the emperor. [You have to whet a prospective buyer's appetite.] Such an effort and Russian influence here at home lead me to think that one day I may have this correspondence stolen from me. This fear finally made me decide to part with it, and I am offering it to you. Unquestionably it is the finest lot of documents obtainable, for, in addition to his correspondence with me beginning on 25 Nivôse of the Year VII and running through the end of 1806, I can also provide the correspondence between Bonaparte and M. de Champagny in 1807 and 1808 and between Bonaparte and Maret in 1813. [Not just his own letters but also those of his successors. One can see that he might have hung onto his own. But the others? He stole them.] All are originals, signed by him, comprising twelve thick packets. I am sure that England and Prussia would be happy to make such an acquisition and would readily pay for it with a healthy portion of their taxes. I speak of England and Prussia because nothing could make me give it to Russia. ["Give"?]
>
> Kindly submit my proposal to your emperor, my dear Prince. You may reply through M. de Binder [the intermediary] . . . you know that I am a Frenchman first, and after that, I am closest to being an Austrian. I feel that I should like this previous and often compromising part of our modern history to be in your hands.

This is one of Talleyrand's most deplorable and contemptible schemes. It made him no fortune because Metternich duped him. When the Austrian diplomat replied that the affair interested him, Talleyrand assumed a deal was on. He turned over the parcels to Metternich's messenger and set the price at 500,000 francs. He was advised that the goods had been delivered safely, but there was no word about the price or when he would be paid.

The tale then becomes sinister. Fifteen months later Metternich returned the parcels to Binder, having copied them in the meantime. Talleyrand had been tricked.

Chateaubriand found out all about it during his tenure as foreign minister. He would certainly have raised a howl if the precious correspondence had been missing. He wrote instead: "There is not a single old document in our archives which he has not tried to turn over to Austria; this time he was taken in by M. de Metternich, who returned the letters religiously after copying them."

As a matter of fact, he did not return them all; some of Bonaparte's originals remain in Vienna. The ones he sent back to Talleyrand were stolen by the latter's secretary, Perrey, along with other papers. The thief's thief fled to London in 1827, where he sold the documents to autograph collectors. The letters thus were scattered if not lost. A group of them were saved and taken by the duchess of Dino to her château at Sagan in Silesia, which was ransacked and burned during the Russian invasion.

So potent was Talleyrand's yearning for power that he read into every little gesture from the Tuileries a sign of favor. But he was wrong. The smiles were calculated not to beckon him on but to put him off. "Every day for a week now they have hinted at a reconciliation to which I always reply that I am going to the country soon for a long stay." [2] Exactly what the King wanted, without saying so, and exactly what Talleyrand did not want, though he kept promising to leave.

As a gesture of good will to the Bonapartists, and a slap at the royalists, he was conspicuously in attendance at General Masséna's funeral. "They were very glad to see me there. I am sure that those good people appreciated my coming," [3] he wrote to the duchess on March 14. We are not so sure that Napoleon's partisans were quite as warmly inclined toward the former prince of Benevento. Anyway, how important were feelings? He continued his balancing act, making overtures to the opposition. He sighed. Under Bonaparte, at least one never had time to be bored. Now he was coming to know the occupations of retirement, the solitary readings by the fire at night. The young women had gone to a ball. "I read good old Plutarch who is worth more than all the moralists and doctrinaires you find in the newspapers." [4] But there was no substitute for those gala evenings in Vienna, and Plutarch (replacing Le Portier des chartreux) held out a bleak future for the Bourbon régime. Talleyrand predicted its downfall: "It is painful to watch an establishment for which one has worked so hard perishing before one's eyes," adding slyly: "It saddens me very much."

As if exclusion from the great events of the day were not enough, he found his involvement in petty ones exceedingly unpleasant. We may recall that strange and alarming adventurer named Maubreuil. He returned with the tide. Summoned once again to appear in court, he took the opportunity to reiterate that Talleyrand had hired him to assassinate Napoleon. It was not true, but some people thought it might be, and even disbelievers gossiped about it. When he could no longer stand these rumors, Talleyrand withdrew to peaceful Valençay.

He had other reasons for liking the countryside. For some time now he had been intriguing—unsuccessfully—to get Louis XVIII to declare his property at Valençay a duchy. Actually, it was not for himself that he sought the title of duke, but for his brother, Archambaud, and the latter's son Edmond. Of course, this would make Dorothée, Edmond's wife, a duchess. Talleyrand kept pestering Pasquier to press "the prankster king" for the coveted duchy. To discourage his importunate grand chamberlain, the king came up with a response matching the best his petitioner might have to offer. His Majesty was terribly sorry, but if he made Valençay a duchy, the king of Spain might be offended by the aggrandizement of that site of his humiliation. So they must first consult the king of Spain. Disheartened, Talleyrand began preparing for the trip to Valençay.

When he went to say good-bye to Madame de Rémusat, he was visibly dispirited. "We embraced. He is unhappy and bored. His departure draws absolutely no attention," she wrote. Public indifference was fatal to a star of his caliber.

He spent the month of May at Valençay. Peace of mind came to him and, believe it or not, a paroxysm of virtue. "What I need is not rest, but liberty. To do as one wishes, think as one likes, follow one's bent instead of searching one's way [a poetic lie, since he made a practice of exclusively following his own bent]. That is the true kind of rest I need, and that, I find at Valençay. When one's eyes are not quite shut and it is essential to see, it is better to view objects of disgust from afar rather than at close range; today's men of ambition are sad figures indeed." What filled him with disgust? The ministry for which he yearned so badly. And the men jockeying for position in 1817, were they different from those of 1789, 1798, 1800, or any other year? Oh, Talleyrand, your sarcasm was so much more becoming than your hypocrisy.

Nursing his spite, he went off traveling with Dorothée and Countess Tyszkiewicz. Dr. Andral was now part of his permanent retinue; Courtiade, the ladies' maids, and a ton of baggage rounded out the expedition. Instead of Bourbon-l'Archambault, they headed for the Pyrenees. Deprived of his ministry, Talleyrand was inaugurating long-distance touring. On the way through Périgord, he stopped off at Chalais. It was a moving experience for him. The townspeople greeted him cordially; they still remembered his great-grandmother, the princess. In Bordeaux, the prefect received them royally, very different from that prefect of the Indre who came to spy. "The prefect, M. de Tournon, was extremely polite to us. Anyone can tell that he is a man of breeding. He inspires love for the king and his person."

Then they reached the mountains. Tastes had changed: mountains, once considered "hideous," now were judged terrifying and their terror appreciated. The heavy coaches struggled along, climbing up among the rocks, then winding their way down into the valley of Cauterets amid its thundering mountain torrents, called *gaves*. They arrived at this thermal station on July 7 and stayed at the hôtel de France until August 26. The daily round of showers, gargling, and baths began. Talleyrand indulged to his heart's content in sniffling up water. Every afternoon he was carried in a sedan chair to springs farther up the valley, at La Raillère, for a diligent repetition of the morning's routine. He adored this hydrotherapy. At the end of July, Dr. Andral halted the cure and they turned once more to sightseeing. Again in a sedan chair, no doubt. What he saw delighted him: "I do not think that any region can give an idea of this one. It resembles no other mountainous region."

They had a guide who, long after they had moved on, remembered his strange and rich clients. He said that he had shown the sights to "a lame old man who was taking the waters to heal his leg." But he had forgotten the man's name: "Taille . . . Taille . . ." he fumbled, until someone reminded him: "Oh, yes, prince de Taille et rang," which confirms once again that the pronunciation in that day was in fact "Tie-uh-rawn." Talleyrand's name had slipped his mind, but not the 500 francs received from him, plus the pension which the poor fellow had been trying to get his hands on and Talleyrand obtained for him. On July 29, 1817, the caravan was at Bagnères-de-Bigorre. The inn where they stayed took them all for princes and princesses. The innkeeper, a good woman named Bellegarde, must have found it entrancing to inscribe in her register: Prince Talleyrand, princesse de Périgord née princesse de Courlande, and "Tyskainvins" (Tyszkiewicz) Princess Poniatowska. From there they journeyed on to Pau, visited Henri IV's château, and spent the night at Coarraze where the king had frolicked and where—fortunately with no ill effects—they tipped over into a wide ditch. Talleyrand suffered a sore shoulder and said that the accident would make his "handwriting worse than usual."

They were back in Cauterets on August 25, the feast of Saint

Louis. All this traveling about from inn to inn was not entirely uneventful. On arriving at a hostelry with his large household, Talleyrand
made it a practice to have a lump price quoted for the party. Some
places tried to tack on extras. When it came to settling his bill, however,
our hero would not hear of extras and insisted on paying the agreed
price. As a result, their leavetakings were not always serene.

The combination of hydrotherapy, mountain air, captious inn-
keepers, and vehicular upsets restored our hero's composure. Some good
news also helped: his uncle, the archbishop, was made cardinal. "It has
been a long time since anything good happened to us. I am delighted
to see the life of this excellent man crowned by the prestige of his estate."
If the excellent man had not added distinction to the family, surely his
virtues would not have been so generously extolled.

He missed the duchess, who had now gone to straighten out her
affairs in Germany. "How far away November is," he wrote to her. And
his comments on the political scene were discouraging enough: cabinet
posts changing right and left whilst nobody gave a thought to his services.
He hoped the king's health would improve, but could not say the same
for Decazes's. In any event, Cauterets raised his spirits.

The best news of all, however, was the royal decree of August 31,
1817, making Talleyrand a duke and peer of the realm; shortly thereafter, this hereditary dukedom was declared transmissible to his brother,
Archambaud, who thus came to originate the ducal branch of the
Talleyrand-Périgords. The title passed to Edmond and to Edmond's
eldest son, Napoléon-Louis.*

Honors, like misfortune, never arrive singly, and on December 2,
1817, King Ferdinand of Naples granted him a second dukedom and
a yearly income of 60,000 livres. The title attached to the tiny island of
Dino off the coast of Calabria. Talleyrand gave the title to Edmond
and kept the income. For some time now he had been wanting Dorothée
to have the title of duchess. At last it was so. Henceforth, she was always known as the duchess of Dino. The title was mere tinsel, but it

---

* The son of Napoléon-Louis (1811–1898), third duke of Talleyrand-Périgord,
was Boson, the fourth duke (1832–1910). The fifth duke, Hélie, son of Boson
and Jeanne Seillière, married Anna Gould on July 7, 1908 (divorced wife of
Boniface de Castellane). They had two children: Howard, who died in 1929,
and Hélène-Violette, married first to the comte de Pourtalès and then to Gaston
Palewski.

In 1829, Valençay became a duchy and Napoléon-Louis, Dorothée's and
Edmond's son, its first duke, who thus claimed all the titles of his great-uncle.
Napoléon-Louis had the further distinction of marrying Alix de Montmorency.

gave her standing at court. Talleyrand stoutly upheld the dignity of his latest duchy: "It bears the name of a royal property in Calabria . . ." he advised the duchess of Courland, who was still at Sagan. Actually, the property was neither royal nor ducal. It was a barren, deserted island, separated from the Italian mainland by a strait where the anchovy fishing was good. No one had ever heard of the place until Talleyrand's niece bore its name. It sank back into oblivion when death ended the liaison between the duchess of Dino and her uncle.

During that summer of 1817, death took three persons for whom he cared or had once cared. It distressed him little enough; hardly at all in the case of Suard, whereas the two others, Choiseul and Madame de Staël, deserved more than a plain listing as "persons with whom I was more or less associated." The loss of Choiseul, he admitted, was a blow. "He was the last of the people with whom I grew up. Now I am the last of that generation; how sad it is." He was sorry for himself primarily. When it came to Germaine, he was cruel. His acid remarks about the passing of a generous friend are utterly indecent: "Paris is intensely interested in Madame de Staël's death and in her marriage, which no one knew about until she no longer existed." Yes, passionate Germaine had committed one final folly by secretly marrying her lover Rocca. "For years she had been Madame Rocca and did not have the courage to say so." He, of course, had been brave enough to tell the world that Madame Grand was the wife of the bishop of Autun. Now he plays the odious hypocrite: "None of this is very savory, especially the matter of having produced a small Rocca now eligible to claim one-third the estate and whom she never mentioned at the time of Madame de Broglie's marriage [her daughter]. I was decidedly right to say that she had no tact. . . ." We can understand why he acted this way, like a sanctimonious prig: the public expected and approved this kind of moralizing. He was trying to win acceptance from the smug and strait-laced doctrinaires of the Restoration. He found himself currying favor with the very objects of his contempt. Again, his sarcasm is preferable to this.

Instead of returning to Valençay, the caravan meandered through the south of France. We find them at Montpellier. Talleyrand hastens to point out that one of his great-uncles, a Périgord, had been governor of Languedoc for twenty-five years and the name was still highly respected there. He never lost a chance to exalt the family. At Nîmes, something else was on his mind, neither politics, finance, or genealogy, but perfumes. Knowing his fondness for them, it is not surprising that he stocked up on quantities of heady essence, unguents, and toilet water— enough to perfume the town and its suburbs for the next ten years.

They went on through Marseilles as far as Hyères, then turned north. On September 18 they reached Bourges.

The grand chamberlain paid his respects to the king at the Tuileries on October 30. Madame de Rémusat saw him that day and reported that his ideas seemed to have a decidedly liberal twist, which is no surprise. The real surprise—or grief, in the case of an ambitious man—was that his return to the capital evoked no more concern than his departure. Patience. Give him a chance to attend and to give a few dinner parties, to preach to his harem. The men in power would soon acknowledge his presence, though the fact that the duchess of Courland had not returned detracted somewhat from the pleasure of rejoining his circle of female admirers.

The ultra-royalists suddenly took note of his existence. Fear jolted them out of their indifference when Talleyrand effected a spectacular reconciliation with the House of Orléans.

Dorothée and he were invited to the Palais-Royal as if they were a married couple. The duchesse Amélie greeted them cordially. With Mademoiselle,* who liked to discuss politics, he renewed a friendship begun in London back in 1792. It is true that he had always preferred this younger, more liberal, more outspoken branch of the royal family, and in 1816 he proved his loyalty by seeing to it that their vast holdings were restored to them. It had taken some doing, for the elder branch had no intention of allowing its rivals to live in opulence. Thanks to Talleyrand, they were doing so. After this visit, he wrote: "The dinner was splendid and the house looked very well. All the old valets of the House of Orléans make quite a sight in the antechambers." Talleyrand valued the display of wealth—especially as he had helped restore it—in a party to which, at some later time, he might wish to look for support.

The royalists were up in arms, convinced that a conspiracy of "the Orléans faction" must be in the wind. Why stir up fears that Talleyrand wanted to put Louis-Philippe on the throne? It was foolish.

Passions were roused. People who had appeared to ignore the prince suddenly began fighting for invitations to the rue Saint-Florentin when it was learned that as of November 10, Prince Talleyrand would give a series of great dinners once a week.

We can understand why it was so difficult to ostracize a man like Talleyrand. Charles de Rémusat tells us that just a few days after his return to the capital, the prince "was already holding court in the grand manner." He found him "cheerful, in good spirits, and lively." What a

* "Mademoiselle" was a title of respect given Louis-Philippe's sister, Madame Adélaïde—Trans.

521

marvelous cure he had taken! Apart from the waters, he had had that succession of duchies and excellent results from the sale of his picture gallery with its Breughels, Teniers, and other treasures. Money, always money. Even on the fringes of power, he was deluged with money and honors; in the seat of power, with more money. In both cases his profits were safe; only his pride and ambition suffered when the king barred his return to the government.

Wounded pride then pushed him into a harebrained scheme at which genuine pride should have balked. He asked a banker named Laffitte to join him in overthrowing the government. Though highly flattered at being approached by so eminent a personality, the banker nevertheless declined and Talleyrand, having nursed the man's vanity, ended up looking ridiculous. Ambition and resentment against the Bourbons had caused France's most level-headed statesman to lose his head.

Now and then people talked about the Empire. When Maria Walewska died, perhaps it reminded him of the evening when he, with a napkin over his arm, had presented her to Napoleon. Did he know that Edmond de Périgord had enjoyed the favors of Countess Walewska? He may have assumed it was his right as nephew of the procurer. There was much talk of Napoleon's illness on St. Helena. "A cannon ball," Talleyrand observed, "four or five years ago would have put a better end to this extraordinary career." He was mistaken about that; a glorious death on the battlefield, though more aesthetic, would have deprived Napoleon of the legend he was then creating.

Anyway, Edmond continued to deplete his own fortune as well as his wife's. As head of the family, Talleyrand studied the situation. He had been able to forestall the sale of Rosny, the beautiful château which Edmond wanted to dispose of in order to satisfy his creditors. Talleyrand prudently advised that the couple seek legal separation of their estates, and a court ruling granted this on March 24, 1818. From then on, Dorothée and her husband saw less and less of each other; with the financial differences settled, their relationship lost some of its bitterness. Actually, all they had in common was a name. For convention's sake, they made it appear that they were living together on the rue d'Aguesseau. In reality, Dorothée and her children never lived there; the rue Saint-Florentin was their home. In 1822, it was Edmond who came to live with them under his uncle's roof—temporarily, and not by choice.

Talleyrand made all family decisions. He engaged Monsieur Thierry as tutor to seven-year-old Napoléon-Louis, who one day would inherit all his great-uncle's titles and property. His authority over the family was never questioned or imposed. He decided, they accepted.

He missed the duchess of Courland very much. She could never decide whether or not to return to Paris. On February 1, 1816, he wrote her that he had given the last of his great Monday receptions, "my great and necessary Monday task." He would entertain five hundred guests at a time. Then there were the great Tuesday night dinners, "Carême's great banquets," as he described them. One is not surprised to learn: "I really ought to save money and go to Valençay as the winter has been very expensive." Each reception cost a fortune. Why did he spend all this money? Because he enjoyed it, and also because he counted on making a spectacular comeback. What he did not count on was the king's stubborn resistance.

During the winter he championed the honor of some of the aging beauties in his seraglio. There was much talk about the impending publication of the duc de Lauzun's Memoirs, dear Biron, the dashing rogue who had been one of Talleyrand's steady companions during the early years of the Revolution. The pages of his Memoirs, which passed secretly from hand to hand, were, as one can imagine, utterly scandalous. Lauzun recounted his exploits in war and in the bedchamber, leaving many of the Restoration's virtuous widows trembling lest the record of their exploits in 1789 come to haunt them in 1818. Madame de Laval had a star role and therefore the most to lose. More than Robespierre's guillotine, she feared the Congregation's * scandalmongering. Talleyrand took up not his sword but his pen in her defense, and on March 27, 1818, sent a note of protest to *Le Moniteur* in an effort to establish "the truth." "The duc de Lauzun, whose friend I was, wrote his Memoirs. He read them to me. I do not know who has laid hands on some copies of them; what I do know for certain is that they have been horribly falsified. I would not speak of this deed of darkness if I did not have reason to believe that this so-called manuscript is about to be printed." [5] The dignity of his lying is in itself something of a marvel. Talleyrand knew perfectly well that Lauzun had given a truthful recital of his exploits. But he managed to destroy any interest there might have been in "this so-called manuscript" which, reduced to a "deed of darkness," fell into obscurity. The ladies were saved.

His adoring women showered him with tributes. On reading *Le Moniteur,* the duchesse d'Escars rushed to convey her gratitude to the gallant knight: "I desire, dear Prince, that everyone should know the magnitude of the service you have rendered. As a letter from you strips

---

* A secret society for Catholic propaganda—Trans.

his Memoirs of their authenticity, and destroys them . . . people will take them for a romance. The day before yesterday they were highly dangerous; today, they are no longer so."

The thanks rival the service rendered; they suggest the impact of Talleyrand's words on the society of his time.

A minor scandal grazed him, Madame de Staël's posthumous revenge. She had left behind a manuscript which was published in May, 1818. In it he found himself attacked for his witty and widely appreciated commentary on the duc d'Enghien's death: "It is far worse than a crime; it is a blunder." Germaine observed: "I have the deepest contempt for politicians whose cleverness consists in rising above virtue." Actually, it is difficult to take all these upholders of virtue seriously. Madame de Staël was not avenging virtue any more than was Talleyrand in condemning Germaine's conduct. The revenge she took was for Talleyrand's attacks on her father. "Madame de Staël wishes to establish a cult of Necker," said Talleyrand, who was not inclined to idolize anyone, least of all Necker, whose financial genius he had long disputed, though not his competence. Germaine never forgave him for this opinion.

Winter passed with its dinners and skirmishes, and spring called Talleyrand and his retinue back to Valençay. It was rumored that they had taken passports for Naples intending to thank King Ferdinand for unwittingly having made Dorothée the duchess of Dino. The exodus took place on May 16. Madame de Rémusat had a long talk with him the previous evening; she found him in good health and good spirits. He hacked a number of ministers nearly to shreds. "I spent two hours with him and was thoroughly entertained," she told her son.

Those ministerial vivisections must have been spicy indeed. Instead of Naples, Talleyrand's trip with Dorothée and Countess Tyszkiewicz took them to Bagnères-de-Bigorre where we find them on August 17. We learn that Thierry, the "Dinot" children's tutor, accompanied them, as well as Dr. Andral and a Monsieur Samuel, a business agent employed by "Mgr. Téleran." They returned to Valençay via Toulouse, and on August 24 celebrated the feast of Saint Louis, patron of French monarchs, at the château: *Te Deum*, fireworks, the village decked out with white bunting. Dorothée lit the bonfire, and there was a ball in the courtyard of the château. For once, the prefect had a clean report for the chief of police.

On November 11, they were back in Paris. Talleyrand paid his respects to the king and, on November 17, His Majesty's birthday, performed the duties of grand chamberlain. One swallow does not make a summer.

False Hopes of Blind Ambition

The purring gave way to fresh recriminations. Word that the Congress of Aix-la-Chapelle was proceeding without him cut Talleyrand to the quick. His hatred grew fiercer for Richelieu, who, he said, had "neither talent nor ingenuity." Added to that was the mortifying acknowledgment of his rival's stunning success. Indeed, the duc de Richelieu succeeded with dignity and conviction in freeing France from allied troops. Richelieu was the man who lifted the crushing burden and humiliation of occupation. Spiteful tongues whispered that Talleyrand was as likely to betray Louis XVIII at Aix-la-Chapelle as he had betrayed Napoleon at Erfurt. It was pure malice to suggest that he would have lifted a finger to delay the liberation of France. He was resentful, however, at having Richelieu steal his thunder.

The Ultras tried to use Talleyrand in their attempts to unseat Richelieu. The comte d'Artois engineered the affair. His plan—if you can call it that—was to seek help from the czar. First, they needed a memorandum on current conditions in France to submit to him. Of course, Prime Minister Richelieu, Alexander's great friend, was ignorant of these efforts. Monsieur thought that Talleyrand could serve as intermediary. Vitrolles, Monsieur's confidant, was very close to Dorothée and thus, in the course of conversation, could broach the matter to her. She listened. Although Vitrolles spoke cryptically, those flashing violet eyes conveyed her understanding: "Her mind moved swiftly," said Vitrolles, "and needed fewer words to understand than do most women's." She bore the marks of Talleyrand's schooling. Vitrolles asked her to prevail on her uncle to send a spokesman to the czar at Aix-la-Chapelle with the comte d'Artois's note. Also, to instruct his emissary on how to conduct himself with the sovereigns and their ministers, whom he, Talleyrand, knew intimately. Prudently, Dorothée persuaded Vitrolles to take up the question personally with her uncle, promising to follow it up later.

So Talleyrand had been replaced on the stage of world affairs. How would he turn the situation to his own account?

He listened. Vitrolles wondered why so clever a man should take so long to grasp the point, plying him with a thousand questions to boot. But the real wonder was why Vitrolles failed to realize that Talleyrand was making him spill out the whole story. On top of that, the prince asked for two days to think it over. Vitrolles returned. Gloomily, Talleyrand told him that after carefully considering all his friends, he saw no one reliable enough for this delicate mission. Taking him at his word, Vitrolles replied patronizingly as if Talleyrand hadn't a friend in the world: "How do you explain, my dear Prince, the emptiness around you? In your long experience of power and momentous events, just think how many men you must have met, how many fortunes you must have made or shaped. Do you mean to say that not one of them deserves your confidence?" [1] Having underscored the solitude and ingratitude surrounding the prince, Vitrolles proceeded to brag about his own numerous and devoted friends. This cocky Marseillais then felt his superiority established. Actually, Talleyrand was leading him on, having no intention of getting mixed up in the comte d'Artois's harebrained and futile scheme, much less asking his friends to do so. He was determined not to accept or to reject Monsieur's proposal, and Vitrolles played right into his hands.

Czar Alexander came to Paris at the close of the Congress. Talleyrand kept expecting his visit. "I am certain that he will not pass this door on the rue Saint-Florentin without recalling that he owes his present glory to favorable decisions affecting the monarchy which he made in this house."

In fact, the czar did not wish to see him. Ever since the Congress of Vienna he could not bear to be reminded of Talleyrand. Never would he forgive him for the Triple Alliance.

In November, Madame de Rémusat, whom nothing escaped, saw Talleyrand again. In March, his rancor had seemed to be subsiding; in November, he was altogether benign. What else did she see? To her utter astonishment, the duchess of Dino and Baroness Alexandre de Périgord (Charlotte) actually visiting Madame Decazes! Their valid excuse for this social call was the fact that Madame Decazes, née Saint-Aulaire, came from an old Périgord family distantly related to Talleyrand. Still, it was only an excuse. "I saw M. de Talleyrand yesterday," Madame de Rémusat reported; "he mentioned M. Decazes rather flatteringly, and considers him the only able member of the cabinet." The wind had shifted.

The explanation was that Richelieu seemed determined to resign over the issue of an electoral law which he favored and Decazes opposed. Talleyrand also opposed it and sensed that this was his chance to bid for power. Hence the social calls and the affable remarks. It did not rule out inviting Richelieu to dinner, a lavish banquet to commemorate the burial of a cabinet. Richelieu knew the reasons for the Decazes-Talleyrand alliance. Still, the prince told everyone that he had no plans beyond enjoying his peaceful life in the country. The court only wished that were true. He should have heard what was said about him in the Tuileries. When Richelieu spoke of resigning, the king objected: "You reduce me to the deplorable extremity of calling back M. de Talleyrand whom I neither like nor esteem." And Monsieur, who was perfectly willing to involve the prince in his impractical schemes, implored Richelieu "to spare the king and France the shame and misfortune of summoning M. de Talleyrand." [2]

Richelieu resigned the premiership and was replaced by General Dessolles. No one even mentioned Talleyrand's name. It was a cruel blow to a man who "was made ill by the sight of a foreign minister," as his friend Castellane remarked.

Talleyrand's bitterness should not be condemned too harshly. Frustrated ambition certainly accounted for a good deal of it. In addition, he found it painful to watch legitimacy slipping down the drain, depriving the country of progressive leadership and driving it needlessly into new crises. The court ought to have heeded the advice of a man "who sets a curse on governments that neglect him."

After this fresh rejection, he assured the duchess: "I don't need to be involved in affairs of state. I have enough to do just thinking about all I have seen and done. There is enough of that to fill a lifetime far longer than mine will be. . . . I love you, dear angel, with all my heart" (April 20, 1818). Except for the final tender words, the sentiments in this letter are questionable. More avid than ever for power, he took to musing over the past only because the power to act was denied him.

He put on the great mantle and the gold-and-diamond encrusted collar of the Golden Fleece to attend the duc de Mouchy's reception into that illustrious order; in attendance were the comte d'Artois, the dukes of Berry and Bourbon, and the lesser dukes of La Vauguyon, Croy, and Fernand-Nuñez. This did not assuage our hero's thirst for power. He possessed the highest titles and distinctions, but they were hollow honors. Instead of a minister, they made him an errand boy. He was delegated to provide the visiting duke of Gloucester with a guided tour of Fontainebleau. And if that honorable duty did not suit him, what about his appointment to the Commission to Improve Prison Conditions?

Louis XVIII was forever talking about having a coronation but never did anything about it. The idea bored him—Talleyrand too. In the spring of 1819 Talleyrand returned to Valençay, where Spain's General Alava visited him. Talleyrand gave him a splendid reception and they talked about the captivity of the Spanish princes. Like Alava, the king of Spain and the infantes had only kind words for Talleyrand, who received a portrait of Ferdinand VII shortly thereafter. A new sovereign joined the royal portraits in Valençay's picture gallery. Napoleon in coronation robes, painted by Gérard, already hung there. Next to him, yet totally unembarrassed, was Louis XVIII in his blue robes of state dotted with white lilies, by Gérard. The artist stopped there. A full-length portrait of Louis-Philippe by Hersent was the next addition.

He returned to the capital with a flicker of hope: the Dessolles cabinet had fallen. But instead of Talleyrand, Decazes was called on to form a new government. Talleyrand's last hope vanished, for the king's unstinting favor made the new premier's position invulnerable.

The monotony of social engagements plus a few new faces in his entourage still did not satisfy our hero's needs. That summer he went with Montrond to take the waters at Barèges. Madame de Souza (formerly Flahaut) called Talleyrand and his retinue "a bad lot" and made her son Flahaut promise not to go near them. How people change!

By way of compensation, certain favors he did for the new archbishop of Bourges, a post for which he had vainly connived in 1787, brought him compliments. The two men spoke of Talleyrand's uncle, the archbishop of Paris, and his coadjutor, Monseigneur de Quélen, a good and virtuous man destined to influence Talleyrand's life. In reality, he always enjoyed the company of clerics. Madame de Rémusat, who was turning critical of him, said at the time that Talleyrand ought not to be given a ministry without a staff of industrious and principled persons in order "to neutralize the conniving and perfumed portion of this curé."

There followed another flash of hope: he starred in a tragedy. Louvel's assassination of the duc de Berry, an heir to the throne, on February 13, 1820, was a great shock to the royalists. Decazes was forced to resign because of the incompetence of his own police force. Talleyrand thought he saw the dawn of his return to power. But no one else saw it. The king remained intractable, and Decazes backed his resolve to employ anyone rather than Talleyrand. Richelieu was proposed, then Molé, Pasquier, and Villèle. Our hero nursed his illusions while the crowd in the Tuileries swore that he had sharpened Louvel's dagger. He invited Villèle to dinner, intending to present him with a list of potential cabinet members. Villèle never bothered to answer the invitation. The king chose Richelieu as premier and Talleyrand was heartbroken.

But the most unexpected part of this whole painful affair was the consolation he found. One night he read a slender volume which his friend the princesse de Talmont had sent round to him that day. It was a book of poetry, the first efforts of a young unknown. Talleyrand grew excited, then euphoric over verses that flowed like a gentle breeze. It was Lamartine's *Méditations*. This new poetry did not resemble Delille, or Chénier, or Jean-Baptiste Rousseau, or Voltaire, and really had nothing familiar to communicate to a man of his age and background, accustomed to clear, concise language and cold reason. It is curious to think of this aging satrap, devoid of romantic sentimentality or rhetoric, and, on top of that, embittered and sarcastic, bewitched, spending the whole night poring over those plaintive incantations, those weightless, colorless verses, verses flowing from some insubstantial source, transparent as the clearest water yet lighter, more like a zephyr than a distinct song, but rich in indescribable resonances, in secrets winning the heart by some enchantment at once feminine, irresistible, and melancholy. Who would expect a man like Talleyrand to express this opinion of Lamartine in the note of thanks he penned that very night: "Princess, before going to sleep I am returning the little volume you lent me yesterday. Suffice it to say that I could not sleep and read it until four in the morning, only to read it again. I am no prophet and do not know what the public will say; but my personal opinion is what I feel in the privacy of my own bedchamber: There stands a man. Let us talk some more about it." [3]

In the years to come, and despite their totally different feelings and attitudes, a strong bond of mutual admiration linked the prince and the young poet. It was a miracle of poetry.

Talleyrand Recovers His Fine Voice and Slips Deeper into Disgrace

Lamartine was only an interlude. What were the prince's political notions? Madame de Rémusat baited the conversation to make him talk, mentioning the duc d'Orléans "to test his response." Did she expect him to divulge his plan to put the Orléans family on the throne? In any event, at that time he had no such plan in mind. But if Madame de Rémusat thought he did, she was probably not the only one. Public spite was far more active than Talleyrand's. Realizing what that impudent woman was after, Talleyrand was on his guard. "He immediately rejected any such idea," she wrote; "he returned to it with such tenacity that I could not help thinking that he wanted to dispel any possible suspicions." So many plots and betrayals were attributed to him and remain so unjustly. Frustrated ambition did not make Talleyrand a ruthless enemy of the Bourbons. He had established their rule and would have preferred to maintain it if they had allowed him to improve it and to inject into the monarchy what it most needed: life, and a sense of reality as a basis for building the future. His continued attachment to the principle of legitimacy is revealed in what he told Madame de Rémusat: "His latest theory," she wrote, "is that the idea of a child will strike a common chord among all Frenchmen if Madame la duchesse de Berry has a son; but that if she has a daughter, the ties will vanish." Madame de Rémusat found his thinking a shade too pessimistic and argued that France was fundamentally royalist because the country needed peace and had forgotten the Revolution. In any case, she contended, the nation "does not understand the situation at all." The choice of words could only irritate a man who could not accept ignorance as an excuse for anything. He retorted: "France will understand this year because the cost of bread will be high." Pessimistic perhaps, but, as Renan said, "truth is depressing."

Talleyrand's political thinking is known to us by remarks he made at the time a kind of revolution broke out in Naples in June, 1820, forcing King Ferdinand to grant his people a constitution. Talleyrand found this quite normal, expressing regret that sovereigns did not themselves promote constitutions, which tend to strengthen rather than uproot monarchy by disarming revolutionary minorities. "I believe that in every country in which the administration is firmly convinced that this is the line it must follow, the minority for whom anarchy holds no terror can easily be contained." [1]

His definition of "legitimacy" was in sharp conflict with ultra-royalist thinking. The Ultras read a quasi-mystical meaning into the term, a divine right to rule, both indisputable and unrestricted. In contrast, Talleyrand wanted the principle of legitimacy, the one true source of power, to be applied rationally, moderately, and lawfully. He affirmed: "The legitimacy of kings, or rather of governments, is the safeguard of nations; for that reason it is sacred." The power of legitimacy did not stem from the fact that the Holy Ghost sent a dove bearing a vial of oil for the anointing of kings. Yet if it was not sacred for supernatural reasons, it was so for human ones. "The mysterious power of legitimacy," as he called it, is mysterious only for the sake of maintaining an aura of majesty. Actually, sovereign power derives its strength from the force of law incarnated in the sovereign's august person. Neither a sovereign's will nor whimsy is sacred, only the law of which the nation makes him the repository. The sovereign so chosen is sacred, but the royal personage is only the reflection of the law. The power of law transcends all else—including kings. In short, Talleyrand regarded legitimacy as the perfection of legality. His was the voice of the Enlightenment. By guaranteeing the peace and continuance of peoples, legitimacy also guarantees their happiness. He is Dr. Pangloss defending the throne of France not in the style of Renan, but of Voltaire.

The Bourbons and Ultras of 1820 could not accept these ideas. But the time was approaching when Talleyrand could no longer associate himself with their backward march through history. He wanted a legitimate monarchy to guide the nation forward. "That is the task," he wrote, "to which this House must dedicate itself." Henri IV would have understood; but Henri IV was dead and Henry V about to be born. In any event, a divorce was on the way between Talleyrand and the Bourbons.

On August 9, 1820, Talleyrand wrote: "It is such a momentous event for the House of Bourbon and for France, this boy which I hope Madame la duchesse de Berry will have, that nothing could keep me away from Paris at the time of her confinement."

His excess of leisure made him clutch at mountains and molehills. Did he not send a message to Fouché, the forgotten exile of Trieste, the once terrifying duke of Otranto? He even promised to send him a charming messenger. Fouché scoffed at both message and messenger, the prince's spell having ceased to affect him. "Talleyrand," he wrote to Princess Elisa on May 2, 1820, "pays me compliments. I was not prepared for such attentions. He announces that an anonymous lady friend of his will visit me. He is probably presenting me with one of his old mistresses to while away my exile." [2]

Who was this lady dispatched from the seraglio on an intelligence assignment? We have no idea.

Talleyrand left Paris at the beginning of July. "Paris is becoming deserted. Even the ambassadors are leaving. I am only too happy to go. Everything is distasteful here," he wrote to the duchess on July 2. We know the rest of the tune. "My plans are to concentrate on Valençay, which does not yield what it should; but I don't believe I have much talent for agricultural management." He was feigning modesty, for Valençay was extremely well run.

The duchess's prolonged absence was becoming alarming. He had been waiting for her to return now for two years. Her letters were always affectionate, but . . . Did life in Paris no longer attract her? Is it too bold to suggest that Dorothée's position as mistress of the rue Saint-Florentin—the household over which her mother formerly ruled—had something to do with the duchess's reluctance?

Talleyrand left Valençay in great haste on September 27, 1820. It was time for the "miracle child" to appear, the duc de Berry's posthumous son born on the twenty-ninth. The royal family and the royalists were ecstatic; their lilies were blossoming. Louis XVIII was so overjoyed that he lost no time in naming thirty-five new knights of his orders. And for having appeared so opportunely to rock the cradle of Henri V, Talleyrand was made a knight of the Holy Ghost. He loved decorations; the older the order, the better he liked it, for it linked him to a long chain of illustrious forebears. Though ahead of his times, Talleyrand, one must always remember, was deeply rooted in the past—up to the neck—but with his head above ground, looking far, far into the future.

Like women and actors, he enjoyed putting on the majestic black velvet mantle incrusted with gold and the wide blue ribbon from which hung a gold cross supporting the holy dove. Castellane tells us that when arrayed in his finery, the prince looked "like a gilded pill." No one in all Europe except the Austrian emperor and the czar possessed such a variety of sumptuous ceremonial attire as prince de Talleyrand.

He left the infant prince to his nurses, his mantle to the embroideresses, and went to drink in the autumn air at Valençay. By November he was back in Paris and had taken his seat in the Chamber of Peers. His colleagues named him to the Commission of Seven Peers constituting the High Court empowered to try treason cases involving state officials, from the royal family to diplomats.

Occupying the seat of a high judge was not enough. One fine day he made a speech. On July 24, 1821, in what was to prove a memorable session, Talleyrand took arms in defense of freedom of the press. His address was so remarkable that even his colleagues in the opposition did not object to printing it. The text of it is still worth reading.

He began by complaining that the Chamber of Peers alone seemed willing to uphold reason and respect for the Constitution whereas the Chamber of Deputies was controlled by a party of hotheads who stifled debate and scoffed at the law. This preamble undoubtedly kindled royalist fires.

He then affirmed this principle: "Without liberty of the press, there is no representative government." Applying the infallible system acquired in the seminary and practiced ever since, he split his central theme down the middle, demonstrating first that "freedom of the press is a necessity of the times," then that "a government exposes itself when it rejects obstinately and persistently what the times have declared necessary."

In the face of a royalist régime, he had the temerity to extol the liberties achieved by the Revolution, acknowledging also the errors and outrages of the Jacobins who seized power from the reformist Assembly. Considering the émigré attitude in 1821, it is amazing that with quiet courage he dared even to suggest such ideas: "Open the *Cahiers* of the different estates. Whatever then represented the considered will of our nation's enlightened men, this is what I call necessities. The Constituent Assembly simply acted as interpreter in establishing freedom of worship, equality before the law, individual liberty, the right to a public trial, and liberty of the press."

Because a free press was "a necessity of the times," it was madness to deny it. It had become a human right. Then he warned that only force could deprive a country of this right. But a greater, irresistible force would inevitably triumph over any government that ignores reality. "In our time, sustained deception is not easy. There is someone smarter than Voltaire, smarter than Bonaparte, smarter than each of the Directors, than each of our past, present, and future ministers: it is Everybody." Thus far no one had ever defined public opinion quite that way, or stated the principle that there can be no government without the consent of the governed. That is Talleyrand at his grandest.

Only one person understood him, Louis XVIII, but he was hopelessly committed to the opinion of his family and court. Moreover, he was tired, ill, and too intelligent for his advisers. He was also prone to sulk and would have cut his own throat rather than admit that the "monster of Autun" was right. Thus Talleyrand's warning and freedom of the press faded into indifference. Nine years later, the monarchy did the same.

Sorrowful Losses and a Miraculous Birth on the Rue Saint-Florentin

One speech cannot fill a whole year; 1821 was another empty year. In March he saw Fontanes into the grave: "I miss him very much; he was a fine man, conscientious, and attached to me for forty years, one of the country's ablest men." Retirement and the easy life had played on our hero's heartstrings—overplayed, in this instance. Fontanes was primarily an ideal courtier under Napoleon. His greatest devotion was probably his servility.

A more celebrated death caused him less emotion but seemed to inspire him with a better choice of words. One July evening in 1821 he was dining with a certain Mrs. Crawford in Paris. The emperor's death on May 5 at St. Helena was announced. It had taken two months for the report to reach the capital. Greatly upset, the hostess exclaimed: "What an event." Talleyrand at once corrected her: "It is no longer an event, Madam, it is news." Those who had been close to the emperor described their impressions of him. Lord Holland, an old friend of Talleyrand's, was at the table and heard and noted the prince's remarks about Napoleon:

> His genius was inconceivable. Nothing could match his energy, his imagination, his intelligence, his capacity for work, his facility to produce. He was also sagacious. In the area of judgment, he was not too strong; then again, when he took the time, he knew how to utilize the judgment of others. Rarely did he exercise bad judgment, and then always because he had failed to consult others [meaning Talleyrand, no doubt]. He had a sense of grandeur but not of beauty. His career is the most astonishing one we have witnessed for a thousand years. He made three crucial mistakes which caused his downfall, scarcely less amazing than his rise: Spain, Russia, and the Pope. Aside from those three things, he made few political errors, surprisingly few considering the multitude of affairs he had to handle, and the scope, importance, and rapidity of events in which he participated. He was certainly a great man, an extraordinary man, extraordinary almost as much for his endowments as for his luck . . . in my opinion the most extraordinary man of our times or of many a century.[1]

Those remarks are less significant for what they tell us about Napoleon than for what they reveal of Talleyrand. His estimate of the emperor's genius is absolutely impartial. He refrains from assessing his personality, habits, or emotions. And, least expected, he has nothing to say about the value of Napoleon's policies and their effects on France and the whole of Europe. He captures the brilliance of the Napoleonic adventure but completely ignores the subject of greatest concern to a diplomat and statesman. Talleyrand concealed his true opinions behind a curtain of generalities, like his eyes behind their half-shut lids.

Grief came to him that summer at Valençay with the news of the duchess of Courland's death on August 20 at Löbikau. She became ill in June and was slightly improved when she wrote him on July 24; it turned out to be her last letter. On hearing of her failing health, he replied: "Perhaps I have never realized how much you mean to me. You are so good, so protective, so giving, that anyone who knows you must worship you. Good-bye angel of goodness and sweetness." He did not know it was to be the final adieu. He never got over the grief of her loss. Strangely enough, he shared his cultlike devotion to this woman with her daughter. One day as he and Dorothée bent over a portrait of the dead woman, he was moved to tears and murmured: "I do not think a woman ever lived who deserved more to be worshipped."

Thus he went on loving, this man whom others regarded as un-feeling because, in an age of sentimental outpourings, he had nothing to say. Talleyrand expressed his hostility with sarcasm and made no effort to hide his physical ailments, but his deepest feelings and emotions were never revealed to his contemporaries.

One death followed another that year. The very day that Dorothée had a memorial service held for her mother in the Lutheran church of Paris, Talleyrand's uncle, Monseigneur de Périgord, archbishop of Paris, who died on October 20, 1821, was buried with great pomp and cere-mony. Before departing at the age of eighty-five, he had taken pains to write to his illustrious and disquieting nephew begging him to return to the faith "which you have never abandoned because you are an honest man." This saintly old man had a very personal notion of the meaning of words. Even with the wrong signals, however, a saint can often ac-complish miracles. After all, the last threads of a cassock still clung to Talleyrand. Perhaps his uncle realized it. He made his coadjutor, Monseigneur de Quélen, pledge to save the soul of his apostate nephew. Time was in their favor, needing only their helping hands. At least they could hope . . .

Why shouldn't they hope? At his uncle's funeral, Talleyrand showed unexpected grief and devotion. Perhaps as he wept and prayed he was also thinking of the duchess. In any case, knowing the im-portance of family ties in our hero's life, and with two deaths following each other so closely, the prince must have been grief-stricken indeed. Paris gossip treated it as a rare spectacle.

The fact is sometimes overlooked that he had kept in touch over the years with some of the professors and seminarians of Saint Sulpice. He was particularly close to Monseigneur Bourlier, bishop of Evreux and member of the Chamber of Peers, who was a frequent visitor to the rue Saint-Florentin as well as Valençay. He died in 1821 after writing Tal-leyrand much the same kind of letter as the archbishop's. It touched him deeply. This series of deaths, and one appeal after the other to return to the faith, left a mark on him. In his funeral elegy for Monseigneur Bour-lier in the Chamber of Peers, Talleyrand stressed that the deceased had entered the church at the time when "M. de Voltaire was beginning to dominate the past century, making M. Bourlier's chosen career more difficult and consequently more brilliant."

The remark might seem an oddly roundabout way of commending his friend unless we recall that just after his ordainment, the young abbé de Périgord went to ask Voltaire, the prince of skepticism, for his blessing. Talleyrand concluded his address with a melancholy and moving appeal on behalf of old age: "A beautiful old age is a great force. Its advice does not offend because rivalries have faded. . . . Let us hope that the old men still among us in this Chamber will remain here for a long time. . . . Their presence is a constant warning: they tell us to take time in our affairs, use taste in our decorum, and to savor without illusion all the things in life. . . ." This wise old man was none other than himself. By evoking Monseigneur Bourlier, he spoke about himself, for himself.

In December, 1821, another death brought new sorrow. Madame Rémusat was no more. The passing of his dear, malicious-tongued confidante left an emptiness in his life. She knew him like a book. "Something sardonic in his smile combined on his lips with an obvious desire to seduce," she once wrote of him. Another time, after he had just said something delightfully touching, she exclaimed: "Dear God, what a pity that you have indulged yourself so wantonly, for I do believe you are worthier than you seem."

The autumn was sad indeed with its procession of caskets—and not one portfolio in sight. The Ultras were bent on getting rid of Richelieu and replacing him with Villèle.

Once again Talleyrand took hope, fluffed out his plumage, gave a series of gala dinners, and tried to win a nod from the Ultras. He had his list all prepared: Chateaubriand, Molé, the duc de Broglie, and, of course, himself in the foreign ministry. The king chose Villèle as premier. Under pressure from the comte d'Artois, the monarchy was hastening its backward march. No question of Talleyrand joining the king's council. He commented dryly: "M. le comte d'Artois discounts his royalty." Yes, at usurious rates.

It so happened that Talleyrand ran into Richelieu as the latter was going into the palace to receive his dismissal, and Villèle was coming down the same steps, beaming at the good news he had just learned. Talleyrand took in the situation at once and described it thus: "See now, the one descending is rising; the one rising is descending."

It was a year of grief, for departed friends and frustrated ambitions. Yet it ended with an addition to the tribe. The event warrants attention. On December 29, 1821, Dorothée gave birth to a daughter who was named Pauline. The year before, Edmond de Périgord had left his apartment on the rue d'Aguesseau and come to live for several months in his uncle's house. This cohabitation neither indicated a reconciliation nor altered the relations—or lack of them—between the couple. It was rumored that the infant's father was Talleyrand, and that Edmond's temporary presence in the house was only intended for appearance's

sake. At what price did he consent? We know for certain that Edmond
did not come willingly. Yet how could he refuse? Was he not the presumptive heir to his uncle's titles and property? In the meantime he
managed to collect some in advance. On May 9, he submitted a request
for the title of grand officer of the Legion of Honor. Talleyrand helped
to get it for him. Edmond left for England as soon as Pauline was born;
on his return, he resumed his bachelor's life on the rue d'Aguesseau.
Once again, there is no formal proof of Talleyrand's paternity, merely a
good deal of circumstantial evidence. Talleyrand had paid off all his
nephew's debts in November, 1820—which was no small matter. And
while this did not appear to improve Edmond's disposition, it kept him
quiet at least, and tractable.

And finally, Talleyrand treated Pauline much the same way he
treated Charlotte, but with even more pronounced tenderness, a kind of
wide-eyed admiration for this second "miracle child" who brightened
his later years. Pauline de Périgord was not only a beautiful child, but
she had an air of innocence, a depth of feeling that fascinated those
around her, most of all Talleyrand. Physically, she resembled her mother,
but when she came to have children, one of them, Marie de Castellane,
bore a striking resemblance to Charlotte, another daughter of Talleyrand.

The new cabinet gave him unexpected satisfaction. As he was an
outsider, however, the satisfaction was purely platonic. Villèle, having
been duly impressed by Talleyrand's defense of a free press, withdrew
the bill on censorship. This infuriated the Chamber of Deputies, which
then redoubled its attacks on the press by bringing suit against various
journals for defaming public officials.

Talleyrand took the offensive on February 26, 1822. Openly opposing the government was a bold and dangerous step, considering the
rebellious mood of liberals and republicans in Paris as well as in the
provinces; it meant siding with the enemies of the throne and the church.
That was not Talleyrand's aim, but as a fundamental human right was
at stake, he resolved to defend it—for the sake of the monarchy and
against the Ultras.

Though not as dramatic as the one he had given on July 24, this
speech was nonetheless artful and persuasive. He argued that the proposed measure was contrary to the spirit of the Constitutional Charter,
that is, contrary to the king's oath and to the popular will. So much for
the present. Then, turning to history to give weight and a sense of
continuity to his theme, he recalled the noble figure of Malesherbes, who
defended freedom of expression in 1758 on behalf of his Encyclopedist

friends, yet lost his head for defending Louis XVI at the latter's trial. The antithesis between an excited mob of petty politicians bent on depriving the people of one of their rights and a great and noble statesman like Malesherbes left only one conclusion: "I vote with M. de Malesherbes against this law." The Chamber was stunned.

Only the duke of Fitz-James rose to answer Talleyrand. Instead of refuting his arguments, he launched a vicious attack on the prince's career, his disorderly life from the Revolution on up through the Directory and the Empire, when he made a fortune, just as he had made one under the Restoration. It was the first time anyone had attacked the prince publicly. All eyes in the Chamber were on him. What was he doing? Following the speech intently. Now and then he scribbled something. Probably notes for his rebuttal. Everyone expected and looked for it. Having finished his tirade the speaker took his seat. Talleyrand reacted no more than if the duke had just finished a lecture on how to improve siliceous soil. Leaning toward his neighbors, he said clearly enough: "The duke has real talent; except for a few uncalled-for annoyances, his speech is very good." As if the whole incident had never existed.

He did not answer the duke or a single one of his detractors. To do so would have meant making a spectacle of himself before a public hungering for spectacle.

The government subsequently came up with another attempt at censorship under an exotic name: "The Law of Justice and Love." Incensed, Chateaubriand dubbed it the "vandal law." When asked his opinion, Talleyrand said that the measure was both stupid and dangerous: "I think it cannot be French; it is inane." In 1830, the country agreed, rejecting it along with the régime.

That was the most notable happening during the winter of 1822. Spring took the prince back to Valençay. The château was filled with guests, who, he tells us, enjoyed themselves. Plays were given, as at Ferney. During the day, there were walks in the vast park or in the forest with its marvelous views, reading, and conversation; at night, supper and, of course, gambling. In an invitation addressed to one of his lady friends on September 18, 1822, he mentioned that his health was not good but that this did not dampen the pleasures of Valençay: "We miss you. Come quickly. You can join us on the twenty-second, the feast day [his name day, the feast of Saint Maurice, which he always celebrated]. It seems that a lot of amusing things have been going on here lately. Alas, I know this only by hearsay, as my legs are so bad that I scarcely leave my bedchamber. On Thursday we are going to put on a nice little improvisation that everyone is now busy arranging. So come quickly, Madam, and don't resort to some vain excuse." [2]

The delights of country life did not close his eyes to political realities. The liberals were sulking, the Ultras spurned him, so he turned to a tiny group of moderates without much political clout but all honorable. They supported the Charter, were respectable men, and, because they took themselves very seriously, were also rather stuffy and depressing. They were the Doctrinaires; Royer-Collard, Guizot, Broglie, Jordan, and old Beugnot comprised the party's leadership—and membership. Charles de Rémusat mocked their meager ranks with equally meager verses:

> When the party assembled,
> The entire thinking faction
> Shared a single couch.

In less trying times, Talleyrand would never have associated with such a group, but the political leadership, the court, and the social élite were so conventional and myopic that he had little choice.

And lest we forget, the government handed him one more insult at Valençay. The chief of police for the Valençay district was removed from his job because "he was completely devoted to the prince de Talleyrand and made it impossible to effect the surveillance which must be exercised currently over all gatherings at the château de Valençay." [3]

That was the price a trusted officer of the law had to pay for yielding to the prince's spell. It indicates the government's total distrust of him.

His overtures to the Doctrinaires were soon to bear fruit. The brains behind this party, Royer-Collard, lived at Châteauvieux, about 15 kilometers from Valençay. Madame Royer-Collard, née Forges de Châteaubrun, had inherited the property from her family. Talleyrand resolved to make the acquaintance of his austere neighbor. They had nothing in common except the fact that both belonged to the opposition. Royer-Collard gave a very cool reception to Talleyrand's advances. Our hero was prepared for this, knowing that the virtuous Royer-Collard went about the capital declaring: "There are two creatures on earth the sight of whom turns my stomach: a regicide and a married priest." Still, he "saw" the married priest. Putting convention aside, Talleyrand announced that he and the duchess of Dino would visit Châteauvieux and was promptly informed by the forbidding Doctrinaire that his wife was ill and therefore would not return the courtesy. But Talleyrand was resolved to go and they went. Over sunken roads, through forests and ravines they jolted along and finally reached Châteauvieux, grim as a fortress in its rocky surroundings. This feudal setting provided Talleyrand with his opening remark to the master of Châteauvieux. With a wry smile, he told him: "The approach to you is indeed forbidding."

Whereupon, by deploying all their charms, uncle and niece succeeded in conquering the recluse of Châteauvieux; within a few hours they established a relationship of respect and admiration, curiosity, and a desire to meet again and even to help each other. Another diplomatic success.

Dissimilar as they were, these two men supported each other in opposing the French intervention in Spain which ultra-royalist folly was soon to promote.

Chateaubriand Wages the Spanish War Against Talleyrand

In 1820, King Ferdinand had been forced to join the throng and grant his subjects a Constitution, which restricted his power by providing for two elected legislative bodies, the Cortes. In 1822, the forces of reaction set off a civil war in the northern provinces aimed at expelling the Cortes and abolishing the Constitution. Whereupon, the French Ultras sprang to the defense of the Spanish royalists, calling for French armed intervention to restore absolutism in Spain.

Would this touch off the second installment of the terrible Peninsular War which Talleyrand considered among Napoleon's major errors? Only the Ultras favored armed intervention, but the Ultras were in power. On October 20, 1822, the members of the Holy Alliance met in Verona to discuss the advisability of intervening in Spain.

With the threat of civil war in Spain, Talleyrand returned to the capital earlier than usual. He lined up opposition to a Spanish expedition: Molé, Saint-Aulaire, and Manuel joined forces with Royer-Collard and himself. Next he went looking for support where he had no reason to expect any since his clash with Alexander, from Pozzo di Borgo, the Russian ambassador to Paris. It was also a good chance to court favor with the czar.

Unfortunately for the nation—and also for the king—the government sent Montmorency and Chateaubriand to Verona, two staunch advocates of intervention. The former was a block of wood, the latter a fountain of words. Both wanted to launch the nation on a new crusade. Chateaubriand was suffering from the same delusions which prompted him to write Le Génie du christianisme, but this time war, not a sermon, was involved. Chateaubriand thought he was indulging in political action at Verona when actually it was simply a romantic stunt.

The Congress of Verona broke up on December 14. Chateaubriand and Montmorency had pursued their own line of thinking rather than Louis XVIII's moderate instructions. At least they had satisfied their party. As Montmorency had resigned from the ministry of foreign affairs, the Ultras, delighted by Chateaubriand's fiery approach to politics, proposed him for the vacant office. Talleyrand refused to believe that the king would yield. He did. And on January 28, 1823, the king proclaimed that an army would be sent to Spain.

At once Talleyrand became leader of the anti-intervention camp. From then on, Chateaubriand considered him a personal enemy. This active struggle fired Talleyrand's blood. Resuming his old habits, he visited the salons, building a circle of admirers, a court which he rehearsed and then dispatched all over town to spread his subversive opinions. He also let fly his famous puns and witticisms, which the government would prefer never to have heard. When someone asked him anxiously: "The king has been in council for three hours, what has been going on?" he replied: "Three hours." Of Blacas, the king's favorite, he said wryly: "On a salary of 150,000 francs he manages to save eight million."

He did more than sound out public feeling; he encouraged and inflamed it—highly dangerous to an insecure government. One day the ailing Count Ferrand entered the Chamber of Peers on the arms of two servants: "Look at Ferrand," said Talleyrand in a loud whisper, "he is like the government. He thinks he is walking, but they are carrying him."

He held court that winter in the salon of Countess Bourcke, a former actress and courtesan who ended up decorating the household of a Danish count. She was hostess to all opponents of current policy: General Foy, Molé, Dalberg, General Sébastiani. Some of these gentlemen did more than curse the government; they extolled the duc d'Orléans. Not in any casual fashion either, for they expected Talleyrand to carry the message to the Palais-Royal. Though a great convenience, this salon attracted a rather motley, conspicuous crowd. The minister of the interior had the Bourcke woman banished. With the shop shut, Talleyrand lost its patrons.

At that time he encountered a new personality, a product of the new times, unknown, all fire and brimstone, a man no higher than one's bootstraps, who was brazen, ambitious, unscrupulous, unmannered, and irrepressible. His name was Adolphe Thiers, and the height he lacked was more than compensated for by abundant intelligence, scholarship, and the discourse tumbling from his lips in the accents of Marseilles.

To win Talleyrand's favor, Adolphe Thiers did a very clever thing. He managed to write the only enthusiastic press comments on the work of Eugène Delacroix, whose canvas "Dante and Virgil in the Underworld" was exhibited in the Salon of 1822. Thiers was a political writer, not an art critic; in declaring Delacroix a genius, he was exercising not his taste for romantic painting but his very astute and informed ambition. The painter Gérard, a friend of Thiers and also of Talleyrand, had told the newcomer all about Eugène Delacroix's parentage. The genius attributed to the son was primarily an homage to the father. Also an entrée to the rue Saint-Florentin. After reading the article, Talleyrand invited the author to visit him. Thiers came running. Having once set foot in the house, he made himself permanently at home.

Thiers was of immediate interest. This vibrant political writer had just returned from a trip to Spain and was therefore in a position to judge the situation and tell the people that they had been sold down the river. Talleyrand was captivated. Though he had every reason to shun a person of Thiers's background, Talleyrand saw him often, and had long, even informal, talks with him.

Talleyrand was constantly amazed by Thiers's mental agility, especially his ability to interpret events to suit his own interests. They did not see eye to eye, for Thiers, an opportunist currying favor in government circles, supported the Spanish expedition. Talleyrand warned: "We will have to struggle against civil insurrection, the worst kind of war. I predicted that some time ago when I tried to dissuade Napoleon from interfering in the affairs of Spain. Napoleon did not listen to me and ventured into a hornet's nest, shamefully squandering his army . . . well, if we insist on going to Spain, it will be the same story all over again. We are headed for disaster." [1]

The prince was remarkably tolerant of a young man who, unhesitantly, would answer him thus: "I don't think so. The Spaniards remember all too painfully the toll of guerrilla warfare. . . . They will not risk another such ordeal." He ended his remarks with the kind of arresting phrase so dear to journalists, and which caught the public eye because the memory of the Chouan rising in the Vendée still haunted France: "Spain is a burned-out Vendée."

Talleyrand may not have appreciated Thiers's position, but he at once spotted the man's extraordinary intelligence.

Talleyrand had a second rostrum from which to plead for non-intervention: the Chamber of Peers. He prepared a speech. If he had given it, the Chamber might have altered its views on the war in Spain.

But it was never heard, for the government forbade the opposition to address the Peers. Talleyrand's speech was not printed until February 3, 1823. It can be read but was never delivered.

This speech is quite as remarkable as its predecessors. As always, a principle is invoked: "The people have the right to elect and to shape the political régime under which they choose to live." In return, neighboring states have an obligation—which is, at the same time, in their own interest—to eschew armed intervention in the internal affairs of other states. He reiterated what he had told Thiers about his opposition to Napoleon's Peninsular War, professing to have voiced that opposition from the very outset, though we know that his initial posture was highly ambiguous. Listen to how he diminishes his own responsibility in the affair: "Sixteen years ago, when summoned by the then ruler of the world to give him my opinion on engaging in a struggle against the Spanish people, I had the misfortune to displease him by unveiling the future to him, by revealing the many dangers that would result from an act of aggression no less unjust than foolhardy. Disgrace was the fruit of my sincerity. It is a strange destiny that, after such a long lapse of time, leads me to renew the same efforts and give the same advice to the legitimate sovereign."

At the very end he takes a clear position—none too pleasant for Louis XVIII. The king was in danger of repeating one of the "usurper's" blunders. Talleyrand offered this warning: "The will of France, needless to say, the will of the entire nation is for peace. Surfeited with military glory, she was led to believe, under the rule of her king, that in peaceful pursuits she was healing the wounds of thirty years of war. . . ."

Who could quarrel with him? Talleyrand spoke for the whole nation. He represented the nation, not one faction. In 1815, Frenchmen had greeted the king's return as a promise of peace. If he now were to default from that promise, there would be trouble. In short, why this war? Was Spain threatening France? Did France want something from Spain? This military action had no purpose, except to reform the Spanish Constitution: "A strange lot of reformers," he commented, "100,000 soldiers, soon to be reinforced by 100,000 more. Whom is this political quixotism meant to impress?"

Recalling his age, his share in the Restoration, and his love of France, he declared that he would do his utmost to "prevent the achievements of wisdom and justice from being jeopardized by insane and foolhardy passions . . ." meaning the passions of Chateaubriand and the Ultras.

TALLEYRAND

The new post offered to Chateaubriand as an outlet for his "insane and foolhardy passions" gave him the satisfaction of calling the expedition a success. The Iberian peninsula did not burst into a new civil war, and the proud viscount could claim a victorious assault on the Trocadero. He boasted about this very minor success, which history, in the long run, has relegated to a footnote. The whole business could have turned very sour; it certainly was not glorious. Its costliness went hand in hand with a first-class financial swindle. The ineffable Ouvrard supplied the expedition and dealt with its commander, the duc d'Angoulême. This courageous Bourbon prince was not terribly bright; being simple-minded and honest, he was badly cheated. Talleyrand summed up the situation: "In this affair, there is only one innocent party."

Chateaubriand meant to revenge himself for Talleyrand's opposition and took another stab at him in the *Mémoires d'outre-tombe*. There he describes—as if he had actually seen and heard him—Talleyrand addressing the Chamber of Peers on February 3, 1823. The satanic words of the Prince of Darkness are engraved in his memory. In turn, he bewitches us into seeing and hearing: "When the purveyor of these imperturbable assertions steps down from the platform and returns impassively to his seat, you watch him half in horror, half in admiration; you ask yourself whether this man has not been endowed by nature with some authority entitling him to recast or to annihilate the truth."

Who could resist these accents of sincerity? As we have said, the speech never was given. No matter: the last sentence is such a masterpiece that it has persuaded thousands of readers to accept this nonexistent scene as gospel truth.

Let us look for a moment at these two illustrious masters of deception. Chateaubriand is a consummate liar, operating baldly with full choir and orchestra. Talleyrand weaves with half truths that are silken, transparent, inconspicuous: the hidden side of the mirror. He is as deceptive as Chateaubriand, though he uses fewer lies, but is a greater master of the art because Chateaubriand's mendacity is passionate, in search of dramatic effects, whereas Talleyrand's is serene. Chateaubriand excites the reader's passions because he himself is impassioned and, in the end, both become victims of a spell. Talleyrand is never taken in by his own game; he cheats only to win. The very economy of his deception raises it to a level of perfection which ought to be the envy of a Chateaubriand. He works with a minimum of words, without images, colors, or music. Still, both are masters of an art; at this level of perfection, mendacity resembles a new branch of poetry. The sometime bishop and the author of the *Mémoires d'outre-tombe* both succeeded in collapsing the

544

cardboard roof sheltering current standards of morality. Their art of dressing up the truth or making it disappear is no more morally objectionable than the art of fugue or counterpoint.

Louis XVIII was not overjoyed at reading this speech. The reminders of Talleyrand's part in restoring the monarchy were irritating. Passion also ran high among the populace, while the very sight of Talleyrand angered the Ultras. Moderates were losing patience. Talleyrand and the duchess of Dino were invited—as if married—to a dinner at the duchesse de Broglie's (Madame de Staël's daughter). Dorothée became uneasy at the presence of La Fayette, fearing that he and her uncle would clash. Generals Foy and Sébastiani were there denouncing a speech of Manuel's, in which the latter had mentioned regicide without also condemning it. They began talking about the Directory; Talleyrand remained silent. Here was a subject he knew inside out, but a fierce debate erupted and he remained aloof. Dorothée sat there anxiously biting her lips. The dinner became intolerable and Dorothée took no pains to conceal it. Her hostess saw this. The duchesse de Broglie did not like Talleyrand or his niece—and with good reason. His remarks about Madame de Staël could hardly be expected to have pleased her daughter, who, moreover, had become a convert to Catholicism—during the Restoration—and more rigid than the Pope. The former bishop of Autun's civil status horrified her, prompting remarks like these about him and his niece: "She fancies herself raising revolutions with her crepe gown and silver turbans, inciting the mob with clever words, and rocking society without disrupting her evening entertainments. She is an odd person, always on the defensive. Her wit is keen and precise, but there is a great deal of it." [2]

Dorothée may have seemed "odd," but making her into a revolutionary is odder still. Madame de Broglie rebukes her for showing ill humor during dinner, "which she makes no more effort to disguise than a totally naïve person who never learned to hide his feelings."

Dorothée naïve? That least of anything. The hostess had allowed her guests to transform a boring meal into an acrimonious political debate and deserved to be told so. Madame de Broglie also made a practice of trying to steal Talleyrand's friends and lure them to her own house. She invited Barante to visit Coppet: "Why go to Valençay? What purpose does it serve? One ought not go to such a place unless it is useful, for duty never sets foot there. . . ."

Barante stayed true to Valençay, which offered something more appealing than utility: the conversation of a man not destined for sainthood or even a ministry, but whose wit and learning, whose knowledge of men and events, whose urbanity made his company advantageous or simply pleasurable.

That summer, Talleyrand got to know Royer-Collard better. A letter dated September 17, 1823, from Talleyrand to his neighbor at Châteauvieux suggests the tone of their relationship: "Gourville says somewhere that on arrival at his estates, the first thing he did was to spread word among the prominent persons in the district that he was now residing there. I follow his example except for one thing: he did not like prominent persons, and I do." [3]

An old friend turned up again: Montrond. He had just left London and came to stay at Valençay. What was he doing in London? Was he on a mission of some kind for his illustrious friend? Neither he nor Talleyrand said a word about it. Talleyrand told Montrond just what he thought of his successors in the foreign ministry, their incompetence, their lack of training and information. Pasquier struck him as a dunce: "M. de Nansouty probably gives him a framed copy of the Treaty of Westphalia for a New Year's gift." This would be a fine discovery for such a grand master of diplomacy.

But all that was just to kill time. Dorothée was on a trip to Germany, their first separation since 1816. She had gone to look after her estates in Saxony, stopping in Baden-Baden to recover her strength. She was in poor health, probably owing to consumption as she suffered from constant colds and spat blood. Writing to the historian Barante, her chaste and discreet confidant, she said: "Farewell, Monsieur, I shall bring back from Germany a little of the strength imparted by one's native air, but more certainly a frame of mind and heart all to the advantage of my second homeland; though forced upon me at first, I have since adopted it and have no wish to find refuge and repose in any other." The "refuge and repose" was Talleyrand, who was also the antithesis, equally essential to Dorothée: ambition, the drive to play a part in world events, and the need to dominate someone.

"Our Acts Pursue Us," Said Paul Bourget: The Duc d'Enghien Rises Again, and Louis XVIII Vanishes

In 1816, a dangerous phantom threatened to ruin Talleyrand: the ghost of the ill-fated duc d'Enghien. One day our hero happened to meet the venerable prince de Condé at court and had the audacity to address him. The duc d'Enghien's grandfather did not turn it into the scandal that certain parties may have anticipated. Handling it in his own fashion, Condé pretended to confuse Talleyrand with the latter's uncle the archbishop and asked if he had heard from his nephew, that "wretch," that "scoundrel," "that good-for-nothing from Autun." Talleyrand swallowed the insults without twitching a muscle. Here is his account of the same incident in the *Memoirs:* "He spoke to me in a gracious manner which I shall never forget about French successes at the Congress of Vienna." Insults slid right off his back. That was the only revenge the old man bothered to take for his grandson's death. He retired to Chantilly, where he died in 1818. His son the duc de Bourbon returned from exile, took the title prince de Condé, and lived at Chantilly. Would he not try to avenge family blood? It was to be feared that he would. He made no move; neither did Talleyrand. Still, the return of the last of the Condés set tongues wagging and stories circulating about the three principal actors in the tragedy, Talleyrand, Savary, and Caulaincourt.

Caulaincourt's widow, the duchess of Vicenza, resolved to preserve her late husband's good name. Before doing anything, she sought Talleyrand's advice. The foolish woman actually had planned to explain to Condé that neither Savary, Caulaincourt, Talleyrand, nor even Bonaparte had any hand in what Savary modestly called "the catastrophe of the duc d'Enghien." "What shall we do?" implored the unhappy woman. "Nothing," was all Talleyrand had to say. It was sound advice. But Madame de Caulaincourt was bent on defending her husband's honor. She made a suggestion. She knew that Condé's mistress, Madame de Feuchères, exercised great influence over him. Why not use her to approach Condé? On hearing the mistress named, Talleyrand drew himself up, exclaiming scornfully: "Madame de Feuchères? Fie on you! How could you stoop so low?" Taken aback, the poor widow exited hastily and maintained strict silence. Talleyrand had won half the battle; the other half was keeping the Condés quiet.

The scheme to recruit Madame de Feuchères, which he had disdained on presentation by Madame de Caulaincourt, suddenly appeared excellent. But how was he to approach Condé's mistress? He decided to employ the comte de Durfort, a reliable gentleman close to Condé and Madame de Feuchères. He invited the count to dinner and crammed him with food and attention, whereupon Durfort was so flattered by the whole performance that he turned to putty in the prince's hands. The two suddenly became fast friends and Durfort found himself listening open-mouthed to Talleyrand's whispered account of that fatal night when the duc d'Enghien had met his end. Talleyrand informed his companion that on the night preceding the abduction, by superhuman efforts he had managed to get a message through to the unfortunate prince urging him to flee at once. He, Talleyrand, had jeopardized his own life to save "so beloved a head." Durfort was stunned with gratitude and admiration. Without bothering to find out whether any trace of the message, its contents, or its bearer existed, he rushed over to repeat the story at Chantilly. Before letting him go, Talleyrand had advised Durfort to speak to Madame de Feuchères and win her over to the notion that Talleyrand was devoted to the House of Condé. Madame de Feuchères agreed to so advise her lover, Condé, and Durfort brought her to the rue Saint-Florentin. There she received the same treatment which had worked so well with Durfort; Madame de Dino dropped "that woman" a curtsey low enough to make her think she was a Bourbon princess. After that, the Feuchères woman was ready to undertake almost anything.

So thoroughly did she do what was expected of her that Talleyrand found himself a guest at Chantilly. In turn, he invited Condé to Valençay in the hunting season. Society talked of nothing else.

Now the duc d'Enghien was buried once and for all. Talleyrand rinsed out the bad taste of this affair with a few lines in his *Memoirs* describing several fine dinners, several compliments worthy of Voltaire, and—least important of all—several "gifts" to the Feuchères lady to cover expenses she had run up for dresses and jewelry. That had occurred in 1818.

Five years later, on October 9, 1823, a newspaper article appeared in *L'Oriflamme* and revived the whole affair. Talleyrand, Savary, and Réal were attacked for their part in the duc d'Enghien's murder. A grim reminder. Would it not have been wiser to ignore this article by a little-known writer? Savary did just the opposite by publishing a pamphlet entitled *Extracts from the 'Memoirs' of M. le duc de Rovigo Concerning the Catastrophe of M. le duc d'Enghien*. To absolve himself, he placed all the responsibility with Talleyrand. "I will not allow odious suspicions to weigh on my conscience while the real culprits strut about with their medals and high offices."

The pamphlet achieved its purpose; everyone recognized the "real culprit." Talleyrand was aghast. He had been so careful to cover up this affair, to burn every scrap of evidence, as we recall. Savary's pamphlet was a fatal snag in his plans. He sensed that lightning was about to strike; for the first time in his life, he had trouble sleeping. On November 3, 1823, he left Valençay in a rush, resolved to be in Paris when the storm broke. An extraordinary decision on his part, for usually he let the rain fall. "I am an old umbrella, rained on for over forty years. What difference does one more drop make?" he would often say. This time, instead of a shower, it was thunder and lightning. Luckily, he had support and encouragement from Royer-Collard. Dull friends often turn out to be dependable. Talleyrand had gone, leaving Dorothée to pack and follow with the trunks. She rejoined him on November 5. To Barante she complained bitterly that Paris was "the center of the most odious calumnies, of the most monstrous creations of a hideous mind." It recalls the *Comédie humaine;* indeed, Balzac lurks in every corridor of the history of his times.

This year an ominous cloud hung over their return to Paris: "the winter promises to be a bad one," Dorothée wrote. She urged that they follow Royer-Collard's advice and "act at the highest level," meaning the throne. Shortly after his arrival, Talleyrand sent a letter to the king calculated to offset the pamphlet's damaging effects and explaining the death of the duc d'Enghien, Louis XVIII's cousin. Never had this disciple of Voltaire written such an involved, confused letter. Was he in too much of a rush, or under stress? Did the subject demand it? It seems most likely that he deliberately obscured his thinking. His conscience hurt him. He asked the king to have Savary tried by the High Court. Had he lost his wits? Did he not realize that any trial involving the assassination would have turned into a political confrontation? What a circus that would have been, what an invitation to chaos! The barricades would have been up within a week. Could he not see what he was asking for? He reacted to Savary's pamphlet like a country squire whose hunting rights have been poached upon.

Louis XVIII behaved as a sovereign should by saving Talleyrand and maintaining order. He refused to lay this matter before the court and reaffirmed confidence in Talleyrand. "His Majesty desires to forget the past and remember only the services rendered to France and to him personally. Your eminent position at court, Prince, is positive proof that the charges which offend and wound you have made no impression whatsoever on His Majesty."

With those few lines Louis XVIII restored to Talleyrand his throne on the rue Saint-Florentin, his kingdom of Valençay, and his sovereignty over public opinion. The king saved him. Now they were even.

On November 17, 1823, the newspapers carried this official note: "The king has forbidden the duke of Rovigo [Savary] to appear at the Tuileries."

Talleyrand breathed easy. Then, characteristically, he casually dismissed the source of his discomfort and embarrassment. Writing to Dalberg, he said: "The duke of Rovigo's attack does not warrant too much attention. The public has done me justice in full. The verdict is in: this whole affair is over and done with." [1]

TALLEYRAND

The duchesse de Broglie coolly told Barante: "M. de Talleyrand emerged white as snow from this affair; you have to admit that in his case calumny brings good fortune." Talleyrand also wrote to Barante, even more coolly, insisting that history had absolved him, the most telling evidence of which was, according to him, Napoleon's own statement: ". . . the phrase in Napoleon's will asserting that he alone is responsible for the duc d'Enghien's murder and that under similar circumstances he would again act as he did then." [2]

Hail Caesar for accepting the burden of guilt; not that it removed any doubts about the guilt of his confederates. But for Talleyrand, nothing was quite as trivial as a doubt. It left his happiness untarnished.

Yet can a lull be called happiness? Talleyrand was seventy. His lameness caused him increasing pain; age was bowing him down. His answer to that was to loop his cravat once or twice more around his neck to hold his head as high as ever. The same cloud of perfume announced his presence in the salon or in the death chamber. That year, 1824, saw the passing of Cambacérès and Louis XVIII. When the former archchancellor died on March 8, the police impounded his papers. "Ah," said Talleyrand, "that is a warning from the Tuileries to the rue Saint-Florentin." He had not waited for the warning to turn his own papers into ashes.

The king died in September, but before that Talleyrand gave him fresh cause for displeasure. By clever scheming, our prince was able to round up a majority of votes in the Chamber of Peers defeating Villèle's proposal to convert government bonds from a 5 to a 3 per cent rate. His tactics, as usual, involved the services of a woman, in this case, Madame de Dino. The incident is worth a pause. Talleyrand sent Dorothée, whose devotion was beyond question, to try to persuade Monseigneur de Quélen, now archbishop of Paris, and his clergy to oppose Villèle's measure. Madame de Dino frequently saw the archbishop, who was himself eager to become closer to Talleyrand in order to reconcile him to the church. In the interest of preserving the bond rate and of her uncle, the duchess of Dino may have gone too far, for she succeeded in making the prelate fall madly in love with her. But "a treacherous woman friend of the duchess's informed him of the mischievous prank being played on him before he had completely succumbed. He took his remorse to the foot of the altar." [3] Repentance undoubtedly fortified the archbishop's resolve to assail Talleyrand with every weapon of the faith.

When the Chamber rejected the motion, Dorothée was in Silesia. Still, it gave her pleasure to think that she had done her part to embarrass Villèle.

Chateaubriand paid for everyone else. He too had schemed against the premier, and now Villèle turned him out of office. He was "sacked like a valet." It was a crushing experience for a man who set such store by his own genius. Talleyrand knew of the impending dismissal before it was announced to the champion of the Spanish expedition. Our limping prince thought nothing of paying a courtesy call on his sworn foe just for the satisfaction of seeing the look on so vain a minister's face the day he was turned out. The spectacle delighted him; he made sure that Chateaubriand knew this.

He had another more private and less cruel satisfaction. Delacroix exhibited his "Massacre of Chios" in the Salon of 1824. It caused a terrific scandal, with those greenish bodies piled up like real corpses. Scattered all over the place; not at all the way one was taught to arrange the bodies of dead heroes at the Academy of Fine Art. It was just too much. The official critics wanted to be done with this revolution of the palette and its proponent, Delacroix. The result of all the scandal was that the revolutionary painting was bought for the nation for 6,000 francs, a prodigious sum for an unknown, much-abused painter. Delacroix's friend Gérard had made overtures to Sosthène de La Rochefoucauld, who was responsible for state acquisitions. Talleyrand, as we know, was very fond of Gérard, not to mention Delacroix.

To be able to enjoy the country without making the long trip to Valençay, he bought the duchesse de Duras's modest house near the Forest of Montmorency. Madame de Duras and her friends were welcome there—except for Chateaubriand, whose literary "sister" she was. Talleyrand had become very fond of this lady. Her tearful novels attracted considerable attention at the time when salon-goers were eager to drink their fill of the melancholy Mississippi. Talleyrand preferred Rivarol.

Royer-Collard continued to work half-heartedly with Talleyrand against the Ultras. But the unapproachable Doctrinaire did not care much for society. All Talleyrand's cajoling failed to lure him into the magic circle of the rue Saint-Florentin.

Finally, deploying their joint charms, Talleyrand and his niece prevailed on Royer-Collard to attend a dinner in honor of the heir to Saxony's throne. Talleyrand and his nation were always on the best of terms with Saxony and its sovereigns. Our hero wanted to acquaint the royal prince with the most illustrious personalities in French arts and sciences. Royer-Collard must be there to represent oratory. The notion of being a symbol must have tickled the recluse's vanity, for he came.

Finally, in September, the grand chamberlain cut short his cure at

Bourbon-l'Archambault to attend his ailing sovereign. He visited the Tuileries every day. A sad spectacle indeed, the dying king and a wasted old man, two relics of another century, another society, so close yet so antagonistic, thrown together now by the appalling presence of death.

Madame de Dino grew anxious about her uncle. If the king's illness were to drag on, Talleyrand's strength would fail. He was obliged to stay on his feet while administering "the most painful and repulsive services for a man of M. de Talleyrand's age and infirmity. It is more than enough to make me fear for his health," Dorothée wrote.

The king was given the sacrament on September 13. When asked how His Majesty had acted, Talleyrand replied: "Most fittingly."

On September 23, Louis XVIII was buried in Saint-Denis. The grand almoner and the grand chamberlain bore the king's heart on a cushion. At the official funeral on September 25, Talleyrand stood by the casket holding the white flag of the monarchy, like Joan of Arc!

After this exhausting experience, he returned to the peace of his own household, where tenderness tinged with admiration and respect always awaited him. It was a curious household, though. He, the old satrap, took charge of educating his nephew's children and lavished affection on his nephew's wife. She, as mistress of the capital's most sumptuous and elegant house, was admirable. Life on a grand scale, but with danger signs. They became apparent after November 6, 1824, on which date a legal separation was granted to Dorothée and Edmond. But why did Talleyrand and Dorothée take Edmond to court; why this writ which in no way altered the situation? The Périgord clan, well connected at court, close to the duchesse d'Angoulême (Louis XVI's daughter), was up in arms over Dorothée, fearing that Talleyrand would leave her part of his fortune. The Tuileries and the faubourg Saint-Germain made it clear that the duchess of Dino was unwelcome. Certain doors were closed to her, notably Madame de Castellane's. Parisian society had never seemed more odious and Talleyrand spent more and more time at Valençay.

The King Changes, the Boredom Remains:
The Régime of Boredom

Another king . . . Another coronation. The Mass, the royal pageantry, the plumed hat, the mantle heavy with gold, yet less heavy than the weight of age and the sadness of disillusion. A king! Talleyrand knew that kings, like other men, could be caught in a web of intrigue.

The comte d'Artois was crowned as Charles X at Rheims on May 29, 1825. He had been ruling since September 24, 1824, in which interval his ministers had made themselves thoroughly unpopular with such legislation as the Law of Sacrilege and the law indemnifying emigrants dispossessed by the Republic.

To take him to the coronation of this king whose reign had got off to such a lame start, Talleyrand bought himself a splendid coach. His coat of arms was prominently displayed: the three lions langued and crowned baring their claws on crimson and gold leaf. It was a monument, that coach; he rode in it until the end of his life on all state occasions. It rumbled through Paris when he called at the Palais-Royal to pay court to Louis-Philippe d'Orléans. It bore him, smiling and submissive, to Rheims for the coronation of Charles X; then a few years later, with just a tinge of irony and bitterness but still smiling and submissive, it carried him to the monarch who dethroned Charles X.

The coronation was torture, as it kept him standing at the king's side for hours, laden down with his robes of state, his seventy-one years, and his burden of poignant memories. Beneath those cathedral vaults, did he visualize his father fulfilling his priestlike function, his uncle the archbishop, the fresh young faces of Madame de Laval and Madame de Brionne? Today he could recognize the former bishop of Nancy, Monseigneur de La Fare, now archbishop of Sens, and a few other faces ravaged by time and the rancors of emigration. Even the king was a wizened old man. This coronation, meant to symbolize resurrection, turned out to be a frightful ode to decay.

Gérard, the court painter, rejuvenated all these relics so that the official painting of the coronation presents Talleyrand as a lively abbé de Périgord, whereas his contemporaries referred to him as a walking death's head. His livid complexion suggested it, and an expression of hopeless desolation.

The next day, he had to stand once again during an incredibly medieval pageant involving victims of scrofula, 120 ragged sufferers of this disease filing in front of the king, who touched their sores pronouncing each time the sacramental words: "May God cure thee; the king touches thee."

In gratitude for Talleyrand's inestimable service during the coronation, Charles X sent him his own portrait by Gérard, another royal face for the picture gallery at Valençay.

The festivities continued in Paris. Talleyrand was exhausted. Returning from a performance of *Pharamond* at the opera, he commented sarcastically: "Life would be bearable without entertainments." The opera was in fact a terrible bore, followed by a no less tiresome ballet. In deference to the prudish attitudes of the Congregation, the dancers' tutus had been lengthened and the gauze replaced by opaque fabric. Ladies of virtue thus need not be offended at the sight of those pirouetting "creatures," and could still secretly hope that the new monarch would force them into burlap from head to toe.

People noticed that the exhausted prince limped worse than ever. About that time he came to be called "the limping Mephistopheles," a nickname which clung to him permanently. So, dragging his foot painfully, he went off to the country, not Valençay this time, but the château de Rochecotte, his niece's newly acquired property in Touraine, near Langeais. Among the very first guests there was Adolphe Thiers. By now Thiers knew the prince extremely well, and the duchess of Dino perhaps even better. "You know that you are our best friend as well as our favorite," she wrote to him. Thiers had already established his reputation as a historian of the Revolution and was using it to further his political ambitions. "We think of you often and talk about your future; it interests us very much and gives us great expectations," she assured the young man. Talleyrand called him "a youngster with the sacred spark." Thiers learned from the experience of the old satrap. When someone ventured to comment in Talleyrand's presence that Thiers was a cheeky parvenu, the prince corrected him: "No, sir, Thiers is not a parvenu; he has arrived."

Another friend whom Talleyrand and Dorothée valued in a different way was Prosper de Barante, chronicler of the dukes of Burgundy. Barante was younger, the same generation as Lamartine and Alfred de Vigny. He was scholarly, mournful as an autumn evening, a perfect gentleman.

In July, 1825, Talleyrand gladly would have gone out of his way to visit Barante at his country estate and enjoy, as he put it, "the simple, rich, elegant conversation, which, in the very heart of Paris, makes our friendship such a pleasure." But he had to go to Bourbon to treat his ailing legs and be utterly bored. That year he happened to meet a young priest at the spa who confessed his regrets at having chosen the wrong vocation: "He is to be ordained in September and is angry at the decision he took." The private utterances entered sympathetic ears. "He is well educated, imaginative, and a bit harebrained," Talleyrand wrote to Barante. But the young curé seemed less troubled by his ill-chosen profession than by a wart on the sole of his foot which the mineral baths were supposed to cure. In between these confessions, Talleyrand read the marquis d'Argenson's absorbing Memoirs.

After a short stay at Valençay and another glimpse of Royer-Collard, who had to be visited at home as he was rarely willing to come to Valençay, Talleyrand, Dorothée, and Countess Tyszkiewicz decided to winter in the south of France instead of Paris, where the reception had been frigid the previous year. To liven the adventure—for in 1825 it was quite an adventure to explore the Midi, which was ill-equipped to handle travelers and had little to offer anyway, except sunshine—the trio decided to split up, each to roam at pleasure, meeting only in the main centers. Geneva was the first of these. Talleyrand wrote to Royer-Collard on October 31, 1825: "While roaming through Switzerland, where the weather has been superb, I have done a bit of botanizing in your behalf. I sent you the pick of the crop; I think it is a plant rarely seen in Paris and which may prove useful against winter ailments." [1] A surprising hobby for Talleyrand. Is it possible that the herb-collecting craze launched by Rousseau had made permanent converts of people who were only twenty in 1774? Who would imagine the prince de Talleyrand dabbling in herbal infusions? They tried to call on Madame de Staël's son, but found Coppet deserted. With the advancing season, they decided to work their way south and meet next in Marseilles, "a good shelter for the months of November and December."

They entered Marseilles on October 28, with the local press announcing their arrival. Instead of an inn, they were offered the use of a private house. Marseilles's officials and notables gave the party a cordial welcome. As a matter of fact, Talleyrand would have preferred fewer solemn Masses and statues unveiled, but that was the price of glory. With his train of ladies, he was treated like a visiting potentate. A comment of his brings to mind Stendhal: "Only in France can one know the full horror of provincial life." Despite his aversion to the red-carpet treatment in Marseilles, he seemed rested, relaxed, and hopeful that he could overcome an incurable urge for the rue du Bac. Dorothée declared that her uncle looked much younger: "Exercise, fresh air, no other heat than the sun's, the sea air which allows him to add to his dinner a good breakfast, all these things have worked miracles." [2]

There was never time to be bored. They met a banker friend of baron Louis's, as witty as he was rich, who told scandalous tales about Louis the former priest, and whose local accent and fund of anecdotes amused Talleyrand. They visited another fading spirit, General Suchet, who died at the beginning of January; and a certain General de la Briche often played écarté with Talleyrand. Our hero made a number of interesting observations about the spirit of enterprise prevailing in Marseilles. In the Greek struggle for independence from Turkey, the Phocaeans prudently sided with both parties. They lent the Greeks money to arm themselves against the Turks, and sold ships to the Turks for use against the Greeks. "The same merchant," Talleyrand noted, "acts as their pay-master [the Greeks'] and also shipbuilder to Egypt's pasha." Talleyrand stated this quite matter-of-factly. To him, the line between commercial and diplomatic trading was extremely fine.

Despite invitations to concerts and a box at the opera which the prefect put at their disposal, the trio fled at the first sign of the mistral. Hyères was their first stop, on January 26, 1826. There, as in Marseilles, they had the use of a private house, the handsomest one in town. Their greatest delight was the enormous, sun-bathed garden sloping straight down to the sea. Having declared the mistral to be "the nastiest and most unhealthy thing in the world," Dorothée was enchanted by the climate of Hyères. ". . . The weather is such that I am writing you next to the open window [January 31] with the blinds lowered to pre-vent the sun from burning my face. And evening walks like August in Paris. . . . I know no other place where life seems sweeter." *

One serious drawback developed in this otherwise pleasant region and made them decide to move on: people around them were dying like flies. In those days, doctors sent their consumptive patients down to the coast. "There you see only the dying, you meet only funeral processions, you hear of nothing but lung disease."

Countess Tyszkiewicz was sent ahead to scout for lodgings in Nice. As it turned out, just as many people were dying there, but the town was large enough for funerals to pass unobserved. Still, the spell of the Midi had been broken. At this point, they learned that Talleyrand had just been named mayor of Valençay. There is no doubt that with all his titles and distinctions, our prince was elated to become mayor of his village. They packed for the return to Valençay. The journey to Prov-ence thus ended on visions of sun-drenched funeral processions and the hope of getting home in time to celebrate Talleyrand's name day, the feast of Saint Maurice.

They went first to Paris, settling into their old, rather monotonous routine. A social circle embracing the same old faces. The same rigid, hypocritical conformism ruled salons peopled by survivors and ghosts. And the youth? What were the Restoration's young people up to? They were all mad, off somewhere declaiming evanescent verses by that

* In Hyères, Dorothée is said to have given birth secretly to a daughter. Alphonse Denis, mayor of the town, has left a documented account of this affair which took place right under Talleyrand's nose. The father is reputed to have been Piscatory, a known lover of Madame de Dino, though she had others who remain unknown.

Lamartine fellow whose every stanza died away in a whisper; or listening ecstatically to the music of someone named Chopin who left them in tears, ready to die of consumption under a weeping willow.

Officialdom went on chanting lugubrious *Te Deums*, burying its dead, and, to relieve the monotony, wrangling over politics. The Ultras were determined to wipe out every vestige of the Revolution, the others, every survivor of the Ancien Régime. All were equally pedantic and opinionated. None had learned a thing from Voltaire. Indeed, the Enlightenment was all but extinguished in France. Talleyrand was its last flickering candle.

The prince made another public appearance on May 3, 1826, at the side of Charles X. The king placed the cornerstone of a monument to the memory of Louis XVI and Marie Antoinette on the site of their execution. The ceremony was impressive but morbid. Official sentiment dwelled on what was dead and gone. The sanctuaries of Paris gave up their most precious relics, the nails from the Cross and the Crown of Thorns, to be carried in procession. The long line of marchers included churchmen, led by Monseigneur de Quélen, princes, generals, peers, dukes in flowing mantles, deputies in scarlet uniforms, and the king heading the solemn procession. Talleyrand followed a step behind, the focus of attention, like a statue, attesting to the presence and permanence of the nation in the face of shifting governments and revolutions.

A fresh note was injected into this society of boredom by a handful of foreign visitors. Sidney Smith, an English canon and friend of the duke of Bedford, came with the duke to the rue Saint-Florentin and proved most entertaining. He reminded Talleyrand of a remark our hero had made in London in 1792 and which had amused his English hosts. Sidney's brother, an English cabinet member, had told the young priest that he would help him obtain a good benefice, but that first "I shall make you commit every loathsome act to which priests readily stoop." Like a true connoisseur, the bishop of Autun pricked up his ears and, with the countenance of a saintly hermit, replied: "What enormous leeway!" The remark and the expression on his face were remembered long afterwards.

Sidney also told the story of a terrible blunder he had made at a dinner party when he mistook his neighbor's name for Barras, whom all the world knew to be a sink of corruption. Scrutinizing the face of this wily and infamous Jacobin for signs of his vices, Sidney managed to find what he took for a few of them. In any event, he had the wrong name, and the person sitting opposite him was none other than Barante, the respectable, chaste, and mournful Prosper. Dorothée and Talleyrand found the story hilarious; if poor Barante had known that someone had taken him for Barras, he too would have turned consumptive.

This miserable fate might have awaited Dorothée if she had been obliged to live at Pont-de-Sains,* where Talleyrand brought her in July, 1826. Accustomed to the unwholesome Pomeranian countryside, she found this even worse. Montrond visited them in their moss-covered retreat. Then came the return to Paris, with Dorothée traveling by way of Dieppe so that she could bathe in the sea, a new fad launched by the duchesse de Berry; by temperament Dorothée needed the stimulus of an occasional escapade.

The rue Saint-Florentin reopened its doors in July with a fresh series of dinners. A young German soprano was threatening to dethrone Madame Malibran. As Fraulein Sontag's virtue presumably exceeded her vocal gifts, she began appearing in the salons of the faubourg Saint-Germain. Such was life in a jaded society.

Talleyrand Receives a Slap, Which Fails to Arouse the Nation from Its Torpor

At the end of August, the whole caravan set out for Valençay: the three Dino children, their tutors, and the servants. Dorothée nicknamed it "the high school"; Talleyrand, "normal school." The new mayor of Valençay's piety apparently had gained him this honor, according to the prefect's edict, which was posted for all to read. Here is the text, complete with its odor of sanctity: "His Serene Lordship has been designated because his desire to cooperate with the administration was demonstrated by the pious, useful, and charitable establishment with which His Lordship has endowed the village." The Chapel of Saint Maurice was referred to, not the Dino "high school."

When entertaining, Talleyrand mercifully warned his guests if the mischievous youngsters were about. Actually, they were a source of amusement to everyone, himself most of all. And when a rainy day kept them all indoors, Talleyrand apologized to Royer-Collard for not driving over to Châteauvieux: "Madame de Dino, our whole normal school, and I are very sorry to have to put off until early next week our much anticipated visit to our very dear and highly respected neighbors."

* This large estate, yielding a good income and far less dreary than some have said, was given to Pauline, who, upon her marriage to the marquis de Castellane, transferred it into his family.

Less than a week afterwards, on September 16, 1826, he was obliged to be back in Paris for the celebration in Saint-Denis of the anniversary of Louis XVI's birth. He offered to attend to whatever Royer-Collard might need in Paris, assuring him by letter that no favor was too small for such worthy neighbors. After spreading on the honey, he spoke of the king, whose politics he despised, but whose hunting exploits deserved some attention: "What do you think of the king's hunting record? In a single day he shot 1,793 pieces of game, which no other king of France had done before. What a boon to civilization!"

The remark throws light on his reply to Charles X's assertion that the Ultras would save the country: "Sire, it was never my impression that the Capitoline was saved by a flock of geese."

Barante visited Valençay: "Here I am in this great château with its magnificent hospitality and lavish elegance, of which there is no longer, or is not yet, another example in all of France. . . ." Everyone found him delightful company. Dorothée confided to him one day: "There is a breach between myself and Paris that may never be mended." Actually, things were worse than she said: her one link with Paris was Talleyrand. After that, an abyss.

They took up residence in Paris at the beginning of November. The fourth was the feast of Saint Charles, the king's patron saint. Another High Mass, another tiresome procession to the Tuileries of government officials and the diplomatic corps. A diet to induce political starvation. Yet the public was about ready to bare its teeth. A minor incident could shake the government. On his deathbed, Talma, the celebrated actor, caused a great scandal by refusing to see a priest. He was given a civil burial. Defying the authorities, a huge crowd of silent mourners trailed after the tainted casket. The government, the Congregation, the leaders of society all caught the message of mute opposition. But, they assured themselves, it was only a funeral. Paris slumbered on like a fly in the sun. Life on the rue Saint-Florentin was just as tedious as the surrounding society. Louis de Périgord's graduation at the top of his high school class was the theme of general rejoicing in the household. Where were the Congresses of yesteryear? Talleyrand was growing sluggish; he toyed with the notion of retiring permanently to Valençay, but the assurance of damp and chilly winters finally dissuaded him. Dorothée had her moods; she too was depressed and sometimes disagreeable. Apathy reigned. And how did the government propose to shake the nation out of its torpor? By shrouding it afresh in ashes and black crepe for a memorial service in Saint-Denis on January 20, 1827, to commemorate Louis XVI's death.

TALLEYRAND

The grand chamberlain stood beside the king. At the close of the ceremony, the marquis de Dreux-Brézé opened a path for the royal family. Talleyrand led the way out for the duchesse and duc d'Angoulême—the dauphin and his wife—escorting them between two rows of guards to their carriage, where he waited, still and straight as a statue, until it drove off. At that moment, a fanatic elbowed the guards aside, flung himself upon Talleyrand slapping him with the full force of a man still young and robust, sent him spinning to the ground, then kicked him several times. The whole thing occurred in a flash, without a word or cry.

People standing near the prince thought he had been murdered. They bent over him, helped him to his feet, and only then realized that he had received a staggering blow but no wound. They carried him home with great to-do and put him to bed. Visitors began pouring in. Their one distraction, no doubt. In fact, that resounding slap reverberated far and wide.

The assailant, Maubreuil, was easily apprehended, almost as if he wanted to be. When questioned like a common drunk or madman, he promptly established his sanity: "I intended to thrash prince de Talleyrand; he wronged me and my family." The man is no stranger to us: Maubreuil had intruded rudely once before in our prince's life. Marie-Armand, comte de Guerry-Maubreuil, marquis d'Orvault repeated the accusation he had made in 1815, that Talleyrand hired him to assassinate Napoleon and to attack the queen of Westphalia's carriage and rob her of a fortune in gold and diamonds. He stole the diamonds but refused to kill Napoleon. His sentence was five years in prison for armed assault and robbery. Now behind bars once again for the Saint-Denis incident, Maubreuil lashed out at Talleyrand in a manifesto addressed to the police commissioner, declaring that he acted to avenge his family's honor. He also spoke of detesting the "apostate priest," an insult calculated to please the Congregation and which recurred in every other sentence. He claimed to have slapped Talleyrand in order to disgrace him publicly. Maubreuil's parting epithet was "Astaroth," * which, in his vocabulary, apparently was the ultimate invective.

Talleyrand lay in his bed. The occasion really warranted those unguents so dear to his heart. His conduct in this affair frequently seems to puzzle his biographers, though it need not. Stretched out with a swol-

---

* Astaroth, Astarte, or Ishtar all correspond to Aphrodite. The image of Talleyrand as a Chaldean Venus seems rather bizarre. Perhaps Asmodée is intended, the central character in Lesage's *Le Diable boiteux*.

len cheek, black and blue ribs, and an aching back, this old man of seventy-three remained true to character. His way of handling a painfully humiliating ordeal was to minimize it, to pass it off as one of life's inevitable discomforts, which social intercourse, crowds, and occasional lunatics visit upon men of distinction who must go forth to the market place. To the prince of diplomats, an attack, whether on his life or his honor, was one of the risks of the game. So why all the fuss about someone jostling him? Bruises he could accept as the price of fame; but as to having been insulted, nothing of the sort! Physically, even, he obliterated the episode. When the examining magistrate came to take his deposition on January 26, 1827, Talleyrand insisted that he would be up and about before the twenty-day period was over (the law provided that if the victim of an assault remained physically incapacitated for more than twenty days, his assailant was liable for solitary confinement with hard labor). He wanted to forget. This slap had no place in the life of Monsieur de Talleyrand. A hundred onlookers had witnessed it, 100,000 discussed it, 500,000 read about it. No matter, there had never been any slap in the face.

Shortly thereafter, the king, when inquiring about his grand chamberlain's health, added, rather obtusely but with the best intentions, that the odious person who had slapped him was to be punished. Stiffening as if from a fresh slap, the prince retorted imperiously: "Sire, it was a blow of the fist." Périgords did not receive slaps.

Propped up among satin and lace pillows, our prince received his friends. At regular intervals he would ask to see the guest register from the vestibule so as to examine the list of callers. He paid less attention to the names of those who came than to the ones who stayed away. The police prefect was among the latter, prompting Talleyrand's remark to Dorothée: "Well, now, Delaveau shows little enough curiosity for a prefect of police." Indeed, Delaveau, staunch supporter of the Ultras and the Congregation, had no use for Talleyrand, who returned his antipathy and frequently ridiculed his attempts to root out vice. This eagle-eyed officer of the law had noticed that masked balls at the opera were encouraging moral license. Fancy that! And closer observation revealed that the guilty couples were arranging assignations under the great clock: a policeman was dispatched straightway to immobilize its hands. Talleyrand commented that Delaveau's eagerness to make arrests included "dispatching an agent to arrest the hands of the opera clock."

The brunt of his scorn for the Congregation fell mainly on the Jesuits. One day he said to the eminent Cuvier: "I wager that Europe's most renowned naturalist does not know which animal is the most grateful of them all." Anticipating a joke at his own expense, Cuvier backed away. "No, really, I'm serious," Talleyrand insisted. Cuvier had no answer. "You don't know? Well, then I'll tell you: the most grateful animals are turkeys. The Jesuits brought the first turkey to France; now it is the turkeys * who are bringing back the Jesuits."

Of course, Talleyrand came in for his own share of derision following the Maubreuil episode. He prepared an exquisite letter informing the magistrate that he wished to waive charges against his assailant. Friends and sycophants took copies of it and went about proclaiming his magnanimous gesture. Someone supplied a fitting title to his literary effort: "On Indifference in the Matter of Slaps," by Monsieur de Talleyrand. That did the trick, apparently, for the letter vanished and never reached the magistrate.

The affair came to trial on February 24. Half the faubourg Saint-Germain was there to snicker. Maubreuil repeated his accusations, specifying that Talleyrand had offered him an annual allowance of 200,000 livres . . . the title of duke . . . the rank of general, "for the infamous mission of assassinating Napoleon and his family." Maubreuil's dagger was for hire at a far cheaper price. A heavy sentence was imposed: five years in prison, ten years under police surveillance, a fine of 500 francs, and 3,000 for bail. The court really wished to punish him for perpetrating his assault in a place like the basilica of Saint-Denis during a religious ceremony attended by the dauphin and his wife.

Once again Talleyrand made an effort to avoid public exposure, claiming that he attended the ceremony as a private citizen, not as a high dignitary of the crown. Who would believe such a story? The court believed the evidence that Maubreuil had struck the grand chamberlain during the performance of his duties. Ever since the duc de Berry's assassination, the police were haunted by fear of others. The fact that Maubreuil could easily have killed Talleyrand, not to mention the dauphin, right next to him, sent shivers through the ranks of law and order.

Maubreuil appealed the case and demanded the right to call a host of witnesses, one of whom, Roux Laborie, Talleyrand's secretary in 1814, supposedly had recruited Maubreuil for his chief. Maubreuil was attempting to bring the 1814 affair to trial; the Saint-Denis slap was simply an excuse to do it. In ruling on the appeal on May 11, 1827, the court confined itself to the incident in the cathedral. No witnesses were called and the case was adjourned until June 15.

The audience was disappointed after taking the trouble to come

* In French, "turkey" can mean "Jesuit" as well as "a vain and stupid man"— Trans.

there. Even scandal began to pall. On June 15, however, the courtroom was jammed. There stood Maubreuil in all his glory. He was unchained. He cursed the world, not forgetting the czar, whom he assailed as "an assassin, son of an assassin." The bishop of Autun came in for his usual share of invective, but no more than everyone else. As Maubreuil refused to testify unless his witnesses were present, the hearing was adjourned once more.

Maubreuil's conduct during the hearing worked to Talleyrand's advantage. What had everyone seen? A fanatic bent on blackmail. "Nobody gives him money so he creates a scandal. If you call scandal the vulgar abuse leveled by a highwayman at persons on whom he has never set eyes." That was Talleyrand's synopsis of the whole affair.

On August 29, there was a new hearing and a new outburst from Maubreuil. In addition to all his previous charges, he now accused Talleyrand of assassinating Mirabeau. The evidence? An Englishman told him so. Again he referred to Talleyrand as "unfrocked" and "Astaroth." Realizing that the court was penalizing him only for physical assault, the defendant proceeded to minimize it. The slap disintegrated. Without knowing it, Maubreuil played right into the hands of the man he wanted to destroy. He assured the court that as "it would have been improper to strike an old man," he merely pushed him on the chin with the palm of his hand, just a push. "I hadn't intended to slap, just to insult in some fashion," he said, adding glibly: "I am sorry I slapped him; I only meant to spit in his face." Charming. Then came another angry outburst: "I slapped because I was in a hurry . . . how should I know, as I headed for Saint-Denis, whether there would be time to curse him out, to spit in his face, to kick him in the ass, or to slap that rascal Talleyrand, that vile renegade priest." [1]

This time the court ruled out premeditation and reduced Maubreuil's sentence to two years in prison and a fine of 200 francs. The incident seemed closed.

Paris became too unpleasant, and Talleyrand left at the beginning of May. As usual, he divided his time between Valençay and Bourbon-l'Archambault.

The Régime Ages Faster Than Talleyrand

Toward the end of the Restoration, Talleyrand wrote rather frequently to comtesse Mollien, the wife of Napoleon's minister. She was not of the "seraglio" but enjoyed a special, privileged rank outside it. She lived in the château de Jeurs. This correspondence allows us to trace the events of the summer of 1827. Talleyrand took his annual cure at Bourbon-l'Archambault accompanied by Pauline, now six and a half, who was his constant delight. Dorothée was at Néris; she was restless and needed to move about. Since he could not bear Néris, the arrangement suited her perfectly. "The princess [Countess Tyszkiewicz] is going to Néris to-morrow just for a day. I am glad as she can then tell me how Madame de Dino is. I will go later on."

In another letter to Madame Mollien he described Countess Tyszkiewicz's latest extravagance. She had a passion for gray horses, and having spotted a fine pair, bought them at once. She could not wait to parade her new acquisitions, but, as Talleyrand explained: "They were delivered to her by a coachman wearing a cotton bonnet that must stay on his head as he has mange [more likely tinea?]. This offended her sense of elegance and amused me."

The painter Gérard was also at Néris. Talleyrand invited him to Valençay in a letter such as a great eighteenth-century nobleman might have written to an artist: "They say you are at Néris, and I am glad. First because the waters of Néris are beneficial to nervous disorders, and then because the return journey takes you through Bourges, and by leaving early enough, you can easily reach Valençay in time for dinner, where I shall be happy to see you. After taking the waters, it is advisable to have a few days' rest, and it strikes me that you ought to take that rest in the company of someone who has loved you these past twenty-five years." [1]

Instead of tending to the vital business of winning public confidence, the government, in its meddlesome fashion, preferred to spend its energies tampering with the letters of Talleyrand and his friends. Montrond's movements were particularly alarming to the police. Why did Talleyrand send him back and forth to London so much? Who was he seeing there and what did he report back? Irritated by this surveillance, Talleyrand wanted the authorities to know that when letters reached him after a week's delay, he was well aware that they had been intercepted. This is the note he sent to Barante so that the minister of police would read it: "It is a good thing that the postal budget was increased as this enables us to pay a few more employees for opening a lot more mail, thus making it possible for a letter from Barante posted on June 6 to arrive at Bourbon on the nineteenth." [2]

Bourbon seemed deserted in the summer of 1827: "This year there is no known case of rheumatism," he reported.

Paris, however, was in a fever. Instead of calming public fears, the government further aggravated them with absurd legislation. The national guard was dissolved, inciting a student riot. Whereupon the prime minister threatened to restore censorship. The repression was senseless. Talleyrand refused to think—though he dwelled on it incessantly—how this intolerable, insoluble situation would end. "Never have I been away from Paris and prey to such anxiety over public affairs. Without predicting what they will do, I fear that despite our apathy, we may be hurled into some revolutionary high adventures if they cannot resist the lure of censorship. [Precisely what happened three years later, in July, 1830.] It is the first link in the chain that drags everything to the edge of the precipice. But what can one do?" [3]

Had he not warned the king and the persons in power? The régime was cutting its own throat. Talleyrand was perpetually amazed by such pretentious stupidity. The situation was beyond repair: "Truthfully, I cannot see that it is anyone's loss." Those final words were so characteristic of him. He had made up his mind; when this foolish government collapsed, no one would be the poorer. Anyone with a head on his shoulders ought to be thinking about the next one and how to avoid the same follies.

On the way to Paris in July, he stopped at Jeurs, in the Seine-et-Oise district, to see Madame Mollien. They discussed the Memoirs of Empress Joséphine—written by a certain Mademoiselle Lenormand—about which Talleyrand had nothing kind to say.

The sudden death in Lord Lansdowne's London house of George Canning, whom Talleyrand had met in 1792, did not upset our prince to any great degree. Canning was an important figure, but in Talleyrand's view, the political past was unreal. In a letter to Madame Mollien on August 14 he made this brief comment on the English foreign minister's death: "The city of London is in a state which does credit to the English nation. For the past twenty-four hours, no commercial, professional or private activities of any kind have taken place." [4]

Even the political present tended to lag, he felt. On this score he attacked Villèle vigorously: "Read *Le Moniteur* every day; it is almost amusing. One actually learns that our country's material prosperity derives from the genius of ministers whose names France never knew in 1816 and who are paying her back by not knowing her today." A scorching commentary on the ultra-royalist régime, which, in fact, was governing a nation of strangers. It refused to recognize that something had happened in France between 1789 and 1815. "What blinds all those gentlemen is that with little or no fuss, France pays out a billion francs," a reference to Villèle's law of 1825 indemnifying emigrants. But the nation's silence did not necessarily indicate assent because public opinion had no outlet. Talleyrand was not fooled, however; he knew what seethed beneath the silence.

Returning from the journey to Paris and Jeurs on August 26, he found Valençay empty, dreary. The duchess of Dino kept moving from spa to spa, from Bagnères-de-Bigorre to Bagnères-de-Luchon. Was she alone? Why was she feeling unwell? Had there been another accident, like the one in Hyères? A strange woman, that Dorothée. Piscatory, her current lover, was probably with her. At just about that time, Stendhal reported: "She is deeper in love than ever with Piscatory." Fortunately, Talleyrand had Pauline.

A man of Talleyrand's stature had to contend with a variety of outrages. The Maubreuil affair was barely settled when a new one came along. Perrey, the secretary longest in his service, well informed and very reliable, absconded to England with certain of his papers and the opening section of his *Memoirs*. The thief sold them in London, where copies were already circulating. As Perrey had mastered the art of duplicating our prince's signature, and indeed had been asked to write and sign any number of his letters which passed for autographs, Talleyrand spread rumors that the manuscripts sold by Perrey were fakes turned out by a thief and a forger.

In Switzerland people were reading *Memoirs* by Talleyrand, presumably authentic and highly entertaining. Madame de Chavagnac, a friend of his living in Switzerland, sent her compliments. The response was not what she anticipated: "I laugh heartily to see that in remote Switzerland you are amused by charades invented here, where, I assure you, everyone claims to have read excerpts from *Memoirs* allegedly stolen from me." He used the same tactics repeatedly, denying or minimizing unpleasantness and disgrace. Why the "allegedly stolen"? "I would be curious to know what the handwriting was like on the copy you read for there must be a dozen floating around, all equally mendacious and silly. I shan't give it a moment's thought. . . ." That settled the whole matter. "Laugh, I beg you, as I do if anyone tries to sell you another piece of nonsense. . . . Try to find out where it comes from. It might help me."

He shifted to pleasanter subjects—such as vegetable seeds. The Swiss ones were excellent. He would like to have some carrot, escarole, and salsify seeds for the garden at Valençay. Other statesmen, other authors might have had a stroke over such a theft.

He made no effort to retaliate against his secretary; prosecuting the man would have caused him more anxiety than the loss of his papers.

If Canning's death was merely a news item, the question of his successor was far more than that and would determine the course of European diplomacy. Talleyrand was glad to hear Lord Lansdowne's name proposed for the Foreign Office. Having known and admired the marquess's father, Talleyrand thus could count on the friendship of England's key official.

Valençay had a rainy summer. Dorothée lingered in the Pyrenees. Pauline's governess became seriously ill and, with only a country doctor in Valençay, Talleyrand was obliged to look after the patient. "I stay to care for the doctor," he told Royer-Collard. Dorothée's prolonged absence vexed him, as well as the dearth of news from Paris and the insipid press coverage. Finally, there was an event! The elections dealt Villèle a severe rebuff. He had dissolved the Chamber of Deputies in response to ultra-royalist defections, hoping to re-create "the vanishing Chamber." But he judged the popular mood very poorly, for the voters returned a liberal Chamber. Villèle was forced to resign. That autumn, Talleyrand returned to Paris thinking that a liberal cabinet would have a place for him. He might have been the only person capable—if left free to do it—of saving the monarchy for the third time. But Martignac became premier and named his cabinet on January 5, 1828. The faint, hopeful smile hovering on our hero's sarcastic lips ever since Villèle's resignation vanished.

Royer-Collard was elected to the French Academy on November 13, 1827. Talleyrand was at Valençay and did not attend the ceremony, but in January he read the new member's address and sent him his compliments: "While sending you my thoughts, I ought to say, as did La Fontaine:

> Our viands, we confess, are less than delicious,
> But, when we are kings, what can we offer gods?

Your speech at first glance is admirable; read leisurely, it is excellent and masterly."

As Dorothée had been in Paris, she attended and enjoyed the ceremony at the Institut. She wrote to Barante: "M. Royer and I are madly courting . . . and for my part, I love him dearly."

The grand chamberlain attended Charles X at the opening of parliament which took place in the Louvre on February 6, 1828. The day before he had attended High Mass at Notre Dame. The duc d'Orléans was there also among the royal family. Everyone admired the seven-year-old boy, who seemed content to appear for the first time in his robes of state, the "miracle child," styled "Henri V," the heir to the throne. The speaker extolled the naval victory at Navarin which restored Greek independence. Talleyrand paid scant attention; it was not something he had predicted. So much for Navarin.

Facts he chose to ignore did not totally lose their reality for him. We may recall how easily he managed to blot out his wife. Yet she was still there, immensely so, corpulent and helpless in her seventieth year. She lived at 87, rue de Lille, never went out, and rarely had visitors. Having lost her looks, she could offer only the last vestige of her glory for admiration: the grand cordon of the Royal Order of Maria Luisa bestowed by the queen of Spain "in gratitude for her efforts to mitigate the circumstances of His Majesty Ferdinand VII during his stay at Valençay." Such outstanding services surely warranted that distinguished citation. By coincidence no doubt, a regular visitor at Madame Grand's was the duchesse d'Esclignac, Boson's daughter and Talleyrand's niece. The second faithful Achates was the duke of San Carlos, her lover, once equerry to the Spanish princes, more recently Spanish ambassador to Paris. When San Carlos met his pious end in July, 1828, our hero reacted most unconventionally. Even Dalberg, a man of the world, was amazed. "I shall miss the duke of San Carlos; his death truly grieves me." Elaborating on this attachment which Dalberg appeared to question: "Let me explain: the duke of San Carlos was my wife's lover; he was an honorable man and gave her good advice, which she needs. Now I must worry about her falling into someone else's hands."

One is forced to admire such lucid reasoning. That year Savary decided to publish eight volumes of Memoirs. "For a history of France, it is far too short," observed Talleyrand; "for a history of the duke of Rovigo, it is far too long."

Spring took the whole tribe back to Valençay, then to Bourbon. They left Bourbon on August 18. Pauline, now seven and a half, was the sole ray of sunshine in another gray and rainy summer. "Tonight I leave Bourbon," he wrote. "The weather has been so bad for two weeks that I cannot tell whether the waters have helped me or not. Pauline has been my only pleasure. There is great charm in the gentle attentions of a sweet child. . . ."

Another less creditable source of charm for him were the verses which General Dupont, who lost the Battle of Bailén, took to scribbling at Bourbon. His poetry was even worse than his military strategy. Our prince's admiration for such bad poetry is a rare exercise of poor taste on his part.

From August 28 until November 4 they stayed at Valençay prior to returning to Paris for the king's birthday celebration. Those were empty days. Charles de Rémusat married Mademoiselle de Lastérie that year. He was all afire, they said. Apparently, even Doctrinaires could fall madly in love. The austere Guizot also conceived a passion for his late wife's niece, Mademoiselle Dillon. Another newsworthy item was Chateaubriand's departure for Rome, where he had been appointed ambassador at a salary of 300,000 francs.

On the way to Paris, Talleyrand and Dorothée paused briefly at the latter's château, Rochecotte.

At the age of seventy-four, the prince's habits were unchanged: to bed at dawn, a public levee at noon, his only meal of the day a formal dinner, climaxed by an evening of conversation and gambling. Montrond was his constant shadow. Too constant for Dorothée's taste. She never liked this man who had shared Talleyrand's life before she was even born. When Montrond had Talleyrand's ear, Dorothée felt shut out. Her uncle would never accept such informality from anyone else, even going so far as to smile at certain things he would have frowned upon in anyone else. Dorothée did not always hide her irritation. Talleyrand was deaf to her complaints: Montrond was his trusted agent, friend, and reminder of his youth.

Ary Scheffer painted Talleyrand during the winter of 1828. It is a romantic, exaggerated portrait of a disenchanted, grim, disquieting personality. The 1828 painting snuffed out the eighteenth-century Talleyrand, who, nevertheless, was very much alive. He is all in black, hunched into a bulky dress coat tinged with bronze, wearing a cravat that seems to be choking him. The features are blunted, the planes enlarged, the nose upturned, the eyes cavernous. An eerie pallor bathes the whole countenance; the drooping lips despair. Rather than a portrait, it is an indictment.

Chateaubriand's comment that "with age, Monsieur de Talleyrand has turned into a death's head," conveyed a common impression among his contemporaries. People whose contact with him was purely official found his icy expression appalling. Talleyrand returned his acrid critic's fire, though more humorously. The English would have adored this sally: "When no one is talking about him, Monsieur de Chateaubriand thinks he has gone deaf."

For lack of weightier responsibilities, he became involved in educating his nephews. Louis, Dorothée's elder son, passed his examinations brilliantly. His uncle decided to let him travel in Italy and Germany; the younger boy, who wanted to be a sailor, was sent to the naval academy at

Brest. The "high school" was no more. Summers at Valençay would be rather dismal. Happily, Pauline was still there. As part of the "family," Talleyrand received Flahaut and his wife at Valençay. Talleyrand was very fond of this son of his, whom he had protected in 1815 when Flahaut continued to support Napoleon—even after Waterloo. When Flahaut was threatened with exile, Talleyrand advised him to keep silent and stay away from Paris. Flahaut chose exile in England. There he made a rich match with the daughter of Lord Keith. Unfortunately, the contract stipulated that only male offspring of the couple could inherit Lord Keith's estate. Flahaut had six daughters and consequently no inheritance.

Barante became a member of the French Academy to the great joy of his friends at Valençay.

It was Talleyrand's idea to open a "circle" in Paris modeled after the English type; he did not call it a "club" though he spoke excellent English. The resulting "Cercle de l'Union" was, along with the Jockey Club, the bastion of elegant society until the First World War.

All this could not nearly fill needs of so talented a man. Like the rest of his countrymen, he dozed. Unlike them, he kept his finger on the nation's pulse. His idleness did not signify decrepitude. In reality, Napoleon's minister was not in a torpor; he was keeping the night watch.

At Seventy-Six, Talleyrand Reflects on the New Régime and a New Career

How could he not foresee the crisis? "In 1829, when Charles X foolishly resolved to alter his cabinet and form a council of the country's most unpopular men, whose sole merit was subservience as blind as the hapless monarch's obstinacy, it was no longer possible to deny that we were bound for disaster." [1]

Neither Talleyrand nor the French nation was prepared to go down with the ship. The Ultras said that he betrayed them. Surely he warned them in telling Vitrolles: "Beware, Monsieur de Vitrolles, the duc d'Orléans treads upon your heels."

Liberals turned to the House of Orléans because Charles X was leading the country up a blind alley. But open rebellion would only have induced repression, further entrenching the régime and making it harder to dislodge. It was best therefore to let the existing power suffocate in the vacuum it had thrown up around the monarchy. In 1829 Talleyrand already knew what the change must be. But he was not going to impose it on the nation. He knew his countrymen too well: the mere suggestion that the elder Bourbon branch should be replaced by the Orléans one would have turned the people against it.

If Talleyrand favored this solution—and it had always appealed to him—it was, as he put it, because "the idea was roaming the streets" in 1829. Ideas that roam the streets are sure winners, so it was just a matter of exploiting this one at the right moment. Meanwhile time, his unfailing ally, would do its work.

But this uncanny intuition of Talleyrand's rested upon sound, reliable information. Montrond went everywhere and supplied a variety of news. Among his many contacts was Madame Adélaïde, Louis-Philippe's sister. And, of course, Talleyrand had his "seraglio," his eyes and ears in the heart of prominent society, the court, government, and diplomatic circles. The siphoning of this precious information was never directly attributed to Talleyrand, but to some impersonal pronoun, or specifically to the duchess of Dino. But the grammar of it fooled no one. Dorothée was hostess to Thiers, Mignet, General Foy, Sébastiani, the ranks of the liberal opposition. These gentlemen might well have assumed that their invitation to the rue Saint-Florentin came directly from the prince. But the prince corrected this notion as he stood at the head of the stairway greeting guests and directing them to his niece's apartments at the left, not to his own. After that, who could say that he was entertaining the opposition? The duchess of Dino was a social celebrity in her own right; she received whoever she pleased. The prince, of course, was at the dinner table. Pale intrigues of this sort reflected the dismal climate of the times.

In January, 1829, Talleyrand married his nephew Louis to Alix de Montmorency. The young man was eighteen. His uncle prevailed on the king to create the new title duc de Valençay for Louis, who was to inherit Valençay after his uncle's death.

Instead of returning to Bourbon-l'Archambault, where the weather had been depressing in 1828 and the cure not very helpful, he decided the next year to try the waters of Aix-la-Chapelle. Madame de Dino did not go with him as she preferred Rochecotte, the place she had come to love best. Pauline had been sent off to Boulogne in hopes that the salt water and sea air would improve her blotchy complexion. The lonely old man missed the child. Again that year, his letters bemoaned the downpour:

> My dear child, the rain is continuous here, making me somewhat vexed about Aix-la-Chapelle, but much more so about Boulogne which

interests me more than Aix-la-Chapelle. I fear that unless the sun returns you will have to spend a few days more in Boulogne, for once having undertaken the trip there, you ought to get some benefit from it. I think the waters are helping me. If you were in Bourbon-l'Archambault, I would regret not having spent my summer there, but as you are in Boulogne and I am not with you, I prefer being here. Every day I visit the well-preserved ruins all around Aix-la-Chapelle. When I went back to the cathedral, I was told that Emperor Napoleon had gone there in 1805. The tomb [of Charlemagne] is in the center of the church with no other inscription than the name Charlemagne. When the persons preceding the emperor walked upon the tombstone, the emperor shouted: "Walk around it." He himself avoided stepping on the burial place of the great man. Everyone was highly impressed by this mark of respect. Good-bye, dear child, I embrace you and love you dearly.[2]

A delightful and inspiring topic calculated to awaken Pauline's admiration for great men of the past. The same is true of his letter of July 14: "All the great changes in modern civilization date from the fourteenth of July. When you are ready for it, I shall teach you that part of history. . . ." History that he had lived through, had helped to shape, and would never abjure. The great aristocrat of Valençay went on maintaining, well into the nineteenth century, not only the extravagant splendor of a bygone era but also the fervent conviction that the great changes in modern society stemmed from July 14, 1789. Changes he had worked for in 1789 and still advocated in 1830. His devotion to the ideals of the Revolution co-existed alongside a profound attachment to the world of Chalais. He observed the mores and urbanities of the Ancien Régime while rejecting its institutions. Realizing that his extravagant life style ran counter to changing economic conditions and moral standards, he succeeded nevertheless in preserving the best of the old world and the sturdiest of the new. He bridged the gulf between the monarchic tradition and the age of democracy.

When he returned to Paris after spending the autumn at Valençay, people whispered that his health must be failing. It was even proclaimed that he had one foot in the grave. Genoude, a friend of the Congregation and the Ultras, a pillar of piety, cheerfully announced: "M. de Polignac will leave the foreign ministry and become grand chamberlain in place of M. de Talleyrand, who will die. . . ." That was rushing things a bit, forgetting that Talleyrand did nothing in a hurry. Though ailing, he was not beyond perpetrating some mischief of his own. He inserted in the press the list of a brand-new, imaginary cabinet of his own choice, which the reading public took to mean that the existing one had been dismissed. There was not a word of truth in it, but the government and the court were furious to see Royer-Collard named as the future prime minister. Rumors spread, and while the authorities were hotly denying them, Talleyrand was calmly preparing for the journey to Rochecotte.

There, in late November, he found repose, the companionship of his niece, and a highly dangerous plaything calculated to wreak havoc on the government. This toy was the creation of Thiers and, to a lesser degree, Mignet. Thiers detested the violently anti-liberal politics of prince Jules de Polignac, the prime minister. To combat him, Thiers, Mignet, and Armand Carrel founded a crusading newspaper called *Le National*. When Talleyrand arrived, the three firebrands were already at Rochecotte, brought by Piscatory, another ardent Orléanist. Piscatory, we recall, was romantically involved with Dorothée at the time, and as she shared her uncle's political views, we may safely assume that any Orléanist gathering at Rochecotte was fully sanctioned by Talleyrand. *Le National*, launched under the duchess's roof, could rely on his moral and financial backing.

If anyone was taken in by this affair, it was Armand Carrel, a staunch republican who did not contemplate installing a new dynasty on the throne.

At that time Dorothée invited her old and dear friend Vitrolles to spend a few days at Rochecotte. Vitrolles loved Dorothée. She had refused to be his mistress but had managed somehow to remain a close friend of this confirmed Ultra. Her attempt to lure him into her Orléanist beehive suggests a test of their relationship. He would not come, and the friendship ended there.

Le National was ready to start publishing in January, 1830. A bad year for the cause of legitimacy.

When in Paris, Talleyrand performed the duties incumbent on a grand chamberlain, which included playing cards with the king. One evening, playing against Charles X in a whist game, he sat for a long time holding his discard, uncertain as to whether or not to put it down. Losing patience, the king spoke up loudly: "Come now, Monsieur de Talleyrand, and be done with your Dominus vobiscum." Only then did he realize that mistakenly he had roused the bishop of Autun. His courtiers tittered appreciatively at the blunder. Playing deaf, Talleyrand sat there holding his card and did not put it down until he was good and ready.[3]

His health grew worse. A painful inflammation of the eyes left him disfigured and nearly blind for weeks. Swathed in poultices, he endured stoicly, unable even to forage his bookshelves, as Madame de Coigny had often seen him doing: "He picks up books, puts them down, sets them aside to return to later, examines them as if they were living things, and this exercise, while enriching his mind with the experience of history, endows these texts with charm ordinarily wanting in their authors." Nevertheless, he read and admired a book which caused quite a stir during the winter of 1830, Saint-Simon's *Memoirs*. For the public, it was an eye-opener. Saint-Simon's pitiless exposure of court life was a far cry from the idealized picture of a pure and pious Versailles which the Ultras and the Congregation desired to promote.

Writing from Rochecotte on January 11, 1830, Talleyrand told Barante: "I have not written to you for a long time because my eyes are very swollen. I could not read or write . . . I picked a good time for this eye trouble because I don't think there is much worth reading; except for Saint-Simon's *Memoirs,* I see nothing published which I would want to send for from Paris."

In the capital, they proceeded openly to bury Talleyrand. Guizot called him "a dead lion," adding: "He is old, without influence at court, and in a government which opens everything to discussion, he is not one to discuss things."

Patience, Guizot; governments come and go. If Talleyrand had no influence at court, it simply meant that the court did not amount to much. The real power now resided in public opinion, and upon that Talleyrand had a certain impact. Guizot had not yet grasped that reality; one day his ignorance would cost him dear.

Molé, who also looked on the prince as a fossil, bewailed the obscurity of "this historic old man."

About that time the "historic old man" came forth with one of his historic sayings. Vexed by violent opposition to Polignac's reactionary policies, Charles X, summoning every ounce of his royal dignity, exclaimed impatiently to Talleyrand: "A king who is threatened has no choice but to mount his horse or the tumbril." To which Talleyrand replied softly: "Sire, Your Majesty forgets the post-chaise."

Charles X opted for that vehicle in July, 1830. If, as Chateaubriand declared, Talleyrand never made history, he predicted it very well.

Why disguise his feelings if the final outcome was perfectly apparent? When the Ultras attacked him for conspiring, in the late winter of 1829, to put the duc d'Orléans on the throne, Talleyrand made his position clear: "The principle of legitimacy served in Vienna to curb allied ambitions. Today, by sacrificing legitimacy we can preserve and even fortify a liberal monarchy."

Principles must change with changing conditions. The legitimists were the main foes of the monarchy as well as the nation. The one immutable demand upon the monarchy was that it must incarnate both the continuity of power and the flexibility of uninterrupted development in the direction of the Revolution's ideals. "Once legitimacy itself betrayed its own principles by breaking its oaths, it became necessary to seek the salvation of France at random and to rescue at least the monarchic principle, independent of legitimacy, from the tempest stirred up by the latter." He is being honest here, except when he speaks of searching "at random." In Talleyrand's scheme of things, nothing is left to chance. "Random" went by the name of Louis-Philippe d'Orléans, destined to reconcile the monarchic principle with the ideals of 1789.

Another death: in February, Talleyrand lost his younger brother Boson, whose anti-Bonapartism had furthered his fortunes under the Restoration. His daughter Georgine, the duchesse d'Esclignac, was Madame Grand's closest friend.

A first-hand observer provides an unexpected close-up of Talleyrand and his niece in the privacy of their home.[*] During the winter, a young poet from Montauban named Mary-Lafon appeared a number of times at the rue Saint-Florentin to recite verses in langue d'oc [†] for Madame de Dino's enjoyment. He had been introduced by Daure, Talleyrand's secretary, a former seminarian and also a native of Montauban. Daure was of humble birth, and his native city could not forgive an innkeeper's son, employed as gravedigger, for aspiring to write poetry. He tried his luck in Paris and landed the job with Talleyrand. This sensitive and tormented young romantic fell desperately in love with Dorothée, who wrongly treated his passion as something of a joke. The other poet, Mary-Lafon, turns a glaring spotlight upon the duchess of Dino and prince de Talleyrand at their fireside. "In front of the fireplace were two people," Mary-Lafon writes, "the prince on one side, half-reclining in his armchair, and a woman, still beautiful though approaching middle age. . . ." Dorothée was thirty-six at the time. She darted at the poet "one of those bold, meaningful glances characteristic of women in high society, acknowledging with a quick nod my respectful bow." Silently, the prince motioned to him to sit down. "Despite his secularization, M. de Talleyrand, his hair white with powder and age falling in

* Mary-Lafon, born at La Française (Tarn-et-Garonne), 1810–1884. Precursor of the *Félibrige* [a literary society founded in 1854 with the aim of preserving the Provençal dialect—Trans.]; poet, journalist, essayist, author of *Histoire littéraire du midi de la France* (1882).

† Literary language of southern France during the Middle Ages, in which *"oc"* meant "yes," rather than *"oïl"* (*"oui"*) as in northern France—Trans.

thick ringlets around his neck, his chin thrust into a high Directory cravat, was the very image of an elderly parish priest."

Talleyrand spoke to the poet directly and cordially, warning him of the difficulties of a literary career. Madame de Dino then interrupted, asking the young man to recite his verses in dialect. The prince and his niece were amused at his timidity; tea and cakes arrived, but Talleyrand preferred a slice of buttered bread with pepper. The conversation was easy and natural, so natural in fact that it appeared supernatural to this provincial poet, whose reluctance to pronounce the word "breast" in Madame de Dino's presence made her and her uncle laugh. At that moment, reported the blushing poet, Madame de Dino, who was standing "with her back to the fire, suddenly scooped up her skirts and petticoats, raising them halfway up her back, and, right in front of us, calmly proceeded to warm the part of herself which earned Callipygian Venus that epithet."

The poet was both flustered and astounded, as much by what the duchess was exposing to the fire and all eyes as by her tranquil self-assurance and Talleyrand's total indifference. Life in Montauban had not prepared him for such an exhibition and he was hopelessly embarrassed. The prince reassured him: "A Russian custom," he said, stretching lazily in his chair. Then to Madame de Dino: "You always forget, my dear, that Daure, the master of my secrets, is a former seminarian.

> By such things are souls wounded
> And guilty thoughts evoked

in this young man who was blushing a moment ago while reciting for you the verses of Despourins."

The two men left. Daure was in a fury, "claiming, and rightly so, that by appearing to ignore the fact that he was a man, she was treating him the way St. Petersburg ladies treat their muzhiks."

Dorothée's predilection for "Russian customs" and her inexplicable confusion between muzhiks and Parisians suggest why, despite great intelligence and culture, Madame de Dino did not encounter more friendly faces in the French capital. As for poor, blindly infatuated Daure, he committed suicide four years later among the ruins of the château de Pennes, not far from his birthplace. One wonders whether it was for love of Dorothée or of romanticism that he resorted to this extremity; Talleyrand's advice would have served him better.

Dorothée and Talleyrand left their fireside on the rue Saint-Florentin earlier than usual to reach Valençay in April. The prince saw the approaching storm and did not want to be in Paris when it broke.

On June 11, 1830, he wrote to the princesse de Vaudémont from Valençay telling her that hope was lost: "There is no averting the shipwreck."

Writing to Barante on June 14, he predicted the government's collapse: "Tomorrow I leave Valençay to coax a little strength into these legs from the waters of Bourbon-l'Archambault where I shall arrive on the seventeenth. . . . We are heading toward an uncharted world, without compass or pilot; one thing alone is certain: all this will end in disaster. . . . The English revolution lasted half a century. As ours is but forty years old, I cannot possibly foretell its outcome. I doubt that even the present generation can tell. . . . We are engaging in new perils."

Still courting the clergy, he was host to the archbishop of Bourges during the latter's confirmation tour of Valençay. Monseigneur de Villèle confirmed between five hundred and six hundred children. "He condemns everything they are doing," Talleyrand noted, referring, of course, to the politicians. Not all Villèles were Ultras, apparently, and in Talleyrand's view, this one, the archbishop, would have made a better minister than the other.

How much longer could he endorse the Bourbons? They managed to insult him outrageously. The last such incident occurred only a few weeks before the July Revolution. We may recall that Talleyrand had gone to great lengths at the Congress of Vienna to restore the Kingdom of Naples to its Bourbon ruler Ferdinand IV, and later had proposed a match between Ferdinand's granddaughter and the duc de Berry, an heir to the French throne. This is how Ferdinand's successor, the duchess of Berry's father, expressed his gratitude. Traveling through France in May, 1830, he stopped at Blois. Talleyrand, who was at Valençay, felt that in deference to the royal House of Bourbon, he ought to pay his respects to this sovereign. So at the age of seventy-six, crippled and ill, he made the journey to Blois. When the prefect of Blois solicited an audience for our prince, the king of Naples's reply was delivered by Count Blacas: "We have no liking here for unfrocked priests." It was a little late to make an issue of this distaste. Had they not already accepted a crown from the unfrocked priest? Had they not created the title duke of Dino so that his niece and concubine could become a duchess? Had they not paid him off royally? Though an Ultra, the prefect was shocked by this treatment and insisted that prince de Talleyrand be received. The response came back, grudgingly, that the renegade priest might appear at seven on the following evening. Talleyrand was thus obliged to spend twenty-four hours waiting in a town where the king of Naples had no reason to stay. The following day he presented himself at the rather shabby inn where the sovereign was holding court. Only a few minutes after he had left his prefecture for the inn, Lezay-Marnesia was surprised to see the prince returning. Talleyrand described his reception by the Neapolitan court as something "entirely unique and unfamiliar to the many sovereigns I have been privileged to attend. After obliging me to climb the filthy stairs of that filthy inn where His Majesty has seen fit to lodge, the gentleman of honor kept me waiting on the landing, turning it into an antechamber for the occasion, saying that he would announce me to the king who would appear shortly." The prince had to remain standing at the head of the stairs, sheer agony at his age and with his infirmity. A door creaked; he caught sight of "someone they said was the king in the aperture." A head nodded; the door slammed shut. Talleyrand had seen the king of Naples. The audience was ended. Talleyrand, who was rarely flustered, confessed that he stood there "in amazement." He concluded his account with this pointed observation: "No one will ever say of that prince: 'The sight of him revealed to all the world its master.'"

Though Talleyrand nursed no grudge, this offensive treatment cannot have encouraged his support of a dynasty so inadequately represented at a crucial moment in its destiny.

In 1830 he ceased to be mayor of Valençay; instead, he became district councilor for the Indre by royal appointment, remaining municipal councilor of Valençay. Not surprisingly, we find him asking Barante to get him books on local administration so that he could keep abreast of town council debates and participate intelligently.

When the court was attempting to make certain changes in the cabinet, Talleyrand wrote to Barante saying that any such efforts were now futile: "Whatever these gentlemen promise is worthless; they ought to be reminded of the English saying: 'Only a gardener can give good gifts.' One of your children might translate it as: Only decent people can give good gifts. I plan to go straight to Paris from here [Bourbon-l'Archambault], arriving July 24. Once again the waters seem to have little effect on my old body."

Having left the capital to avoid the storm he saw coming, he managed to be back there just as it broke.

On one point he showed poor judgment. He was so wrought up against the Polignac ministry that nothing it did, including the capture of Algiers, was right. Talleyrand noted: "The Algerian expedition is turning into a careless blunder which perhaps may have serious consequences." He called it a "careless blunder" because the operation, as he saw it, was merely a diversion, a mock war permitting the government to boast of an easy victory in order to offset mounting domestic strife. Talleyrand felt that it would have made more sense "to reduce taxes. They have gone up more than 200 million since the Empire, whereas England has reduced hers by 400 million francs. . . ."

Good advice, but if Talleyrand had been premier would he have practiced what he preached? He knew very well that in 1815 France was saddled with an enormous debt resulting from the Napoleonic Wars, their devastation, the allied demands for indemnity, the cost of maintaining foreign armies of occupation, and the billion francs for émigrés. To compare the situation with England's was not realistic. In the area of finance, the Restoration government conducted its affairs very competently. Talleyrand knew this even if he would not admit it. But in July, 1830, the government was beyond help.

Behind the Scenes of a Revolution, the Prince Stages a Spectacular Comeback

Though heartily opposed to the Ultras, Talleyrand did not greet their downfall with any measure of enthusiasm. By now, he had little confidence in "the fortunes" of revolution. He did not look forward to another upheaval, a view shared by many of his countrymen. "That is what worries everyone," he wrote, "everyone of every class." He himself "nursed the expectation of dying peacefully in the shadow of a throne which my own efforts had helped in some way to restore."

These doubts and anxieties scarcely fit the Mephistophelian portrait invented by his critics of some sinister villain spinning out a melodrama in which the victims are Louis XVI's ill-starred brother and the French throne. In reality, no one was unhappier than he at the pathetic record of legitimacy.

Just as a clever man turns every situation, even a risky one, to his advantage, so Talleyrand, on hearing that Charles X was at Saint-Cloud consulting with Polignac on the Ordinances fated to destroy his throne, gambled on a sharp drop in the price of government bonds. Excellent guesswork, as it turned out—at least for him.

On July 27, the first day of the uprising, all was quiet on the rue Saint-Florentin. It was too soon to act until the outcome of the street fighting could be known. On the twenty-eighth, based on reports brought to him from all sectors of the capital, Talleyrand could see that Charles X would fall and the rebellion triumph. As bells tolled in the afternoon, Talleyrand learned that the crowds had captured the City Hall. The clock was just striking five as he made this prediction: "A few minutes more and Charles X will no longer be king of France." Few would have agreed with him at that moment. He had planned to convene the Chamber of Peers, but not many of its members saw what he saw. On the twenty-ninth, they would see it. He surpassed his contemporaries just for that reason: he could see into tomorrow. He prepared the event itself and its outcome. On the twenty-eighth, he removed the sign reading "hôtel Talleyrand" above his door. The insurgents were approaching the Tuileries, close by the rue Saint-Florentin. Though the Bourbons chose to ignore the fact that Talleyrand had given them back their throne, there were revolutionists in the crowd who did not, and who might prove far more vindictive than the Bourbons had proved grateful.

On the twenty-eighth, the situation was still uncertain except that the king was sure to fall. As the tocsin tolled, Talleyrand said: "Listen to the tocsin! We triumph!"

"We?" someone queried, "who are 'we'?"

"Sh-h-h-h! Not a word! Tomorrow I will tell you."

What a marvelous actor he was with that fabulous gift for tossing out his innermost thoughts in a cryptic phrase. In any contest, it was essential to pick the winning side, in this case, the France of tomorrow.

His callers that day are significant. Lord Stuart de Rothsay, England's ambassador and a confirmed Orléanist, came to the rue Saint-Florentin. In Vienna in 1814, in Paris in 1815, and again in July, 1830, whenever a crisis loomed, Talleyrand had private talks with the English ambassador. During his visit, the latter met General Sébastiani and Bertin de Veaux, friends of the prince by virtue of their Orléanist leanings. The duc de Broglie looked up and saw Talleyrand standing at a window overlooking the Tuileries, watching the fighting. He went in to give the prince news of the street battles and stayed for dinner. During dessert, the English ambassador casually dropped by again and they discussed quite openly what to do next. They agreed that the younger Bourbon branch must take the throne. The duc de Broglie noted: "What they said about what was bound to happen surely was not the talk of people discussing a subject for the first time."

On the twenty-ninth, the fighting still raged, though uselessly, for Charles X had already abdicated and gone from Saint-Cloud to Rambouillet. Once again he was preparing for exile. Thus Talleyrand could claim: "It is not I who abandoned the king; it is the king who abandoned us."

He dispatched Colmache, a secretary, to the Orléans residence at Neuilly with a note for Madame Adélaïde, Louis-Philippe's sister, who was far more ambitious and daring than he. The message simply introduced the bearer, who sought to deliver the prince's counsel. Talleyrand urged the duc d'Orléans to come immediately to Paris and head the rebellion if anarchy was to be averted. Madame Adélaïde had such confidence in Talleyrand that already she imagined the crown safely upon her cherished brother's head: "Ah, the good prince," she exclaimed exultantly, "I knew that he would not forget us." Independently, the duke would never have had the courage to lead the rebellion; he did so under the prodding of his sister and Talleyrand. He returned to the Palais-Royal in the midst of the insurrection—the victorious insurrection, we might add, for this detail is of some significance. At Cherbourg, Charles X was embarking for England, having abdicated in favor of his grandson, the duc de Bordeaux. A clever move, and rather embarrassing for the duc d'Orléans, whom the departing sovereign delegated to oversee the transmission of power. The duke had already been prevailed upon by a group of deputies to assume the title of lieutenant general of the realm, but his power was only temporary. If he kept it, he would be dethroning the legitimate heir. Louis-Philippe hesitated.

There are times when hesitation amounts to refusal. On that particular day, hesitation would have been fatal, for what was possible at noon was impossible twelve hours later.

On July 31, Talleyrand played Louis-Philippe's hand; he dealt him the cards, saw to it that he took up power—and did all this without showing his face publicly and without anyone, friend or foe, mentioning his name. His chosen spokesman was Adolphe Thiers, who rushed between Paris and Neuilly carrying out Talleyrand's wishes on behalf of Louis-Philippe. On behalf of Thiers, too.

At eight on the morning of the thirty-first, when the deputies gathered at the Palais-Royal and offered the crown to the duc d'Orléans, he asked them to let him think it over for an hour. At once he dispatched General Sébastiani with a message for Talleyrand. "Let him accept," was the prince's only reply. Armed with this sanction, the duke made his way to the City Hall where the insurgents themselves acclaimed him in something of a spontaneous plebiscite—the source of that abusive epithet "King of the barricades," which legitimists flung at Louis-Philippe. The duke stepped out on the balcony holding aloft the tricolor flag of the Republic while La Fayette led the ovation.

It was 1789 all over again on the very stage where these events had unfolded forty-one years before.

When the crowds and the soldiers had done with their cheering and salvos, and after the tumult had died down, Louis-Philippe d'Orléans, king of the French by virtue of an ecstatic mob, returned, weary but content, to the Palais-Royal.

Very late that night a heavy coach rumbled into the palace courtyard, depositing the prince de Talleyrand, rumored a dozen times over in recent months to be headed for the grave. With the grace and dignity of a grand seigneur, with a tinge of irony and perhaps of condescension, he arrived, first among his countrymen, to pay court to the new ruler who, like his predecessors, owed his throne to him.

The Charter was revised in the most liberal spirit.

Happy to have weathered the crisis, the two Chambers did what they were asked, proclaiming Louis-Philippe king of the French. The mastermind behind these events had counted on bourgeois panic to render these politicians tractable. They heaved a sigh of relief when Louis-Philippe embraced La Fayette, that venerable darling of the Paris circus, recalled for one last walk-on role at the end of his life. Did he not tell Louis-Philippe: "You are better than any Republic we might have had"? Talleyrand had no such illusion, and to one of the rejoicing throng, observed: "Monsieur, what all this lacks is a touch of conquest." And, in fact, the transfer of power had occurred too effortlessly, it seemed, in front of the City Hall, on the heels of a night of rioting. Some went so far as to say that the crown had been "filched." Whatever you chose to call it, the method used was not particularly heroic, or legal, or even legitimate. In any event, France needed leadership, so Talleyrand provided it. Louis-Philippe may have lacked stature, but he stood for temperance, peace, and the protection of civil liberties.

Our prince is too modest in his *Memoirs* when he claims to have had no part in crowning Louis-Philippe. Perhaps he really meant in ousting Charles X. If so, he was right. But his effort to minimize his control of events on the third day of the July Revolution was simply his way of pacifying the legitimists. As we have seen, he made a practice of appeasing his enemies, and disliked them even less when their power was fading. Furthermore, he was not at all eager to magnify his discreet but decisive promotion of Louis-Philippe. Why alienate the left by proclaiming his choice of a new monarchy over a Republic? The letter written by Dorothée, with her uncle's approval, to the king's sister casts away any doubt as to Talleyrand's role:

> Mademoiselle, I and the whole of France hasten to greet you as our good angel. Yes, Mademoiselle, you showed yourself to be just that in a time of crisis.
>
> To tell you, Mademoiselle, that this wondrous event was our dearest wish is superfluous. You have long known it.

How could one know you, and how could one be bound eternally to M. de Talleyrand [a remark far more superfluous than the other!] without ardently desiring the triumph of your virtues and your cause, which is also the nation's.[1]

It was Talleyrand's cause as well, and on August 8 he himself declared: "Now we are established. The fourth dynasty begins. . . ." The "we" speaks for itself.

And indeed the new establishment promptly re-established Talleyrand's career. A man can be seventy-six and crippled yet still respond to the lure of ambition. Why did Louis-Philippe not appoint him to the foreign ministry, the natural abode of a prince of diplomats, instead of sending him to the London embassy? Because the London assignment was far more important to the new government. Yet Talleyrand refused it, saying that he was too old and feeble. Molé, the new foreign minister, kept after him, insisting that "the king desires it, not to say 'demands,' more than I can tell you. See him and judge for yourself." Did Molé guess what a problem he was shouldering by taking "under his command" an ambassador destined to eclipse his superior?

The king finally persuaded Talleyrand to accept: "I believed that the new government could gain stability only by preserving the peace, and though at the time everyone opposed me in thinking that war was inevitable, I was convinced that my name, my past services in Europe's behalf, and my efforts perhaps could stave off the ultimate tragedy, a universal, revolutionary war. I am glad to think that I achieved this before the end of my career." [2]

All that was true. As London held the key to the new government's foreign policy, there must France strengthen her position. Talleyrand had other personal reasons for accepting the post. The game of diplomacy still intrigued him, with its promise of power and riches. Then, too, he loved elegant society and official entertaining, but most of all he loved London. At the end of his life he found himself reoccupying the post he had held in 1792. His career made a perfect circle. The dream that began in 1792, only to end in failure, not to mention deportation, was to be fulfilled in 1830. For Talleyrand, it was never too late. He walked into an extremely precarious situation and, by his adroitness and prestige, transformed that final mission into a triumph.

Still, his good reasons for accepting the embassy would not have sufficed to crank up once again an aged, wheezing, creaking machine if Dorothée's presence had not provided fresh energy. An intensely ambitious and passionate woman, the duchess of Dino was enjoying the autumn of her youth as best she could while attached to this old man, admiring him greatly, basking in the prestige of his eminent position, but bound nevertheless to share the slackening pace of his declining years. She escaped whenever she could, roaming the spas in search of casual adventures. To her, the London mission meant a chance to free herself from the heady magic of the rue Saint-Florentin and Valençay and to channel all her passions into the one passion she could indulge openly: ambition. She would fulfill herself, her boundless aristocratic pride, by playing a vital political role in a splendid setting. The Paris she detested would be far away. The prince, whose secretary, confessor, and adviser she had become, would be hers alone. She would rule his life, his affairs, his salon, his table. She would be the very heartbeat of the London embassy. Because of her, the prince's career would reach its climax; he, in turn, would give meaning and direction to her life. Disillusioned by love, family, and society, she would find fulfillment in politics.

Talleyrand was the target of too much envy in Paris for the king's choice to receive wide support. People spoke of the prince's unpopularity. Where? In certain political backrooms, in legitimist salons, in so-called anarchist quarters—in the French capital, of course. For in the other European capitals it was a different story: Talleyrand was the man of France. Mademoiselle, the king's sister, pressed for the appointment as insistently as her brother. It was to her that he addressed his acceptance: "As Mademoiselle's ambassador, I fear that it might distress her were I to give up the place she chose for me."

On hearing the good news, the king declared: "He will cast the dice." And indeed he did. Official notice of the appointment appeared in *Le Moniteur* on September 6.

The July Monarchy had little credit abroad. Czar Nicholas I had refused to recognize any government born of a riot. But he changed his mind on hearing that Talleyrand was going to London: "As M. de Talleyrand is associated with the new French government, that government must have some chance of survival." Aside from its sarcasm, the comment tells us that Talleyrand's name served as credential for the new régime.

In Paris, some of the prince's foes such as the legitimist Montlosier, whose hostility had not blinded them completely, were willing to admit, after voicing all the familiar complaints about his apostasy, his marriage to the Grand creature, his betrayal of everything under the sun, that Talleyrand would make a good ambassador to England: "He can create a favorable impression in England . . . " said Montlosier. "First of all it will convince them that our government is solidly established if a man as circumspect as the bishop of Autun associates with it. Also they will think that we strive for peace abroad if we send as envoy to one of the great powers the man who has done most to institute civil liberties in Europe." [3] A splendid tribute from an adversary.

Talleyrand had made overtures to Vienna well in advance. While musket fire was still crackling near the Tuileries, he sent an emissary to reassure Metternich. A wise precaution. Champion of the Holy Alliance, the Austrian chancellor thought that Europe was on the eve of a new bloodbath, about to explode. Nor were Metternich's fears exaggerated, for the Jacobins of 1830—who then styled themselves "anarchists"—had publicly declared during the recent insurrection that they intended to take up arms again in order to liberate the peoples of Europe and to regain territories conquered under the Revolution and the Empire. These bellicose threats greatly discredited the July Revolution in the eyes of London as well as Vienna. If France once more fell under the sway of fanatics, would she launch another general war? Was it 1792 all over again? Or 1802? Being the ambassador of a government born on the barricades was rather uncomfortable.

Talleyrand's appointment came as a balm to Wellington. He read and reread with delight the reassuring message from his old friend: "Together, the two of us will preserve the peace against France's anarchists and Europe's agitators."

That was Talleyrand's immeasurable service to the July Monarchy and to his nation. In *Le Père Goriot,* Balzac puts these words in the mouth of Vautrin: "The prince saved France from dismemberment; she owes him crowns, she pelts him with mud."

In fact, from 1830 onward, Talleyrand was slandered unmercifully. Lord Grenville, England's representative in Paris, voiced the joy, the admiration, the hope which Talleyrand's mission to London had kindled there and everywhere on the continent. But Paris reviled her ambassador.

A Dream of Youth: London, Where Life Began Anew

Talleyrand left Paris on September 22, 1830. A few days before, he paid a farewell visit to the king, still living in the Palais-Royal while they dusted out the Tuileries. He went there like a prelate to his induction and in fact it was the last of many state rituals he had observed in his lifetime. He was never casual about such matters. Loving court pageantry, he came before the king decked out like a church treasury, laden with orders and decorations, his hair meticulously powdered and curled. It was his way of preparing for battle.

Whereas Paris greeted his departure with insolent cartoons, notably one by Daumier depicting him with a weathervane for a hat and identifying him as "Monsieur Bienauvent," * the reception awaiting him at Dover was nothing short of brilliant. A guard of honor commanded by the duke of Wellington's son Wellesley waited at the dock to escort him to London. The guns of Dover fired a cannonade worthy of visiting royalty.

Before embarking at Calais, he talked with Ouvrard the banker, that familiar figure in his life who always had some new business to offer the prince. There in Calais Ouvrard had just received word that the Belgians were revolting against the king of Holland, whose rule had been imposed on them in 1815. Surely England would view this as an offshoot of the July Revolution, perhaps operating with the new régime's blessing. The Belgian affair was going to complicate Talleyrand's mission, his efforts to "establish at last that union between France and England which I have always considered the firmest guarantee of the security of these two nations and of the peace of the world." He thought of the difficult task ahead as he entered London, with crowds cheering and surging about the coach of "Old Talley." "Thoughts assailed me on my journey through beautiful England, so rich, so peaceful; and on my arrival in London on September 25, 1830. Fortunately they did not shake my resolve or my convictions." [1]

His entrance on the London stage was somewhat theatrical, under reams of tricolor ribbons and streamers, with an enormous revolutionary cockade planted in his hat, and three sans-culottes in tow. This exhibition was followed by a long speech declaring himself the representative of a popular government. Symbolically, he compelled respect for the July Monarchy. The crowd cheered his performance; he won their sympathy.

That evening, Wellington came in from the country expressly to host a dinner honoring the prince, who appeared in his silk dress coat, his stockings with gold clocks, well powdered, and decked out with the ribbons and badges of his orders. Gone were the tricolor cockade and ribbons, for he had already conquered the crowd. Now he must conquer the salons.

On September 30, Dorothée arrived to reinforce him. London society opened its doors to the duchess of Dino; the relationship between uncle and niece caused no scandal. Dorothée at once felt comfortable there, as she had never felt in Paris. Her first reception, at the duke of Wellington's, brought out her sparkle. It reminded her of happier days in the Vienna of 1815; she saw Prince Esterhazy again, the Austrian

---

* I.e., Mr. "sailing with the wind"—Trans.

ambassador, and Bülow, Prussia's envoy and Humboldt's nephew. When someone asked flippantly how her husband was, she replied matter-of-factly: "I really don't know anything about him." And that was that. Dorothée's reputation was decidedly flimsy, yet Lady Grey, London's arbiter of morals, silenced wagging tongues with this manifesto: "I like Madame de Dino very much; she is always good-humored and good company. As she never says anything to offend me, why should I care how many lovers she may have had? I take no credit for being different from her. I have simply been lucky."

Talleyrand's success mounted steadily. Madame de Boigne, whose father the marquis d'Osmond previously had held the same post somewhat ingloriously, admitted grudgingly: "The position adopted by M. de Talleyrand in London had immediately placed the new throne very high on the diplomatic scale."

The French embassy at 50, Portland Place quickly became London's most fashionable address: "He kept a very large house, over which the duchess of Dino ably presided. Both had succeeded in becoming leaders of whatever was currently in fashion."

Prosper Mérimée, who visited London about this time and left some interesting notes on how the prince practiced his impressive diplomacy, mentions this: "Wherever he goes, he forms a court and makes the law."

With considerable pride, Dorothée informed her friend Barante that her dinners "were making gastronomic history in London, but they are costing a fortune and M. de Talleyrand is alarmed at the expense."

Louis-Philippe had chosen to continue paying him the 100,000 francs attached to the office of grand chamberlain, though Talleyrand no longer held it. But that was nothing when the embassy cost him a million annually. Visitors from the Continent found the cost of living very high in London. Dorothée noted: "Even Prince Esterhazy, despite his vast personal fortune and his large salary, has managed to run up a million francs' worth of debts."

Talleyrand, as we know, chose to work only with people he had known and trusted for years, whose devotion or, if you will, collusion was thoroughly reliable. During his long eclipse between 1816 and 1830, most of his old colleagues had scattered or died. For that reason, Dorothée became his confidential secretary in London. Molé, the foreign minister, had assigned him a staff of subordinates, and these he did not want. He sent for Bacourt, whom he knew to be trustworthy and whom his niece knew even better. By working hard, the three of them managed to get everything done, successfully at that. Subordinates did next to nothing.

Also doing his share was the ever-obliging Montrond, who frequented London's most elegant houses, and a few not so elegant ones. He acted as liaison between the French ambassador and English officials, from whom he received excellent tips on the stock market. Talleyrand never could resist the pleasure or the profit of speculating. In 1832, a bad tip cost him 800,000 francs in a single day (300,000 old francs). A good tip could bring him in just as much.

In presenting his credentials to William IV, the prince at once began to wonder how things would turn out under a sovereign not overly blessed with either intelligence or manners. Custom permitted new ambassadors to make a little speech to the sovereign. Talleyrand composed one while Courtiade arranged his hair. Dorothée came in and he said to her: "Now, Madam, sit yourself down, think up two or three sentences for me, and write them out in your biggest hand." She did so and handed him a slip of paper; he revised it, as was his habit, inserting this seemingly innocuous allusion to the king of England: "descendant of the illustrious House of Brunswick." It was a reminder that if Talleyrand represented a monarch of the cadet branch who came to the throne astride insurrection, it was also true that the Brunswicks had usurped the Stuart throne in 1714. That more or less evened the score.

In addition to the "allusion," his little speech conveyed some interesting facts to those alert enough to grasp them, among which, that the July Monarchy "had been elected unanimously by a great people." In fact, the Chambers had chosen Louis-Philippe by a vote of 308 to 234. That was not unanimous, and the Chambers did not represent the popular will. But "the people" had to have their say, and whatever was best for them to say was said eloquently, coming from Talleyrand's lips. Napoleon admired that particular quality in his minister: "Talleyrand is a philosopher, but a philosopher whose philosophizing comes to a timely halt." Undoubtedly that was why the philosopher got along so well with the English. He wrote to Madame Adélaïde, the king's sister, that during the audience: "In speaking of the king of France, my voice rang out as it once did before the Constituent Assembly." At every turn he demanded respect for his country. One day when Wellington mentioned "the unfortunate July Revolution," Talleyrand cut him short. Wellington smiled and retracted the expression. Princess Lieven, wife of Nicholas I's ambassador, was vexed to see Talleyrand and his niece stealing London's diplomatic and political stage. In her efforts to discredit the French ambassador, she even told the English monarch: "A man who has spent seventy-five years in intrigue does not forget his trade in his seventy-sixth."

Talleyrand's fascination for Wellington struck her as absurd: "The duke of Wellington has fallen hopelessly under M. de Talleyrand's spell. You should hear him solemnly maintaining that he is a very honorable man and that any remark to the contrary is pure calumny. M. de Talleyrand's integrity reminds me of M. de Polignac's wits [he passed for something of a simpleton]. No portrait of the duke of Wellington can be inspiring." Talleyrand silenced her acid tongue at the first opportunity. When she proclaimed that the Revolution of 1830 was a usurpation, he snapped back: "You are right, Madam, and the only regrettable part is that it did not occur sixteen years sooner . . . as the czar, your master, desired and wished." The princess dropped the subject of usurpation.

Like Wellington, Lord Aberdeen was delighted to have Talleyrand in London. Our prince told the duchesse de Vaudémont so; after making the rounds of the "seraglio," the letter ultimately reached the king and Madame Adélaïde: "I am perfectly satisfied here with the candor and loyalty of the English cabinet and especially of the duke. We may and we ought to trust the duke if we expect to achieve anything of lasting value. . . . I wish the king and Mademoiselle would believe this. I don't care about Molé because once he sees that it is to his own interest, he will go along." So much for Molé. That was only the beginning.

Talleyrand would have moved mountains to maintain England's friendship. As he wrote to the princesse de Vaudémont on October 22: "England's attitude toward us will determine Europe's attitude, and it would be a great mistake for us to look elsewhere for support."

Dorothée reported with relish that the daily press was giving extensive publicity to the French ambassador, that Talleyrand was delighted with this, and that both he and she were invited everywhere. On November 2, as he came out of Westminster, Talleyrand received an ovation from the crowd. A far cry from the days when Londoners had treated spokesmen of the French Revolution like lepers. Today King William IV prepared a special dais for the prince de Talleyrand so that, contrary to etiquette, he might sit during the ceremony. Talleyrand thanked him but chose to stand along with the rest of the diplomatic corps. The royal gesture was regarded as something of a miracle. Talleyrand painted a glowing picture for Louis-Philippe and his sister of his relations with the English: "His Majesty has many admirers here and many people who love him; his praises are on every tongue," he assured them. And to prove that England's government was well disposed toward the July Monarchy, he observed that Charles X had been assigned a residence "fifty miles in the interior." That was an attempt to prevent any intrigue on the French coast from reaching out to whatever coastal city the king might have chosen to stay in.

Unfortunately, Talleyrand's relations with his own ministry of foreign affairs were far worse than with London. Between Molé, the foreign minister, and his ambassador to England, communications came to a standstill. The friction was inevitable, for Molé wanted to run his own ministry, yet Talleyrand held the key position in determining foreign policy for the new government—indeed for Europe. In London, foreign representatives held their breath when Talleyrand, at the close of a dinner, drew aside Wellington or some other key figure for a private word. History was being made in London, not in Molé's office. Unfortunately, Molé refused to understand that and, overwhelmed by the prestige of his colleague, he balked.

Their first clash occurred over the Algiers question. Intent on winning England's friendship, Talleyrand wanted to end the conquest of Algeria and prove to the English that French intentions in Europe were truly peaceful, then bring about a permanent alliance between the two nations. Molé protested, threatening to resign if Algiers were abandoned. The French kept Algiers and Molé kept his post, but Talleyrand felt that the foreign minister was interfering spitefully.

After that, their relationship became increasingly hostile. In the matter of Belgium's revolt against Holland, Talleyrand thought that he could best handle this delicate affair directly with Wellington and his own friend Bertin de Veaux, French ambassador to The Hague, a critical post under the circumstances. Because of their longstanding friendship, Talleyrand felt he could deal directly with Bertin instead of through Paris. This meant that one day Molé would wake up to find the Belgian affair settled; his only function being to sign the papers. Molé would not stand for such treatment and ordered Bertin to report to Paris. He had a right to demand it; on the other hand, he had no right to keep Talleyrand entirely in the dark as to what was going on between Holland and the Belgian rebels or what attitude Paris was taking. He was alienating the one man capable of dealing with a situation threatening to spark a war involving England and Prussia. In retaliation, Talleyrand was sending Molé insignificant dispatches about customs duties on port wine entering England. The duchess of Dino, the ambassador's right hand and spokesman, complained: "We are displeased with the tone of M. Molé's dispatches."

Talleyrand was angered by Molé's refusal—backed by the king—to publish his speech to William IV. Undoubtedly, they felt that what it was wise to tell the king of England it was not wise to tell the French public. "The unanimity of a great people" would have been a bit too much for legitimists and republicans to stomach.

Talleyrand blamed Molé for the snub. Dorothée decided to avenge it by sending the speech to Adolphe Thiers, "her best friend." Thiers, battling the current cabinet in the hope of joining the successive one, published Talleyrand's speech in *Le National*. And while Dorothée campaigned against Molé through Thiers, "Talley" did the same through Mademoiselle, the king's right hand. To her he expressed the opinion that "a certain lack of experience was revealed" in the way Molé bypassed his ambassador by corresponding directly with Wellington. This he characterized insultingly as a trivial "blunder" on the part of a pretentious fellow bent on asserting himself, adding that Wellington told him about the "blunders" anyway. Molé lost patience before Talleyrand and submitted his resignation to the king: "Nothing could make me stay as long as M. de Talleyrand refuses to subordinate himself to my control like any other ambassador. . . ."

One gets the feeling of exasperation as well as exaggeration. In principle, the minister was correct. But in reality, could he ever expect Talleyrand to play second fiddle? By demanding blind obedience of his subordinate, Molé lost out on valuable information which he could have obtained by treating Talleyrand with the deference he deserved.

When Louis-Philippe refused the resignation, Talleyrand wrote an excellent letter to Molé, addressing him not as minister and superior, but, much more subtly and intelligently, appealing to their long friendship and common aspirations:

> Why not pull together as we go? Something is going on which I do not understand; I trust it will be only temporary.
>
> Our correspondence is neither friendly nor ministerial; I feel that between the two of us this should not be. If my way of handling affairs is outmoded, tell me so plainly. . . . We can only succeed if we act with the fluency born of mutual confidence . . . I realize that France no longer embraces the old tradition, being caught up in what is known as "progress."

And he proceeded to defend the right to move slowly. Haste "is so foreign to English custom that it diminishes whatever importance we necessarily ascribe to all our efforts."

Sheer wisdom, and a warning that Molé's "levity" was cheapening French diplomacy. In another letter dated October 29, no longer was he criticizing levity and improvisation but still another defect: prolixity. There he reveals the spirit of *Candide*, the disciple of La Fontaine and Rivarol. He recalled that Napoleon could not tolerate longwinded ambassadors; they were simply trying to curry favor with their government, he felt, and really had nothing new to say.

Friction continued between the minister, who kept wanting to resign, and Talleyrand, who kept talking of returning to Valençay. Dorothée wrote to Thiers on October 26: "Once the Belgian affair is settled, whatever the outcome, we are leaving England. M. de Talleyrand does not fancy and is not accustomed to executing the wishes of a hostile cabinet. He does not intend to exhaust either himself or his funds here. And the latter is unavoidable, for you cannot imagine what it costs to live here or the niggardly treatment accorded us by the foreign ministry." That was another aspect of the cold war; Talleyrand may have been spending too much, but Molé retaliated by cutting his allowance.

Things looked up when Molé stepped down. His successor, General Sébastiani, did not attempt to interfere with the prince of diplomats. Diplomacy was not his trade, and he had the good sense to stay out of it. Talleyrand counseled him thus: "We must seek closer ties with the most highly civilized nations, where our embassies find true kinship," instead of the fickle cousinship of kings. "This brings us naturally to regard England as the power with which we should engage in the closest relations . . . England is the only power which, like ourselves, truly desires peace. The other powers recognize some form of divine right; France and England no longer attach their origins to that."

The old aristocrat was assailing the outworn principle sustaining the Holy Alliance. Speaking of certain sovereigns ruling by divine right, in a dispatch dated November 27, 1830, he said: "They uphold their right with cannon. England and ourselves, we uphold public opinion with principles. Principles spread in every direction; cannon are known to have a limited range. . . ."

Those very principles guide Europe's leading nations in the twentieth century. Talleyrand invoked them, to his eternal credit, on English soil, where they were bound to be appreciated.

In London, Talleyrand Has a Right to Say:
"I Have Done Some Good; This Is My Finest Achievement"

Talleyrand did not establish lasting peace or a permanent Franco-British alliance; he did, however, maintain peace in Europe, lay the foundations of the Entente Cordiale, and settle the issue of Belgian independence. The last was the most serious threat to European peace and to the stability of the July Monarchy.

At Vienna, Talleyrand had protested Holland's annexation of Belgium. When the Belgians revolted against their oppressors on August 25, Talleyrand was not the least surprised. Still, by taking arms against the king of Holland, the Belgians dealt a mortal blow to the balance of power established by the Congress of Vienna. Every capital in Europe watched the situation anxiously, members of the Holy Alliance with alarm, and the partisans of revolution with enthusiasm. In Paris, the latter were demanding outright union with Belgium: the tricolor flag floating over Paris must also float over Brussels. Doing this would have invited a new European coalition. Two countries were particularly apprehensive of the new situation created by the Brussels revolution: Prussia, fearful that France would regain a foothold on the Rhine, and England, that she would recapture Antwerp.

That was the dilemma facing Talleyrand in London.

By at once reaffirming the principle of non-intervention, he was able to convince the English—though not his French detractors—of his sincerity. The English trusted him, and rightly so. Wellington and he proposed holding a European conference to iron out the Belgian issue. That in itself constituted recognition of Belgium's existence. The next question was where to hold the conference, and after eliminating the various choices, they selected London. Out of vanity, Talleyrand's critics blamed him for not bringing the talks to Paris. He had excellent reasons for wanting them in London, beyond the reach of scheming Pozzo di Borgo, Russia's ambassador who had won Molé's confidence, and also because the violent street demonstrations in Paris would have had an impact on the proceedings. In London, Wellington's conciliatory, moderate posture matched that of Talleyrand, and these two men, determined to understand each other, would decide the issue.

On November 4, the prince arrived at the conference without the customary retinue of secretaries and file-laden councilors, without pomp or pretension; he seemed more like an aristocratic old gentleman entering his club, confident of finding urbane peers with whom to discuss grave and complex matters, which would become less grave and less complex as a result of their common efforts and understanding. Such discussions had no place for rhetoric, vanity, nationalism, or other such nonsense.

The prince's opening remarks set the tone of the conference: "Mine is not the voice of French diplomacy; there is no more French diplomacy. I am simply a man of some experience sitting down with old friends to talk about things in general."

The very first day he was able to impose a cease-fire between Dutch troops and the insurgents. With each side claiming its own territory, an independent Belgian state was already in existence. The only question was who would rule the new country. Louis-Philippe sent a personal letter to Talleyrand asking him to inform the London conference that, on behalf of his son the duc de Nemours, he declined the crown which Belgian leaders had offered the young French prince. Upon reading this, Talleyrand wrote to Madame Adélaïde: "I am struck by the lofty reason and profound wisdom marking this [report]." The king and his ambassador agreed that peace and common sense demanded this sacrifice.

Louis-Philippe's government dispatched a surprise emissary with secret instructions for Talleyrand: the comte de Flahaut. Behind the prince's impenetrable gaze, what memories welled up as his own son appeared before him? As usual, his *Memoirs* are silent, except for a vague, imperceptible allusion to something the visitor called to mind: "It might be supposed that the kindly protection I had shown M. de Flahaut at the start of his career [under the Empire] would make his presence agreeable to me in the present circumstances."

Unfortunately, this was not to be. The plan presented by Flahaut appeared indefensible to Talleyrand, contrary to the interests of France, inherently unjust, and unacceptable to several nations. The plan came from Sébastiani, the foreign minister, and was no more than a crude proposal to partition Belgium between Holland, Prussia, and France. Talleyrand would not hear of such butcher's diplomacy.

Nicholas I took a different view, preferring to let his Cossacks teach the Belgians a lesson. Fortunately, the Poles rebelled on November 29. Belgium benefited from Russian efforts to quell the disorder.

In London, Wellington, a Tory, was replaced by a Whig, Lord Grey. As luck would have it, Talleyrand was a friend of the new prime minister; the two saw eye to eye. On December 20, Talleyrand, backed by Lord Grey, put through a protocol aimed at reshuffling the balance of European power and containing the words "independence of Belgium." The hardest part was getting the Russians to sign it, but finally he succeeded. As the year drew to a close, the conference seemed to bog down. In Paris, as one cabinet succeeded another with the opposition growing more and more vociferous, Louis-Philippe probably prayed for the London talks to wind up—rapidly if possible—with a French triumph. Did he think he could hasten a settlement? He sent Flahaut back a second time with his proposal to cut up Belgium, instructing him secretly to push it through himself. Talleyrand sensed immediately that Flahaut was bent on overriding him. The call of kinship gave way to hostility. He rejected any and all plans to partition the new state. On January 21, 1831, he obtained ratification of the famous Article Five guaranteeing the perpetual neutrality of Belgium and the inviolability of her territory.

Talleyrand informed Sébastiani of these developments, stressing that the long and difficult debate had lasted eight and a half hours. The negotiations had left him weary but triumphant. He summed up the gains for France and for Belgium, "placed in the same position as Switzerland": the kingdom of the Netherlands, which the Congress of Vienna had created "out of hatred for France" and installed on her northern border, was dissolved; "The thirteen Belgian fortresses menacing our northern flank are virtually demolished as a result of this resolution."

Talleyrand saw this as a requital for the harm done in 1815, the kind of requital he appreciated, arrived at through peaceful negotiations. He wrote to Madame Adélaïde: ". . . yesterday was one of those days which seem to warrant an important place in my life." Louis-Philippe was delighted with Article Five, calling it "a great achievement of M. de Talleyrand." But Paris was full of malcontents; the "hawks" felt cheated out of a war, the "patriots" out of a new conquest.

London hailed the conquering hero. The Lord Mayor gave a great dinner to honor the triumph of wisdom and peace. All the guests were English except Talleyrand, who toasted the unity of the two nations which had "the rare privilege of offering Europe the spectacle of liberty protected by law, guaranteed by the popularity of their rulers who recognize the advantages of peace and turn their efforts to maintaining it."

A storm of applause greeted his words. Here at least, he was understood.

Contrary to some opinions, Prussia's subsequent violation of Belgian neutrality did not invalidate Talleyrand's work. It simply proved that certain people—the ones Talleyrand always distrusted—regard bayonets as the only valid instruments of negotiation.

Final settlement of the Belgian question awaited a formal renunciation of Belgium's throne from the French monarch. This occurred at the Tuileries on February 17, 1831, in response to Belgian envoys asking for the duc de Nemours, Louis-Philippe's son, as their king. Here again, Talleyrand's critics blame him for betraying his country's interests. But he, far more than the frenzied patriots, could see what these were. "Belgium may come to us perhaps, but later on," he told the princesse de Vaudémont, "today she is of secondary interest. The pressure of events drives her closer to France, but France can develop wisely and surely only in concert with the great nations which today claim her friend-ship. . . ."

Peace alone would allow France to take her place once more in the community of great nations and damp the distrust smoldering in the wake of Napoleon's adventure. After fifteen years of waiting and watching, Europe was ready to welcome France. It was no time to launch an invasion of Belgium.

Finally, on June 4, 1831, to everyone's relief, the conference chose Prince Leopold of Saxe-Coburg to rule Belgium. Talleyrand and his fellow diplomats assumed that the situation was settled for good. But no, Belgium now wanted her borders redrawn, making such a bitter issue of it that a few acres of land threatened to undo months of negotiations.

Already tired and overworked, Talleyrand lost patience. In an effort to wind up the conference, he proposed an absurd plan of his own for partition. Had the storm of abuse from home demoralized him at the time he and Flahaut had quarreled over Sébastiani's proposal? His reversal damaged his image abroad, especially in Belgium, where gratitude for all his efforts suddenly gave way to anger at his one burst of petulance. No longer thankful, Belgium would not bestow the Order of Leopold on Talleyrand. Yet Belgium existed.

Talleyrand tried to get England's help in settling the problem of Poland. During the Empire and the Congress of Vienna, he had shown no enthusiasm for reviving that unfortunate country, but Countess Tyszkiewicz and Dorothée, who supported the November uprising, changed his views. In 1830, however, neither England, Prussia, nor Austria would follow his lead. Russia was master in Warsaw. And as Princess Lieven had totally captivated England's prime minister, Lord Grey, Talleyrand lost that hand to the Russian ambassador's wife. It was Poland's loss as well, for the sack and martyrdom of Warsaw became history. So did Sébastiani's inane comment to the Chamber on these events: "Order reigns in Warsaw."

*London at One's Feet Can Be as Tiring
as London on One's Back*

Talleyrand's political success was merely the corollary of social and personal success. As one English journalist reported: "He had everyone here at his feet; all the nobility of England eagerly sought his society; diplomats of every nation bowed before him."

Perhaps even more than his diplomatic efforts, his daily life and his conversation—at least what we know of it—hold the secret of this extraordinary old man's vitality.

Lamartine visited him frequently in London in the spring of 1831. Surprisingly enough, the century's most idealistic poet and the least romantic of statesmen understood each other, respected and admired each other. Lamartine was a man of great integrity; he was aware of the odious slander which had hounded Talleyrand since his youth, amplifying with the years, with the honors, titles, and riches he accumulated—as well as the services he rendered to France. Talleyrand had sensed that within this poet's soul lodged an unborn statesman and resolved to win his support for Louis-Philippe. But Lamartine pleaded loyalty to the legitimist cause and refused to be wooed. Talleyrand suspected other motives, and one evening after dinner, in a private monologue bordering on prophecy, he told the poet: ". . . I think I understand you. You want to reserve yourself for something fuller and grander than the substitution of an uncle for a nephew on a baseless throne. You will succeed. Nature made you a poet; poetry will make an orator of you, tact and reflection a statesman."

He was anticipating the Lamartine of 1848. This servant of the July Monarchy, which he termed a "baseless throne," perceived with frightening lucidity that Louis-Philippe lacked both legitimacy and popular support. And Talleyrand upheld his rule only because the peace and prosperity of France and of Europe *momentarily* necessitated it.

He continued his visionary monologue: "I can tell you about men. I am eighty years old, I see far beyond my field of vision. You will play a great role in the events that follow This. ["This" being the already shaky rule of Louis-Philippe.] I have watched the maneuvers of courts, you shall see far more stirring movements of the people."

How superior he was to his old colleague Metternich, who thought that clinging to the past was the way to face the future. Talleyrand foresaw that stirrings of the masses could bring down governments. Henceforth one had to reckon with the people. "Put aside your verses, much as I adore them. The age is past." He was far ahead of romanticism's great preachers, who thought the age of poetry had arrived, though socialism and the machine were emerging right under their noses. He praised the greatness of Mirabeau, that strange political animal whom he regarded somewhat as the precursor of future statesmen. In 1830, no one but Talleyrand had evinced any understanding of Mirabeau. With uncanny intuition, Talleyrand discerned his chief flaw: "He was a great man, but he lacked the courage to be unpopular."

Mirabeau was still too much of an aristocrat to fit the modern image of a statesman: the tribune of the people.

Then, for once, Talleyrand spoke about himself, choosing to make this sincere, plainspoken confession to a poet. "In contrast," he resumed, after discussing the personality of Mirabeau, "I am more manly than he; I expose my name to every interpretation, to every outrage from the crowd. I am called immoral and Machiavellian when I am merely impassive and disdainful. I have never given perverse advice to any government or sovereign, but I do not founder when they do. Shipwrecks call for pilots to rescue the survivors. With my steady nerves, I tow them to the nearest port; which port does not matter, so long as it offers shelter." How clearly this explains the progress of his own career. He never expected gratitude from those he saved from anarchy, civil war, foreign invasion, partition, or occupation. "They will curse me in the French press. Then they will bless me later on. My conscience is my acclaim; my career in public life has turned out well . . . you are one of the few persons by whom I desire to be understood."

The rest of this confession, included in Lamartine's *Entretiens familiers de littérature,* is no less astonishing. Lamartine had just told the prince bluntly that certain official dealings of his appeared dishonest and that he condemned them. Unoffended, Talleyrand replied: "For a statesman, there are many ways of being honest; mine is not yours, I can see, but one day you will respect me more than you think. My alleged crimes are the dreams of idiots. Does an intelligent man need to commit a crime? Political blockheads alone resort to that. Crime is like the ebb tide: retracing its path, it engulfs. I have had failings—some call them vices—but crimes? Fie!"

Pure Talleyrand. He evokes an astounding and perfectly valid argument in defense of his own record. Crime, he says, like war, is the last resort of imbeciles, who kill because they do not know how to negotiate or persuade; Talleyrand is incapable of such stupidity. Voltaire employed the same logic when accused by his critics of composing infamous verses: "How could they be mine if they are bad?"

Despite fatigue, his triumphs kept his strength up. Finally, however, after having been "serene, calm, hopeful, and as undiscouraged as he was during the first week here," his niece reported, he began to fail. On April 8, Dorothée wrote to Madame Adélaïde for support: "The bad cold and fever he had is fortunately over. I was hoping that he might spend Easter recess in the country and get some fresh air, but unfortunately he is all alone in the embassy at the moment and could not get away. . . ." What's this? Talleyrand detained at the age of seventy-eight by administrative details which he had never had to attend to before? Dorothée painted a grim picture. Talleyrand had the poorest staff of any embassy. Every other ambassador had three secretaries. He had none. Monsieur Bresson had left (Talleyrand did not want him); Monsieur de Bacourt, the very soul of perfection, was ill in bed. (She neglected to mention that while the charming young man was under her care, she proved a most devoted, tender, and demanding nurse.) Finally, there was Monsieur de Laborde, just a beginner and no help at all. "Which leaves the entire political burden and others—for we have all kinds here—entirely on M. de Talleyrand's shoulders. It is more than he can take. I think he looks badly, yet his zeal and activity have not slackened."

London's diplomatic climate was less serene now than when he had arrived. Lord Palmerston, the new foreign minister, did not share his predecessors' enthusiasm for "Old Talley," as he called him. Still, he listened to him and took his advice, until the day, that is, when a political cartoonist engraved a highly successful plate depicting two figures for all the world like Talley and Palmerston, bearing the legend: "The lame leading the blind." Palmerston was highly indignant at the image of himself as a sightless pawn in the hands of the Frenchman. After that, the Talleyrand magic ceased to operate on the English government. Palmerston recovered his sight, but only to pick out Old Talley's vices.

August brought a new alarm when Belgium decided to annex Luxembourg. Talleyrand tried to stall the Belgians, but anxious Holland lost patience and invaded the new state. In a matter of weeks, then, and despite Article Five, Belgium's neutrality was violated. At Talleyrand's instance, French units moved into Belgium. Holland's army withdrew. "I do not like this ending at all. The whole thing bores me to death," he wrote to Madame de Vaudémont.

Another troublesome incident awaited him in London. Too much good fortune sometimes brings on the bad. Palmerston was already bristling. Talleyrand's influence aroused jealousy and piqued more than one Englishman's national pride. Talk against him was encouraged partly by the Tory opposition but also by foreign diplomats, chiefly the Russian ambassador's wife, Princess Lieven. This talk reached the House of Lords, where, on November 29, 1831, it caused a scandal. The marquess of Londonderry began upbraiding "the astute diplomat who has served four régimes [at least]. . . . The sight of English ministers rushing pell-mell to consult such a person fills one with perfectly understandable disgust." Wellington rose to dissent, a gesture noteworthy in itself, for he and Londonderry were both Tory members of the opposition: ". . . I feel it my duty to declare that never has the public and private image of a man been so distorted as has the public and private image of this illustrious personality." The House of Lords applauded him. Lord Holland then rose to second Wellington, saying that he had known Talleyrand for more than forty years, over a period "peculiarly fraught with calumnies of every description; there had been no man's private character more shamefully traduced, and no man's public character more mistaken and misrepresented, than the private and public character of Prince de Talleyrand." [1]

Remember that these words were uttered in the English Parliament.

Hearing about this brought tears to Talleyrand's eyes. "I am all the more grateful to the duke as he is the only statesman who has ever spoken kindly of me." This token of esteem and friendship moved him far more deeply than the preceding insults had hurt him.

On November 15, 1831, the final treaty deciding Belgium's fate was signed. Talleyrand had thought that he could dispose of the whole business in two weeks, and here he had been struggling with it for over a year. He wrote to Madame de Vaudémont on November 16: ". . . I believe that the Tuileries will be pleased with my dispatch announcing this treaty. It will be the first one the king has made; it serves France by protecting her borders and Belgium by establishing her independence." Two lines defining, not exalting, his success.

The king and his sister acclaimed him in twice that number. But opinions carried in the press extended to a torrent of vituperation, mockery, and ugly slander. The legend of the diabolical prince grew and flourished in verses such as these:

> Now what do you think they are up to in London? What
>   are they up to?
> Why, it's clear from the man they sent there
> To work their secret diplomacy.
> Falsehood incarnate, perjury in the flesh
> Talleyrand-Périgord, Prince of Benevento.

The author, Auguste Barthélemy, was a warmongering Jacobin eager to seize Belgium and carry the flag of the Republic to Berlin, Warsaw, and beyond. Atheist and revolutionary, he echoed the charges of ultraroyalists and the Congregation against Talleyrand.

> Impenitent Judas, sanctified faker,
> He began his career by betraying his Maker.

Epithets such as "limping Proteus," and "Satan of the Tuileries," not to mention the charge: "Republic, emperor, king: he has sold them all," filled every line of this widely read, virulent poem entitled "Nemesis" (meaning Retribution). The only positive thing it produced was an admirable response from Lamartine. Talleyrand's critics and people who did not know him wallowed in this arrant nonsense. And Talleyrand, for whom "retribution" had no meaning, contented himself with a single scathing comment: "Corruption engenders verses."

At the same time, Charles de Rémusat wrote this during a visit to London: "What they say about M. de Talleyrand's position in London is true, less than the truth rather than exaggerated. His position is admirable. It is a fortress for France." A fortress which the majority of the French people apparently were resolved to demolish. Cartoons depicted him as Judas, or as a priest celebrating Mass, holding up, in place of the Host, the pear-shaped head of Louis-Philippe. And with all that they accused the apostate of defending Jesuits and the Congregation, who detested him more heartily even than the revolutionists.

Yet no one bothered to mention that the prince took pen in hand to remind Belgium's new king of his commitment to demolish fortresses installed by the Holy Alliance along the Belgian border facing France. The "patriots" had barricades on their mind; the "traitor," national security.

He got what he wanted in January, 1832. This is how he passed on the news to his old friend Madame de Vaudémont: "A reply has come in from Holland, forty pages long. I can assure you that I would much prefer forty pages of your own bad writing which I love because I love everything about you. . . . The principle of demolition is established and acknowledged; the injury to France has been repaired and the 45 million which the fortifications cost the allies have been lost. . . . Good-bye, angel or demon, I love you."

Quietly, with no extravagance other than his dinners, Talleyrand was undermining the Treaty of 1815. He felt sure that, with patience and peace, France could regain all she had lost. Stable government and economic prosperity would soon follow.

He was shocked when Casimir Périer, president of the council, yielding to pressure from interventionists, sent French troops to occupy Ancona against Austrian encroachment. Talleyrand publicly denounced "a foolhardy expedition void of common sense." All over Europe the fear of French aggression revived. On March 22, Talleyrand wrote to his foreign minister not as an ambassador but as a sovereign: "Let us be done now, I entreat you, with this Ancona business, and pin the blame for it on subordinates too easily reminded of revolutionary times. . . ."

In May, after manning the fort day and night for two years, the old man asked permission to return to France: "I must think of my legs, of my eyes, and I must look after my affairs," he wrote to the princesse de Vaudémont, the old friend in whom he confided his political views. Because a friend of his had been denied the peerage owing to official fears of offending legitimists, Talleyrand deplored the régime's spinelessness: "They seem frightened to death of the Faubourg where there is no real strength. That side of the river is absolutely pitiful." Neither a political nor economic force, legitimacy, as he well knew, was now only a memory.

In another letter he confessed to her his fears for the future. The rest of Europe was bent on driving a wedge between England and France. Their success would mean failure for the July Monarchy; with Ultras on one side, revolutionists on the other, France once again would be thrown into turmoil. "I think this letter would be better off in your fireplace than in your writing desk. Please write me: I have obeyed." Princesse de Vaudémont did not obey.

During the year 1831, old ghosts had reappeared. He did not send them away. Queen Hortense, duchess of Saint-Leu, asked him to obtain a passport for her. He did so readily for the mother of his own grandson, the duc de Morny. Montrond saw her, though Talleyrand would have done so had she requested it. He had not refused to see Lucien and Joseph Bonaparte, Napoleon's brothers. He described his position quite simply to them: he remained forever grateful to the emperor but continued to regard him as a menace to France and to Europe. But, as he put it, "that has no bearing whatever on my political views," or, as he might have added, on the courtesy due members of the Bonaparte family.

Charles de Rémusat made a special trip to London in hopes of persuading Talleyrand to head a new cabinet. His Doctrinaire friends—a group known as the "Juste Milieu"—asked Rémusat to do this. Madame de Dino wrote on May 25, 1832: "M. de Talleyrand's resolve not to participate in any administration is far too firm to be shaken on that point."

Despite the urgings of Rémusat, Royer-Collard, Guizot, and their cohorts, Talleyrand refused: "I say that softly and dispassionately, as when one's mind is made up." In truth, the king had not joined the appeal.

His leave granted, Talleyrand left London on June 20, 1832. Even Palmerston wished him well: "Take good care of your health, recover quickly from your long and fatiguing conferences, and above all, come back to us soon."

Did Palmerston fear the eternal parting? The fear was not unfounded, for Talleyrand was indeed weary. Paris gossips had a field day, with every devil's disciple proposing a more venomous motive behind the prince's return: he was about to seize power, make a quick fortune, and betray the government. His response was: "They take me for a fool in thinking that I want to be president of the council. I don't want to incite any riots in the rue Saint-Florentin."

Just as he had promised, he went off to Bourbon-l'Archambault to look after his legs, "to go to bed early [at two, probably, instead of four], to eat only what is necessary, and to not have occasion to utter a single word of interest to anyone."

The fact was that in London, just as in Paris, people construed mountainous falsehoods out of certain things he said. Princess Lieven, for one, claimed to have had the following conversation with Talleyrand. At a dinner party one evening, she noticed him sipping his coffee alone in a corner. Now why, she asked herself, should a man lionized by society stay off in a corner by himself? Invading his solitude, the astute ambassadress sought to rouse him with a saucy challenge: "Well, Prince, tell me something amusing!" And without waiting, she broached a burning issue: "Let's talk about our two armies. What do you think of it?" (She was referring to the Dutch army which had invaded Belgium, with the French following suit.) Deriding his efforts in behalf of the Belgians, she went on: "You have gone to a lot of trouble for something that will not last."

"Do you think so?" Talleyrand responded.

"And you, Prince?"

"I hope so."

"What? You really mean that your kingdom of Belgium and your king of the Belgians . . ."

"Will not survive," he cut in. "Look, it is not a nation, nor will two hundred protocols ever make it one; Belgium will never be a country, it will not hold together."

These are incredible statements. Why would he call his herculean labor a waste of time, especially to the one person who had fought him tooth and nail and whom he knew to be his worst enemy?

The rest of the dialogue is even more hair-raising. With a little prodding from the clever princess, Talleyrand is supposed to have come around to "naïvely" confessing that Prussia would take a piece of

603

Belgium, Holland the lion's share, France a tiny morsel . . .

"After that?" persisted the princess.

"Who else?" from Talleyrand.

"Oh, something for England—Antwerp, for instance." Whereupon, she tells us, Talleyrand flew into a rage, pounding the table with his fist and the floor with his cane, making such a scene that everyone in the room turned to stare (how unlike Talleyrand), and shouting: "Antwerp! Antwerp to England? Do you know what an outrageous thing you are saying? What, England on the continent? Madam, as long as France exists, small as she is, England cannot, shall not have a foothold on the continent. You shock me . . . this is abominable." [2]

According to the princess, she then told him that it was all a joke and he took it in good humor.

What are we to make of this account? How is it that in a room full of people, not one of them reported his angry outburst against England, or that the press never heard about it? That Dorothée did not intervene? The truth is that the whole scene was a piece of fiction invented by the czar's representative to sow discord between Talleyrand and his English and Belgian friends.

At Bourbon, though he had no such perils to face, the season nevertheless was rather gray. He was alone, his niece having returned to Rochecotte. Right in his own room, two people suffered seizures. The experience was profoundly disturbing. Finally, he took a fall and came down with "a heavy cold for which they made me take an emetic yesterday. So that's how I am," as he wrote to Royer-Collard on August 14, 1832.

In Paris, cholera broke out, taking a terrible toll. During the summer the epidemic spread to the countryside; by August, it reached Selles-sur-Cher, 15 kilometers from Valençay. At the end of August he joined his niece. "The air of Rochecotte is good enough to act as a remedy," he wrote. He spoke of returning in October to the London embassy and scoffed at rumors of revolution coming from Germany. "Five-sixths of the German people do not want it." He was a better judge of national character than government advisers, who would exaggerate or twist the news in order to embarrass the régime and excite the public. To give warmongers pause for reflection, he warned that if France mobilized her forces, "Vienna, Berlin, and St. Petersburg can raise 400,000 men in twenty days." Who would save the country then? Barthélemy with his "Nemesis"?

The visit to Rochecotte was pleasant. He wrote to Bacourt, who was running the London embassy in his absence: "Madame de Dino feels fairly well and is improving; as for me, I think my strength is returning and that I sleep better" (September 10, 1832).

On October 14 he was back in London with new problems to face.

Every Fresh Start Has Its Disappointments

The king of Holland's unwillingness to submit to the decisions of the London conference postponed final settlement of the Belgian issue. He refused to give up Antwerp. He had gone on occupying it for two years now despite the treaty; to tolerate this any longer meant denying Belgium's sovereignty.

Talleyrand would not tolerate it. It was then that Europe's great exponent of non-intervention called for armed intervention against the Netherlands.

This incident of course unleashed a flood of sarcasm as to his immutable principles. Actually, his attitude toward each new situation was strictly pragmatic. In this case, he felt that in the interests of peace and the general welfare, the treaty had to be enforced. Instead of denying a principle, he was insisting that it be observed. History has shown that peace often must be conquered by force. When an Englishman slyly inquired what he thought of non-intervention, the prince earnestly replied: "Non-intervention is a metaphysical and political term meaning almost the same thing as intervention."

Palmerston upheld Franco-English unity. A squadron of English ships blockaded the Dutch coast while French troops besieged Antwerp. Holland gave up the city and handed it over to the Belgians on December 23, 1832. Belgium was a reality and Talleyrand had demonstrated the validity of a principle he had enunciated in 1792: that unity between France and England could ensure peace in Europe. Together, the two powers had enforced a treaty. Shortly after Talleyrand's arrival, Dorothée joined him in London. The round of social life began afresh, with its smiles and disappointments, its sweet and bitter moments.

That winter, Talleyrand and his niece had to deal with the hostility of Flahaut and his wife. Talleyrand finally admitted it: "At present, I am forced to consider myself an imbecile when I rejected as slander everything I heard about that couple." Madame de Flahaut was especially insulting to her "father-in-law," who had disappointed her ambitions. It was her intention to see Flahaut installed as ambassador during Talleyrand's absence. Instead, Bacourt was chosen, because he was fully acquainted with embassy business, knew Talleyrand's mind—and his niece's even better—and was the soul of probity. There was every reason to choose him. Thus Flahaut did not become his father's diplomatic rival, a great loss to the vanity of this ambitious couple. To his great regret, Talleyrand was obliged to keep them at arm's length. Palmerston became no less unfriendly. He claimed that when Talleyrand came by to discuss business, Montrond would wait in the coach for him to return and then go off to buy or sell government bonds. Very likely; but after all, Palmerston was providing the "tips," wasn't he?

Another ghost from the past appeared: after his release from prison in 1829, that sinister personality Maubreuil brought a further suit against Talleyrand. It was adjudicated in 1832 and never made much of a stir. "The case will be dismissed," Talleyrand predicted. "Anyway, it does not put me out or worry me." The prophecy proved correct; the plaintiff had to pay costs.*

By contrast, the princesse de Vaudémont's death gave him a terrible shock. Montrond, who was there when the prince heard about it, witnessed a unique spectacle: Talleyrand in tears. "Hell's Christchild" shuddered. "I lost a friend," Talleyrand noted, "to whom I had been very close for fifty years; I met her at her mother-in-law's, the comtesse de Brionne, where I spent the best years of my youth. . . ."

For whom did he weep? Surely for this friend whose warmth, wit, and elegance he cherished. He loved her dearly. Together they had shared simple, gracious pleasures born of absolute trust. He wept for her, yes, but also for the part of himself that died with her, for the last radiance of a shimmering world, the world he knew at twenty in 1775.

Next came Dalberg's turn, another painful blow. Two years later, Talleyrand still felt the loss.

Social and diplomatic triumphs now served to mute irreparable griefs. The prince was encircled by death. Yet no one noticed the slightest sign of despair on his face or in his manner. No one read the meaning of his detachment; he was, as always, inscrutable. His dinners had never been more lavish or frequent, his receptions more brilliant, his gambling

---

* Maubreuil deserves further mention just for being such an odd personality. He had no money but was clever enough to land himself a state pension. On what basis? Guizot terminated it, Napoleon III restored it. In 1866, at the age of eighty-two and armed with the title marquis d'Orvault, he married a woman named Schumacher who had a rather broad and casual circle of friends. In 1867, he was again involved with the law as a result of an attempt on his wife's life. They were living miserably in a furnished hotel in the 18th arrondissement. He died in 1869, but his wife lived on until 1910. She joined him in far better shape than she started out, with a carriage and a luxurious apartment on the rue de Rivoli. Who knows how she came by them? She left all her money (a million francs in 1910) to the Institut Pasteur—Virtue rewarded at last.

more persistent, rash and costly. His limp was more pronounced now and more painful.

Prosper Mérimée was living in London that winter and became a regular visitor to the French embassy. His rapid sketches of the goings-on there are among the liveliest of the period. In a letter dated December 14, 1832, to a friend who had just sent him a note of introduction to Talleyrand, he replied: "The introduction has already been made, but your letter will give me the pleasure of seeing more of this truly extraordinary man. I am lost in admiration for the profound meaning behind everything he says, his simple, impeccable manners. He is the ultimate aristocrat. The English, who claim to know something about elegance and propriety, cannot hold a candle to him."

With his critical, satiric eye, Mérimée caught the whole astonishing spectacle of the prince holding court, noting in particular: "Nothing is quite so amusing as the sight of him surrounded by the most prominent members of the House of Lords, obsequious to the point of servility."

The sly-humored author of *Carmen* and *Colomba* relates the following scene, incredible but true as it is supported by other accounts not nearly so vivid as this:

> Now the prince has an odd habit. After dinner, instead of rinsing his mouth according to the custom in London and Paris, he rinses his nose, and in the following manner. After something resembling an oilcloth napkin is tied under his chin, he sniffles two glasses of water up his nose, passing it out through his mouth. This operation, accompanied by loud noises, takes place at a sideboard right next to the dinner table. Even yesterday, during the course of this singular ablution, the entire diplomatic corps stood with eyes lowered, waiting silently for the operation to end, while Lady Jersey, towel in hand, stood behind the prince, following the voyage of each glass of water with respectful interest. Had she been bolder, she could have held the basin. This Lady Jersey is the haughtiest, most impertinent lady in all England; she is very beautiful, very witty, very well educated, and very well born to boot. The prince must have uncanny charm to wring such condescension from her. "It's an excellent habit, Prince," Lady Jersey said. "Nasty, very nasty!" insisted the prince. And he took her arm after keeping her waiting for five minutes.

At dinner they talked about everything under the sun without dwelling on any one theme or delivering impassioned speeches. Mérimée went on: "They talked politics, literature, cooking, and it appeared to me that the prince was equally in command of all three subjects." Talleyrand commended Mérimée for doing his literary apprenticeship in the business world. At which point he cited the example—to be avoided strenuously—of Chateaubriand, who had no knowledge of human nature, no talent for business (his own or the government's), and who depicted a world known only to himself. But the *coup de grâce,* which René never forgave and which earned the prince a coffin in Hell—at least in the *Mémoires d'outre-tombe*—was Talleyrand's comment: "Chateaubriand did his writing with a crow's feather." As our hero frowned on feathers of any kind, he attributed the saying to Madame Hamelin. Mérimée commented: "I suspect that he made it up himself." We agree. Continuing the gossip in his letter, Mérimée spoke of London's most elegant women in the season of 1832, naming duchesses, peeresses, and then suddenly: "Speaking of whoring, when Madame de Dino came to London, she was preceded by a reputation for enjoying gymnastic exercises which shocked all the ladies and made them declare their intention to shun her, 'to cut her,' as they say here." The ensuing tale throws some light on the silent war which Dorothée and Montrond were waging behind the prince's back. Mérimée tells it:

> Montrond, wanting to even the score, took Lord Palmerston's nephew in tow, a six-foot hulk of a dandy, and told him: "You have no mistress, silly fellow; you shall have one, and a famous beauty at that. I have just what you need, Madame de Dino. But if you would take her, you must do it boldly. This is how: when you are alone with her, shut the door and lock it, throw her down on a couch or the rug, and go to work, but whatever you do, don't waste time talking to her." His mouth watering, our young giant set off at once to accost the damsel in her chamber, reduced her gown to a mask, and proceeded to board her. And she to shriek and scratch at her ravisher, on whose cheeks her nails left ten distinct imprints. After a brief skirmish, the Englishman was repulsed and departed to lick his wounds, while the duchess, mistress of the fray, became known as a dragon of virtue.[1]

In a letter dated January 21, 1833, Mérimée spoke once again of Talleyrand's gift for conversation: "He was extremely gracious to me. . . . He is a great wad of flannel encased in a blue dress coat and surmounted by a death's head overlaid with parchment. . . . Witty for the most part, but I noticed that his wit never queens the pawn of common sense. Rare, isn't it, for a Frenchman?" But the prince's graciousness had a purpose. Suspecting that his visitor was a journalist, he was cajoling him out of distrust. "Hence my concern and my attempts to subdue this young tiger in order to avoid being clawed. He comes from a long line of tigers. . . ." They became friends, and Talleyrand offered to introduce Mérimée to Lord Holland. "Now the ultimate sign of favor is being introduced to someone by the prince." In the carriage taking them to Lord Holland's, Mérimée asked whether Talleyrand thought the Revolution had had a good or bad effect on France: "There was debauchery before the Revolution, but there was elegance. There were rogues, but they were witty. Today, debauchery is vulgar and rogues are a bore."

Maxime du Camp saw him in London in 1833 and left these notes on the prince: ". . . livid pallor, a drooping lower lip, shoulders hunched forward; his limp was so pronounced that at each step his body swayed from side to side as if it might keel over." The old man, who seemed on his last legs, managed nevertheless in May, 1833, to do the honors of London for the young duc d'Orléans, eldest son of Louis-Philippe and heir to the throne. Talleyrand was anxious to cement relations between the two countries; in the eyes of Europe, this state visit affirmed the success of his mission. It also depleted his energy. Alexis de Saint-Priest, a contemporary observer, wrote on May 16: "I have never met a man more eminent or more esteemed. He derives nothing from his party [the July Monarchy], but enhances it instead with his dignity, with the full weight of his own existence. The July Revolution sometimes appears slightly bourgeois in Paris, yet in London, thanks to M. de Talleyrand, it has great elegance. Madame de Dino also plays her part very well." Flahaut was to have been in the duke's retinue; Talleyrand had him replaced because of his wife's rudeness.

The visit gave him satisfaction but wore him out. Satisfactions had a way of vanishing in the wake of new problems, but the weariness stayed on. Palmerston avoided him; the prime minister would not attend any of Talleyrand's receptions. Holland was constantly harassing Belgium, refusing to recognize her sovereignty. In the old days, he would have risen above such things. But not at the age of seventy-nine. He asked for a leave of absence in September, thinking that it would be his last. Neither the king nor the foreign minister shared that anticipation. Talleyrand was too valuable in London to be allowed to retire. On September 26, he was back in Paris. Archambaud was very ill. After that he went on to Valençay to be away from politics and pressure from the throne and from the foreign ministry headed by the duc de Broglie. In December, when he returned to the capital, he finally yielded to them and agreed, without enthusiasm, to go back to London. He wrote to Barante on December 13: "I am returning to England for several months. There seems to be a feeling, greater than my own, that I am of some use there; I yield. Madame de Dino leaves in two days and I in three. My plan is to return to France in April and to retire permanently in May; I have served more than my term. . . ." Retirement was now no longer merely an idle thought in the back of his head. He painted a rosy picture of the situation at home and abroad in order to reassure himself and to make others think that he was leaving an orderly house behind. It relieved his conscience.

During the four months he was away, Bacourt once again acted as chargé d'affaires. But something happened and Bacourt was no longer perfection. Talleyrand found fault with him. Bacourt complained to the duchess of Dino; unlike Talleyrand, he did not address her as "Madam" but instead as "my angel, my pretty one-eyed magpie." He told her that the prince's return filled him with apprehension, that he felt "a great dislike for having to bend once more beneath the yoke of M. de Talleyrand's ill-humor. Tell me as often as you like that he has become gentle as a lamb; a rift has come between us that cannot be mended. . . ." It would be hard to imagine the conflict as being of a political or professional nature; Bacourt was above reproach. What was it then? Could not this ill humor be caused by just a touch of jealousy? True enough, Talleyrand had never shown it for other lovers in his niece's life, Piscatory least of all. But Piscatory came and went, whereas Bacourt lived under the same roof with them. Though Bacourt was a perfect gentleman, a host of little things, day after day, may have irritated the old man who still loved his niece dearly. When he returned to London, he was his customary self, serene and good-humored. Bacourt became the lamb, and the *ménage à trois* picked up where it left off, living and working together in harmony.

During this last trip, Talleyrand was able to solidify the Franco-English entente with a treaty: "The dearest wish of my career from beginning to end has been for a close alliance between France and England, for I am convinced that world peace, the strengthening of liberal ideas, and the progress of civilization must rest upon this foundation." [2]

Palmerston was not hostile, simply cool. By April, 1834, nothing had yet been done. There was no lack of good will, or for that matter of intrigue on the part of governments interested in alienating the two powers. Palmerston proposed that Talleyrand support England's desire for an entente with Spain and Portugal in order to bolster legitimate rule against the claims of pretenders in those two countries. Talleyrand turned the entente into a treaty to which France became an actual party. The Quadruple Alliance was signed on April 22, 1834, with no time lost. It was Talleyrand's last masterpiece. Admiral de Rigny, the new foreign minister, expressed the nation's gratitude.

Pauline, his adored "great-niece," was in London, where she made her first communion in March, 1834. In the morning, wearing her white veil, she knelt to receive the blessing of her great-uncle—who was something more than an uncle, and a bishop in the bargain. Pauline's innocent piety stirred the old man's heart, prompting the comment: "How touching is the piety of a young girl, and how unnatural is unbelief, especially in women." His uncle the archbishop must have trembled with hope in his grave.

In May, 1834, he learned that La Fayette, for whom he never had much use, was dead. Privately, he used to call him "Gilles le Grand" (Rivarol's version was "Gilles César"). Still, as Dorothée observed, Talleyrand was not totally indifferent to the event. "Beyond the age of eighty-four, it seems that all contemporaries are friends." [3]

On August 18, for the last time, he added his signature to a codicil of the treaty. Four days later he was back home on the rue Saint-Florentin, his career at an end. He had forgotten to bring with him from London the gold key on a red ribbon which opened his portfolio. He wrote asking Colmache, his secretary, to return it.[4] With that, prince de Talleyrand had nothing further to do with 21, Hanover Square, the French embassy in London in 1834.

The Art of Making an Exit

No triumph awaited him in Paris. Instead, a volley of insults greeted him—the old familiar ones. The *Tribune des Départements* had this to say: "Talleyrand, laden with the ignominy of nine governments that have rolled over France [the 'patriots' made France sound like a camp follower] for half a century, traitor to God and man, who has wasted a lifetime bartering morality, selling consciences. . . ." Grandiloquence in the service of bourgeois virtues.

On September 6 the *Charivari* served up the same dish without varying the sauce, labeling Talleyrand a "Jacobin" (he had left France to escape the Jacobins), "regicide" (in 1793 he was in America), "royalist conspirator" (in other words, they were saying that he murdered the duc d'Enghien), "émigré" (not so), and "Blücher's minister" (when he consistently opposed Prussian ambitions). Not one word of his achievements. That he served France, created an independent Belgium, broke up the Holy Alliance, made England an ally, and upheld liberty apparently were facts of no significance. Legitimists and revolutionists alike declared open season on him for having managed "to win sovereign rights in Europe" for the government of Louis-Philippe, whom they exe-crated. What had party rivalries to do with the nation's safety, security, and honor? The *Charivari* depicted the ambassador as merely an adjunct of the men in the Tuileries: "The taint of their collective corruption is concentrated in this man who has known every kind of corruption. . . ."

While the left pelted him with nettles, the Most Christian spokes-man of the legitimist right, Chateaubriand, reserved for him this Crown of Thorns: "Before descending to the tomb, his mummy was placed on temporary exhibit in London as representative of the skeleton of royalty now ruling us."

That was the image of Talleyrand which many Frenchmen ac-cepted. That was the result of four years of painful negotiations ac-claimed by the rest of Europe. Outside France, Talleyrand gained the reputation he aspired to and described in his *Memoirs:* "In the eyes of that part of France so unforgiving when its national vanity has been wounded, I was just what I had always wanted to be: the man of France."

Even Metternich, who had no reason to love Talleyrand for break-ing up the Holy Alliance, paid him this tribute: "As an individual and as a symbol, M. de Talleyrand truly represents France as she is, whereas the majority of foreign envoys often represent a political party at best and very often just themselves."

Talleyrand, as we know, paid scant attention to calumny, and the current crop of it took less of a toll on him than his London triumph. Dorothée was at Valençay; he thought he would join her there and re-arrange the palatial dwelling for a long and comfortable stay. She feared, however, that her uncle would heed appeals from the king, from Ma-dame Adélaïde, or from Broglie in the foreign ministry. To keep the political sirens from luring him back to London, she wrote him a long, deliberate letter in the hope of persuading him to retire. She had seen enough of London, where, in recent months, a host of new issues were coming to a head and her uncle's position was becoming tenuous. In short, she felt that now was the time to make a brilliant exit rather than a forced retreat later on. "In youth," she told him, "one moment is as good as the next to step into the fray; in age, all that matters is choosing the right moment to walk away from it."

She asked him to recognize that his only future was the one history would decree: "As you know, [history] judges the end of a life more harshly than its beginning." Her last line was stunning: "Assert that you are old before others say that you are aging; say nobly, simply to all the world: the time has come!"

Dorothée had the courage to say that and Talleyrand the courage to face it. When she rejoined her uncle, they were of one mind. Now they must decide how to "end his career with dignity." As a first step, the prince handed in his resignation to the foreign minister with the reminder that he had accepted the London post—despite his advanced age —only to accomplish a specific mission. Having done so in the best interests of the government and the nation, he was entitled, by virtue of his age and his infirmities, to rest.

The duchess wrote out the letter; Talleyrand went over it, making a few minor corrections. It was then given to Royer-Collard, who changed a phrase. After that, Talleyrand decided that it was ready to go out.

At the same time, Dorothée advised Thiers that the letter of resignation was on its way. Modestly, she concluded: "Soon we shall be forgotten; indeed, this is our wish. Our true friends will still be with us, especially you, I know, and for this I thank you."

Talleyrand also wrote to the king. He flattered himself that the London mission had been highly successful, ending thus: "The king, in his bounteous indulgence, often forgets my old age; he forgets that no octogenarian is allowed to commit an imprudence, for what makes the errors of old age so sad is the fact that they are irreparable" (November 23, 1834).

He felt compelled to write also to Madame Adélaïde, who had helped so much to advance his career. This letter conveyed something more personal touching on the real reasons for his retirement: "By prolonging my activity, now to no avail, I would not be serving my country and would only be damaging my own reputation." This motive, which Dorothée had put forward so convincingly, was the decisive one: fear of lowering his prestige.

Louis-Philippe responded above and beyond the level of official regrets; he felt that he was losing a pillar of the régime. "It is my keenest desire that you return to Paris as soon as possible. I am anxious to hear from and to be heard by you; I feel the need of your experience and especially of your friendly counsel, which is so valuable to me. I assure you once again that you may rely on mine and on my long-established feelings for you."

One piece of advice offered by Talleyrand was not adopted. He wanted Rayneval, whom he trusted, to head the London embassy. Instead, the government sent over old Sébastiani. It was ill advised, if not ludicrous, to replace one lame but lucid octogenarian with another incompetent, obtuse one. Daumier satirized the situation mercilessly. Two open carriages meet on the Calais road, each with its moribund occupant propped up on cushions. One is Sébastiani headed for Calais, the other Talleyrand going the other way. The legend: "Apoplexy off to Replace Dropsy in London."

Shortly before Talleyrand resigned, he had the signal honor of receiving the duc d'Orléans at Valençay. Possibly Madame Adélaïde prevailed on her nephew to make this quasi-royal visit to the old statesman in hopes that he would change his decision to retire. We do not know. In any event, the heir to the throne certainly did not put himself out just to inspect twenty-eight canvases of the sovereigns with whom the old prince had dealt during his lifetime. Or to admire Valençay's great gallery, its gardens, and wild rabbits; or to hunt as he did in the immense forest preserve, or to dine in splendor with all the protocol due a royal guest by a host who dazzled the duke even more than he honored him. The heir to the throne was taken on a tour of the church, the school, the infirmary, and the pharmacy, all put there by the master of Valençay. He saw the ironworks and the stocking factory which Talleyrand had introduced with an eye to increasing prosperity in the region. The duke may have been astonished to see a display of plaster casts of the legs of our prince's lady friends. One of the courtesies extended to members of the harem was a lifetime supply of made-to-order hosiery! In an age when it was indecent for a woman to show her ankles, this exhibition of nude limbs aroused the duke's curiosity, especially as the originals belonged to the elegant set of the faubourg Saint-Germain. The duc d'Orléans took with him at least that one memory of Valençay. The memory he left behind was of a very open and engaging personality.

In order not to be deprived of Talleyrand's services, the government offered him the embassy in Vienna. Everyone knew how famously he got along with Metternich, who would have been happy to see him. He declined, claiming that he had but one ambition: "To retire to my lair and fall into a torpor is all that interests me at the moment." Bitter words from a man whose ambition had always spurred him into the thick of world events in a century of tumult. It was all over. Talleyrand had decided irrevocably that from now on he was going to be old.

A Sumptuous "Lair"

Valençay, that elegant "lair" of his, might have been a royal château. He loved its solitude amid the surrounding woods, its magnificent views of ancestral forests. Apart from beauty and splendor, it offered him something unique: the unqualified affection of everyone living there. Even at a distance, he had always looked after his estates, his tenants, and retainers. The lesson learned at Chalais at the age of six stayed with him throughout his life. He rebuilt the town hall, founded a school for girls run by the Sisters of Saint Andrew, and restored the church belfry on which the date 1836 can be seen. The infirmary distributed free medicine. He also distributed bread, firewood, clothing, and money. At Valençay, he was a totally different personality from the man on the rue Saint-Florentin, abandoning himself to the warm and human elements of his nature. He loved visitors, whom he entertained with cordial, lavish hospitality. Madame de Dino was right when she told Barante: "Come to Valençay; I assure you that you will not regret it. M. de Talleyrand is his most charming self, and if I have any merit at all, then it is there too." [1]

In Paris, he was looked upon as Machiavelli, the Prince of Corruption; at Valençay, a mild and benevolent patriarch.

He had made many changes in the vast château, which, when he acquired it, still possessed reminders of its fortress and convent past. He tried to give it light and air, to make it cheerful and more modern. He supervised all the work, including the gardening, landscaping, and planting of crops. As he loved peaches, the walls of the kitchen garden were covered with espaliers. The rabbit warren and game park kept his table well provided. He served a great deal of cheese. Brie, as we have already learned, once earned him a diplomatic triumph in Vienna. He called it "the king of cheeses"—Eugène Sue commented: "The only king he did not betray." Talleyrand might have countered that Brie upheld its reputation more consistently than kings the constitutions they signed into law.

He had Bacourt send him Scotch Pine seeds from London so that Valençay could have a forest of saplings.

Parish priests in the region confessed astonishment to abbé Dupanloup at the fact that an eminent statesman should spend so much time and effort on so-called menial occupations.

On November 2, 1834, shortly after Talleyrand returned from London, death paid a visit. Countess Tyszkiewicz died in Tours, Princess Poniatowska, his beloved Maria-Theresa whose warm devotion made up for her lack of beauty. She had permanent rooms at Valençay. In Paris, though she might as well have lived in the hôtel Talleyrand where most of her time was spent, she preferred keeping an apartment close by on the rue Saint-Florentin. But Valençay was her last refuge; she was buried in the Chapel of Saint Maurice next to the tomb of the man to whom she devoted most of her life. Her generosity was legendary. Having seen two handsome porcelain pillars at an antique dealer's which he wanted very much but felt were too costly, Talleyrand found them at home that evening. She had paid about 30 million old francs for them. To the Chapel of Saint Maurice, her resting place, she presented a gold ciborium, a papal gift to her uncle, Cardinal Poniatowski, archbishop of Cracow, which she had brought from Poland. Her death was a cruel blow to Talleyrand. Dorothée hesitated to tell him. "What makes it worse," she wrote, "at M. de Talleyrand's age, it is not only a great tribulation to bear but also a warning. It grieves me more than himself."

The prince wrote to Lady Jersey: ". . . twenty-seven years of absolute devotion make her death a cruel loss. Although I knew for some time that the end was approaching, still, the moment of eternal separation is very painful. Affection is never prepared for that final hour. I feel compelled to express my sentiments to someone I have loved for twenty years, and that is why I write you now."

He saw her buried on November 20. Her home was also his. They rest side by side. November was a sad month; his niece, Archambaud's daughter, comtesse Just de Noailles, duchesse de Mouchy, princesse de Poix, also died. He wrote to one of the ladies of the "seraglio," his "stars" as he called them, princesse de Baufremont: "So many people are falling around me!" (November 24, 1834).

Infirmity and failing health would not allow him to forget that death waited. Caring for himself was time-consuming; but Valençay's leisurely pace gave him all the time he needed. He experimented with new cures: having his ailing legs rubbed with a mixture of spirits of alcohol and boiling water. Bacourt advised bathing them in bouillon; he used quantities of it. Unfortunately, he took to reading medical books, and in addition to very real ailments, he invented a "polyp on the heart" which caused him considerable suffering.

Still, he confessed: "Our life here is very orderly, which makes the days very short. At the close of each day we find ourselves without a moment's languor. This morning our readings in the salon were interrupted by the arrival of a wolf which the watchmen had just slain. A great event in the day. I work for several hours every day and feel very well." [2]

He rose late. As his legs grew progressively weaker, he no longer walked in the park, but took the air instead in a curiously constructed wheelchair of sorts, a gift—not costly but precious all the same—from Louis-Philippe. It had belonged to Louis XVIII and was discovered at the

Tuileries; Talleyrand could exchange secrets with this paltry throne of a rejected monarch.

Returning from his outing, he took a glass of Madeira in which he would dip a biscuit. If there were other players, he would have a game of whist. Sometimes he sat musing alone in his room, with more than enough memories to occupy his mind. Or write a few pages of the *Memoirs*. He read a good deal: "Reading," he said, "is much more agreeable and leisurely than writing." He read classics, especially Bossuet, yet his writing does not reflect the latter's influence. Not for anything in the world would he miss Sunday Mass, where he never listened to a word, but sat there absorbed in Bossuet's *Funeral Orations* or his *Discourse on Universal History*. He was so fascinated with Bossuet that one day he called Dorothée into his room, saying: "Come in, I want to show you how mysteries should be treated. Read this, aloud and slowly." She goes on to describe the scene in her Diary:

> I read the following: In the year 4,000, Jesus Christ, temporal son of Abraham, eternal son of God, was born of a virgin.
>
> Memorize that passage, M. de Talleyrand told me, and see with what authority, what simplicity all mysteries are concentrated in a few lines. That is the way, the only way to speak of religious matters. They must be imposed, not explained; that is the only way to make them acceptable; any other is a waste of time because doubt enters once authority is wanting; authority, tradition, stewardship are adequately revealed only in the Catholic church.

With all due respect, someone might have pointed out to Monseigneur d'Autun that in his case, surely the church failed to reveal sufficiently its authority and tradition, neither of which had rubbed off on him. Also, the qualities he admired in the quotation from Bossuet—compression, clarity, restraint—were stylistic ones not particularly representative of the great churchman's religious prose.

More likely, the lesson in style indicates a burgeoning of religious feeling, which had occurred once before in London at the time of Pauline's confirmation. It was not faith certainly, or even a religious frame of mind; but for lack of a better definition, for the moment let us call this interest in devotional literature a return to Catholic discipline, meaning a predilection for a particular moral and social order in the universe, inseparable for him from human dignity linked to a system of values, which was embodied in the Catholic church.

Among the visitors to Valençay were the duc de Noailles; the prince de Laval; the duc Decazes with whom Talleyrand was now reconciled; Lady Clanricarde, Canning's daughter; Mignet, the historian; Cuvillier-Fleury; the much-welcome Adolphe Thiers and his wife; and John Hamilton, whose father had invited Talleyrand to his Philadelphia home in 1793. Valençay also was host to occasional birds of passage, unexpected visitors such as Princess Lieven, with whom Talleyrand had made peace. She was an impossible houseguest, perpetually bored, and shifting to different rooms every day. Still, her leavetaking was tender: snipping off a lock of her hair, she handed it to Talleyrand, who did the same.

Royer-Collard, his esteemed neighbor at Châteauvieux, was by now a willing visitor to Valençay, having discovered the fascination of Talleyrand's conversation. When the prince recalled the past: "M. de Talleyrand no longer invents; he simply relates his own life," said the old Doctrinaire.

There was also a lady from Sainte-Algegonde with two distinctions: one was having been married to General Augereau in the epic days of the Empire; the other was a pair of exceptionally black and well-tufted eyebrows atop singularly lusterless eyes, which prompted Talleyrand's comment: "They are bows without arrows."

But arrows did strike at the lord and lady of Valençay one September afternoon. in 1834. Returning from an outing, Talleyrand and his niece found the château filled with strangers busily inspecting everything, and noisily commenting on what they found. The servants identified two of them as a Madame Dudevant and a Monsieur de Musset. No one had ever heard of them. Madame d'Entrague, a guest of Talleyrand at the time, whispered to her host that Madame Dudevant went by the name of George Sand, and that the man was neither Alfred de Musset nor his brother Paul, but Alfred Rollinat, a local poet of some distinction. He belonged to the horde of admirers clustered about Madame Sand whenever she melted into the solitude of Nohant. Dorothée showed the queen and her swarm around the château and received them in the drawing room. They left.

No note of thanks followed this visit; instead, a long article appeared on October 15, three weeks later, in the *Revue des Deux Mondes*. An astounding piece, it is the most defamatory estimate ever written of Talleyrand and his niece. And by the woman who called herself George Sand, who descended uninvited at Talleyrand's doorstep, poked through his home, questioned his servants, and was courteously received by his niece.

> Don't you know that for sixty years the man living there has been juggling nations and crowns on the universal chessboard. . . . That narrow, curled lip, like a cat's . . . like a satyr's, blending deceit and

lust . . . the arrogant nose, the snakelike eyes . . . a man destined for great vice and petty acts [Wasn't she just saying that he gambled with nations and crowns?], a heart that has never known a warm impulse . . . a unique monstrosity . . . what bloody struggles, what public disasters, what shocking extortions has he averted? . . . Let me curse this enemy of mankind. . . .

Having apostrophized a chorus, she now addressed an octogenarian fox: "As for you, you will die slowly and reluctantly in your nest, sated old vulture. . . ."

To give the readers of her day the ultimate thrill, she looked for a resounding antithesis to the fox-vulture image and came up with a shining symbol of purity: a lily on a dungheap. Here is the lily, the duchess. "Dressed all in white like a young girl, like a nymph of Diana . . . the most beautiful eyes in France . . . with magic sparkle. Ah, that must be the duchess. . . . They say that . . ." Here Madame Sand pauses breathlessly. Could she have understood? Could she, the soul of innocence, dare to suggest "tainted relations" . . . "can the world contain such monsters?" Wringing her hands, Madame Sand protests in horror: "Repeat it no more: spare my imagination these hideous visions, these awful doubts. . . . If rampant debauchery and sordid avarice inhabit such beguiling creatures and conceal themselves beneath such chaste forms, let me be ignorant of it, let me deny it. . . ."

In 1834, rampant virtue could produce just such results. Madame de Dino was stunned; so for once was Talleyrand. As usual, he kept silent. Only his closest intimates knew that he was deeply offended. When told that her article had proved hurtful, the lady of Nohant seemed surprised. Why, a little thing like that? "It was only an impulse." An impulse typical of its author.

They put on plays, for Madame de Dino and Pauline were mad about acting. Because Talleyrand said they were stars, all his friends repeated it. The plays were purely for their own entertainment. The villagers enjoyed them too; *La Farce de maître Pathelin* drew such roars of laughter that Dorothée actually became frightened of the audience. Reports said that they also played *Les Femmes savantes* to perfection. La Besnardière attended the performance and declared that it was better than the Comédie-Française. The satrap's former collaborators were now his aged courtiers.

Sometimes they would listen to music. Talleyrand's household always included a musician. The last one he employed at Valençay, Nedermann, was a harpist, willing to put up with provincial boredom for 600 francs a month, plus travel expenses, a very generous sum.

Then, of course, there was Montrond, like a permanent fixture. Unfortunately, he had lost his good looks and was aging badly. He complained about everything and everyone. Behind tinted glasses he railed at the world, including the dinner menu and the guests. Talleyrand said nothing, as usual. The small-scale war between Montrond and Dorothée had even amused him, but at Valençay Montrond became impossible. After Dorothée refused to put up with the old rake any more, Talleyrand gave him to understand that the climate of Valençay was bad for his health and he would be far better off in Paris. So Montrond left in October, 1834. Hurt, he complained that Talleyrand had not treated him "kindly as an old friend, or politely as the master of his house." A reply from the duchess told him that the master of the house had failed to discern in Montrond the deference of a guest. "In what other house would you have found fault with everything as you do here? You criticize his neighbors, his servants, his wine, his horses . . . if he has been rude, you have been peevish. . . ." With Montrond gone, Dorothée could breathe again. On a trip to Paris, Montrond met Talleyrand in a salon and did not greet him: "Now why doesn't he greet me?" the prince noted. "Evidently I brought him up badly." Montrond was reprieved and re-entered the rue Saint-Florentin on the arm of his inseparable companion. Dorothée did not rejoice. What could she do? "Hell's Christchild" and "the limping Mephistopheles" were wedded for life.

Talleyrand would conduct his visitors all over the château, showing them his paintings and statues and his 10,000-volume library. He owned a picture representing the tomb of Charles X which Dorothée had won in a lottery and given to him, thinking it would please him: "You are right, niece," he said, "Charles X was the most incompetent king in terms of ability and made the greatest number of mistakes. Yet I have always regarded and loved him as the most loyal, the best man I have known."

In good weather, he would follow the hunt in an open carriage. Sometimes he simply accompanied his guests in a landau, pointing, with the tip of his cane, to deer fleeing in the underbrush.

During an outing in his historic wheelchair, capricious as the fate of thrones, he took a tumble. Like a king, he fell, but though his head struck the ground, he did not lose it. They thought he was dead. At eighty-two and in his weakened condition, the fall could have been fatal. "He should have been killed," the duchess wrote, "in fact he just has a scratch on his face."

The fall bothered him less than the stubborn prefect of the Indre who refused to authorize the planting of trees. Talleyrand insisted that he lift the restriction in defiance of a certain ruling. Mounting his high horse, the prefect replied that he was "astride" ("an expert on") the regulations. "You ride a proud beast," retorted Valençay's haughty planter.

Every year brought regal celebrations on the name days of his two saints, Maurice and Charles. He set great store by this ritual, recalling Chalais, the only time in his childhood when anyone bothered to celebrate his saints' days. The festivities on September 22, Saint Maurice's Day, were more elaborate. The morning began with a bugle call by the local militia, followed by Mass at the château, after which the schoolchildren came to recite their greetings and present flowers. Pauline presided over a great banquet for the poor, no almshouse repast but a lavish feast flowing with wine. At dessert time, Talleyrand made his appearance, presenting each guest with a new suit of clothes for the winter. In the evening, the towers and keep were illuminated and the whole village invited to watch fireworks.

He was very conscious of manners in his guests. Bad manners offended him more than ingratitude or hostility. "You receive someone according to his name or the clothes he wears," the prince once said, "you show him out according to his behavior." His door closed permanently behind certain visitors. Generally, he seemed not to notice things, but later on he would pick out faults. The lessons he gave are a self-portrait. His advice, for instance, to a casual visitor who had just gulped down a very fine cognac which Talleyrand had served to him. The prince instructed him on how to treat a work of art: "Cup the glass in your hands, warm it, agitate it gently in a circular direction so that the liqueur gives off its bouquet. Then, bring it to your nostrils, breathe it . . . "

"Then what, Monseigneur?"

"Then, sir, put down the glass and converse. . . ." Everything is there except the prince's tone and the look on his face, which would have crushed any lemonade-gulper.

Besides visits to neighboring Châteauvieux there were occasional long periods of residence at Rochecotte. A letter he wrote on April 20, 1835, to the Austrian diplomat, Baron von Gagern, reveals not only the charms of Rochecotte but also the writer's sensitive regard for old friends:

> Long-standing friendship prompts your inquiry about my health; I would say that it is as good as my advanced years will allow, that I live in a delightful retreat, that I share it with those dearest to me, and that my unique occupation is sampling the full range of *dolce far niente*:

TALLEYRAND

When one has explored everything
Done everything or at least tried to,
How sweet it is to do nothing . . . etc.

You do not know Rochecotte, otherwise you could not ask "Why Rochecotte?" Even as I write I am looking out on a real garden two leagues wide and four leagues long, watered by a great river and flanked by wooded slopes which, because they are sheltered from northern winds, show signs of spring three weeks earlier than in Paris and are now a mass of greenery and flowers. Besides, there's another thing that makes me like Rochecotte better than anywhere else. Here I am not only with Madame de Dino, but also in her home, which for me is an added pleasure.

They made one excursion to the château de Courtalain in the Eure-et-Loire district, home of the duc de Montmorency, where they made the acquaintance of Sabine de Noailles, daughter of the princesse de Poix, Talleyrand's niece who had died in 1834. This great-niece of his was something of a tomboy, described by Dorothée as having "coarse good looks, a masculine voice, a good head on her shoulders, well-educated . . . and rather brusque manners." She revealed the last during dinner. Raising her glass, she called out loudly to her uncle at the far end of the table: "Uncle, will you drink a toast with me?" "Gladly, nephew," the prince replied softly.

Life at Valençay, despite its many pleasures, at times engulfed the old man in sorrow. He suffered badly from insomnia, yet was reluctant to wake others for a game of whist or to have Bossuet read aloud to him. So he would write a few more pages of his *Memoirs,* or the maxims or "pensées" he jotted down on odd sheets of paper or in a thick little red notebook he kept in his pocket.

The following lines, taken from his intimate journals, cast a curious light on his old age: "Here at Valençay, I arrange to make my life monotonous. I want to closet myself in the routine of a shut-in. I am not happy, I am not unhappy. My health is not good, it is not bad. I have no pain or illness. I am getting weaker gradually, and if this languorous condition does not cease, I know where it will end. I am not distressed by the thought, nor am I afraid. My business is done. I have planted trees, I have built a house, I have done many other foolish things; is it not time to make an end of all this?" [3] The last sentence might have come from Voltaire's pen. Yet it is less arresting than his suspended apprehension, a kind of stoic or Hindu ataraxia: the experience of non-being.

The "pensées" which he wrote as only a great nobleman could—not caring a fig for their composition or possible publication—are not gilt-edged, though their edge be sharp and subtle, suggesting a kinship with Rivarol or Laclos rather than Pascal and La Rochefoucauld, as unthinking critics impulsively proclaim. They possess the sparkle of infallible reason, the profundity generated by a supreme understanding of human nature, and the piercing, almost desperate consciousness of time's fatal usury.

"Fathers are forever trying to spare young people the experience of pleasure," that from an old man of eighty-two.

On politics: "In France, nothing eases the strain of obedience as readily as epigrams." Mazarin had already discovered that when he said: "They sing, they will pay."

"The more unstable a nation's character, the more strictly its institutions of government must be enforced." No one could question his competence to assert that.

"Bankers do their best business when governments fail to do theirs." His friend Ouvrard must have inspired that maxim.

He was the arbiter of manners: "Elegance and simplicity combined are, for all things and all persons, the hallmark of nobility."

Occasionally, when shifting from abstract speculation to concrete events, he showed by his marksmanship what an effective pamphleteer he might have been. Yet instead of publicly denouncing his revilers, he chose to scribble a few lines which ended up in a drawer. He had friends among the Doctrinaires, but also spiteful foes such as Molé and Broglie. With penetrating insight he exposed those austere, self-righteous individuals who created vexations and, in the long run, displayed only arrogant incompetence.

"Until the present one had the impression that France was not prepared to forgive importunate ministers; now she seems accustomed to them." In 1848, she would no longer tolerate them.

One more slap at members of the "Juste Milieu": "They are people whose existence is sandwiched between courtyard and garden; they never look into the street." Here was a bulwark of the old aristocracy advising those earnest young members of the bourgeoisie that government could not afford to ignore the public. This meant that one must govern with the "street" but not in it. Another scrap of paper clarified the point: "Public opinion is a useful check but a dangerous guide for governments." Public opinion can tell you where not to, but not where to go. On society and the people one encounters: "I forgive others for not adopting my opinion but I cannot forgive them for renouncing their own." The very thing he was accused of doing because people judged only outward appearances; he had changed masters but not principles. In changing his shirt, does a man also change his skin?

And this comment which he must have dedicated to himself: "Marriage is such a beautiful thing that it deserves lifelong deliberation." Indeed, he had thought constantly about his own since 1798.

We get another personal glimpse of him in this optimistic maxim: "With time and patience, blackberry leaves turn satiny." By sticking to one's ideas, lo and behold! enemies become friends, creditors debtors.

Such were the fruits of his insomnia and daydreams. There was no diminution of his intellect; he retained his powers right to the end. His withdrawal from public life was a question of will and propriety, not to mention pride. As a great nobleman and a great statesman, he could neither be part of a world in which his political role was curtailed or live entirely outside it; he was a prince in retirement. So he retired in princely fashion. It was a matter of good breeding, of taste, and of dignity. From the very outset, it was a stern discipline to impose on a life of ease and luxury.

"Renunciation" for Talleyrand
Is Almost Equivalent to "Attachment"

Winter found Talleyrand back on the rue Saint-Florentin, entertaining as regularly as ever. With false modesty he protested: "We have become thoroughly bourgeois." The language of the times. Twice a week he received visitors on the mezzanine. Enthroned in a monumental armchair, sitting very straight and still, like some ancient god-king yet completely himself, his hair carefully powdered and curled, his neck sunk in the high collar. "His short, rounded foot, clubfoot, like a horse's hoof," reports Madame de Mirabeau, rested on a stool in front of the throne. Society's ranks filed past the cushion displaying the deformed foot, at once fascinating and repellent. The old satrap's vivid conversation, his elegant manners, his dazzling career exerted a fascination at the same time that his infirmity and reputedly licentious past caused dismay. One reinforced the other, casting the crippled and retired prince in the role of an enchanting spirit dispensing some vaguely pernicious but irresistible magic.

To most visitors he remained aloof, but if a face caught his interest, his own would come alive, and with it his mordant wit and gracious manners. D'Argout described him as frequently taciturn: "Then suddenly he grew animated, his conversation sparkled, became ingenious, brilliant, profound, his dazzling wit captivated listeners who hung on every word. Yet he spoke with no attempt to please his admirers . . . he yielded to whatever impulse stirred him, to his mind's need to release its sparks. . . . At all times he spoke with authority, constantly dominating his interlocutors."

Madame de Dino commented that he was often sarcastic but never indulged in backbiting: "Scandalmongering offended him. He turned a deaf ear to malicious gossip, and I doubt that any household in Paris heard less of it and despised it more than his own." But he could unleash stinging volleys against absurdity or bad taste. A skinny woman whose outrageously low neckline bordered on a dismally flat landscape came in for this: "It is impossible to uncover more and reveal less." Returning to the rue Saint-Florentin with Montrond one day, he found a visiting card from a stranger, a would-be member of the French Institut. "What are his titles?" Montrond asked impatiently. "Didn't he write anything?" "Pardon me," Talleyrand replied, holding out the card, "he wrote his name."

He rarely thought twice about his own flashes of wit, which never conveyed spite or anger. He was not contentious: "It is easy to quarrel; I can do it as well as the next man, but why should I when it ruins business and creates problems? Besides, I am too lazy to do it, and perhaps too clever. One should not put others at ease by arguing with them or permit oneself to be quarreled with at will."

He never turned upon his detractors; why would he do so against chosen targets of his ridicule? In any event, his mordant wit was calculated to amuse an audience rather than claim a victim. Like that toothless Madame X (her name has been lost) whom people compared to the actress Mademoiselle Duchesnois, a woman of no great beauty but possessed of her own albeit decaying teeth. Talleyrand said: "If Madame X . . . had teeth, she would be as ugly as Mademoiselle Duchesnois." Most of all, he took rudeness to task. General Dorsenne le Paige arrived late for dinner at the rue Saint-Florentin, after everyone was seated at the table. Without excusing himself, the general calmly announced that he had been detained by a wretched *"pékin"* (civilian). Talleyrand addressed him acidly: "And what may I ask, General, is a 'pékin'?"

"We usually use it for any non-military person," replied the general.

"Just as we call any uncivil person a military man," retorted Talleyrand.

On the other hand, he was endlessly indulgent. For eighteen years he kept on a manservant with a decidedly hang-dog look which was not deceptive, for the fellow was finally arrested and sent to prison on various charges of thievery and fraud. News of the man's arrest did not surprise Talleyrand: "For the past eighteen years, every time his razor approached my face, I wondered whether he was about to cut my throat." It was said that he rehearsed certain bits of repartee before going out to dinner, but others, such as the following, rolled spontaneously off his lips. Listening to an incredibly long-winded German diplomat, suddenly, without interrupting the speaker, his face took on a hopelessly exhausted look. "What are you waiting for?" someone asked him. "The verb," he sighed.

The lure of political intrigue assailed him the moment he was back in the capital. To promote his protégé Adolphe Thiers, he tried to undermine the government. Molé sensed the fresh wave of hostility the day Talleyrand returned to Paris. "The rue Saint-Florentin is active indeed, a den of glowing intrigue," he wrote in February, 1836.

The prince continued to visit the king and Madame Adélaïde at the Tuileries. There he met the celebrated chevalier d'Orsay, whose description of the prince more or less coincides with the impressions of most of his contemporaries. Being a dandy, however, he observed that the prince's dress coat was too big and his top hat too broad. There was one further detail: the cane, that cane with which Talleyrand tapped on the painful iron brace supporting his right leg, its metallic ring denoting the prince's approach, heralding it just as clanking chains announce the appearance of ghosts. At the sound, people whispered: "The prince! The prince!" That cane was his scepter.

On December 13, 1834, he attended Thiers's reception into the Académie Française. He wanted to hear his protégé's speech and to support him publicly. Our prince made a spectacular entrance on the arm of his great-nephew the duc de Valençay, escorted by a bevy of elegant ladies: the duchess of Dino, Lady Clanricarde, the comtesse de Castellane, the comtesse de Boigne, and others. To the audience he was a symbol of grandeur, bearing on his shoulders the whole epic of France and of Europe for the past fifty years. So radiant was his presence that at his entrance the Chamber rose to its feet. Evidently, *Charivari* did not represent the only opinion in the capital. Thiers gave an excellent speech, his eyes fixed on the two men in the audience whom he particularly wanted to reach: Talleyrand and Royer-Collard.

In the spring of 1835, he decided to travel. Before returning to Valençay, he visited his estates and his ironworks at Pont-de-Sains, first passing by Rochecotte. He accompanied Louis-Philippe on an exhausting tour of Versailles which the king intended to restore. The château had been untenanted for forty years, and pillaged for a number of them.

The pilgrimage was painful to his aching legs as well as his memory. There is no mention of it in his *Memoirs*.

That year he forsook the waters of Bourbon-l'Archambault for those of Bourbonne. After reaching Valençay, where he attended a meeting of the district council, he was able finally to rest. His ailing legs made walking increasingly difficult. "My balance is as shaky as Europe's." An added misfortune in December, 1835, when he was back in Paris, was the death of his doctor, Bourdois de la Motte.

But his doctor's funeral was not the most talked-about one. On December 10, his wife, the princesse de Talleyrand, whom we have neglected almost as completely as he did, died on the rue de Lille. Madame Grand's fate had been settled, as we may recall, according to Dorothée's prudent advice. Rather than lose an income for life, the unfortunate princess led a secluded, pious existence. Talleyrand expected all this to change after the duke of San Carlos died, but, to his surprise, she continued to conduct herself discreetly. Gone were the days of the Empire. Madame Grand had died long ago. On December 10, it was the princesse de Talleyrand whom they laid to rest officially in the arms of the church. Her friend Madame d'Esclignac had seen to it that the archbishop of Paris, Monseigneur de Quélen, administered the last rites. Her death was sheer perfection. Did the good archbishop perhaps regard the princess's exemplary demise as heralding a far more spectacular reconciliation between the lady's husband and his Maker?

When news first reached the rue Saint-Florentin that the princess was dying, Dorothée hesitated to tell her uncle, not, however, from fear of bringing him grief, for as she well knew and expressed it herself: "I was not afraid of causing him any distress of heart, as that was in no way involved in the matter." Dorothée understood him perfectly. He listened to what she told him, then changed the subject as if he had heard nothing. The next day he broached the matter, mainly with regard to arranging the funeral and sending out death notices. Nor did he forget his will, for under their marriage contract whatever part of his fortune and estates she enjoyed during her lifetime was to revert to him upon her death. The idea of going to her never occurred to Talleyrand. That was all in the past. That afternoon, Dorothée heard her uncle humming. Taken aback, she asked him if the prospect of becoming a widower was making him so cheerful. The question seemed to irritate him, as if it had disclosed a private secret. When Madame de Talleyrand actually died, Dorothée was again reluctant to inform her uncle. She need not have been, for he responded thus to the news: "That simplifies my position a great deal." Such was the funeral oration honoring Madame

Grand, prince de Talleyrand's wife. The funeral was in impeccable taste, the "family" presenting a united front to stave off any gossip. With the prince's nephews acting as chief mourners, the princess received a dignified burial. A "legitimist" newspaper had the effrontery to speak of a "funeral scandal." The two nephews, Louis and Alexandre de Périgord, called on the editor, offering him a choice between retraction and a duel. The damaging article was withdrawn and another, suitable to "family" demands, took its place. Only the principal party remained invisible and silent. That day he was suffering from palpitations.

There was some unpleasantness over two caskets containing papers which the princess had left to the archdiocese and which belonged to the prince, together with all his wife's possessions. Afterwards the princess's name sank into oblivion.

During the winter of 1836, Thiers had a hard time keeping his government afloat. He complained bitterly to his adviser of incessant attacks and useless, recriminatory votes from the opposition. Talleyrand told him: "Remember, dear fellow, that for forty years I was the most morally discredited man in Europe, yet I was all-powerful in the government or on the threshold of it." He had few illusions about his own success or what others thought of him. Yet officials came in droves to the rue Saint-Florentin to greet him and seek his advice.

He was still dining out. After attending a dinner given by Thiers and finding the company motley and the service inferior, he shrugged it off as "a Directory dinner."

He much preferred invitations from Princess Lieven, a glutton for any kind of intrigue, an intolerable woman, but lively and witty. The gossips reported that he visited her regularly to collect bribes from the czar. Highly improbable, for if Russia's rulers had never been willing to pay for favors in the days when Talleyrand was in a position to do them, why should they pay when he wasn't?

The old prince was now experiencing a new life, a new love, the warmth of pure affection for his beloved Pauline. This tender "naïveté" reveals a different man from the one seen through the eyes of Chateaubriand and the journalists and political figures of his time. In fact, the warm, responsive side of Talleyrand's nature was always there; his brothers, his nephews, his "harem," his secretaries and servants, the townspeople of Valençay all were familiar with it. But their whispers were lost in the swollen chords of the *Mémoires d'outre-tombe*. Shrewdness and pride made him lock away this inner life in the recesses of his heart. An octogenarian, with nothing to lose, he released his tender affections for the exquisite child who was the delight of his old age.

Even Sainte-Beuve, who detested Talleyrand, admitted this: "If there was a good side to M. de Talleyrand at the end of his life, it was that niche of pure affection."

He wrote charming little letters to Pauline about things sure to please a child. Summers were always sad for him when she was sent away to the seashore:

> I am anxious to see you, but even more anxious to know that you are well, and if a few more dips in the sea will do you good, then take them. Anyway, that is Mimi's decision. When you come back to Paris, I will take you to see the king of Siam's elephant. He performs exercises with remarkable skill. His great size does not prevent him from being agile. You know that when an actor pleases us we call him back after the play to applaud him. At the present time he is called back after each performance and comes to the front of the stage where he thanks everyone and says polite things with his trunk. I am sure he will amuse you. Good-bye, dear child; I embrace you and love you with all my heart.

He worried another time because "the angel of the house" was about to visit the dentist: "I have thought a great deal about your visit to the dentist lest my dear Ninette suffer. I only hope it is not a visit that calls for another one soon again. Take courage. I have little enough of it to give you. . . ." He told her that he had seen the king the day after a young radical tried to shoot him. When he went to the Tuileries, he said, he heard that the queen had faced the crisis very bravely: "She removed from the king's hair the wad from the firearm with which they tried to assassinate him as he stood at her side. What a situation! . . . Everything I write you is sad. Dear child, I should like so much to be with you. . . ."

The attempted assassination delayed the inauguration of the newly completed Arc de Triomphe. He wrote to Pauline: "The Arc de Triomphe is superb; it is 152 feet high, 138 wide, and 68 feet around. . . . " Talleyrand was always fond of figures.

He planned Pauline's education very carefully, and like a true son of Voltaire, did just as Voltaire had done with his adopted daughters: made sure that she received proper religious training. Talleyrand sent Pauline to her confessor, abbé Dupanloup, in his own carriage. Madame de Dino wrote: "In the end he came to pride himself on Pauline's piety and was flattered that, under his guidance, she too had received a religious upbringing."

In December, 1835, Pauline turned fifteen and began attending balls. Talleyrand advised her mother to pay close attention to the modesty of the young girl's attire: "When what you display is attractive, then it is immodest; when what you display is ugly, it is hopelessly ugly."

Sometimes he set out with Pauline to explore the Paris of yesterday, the districts then out of fashion and forgotten except by him. Would he still be able to pick out his nurse's humble cottage, or the deserted field in which his uncle had found him looking like just another ragged neighborhood urchin, he who was now one of Europe's most illustrious men, among the noblest and richest in France? With Pauline he would relive this ancient history. They would stop in front of the Sorbonne, facing the Lycée Saint-Louis where the old Collège d'Harcourt once stood, his preparatory school where he had been happy. They went to Saint-Sulpice, and on the rue Garancière he showed Pauline the windows of the house where he was born. In the rue Férou, onto which the window of his seminarian's cell looked out, did he imagine the ghost of the first Dorothée? One evening they entered the church; he stood very still for some time. Pauline began to shiver; she snuggled up to him and was afraid. He told her: "This is the place where I was baptized." That simple sentence transfixed Pauline.

He talked to her about his uncle the archbishop, which in turn led to the subject of Monseigneur de Quélen: "I think of Monseigneur de Quélen as a legacy of my uncle the cardinal; he loves us, he loves our name and everything associated with the cardinal. We must always treat him as our kinsman."

He cultivated in her the same respect for family ties which meant so much to him, ties which, in this case, happened to be religious as well. The things he told Pauline filtered back to abbé Dupanloup and thence to the archdiocese.

They returned to Valençay and, in the autumn, to Rochecotte where, among others, Balzac visited them. In one of his novels he speaks of "a certain prince crippled in one foot, whom I consider a political genius and whose name will live on in history." Balzac delved deeper in this comment of Vautrin's: "A man who boasts of never changing his opinions is a man who commits himself forever to walk a straight line, a fool trusting in infallibility. . . ." Balzac went on: "There are no principles, there are only events; there are no laws, there are only circumstances. . . . The superior man espouses events in order to direct them. . . . No man is expected to be wiser than a whole nation." Especially, he might have added, if that nation is at once the most inconstant and the most hostile to inconstancy.

The words touched Talleyrand in just the right spot. The duchess threw open the doors of Rochecotte to *Père Goriot*'s creator. In a letter dated December 13, 1836, Balzac wrote to Madame Hanska about the memorable visit. Dorothée did not care for this great hulk of a man, scarcely her type, but Talleyrand found him enchanting and invited him to Valençay. "If he lives, I shall go," Balzac wrote. "I still have Wellington and Pozzo di Borgo to see before my collection of antiques is complete." The meeting left him with a vivid memory of the prince's fine, deep, cultured voice and "two or three spurts of prodigious ideas." He had eyes and ears only for Talleyrand, which may explain why Dorothée never took to him.

Fatigue caused Talleyrand to sever one more strand of public activity in Valençay. He resigned as councilor general of the district. In 1834 he had made a will. Now he made a new one, the opening sentence of which is highly significant: "I declare first and foremost that I die in the Catholic, apostolic, and Roman faith." Retracing the events of his life, he asserted that he had married in the belief that he was free to do so. A brief outline of his political career allowed him to present a highly simplified, flattering picture of his conduct. "My position [after resigning his bishopric] barred me from seeking my own path. I walked alone because I did not want my career to depend on any party." It was true. He had always been independent. He never looked to any political faction for support; none sponsored, but all assailed him.

"I thought about it for a long time and came to the conclusion that I would serve France in whatever situations France happened to be; she needed help in all of them. And I do not reproach myself for having served every government from the Directory until the present one."

Sheer logic, which Balzac had no trouble understanding. Of the governments he had served, Talleyrand went on to say: "I did not abandon a single one until it abandoned itself." Never, he stressed, had he allowed his own or any party's interests to compete with "the real interests of France, which, in my opinion, are never in conflict with the real interests of Europe." That consistent position of his is still espoused by knowledgeable Europeans, and perhaps deserves wider credence.

After a host of generalities, one is rather surprised to encounter a lengthy expression of gratitude to Napoleon. Recalling complacently that he had made a fortune under the emperor, Talleyrand urged his heirs never to forget it. "To my last hour, I shall not forget that he was my benefactor and that the fortune I leave my nephews comes to me in great part from him. My nephews ought to remember this as well as teach it to their children and their children's children, with the memory of it stretching from generation to generation, so that if ever a person named Bonaparte should find himself in need of aid and comfort, he shall receive from my direct heirs or their descendants every assistance they are able to give."

Why this flood of gratitude? Was it sincere? What was behind it? Talleyrand hoped that when he died no one would start poking around after the sources of his "immense fortune." In the course of our hero's career, we have come across several secret sources of income. Others remain secret, though we know they existed. He had his own underground system for bringing in the "sugarplums" from faraway places. However, it has been possible to estimate his total receipts from Napoleon. The emperor was generous indeed, but not generous enough, as we have seen, to satisfy the luxurious tastes of his minister. Apart from Valençay and his house on the rue Saint-Florentin, in 1814 Talleyrand had spent nearly everything Napoleon had provided. So the fortune he built after 1814 remained unaccounted for, the fortune involved in his will of 1836. To explain the inexplicable, he decided that it would be both touching and astute solemnly to attribute all his wealth to Napoleon's bounty.

As he nears the end of his life, we may well ask what was Talleyrand's attitude toward money. The rich inheritance he left Dorothée, his nephews, and Pauline was only a shadow of what he had spent during his lifetime. Gambling swallowed a good deal of it. And the rest? The rest was spent. Not squandered. Our prince felt that lavish expenses had a purpose and everything a price. His generosity and his sumptuous style of living were great, even grandiose at times, but never excessive. His household and entertaining expenses were carefully tailored to express his station in life, his high birth, and his personal aims: "Opulence," said Lamartine, "for Monsieur de Talleyrand, was a policy as much as a style of life." In that respect he differed from his nephew Edmond, duke of Dino, a hopeless wastrel who squandered his money aimlessly. In London, Edmond was nearly imprisoned for debt; the duc de Laval paid his creditors. Once back in Paris, Edmond proceeded to run up more debts. Talleyrand intervened to prevent his nephews from throwing their money away to pay their father's debts. Edmond went to prison. On his release, he settled in Florence with a yearly allowance of 40,000 francs from his wife. Talleyrand was interested in building the family fortune, not in subsidizing a nephew bent on wrecking it. Still, he must have spent ten times more than Edmond. But in a different way. We get a glimpse of the precise, orderly routine of the Talleyrand household from a letter he wrote from Valençay to his steward on the rue Saint-

Florentin where his niece Charlotte, Baroness Alexandre de Talleyrand, and her daughter Marie Thérèse were planning to spend a few days:

> My dear Couslier,
>
> Charlotte and her daughter will be in Paris on November 30 or December 1 and will occupy the same apartment they occupied last spring, nothing more. . . . Charlotte's apartment should be thoroughly cleaned and provided with sheets, towels, dusters, candelabra, candlesticks, and andirons. That is all you have to supply. Silver candelabra and candlesticks will do. Logs and candles are her concern. Simply say, if you are questioned, that you never provide such items, very politely and without further discussion. If she is hiring horses, the driver is not to be lodged; the horses should go back every evening.

For all his nonchalance and generosity, this great nobleman condemned inattention as a mark of vulgarity.

Enough about money. The conclusion of his will dealt with more personal matters. He left the manuscript of his *Memoirs* to Bacourt, with instructions not to publish it for thirty years after his death. In fact, the *Memoirs* did not appear for fifty years, in 1888. To his niece he addressed this touching farewell: "I beg Madame de Dino to accept my heartfelt gratitude for the happiness she has given me, and which I acknowledge as wholly due to her, for the past twenty-five years. . . ."

He wrote these thoughts on February 2, 1837, his birthday:

> Eighty-three years gone by! I am not altogether satisfied when I think back over the record of so many years. . . . What useless agitation! What fruitless efforts! tiresome complications! overblown emotions! wasted energies! squandered talents! . . . Leading to what? To moral and physical weariness, to disillusionment in the future and intense loathing for the past. Plenty of people have a talent or failing for never taking stock of themselves. I have just the opposite misfortune or distinction; it increases with the solemnity of advancing age. . . .[1]

Despite a vague, oppressive listlessness, he attended the wedding of the duc d'Orléans and the princess of Mecklenburg at Fontainebleau on May 30, 1837. Louis-Philippe assigned Madame de Maintenon's apartment to prince de Talleyrand. Cheered by the pomp and pageantry, the old man appeared to survive the exhausting ceremonies in good spirits. "Fontainebleau was enjoyable enough not to be too tiring," he wrote to Montrond several days later. Instead of following the king and court to Versailles for the inauguration of Louis-Philippe's new museum, Talleyrand returned to Valençay to receive the archbishop of Bourges on his confirmation tour. A great dinner honoring Monseigneur de Villèle, the prefect, curés, and notables of the district, followed by a village feast, were the climax of the day. These festivities gave him pleasure; he lavished his bounty, receiving touching tokens of affection and respect. With death approaching, these warm feelings and Pauline's love meant everything to him.

He left Valençay in the autumn of 1837, saying: "It is so excessively and extraordinarily distressing to tear myself away from Valençay this time that it strikes me as an omen." His instinct was uncanny; it was his last farewell to Valençay.

The Road to Heaven Also Has Its Meanders

He had only a few months to live. As with every other undertaking of his, he left on that space of time the imprint of his impeccable taste and astounding mastery of men and affairs. He approached death as serenely as the events which life had dealt him. He contracted with death as with a peer to whom he must surrender, claiming the right to dictate the terms and rites of surrender. If certain incidents have cast doubt upon the nobility of his spirit, all such doubt vanishes in his final hours. Talleyrand bargained as an equal with eternity.

His serene courage, his sublime indifference to danger, to calumny, to failure, was not a mask; it was a basic element of his character. At the end he was again Talleyrand standing up to Napoleon's threats and invectives.

Madame de Broglie, watching and waiting for him to yield his sinful soul to eternal torment, produced a witty remark probably not conceived in charity. To a raving admirer of the prince's inimitable savoir-vivre, Madame de Staël's daughter replied: "What he needs now is to know how to die."

Let us retrace the last four months of his life, a gently curving path along which, in recent years, his star had been drawing closer to the Catholic church. He had retained a number of long-standing ties with members of the clergy, ties of courtesy and deference, rather formal, but nonetheless sturdy ties. His niece often reminded him of his ambiguous position with regard to the church. Though Madame de Talleyrand's death had made his position simpler, it was still awkward.

He might be deeply moved by "the touching piety of young girls," but he was at heart an apostle of Voltaire. Pasquier describes having heard him declare the following publicly: " 'I maintain,' said M. de Talleyrand in an impressive burst of vigor, 'I maintain that if Ferney had not been awarded to France, I would never have signed the Treaty of Vienna.' " [1] So spoke, on the brink of death, a man condemned by so many as the arch-betrayer, just as we in our times brand as "traitors" the advocates of unpopular ideas.

His eighty-fourth birthday found him in bed, recovering from a fall he had taken on his way from a dinner given by Lord Grenville at the English embassy. He talked to the duchess about his past life. His offenses against the church, he assured her, had not been willful, nor had he ever adopted a heretical posture. He had simply acted heedlessly. Both of them felt that this improved his position.

He attended Mass regularly, read the *Imitation of Christ* and advised friends to do likewise. One day Dorothée asked him how he felt watching a priest, like himself, officiate at the altar. He gave the impression of being firmly convinced that the church had absolved him of all his vows. He replied to her that he listened the same way everyone else did, and that having been secularized made him just another worshipper. Dorothée conveyed all such remarks to Monseigneur de Quélen.

He experienced recurrent bouts of almost childlike piety, especially for the Virgin. Madame de Dino recounted that one day he asked which was her favorite prayer; The Lord's Prayer, she told him. " 'Say the Salve Regina too,' he counseled. 'It will comfort you. Come sit down and I will teach it to you, for I know it by heart. I will teach you the Latin and explain what it means.' " Dorothée listened as her uncle, adopting his priestlike solemnity, began to recite in a firm, mellow voice the words of hope, pausing to explain as he went along. " 'Do you know anything so sweet, so comforting? *Salve regina, mater misericordia*: they are rapturous words. *Vita, dulcedo et spes nostra, salve*: our life, our joy, our hope. Learn them and say them often, they will help you.' Whereupon he made me repeat them several times in his presence to engrave them in my memory. Today I know them by heart, yet I never read them in any book. He alone taught them to me." [2]

Humble parish priests and nuns in their cloisters sent word to the old man that they prayed for him every day. He kept a portfolio at his side containing these touching messages invoking God. "Good souls do not despair of me," he said. "Does this not make me better than people think?"

None of these private ruminations crept into his public life. Yet Monseigneur de Quélen watched for them day and night. The saintly man may not always have gone about his task in the most adroit fashion

—sometimes he pressed too hard—but for the moment, his caution outweighed his virtue and constituted his strongest trump. Talleyrand revered him but kept him at arm's length: "Yes, yes," he would say impatiently when someone sang the archbishop's praises, "I know he would like to salvage my soul and present it to the cardinal." [3]

Madame de Dino began to fret when her uncle seemed to be making little progress along the Heavenward path. She wondered what the official attitude would be toward a former bishop who died unreconciled to the church. Monseigneur de Quélen wrote to Rome to find out, and was informed that if the dying man accepted the sacraments, he would not be refused a Christian burial, provided that he made proper atonement. This implied repentance and a public retraction, for the ex-bishop of Autun had generated a scandal known the world over.

Monseigneur de Quélen drafted a retraction and gave it to Dorothée. The curate of the Madeleine was notified that he might administer the last sacraments to the prince and bury him if the dying man first signed the retraction. Everything was in order. The one essential ingredient was missing: Talleyrand's signature.

Negotiations thus opened between the two litigants, God and Talleyrand. The prince had not rejected Paradise; he had not accepted it. On the sidelines, many people, including Adolphe Thiers, chuckled to think of old Talleyrand cajoling the archbishop with pious words and then putting one over on him in the end. Talleyrand said nothing. He was determined to choose the hour and the terms of his surrender, and not to pay too high a price for it. Actually, he had made a decision long before. During a talk with Metternich in 1825, when the Austrian had reminded him that he ought to wind up his lifetime doing credit to his career and his family, Talleyrand assured him that he had already thought about it and would give no one cause for embarrassment.

Through Pauline, he took the decisive step of becoming acquainted with abbé Dupanloup. The duchess and Pauline had often painted glowing descriptions of this priest, then superior of the little seminary of Saint-Nicolas-du-Chardonnet. Talleyrand expressed a desire to meet him. Madame de Dino invited the abbé to dinner on February 6, 1838. The abbé found himself in a very awkward situation, having been weaned on the diabolical image of the prince fostered by the Congregation. The old man's career, his reputation, the way he made his fortune all combined to make the abbé shy away from him. He declined the invitation. Talleyrand was surprised: "I had heard that the abbé Dupanloup was a man of wit; if that were true, he would have come. He would have realized the importance of entering our house."

Dorothée had an idea. She paid a visit to the archbishop, after which Monseigneur de Quélen, deploring the incident, delivered a stern lecture to abbé Dupanloup. An opportunity had been lost; would there be another one? They underestimated the prince, who had his own plans. Abbé Dupanloup received a second dinner invitation in Talleyrand's own hand. He hastened to accept; the situation changed completely, with Talleyrand calling the tune.

Dupanloup was thirty-six, an ardent believer, decisive, and outspoken. The prince liked him. In the course of the evening, the abbé's doubts about his host vanished one by one. Talleyrand's compelling fascination never failed to amaze newcomers. The abbé was converted to Talleyrand sooner than Talleyrand to the idea of a retraction. Abbé Dupanloup, who left a scrupulously detailed account of all his efforts, conversations, and correspondence with the rue Saint-Florentin during this period, tells us: "The prince received me most cordially." He sat enthroned in an enormous armchair, "whence he dominated so completely yet so courteously everyone around him, with his lofty gaze, his brief, rare, witty, and strongly accented syllables: I can imagine no king more supreme in his own house than M. de Talleyrand in his salon."

His authoritative manner was too natural to be trying. The prince guided the conversation, invariably onto religious subjects in order to give the abbé a chance to express his ideas. After dinner, the prince reminisced about Saint-Sulpice, his teachers, and Pope Pius VII, to whom he attributed this comment: "Ah, yes, Monsieur de Talleyrand! May God keep his soul; still, I am very fond of him."

The abbé confessed to having succumbed to the spell: "I was, I admit, staggered, stupefied, nearly swept away! As I left, I could not help thinking that surely it was one of the most edifying conversations one could expect to find anywhere in Paris today. . . ." He must have been thinking, too, that except for his pectoral cross, the bishop of Autun was present indeed.

It was a revelation and a burden on the conscience of this highly intelligent and scrupulous priest. He had discovered a Talleyrand unknown to the world. A while ago, he had rejected him just as he had been taught to do. Certain facets of the prince's extraordinary personality impressed him. Here was a shining example not only of benevolent nobility, but also of "the respect, the attentiveness, the tenderness, I might almost call it the cult of family and friends" which sheltered Talleyrand "from the storm of outrageous abuse leveled at his public self."

Dupanloup realized that the prince endured abuse "with utter tranquility," knowing that a private refuge of affection, respect, and tenderness was his to fall back on. "Because one thing I did not know, and people generally ignore, is that prince de Talleyrand was revered and cherished by everyone he met. And as this reverence and deep affection persisted throughout his quasi-secular life, it must mean, I told myself, that people who never had a good word to say about him were somewhat mistaken, having not grasped the whole picture." [4]

That is one of the most interesting revelations of Talleyrand's last days. Will his critics persist in calling him heartless? Was he not endowed with the capacity to cultivate lifelong friendships? This called for extreme thoughtfulness and sensitivity to the personalities of his friends, qualities far superior to the sentimentalism prevalent in his day. Talleyrand himself summed up the evening's success: "I like your abbé; he has breeding."

Glowing with admiration—and with hope—abbé Dupanloup felt sure that he had salvaged a soul.

The prince thought it would be fitting for him to bid farewell to the public and the capital before leaving them forever. He had been a member of the Institut's Academy of Arts and Science since the Directory, at which time his "Memorandum on the Usefulness of Colonies" had earned him considerable acclaim. Forty years later, in 1838, his farewell appearance brought even greater applause. How well-contrived his life had been! Returning from emigration, he had made his political comeback on the stage of the Institut. Now he was about to take his exit from the same stage. His final offering to that august body was a eulogy of Count Reinhardt, a native of Württemberg who became French and a professional diplomat. Talleyrand had seen a great deal of him, respected him, and made him work very hard. Reinhardt had just died at the close of an honorable career. Though the occasion was not a brilliant one, it offered the speaker a priceless opportunity to put Talleyrand on show for the last time.

Family and friends tried to discourage him from making this effort. The doctor warned that he would not answer for the consequences. "Who asks you to answer for them?" the prince said to him. "It is my farewell address to the public. Nothing will keep me from making it."

A great crowd jammed the Institut on Saturday, March 3, 1838, eager to hear the eulogy of an obscure public official delivered by Europe's most illustrious citizen, the century's most impressive political personality after Napoleon.

Chateaubriand commented maliciously that the prince went "to perform a feat of strength" and to "deliver before the Institut the eulogy for a pair of German jaws for which he didn't care a rap. Despite the surfeit of spectacles to which we are treated, people lined up to see the great man go by."

A vast and select audience. The greatest academicians of the day were there: Tocqueville, Victor Cousin, Mignet, and Guizot, as well as the prince's good friends Royer-Collard, Pasquier, Thiers, Noailles, Barante, Molé . . . His entrance was regal, the painful limp simply adding to the drama. Two servants in full livery helped him up the stairs. He wore a black redingote, his concession to current fashion; but his head, forever powdered and curled, emerged from the high cravat popularized by the "incroyables." As he approached the door opening into the hall, the usher cried out: "The prince!" The audience rose. For half an hour, and without spectacles, he delivered a eulogy of Count Reinhardt in a voice still firm and resounding. He had worked and reworked the speech carefully with the help of his niece.

In no time, the audience recognized more of Talleyrand than Reinhardt in his picture of an ideal diplomat. Reinhardt had served "under three reigns," all of which, as he casually put it, were "very different." The audience held its breath. Recalling that Reinhardt had been a theology student—what a coincidence—he went on to recommend the seminary as an excellent apprenticeship for diplomacy. His ideal combination of statesman and theologian had all the earmarks of a self-portrait. Each brushstroke touched in a precise and perceptive detail, culminating in a final exaltation of "the religion of duty." It was a triumph. Expressionless, the prince acknowledged the president's thanks and left the hall on the arms of his two servants, plowing their way through throngs of admirers. He was leaving forever, he knew; that was the way he had planned it.

The press proved unusually kind. Everyone saw this academic rite as the prelude to the ultimate, painful one.

Never prone to indulgence, Sainte-Beuve has this to say in his *Nouveaux Lundis* about Talleyrand's address to the Institut: ". . . he outlined the triple ideal of a perfect foreign minister, a perfect administrator, a perfect consul general." One could identify "the pen of M. de Talleyrand when he praised or chastised himself."

On the rue Saint-Florentin, family and friends were content. The withdrawal was going well.

The speech was published; he sent copies to Monseigneur de Quélen and abbé Dupanloup. The copy for dear Bacourt contained a note saying that he was ill, had a blister on his arm and was drowning in perspiration.

The abbé came to thank him personally for the speech. When asked if he would receive him, Talleyrand replied: "I shall be delighted." Pauline brought her confessor to her uncle's bedside and left them alone together. The prince told the priest that he had mentioned "the religion of duty" with him in mind. He went on to speak of his ailments and the treatments he was taking; foot baths in beef broth, leg baths in alcohol. But nothing helped. He joked about the hypochondriacs people always talk about, and the others no one talked about whose good health is only imaginary and who are far worse off. Not a word about retraction. Pauline and her mother prayed earnestly that he would make his peace with the church.

On March 17 he felt so weak that he asked to see his will. Once again he designated Madame de Dino as his residuary legatee to take charge of his property and papers and to dispose of them according to instructions he had given her. He left a diamond valued at 50,000 francs to Edmond de Bacourt as a reminder to publish his *Memoirs*. Each of his servants was to receive a pension, and in the case of an old retainer who liked his drink, the pension was to increase with any rise in the cost of wine.

Abbé Dupanloup sent the prince his copy of Fénelon's *Le Christianisme présenté aux hommes du monde*. Was it not his attempt to revive their spiritual discussions? The prince enjoyed the book and asked the priest to come dine with him again soon. Talleyrand lingered over Fénelon and the letter accompanying it, which touched him. He called his niece and asked her to read it aloud. Suddenly, for the first time, he broached the subject: "Do you think abbé Dupanloup would come if I were gravely ill?" Dorothée said that she was sure he would. He then confessed that he had been thinking about making his peace with Rome. Since when? she asked him. Since the archbishop of Bourges's visit to Valençay, he told her, adding that he could not understand why the archbishop had not offered to help. He did not dare, Dorothée pointed out. Talleyrand told her that he was prepared to do something, but wanted to know what Rome expected of him. She said that she had a letter of retraction on hand. He paused to meditate. Then the negotiations began in earnest. He was prepared to acknowledge his errors with regard to the oath of the Clergy to the Civil Constitution and also the consecration of constitutional bishops, whom he had once called "those queer fish." But when it came to his marriage, he insisted: "I was free! I was free!" Madame de Dino referred to the interpretation given in the pontifical bull, which Monseigneur d'Autun had reinterpreted in his own fashion and not Rome's. Knowing that perfectly well, he persisted in quibbling. Finally, he surrendered on all fronts, but expressed the fear

that gossip would attribute his submission to senility. "I do not want anyone saying that I am in my dotage. I must do what I have to do in the
same month as my speech to the Academy."

Surely he feared God less than the scandal of a civil funeral, another point on which he and Voltaire agreed.

He wrote to abbé Dupanloup saying that he was sending him a
fine edition of the *Imitation of Christ,* and invited him to dinner again.
The abbé came a few days after Easter. They spoke of Holy Week, but
nothing positive transpired.

On March 28, Archambaud died. His title, duc de Talleyrand,
passed to Dorothée's husband Edmond, and she became the duchess.
His brother's death was a great shock to Talleyrand. "Another warning,"
he observed. Besides, Archambaud had died too suddenly to receive the
last sacraments. Abbé Dupanloup came by to offer his condolences. They
talked at length. Talleyrand mentioned his mother and also Monseigneur
de Quélen, who, since the sacking of his palace in 1831, had been reduced to living rather awkwardly. Talleyrand cited Montlosier's comment before the Constituent Assembly: "A wooden cross is what saved
the world."

The conversation had been very pleasant and breezy. Abbé Dupanloup came away with a sense of progress, but the race was still not won.

In April, the prince felt stronger and began planning some travels.
He would go to Pont-de-Sains on May 1 and spend the summer there;
then to Nice on September 1; in the spring he would return to Valençay.

Still, he had not definitely abandoned the idea of a retraction. One
day when his niece was about to leave for a visit to Monseigneur de
Quélen, he gave her a letter to the archbishop—or at least a draft of one.
"Here, this will make you welcome where you are going. Let me know
what the archbishop has to say about it."

On her return, Dorothée told him that Monseigneur de Quélen had
found the letter very moving but felt it ought to be shorter and worded
more formally. This seemed to offend her uncle, but he said nothing,
except to remind her that the retraction must be dated the same week as
his appearance before the Institut: "I will not have people say that I was
in my second childhood."

Talleyrand Negotiates His Last Great Treaty and Departs

Who would say such a thing? Didn't he ride out in his carriage and
exercise his wit after dinner? On May 10, he walked in the parc Monceau enjoying the sunshine. But on the twelfth, after dining with

Alexandre de Talleyrand, Noailles, Princess Lieven, and Montrond, he began to tremble violently, although there were fires in the grate. They took him to his bedroom. He felt faint, drank some tea, then seemed as well as ever. He shared in the conversation as if nothing had happened; they were discussing the newly published *Chute d'un ange*, whose author, Lamartine, had dined with the prince the day before.

It was a bad evening. Cruveilhier, his doctor, diagnosed an anthrax in the lumbar region. It was decided to operate. We can imagine the caliber of surgery practiced in those days. It was atrocious. Talleyrand endured the butchery with incredible forbearance. At one point, the pain was so severe that he turned to the surgeon and whispered with utmost courtesy: "Do you know, sir, that you are hurting me terribly."

Once the torture was ended, he gathered himself together and asked to be taken into the salon. He was returning to the stage; the show would go on. "The prince's face was altered; one could see that he had suffered greatly and was suffering still, but his voice was calm and soft, his mind clear and composed. . . ." He ordered tea served to the visitors. Bacourt, who knew him well, was nevertheless impressed by this astounding display of self-control, commenting: "M. de Talleyrand is a firm believer in the authority and power which moral actions can exert over physical nature."

This supremacy of mind and will over bodily suffering was another extraordinary quality of Talleyrand's.

Abbé Dupanloup came again the very next morning, May 15. The prince was glad to see him, though he had hardly slept the night before. The priest mentioned the retraction. Talleyrand replied that everything he wished to say was in his own letter and that anyone reading it would understand what he meant. The abbé repeated the archbishop's words: many people have a habit of reading whatever they wish into a text. A short, precise letter would rule out loose interpretations. When Talleyrand nodded his assent, the hopeful priest assumed that he was prepared to accept the archbishop's text, which he had with him. He handed it to the prince, noting that it respected the spirit of his own letter and even retained some of its expressions. He offered to read it aloud. "Give it to me; I shall read it myself." And the evasions began anew. The prince sat up painfully on the edge of the bed as he could not remain prone for long owing to the huge, agonizing abscess in his back. With his head resting on his hand, slowly and attentively he read the retraction framed by the archbishop. "Monsieur l'abbé," he announced, "I am very satisfied with this document." Having anxiously awaited the verdict, the priest could now breathe again. Thinking the matter settled, he was aghast to

hear the prince of diplomats add: "Would you mind leaving this document with me? I would like to read it through again."

The disheartened priest did as he was asked. Actually, the negotiations had merely entered a new stage. Now, with utter equanimity, they
talked about suffering, death, and divine absolution. The abbé went
away without a signature or any assurance of getting one.

During the night of the fifteenth, the prince grew worse. Past midnight he suffered a heart attack. On consulting the doctor, he was told
that it was the hour for a good Christian to put his affairs in order. As if
by magic, the abbé appeared. Dorothée and her family waited anxiously
in the wings; if her uncle died unreconciled to the church, it would be a
terrible scandal for the whole family. The prince was at death's door. He
must sign. They had one last trump and decided to use it: Pauline. She
alone could make him see that he must not falter. The duchess prevailed
on her daughter, now eighteen, to approach the dying man. Out of piety
and affection for the old man, who loved her dearly, Pauline agreed.
After obtaining abbé Dupanloup's blessing, she went to her great-uncle's
bedside. The magnitude and gravity of her task were not lost upon her.
She knew what she was doing and that it was the right thing. She spoke
privately to the prince. Then the abbé went to him but could not get
him to sign. Talleyrand called for Dorothée and asked her to read aloud
the archbishop's retraction. He repeated clearly several times that he
wished to die in the arms of the church: "I want it . . . I want it . . ."
Yes, he would sign, but later. Later? There would be no later. "Now,
Prince, while your hand can still do it." It was useless. They watched
him grow weaker every hour; his mind remained clear, but at any
moment he might slip from them. If that happened, they would have to
bury him secretly. With perfect composure, he repeated to them what he
used to say in the foreign ministry when putting off sending an urgent
dispatch: "Rest easy, I shan't be long."

Bets were on in the capital. Would he sign or wouldn't he? The
main floor of the rue Saint-Florentin was host to a permanent invasion
of visitors debating the prospects of sin *versus* redemption, calculating
the curability of a festering abscess *versus* the stagnancy of absolution.
Talking and joking, they managed to enjoy themselves. If Dupanloup
seemed to have carried the field, the Voltairean faction retreated behind
a volley of jeers aimed at the still powerful Congregation and the hypocrisy it fostered. If Dupanloup went home empty-handed, Voltaire
gloated; the prince was playing one last trick on God and the priestly
crew. In short, until the very end, Talleyrand remained the object of
controversy he had always been.

But why all the quibbling and evasions on his part? In his condition, why not sign the retraction, having decided to do so long ago? The best answer comes from Montrond, friend of so many years, whose thinking defied political or religious bias. Of all the people hovering over the dying man, Montrond knew him best and saw his behavior as consistent to the end. The prince simply was unwilling to be hurried in this or any other situation. He intended his death to unfold at a proper, decorous pace, in the lingering, sinuous rhythm prescribed at birth by his station in life and which marked the progress of his entire career. This rhythm would carry him to the end. The stately pace had a majesty all its own.

Absolution "had encountered obstacles worthy of Satan," Monseigneur de Quélen wrote. What were they? The resolute character of Talleyrand, determined to do as he pleased—take it or leave it. The church would have to accept what he chose to offer. His delaying tactics served to ensure that he would not survive the retraction. How ridiculous he would have looked playing the part of a penitent old man! Such hypocrisy was too bourgeois for words. No, he must obtain absolution and die, leaving the priests to claim only his body. He acted like an ambassador, "contending with God for his soul," as Duff Cooper puts it. He treated his conversion like an international agreement, between God on the one side, with His deputies the archbishop and Dupanloup; and the prince on the other, representing not just a soul to be saved but an entire clan as well, for the social prestige and fortune of the Périgords were at stake. That was still another complex affair, for the soul of an apostate bishop was but one element of an issue which history and ambition had ballooned into a tangled tale of impiety, revolutions, schism, wars, treaties, and money—huge amounts of money. All these matters had prompted Quélen's missives. Perhaps God, too, was somewhere in the picture.

"Two motives guided him: to avert the scandal of a funeral without religion's last rites, and to delay his conversion until the last minute in order to escape society's scorn." Montrond was not mistaken. No matter what he did, Talleyrand inevitably found himself the center of controversy.

The last stir he caused, involving a display of almost superhuman self-discipline which seemed to give him an edge over death, was to set the hour of his own death.

Abbé Dupanloup did not stir from the dying man's bedchamber on Wednesday, May 17, 1838. At eight in the evening, he made a fresh attempt: "Would you like to sign your declaration?" he asked him, in between references to the good wishes and prayers of Monseigneur de

Quélen, now beside himself with impatience. "Thank the archbishop for me and tell him that everything will be done," the undaunted old prince answered. He was not yet ready to sign.

Pauline went in a second time. She implored him: "But when will it be, good uncle?" Entreating him thus, she finally obtained this simple, dramatic reply: "Tomorrow morning between five and six." Tomorrow seemed so improbable that she repeated incredulously: "Tomorrow?"

"Yes, tomorrow, between five and six."

Eager to rush off and inform the archbishop, Dupanloup asked: "May I now convey this hope, Prince?"

Talleyrand corrected him impatiently: "Don't call it hope, call it certainty. It is a positive fact." The archbishop and death had best comply.

The prince spent such a bad night that by eleven, death seemed bent on defying him. A false alarm, as it turned out, but once more Pauline approached the dying man's bedside to implore him to sign two documents, the retraction and a declaration of submission to papal authority. Gently but firmly, he sent her away: "It is not yet six o'clock. I told you that I would sign tomorrow morning between five and six; I still promise to do it."

He was in agony, his strength waning, yet he dominated his tortured flesh, his pain, and the needs of those dependent on him. During the night, in a conversation with Bacourt, he spoke not of himself but of Pauline's piety and of the coldness of Protestant doctrine.

At four in the morning, abbé Dupanloup was at his side as well as the duchess and Pauline. One by one the witnesses designated by the archbishop arrived. "It would have been difficult to choose men of greater integrity and authority," Dupanloup observed. Each presided like a deity over his own specialty: the prince de Poix stood for the aristocracy; Saint-Aulaire and Barante, ambassadors to Vienna and St. Petersburg respectively, for diplomacy; Royer-Collard for virtue; and Molé, president of the council, for politics.

From then on, the prince's bedchamber became the theater of Death—the century's most theatrical death. The five grim witnesses entered with solemn step, their imposing presence lending depth and substance to the funereal act about to envelop them, the echoes of which they would transmit directly or indirectly to all levels of society and even beyond the borders of France. Hélie, senior valet of the household, was also present. Talleyrand had insisted on it. Hélie, too, would bear witness.

Only Balzac could convey, in the somber mood of the period, those five statues of social power. The witnesses were barely visible behind a tapestry partly covering the doorway of a small room adjoining the dying man's bedchamber. Unseen, they watched and listened, charting the progress of death and of the negotiations. They were not to appear before the satrap until that fatal moment when, with a nod of his head, a flourish of his pen, and a sigh, he would say Yes to God. Their only function was to certify the transaction.

For two hours the faithful witnesses stood waiting, immobile, watching for a sign from the abbé.

Never was death treated so arrogantly, forced, as it was, to come to terms with its victim. The bedchamber, sumptuous as a king's, was also a torture chamber. Ropes and pulleys attached to the ceiling served to raise and turn the anguished body propped up on cushions in order to isolate the hideous, gaping sore, like a crater, reaching from his back straight through to his intestines.

Surmounting those horrors was the head, his unblemished, pow-dered, immutable, regal head. He opened his eyes and asked the time. A well-meaning voice replied: "It is six o'clock." It was not even five. Abbé Dupanloup intervened; any hint of deceit would constitute sac-rilege. "Prince," said the abbé, "it is not yet five." "Good," responded the dying man, with the calm assurance of someone who has no intention of advancing his schedule.

Suddenly, as if sprung from some stage manager's whimsy, an elf, a charming, gauzy little creature all in white, slipped into that cavern of pain and suffering, with the lavish gold fittings, the mahogany, the heavy, fringed velvet drapes so fashionable at the time, that cavern where five ominous men stood while a priest and praying women knelt at the foot of the monumental bed. It was Charlotte's daughter, Marie-Thérèse de Périgord. In her white satin dress and tulle veil, she came flitting into the midst of death, seeking the dying man's benediction before taking her first communion. She knelt as Talleyrand blessed her and murmured fond words. Then the little creature took flight to join the living. Talley-rand was touched by her visit: "There indeed are the two extremes of life: she is about to make her first communion . . . while I . . ."

Six o'clock at last. Pauline asked if he would like to have the papers. He nodded. He took the pen. Madame de Dino asked if he wished the two letters read to him one last time. "Yes, read them," he answered. The duchess read the retraction first:

Faced with ever increasing concerns, forced to assess dispassionately the consequences of a Revolution which swept everything in its path and has lasted for fifty years, I have come to the point, in extreme old age, and after long experience, of repudiating the excesses of the century to which I belonged, of condemning openly the grave errors which, in the course of those many years, disturbed and distressed the Catholic, apostolic, and Roman church and in which I had the misfortune to share.

If it is pleasing to my family's esteemed friend, the archbishop of Paris, who has assured me of the Holy Father's compassionate regard for me, to convey to His Holiness my respectful gratitude and the assurance of my complete submission to the doctrine and teachings of the church, to the decisions and judgments of the Holy See governing the ecclesiastical affairs of France, I trust that His Holiness will deign to accept them graciously.

Very general statements, as much political as religious. It would seem that to have summarized all that in a few sentences backed up by some specific facts would have been more satisfactory. Actually, he was getting off very lightly.

At the end, the tone grew more personal, yet repentance did not attach to anything specific. Sins and transgressions were all lumped together in one innocuous phrase, "the acts of my life":

"Granted dispensation later by the venerable Pius VII from the exercise of ecclesiastic duties, I sought occasions, in the course of my long political career, to render all services in my power to religion and to many honorable members of the Catholic clergy. Never have I ceased to look upon myself as a child of the church. I again deplore the acts of my life which have saddened her, and my last thoughts shall embrace her and her supreme leader." Having listened intently to every word, Talleyrand took the pen, dipped it in the inkwell and, with a steady hand, set his most official, treaty-maker's signature on the document: "Charles-Maurice, prince de Talleyrand."

He also asserted that the document did not say all the things he wished to say. The duchess assured him that they were contained in the second document addressed to the pontiff.

It repeated the same expressions of obedience, attachment, and affection for the Pope. It blamed extenuating circumstances—times of general disorder—for failures which he never defined. Finally, in one, brief, amazingly restrained phrase he mentioned for the first time, on the brink of death, how he had happened to enter the church: "The respect I owe to those who bore me does not prohibit me from saying that my entire youth was directed toward a profession for which I was wholly unsuited."

It would be hard to imagine a more benign allusion to the agony deep in his soul since the black days of his childhood. Now at last, on May 17, 1838, with all the loose ends securely tied, he ventured to acknowledge it. And like Racine, he condemned by omission. Besides, was his death not as tragic, as pageant-like, as ghastly as that of Phèdre or Athalie? The motionless splendor, the silence, the resolute mastery of suffering and death combined to make the prince a tragic figure, whose lofty indifference was a challenge to heroes and the authors of melodrama. In signing, he did not forget the matter of a date: "What is the date of my speech to the Academy?" he asked.

"March the third."

"Well then, date it the tenth so that it falls in the same week."

That was why the two letters signed on May 17 bore a different date.* They were taken at once to Monseigneur de Quélen, who dispatched them, like victory bulletins, to Rome.

About seven in the morning, Talleyrand began to sink rapidly. A little later he rallied. Around eight he felt better, and a stir was heard downstairs. The king was announced. Louis-Philippe and Madame Adélaïde had come to pay their respects to the dying man. "It grieves me, Prince, to see you suffering so." Despite such trite expressions, the king and his sister were visibly distressed. They knew whom they were losing. Talleyrand addressed the monarch with courtly deference: "Sire, you have come to witness the last moments of a dying man. The king has bestowed a great honor on this house by coming here today." Then, performing his duties as grand chamberlain for the last time, he observed the rule of court etiquette calling for the identification of all persons in the king's presence. He named everyone in the room, including Hélie. It was all part of the drama, part of his design for a death as ambitious as life. The king withdrew. Madame Adélaïde lingered a moment. Talleyrand said to her: "Madame must find it very chilly here." She pressed the dying man's hand. He assured her: "Indeed I do love you." She turned and went out.

After another lengthy relapse, he opened his eyes to find abbé Dupanloup standing at the bedside. He knew it was time to confess and repent. Not since 1789 had he made confession; fifty years. He tried to raise himself. With the aid of the ropes, they maneuvered him to the edge of the bed, and bolstered him with pillows, his legs dangling, already numb. All his strength was concentrated in his hands, which

---

* Gregory XVI kept the letters until his death. In 1842 he showed them to Pauline, then Madame de Castellane. Subsequently they disappeared.

clutched the abbé's in a viselike grip. The two were alone in the room. The abbé was barely able to free his right hand in order to grant absolution. The meek and penitent tone of the confession surprised the priest; it was far more convincing than the two documents.

They spoke of the archbishop, who had declared that he would give his life to save the prince's soul. "Tell him that he has better things to do with it," answered Talleyrand.

News of the prince's retraction had begun to spread. During confession and the royal visit, the house slowly filled with visitors. In the courtyard, on the stairs, in the salons, the mounting murmurs of society's élite seemed to signal an approaching revel. Now and then a burst of laughter escaped before someone could stifle it. A young duchess reclined on the sofa surrounded by gossiping dandies perched on pillows. When the grim witnesses emerged from the bedchamber, they were besieged by a chattering, curious crowd: What was in the documents? What had the dying man said? How did he look? In search of scandal, they were making it at will. A truly thrilling morning for privileged society.

After confession, the bedchamber suddenly filled. The abbé administered the last sacraments. It was then that the prince launched his final sally. When the priest was about to apply the unction, Talleyrand held out the knuckles of his clenched fists rather than the palms to receive it, saying: "Do not forget, Monsieur l'abbé, that I am a priest." Indeed, he had received the episcopal unction on his palms in 1789. Thus, by his own admission, he died a bishop; the church was right—a shining tribute from an apostate.

A chorus of over forty voices joined abbé Dupanloup in reciting the prayers for the dying. During the litanies of the saints, the names of Maurice and Charles caused the prince to open his eyes. Pauline, all but overcome with grief, stayed until the end. She wrote: "As his strength failed him, his poor head bobbed forward, then to the right, then to the left, for lack of support . . . , M. de Bacourt, abbé Dupanloup, and the valet took turns holding him up, and thus he breathed his last." At 3:35 in the afternoon, he squeezed Bacourt's hand convulsively and died.

"The rest of our family were kneeling at our poor uncle's bedside, praying and weeping by turns. When the doctor declared him departed from us, we kissed a hand already grown cold."

He died publicly like a king.

The news went out with the horde of flies, hornets, and wasps swarming about the house, which emptied, in the twinkling of an eye, forever. The glorious days of the rue Saint-Florentin were ended.

TALLEYRAND

Did the Church Strike a Better Bargain Than Talleyrand?

The capital could talk of nothing else. The greatest wits of the day invented clever sayings about the prince's death. In legitimist circles, this one was all the rage: "After tricking everyone, in the end he managed to trick God as well." Surely an involuntary tribute to a new Prince of Darkness. In the same vein, Pozzo di Borgo had a livelier anecdote: on Talleyrand's arrival in Hell, Satan paid him the highest honors, yet hastened to point out: "Prince, you exceeded my instructions." In opposite circles, Adolphe Thiers, using the conversion as an excuse to absolve himself of any obligation to the man who had cultivated, promoted, and protected him, said this: "Prince de Talleyrand has spoiled his whole life by this sermon." He never offered condolences or showed his face again to Madame de Dino, to whom he owed so much.

The duchesse de Broglie was not convinced; it seemed like such an "odd" ending. She might have given him credit at least for his courage. But she wanted much more: Monsieur de Talleyrand should have dealt directly with God. "God must have spoken personally to his soul," she told Barante.

Alfred de Vigny related someone's remark after hearing of Talleyrand's death: "France simply has one less dishonest man."

Even the king's visit came under fire: Talleyrand was supposed to have told him: "I am suffering the tortures of the damned." To which the king replied: "Already?"

Other, more dignified voices, were heard. Royer-Collard, not one to compromise with virtue, said: "I have seen M. de Talleyrand ill, I have seen him dying, I have seen him dead; that great spectacle will long remain before my eyes. M. de Talleyrand died a Christian, having satisfied the church and received her sacraments. He was the last cedar of Lebanon, the last of a breed of cultivated, enlightened nobility." Talleyrand conveyed precisely that in his final hours.

The reaction of abbé Dupanloup, who was closest to the scene, turned out to be far briefer and kinder than any sentiments voiced by the faithful or the skeptics. After hearing Talleyrand's confession, he wrote: "God knows the secrets of the heart." Talleyrand's heart was not easy to read, and we are no more willing than was his confessor to venture an opinion as to the sincerity of his conversion.

All in all, we are better off remembering Madame de Girardin's verdict: "Monsieur de Talleyrand died like a man who knows how to live."

Victor Hugo also was inspired to turn out a bravura passage, beginning thus:

> On the rue Saint-Florentin is a palace and a drainpipe [the antithesis proved far more important than the subject; the trick—for it was an intellectual stunt—was to flush the palace down the drainpipe . . .]. The palace's last tenant probably never noticed that drainpipe.
>
> A strange, awesome, prominent personality, his name was Charles Maurice de Périgord; he was nobly born like Machiavelli, a priest like Gondi, a renegade like Fouché, witty like Voltaire, and lame like the Devil. . . .

The rhetorical exercise builds into a collision of historical names, with the page resounding like an empty barrel; all very amusing, with more noise than danger. The macabre ending is rather good-natured:

> Well, the day before yesterday, May 17, this man died. Doctors came and embalmed the body. In the Egyptian tradition, they removed the entrails from the abdomen and the brain from the skull. After that, having transformed the prince de Talleyrand into a mummy and nailed the mummy into a white satin casket, they went away, leaving the brain on the table, that brain. . . . After the doctors had gone, a valet entered and saw what they had left behind: "Well now, look what they forgot. What shall I do with it?" And recalling the drainpipe in the street, he went out and tossed the brain down the drain.

Victor Hugo thrilled his readers.

The worst is yet to come. While Talleyrand lay dying, Chateaubriand crouched on the rue du Bac distilling his venom, whetting his scalpel for the autopsy. Rarely has a writer been blinded by envy to the point of flinging himself savagely on a still-warm body. Of all Talleyrand's critics he alone offends, he alone wounds because he is at once the most cruel, the most unjust, and the most sensitive. He alone is both admirable and dangerous. He endows his hatred and his lies with the colors, the music, the magic of supreme genius, and with the aura of irresistible sincerity. Even today, despite overwhelming evidence of his falseheartedness, Chateaubriand retains his magic spell. To escape it, Talleyrand provides a key: "Whatever is exaggerated has no value." Chateaubriand betrays himself through exaggeration. His overactive malice stifles any capacity of his to experience the anguish of death. He had the audacity to write: "The crowd stood gaping at the funeral of this prince three-quarters rotted away, with a gangrenous aperture in his side, his head sunk onto his breast despite the sling supporting it. . . ."

Beneath the allusion to the repulsive suppuration rotting his enemy's flesh runs a tremor of sordid pleasure. Further along, we read this atrocious image: "Men infested with sores resemble the carcasses of prostitutes: they are so eaten away by ulcers as to be useless for dissection." Chateaubriand was outraged that Talleyrand finally had made his peace with the church; he would rather have seen him die like a dog. He spits on everything, even Pauline, in describing the dying prince "wrangling from minute to minute over his reconciliation with Heaven, his niece playing a well-rehearsed role supported by a deluded priest and a deceived young girl." He insinuates that Talleyrand did not sign the retraction. What about the witnesses? No matter, Chateaubriand provides the kind of testimony that would never stand up in a court of law. Talleyrand, he asserts, "had frightful lapses of memory." More accurately, he himself had an overworked imagination. "Death came searching for him in behalf of God." A hollow, pretentious notion. At the age of eighty-four, death had no need to look for Talleyrand, having already found him. And for a Christian like Chateaubriand, who else but God would dispatch death, even to someone aged twenty? After the claptrap and the lies, he resorts to invective: "Never did pride prove so abject, admiration so foolish, piety so gullible." If pride allowed Talleyrand to die a stoic—not to mention Christian—death, then we can only admire the strength it gave him to face adversity. Yet the proudest Christian of them all assures us that Talleyrand's pride was "abject"! It makes one laugh, knowing that Chateaubriand altered his passport for the sake of adding 3 centimeters not, alas, to his short stature, which remained the same, but to the written measurement of it. And Chateaubriand's grave, is that not a monument to pride?

What gave the author of *Le Génie du christianisme* the right to fling Talleyrand's carcass on the dungheap? Was Talleyrand any more corrupted by pride, envy, and lust than Chateaubriand, whose conduct had focused a good deal of publicity on those three capital sins? What entitled the little viscount to substitute his own for the Last Judgment? His utterances over the body of Talleyrand destroy any confidence one might have in the Christian sentiments of the author of *Les Martyrs*. Nevertheless, those pages from the *Mémoires d'outre-tombe*, which are neither Christian, nor human, nor accurate, are admirable enough to have endowed malice with unlimited credit.

And the church? What did the church think? The reaction was mixed. From Paris, word went out to the Vatican that it was best not to crow about it. The church had not struck as great a bargain as Monseigneur de Quélen and abbé Dupanloup liked to think. Talleyrand had made a stunning exit, having managed to gain a foothold (club at that) on the Heavenly path; but the other foot was not likely to follow. Anyway, as Duff Cooper says, he left with his papers in order, armed with "his credentials and his passport." He left, yes, but where was he headed?

His death generated a vague sense of uneasiness. To the average bourgeois, it was a scandal. It confused more hearts than it stirred. The prince's noble self-possession in the face of death did not arouse sympathy in a society sophisticated by romantic sensibility. Rather than superhuman, he was seen as inhuman. Self-discipline, restraint, and dignity had no meaning for "les enfants du siècle" of Joseph Prud'homme. Why hadn't he torn his hair, wept and moaned, cursed and implored Heaven —or Hell, for all it mattered, as the important thing was to be verbose, extravagant, convulsive, just plain romantic? If, on his deathbed, Talleyrand may not have wished to be judged by God, much less by his fellow men, surely he judged himself. When the surgeon dug up his back with a scalpel, extracting a basin of pus from the fatal abscess, Talleyrand felt neither resigned nor humbled nor even sorry for himself. He remained Talleyrand, comte de Périgord, peer of the Capetians. His death was cruel, indeed, but humility would have made it intolerable. Courage saved him. The Faubourg's senior members, unfamiliar with the new politics and customs but experts on good manners, said: "He died like a gentleman." They might have said, with a trace of pedantry, like a stoic. It was not a genuinely Christian death.

So they said in high places. Monseigneur de Quélen came under attack from Rome. Guileless, he thought he had performed a miracle, only to learn that he had allowed himself to be gulled. Heartbroken, the archbishop died five months after Talleyrand.

In reality, Talleyrand had negotiated with the church as with a tutelary power to which he felt bound by a kind of feudal obligation totally devoid of mysticism. He yielded at the last moment, without a murmur of humility or repentance, without imploring divine mercy. Behaving as he had in other situations, he might just as well have said: "I placed myself at the disposition of events."

Propriety was saved. That was more important than Heaven's demands.

The Last Parade

The prince's funeral took place on May 22 at eleven o'clock. Fittingly, his final appearance was a splendid, cheerful, and orderly pageant. Few tears; a sea of elegant finery. A monumental hearse displayed the Périgord coat of arms with its gold lions crowned and still romping about, its motto "Rien que Dieu" striking a somewhat ironic note at a funeral that attracted everyone but God. The procession stretched out endlessly: a great throng of clergy preceded the flower-strewn hearse drawn by six horses, their headbands decked with a single ostrich feather, their silver-edged caparisons reaching to the ground; the diplomatic corps; the Chamber of Peers; the Institut; six state coaches bearing the royal family; an infinity of black-draped carriages between two lines of soldiers presenting arms to the hearse and to the ducal crown borne on a velvet cushion. Everyone in full civil or military regalia, gold braid, feathers, brocades; a vast display of every conceivable and prestigious decoration, ribbon, badge of merit. D'Argout caught the mood of the occasion: "But for the casket," he observed, "one might have mistaken it for a wedding or a court ceremony." Talleyrand would have found that in perfect taste. The Requiem was celebrated in the Chapel of the Assumption, after which the casket was removed to the crypt pending transfer to Valençay where the prince had asked to be buried. An interminable line of mourners filed past the two nephews, the dukes of Valençay and Dino. Thus ended the festival.

Talleyrand waited patiently until September 2 when the vault at Valençay was ready to receive him. We ought to note, as Victor Hugo did, that the body was embalmed in the Egyptian manner.

Madame de Dino lost no time. On July 3, forty days after the funeral, she sold the house on the rue Saint-Florentin to baron James de Rothschild for 1,181,000 francs. The price was poor, she felt, but added: "At least he is a very solvent purchaser, who pays cash, which is a consideration." On July 9, without further ado, she sold her uncle's library; it was the fourth time his books were dispersed. This niece and residuary legatee had at least one thing in common with Voltaire's niece and residuary legatee: the manner in which each sold off her "good uncle's" legacy.

Madame de Dino's haste can be explained: she disliked Paris and was anxious to leave. It was evident to her that without the prince, she could expect only jealousy and vexation from society. The faubourg Saint-Germain had made this clear; as for the "philosophy clan," Adolphe Thiers already had offered a sample of his hostility.

On September 5 Talleyrand returned to Valençay. He did not journey alone; alongside his casket were those of his brother Archambaud and of his great-niece, dead at the age of three, Yolande de Périgord, Louis de Valençay's daughter. The three coffins traveled in the same munitions wagon which, the year before, had brought Queen Hortense's body back to France for burial. A singular personality, this Talleyrand, who took the air in a wheelchair belonging to Louis XVIII and went to his grave in the same conveyance as Queen Hortense (mother of his grandson, the duc de Morny).

The prince's death was a blow to the whole region. Valençay's inhabitants flocked to the château. Talleyrand was to be buried in the little chapel dedicated to Saint Maurice which he had built. Nowhere in the vast gathering were the archbishop of Bourges or the district prefect to be seen. The faint odor of heresy wafting from his retraction had reached their nostrils. On the other hand, as the prince still possessed the odor of sanctity for Valençay's guardians of the peace and municipal councilors, they were all present. After Mass was held in the parish church and final prayers offered, the three caskets were removed to the chapel and taken down into its crypt. Musketeers fired a salute to the prince as his coffin, followed by those of his brother and his great-niece, descended into the tomb.

There is nothing pretentious about the crypt where he lies buried next to the beloved Countess Tyszkiewicz, whose squinting, fondly admiring gaze followed him about for thirty years, and to the brother who had dispossessed him of the rights of primogeniture.

Talleyrand never evinced the slightest trace of hostility or jealousy toward that brother, never said a word against his parents. It was he, the outcast, who restored the prestige and fortune his family had lost in the fifteenth century. He expected nothing in return; his code of honor stipulated that he owed everything to his family for giving him the name of Talleyrand-Périgord.

He expected even less from his contemporaries. Like all desperate souls, he pinned his hopes on posterity. These are the final lines of his *Memoirs:* "Posterity will hand down a broader, more independent verdict than contemporaries with regard to persons like myself, who, summoned to the stage of world events in one of the most extraordinary periods of history, are entitled, for that very reason, to be judged more impartially and equitably."

His appeal, it seems, has not been widely heard. A century after his death, surely it is easier to paint the man as he was, capable of all things, even goodness.

He won the most difficult struggle of all, self-mastery. He dominated his suffering and humiliations; he tempered his pride with courtesy, his power with humanity, his great wealth with elegance. No instinct ruled his life; he yielded to no passion, yet pursued certain aims passionately. To escape monotony, he indulged in every conceivable inconstancy; he dipped greedily into life, exploring the pleasures of the palate and the flesh, assuming protean postures. None of these distracted him from his goal: a nation of enlightened citizens. If it is true that enthusiasm excites men's minds and controls them, then he never excited or controlled anyone, preferring instead to fascinate and persuade some, to lure others to their own downfall.

He had no system, no hard-and-fast rule for transforming a world he knew to be as unalterable as himself. Through his own person, not his discourse, he transmitted the ancient legacy of civilization. He was not an innovator. Though he looked ahead with greater assurance than backward, he knew that the future needed to root itself in the past. In the society which inherited the Revolution, he stood out like a shimmering, shifting symbol of decadence, ever willing to meet the demands of the future for the sake of survival and the preservation of mankind's achievement. "A great relic of the past and a shining light of the present. . . . That, gentlemen, is what we have seen, and nothing we shall see can approach it."[1]

Still, beneath the splendor of his station, he suffered. On the day he was baptized, adversity began gathering its forces to strike at him. Like most great figures at the end of the eighteenth century, he was destined to live with storm and strife. To him, the storm brought no acclaim, the strife no poetry. They were simply universal forms of brutality and ignorance. And because the world was like that, he learned to live with it and in it, to ride out the gales, to find shelter in whatever port he chanced on, and to step ashore more blithely than to a picnic on Cythera. He found pleasure where others found jobs.

What remains of this matchless splendor and endless misery? A marble tombstone with its factual, official message:

HERE LIES THE BODY OF

CHARLES MAURICE DE TALLEYRAND-PÉRIGORD,

PRINCE-DUC DE TALLEYRAND,

DUC DE DINO

BORN IN PARIS FEBRUARY 2, 1754

DIED THERE MAY 17, 1838

A great name remains carved for all eternity in stone and in history.

NOTES

(*The Memoirs of Talleyrand are herein cited simply as Mémoires.*)

PART ONE

Golden Lions on a Blood-Soaked Field
  1. Grelière, *Les Talleyrand-Périgord.*
The Lioncel Is Treated Like an Alley Cat
  1. Vivent, *"La Vie privée de Talley-rand,"* in the *Encyclopaedia Britannica.*
Fundamentals of the Enjoyment of Living
  1. *Mémoires.*
The Marriage of Revolution and Love
  1. This and the following quotations are from Talleyrand's *Memoirs.*
  2. See Lacour-Gayet, *Talleyrand.*
  3. Lacour-Gayet.
  4. Abbé Letourneau, *Histoire du séminaire d'Angers.*
Time to Take the Plunge
  1. Lacombe, *Vie privée de Talley-rand.*
  2. Lacour-Gayet.
The Abbé Begins to Step Out
  1. Tarbé, *Reims* (historical essay), p. 422.
A Stylish Abbé in 1780
  1. Lacour-Gayet.
  2. Lacour-Gayet.
  3. *Mémoires.*
  4. Correspondence with Rémusat.
  5. Lacour-Gayet.
  6. Lacour-Gayet.
Behind the Scenes of Power
  1. Lacour-Gayet.
  2. Colmache, *Révélations sur la vie privée de Talleyrand.*
  3. Lacour-Gayet.
How to Ignore One's Bishopric
  1. Lacour-Gayet.
  2. Lacour-Gayet.
  3. Grivot, *Autun* (1967).
  4. Grivot.
Monsieur d'Autun Adopts New Ideas
  1. Lacour-Gayet.
  2. Lacour-Gayet.
  3. Grivot.
D'Autun Runs the Machinery of Revolution
  1. Lacour-Gayet.
  2. Lacour-Gayet.
  3. Grivot.
  4. For the Autun period of Talleyrand's career, we have relied chiefly on Grivot's major work, *Autun.*
How to Organize a Festival
  1. Vitrolles, *Mémoires.*
A Few Aspects of Monseigneur d'Autun
  1. Lacour-Gayet.
  2. Lacour-Gayet.
Diplomatic Feelers
  1. Fay, *Politique étrangère française sous la Révolution* (Russian Archives, illustration 1939).
  2. Pallain, Diplomatic Correspondence.
  3. Lacour-Gayet.
  4. Lafforgue, *Talleyrand, l'homme de la France.*

659

Notes

The Matter of a Passport
1. Sorel, *L'Europe et la Révolution française*.
2. Barère, *Mémoires*.

Third Trip to England
1. Pallain, *Ministère de Talleyrand sous le Directoire*.
2. Lacour-Gayet.
3. Lacour-Gayet.
4. Lacour-Gayet.

Monseigneur d'Autun Explores the New World
1. For an excellent account of Talleyrand's visit to America, see Poniatowski, *Talleyrand aux Etats-Unis 1794–1796*.
2. Poniatowski.
3. Poniatowski.
4. Lacour-Gayet.
5. Lacour-Gayet.
6. Madame de Genlis, *Mémoires*.
7. Poniatowski.
8. *Journal d'une femme de cinquante ans*.

The 9th Thermidor
1. Lacombe.
2. Lacour-Gayet.
3. Colmache.
4. Saint-Méry, *Voyage aux Etats-Unis d'Amérique*.
5. Colmache; quoted by Poniatowski.

PART TWO

If You Don't Have What You Like . . .
1. February 18, 1797; quoted by Lacour-Gayet.
2. February 17, 1797; quoted by Lacour-Gayet.
3. Regarding Talleyrand's return to public life, see Lacour-Gayet.

Madame de Staël Knocks on Doors
1. *Mémoires*.

Bitter "Sweets" from America
1. Villemarest, *Monsieur de Talleyrand*.
2. Pasquier, *Mémoires*.

Talleyrand Manages a Coup d'Etat
1. Duchesse d'Abrantès, *Histoire des salons de Paris*.

Tallyerand Nods to Bonaparte
1. Duchesse d'Abrantès.

A Historic Encounter
1. Villefosse and Bouissounouse, *L'Opposition à Napoléon*.

Entertaining in the Grand Manner
1. Lacour-Gayet.
2. Villefosse and Bouissounouse.

A Beauty from India
1. Lacour-Gayet.

The Orient Sets Bonaparte Dreaming
1. Annales historiques de la *Revue Française* (1933), pp. 63–119.

The Former Bishop Comes a Cropper
1. Lacour-Gayet.
2. Lacour-Gayet.
3. Barras, *Mémoires* (III).

Talleyrand Returns to the Foreign Office
1. Aulard, *Paris sous le Consulat*.
2. Lacour-Gayet.
3. Lacour-Gayet.
4. Bertrand, *Lettres inédites de Talleyrand à Napoléon*.
5. Madame de Rémusat, *Mémoires*.
6. Published in the *Citoyen Français*, November 10, 1799; quoted by Aulard.
7. Baron Hyde de Neuville, *Mémoires*.
8. Lacour-Gayet.

Talleyrand Settles Down Comfortably
1. Villefosse and Bouissounouse.
2. Letter from V. Jacquemont to Stendhal; *Correspondance de Stendhal*.

Talleyrand Nobly Executes Ignoble Policies
1. *Mémoires*.

Notes

Make Peace or Make War, but . . .
1. Lacour-Gayet.
2. Villemarest.
3. Cf. Lacour-Gayet.
4. Barras.

Monsieur d'Autun and the Celibacy Issue
1. Lacour-Gayet.

A Striking Resemblance to Monsieur d'Autun
1. Diary of Madame de Cazenove d'Arlens; quoted by Lacour-Gayet.
2. Pichot, *Souvenirs intimes sur M. de Talleyrand.*
3. Villemarest.
4. Lacour-Gayet.

The Cripple Wades in Blood
1. *Histoire du Consulat et de l'Empire* (IV), p. 602.
2. Pasquier.

"The First to Become King . . ."
1. Lacour-Gayet.

"While We Were Marching Through Germany"
1. Bailleu, *Preussen und Frankreich von 1795 bis 1807;* quoted by Lacour-Gayet.
2. Montar, *Histoire du comte d'Hauterive.*
3. Bertrand.
4. Bertrand; quoted by Lacour-Gayet.

How to Become a Reigning Prince
1. Lacour-Gayet.

The Sublime Art of the Double Cross
1. *Mémoires.*
2. On the Dalbergs, see Dard, *Napoléon et Talleyrand.*
3. Lacour-Gayet.

Vexations on the Eastern Front
1. Countess Potocka, *Memoirs;* quoted by Lacour-Gayet.
2. Lacour-Gayet.
3. Bertrand.
4. Lacour-Gayet.
5. Villemarest; quoted by Lacour-Gayet.
6. *Mémoires.*

7. Savary, Duke of Rovigo, *Memoirs.*

Benevento Leaves the Ministry
1. Bertrand.

At Leisure, Benevento Causes Anxiety
1. Madame de Rémusat.
2. Lacour-Gayet.
3. Lacour-Gayet.
4. Madame de Dino, *Notice sur Valençay.*

"Perfidy Is Noble Against Tyranny"
1. *Mémoires.*
2. *Mémoires.*
3. Metternich, *Memoirs;* quoted by Lacour-Gayet.
4. *Mémoires.*
5. *Mémoires.*
6. Caulaincourt, *Mémoires.*

Grounds for Divorce
1. Cf. Villefosse and Bouissounouse.
2. Fouché, *Mémoires.*

Benevento Changes Residence
1. Lacour-Gayet.
2. Lacour-Gayet.
3. Lacour-Gayet.
4. *Mémoires.*
5. Regarding Edmond's marriage and the personality of Dorothée, see Bernardy, *Talleyrand's Last Duchess.*
6. Arrigon, *Une Amie de Talleyrand: la duchesse de Courlande.*
7. Missoffe, *Le Coeur secret de Talleyrand.*
8. Letter dated March 24, 1809; quoted by Lacour-Gayet.

Benevento's Shady Associates
1. Metternich.

The Scene on January 28
1. Lacour-Gayet.
2. Pasquier; Sainte-Beuve, *Nouveaux Lundis.*
3. Lacour-Gayet.
4. Queen Hortense, *Mémoires.*
5. Sainte-Beuve; quoted by Lacour-Gayet.
6. Metternich.

The Repudiated Prince Regains His Freedom

661

1. *Mémoires.*
2. *Le Coeur secret de Talleyrand.*
3. H. de Montlaur.
4. Villemarest.

The Disgraced Prince Forsakes No Pleasures
1. Potocka; quoted by Lacour-Gayet.
2. Potocka; quoted by Lacour-Gayet.
3. Countess Kielmannsegge, *Memoirs;* quoted by Lacour-Gayet.

Sorrows, Rebuffs, and Financial Headaches
1. Lacour-Gayet.
2. Lacour-Gayet.
3. Letter of Napoleon's dated June 22, 1811; quoted by Lacour-Gayet.

The Prince Remains Cool
1. Missoffe.
2. Lacour-Gayet.

The Emperor Thwarts Talleyrand
1. Bernardy, *Le Dernier Amour de Talleyrand: la duchesse de Dino.*
2. Duchesse de Dino, *Mémoires.*
3. Bernardy, *Le Dernier Amour de Talleyrand.*
4. Bernardy, *Le Dernier Amour de Talleyrand.*
5. *Revue des Deux Mondes* (July 15, 1928).

Talleyrand Thinks Ahead
1. Lacour-Gayet.
2. Lacour-Gayet.
3. Lacour-Gayet.
4. Louis Madelin.
5. Madame de Coigny, *Mémoires.*

Rages and Reconciliations
1. Marquis de Noailles, *Le Comte Molé.*
2. Louis Madelin.
3. Lacour-Gayet.
4. Duke of Rovigo, *Memoirs.*
5. Lacour-Gayet.

Talleyrand and Napoleon's Downfall
1. Lacour-Gayet.
2. These conversations appear in Coigny, *Mémoires.*
3. Vitrolles.

"In 1814 . . . Talleyrand Was There . . ."
1. Pasquier; quoted by Lacour-Gayet.
2. Duke of Rovigo.
3. Pasquier.
4. Marmont, *Mémoires;* quoted by Lacour-Gayet.
5. *Mémoires.*

The Vacant Throne Needs an Occupant
1. Beugnot, *Mémoires;* quoted by Lacour-Gayet.
2. *Mémoires.*
3. *Mémoires.*
4. *Mémoires.*
5. *Mémoires;* quoted by Lacour-Gayet.
6. Comtesse de Boigne, *Mémoires.*

The King Presents Himself
1. Lacour-Gayet.
2. Lacour-Gayet.
3. Beugnot; quoted by Lacour-Gayet.

A Caustic Encounter
1. *Mémoires.*
2. *Mémoires;* quoted by Lacour-Gayet.
3. Pasquier; quoted by Lacour-Gayet.
4. *Mémoires.*
5. Villemarest; quoted by Lacour-Gayet.
6. Comte Ferrand, *Mémoires;* quoted by Lacour-Gayet.

The Problems of Treaty-Making, Etc.
1. Lacour-Gayet.
2. Emile Dard and Guglielmo Ferrero are his most searching critics; also Albert Sorel, despite his harshness.
3. Lacour-Gayet.

Talleyrand Disrupts the Coalition
1. *Mémoires.*
2. Cf. Madelin, *Talleyrand.*
3. Paris, November 27, 1814; Vienna, Hanshort und Staats Archiev.
4. Madelin, *Talleyrand.*

Notes

5. Cf. Madelin, *Talleyrand*.
6. Cf. Madelin, *Talleyrand*.
7. Madelin, *Talleyrand*.
8. Madelin, *Talleyrand*.

The Congress Is Entertained
1. Loliée, *Talleyrand et la société européenne*.
2. Loliée.

A Shadow Falls on the Congress
1. With reference to this entirely convincing story, see Bac, *Le Secret de Talleyrand*; Bartel, *Napoléon à l'île d'Elbe*; and Audiat in *Le Figaro Littéraire* (September 23, 1950).

Vanity Is an Ugly Trait
1. Lacour-Gayet.
2. Sainte-Beuve.

Returning the King to His Throne
1. Madelin, *Talleyrand*.
2. Madelin, *Talleyrand*.
3. Lacour-Gayet.
4. Cf. Lacour-Gayet.
5. Chateaubriand, *Mémoires d'outre-tombe*; quoted by Lacour-Gayet.

Talleyrand Mixes Politics and Passion
1. Vitrolles.
2. Lacour-Gayet.
3. Lacour-Gayet.

Talleyrand Believes He Is Indispensable
1. Lacour-Gayet.
2. Lacour-Gayet.
3. Vitrolles.

PART THREE

Retirement from Politics, Matrimony
1. Letter of May 4, 1816, to Madame de Bauffremont.
2. Bernard de Lacombe.
3. Lacour-Gayet.

Spiteful Ambition
1. Comte Molé, *Mémoires*.

Minor Affairs
1. Dard; on the sale of archives from the Foreign Ministry.
2. Lacour-Gayet.
3. Lacour-Gayet.
4. Lacour-Gayet.
5. Lacour-Gayet.

False Hopes of Blind Ambition
1. Vitrolles.
2. Louis Madelin.
3. Lacour-Gayet.

Talleyrand Slips Deeper into Disgrace
1. Lacour-Gayet.
2. Lacour-Gayet.

Sorrowful Losses, a Miraculous Birth
1. Lord Holland, *Diplomatic Memoirs*.
2. Gorsas, *Talleyrand*.
3. Lacour-Gayet.

Chateaubriand Wages the Spanish

War
1. Lacombe, *Conversations avec M. Thiers*.
2. Duc de Broglie, *Souvenirs*.
3. Lacour-Gayet.

"Our Acts Pursue Us" . . .
1. Lacour-Gayet.
2. Barante, *Souvenirs*.
3. Boigne.

The King Changes, the Boredom Remains
1. Lacour-Gayet.
2. Lacour-Gayet.

Talleyrand Receives a Slap
1. Lacour-Gayet.

The Régime Ages
1. Sainte-Beuve.
2. Lacour-Gayet.
3. Letter dated June 20, 1827, to Madame Mollien; quoted by Lacour-Gayet.
4. Sainte-Beuve.

Talleyrand Reflects on the New Régime
1. *Mémoires*.
2. Lacombe.
3. Diary of Castellane.

4. Mary-Lafon, *Cinquante Ans de vie littéraire* (source courtesy of M. Méras, chief archivist for the Tarn-et-Garonne region).

The Prince Stages a Comeback
1. Lacour-Gayet.
2. *Mémoires.*
3. Lacour-Gayet.

London, Where Life Began Anew
1. *Mémoires.*

London at One's Feet
1. *Mémoires.*
2. Letters and papers of Nesselrode; quoted by Lacour-Gayet.

Every Fresh Start Has Its Disappointments
1. Mérimée, *Correspondance.*
2. *Mémoires.*

3. Journals of Madame de Dino.
4. Lacour-Gayet.

A Sumptuous "Lair"
1. Journals of Madame de Dino.
2. Lacombe.
3. Lacombe.

"Renunciation" Is Almost Equivalent to "Attachment"
1. Lacombe.

The Road to Heaven Has Its Meanders
1. Pasquier.
2. Lacombe.
3. Lacombe.
4. Lacombe.

The Last Parade
1. Barante, *Eloge funèbre du prince de Talleyrand devant la Chambre des Pairs* (June 8, 1838).

BIBLIOGRAPHY

A. WORKS BY TALLEYRAND

L'Album perdu. Paris: Les Marchands de Nouveautés, 1829. (This work, published by H. de Latouche as adapted from Quérard, was released in 1835 under the title *Pensées et maximes de Maurice de Talleyrand* . . .)

L'Assemblée nationale aux Français (February 11, 1790). Paris: Imprimerie Nationale, n.d. (By Talleyrand, as adapted from Barbier.) Paris: Baudouin, 1790.

L'Assemblée nationale aux Français (February 11, 1790). N.p., n.d. (By Talleyrand, as adapted from Barbier.) Printed in two volumes, the second of which contains a facsimile: *Les Français à l'Assemblée nationale* (February 12, 1790).

Bericht des Herrn von Talleyrand-Périgord in Namen des Constitutions-Ausschusses, ueber den Schluss des Pariser Departements vom 6ten April jüngst. Strasbourg: P. J. Dannback, Buchdrucken, 1791.

Catalogue des livres très bien conditionnés du cabinet de M. de Talleyrand. (A sale in Paris on April 30, 1811.) Paris: De Bure et Fils, 1811. (Copy bearing handwritten information of auction prices. Two autographed letters of Talleyrand and six engraved portraits are included.)

Communication faite au Sénat dans sa séance du 15 Pluviôse an XIII (by the Minister of Foreign Relations [Talleyrand]). (Including an oath sworn in the same session by the "great Admiral of the Empire" [Murat], a report [by François de Neufchâteau] made to the Senate in the same month's session of the 18th, and further debate.) N.p., n.d. (*Sénat-conservateur,* collected minutes, year XIII.)

Compte de la dépense du ministère des Relations extérieures, sur le fonds affecté par le Corps législatif à l'arrière antérieur au 1er Vendémiaire an V, à commencer du 18 Prairial an VI jusqu'au 1er Vendémiaire an VII, et du 1er Vendémiaire an VII au 1er Germinal suivant. (Rendered by Charles Maurice Talleyrand.) Paris: Imprimerie de la République, year VII.

Compte de la dépense du ministère des Relations extérieures, sur les fonds affectés par le Corps législatif à l'exercice an V (an VII) . . . (Rendered by Charles Maurice Talleyrand.) Paris: Imprimerie de la République, year VII, year IX.

La Confession de Talleyrand (1754–1838). Paris: L. Sauvaitre, 1891. (According to the preface, a pastiche of extracts written by and about Talleyrand by the author of *Mariage d'Alceste* [Ch. Joliet].)

Correspondance du comte de Jaucourt . . . avec le prince de Talleyrand pendant le congrès de Vienne . . . (Published by his grandson, Jean-François Le

667

Visse de Montigny, marquis de Jaucourt. With foreword and biographical note.) Paris: Plon, 1905.

Correspondance diplomatique de Talleyrand. (Talleyrand's mission to London in 1792; his unedited correspondence with the Department of Foreign Relations, General Biron, etc., and his letters from America to Lord Lansdowne. With an introduction and notes by G. Pallain.) Paris: Plon, Nourrit et C^{1e}, 1887.

Correspondance diplomatique de Talleyrand. (Talleyrand's embassy to London, 1830–34. Part I, with an introduction and notes by G. Pallain.) Paris: E. Plon, Nourrit et C^{1e}, 1891.

Correspondance diplomatique de Talleyrand. (The ministry of Talleyrand under the Directory. With an introduction and notes by G. Pallain.) Paris: E. Plon, Nourrit et C^{1e}, 1891.

Correspondance inédite du prince de Talleyrand et du roi Louis XVIII pendant le congrès de Vienne. (Printed from the original letters preserved at the Office of Foreign Affairs, with preface, explanatory comments, and notes by M. G. Pallain.) Paris: Plon, 1905.

Correspondance de Talleyrand avec le Premier Consul pendant la campagne de Marengo. (Published by the Count de la Meurthe.) Laval: E. Jamin, 1892. (An extract from the *Revue d'Histoire Diplomatique.*)

Dernière Lettre que M. Géry, envoyé des Etats-Unis, reçut du ministre des Relations extérieures avant son départ. (Signed: C. M. Talleyrand.) Paris: Laran, n.d. (Bound in the *Propagateur an VI* between the numbers 228 and 229, the 21st and 22nd of Thermidor.)

Discours de M. le prince de Bénévent au Roi (in presenting the Senate to the king at Saint-Ouen, May 2, 1814). Paris: P. Gueffier, n.d.

Discours de M. le prince de Talleyrand . . . sur le projet de loi relatif aux délits de la presse (26 février 1822). Paris: Plancher, 1822.

Chambre des Pairs de France (session of November 13, 1821). *Discours prononcé dans cette séance par M. le prince de Talleyrand, à l'occasion du décès de M. le comte Bourlier, évêque d'Evreux.* Paris: J. Didot Aîné, 1821.

Discours prononcé à la Chambre des Pairs, par M. le prince de Talleyrand à l'occasion du décès de M. Le comte Bourlier . . . (Session of November 13, 1821.) Paris: Me Seignot, n.d.

Chambre des Pairs de France (session of September 8, 1814). *Discours prononcé . . . par le ministre des Affaires étrangères.* (A speech made by Talleyrand in presenting the Finance Bill, adopted by the Chambre des Députés on the 3rd of the same month, to the Chambre des Pairs.) Paris: P. Didot l'Aîné, n.d.

Eclaircissements donnés par le Cen Talleyrand à ses concitoyens. Paris: Laran, year VII.

Royal Institute of France. *Eloge de M. le comte Reinhard, prononcé a l'Académie des Sciences morales et politiques par M. le prince de Talleyrand* (in the session of March 3, 1838). Paris: F.-Didot Frères, 1838.

Mémoire: *"Essai sur les avantages à retirer des colonies nouvelles."* See S. Dutot, *"De l'Expatriation"* (Paris, 1840).

Essai sur les avantages à retirer des colonies nouvelles dans les circonstances présentes. Paris: Baudouin, n.d. (The original title additionally includes:

Bibliography

"Par le citoyen Talleyrand, lu à la séance publique de l'Institut national, le 15 Messidor an V." Drafted by d'Hauterive, as adapted from Quérard.)

Les Etats-Unis et l'Angleterre en 1795. (A letter by Talleyrand.) Paris: E. Leroux, 1889 (second printing). (An extract from the Revue d'Histoire Diplomatique, third year, 1889.)

Extraits des mémoires du prince de Talleyrand-Périgord . . . (Collected and arranged by Countess O... Du C... [Baron E. L. Lamothe-Langon].) Paris: C., Le Clère, 1838–39 (of doubtful authenticity).

Parliamentary Archives, Vol. VIII: Intervention de Talleyrand sur l'article 6 de la déclaration des droits de l'homme. N.d.

Lettres et billets du prince de Talleyrand et de M. Royer-Collart. (With an introduction by Paul Royer-Collart.) Paris: Lahure, 1903. (A miscellany published by the Société des Bibliophiles Français, Section I, Article 3.)

Lettres inédites de Talleyrand à Napoléon (1800–9). (Printed from the originals preserved in the archives for Foreign Affairs, with an introduction and notes by Pierre Bertrand.) Paris: Perrin, 1889 (second edition).

Lettres du ministre des Relations extérieures, à M. Géry (posted from the United States in sending Géry his passports). (Signed: C. M. Talleyrand.) Paris: Laran, year VI.

Liberté des cultes religieux. (A report made in the Assembly's session of May 7, 1791, pertaining to the Department of Paris' decree of the preceding April 6; made by Talleyrand-Périgord in the name of the Constitutional Committee.) Paris: Lottin Aîné et J. R. Lottin, 1791.

Des Loteries. (By the bishop of Autun [Talleyrand].) Paris: Barrois Aîné, 1789.

Mémoires, lettres inédites et papiers secrets. (Memoirs, unedited letters, and secret papers of Talleyrand, with explanatory notes by Jean Gorsas.) Paris: A. Savine, 1891.

Mémoires du prince de Talleyrand. (Published by the Duke of Broglie, with a preface and notes.) Paris: C. Lévy, 1891–92. (5 volumes—I: 1754–1808; II: 1809–15; III: 1815–30; IV: 1830–32; V: 1832–34.)

Le Ministre des Relations extérieures au citoyen Camille Corona . . . (Signed: C. M. Talleyrand.) Rome: I Lazzarini Stampatori, 1798. (Letter dated the 3rd of Germinal, year VI, conveying the congratulations of the Directory to the Roman government.)

Motion de l'évêque d'Autun (Talleyrand) sur les biens ecclésiastiques du 10 octobre 1789. Versailles: Baudouin, n.d.

Motion de M. l'évêque d'Autun (Talleyrand) sur les mandats impératifs. (A statement about the grounds for imperative mandates, read before the National Assembly on July 7, 1789.) N.p., n.d.

Motion de M. l'évêque d'Autun (Talleyrand) sur la proposition d'un emprunt faite à l'Assemblée nationale par le premier ministre des Finances, et sur la consolidation de la dette publique (August 27, 1789). Versailles: Baudouin, n.d.

Notice historique sur le chevalier Don Joseph Nicolas d'Azara . . . (Written by Talleyrand about the Spanish ambassador to Paris, who died there on the 5th of Pluviôse, year XII.) Paris, n.d. (Attributed also to Baron J. F. Bourgouing and to Count A. M. d'Hauterive.)

Opinion de M. l'évêque d'Autun (Talleyrand) sur les banques et sur le réta-

blissement de l'ordre dans les finances (stated before the Assembly on December 4, 1789). Paris: Baudouin, 1789.

Opinion de M. l'évêque d'Autun (Talleyrand) *sur la fabrication des petites monnaies . . .* (December 12, 1790). Paris: Imprimerie Nationale, n.d. (On the freedom of religious cults.)

Chambre des Pairs de France (session of April 9, 1821). *Opinion de M. le prince duc de Talleyrand sur le projet de loi relatif à la circonscription des arrondissements électoraux.* Paris: P. Didot Aîné, 1821.

Chambre des Pairs de France (session of February 26, 1822). *Opinion de M. le prince duc le Talleyrand sur le projet de loi relatif à la répression des délits commis par la voie de la presse ou par tout autre moyen de publication.* Paris: J. Didot Aîné, 1822.

Chambre des Pairs de France (session of December 26, 1820). *Opinion de M. le prince duc de Talleyrand sur une proposition de M. le comte Lanjuinais, relative à la compétence de la Chambre des Pairs . . .* Paris: Didot Aîné.

Opinion de M. le prince de Talleyrand . . . sur le projet d'adresse en réponse au discours du Roi, à l'ouverture de la session. (Session of February 3, 1823.) Paris: Baudouin Frères, 1823.

Chambre des Pairs de France (session of July 24, 1821). *Opinion de M. le prince de Talleyrand sur le projet de loi relatif aux journaux et écrits périodiques.* Paris: P. Didot Aîné, 1881.

Opinion de M. le prince de Talleyrand . . . contre le rénouvellement de la censure. (Session of July 24, 1821.) Paris: Baudouin Fils, 1821.

Pensées et maximes de M. de Talleyrand. Paris: Les Librairies, 1835.

Pétition de Maurice Talleyrand . . . à la Convention nationale. Paris: Vve. A. J. Gorsas, n.d. (The author petitions to come back to France as a returning ex-patriot rather than as an emigré. The letter is dated from Philadelphia, the 28th of Prairial, year III.)

Pétition de Maurice Talleyrand à la Convention nationale. (The 28th of Prairial, year III.) Paris: Vve A. J. Gorsas, n.d.

Précis de la vie de M. l'évêque d'Autun. N.p., n.d.

Précis de la vie du prélat d'Autun, digne ministre de la fédération. Paris, 1790.

Procès-verbal de l'Assemblée générale du clergé de France (held in Paris in 1786). (By the abbé of Périgord, former *agent général,* secretary of the Assembly, etc.) Paris: G. Desprez, 1789.

Projet de décrets sur l'instruction publique. Paris: Imprimerie Nationale, 1791. (Proposed by Talleyrand in further reference to his report on public education.)

Proposition faite à la Chambre des Pairs. (A proposal made by Prince Talleyrand in the session of January 23, 1817.) Paris: J. G. Denty, 1817.

Rapport de l'agence contenant les principales affaires du clergé (from 1780 until 1785). (By the abbé of Perigord and the abbé of Boisgelin.) Paris: F. A. Didot Aîné, 1788.

Rapport fait au nom du Comité de constitution. (Made by Talleyrand-Périgord in the session of May 7, 1791, and relating to the Department of Paris' decree of the preceding April 6.) Paris: Imprimerie Nationale, n.d.

Rapport fait au Premier Consul, en Sénat. (A report, concerning the settlement of German indemnities, made by the Minister of Foreign Relations [Talley-

rand] during the session of the 3rd of Fructidor, year X. Signed: Charles
Maurice de Talleyrand, and dated: Paris, Thermidor, year X.) Paris: Dépôt
des Lois, n.d.

Rapport sur l'instruction publique. (Made by Talleyrand-Périgord in the name
of the Constitutional Committee.) N.p., n.d.

Rapport sur l'instruction publique. (Made in the name of the Constitutional Committee to the National Assembly on the 10th, 11th, and 19th of September,
1791. Plan of decrees on public education. By Talleyrand-Périgord.) Paris:
Imprimerie Nationale, 1791.

Réponse de M. l'évêque d'Autun (Talleyrand) *au Chapitre de l'Eglise cathédrale
d'Autun.* (On the National Assembly's decree of April 13, 1790.) Paris:
Imprimerie Nationale, 1790.

Talleyrand in America as a Financial Promoter, 1794–1796. (Unpublished letters
and memoirs by Talleyrand and others. Translated and edited by Hans Huth
and Wilma J. Pugh; foreword by F. L. Nussbaum.) Washington, D.C.:
U.S. Government Printing Office, 1942.

Talleyrand intime. (After his unedited correspondence with the duchess of
Courland. The Restoration in 1814.) Paris: E. Kolb, 1891.

G. Lacour-Gayet. *Talleyrand et Royer-Collart.* (Unedited correspondence.) Paris:
Editions de la *Revue Mondiale,* 1927.

Talleyrand . . . à ses citoyens (December 12, 1792). Paris: Plassan, n.d.

Two Letters (upon the uniformity of weights and measures). See John Riggs
Miller, speeches in the House of Commons upon the equalization of the
weights and measures of Great Britain (London).

B. WORKS ABOUT TALLEYRAND

ABRANTÈS, Madame d'. *Le Sacre de Napoléon, la cour impériale.* Paris: Bibliothèque Figuière No. 1, Eugène Figuière, Editeur, 1934.

ACTON, Lord. *Essai sur les mémoires de Talleyrand,* in *Historical Essays,* 1906.

ANGEBERG, Count. *Le Congrès de Vienne et les traités de Vienne précédés et
suivis des actes diplomatiques qui s'y rattachent.* Paris: Amyot, 1863. 4 vols.

ARRIGON, L. G. *Une Amie de Talleyrand: la duchesse de Courlande, 1761–1821.*
Paris: Flammarion, 1945 (*L'Histoire et les Hommes*).

AUJAY, Edouard. *Talleyrand.* Paris: J. Tallandier, 1946.

AULARD. *Paris sous le Directoire.*

BAC, Ferdinand. *Le Secret de Talleyrand, d'après des témoignages contemporains.*
Paris: Hachette, 1933.

BASTIDE, Louis. *Vie politique et religieuse de Talleyrand-Périgord . . .* Paris:
Faure, 1838.

BERNARDY, Françoise de. *Le Dernier Amour de Talleyrand. La duchesse de Dino.*
Paris: Hachette, 1956.

BERNARDY, Françoise de. *Le Dernier Amour de Talleyrand, la duchesse de Dino*
(*1793–1862*). Paris: Perrin, 1965.

BERTAUD, Jules. *Talleyrand.* Lyons: H. Lardanchet, 1945. (*Histoires et Mémoires,* No. 8.)

BLEI, Franz. *Talleyrand homme d'Etat.* (Translated from the German by René
Lobstein.) Paris: Payot, 1935.

BLENNERHASSET, Lady. *Talleyrand* . . . Berlin: Paetel. (A translation from the English.)

BOIGNE, Countess. *Mémoires* . . . Paris: Plon, 1907–8. 4 vols.

BOULAY DE LA MEURTHE. *Le Directoire et l'expédition d'Egypte.* N.p., n.d.

———. *Les Justifications de Talleyrand pendant le Directoire.* Angers, 1889.

BOURGOING, Jean de. *Lettres de Talleyrand à Metternich.* (Reproduced from the originals.) R. Inst. "Napoléon," 1965. No. 95.

BOWMAN, Dodd Anna. *Talleyrand. The Training of a Statesman.* London, 1927.

BRINTON, Crane. *The Lives of Talleyrand.* London: G. Allen and Unwin; printed in the U.S.A., 1937.

BROUGHAM, Lord. *Historical Sketches of Statesmen, 1839–1843.* N.p., n.d.

BULWER, Sir H. Lytton. *Historical Characters. Essai sur Talleyrand.* (Translated by Perrot.) Paris: Reinwold, 1868.

CAMBON, Jules. *Le Diplomate.* Paris, 1931.

CAPEFIGUE. In *Diplomates européens.* N.p., 1843.

CARION, Henri. *La Mort d'un grand coupable.* N.p., 1838.

CASTELLANE, Jean de. *Talleyrand.* Paris: Edit. des Ambassadeurs, 1934.

CASTILLE, Hippolyte. *Talleyrand.* N.p., n.d.

CAULAINCOURT, Armand de. *Mémoires du général de C* . . . (Introduction and notes by Jean Hanoteau.) Paris: Plon, 1933. 3 vols.

CHASTENAY, Madame de. *Mémoires de Mme de* . . . *1771–1815.* Paris: Plon, 1896. 2 vols.

CHATEAUBRIAND, François René de. *Talleyrand, La mort du duc d'Enghien.* "Bibliothèque Figuière," Eugène Figuière, Editeur, 1934.

COIGNY. *Mémoires d'Aimée de Coigny.* Paris, 1902.

COLMACHE. *Reminiscences of Prince Talleyrand.* London, 1843. 2 vols.

COMBALUZIER, F. *Le Sacre épiscopal de Roberto Obaldini, nonce en France (3 février 1608) et de Charles-Maurice de Talleyrand-Périgord évêque d'Autun (4 janvier 1789).* Paris: "Ami Clergé," 1967.

COOPER, Duff. *Talleyrand.* Paris: Cercle Historia, 1958.

———. *Talleyrand 1754–1838.* (Translated from the English by H. and R. Alix.) Paris: Payot, 1937. (Published 1968 in the U.S.A. by Stanford University Press.)

———. *Viscount Norwich. Talleyrand.* London: Arrow Books, 1958.

COUCHOUD, Paul Louis, and COUCHOUD, Jean-Paul. *Talleyrand—Mémoires* . . . (Introduction, notes, and comments about the text.) Paris: Plon, 1957. 2 vols.

DARD, Emile. *Napoléon et Talleyrand.* Paris: Plon, 1935.

DESCHANEL, P. *Orateurs et hommes d'Etat.* Paris, 1888. Pp. 253–93.

DINO, Dorothée de Courlande, Duchess of. *Chronique de 1831–1862.* (Published by Princess Radziwill.) Paris, 1909.

D.S., Mademoiselle. *Eloge historique de M. de Périgord.* N.p., year VIII.

DUFOUR DE LA THUILERIE, Sosthène. *Histoire de la vie et de la mort de M. de Talleyrand-Périgord* . . . *avec un grand nombre de documents et de notes historiques, par S. D.* Paris: Librairie de la Société de Saint-Nicolas, 1838. (As adapted from M. Quérard.)

DUPANLOUP, Abbé. In *Revue des Deux Mondes,* March 1910.

DUPUIS, Charles. *Le Ministère de Talleyrand en 1814.* Paris: Plon, 1919. 2 vols.

DUSSORD, Jacques. *Les Belles Amies de M. de Talleyrand.* (Illustrated by Hofer.) Paris: Editions Colbert, 1942.

EARL, John L., III. "Talleyrand in Philadelphia 1794–1796," *Pennsylvania Magazine,* Vol. 91, No. 3 (1967).

EVANS, P. D. *Deux Emigrés en Amérique, Talleyrand et Beaumetz dans la Révolution française.* N.p., 1926.

FABRE-LUCE, Alfred. *Talleyrand.* Paris: Dargaud, 1969. (*Histoire Vérité,* XI).

FERRERO, G. *La Reconstruction. Talleyrand à Vienne. 1814–1815.* Paris: Plon, 1940.

FLEURY, Serge. *Talleyrand, maître souverain de la diplomatie.* Montreal: Les Editions Variétés, 1942.

FLICHE and MARTIN. *Histoire de l'Eglise. XX: La Crise révolutionnaire par le chanoine Leflon.*

FUZIER, A. *Napoléon et l'Espagne.* Paris, 1930. 2 vols.

G..., André. *Biographie des contemporains. Talleyrand-Périgord.* N.p., 1838. Vol. IX, No. 80, p. 184.

GAEVELLE, Yvonne Robert. "*Des Plages du Coromandel aux salons du Consulat de l'Empire,*" *La Vie de la princesse de Talleyrand.* Paris: P.U.F., 1948.

GAJE, J. Antonio de Araujo. "*Talleyrand et les négociations secrètes pour la paix de Portugal 1798–1800,*" *Bulletin des Etudes Portugaises,* 1950.

GARDE, Chambonas A. de la. *Souvenir du congrès de Vienne.* Paris: Appert, 1843. 2 vols.

GENLIS, Madame de. *Mémoires de Mme de* . . . (Preface by Lucas Dubreton.) Paris: Didot, 1892. 2 vols. Section IV: "*Période à Londres.*"

GRAND MAISON, Geoffroy de. *L'Espagne et Napoléon.* Paris, 1908. 3 vols.

GUIZOT, François. *Mémoires pour servir à l'histoire de mon temps. IV: Talleyrand après Waterloo.*

GUYOMARD, Y. *Le Secret de Talleyrand.* Cherbourg, 1934.

GUYOT, R. *Du Directoire au Consulat.* (The transitions in *Revue Historique,* 1912.)

———. *Le Directoire et la paix de l'Europe.* Paris, 1941.

———. *Projet de Talleyrand à la conférence de Londres, 16 janvier 1831.* N.p., n.d.

HAYDEN, Horace E. *French Revolutionary Pamphlets, A Check List of the Talleyrand and Other Collections.* New York: Public Library, 1945.

HOLLAND, Lord. *Foreign Reminiscences.* (Translated by H. de Chousky.) Paris: Rouvier, 1851.

HOUDIN, Maurice. "*Talleyrand à Bry,*" *Bull. Soc. Hist. Archéol.* (Nogent-sur-Marne), 1965.

JOELSON, Annette. *Courtesan Princess. Catherine Grand, Princess Talleyrand.* London: A. Redman, 1966.

KIPLING, R. *Prêtre malgré lui,* in *Rewards and Fairies.* N.p., n.d.

KRAFT, Johannes. *Doctrine politique. Prinzipien Talleyrand in der Aussens—und Innenpolitik.* Bonn: H. Bouvier and Co., 1958.

LACOMBE, Bernard de. *Talleyrand, évêque d'Autun.* Paris: Perrin, n.d.

———. *La Vie privée de Talleyrand. Son émigration. Son mariage. Sa retraite. Sa conversion. Sa mort.* (Revised edition.) Paris: Plon, 1933.

LACOUR-GAYET, Georges. *Le Centenaire d'un soufflet: Maubreuil et Talleyrand.* Paris, 1927. (Extract from the *Revue Bleue* of January 15, 1927.)

———. *Comment on devenait ministre sous le Directoire.* (*Talleyrand*). Paris, 1926.

———. *A propos du mariage de Talleyrand.* N.p., n.d.

———. *Talleyrand.* (Preface by François Mauriac.) Paris: Editions Rencontre, n.d.

———. *Talleyrand 1754–1838.* I: *1754–1799;* Paris: Payot, 1928. II: *1799–1815;* Paris: Payot, 1930. III: *1815–1838;* Paris: Payot, 1931. IV: *Mélanges;* Paris: Payot, 1934.

———. *Talleyrand et la Pologne.* N.p., n.d.

———. *Talleyrand et Royer-Collard.* (Unedited correspondence.) Paris: Garnier, 1927.

LACRETELLE, Jacques de, Jacques Audiberti, Arthur Conte, Marcel Dunan, etc. *Talleyrand.* Paris: Hachette, 1964.

LAFORGUE, Dr. René. *Talleyrand, l'homme de la France: essai psychanalitique sur la personnalité collective française.* Geneva: Editions du Mont Blanc, 1947.

LATREILLE, A. *L'Eglise catholique et la Révolution française.* N.p., n.d.

LAUZUN, Duke of. *Correspondance intime* . . . Paris, 1858.

LESOURD, Paul. *L'Ame de Talleyrand.* Paris: Flammarion, 1942.

LIMOUZIN-LAMOTHE, Roger. *Mgr. de Quélen et la conversation de Talleyrand, documents inédits.* Toulouse: Institut Catholique, 1957. (Containing the letters of Mgr. de Quélen and Talleyrand. Extract from the *Bulletin de Littérature Ecclésiastique,* III [July–September, 1957].)

———. *La Rétractation de Talleyrand, documents inédits.* Paris: Société d'Histoire Ecclésiastique de France, 1954. (Extract from the *Revue d'Histoire de l'Eglise de France,* LX [July–December, 1954].)

LOCKART, J. G. *The Peacemakers.* N.p., 1932.

LORIAN, André. *Un Opportuniste indépendant sous la Révolution, le Consulat et l'Empire.* (Extract from *Bulletin* No. 1 (1963) of the Société des Lettres, Sciences et Arts de la Corrèze.)

LOTH, Arthur. "Talleyrand et l'Eglise constitutionnelle de France," *Revue Anglo-Romaine* (October 1896).

LUENGO, Luis Alonso. *Ochos Vidas de conquista: Jesus, Roger de Flor, Hernan Cortés, Francisco Javier, Francisco de Borja, Enrique VIII, Talleyrand, Bernadotte.* Madrid, 1952.

MACCABE, Joseph. *Talleyrand. A Biographical Study.* London: Hutchinson, n.d.

MADELIN, Louis. *Fouché 1750–1820.* Paris: Plon, 1955.

———. *Les Hommes de la Révolution.* An essay: "*Talleyrand révolutionnaire.*" N.p., n.d.

———. *Talleyrand.* Paris: Flammarion, 1944.

MARION. *Histoire financière de la France.* N.p., n.d.

MASSON, Frédéric. *Le Département des Affaires étrangères pendant la Révolution.* N.p., n.d.

MATHIEZ, A. *La Réforme de la Constitution de l'an III après le coup d'Etat du 18 Frutidor,* in *Annales Historiques de la Révolution Française,* VI (1929).

MENTIENNE, M. *Histoire de deux portefeuilles de ministre du temps de la grande Révolution française, ayant appartenu à Talleyrand et à Fouché dès le temps du premier Directoire.* Paris: Honoré Champion Editeur, 1924.

METTERNICH, Prince de. *Documents et écrits divers laissés* . . . Paris: Plon, 1880–84. 8 vols.

MICHARD, L.-G. *Histoire politique et privée de Charles de Talleyrand, ancien évêque d'Autun—Suivie d'un extrait des mémoires inédits de M. de Sémallé, commissaire du roi en 1814; de nouveaux documents sur la mission qui fut donnée à Maubreuil pour assassiner Napoléon* . . . Paris: Bureau de la Bibliographie Universelle, 1853.

MICHEL, Bernard. *Les Grandes Enigmes du temps jadis.* (Presented by Bernard Michel.) Paris: Amis de l'Histoire, 1968. (XIII: *Talleyrand et le congrès de Vienne, 1969.*)

MIGNET, Auguste. *Sur la Vie et les travaux de M. le prince de Talleyrand,* in *Portraits et Notices Historiques,* 1852.

MISSOFFE, Michel. *Le Coeur secret de Talleyrand.* Paris: Perrin, 1956.

MOLÉ, Count, *Mémoires* . . . Paris: Champion, 1822–30. 6 vols.

NABONNE, B. *La Diplomatie du Directoire et Bonaparte.* Paris, 1951.

NESSELRODE, C. R. *Lettres et papiers du chancelier* . . . Paris, 1906.

NODIER, Charles. *Le Banquet des Girondins.* "Bibliothèque Figuière," No. 1, Eugène Figuière, Editeur, 1934.

OLDEN, Peter Hans. *Napoleon und Talleyrand. Die fruz* (sic) *Politik während des Feldzugs in Deutschland.* N.p., 1805.

OLLIVIER, A. *Le 18 brumaire.* Paris, 1959.

PABON, Jesus. *Talleyrand en el trance decisivo.* N.p., 1963.

PALÉOLOGUE, Maurice. *Talleyrand, Metternich, Chateaubriand.* Paris: Hachette, n.d.

PALLAIN, G. *Correspondance inédite du roi Louis XVIII pendant le congès de Vienne.* Paris, 1881. (*Archives de l'Histoire de France.*)

PICHOT, A. *Souvenirs intimes sur M. de Talleyrand.* N.p., 1870.

PIGUET, Théodore. *Une Enigme dans l'oeuvre de Greuze: le portrait de Talleyrand.* Mâcon, 1954. (Extract from the *Amis des Arts de Tournus,* LIII [1953].)

PLACE, C., and FLORENS, J. *Mémoire sur M. de Talleyrand, sa vie politique et sa vie intime, suivie de la relation authentique de ses derniers moments et d'une appréciation phrénologique sur le crâne de ce personnage célèbre* . . . Paris: Bureau de la Gazette des Familles, 1838.

PONIATOWSKI, Michel. *Talleyrand aux Etats-Unis, 1794–1796.* Paris: Presses de la Cité, 1967.

PORDEA, G. A. *Talleyrand et la couronne d'Espagne. L'Intrigue de Bayonne à la lumière des documents diplomatiques.* Bayonne: Soc. Sc. Lettres, 1967.

POTOCKA. *Mémoires de la comtesse P* . . . Paris: Plon, 1897.

RAOUL DE SCEAU (Le Père). *Guide historique de Valençay, le château, l'église, le tombeau de Talleyrand.* (Preface by Hugues Lapaire. Illustrations by René Roussel.) Châteauroux, n.d.

RÉMUSAT, Madame de. *Les Confidences d'une impératrice.* "Bibliothèque Figuière," No. 1. Eugène Figuière, Editeur, 1934.

RENAUD, Ferdinand. *La Onzième Heure, retouches à 3 portraits, Mgr. Dupanloup, la duchesse de Dino, Talleyrand.* Paris: G. Victor, 1960.

RENOUVIN, Pierre. *Histoire des relations internationales. La Révolution française de l'Empire napoléonien par André Fugier.* Paris, 1954.

675

Bibliography

SAINT-AULAIRE, Count de. *Talleyrand.* Paris: Dunod, 1936.

SAINTE-BEUVE, Charles Augustin. *Monsieur de Talleyrand.* Paris: Lévy, n.d.

———. *Monsieur de Talleyrand.* (Introduction and notes by Léon Noël.) Monaco, 1958.

SALLE, Alexandre. *Vie politique de Charles-Maurice, prince de Talleyrand.* Paris: L.-F., Hivert, 1834.

SAVANT, Jean. *Talleyrand.* Paris: J. Tallandier, 1960. (Bibliothèque Historia.)

SINDRAL, Jacques. *Talleyrand.* Paris: Gallimard, 1926.

SOREL, A. "Talleyrand au congrès de Vienne," in *Essais d'Histoire et de Critique,* 1895.

———. "Talleyrand et ses mémoires," in *Lectures Historiques* (Paris), 1894.

SOREL, Albert. *L'Europe et la Révolution.* Paris, 1946–9. 8 vols.

STENDHAL (Henri Beyle). *Le Rouge et le Noir.* II: Talleyrand as promoter of the restoration of the Bourbons. N.p., n.d.

STENGER, G. *La Société française pendant le Consulat.* (2nd series: *Aristocrates et Républicains.*) Paris, 1904.

TARLE (Evgeni Viktorovitch). *Talleyrand.* Moscow: Editions en Langues Etrangères, 1958.

TERRE (Abbé Marcel). *Prud'hon, portraitiste de Talleyrand.* Auxerre, 1959.

TESSIER, J. *Les Relations anglo-françaises au temps de Louis-Philippe. L' Election du roi des Belges nov. 1830–juil. 1831,* in *Mémoires de l'Academie Nationale des Sciences . . . de Caen,* LIX (1905).

THOMAS, Louis. *L'Esprit de M. de Talleyrand.* N.p., 1909.

TOUCHARD-LA-FOSSE, G. *Histoire politique et vie intime de Ch. de Talleyrand, prince de Bénévent.* Paris, 1848. (The subtitle reads: "Le Plutarque de la Révolution française.")

VANDAL, A. *L'Avènement de Bonaparte.* N.p., n.d.

———. *Napoléon et Alexandre,* I. N.p., n.d.

VILLEFOSSE, Louis de, and BOUISSOUNOUSE, J. *L'Opposition à Napoléon.* Paris: Flammarion, 1969.

VILLEMAREST, Charles-Maxime de. *M. de Talleyrand.* Paris: J.-P. Roret, 1834–5. (Adapted from M. Quérard.)

VITROLLES, Eugène François de. *Mémoires et relations politiques du baron de V.* N.p., n.d.

VIVENT, Jacques. *Monsieur de Talleyrand intime.* Paris: Hachette, 1963.

———. *La Vie privée de Talleyrand.* Paris: Hachette, 1940. (From the series *Les Vies Privées.*)

———. *La Vieillesse et la mort de M. de Talleyrand.* Paris: Ecrivains Contemporains, 1964.

WALDECK, Rosie. *De Pourpre et d'azur.* (Translated from the English by Charlotte Neveu.) Paris: Presses-Pockett, 1967.

WEIL, Commandant H. *Les Dessous du congrès de Vienne.* Paris, 1917.

———. "Talleyrand courtisan, peint par lui-même." (Extract from the *Revue Historique,* CXLVI [1924].)

———. *Talleyrand et la frontière ouverte.* Nancy, n.d.

YEWDALE, Ralph B. "An Identified Article by Talleyrand," *American Historical Review,* October 1922.

Bibliography

Chambre des Pairs (session of June 8, 1838). (A speech given by the baron de Barante on the occasion of Prince Talleyrand's death. No. 106, Vol. III, 1838. From the catalogued minutes, Vol. VI, No. 2, p. 723.)

Le Prince de Talleyrand, sa vie et ses confessions. Paris: chez l'éditeur, 1838.

Notice sur Mme la comtesse de Périgord . . . Paris: H. Simon-Dautreville, 1854.

Bénévent (the principality). Collection of 22 pieces concerning Charles Maurice de Talleyrand's administration of the principality of Bénévent.

Montjeu (in Sarthe). An important charter roll, which pertains to the families of Montjeu, Jeannin, Rolin, d'Harcourt, d'Aligre, Leppelletier de Saint-Fargeau, and Talleyrand, who successively possessed the château from the thirteenth century to the nineteenth; it furnished the materials for a work titled: *Montjeu et ses seigneurs*, by A. Monard and l'abbé Doret. (*Mémoires de la Société Eduenne*, VIII (1879), and following.)

INDEX

(Within entries the initials T, for Talleyrand, and N, for Napoleon, are frequently used. The names of royalty are generally listed under first name.)

Index

PHOTO CREDITS

A NOTE ON THE TYPE

The text of this book was set on the Linotype in Fairfield, the first typeface from the hand of the distinguished American artist and engraver Rudolph Ruzicka. In its structure Fairfield displays the sober and sane qualities of a master craftsman whose talent has long been dedicated to clarity. It is this trait that accounts for the trim grace and virility, the spirited design and sensitive balance of this original typeface.

The book was composed, printed and bound by Kingsport Press, Inc., Kingsport, Tennessee.

Typography and binding design by Earl Tidwell

Hélie

D. 1205 IN THE HOLY LAND.
SEIGNEUR DE GRIGNOLS; YOUNGER BRANCH
OF THE COMTES DE PÉRIGORD.

Hélie

(HIS GRANDSON)
MARRIES AGNÈS DE CHALAIS.

Jean de Talleyrand

SEIGNEUR DE GRIGNOLS (M. DE GRIGNAUX),
VICOMTE DE FRONSAC, PRINCE DE CHALAIS;
CHAMBERLAIN OF CHARLES VIII, LOUIS XII.

Daniel de Talleyrand

RECOGNIZED BY LETTERS PATENT (1613).
COMTE DE GRIGNOLS, MARQUIS D'EXCIDEUIL,
ISSUE IN DIRECT LINE OF THE COMTES
DE PÉRIGORD; PRINCE DE CHALAIS.
MARRIES THE DAUGHTER OF THE
MARÉCHAL DE MONTLUC 1585.

Wilgrin

843–886
COMTE D'ANGOULÊME
AND DE PÉRIGORD.

Alduin

FOLLOWED BY VARIOUS GUILLAUMES,
ADALBERTS, WILGRINS, BEARING THE
SURNAMES TAILLEFER AND TAILLERANG.

Adalbert

COMTE DE PÉRIGORD;
IN COURT OF HUGH CAPET IN 990.

Hélie V

COMTE DE PÉRIGORD;
CALLED TALLERANG IN 1166.

Charles   *Henri*

COMTE DE CHALAIS.
BEHEADED AT NANTES 1626.

Guyonne de Rochefort MARRIES (1)

Archambaud

LATE TWELFTH CENTURY.
ELDER BRANCH OF COMTES
DE PÉRIGORD, UNTIL 1440.

Gabriel de Talleyrand-Périgord

GRAND D'ESPAGNE;
GOUVERNEUR DU BERRY, DU LANGUEDOC.
MARRIES HIS COUSIN MARGUERITE DE CHALAIS.

THIS IS THE FOUNDATION OF THE BRANCH
OF THE DUCS DE PÉRIGORD, PRINCES
DE CHALAIS, GRANDS D'ESPAGNE,
AS CONFIRMED 1815.

Archambaud VI

(15TH DEGREE), D. 1440 IN BORDEAUX.
DISPOSSESSED AND BANISHED
BY CHARLES VI IN 1399.

END OF THE ELDER BRANCH.

Augustin-Hélie

MARRIES MLLE DE CHOISEUL 1807.

Augustin-René Adalbert

MARRIES MLLE ROUSSEAU DE SAINT-AIGNAN 1879.

A DAUGHTER, WHOSE MARRIAGE BROUGHT
THE TITLE OF PRINCE DE CHALAIS
AND THE GRANDESSE D'ESPAGNE
INTO THE GALARD DE BRASSAC DE BÉARN FAMILY.